I0813794

Women Architects at Work

Mary Anne Hunting
Kevin D. Murphy

Women Architects at Work

Making American Modernism

Princeton University Press
Princeton and Oxford

Published by Princeton University Press, 41 William Street, Princeton, New Jersey 08540
In the United Kingdom: Princeton University Press, 99 Banbury Road, Oxford OX2 6JX
press.princeton.edu

Frontispiece: Home workspace of Samuel Eldon and Victorine du Pont Homsey, Lancaster Pike, Hockessin, DE, 1940. *Page vi:* Detail of figure. 6.4. *Jacket images: (front)* John and Sarah Pillsbury Harkness house (1949), Six Moon Hill, Lexington, MA. Photograph by Ezra Stoller / Esto; *(back)* S. (Samuel) Robert Glassford house (1940; now demolished), Jupiter Island Club, Hobe Sound, FL. Photograph by Gottscho-Schleisner, Gottscho-Schleisner Collection, Library of Congress, Prints and Photographs Division.

Library of Congress Cataloging-in-Publication Data
Names: Hunting, Mary Anne, author. | Murphy, Kevin D., author.
Title: Women architects at work : making American modernism / Mary Anne Hunting, Kevin D. Murphy.
Description: Princeton : Princeton University Press, [2025] | Includes bibliographical references and index.
Identifiers: LCCN 2024019953 | ISBN 9780691206691 (hardcover) | ISBN 9780691261508 (ebook)
Subjects: LCSH: Architecture and women--United States--History--20th century. | Women architects--United States. | Modern movement (Architecture)--United States. | Architecture--United States--History--20th century. | BISAC: ARCHITECTURE / History / Modern (late 19th Century to 1945) | SOCIAL SCIENCE / Women's Studies
Classification: LCC NA2543.W65 H86 2025 | DDC 720.82--dc23/eng/20240722
LC record available at https://lccn.loc.gov/2024019953-
British Library Cataloging-in-Publication Data is available

Editorial: Michelle Komie and Annie Miller
Production Editorial: Terri O'Prey
Text Design: Yve Ludwig
Jacket/Cover Design: Yve Ludwig
Production: Steven Sears
Publicity: Jodi Price and Kathryn Stevens
Copyeditor: Lachlan Brooks
This book has been composed in Graphik and Minion Pro
Printed in China

10 9 8 7 6 5 4 3 2 1

Dedicated to our children,
Lilla, Henry, and Mary Ives

And in memory of our friends,
architect Sam Robertson Little
and Joan Underwood

NO PARKING

Preface

COLLABORATION IS AT THE HEART OF THIS BOOK. IT HAS characterized our working method over two decades, and it was also the primary career strategy for the modernist women architects we study. Our collaboration began in the Domesticity and Architecture seminar taught by Kevin D. Murphy at the CUNY Graduate Center, where Mary Anne Hunting wrote a paper about Ethel Brown Power (1881–1969). Trained as an architect, Power was an editor at *House Beautiful* between 1923 and 1933, and introduced to her broad readership European Modernism and its subsequent American variants, incorporating vernacular elements into the imported idiom. Correspondingly, Murphy published an article in the *Journal of the Society of Architectural Historians* focusing on Power's life partner, Eleanor Agnes Raymond (1887–1989), a Boston-based architect who was among the earliest women to be honored with a fellowship (in 1961) from the American Institute of Architects.[1] Murphy described the "vernacular moment" when Raymond modified European Modernism with details from regional settings and traditions in New England—well before the German modernist Walter Gropius arrived in the United States in 1937, although he is usually credited with introducing Modernism into the region's architectural culture.[2]

While we did not initially recognize the tremendous influence that Raymond and Power had as a couple on the development and dispersion of Modernism in the United States, we sensed there was more to their joint narrative. Thus, we centered our early research on the Cambridge School of Architecture and Landscape Architecture (1915–42) in Cambridge, Massachusetts, from where Power and Raymond obtained certificates in architecture in 1919. The records (at Smith College in Northampton, Massachusetts) are remarkably informative—especially the entries in the quarterly *Cambridge School Alumnae Bulletin* that were produced by alumnae between 1928 and July 1942 and also contained writings by students.[3] The *Bulletins* make clear that this formidable institution not only provided academic training paralleling that at Harvard University nearby, but fostered a community that became the lifeblood for students, alumnae, and even faculty.

As we compiled a list of Cambridge School architects and their education histories (see Appendix I), we began to wonder how influential the relationships they forged at the school were in their professional development. Aware of the growing importance of computer-aided analysis in art history, we asked Scott B. Weingart, a digital humanities specialist, to design a network analysis of their educational, social, and professional connections.[4] In addition to the relationships students and alumnae had with each other, we included those they maintained with instructors, trustees, mentors, and, eventually, professional partners. While our decision to focus on the Cambridge School was subjective, we were able to produce compelling visualizations of women architects who networked as intentionally as their male counterparts to achieve professional success and personal fulfillment.

Even though the list of Cambridge School architects anchored our research, we did not want them to be evaluated in isolation but rather as part of a larger body of women architects from varied backgrounds. Some were already familiar to us from publications, and, since 2002, from entries on the Beverly Willis Architecture Foundation's website, *Pioneering Women of American Architecture*.[5] These resources enhanced our effort to create a group biography of modernist women who focused on such critical issues as mass housing, community planning, preservation, racial inequality, and gender bias, and their concerns permeate our text.

Early in our research, we realized that only a small minority of women architects have papers in institutional archives. With a few exceptions—such as the collections in the International Archive of Women in Architecture, established in 1985 at Virginia Tech in Blacksburg—the records of most remain in the possession of descendants.[6] Thus, we traveled from Maine to California and beyond to locate their student work and document the evidence of their practices. In Tamworth, New Hampshire, we tromped off the grid in search of a vacation cabin, the only known (and now dilapidated) building by Florence Hope Luscomb (1887–1985). In Lincoln, Massachusetts, a contractor drove us off the grounds of the soon-to-be-demolished house of Frances "Franie" Baxter Quarton (1918–2017). In Montana, we pored over published histories of the family of Elizabeth-Ann "Libby" Campbell Knapp (1913–90) on the ranches she operated after her father died. In Pepper Pike, Ohio, we discovered the files of Ann Murphy Halle Little (1914–2012) exactly as she had left them in the home she built and shared with her husband, Robert Andrews Little, a Harvard-trained architect.

Women architects also did not leave many revealing memoirs or journals, much less autobiographies. This was not an anomaly; in 1940, Virginia Woolf commented, "I was thinking the other night that there's never been a womans [*sic*] autobiography. Nothing to compare with Rousseau." She supposes that "chastity" and "modesty" were the reasons, but late twentieth-century feminist criticism suggests instead that women's lives were frequently deemed unworthy of recording or publicizing in comparison to men's.[7] Regardless, we sought whatever information we could find, beyond collegiate alumnae updates and surveys. Our interactions with descendants revealed that women architects shared their histories to widely varying degrees, to the extent that some children had no knowledge of what or where their mothers had studied or accomplished. Most, however, expressed deep interest, and with their input we have assembled a portrait of women architects who exerted a decisive impact on Modernism, either regionally or nationally.

During our years of study, slowed by the COVID-19 pandemic, the intellectual and political backdrop to this study changed dramatically. For one thing, the field of gender and sexuality studies expanded so that the identification of "woman" no longer is a fixed notion. Consequently, we historicize how our subjects saw themselves with respect to the categories of male and female. Further, we aimed to understand how those who partnered with other women—personally and professionally—saw themselves in relation to the heteronormativity that dominated their culture. For another thing, the Me Too social movement that started in 2017 brought widespread media attention to the sexism faced by women in entertainment and other industries. An important argument of Me Too is that women lack representation and visibility in culture; the same can be said about women in architecture, as the Women in Architecture Affiliate Group of the Society of Architectural Historians has set out to rectify since 2020.[8] This period also witnessed the rise of the Black Lives Matter movement. The story we present here is one in which white women and predominantly white institutions play outsized roles. Nonetheless, there are scattered examples of women of color who surmounted the obstacles and contributed significantly to the modern movement. Even more than white women, those of color received little encouragement and recognition compared to their white male contemporaries; still, they produced works that introduced Modernism to their communities—from Virginia to New York to California.

While our interest initially was piqued by Power and Raymond, this dynamic pair turns out to be the most visible among a larger, interconnected group of women architects. Early in our process, we decided to bring as many individual biographies as possible into our story—those with recognized work as well as those who labored in obscurity—because they are fundamental to understanding the roles of women in architecture. Our comprehensive approach to studying women architects establishes that women had a considerably larger impact on Modernism than has been previously recognized, in part because many were forced to find jobs related to, but outside of, mainstream architecture. Bringing women into the history of Modernism necessarily entails a willingness to look broadly at their life histories and consider their wide-ranging production. Viewed collectively, these American-based modernists created a transformative cultural movement.

Note to the reader: After the first mention of women's full names, they are referred to by their last names; if they marry, they are referred to by both their maiden and married surnames; if they divorce and remarry, the surname of the first husband is omitted.

Women Architects at Work

Introduction

IN THE FIRST HALF OF THE TWENTIETH CENTURY, THE number of women in the United States who were trained in architecture markedly trailed that of men; but paradoxically, the divergent forms of their practice allowed them to reach a larger and broader audience to advance Modernism. Women in architecture effectively advocated for a particular kind of Modernism in which the International Style—an austere idiom codified by the Museum of Modern Art (MoMA) in New York in its famed *Modern Architecture: International Exhibition* (1932)—was balanced by a more "humanized" expression, as the architectural historian William H. Jordy labeled it. By incorporating historical and regional references, the buildings were intended to be "physically more comfortable."[1] Far from the simplified view presented in the traditional histories of Modernism, and equally far from the caricature advanced by postmodernists, the modern movement was notably diverse. And yet, although women architects promoted it through a variety of means, their contributions are only occasionally documented in period literature or, more often, unacknowledged or forgotten.

The house Eleanor Raymond designed in 1931 for her younger sister Rachel C. Raymond (1895–1971) in Belmont, Massachusetts, exemplified a new type of Modernism that inspired subsequent variations (fig. I.1). Historic images of the house show that it possessed the geometric austerity of the 1920s villas of Le Corbusier and other Europeans with whom Raymond was enthralled, but at the same time, the building incorporated locally familiar materials and accents of strong color, often relating to on-site vegetation. The interior could not have been more of a contrast as it was filled with comfortable furnishings and a hodgepodge of antiques (fig. I.2).[2] The overall aesthetic of the house recalls the way that architectural historian Daniel P. Gregory describes the wood-framed farmhouse designed in 1927 by the Bay Area architect William Wilson Wurster for his grandmother, Sadie Gregory, in Santa Cruz, California: "It represented an in-between stage in the evolution of Modernism: not traditional, not avant-garde, but free-thinking and pragmatic."[3] Similarly, Raymond thought about the Belmont house as a continuation of the experiments in domestic architecture by the Europeans she admired but nonetheless connected it to the landscape and architecture of the Northeast. Moreover, she designed it while working on *Early Domestic Architecture of Pennsylvania* (1931), the publication in which she documented historic vernacular

I.1. House (now demolished) designed in 1931 by Eleanor Agnes Raymond for her sister Rachel C. Raymond, 9 Park Avenue, Belmont, Massachusetts. *Eleanor Raymond Photographic Collection, Historic New England, gift of James E. Robinson III.*

I.2. Rachel Raymond house interior, c. 1932. *Raymond Collection, Historic New England, Robinson gift.*

buildings in photographs that emphasize simple geometries like those of the Rachel Raymond house.

Raymond was interested less in social housing than in designing modest houses for individuals or families. As she once explained, her mission was to plan informal, flexible, and livable spaces "with the owners instead of for them." She was humble and had no intention of creating a monument to herself in a signature style, as male architects tended to do.[4] Raymond carried her design sensibility into the many roles she played as an alumna of the Cambridge School of Architecture and Landscape Architecture—as critic, lecturer, donor, volunteer, alumnae president, and trustee. Informally founded just a year before she enrolled in 1916, the school was incorporated as an educational institution in 1924 and was distinguished for being exclusively dedicated to the professional education of women, most of whom were college graduates, frequently from the Seven Sisters (fig. I.3).[5]

The director, Henry Atherton Frost (1883–1952), also taught at Harvard, where he was recognized for his work with beginning architecture students in graphics (descriptive geometry, isometric and axonometric projection, shades and shadows, and perspective) and freehand drawing, as well as design. The Cambridge School pedagogy progressed over time—from informal tutorials and occasional lectures to structured curricula composed of the histories of architecture and landscape architecture, graphics, freehand drawing, design (which included the completion of numerous "special" problems), construction, and professional practice.[6] By 1941, students were required to base much of their work on actual sites and to produce models that showed the details of construction instead of making elaborate Beaux Arts–oriented drawings of hypothetical buildings, as students had done twenty years earlier. Nonetheless, the school never deviated from its core principle that all entering students share a broad first-year curriculum encompassing the fundamental elements of design, after which they could concentrate on their chosen discipline of either architecture, landscape architecture, or (beginning in 1935) "interior architecture."[7] Students were taught to consider a building and its corresponding landscape as a single design problem instead of two separate assignments, which was the more customary approach in design; a centerpiece of the school's method of training was collaboration.[8] Though influenced by the evolving curricula at Harvard—since many Cambridge School instructors were also employed there—the Cambridge School was different in that its small size and gendered focus made it possible to adapt its curricula to compensate for any perceived deficiencies of the students. For the same reason, the school was able to respond to student demand for more complex problems, expanding beyond the domestic realm, which was the stereotypical assignment for women and an early mandate of the school.

This comprehensive training gave Cambridge School women an edge in that each was prepared to expand beyond her own specialization into other areas of design. Still, none escaped the overarching problem that the field was fraught with sexism—in hiring practices, promotions, titles, assignments, salaries, and construction-site supervision. Women trained in architecture at coeducational institutions such as the Massachusetts Institute of Technology (MIT)—where they were allegedly perceived as a "nuisance"—were vulnerable to prejudice from the time they were first admitted in the late nineteenth century.[9] Regardless of where they trained, many were able to innovate meaningful professional situations in which they could apply their knowledge and skills to move beyond entry-level drafting work. Advancing Modernism in a variety of capacities was the path to their success.

This study considers the ways women created gratifying forms of professional practice without the benefits of male-dominated educational and professional networks. In doing so, it builds on groundwork provided by feminist historians. Linda Nochlin's call to arms, "Why Have There Been No Great Women Artists?" (*ArtNews*, 1971), opened debate on two particularly salient issues: the lack of historiographical attention paid to women artists and the absence of institutional support for them. More than four decades later, when the architectural historian Despina Stratigakos echoed Nochlin by asking another question in her book, *Where Are the Women Architects?* (2016), she recognized that women still were excluded from high-level architectural practice and that they were receiving far too little attention from scholars and critics.[10]

It was not until thirty years after the Cambridge School closed that scholars began to show any interest in the school. In 1973, Doris Cole devoted a chapter to it in her pioneering publication about the history of women in architecture; four years later, Mary Otis Stevens (b. 1928), an architect trained at MIT, referenced the school in her chapter on women's "Struggle for Place" in the catalog for the pathbreaking exhibition *Women in American Architecture: A Historic and Contemporary Perspective*, spearheaded by the architect-critic Susana Torre (b. 1944).[11] In 1987, landscape architect Dorothy May Anderson (1916–93) published a specific history about her alma mater, *Women, Design, and the Cambridge School*, which was informed by a survey she had sent to alumnae; two years later, she contributed a chapter in the publication *Architecture: A Place for Women*.[12]

I.3. Photograph of women graduating from the Cambridge School of Architecture and Landscape Architecture (1915–42), Cambridge, Massachusetts, 1940. *Left to right:* Alice Morgan Carson, Franziska Maria Alma Porges, Katharine Frances Wilson, Priscilla Congdon Gladding, Ann Murphy Halle, and Elizabeth-Ann Campbell. *Private collection.*

Like the scholarship on the Cambridge School, the first studies of women in architecture from the late nineteenth century onward are broad in scope but underscore the women's decisive roles in shaping the built environment. In the only essay to address gender in the well-known volume edited by Spiro Kostof, *The Architect: Chapters in the History of the Profession* (1977), architectural historian Gwendolyn Wright argues that the traditional association of women with the home led some of them to limit their architecture practices to domestic design.[13] One of their roles, according to Wright, was that of the "reformer," a reference that recalls the nineteenth-century women examined by Dolores Hayden in her influential book, *The Grand Domestic Revolution: A History of Feminist Designs for American Homes, Neighborhoods, and Cities* (1981). There, she describes "material feminism," efforts by women to reconceive the built environment, especially the home, to achieve progressive objectives and improvement in the lives of women.[14]

In 1974, both the West Coast Women's Design Conference at the University of Oregon in Eugene and the Women in Architecture Symposium at Washington University in St. Louis, Missouri, demonstrated the attention being directed toward the state of women in the profession, including its multiple barriers to full participation.[15] At the latter, where the psychological and social implications of women practicing architecture were of particular concern, a positive note was sounded by Natalie L'Hommedieu Griffin de Blois (1921–2013) in a workshop entitled Architectural Practice, or The Rewards of Building Buildings.[16] Having achieved the level of associate partner in the Chicago office of Skidmore, Owings & Merrill, she was one of the few women who could reflect on her experience in the design and construction of large commercial projects. Echoing a statement from 1955 by the modernist architect Pietro Belluschi, Gwendolyn Wright referred to Griffin de Blois as "*that exceptional one*," meaning that she was a woman able to have a career in architecture on a par with a man.[17]

Following the initial spate of publications, historians and critics continued to address the role of women as professional architects while also engaging in a broad-ranging recovery of the history of women and the built environment. As a cofounder of *Heresies, A Feminist Journal on Art and Politics*, for example, Susana Torre was instrumental in dedicating its 1980 issue to the theme of "Making Room: Women and Architecture," which addressed the social, political, and economic implications of the involvement (or lack thereof) of women in design.[18] The succeeding discussion of women modernists built upon the literature that followed in the 1980s and beyond.[19] Of note is the pioneering scholarship of the architectural historian Alice T. Friedman, who drew attention to the role of women as patrons of modernist architects in her book *Women and the Making of the Modern House* (1998). As this study also shows, in a variety of capacities, women who exerted an influence on Modernism did so by virtue of their female collaborators and supporters.

While it is important to acknowledge the ways that sex and gender affected how women architects identified themselves as well as how they were known by others, it is also problematic to apply current terminology to earlier periods. The words *woman* and *women* are used advisedly in this text with an awareness of the varied terminologies applied to gender identification at the time of this writing. As far as can be determined from historical records, the women architects examined here were cisgendered rather than gender nonconforming—meaning that their gender identity and senses of self were congruent with the sex assigned to them at birth—and they presented as women throughout their lives.[20]

Some of the women found ways to escape from widely held assumptions about the capabilities of women and men. For example, even though she prevailed in the face of gender prejudice, Ellamae Ellis League (1889–1991) of Macon, Georgia, was among those who outwardly rejected the label *woman architect,* declaring in an interview, "I was always an architect, not a woman architect but an architect. I encourage women going into the profession not to concentrate on being separate as a woman but to concentrate on being a good architect."[21] Correspondingly, when at midcentury the Women's Medical College of Pennsylvania in Philadelphia commissioned Elizabeth "Bess" Hirsh Fleisher (1892–1975) to design housing for its nurses, she insisted, "sex has nothing to do with the design"—despite the fact that women would also own and occupy the building.[22]

On the other hand, some architects appealed to end users precisely because they were women. Historical examples include the Berkeley Women's City Club (1930), one of the better-known buildings by Julia Hunt Morgan (1872–1957) of San Francisco; an English cottage for Tau Zeta Epsilon (a society of arts and music at Wellesley College), designed by Raymond in 1929 in collaboration with two other alumnae, Esther Parsons (Brabson; 1902–92) and Helen Frances Baxter Perrin (O'Rourke; 1903–94); and an award-winning clubhouse in the Bay Region style for the women's ZLAC Rowing Club in San Diego, produced in 1932 by Lilian Jeannette Rice (1888–1938), who was also a crew member and served as club president from 1915 to 1916.[23] There were other situations in which the perspectives of women architects added tremendous value to projects. In the 1940s, based on their previous experience of combining their two families in one house, Jean Bodman Fletcher and Sarah "Sally" Pillsbury Harkness (1914–2013) influenced the layout of Six Moon Hill, the celebrated community development in Lexington, Massachusetts, which is still appreciated for its family-centered plan.

I.4. Eleanor Raymond. *Private collection.*

The occasional woman presented herself with elements of masculine dress or engaged in aspects of practice identified as male. Morgan regularly donned a formal shirt and tie, as did Raymond (fig. I.4). The architect Theodate Pope Riddle (1867–1946) renounced her given name, Effie, at age nineteen to adopt Theodate, the name of her grandmother and one that she could shorten to the more masculine-sounding Theo, by which she became known.[24] Without historical evidence or personal information, it is hard to say more about these instances of gender nonconformity and how they affected the personal lives of women architects.

More often, however, their gender presentations conformed to social and cultural norms. Because training in architecture required a significant investment of both time and money, most women architects came from financially stable backgrounds. Scholarships and grants were rare for women, though Marion Lucy Mahony Griffin (1871–1961) and Natalie Griffin de Blois attended college with the support of generous patrons. In certain instances, women obtained influential positions in architecture by unconventional paths that did not include years in higher education: Louise Blanchard Bethune (1856–1913), one of the earliest professional woman architects in the United States, is an example.[25] Still, the most effective and visible women advocates for modern architecture primarily came from privileged backgrounds and thus conformed to the social expectations for bourgeois women even as they worked against the stereotypes that limited their professional opportunities.

Heterosexual marriage loomed large in their communities, and given that a professional collaboration with a husband could increase the prospect of his wife practicing architecture, many women married men from similar backgrounds. According to the sketch completed by the Austrian-born architect Franziska "Fran" Maria Alma Porges (Hosken; 1918–2006), immediately after she and her female colleagues were allowed into Harvard's architecture department in the fall of 1942 came "the story … [of] newlyweds" (fig. I.5). Some women architects, however, followed bourgeois expectations by abandoning their hard-won careers and devoting themselves solely to the home front. For instance, during World War II, Faith Gregg Bemis Meem (1902–89) proudly parented four evacuated British children in addition to her own daughter.[26]

A significant group of women avoided the expectations of heterosexual pairing by eschewing marriage and partnering with other women. An outstanding example of this sort of household formation is that of Eleanor Raymond and Ethel Power, who spent their adult lives together as partners at their home in Boston and at their summer residence in Gloucester, Massachusetts. Power was one of the succession of editors at *House Beautiful*—"all of them with short tenures and most of

I.5. Page in *The Architectural Sketchbook / Fall 1942* by Franziska Porges. *Franziska Porges Hosken Papers, Frances Loeb Library, Graduate School of Design, Harvard University.*

I.6. Eleanor Raymond, studio of Amelia Peabody, Mill Farm, Dover, Massachusetts, 1933.

them women"—according to historian Monica Penick, who credits her with the magazine's "upward trajectory" prior to the influential editorship, from 1941 to 1964, of Elizabeth Gordon (1906–2000).[27] Yet, unlike Gordon, who was an infamous opponent of the International Style, Power championed Modernism during her decade-long tenure, especially as interpreted by her American contemporaries, Raymond chief among them (see Appendix II).[28] In 1934, *House Beautiful* was sold and relocated to New York, and although a new editor took over, Power continued to contribute articles and shape the content. In "I've Got My Own Ideas," published in September 1937, she creates her own version of a modern house in a story in which she and her fictitious husband "Gregory" receive a windfall of $10,000 that allowed them to commission a family home.[29] The ideas Power presents are consistent with her position as editor; what is remarkable is her need to contrive a heterosexual marriage and family for herself. As such, it demonstrates the societal pressure to conform to heteronormative expectations as well as to the strong connection between concepts of the home and the nuclear family. Despite what she implied in the article, Power, in fact, relished the summer home she created with Raymond, writing in a poem addressed to her in

1967, "I cannot imagine anything lovelier than here, in this place where I am. Here are beauty, quiet, well-being; here is my Sanctuary Hammock; and here are you."[30] Publicly, however, neither Power nor Raymond discussed their relationship. They also did not name their sexual orientation—even late in life when Raymond told an interviewer, "I never wanted a husband or to have children. I wouldn't have the slightest know-how of how to take care of children, nor would I want to take care of them."[31]

Not all relationships between partnered women architects lack documentation: an exception, for example, are the letters exchanged by the African American artist, architect, and educator Amaza "Mazie" Lee Meredith (1895–1984) and her life partner, the educator Edna Meade Colson (1888–1985).[32] The archive of their correspondence and scrapbooks at the historically Black Virginia State University in Petersburg, where they both taught, evinces the passion between the two women; moreover, letters from members of both their families document their acceptance of them as a couple (c.2–3).[33] Historians have argued that Black culture was more open to romantic relationships outside of heterosexual marriage than the white culture from which most modernist women architects sprang. For example, in Harlem, not far from Teachers College, where Meredith and Colson studied, lesbian weddings were known to exist in the 1920s and 1930s, sometimes even involving one member of the couple "passing" (as a man) to obtain a marriage license.[34] Meredith was also the product of an interracial marriage, a type of pairing more tolerated in Black than white communities.

For Power and other women in the period, being a modernist (or "a modern" as they were sometimes referred to at the Cambridge School) often meant something different than it did for men, although in some cases they drew directly on the work of European modernists, just as their male counterparts in the United States did. For instance, in some of the projects that Raymond executed in Dover, Massachusetts, for her most important patron, Amelia "Amy" Peabody (1890–1984), a granddaughter of the founder of the securities firm Kidder Peabody, her understanding of European Modernism exerted a powerful formal impact. Raymond composed designs from simplified geometric forms, avoiding the overt historicism that still dominated architecture, and she incorporated newly perfected materials like steel, concrete, and glass (fig. 1.6; see fig. 2.2). More often, however, women practiced a sort of Modernism that was less formally radical but nevertheless functionally and socially progressive. In some instances, they were practicing in regions where Modernism was unfamiliar or unacceptable to potential clients. Women typically tempered their uses of the forms and materials associated with Modernism with references to local architecture and culture to blend with, rather than disrupt, the existing built environment: vernacular adobe buildings in the Southwest and wood-framed buildings of the seventeenth and eighteenth centuries in the Northeast, for example.

I.7. Florence Hope Luscomb in front of her cabin, Elk Horn Ranch House, Tamworth, New Hampshire, 1940. *Papers of Florence Luscomb, Schlesinger Library, Harvard Radcliffe Institute.*

Even when their designs did not appear modern because they lacked signature formal elements, women nonetheless embraced some of the movement's programmatic aspects. In houses and apartment buildings, women were apt to espouse a commitment to functionalism, an approach perceived as the opposite of so-called Victorian architecture, which ostensibly privileged aesthetics over practicality. For instance, in the modest cabin that Luscomb designed for herself in New Hampshire, she maximized the property, both in- and outdoors to ensure it could accommodate her numerous guests on their getaways (fig. 1.7).[35] The cabin can be thought of as "modern" (and its architect as a modernist) even though it lacks Machine Age materials and visual severity. Similarly, Raymond was recognized for her penchant for functional design: as "a woman of today" dedicated to "making a house work properly," a client reported, Raymond wanted "workable, no nonsense, architecture."[36] No matter how progressive the programs were, buildings that failed to correspond to formal definitions of Modernism tended to be excluded; according to such criteria, Luscomb's cabin and much of Raymond's functionalism would not be considered modern.

The earliest Cambridge School architecture graduates would have entered a profession in which a small number of women had already demonstrated they could have a modicum of success and gain recognition, albeit within parameters established by men. The earlier generations of trailblazing female practitioners born during or just after the Civil War include Lois Lilley Howe (1864–1964), whose eponymous Boston firm, which eventually included her younger partners Eleanor Manning (O'Connor; 1906–86) and Mary Almy (1883–1967), produced designs for suburban houses and other building types, many inspired by the Arts and Crafts movement. All three studied under the historicist French Beaux-Arts system of design at MIT. Theodate Pope, on the other hand, was solely tutored by art historian Allan Marquand of Princeton University and also relied on the large collection of books on historic architecture that she assembled.[37] Despite their commitment to historicism in the broadest sense, these women established a precedent in the early twentieth century for the next generation of modernists by their career choices and styles of living. Doris Cole and Karen Cord Taylor observe in their monograph about the firm of Howe, Manning & Almy (1913–37) that "in their high standards for [domestic] design and in the confidence with which they pursued other projects, they set the stage for subsequent women architects."[38] Similarly, in the article "The Modernism of Theodate Pope," architectural historian James F. O'Gorman describes his subject as "thoroughly modern" primarily because she surmounted the expectations of her family, the traditions of her social class, and the status quo of the profession in order to join "the thin ranks" of trailblazing women fighting for a footing in male-dominated practices.[39] Pope Riddle's work was informed by the Colonial Revival and Arts and Crafts aesthetics, but she was also deeply committed to using architecture to achieve progressive social and institutional ends, a central tenet of Modernism.

Women architects like these often joined the profession by appealing to the conventional association of women with the home. Like their contemporaries Katherine Cotheal Budd (1860–1951) of New York and Hazel Wood Waterman (1865–1948) of San Diego, they did not limit themselves to domestic architecture; however, they did justify their practice as an extension of women's inherent domesticity and published articles to that effect.[40] In contrast, Julia Morgan rejected this notion and instead promoted herself as an architect on the basis of her knowledge of building technology and engineering as well as her professionalism.[41] She relied upon a network of female clients as she moved beyond domestic commissions to public buildings, including campus facilities at Mills College in Oakland (the first women's college west of the Rockies) and buildings for such female-serving organizations as the YWCA.[42]

The younger women architects educated in the interwar period knew their precursors not only through New England buildings but through exhibitions and talks. When in 1931 the Cambridge School mounted the exhibition *Houses and Gardens Designed by Women*, the firm of Howe, Manning & Almy lent examples of its work, and also that year each of the principals participated in alumnae activities as special guests.[43] At the annual alumnae dinner at the Boston Architectural Club, Manning was among the chosen speakers, observing in her toast, perhaps sardonically, "It's easy to be an architect—all you have to do is to do it better than everyone else."[44]

Though Pope Riddle also participated in the Cambridge School's exhibition, she was not present that year at the alumnae weekend. Had she been there, she might have cautioned that superior ability did not necessarily lead to commissions, nor did it ensure recognition for a female architect's work. As O'Gorman shows, Pope Riddle hired the New York firm of McKim, Mead & White, known for its classical architecture, to make detailed drawings of the overall ideas she originated for a house called Hill-Stead for her parents in Farmington, Connecticut. Unfortunately, the plans were erroneously attributed only to McKim, Mead & White when published soon after the house's completion in 1901.[45] The establishment was so reluctant to give credit to women architects that, in 1915, when Nugent Publishing was producing a directory of New York architects, it refused to print a photograph of Pope Riddle. The still unmarried architect wrote to her mother:

You will be most amused to learn that I was called up by telephone … and a masculine voice asked if I were really Theodate Pope the architect, and when I said I truly was, this voice apologetically explained that it would be impossible for them to use my photograph as they had just heard I was a woman. They had not believed the rumor, hence the incredulous voice over the telephone. So you see, although art has no sex, I am discriminated against, though on the merits of my work they had selected me as one of the architects whom they wished to mention.[46]

Pope Riddle was not personally active in Boston architectural circles, but her work was known to Raymond, in whose archive there is a postcard of the Avon Old Farms School (1918–27) that she built near Hartford, Connecticut.[47] The all-male school, like Hill-Stead, was funded by the Pope family's wealth; her investment in the school alone was about $7,000,000, which included thousands of acres and buildings that were part of a larger effort to memorialize her father Alfred Atmore Pope, an industrialist who died in 1913.[48]

The extraordinary financial and moral support Pope Riddle received from her family enabled her to breach the considerable barriers to architectural practice that women often experienced.[49] Yet even if women did not have support from their families in their pursuit of architecture, as men more often did, they could be adept at finding it elsewhere. Most male architects resisted employing and mentoring women, but a few took the opposite approach. George Washington Percy, a professor of engineering at the University of California, Berkeley, mentored Morgan and even offered to help pay her expenses to study architecture on the East Coast or in Europe. Another Berkeley instructor, Bernard Ralph Maybeck, involved Morgan in a small group of talented students to whom he offered special instruction as well as employment following their graduation in the spring of 1894.[50] Howe also benefitted professionally from the encouragement of established architects, including Francis Ward Chandler, a partner in the Boston firm of Cabot and Chandler (1875–88), who had designed a house for Howe and her mother following her father's death in 1887. Howe reminisced, "Always interested in houses, I had wanted to be an architect but had been suppressed by my pastors and masters on the ground that I could not be an architect because I was a woman."[51] Nevertheless, just as Chandler was becoming head of its department of architecture, she was admitted to MIT. After completing a two-year "partial" course in 1890, Howe worked as a draftsperson for Francis Richmond Allen in Boston for about two years before accepting a position with Robert Swain Peabody, a leading Colonial Revival architect in the city who was also a family acquaintance.[52] From him, she learned about the competition for the Women's Building at the World's Columbian Exposition in Chicago in 1893. Howe placed second to Sophia Hayden (1868–1953), the first woman architecture graduate at MIT, but nonetheless won $500, which funded an extended trip to Europe with her mother and sisters. When Howe could not find a drafting job upon her return, she established her own practice with commissions for houses from family friends. Subsequently, in 1901, with the support of her "old friend" Peabody, Howe became a member of the American Institute of Architects.[53]

Male practitioners recognized Howe's talent and passion and were in positions to help her advance professionally. Even so, when she was successful enough to expand her own firm, Howe cultivated only female partners—Manning in 1913 and Almy in 1926. The arrangement stemmed from an early experience in her office, as she recounted: "By 1900, I had an office 'downtown' with two men. They left me high and dry at the end of a year—one of the best things that ever happened to me."[54] Not only did she surround herself with women, but Howe mentored other MIT graduates whom she hired to bring current ideas to her firm.[55] Her ability to create a network of like-minded women was a pattern that became more pronounced as women advanced in the field.

The circumstances of Marion Mahony were different in that she had already met success as the second woman architect to graduate from MIT, the first licensed female architect in Illinois, and the first employee, in 1895, of Frank Lloyd Wright. His son John recalls that Mahony and another woman architect, Isabel Roberts (1871–1955), sported "smocks suitable to the realm" as opposed to the five men in "flowing ties."[56] Unlike Morgan's San Francisco office, in which professionalism was everything, in Wright's office an artistic ethos set the tone.[57] Recognizing Mahony's superb graphic skill, Wright asked her to lead the practice during his absence with Mamah Borthwick Cheney in Europe, beginning in 1909. Although Mahony declined and the responsibility went to Hermann Valentin von Holst, she insisted on "a definite arrangement" with von Holst in which, as she explains, she could have "control of the designing." The house produced for David Moses Amberg and his wife Harriet Houseman Amberg at 505 College Avenue in Grand Rapids, Michigan, stemmed from this arrangement (fig. 1.8).[58] At the same time, the legendary two-volume *Wasmuth Portfolio* (1910), comprising drawings of Wright's work, contains some signed by or attributed to Mahony.[59] She contributed far more than beautiful renderings, however; Friedman is certain that her "progressive, democratic example—as a feminist, artist, activist and intellectual—left a mark on Wright's heart and mind that helped shape his vision for the future and for the community he hoped to create around him."[60]

Despite her talent and promising career, Mahony was eclipsed in the profession by her husband, Walter Burley Griffin, after their marriage in 1911.[61] Their thirty-year working partnership may have facilitated her involvement in more large-scale work than Mahony Griffin would have had on her own, but she often did not take credit for her contributions.[62] Not surprisingly, scholars have underestimated or misunderstood her role.[63] In 1984, Elizabeth "Betty" Bauer Kassler (previously Mock; 1911–98), a former curator in architecture at MoMA, wrote in a letter to a colleague about that "mysterious Mahony woman," concluding that it was "too bad that more is not known about her."[64] More recently, her pervasive influence has been demonstrated by Prairie School scholars including Thomas S. Hines, who contends that even though their designs were credited to Griffin, the couple, in fact, worked as a team with Mahony Griffin being a source of ideas, a design critic, and "always as the renderer and interpreter of his (and their) visions."[65] Thus, Mahony Griffin had a significant role in the self-conscious development of an American modern architecture in the form of the Prairie style.

While the work of Wright and other Prairie School architects continued to exert an influence on American design in the 1920s and 1930s, not all women architects advocated for Modernism. Even though the Cambridge School, for example, increasingly embraced Modernism, there was never just one perspective; instead, students drew from a variety of sources and inspirations—from regional vernaculars (both in the United States and abroad) to avant-gardism (in France, Germany, and the Low Countries), to ubiquitous historical revivals. Still, a common thread united them: they demonstrated a commitment to using architecture as a means of engaging with the communities they created for themselves or their clients. In addition, when they moved beyond the scale of the single house to lay out larger developments (a trend in the postwar period when suburbs and resorts were expanding), their programs fostered evolving lifestyles and functions, and they also facilitated tightly knit communities. When women architects addressed larger-scaled urban and housing issues, they frequently started with human needs rather than with abstract modern principles. Even when women built only a single house (commonly a retreat for themselves), they did so while keeping in mind the friends and relatives they intended to welcome.

This examination of twentieth-century women in architecture unfolds in eight thematic chapters. Chapter I examines their formative years by charting the dynamic evolution of education, including the establishment of the Cambridge School as a professional school for women. It focuses on the school's innovative pedagogy, particularly its emphasis on interdisciplinary collaboration, which influenced the modernization of architecture school curricula elsewhere, including at Harvard.[66] Chapter II revisits the familiar account of Modernism's arrival in the United States and revises it to include women. As it expands on the sources of Modernism, consideration is also given to the Mexican architecture and landscapes that women architects documented. It was not only the European-inspired concrete buildings but the traditional adobe architecture situated in dramatic, colorful settings that Victorine "Vicki" du Pont Homsey, a Cambridge School-trained architect, saw as beautiful in their simplicity (fig. 1.9). Inevitably influenced by the deluge of contemporary publications about Mexico, frequently penned by women, American travelers sent rhapsodizing letters home about their tours, just when, as Keith Eggener described, modernist Mexican architects "began to step away from the International Style toward a site-specific regionalism."[67] Chapter III applies current network theory and computational methods to the activities of the Cambridge School architects whose networking patterns are represented in visualizations of their educational, professional, and social connections (figs. 3.2–4). Despite being excluded from male-dominated institutions, women developed associations that led to professional success, and Raymond and Power excelled at creating domestic spaces in which relationships could thrive. Women who practiced modern architecture often engaged in collaboration, the subject of Chapter IV. Though it often blurred professional and personal boundaries, a substantial number of women architects married and practiced with

I.8. Marion Lucy Mahony, house for David and Harriet Houseman Amberg, 505 College Avenue, Grand Rapids, Michigan, 1909. *Historic American Buildings Survey (HABS), Prints and Photographs Division, Library of Congress.*

men in the same or related fields. Personal and professional coupling, sometimes with other women, afforded women a quality of practice otherwise difficult to attain. Collaboration was also essential to the enterprising women architects chronicled in Chapter V who worked outside of their profession. Unlike male architects, whose professional trajectories were usually linear, women had to re-create themselves in multiple settings to achieve similar longevity. Arguably, through their work in related fields, they were able to disseminate Modernism to a larger and broader audience than they could have done in architecture alone. Chapter VI examines the extent to which women architects led the reinvention of the modern American home—however much they may have objected to their relegation to the domestic sphere. Cambridge School women chafed against this affiliation, particularly those who insisted that the school omit the word *domestic* from its name. Their progressive contributions to residential design, which included solar heating, prefabrication, and innovative materials, countered the perception that Machine Age forms and materials were inhospitable.[68] In fact, women advanced modern concepts on a variety of scales—from an individual object to a city or region, as detailed in Chapter VII—about creating communities. Instead of private estate planning, they focused on urban plans with large housing projects and community

I.9. Victorine du Pont Homsey, *Women at a Pool, Mexico*, watercolor on paper, 1932. *Private collection.*

centers.[69] Their humane approach created designs that brought about community cohesion and supported family life. Chapter VIII addresses projects by women architects that serve as the salient (and sometimes lone) expression of their perspective on Modernism. Since most had limited commissions, these works provided nearly unique opportunities to invent a modern language in which to represent themselves as architects.

The conclusion is a response to the legendary two-part feature published in *Architectural Record* in 1948.[70] The title, "A Thousand Women in Architecture," is both contradictory and paradoxical: on the one hand, it highlights their facility with logical planning and ability to give a building distinctive character; on the other, it counterfactually asserts itself as proof that architecture is a profession in which women were accepted. The lack of opportunity to establish themselves in the prominent architecture firms necessarily meant they had to find alternative approaches. In the end, their work demonstrates an enthusiasm for moving beyond International Style formulae to an American Modernism engaged with the particularities of place. Their professional pathways were far from solitary ramblings but rather entailed deep engagement with the communities in which they worked.

CHAPTER I

Early Experience and Education

THE DYNAMIC EVOLUTION OF ARCHITECTURE EDUCATION for women is illustrated in a comparison of two student drawings: one was created in 1902 by Julia Morgan at the time-honored École des Beaux-Arts in Paris; the other was created by Suzanne Marjorie Stockard (Underwood; 1917–2001) as an art major at Bennington College in Vermont, from which she graduated in 1938 (figs. 1.1, 1.2). Each of them set a precedent for their time: Morgan was the first woman to earn a *certificât d'études* from the École des Beaux-Arts; Stockard was the first woman architect to graduate from Harvard University, in 1943.[1]

Together, their drawings represent the aesthetic progression from Neoclassicism to Modernism as well as the expansion of educational opportunities available to women. While the pedagogy Morgan experienced at the École des Beaux-Arts emphasized mastery of the classical tradition with sophisticated composition and drawing skills, Stockard's training at Bennington, followed by the Cambridge School of Architecture and Landscape Architecture and then Harvard, was oriented toward the invention of design solutions using open plans, abstract forms, and new materials that could meet the needs of clients.

Historically, many Americans—including Morgan—considered their architecture training incomplete without

1.2. Suzanne Marjorie Stockard, student drawing, Bennington College, c. 1937. *Private collection.*

1.1. Julia Morgan, student rendering of a theater in a palace, graphite, ink, watercolor, and gouache on tracing paper, 1902. *Julia Morgan Records, Environmental Design Archives, College of Environmental Design, University of California, Berkeley.*

study abroad, particularly in Paris.[2] Not long after the Civil War, however, aspiring American architects also began to train domestically in institutions inspired by the École des Beaux-Arts. Small numbers of women such as Louise Blanchard Bethune—the first woman admitted to the American Institute of Architects—achieved professional status through the longstanding apprenticeship system, although this pathway largely excluded them until after World War II.

A common misconception is that women were not allowed or had to fight their way into the architecture schools in the United States.[3] At the turn of the twentieth century, however, a range of geographically dispersed schools started to graduate women in architecture, beginning with Cornell University in 1871, Syracuse University in 1881, and MIT in 1885. By 1928, at least twenty-seven accredited coeducational institutions had charters requiring them to admit women into their architecture programs, although they could make up as little as 10 percent of the student body. Women are said to have been "distinctly unwelcome" and given little encouragement in either their studies or their professional development.[4] For instance, at Columbia University, an announcement for the 1910–11 academic year stated, "Owing to the lack of suitable drafting room accommodations, women … are advised to do the work in design elsewhere, upon the same terms as students working in outside ateliers."[5]

Between 1931 and 1940, nearly twenty women earned degrees (mostly bachelor's) in architecture at MIT, but there were already exemplary figures from the school with significant output, among them Marion Mahony Griffin and the professional partners Lois Howe, Eleanor Manning, and Mary Almy, as well as Elisabeth "Betty" Coit (1892–1987).[6] Despite having access to higher education in architecture, women could not always evade marginalization in residential design, nor did they necessarily gain familiarity with Modernism. In contrast to Harvard, at MIT the dean of architecture, Walter Roy MacCornack, reportedly did not permit "the first hint of the modern trend" until 1940–41, when he brought in the Finnish architect Alvar Aalto as a research professor.[7] Even though MIT took on the issue of housing, the school's 1940 catalog shows that architectural history and freehand drawing were still considered important, following the Beaux-Arts emphasis on aesthetics rather than real-world problems. The women's theses in the MIT Museum demonstrate the ongoing concentration on programs disconnected from the most urgent contemporary concerns, for instance, the watercolor of the Gothic-inspired private chapel (1923) by Ida Brown Adelberg (Webster; 1899–1983) and, even later, A Beauty Establishment (1937) by Lillian Polly Povey Thompson (1904–94).[8]

Modernism in Undergraduate Studies

The emergence of Modernism in the United States may have made architecture more compelling for women because it was connected to so many adjunct fields in design, planning, publishing, and education. The women's colleges grasped that an understanding of its concepts could enhance opportunities for their graduates and, accordingly, promoted Modernism in their arts curricula, lectures, tours, and exhibitions. In 1934, the art department at Bennington College, which was established just two years earlier as a laboratory for women, wanted to recruit Josef Albers, a lauded alumnus and instructor at the Bauhaus (1919–33) design school in Germany whose avant-garde pedagogy would have tremendous influence in the United States.[9] Albers declined the offer, despite encouragement from Philip Johnson, chairman of the nascent Department of Architecture at the Museum of Modern Art (MoMA), and by an important school trustee whose daughter, Nathalie Swan (Rahv; 1912–83), had studied at the Bauhaus. Nevertheless, in 1935 Bennington did hire Lila Fairbairn Ulrich (Koppelman; 1910–84), a Bauhaus student between 1931 and 1933, who by then was living in New York and collaborating with another Bauhaus alumna, the German-born architect Hilda Reiss (1909–2002).[10]

Several other institutions also hired faculty dedicated to Modernism. At Wheaton College in Norton, Massachusetts, one of the earliest colleges for women, Esther Isabel Seaver (Burno; 1903–65) allegedly "swept" onto the campus in 1930 "with energy, unconventional ideas, and an almost evangelical devotion to Modernism." As head of the art department and a professor of art, she relentlessly pushed for the construction of a modern building.[11] Although Seaver convinced the trustees to engage in a competition in 1938 for a modern art center under the auspices of MoMA and *Architectural Forum*, she could not muster the funding to support the winning design by Richard Bennett and Caleb Hornbostel.[12] Subsequently, when in 1946 it was announced that the more conservative firm of Perry, Shaw, & Hepburn (1923–68)—responsible for the reconstruction of Colonial Williamsburg in Virginia—would design the building, Margaret "Peg" King Hunter (1919–97) fanned the flames of controversy with a telegram she sent to the *Wheaton News* accusing the college of violating a professional code of ethics.[13] A Wheaton undergraduate who subsequently studied architecture at the Cambridge School and then at Harvard, King Hunter later explained in the *Wheaton Alumnae Quarterly* that it was through Seaver's teaching that she first experienced the "creative thrill of good contemporary design" and that Seaver had "most certainly" influenced her decision to pursue architecture, which she found to be "the most satisfying career in the world."

The Seven Sisters, to varying degrees, also took leading roles in the integration of Modernism into American undergraduate education. Vassar College in Poughkeepsie, New York, hired instructors who would later become prominent advocates of Modernism—Alfred Hamilton Barr Jr. in the academic year 1923–24, Henry-Russell Hitchcock in 1927–28, and John McAndrew in 1932–37—each of whom eventually found employment at MoMA (fig. 1.3). Wellesley College outside of Boston also showed an interest in Modernism when the school newspaper gave front-page coverage in 1929 to a campus lecture by Barr on Walter Gropius's Bauhaus in Dessau, Germany.[14] Barr had already made his mark at Wellesley as an associate professor of art with the legendary, all-encompassing art course Tradition and Revolt in Modern Painting, which he sometimes taught with Hitchcock's assistance, in 1926–27 and again in 1928–29.[15] Barr's course was the first in modern art to be offered in the United States and included field trips to contemporary avant-garde buildings, for instance, the Necco candy factory (1925–27) in Cambridge, Massachusetts.[16]

Radcliffe College in Cambridge also participated in the discussion when in 1933 the continuing education committee organized a conference entirely devoted to modern architecture. Philip Johnson saw his talk there as an opportunity to decry the upcoming Century of Progress exhibition in Chicago, anticipating that most buildings

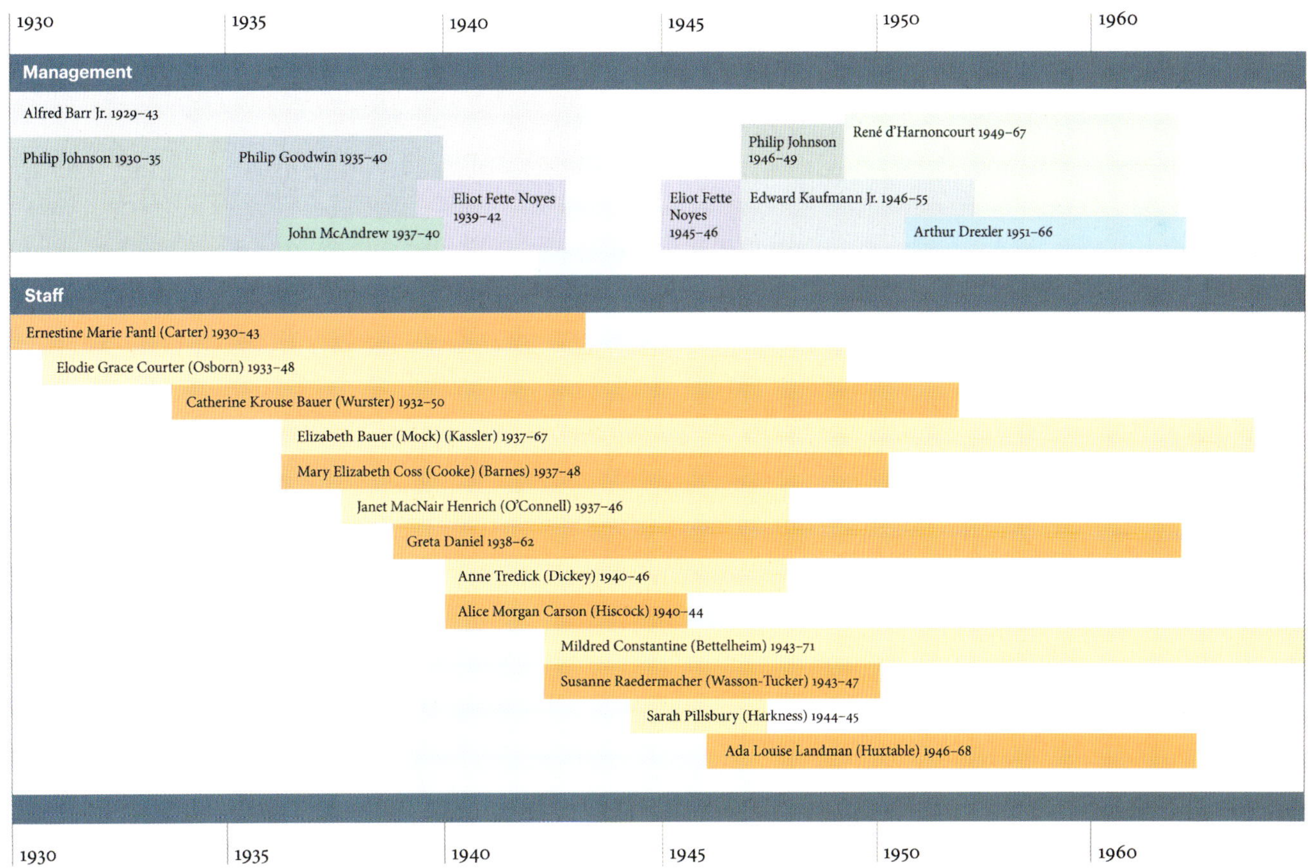

1.3. Timeline of the female staff in architecture and industrial design at the Museum of Modern Art, New York, 1930–68. *Design by Anita Bassie, Group M.*

would lack the influence of the International Style, which he had promoted a year earlier at MoMA.[17] In addition, the occasion included a roundtable on the roles of women in modern architecture, headed by Eleanor Raymond, one of the few architects to have built a modern house by that date (see figs. 1.1, 1.6).[18] As a result of their efforts, women's colleges gave students access to the most current thinking about contemporary design and a conversancy in Modernism that would open up opportunities.

The Educational Program of the Cambridge School of Architecture and Landscape Architecture

A close examination of the architectural education at the Cambridge School shows that its training prepared women not only to excel academically but also to navigate around the educational and professional strictures they would experience. Regardless of whether the women chose to pursue modern architecture, as many did, the recollections of past students repeatedly confirm what Frances Baxter Quarton recalled at age ninety-seven about her education at the Cambridge School: "You have never seen any group of people who were so enthusiastic about what they were doing!"[19]

The Cambridge School was never formally associated with Harvard as some have written; instead, in 1934, it became affiliated with Smith College so that in place of certificates those with undergraduate degrees could earn bachelor's and master's degrees, which the school believed would enhance their consideration in the professional fields of architecture and landscape architecture. Four years later, the Cambridge School was further integrated with Smith to lessen chronic financial trouble (after which the school worked under various names, frequently the Smith College Graduate School of Architecture and Landscape Architecture).[20] Nonetheless, the Cambridge School was intertwined with Harvard's enrollment policies, curricula, and faculty until the academic year of 1942–43, when the Cambridge School closed and Harvard allowed women to enter its Graduate School of Design (GSD)—consisting of architecture, landscape architecture, and regional planning—due to losing nearly two-thirds of its male students to military service (attendance, in fact, hit its low of forty students in 1940).[21]

Consequently, the Cambridge School has sometimes been overlooked in the biographies of women architects who also attended Harvard's GSD. For example, in an account of Anne Griswold Tyng (1920–2011), an acclaimed modernist who worked her way up to associate in the office of Louis Kahn, one critic wrote, "[Tyng] got her undergraduate degree at Radcliffe College in 1942 and went on to study architecture at the Harvard Graduate School of Design, as part of the school's first class to admit women."[22] Yet, as Tyng herself remembered, after she discovered that she could get credit in her senior year at Radcliffe (1941–42) for studying architecture at the Cambridge School, she felt "called to architecture" in the design studio of Henry Frost, whom she "adored."[23] Tyng was actually introduced to the Cambridge School after her junior year when she completed an architecture science course in the collaborative summer school it held with Harvard; during senior year, Tyng completed three more courses (design and graphics) at the Cambridge School, which made it possible for her to graduate from the GSD at Harvard, which she entered in the fall of 1942, in just two and a half years with a master's degree in architecture.[24]

The Cambridge School had a humble launch. In late 1915, a Radcliffe graduate named Katherine "Kitty" Glover Brooks (Norcross; 1892–1989) was denied entrance to Harvard's program in landscape architecture, and she was advised by its chairman, James Sturgis Pray, to be tutored at her home by Frost, a young architecture instructor at Harvard who had not yet completed his master's degree. Early in the following year, Brooks and a few other women wishing to study landscape architecture were tutored by Frost along with Bremmer Whidden Pond, a Harvard instructor in landscape architecture, in their shared office at 4 Brattle Street in Cambridge. Among the architecture students from MIT to join the group were Florence Luscomb and Abby Winch "Winnie" Christensen (1887–1969) of Beaufort, South Carolina, who sent letters to her mother in 1916 and 1917 describing the daily protocol.[25] As she explains, Frost viewed the initial effort as short-term tutoring, but to the students it already was a "little school" with strenuous requirements.[26]

While a more formal curriculum—in design, construction, history, freehand drawing, graphics, mechanical plants, horticulture, and office practice—eventually took shape, the initial instruction was reminiscent of Beaux-Arts ateliers: the women were left to themselves for much of the day until Frost and Pond made their rounds to teach and critique construction, design, and horticulture. They also heard lectures, for example, by

Herbert Langford Warren, the founder of the School of Architecture at Harvard in 1912, whose teaching emphasized the mastery of the classical tradition and the design methods of the École des Beaux-Arts. Warren advised, "A point of departure there must be, and we think it better to found our work on the world's highest achievements, rather than to take as a starting point an imported and debased modern tradition."[27] Even after a modern wing had been built at the school, Frost, who had studied under Warren at Harvard, waxed lyrical about the "eloquence and inspiration" of the talks Warren gave at the Cambridge School during its early years.[28]

According to Christensen's letters, she had to supplement her Cambridge School education with freehand drawing twice weekly with William Felton Brown, a revered assistant professor at MIT, and clay modeling on Saturdays with the sculptor Johan Selmer-Larsen. Christensen's work experience was limited to assisting in the drafting room and cataloging book illustrations in the school's library. Nonetheless, she (like her fellow students) was encouraged by the faculty to question received notions and argue her ideas, an approach that would become customary at the school.

Surprisingly, by the academic year of 1917–18, the Cambridge School was able to offer twenty-two courses to its seventeen students.[29] Though an article in the *Boston Daily Globe* commended the investment of the school in launching their careers, its headline, "Let Women Plan Houses for Women: Mere Man Doesn't Know Where to Put the Closets or Arrange for the Furniture," assumed that women were primarily suited for domestic design because of their predisposition to homemaking.[30] Shaking off this label would prove an enduring challenge. Even so, interest in the school swelled, and by 1922 the thirty-five enrolled students forced it to expand the faculty and move from the small office to quarters twice the size at 13 Boylston Street in Boston, away from Cambridge but near the business district as well as the residential Back Bay neighborhood.[31] The professional partnership of Frost and Raymond, which they formed after her graduation in 1919, was relocated nearby to the Raymond Whitcomb Building on Newbury Street, one of two major commercial thoroughfares in the Back Bay.[32] When in 1928 the Cambridge School needed more space and moved to 53 Church Street in Harvard Square, it was more distant from the offices of many practicing architects in Boston but more convenient to Harvard, where many of the Cambridge School faculty also taught.

Since the education of women in architecture was not widespread, no two women arrived at the Cambridge School with equivalent expectations, much less preparation. Mary Cope Elkinton Duguid (1888–1975) enrolled in 1929, eighteen years after graduating from Wellesley College, so she could become an equitable working partner with her Scottish-born architect husband, William Morrison Duguid. Although federal regulations prevented her from collaborating with him in the mid-1930s at the Tennessee Valley Authority in Knoxville, she claimed to have assisted him in designing houses for the builders of Norris Dam in a community that she considered a forerunner of new town development.[33]

Another student, Faith Bemis, was influenced by the prefabrication experiments of her father, Albert Farwell Bemis.[34] Her 1928 thesis on a suburban development specified that its fifty houses would utilize "one of Mr. Bemis' new types of construction that would allow stucco finished walls" with colored and textured finishes being "the chief feature of the scheme."[35] Although only briefly at the school in 1938, Anne Laurie Westbrook Gould (Hauberg; 1917–2016) was also inspired by her father, the Harvard-trained architect Carl Frelinghuysen Gould, chair of the Department of Architecture at the University of Washington in Seattle. Others who discovered architecture through family members include Anne Tyng, who remembered that when her family lived in China, she watched her father, an Episcopalian missionary, oversee the construction of a school and a church in Changsha, the capital city of the Hunan province; he also designed their brick home, which had interior walls of redwood salvaged from a temple, as well as their mountain cottage of granite in Kuling.[36] While it was not unusual for children of prominent families to be introduced to art and architecture abroad, Tyng was unique in that at age sixteen she traveled the world with her older sister, her most vivid memories being of the great monuments of the past.[37] Margaret Burnham Kelly (1907–95) continued the legacy of her family of architects—her grandfather Daniel Hudson Burnham and two uncles, Daniel Jr. and Hubert—by attending MIT between 1929 and 1933, after graduating from Vassar College. She went on to work as an architect in Rhode Island, both independently and in collaboration with the Columbia University–trained architect James Peter Geddes, whom she married in 1941.[38] At least in one instance a passion for architecture between a mother and a daughter developed concurrently; during the four-year tenure of Mary "Molly" Duncan Weed Noyes (1915–2010) at the Cambridge School, 1935–39, her mother, Mary "Polly" Duncan Walker Weed (1876–1957) also took courses (though not for credit).[39]

Cambridge School students could also have been inspired by the cultural vanguard in Cambridge, an intellectual community that spawned progressive ideas and avant-garde art across the media. Modernism took root there well before prominent émigré architects arrived in the educational institutions. In the Harvard Cooperative Building, for instance, women could have viewed the first exhibition in the United States on the Bauhaus, in 1930–31, organized by the Harvard Society for Contemporary Art (1929–36), a collaborative project of Lincoln Kirstein, Edward M. M. Warburg, and John Walker III, which is now recognized as one of the most important early venues for the presentation of Modernism in the United States.[40] Its pathbreaking exhibition program evidences the standing of Harvard as a cradle of Modernism on a par with the cities of London, Paris, New York, and Chicago.[41]

Women at the Cambridge School flourished due to the vision of Frost and his faculty. After observing their capabilities, he altered his initial opinion that women were best suited to domestic design. In turn, he challenged and motivated them beyond their expectations: "He could tear your solution to a problem all apart and yet leave you on top of the world and ready to begin again with complete confidence in yourself," Gertrude Elizabeth Sawyer (1895–1996) recalled, fifty-seven years after receiving her certificate in architecture.[42] Indeed, Sawyer's "complete confidence" morphed into her prosperous independent practice in Washington, DC, where she designed the boldly curved Junior League Building (1935; now owned by the Hungarian government) at 2001 Massachusetts Avenue NW, as well as the multibuilding Colonial Revival estate of Jefferson Patterson in St. Leonard, Maryland; she collaborated on the latter project with another alumna, Rose Ishbel Greely (1887–1969), a prominent landscape architect.[43]

Greely and Sawyer were at the Cambridge School together before graduating in 1919 and 1922, respectively, just as the school was finding its way.[44] Since there was no formal precedent for an all-women's architecture school, the curricula and related activities were structured to reflect current debates and evolving ideas about what a relevant professional practice could be in the interwar period. Significantly, the pedagogy was based not on a specific model (though Frost and Pond were obviously versed in Harvard's) but rather on the requirements and interests of the students themselves. Since the Cambridge School was the only professional school in the United States to unite architecture and landscape architecture under a single faculty, the students worked cooperatively rather than in isolation and in competition with one another, as was more typical of the pervasive Beaux-Arts–oriented programs.[45] That they learned to visualize their projects comprehensively gave them a broader perspective that could enhance their prospects for practice.[46]

The school broadened its pedagogical approach in 1933 after Albert Evans Simonson, an instructor of history and design, visited the Cranbrook Academy of Art in Bloomfield Hills, Michigan, to observe its postgraduate program.[47] Simonson innovated something similar at the Cambridge School with an all-encompassing, five-month design problem in which about fifty students, under the guidance of some twelve faculty members, participated. Based on a 150-acre site in nearby Middlesex Fells, the hypothetical community they designed—with civic, business, educational, recreational, and housing units—concluded with a 1/20 scale model ten feet square. Published in *Pencil Points*, the award-winning practicum encouraged greater appreciation for three-dimensional studies, for authentic sites and realistic projects, and for collaboration between disciplines.[48]

This emphasis on collaboration had lasting impact on students, as demonstrated by the architect alumna Louise Leland (1902–56), who graduated from the Cambridge School in 1933, and her professional and personal partner, Ann Bruce Haldeman (1903–93), a landscape architect who graduated two years later. Explaining the function of their seven-year "collaborative adventure" to fellow alumnae, Leland wrote, "If we know 'our public,' it is unnecessary to introduce the idea of collaboration between the professions of architecture and landscape architecture, for the School itself has taught the need and demonstrated the worth of this in professional training, in a way that none can surpass."[49] The students enthusiastically embraced the school's view of architecture and landscape as complementary fields, to the extent that some doubled up on their specializations. For instance, after obtaining her master's degree in landscape architecture, Katherine "Katy" Charlotte Gibbs (Ericsson; 1907–91) was granted a scholarship to complete the architecture curriculum. In 1938, she declared: "Lest it should appear that I am wavering in loyalty to my first love, landscape architecture, or wanting in devotion to my new love, architecture, may I say that I believe they are both different aspects of the same professions. The two are one, inseparable, and the one is infinitely greater than either of its parts."[50] The Cambridge School's guiding principles were in certain respects more experimental than at other schools, primarily because they arose from the requirements of contemporary practice rather than established traditions. Hence, the input of the students themselves increasingly carried weight as they forthrightly demonstrated through their ideas, conviction, and courage that they were capable of more extensive challenges than simple domestic problems, which was the school's original mandate.[51] Frost's reminiscence reflects the steadfast determination of the women: "They drove us. They, not we, proposed steps to make the training more effective. ... and then [they] came back with more demands."[52] Consequently, by the late 1930s, the school's mission was expanded to provide more thorough technical training to prepare students to meet "the many and varied needs of civilization."[53]

Likewise vital to the success of the school was the faculty's role in supporting the professional standing of the women. They helped students navigate the restrictions they faced, especially the tendency to marginalize women as house designers and interior decorators. When the discipline of interior decoration was added as a third curriculum in 1935–36, it was elevated to "interior architecture"—as it had been called since 1923 at the University of Minnesota—and only made available to those with advanced standing.[54] Recognizing that the field presented reasonable opportunities for women, the school advanced it as a profession closely associated with architecture, just as it had done with landscape architecture.[55]

While the Cambridge School aimed to provide students with the skills and knowledge to establish themselves in the competitive work arena, at the same time, it drew attention to successful women practitioners in- and outside the school. For example, in 1931, it organized the exhibition *Houses and Gardens Designed by Women* to show their achievements so that "even the most skeptical observer" would realize that women were capable of professional success. Targeted at garden clubs, galleries, and schools, the exhibition highlighted the work of women architects from diverse educational backgrounds: from Elisabeth Coit (MIT, 1919) and Georgina Pope Yeatman (MIT, 1925) to Verna Cook Salomonsky (École Spéciale d'Architecture, 1911–23; Columbia University, 1912–13) and Elisabeth von Knobelsdorff von Tippelskirch (Technische Universität Charlottenburg, 1911), and even Theodate Pope Riddle who lacked a degree.[56] Their presence would have argued against the familiar opinion that careers for women were incompatible with marriage, an alleged stumbling block to professional development. In fact, in 1932, the Cambridge School was able to report that 83 percent of its graduates were active in professional work as independent practitioners, office draftspersons, educators, or writers; of those married, 60 percent continued to work.[57] Given that two years earlier, only about 24 percent of women nationally were employed outside the home, women at the Cambridge School were ahead of the trend for women to obtain paid work rather than to labor for free at home.[58]

The Cambridge School and Harvard

The two architecture schools in Harvard Square, each oriented toward a single gender up to 1942, became important centers for the advancement of Modernism. Although their histories intertwined, each was distinct: at the Cambridge School, students developed their knowledge of modern architecture by examining important examples at home and abroad and then formulated distinctive versions of it in school or professional projects; at Harvard, administrators and faculty, including prominent European émigrés, implemented an influential approach to architectural education that overturned the historicism that had prevailed there.

When Joseph Hudnut took over as dean of the School of Architecture at Harvard in 1935 and began modernizing the Beaux-Arts curriculum, he also visually updated Robinson Hall (1904) by McKim, Mead & White, where the school was housed. As the architectural historian Jill Pearlman notes, "He destroyed the plaster casts of antique building fragments and sculpture that had filled the interior and stripped the walls of Old Master copies and Beaux-Arts envois, repainting them a pristine modernist white."[59]

Hudnut joined the Cambridge School's board of trustees just three months after he began his deanship at Harvard, as his predecessor, George Harold Edgell, had done. The connection between the two schools was further reinforced by the roles that at least twenty-five Harvard educators held at the Cambridge School at various times as instructors, lecturers, or critics.[60] Among the most distinguished was Charles Wilson Killam, who taught his "tough and rough" construction courses intermittently for fourteen years; these were reputed to be among the most rigorous in the country (Edward Durell Stone failed his course at Harvard, causing him to transfer).[61] G. (George) Holmes Perkins led design studios and taught history, which he compiled into the widely read *Comparative Outline of Architectural History* (1935).[62] Charles Augustus Whittemore taught Mechanical Plant of Buildings (heating, ventilating, plumbing, and electrical installation), a course he had been teaching at Harvard since 1924. Walter Francis Bogner, whose first engagement at the Cambridge School in 1931 was as an architecture design critic, later taught Professional Practice (contracts and specifications) after he created that course at Harvard.[63]

The two schools inevitably shared similar points of view about the professional development of students, especially after 1936, when Hudnut reorganized the curriculum and designated the preparatory courses (basic sciences, history, drawing, and theory) as undergraduate courses in the department of Architectural Sciences at Harvard College; this allowed the newly created GSD to concentrate on preparing students for professional competency. The Cambridge School did not have this option, but it did create an architecture curriculum that in many respects paralleled that at Harvard. As an example, in 1940 the schools had comparable requirements for history, graphics, construction, mechanical equipment, and professional practice, and both addressed such contemporary challenges as multiunit housing, social and economic implications of design, and new construction technologies and materials. The two diverged in that Harvard put more emphasis on city planning and the Cambridge School on landscape planning. While the introductory design courses were almost identical at both, intermediate and advanced design at Harvard was taught in three rotating studios, each headed by a different professor so that students could benefit from varied perspectives. Harvard also insisted on three months of practical experience in the building industry; such opportunities were not readily available to women, and so the Cambridge School did not require apprenticeships. On the other hand, the Cambridge School mandated five terms of freehand drawing while Harvard had none at the graduate level. In retrospect, the acquisition of this fundamental skill most likely worked to the advantage of women since they sometimes had no other choice but to seek employment in allied design fields.

A major concern of modernist architects internationally was in housing. While MIT did not put multiunit housing on its agenda until 1934–35 (as part of a course in city planning) and Harvard not until 1938, when Hudnut hired Martin Wagner (at the behest of Gropius) as assistant professor of regional planning, it was a focus earlier at the Cambridge School, illustrated by the subjects of some of the theses.[64] Frost considered the Cambridge School as the first educational institution "to give serious thought to the problem … of housing, individually and collectively."[65] Though he said it was only by "chance" that the Cambridge School focused on housing in advance of other architecture schools, it is possible that his interest evolved from his own experience in World War I, when he served in the federal emergency war housing program.[66] In addition, in 1927, Albert Bemis, the industrial entrepreneur engaged in low-cost housing research, began his nine-year tenure as a trustee at the Cambridge School, where his daughter Faith was still enrolled. The interest of Bemis in housing may have influenced the curriculum, given that he was later recognized by Frost for providing "judgement, foresight, and generosity" to the institution.[67]

A New Modern Wing at the Cambridge School: An Inspiration

Such broadminded modern thinking was put into play at the Cambridge School as early as 1928, when it vacated its small, shabby space filled with dust, dirt, and noise on Boylston Street and moved to an early nineteenth-century wood-frame house on Church Street. The building was purchased by Faith Bemis, who also worked on the remodeling of the house and the design of a two-story brick wing at the southwest corner of the original building (fig. 1.4).[68] The new flat-roofed, rectangular mass (seventy feet long by twenty-eight feet wide)—united with the older house by means of the ochre-colored paint chosen by Raymond—is dominated on the north side by industrial steel sash windows, painted black in order to read as large spans piercing the planar walls.[69] Inside, white ceilings and pale gray walls contributed to a sense of openness in the upper and lower drafting rooms, each fifty feet long by twenty feet wide.[70]

The design process itself modeled the collaborative relationships the school promoted: Frost and Raymond were the architects of record, Bemis created the plan and blueprints and was on site for supervision along with Laura May Cox (1896–1986), an alumna who had been working for Frost and Raymond since 1925 (and would be the only associate in Raymond's own firm); and Edith V. Cochran (1886–1989), an alumna instructor at the school and a frequent collaborator with Raymond, did the landscape plan.[71] The drafting room addition made an impression on students even ten years after it was completed: an example is Elizabeth-Ann Campbell's sketch of the junction of the new and the old buildings as well as of the metal-framed awning windows (fig. 1.5). Her watercolor of one of the two drafting rooms similarly focuses on the windows and piers between them as well as the penetrating light (fig. 1.6).

Frost reported in the first issue of the *Cambridge School Alumnae Bulletin* that some had feared the modern tendencies of the new wing could dwarf or even clash with the Colonial tradition of the older house, but the need for an economical and functional space allowed the group to utilize modern concepts way before the school itself embraced modern design.[72] It would be another year before Modernism was mentioned again in the *Bulletin*, when a tri-city promotional lecture tour on "modern tendencies" in garden design, architecture, and decoration was organized by the Cambridge School.[73] Much was made of the "unusual and interesting" upcoming lectures, but because Modernism was so novel in the United States, no one at the school had much practical experience of it other than the design and construction of the new wing.

Thus, the lecture tour was led by Fletcher Steele, a respected Harvard-trained landscape architect and school trustee, and Jean-Jacques Haffner, a French émigré architect and Prix-de-Rome winner who was a professor of architecture at Harvard and a visiting instructor at the Cambridge School.[74] Given his own Beaux-Arts education, Haffner was surprisingly amenable to Modernism; in one lecture, he paid homage to the functionalism of Europeans Le Corbusier, Auguste Perret, Robert Mallet-Stevens, J.J.P. Oud, Bruno Taut, and Walter Gropius, and even more to the American work of Frank Lloyd Wright, whom Haffner considered a superior architect, writer, engineer, and poet. Acknowledging how powerful the modern movement was becoming, Haffner nonetheless expressed his apprehension about its rapid pace of development in methods and materials, preferring instead to rely on tradition.[75]

During this critical introductory period, modern concepts were not easily grasped: in April 1930, the *Bulletin* declared, "The School apparently has 'gone modern'—whatever that may mean."[76] The lack of understanding about the principles underlying the modern movement is reflected in two thesis titles in 1931: "An Island Estate—Modern" and "A Modern Estate."[77] In both, it is as if the word *Modern* were tacked on to suggest a superficial style rather than an entirely new way of planning and building. It was too early for students or faculty to fully comprehend that modern architecture was not merely a transitory, stylistic mode of building, but a program for an enduring, straightforward approach to design with positive social implications.

1.4. Cambridge School drafting wing, 1928. *Cambridge School Alumnae Bulletin* 1, no. 1 (December 1928), *Cambridge School Records, Smith College Archives.*

1.5. Elizabeth-Ann Campbell, student sketch of the Cambridge School's modern wing, pencil on paper, April 1935. *Private collection.*

1.6. Elizabeth-Ann Campbell, watercolor of one of the Cambridge School's drafting rooms, c. 1936. *Private collection.*

1.7. Walter and Ise Frank Gropius house, 68 Baker Bridge Road, Lincoln, Massachusetts, 1938. *HABS.*

The faculty, many trained in the classical tradition, initially seemed unsettled, based on a comment Frost made in 1931 to Paul J. Sachs, the director of Harvard's Fogg Museum and a Cambridge School trustee, saying that he was "disgust[ed] at the somewhat hysterical attitude" toward the modern.[78] Frost came around, however, likely with the encouragement of his enthusiastic students and later his younger colleagues, I.M. Pei and Philip Johnson, reportedly frequent guests at his home.[79] In fact, Hudnut recognized Frost as the most sympathetic to modern architecture of the senior faculty at Harvard.[80] Frost's shift in attitude toward Modernism, and assumedly the school's as well, is substantiated in a lecture he gave in 1936, when he advised Smith College alumnae "to look favorably on the prefabricated house, upon the steel, the concrete, the glass materials of the 1930s, and away from the 'archeological' and 'academic.'"[81] If Frost's advocacy of prefabrication, modern materials, and anti-historicism indicates the broader acceptance of Modernism at the Cambridge School, it is notable that his transition to Modernism occurred soon after Hudnut began making changes at Harvard and in advance of Gropius's arrival there.

Of course, a few adhered unremittingly to academic historicism. Among them was the Cambridge School alumna Constance "Connie" Mumford Warren (1903–87). Even though she built near the modern houses designed by Walter Gropius and Marcel Breuer as well as Walter Bogner in what is now known as the Woods End Road Historic District in Lincoln, Massachusetts, the house (1938) that she designed for John F. Loud and his wife Mary at 1 Woods End Road is modeled on a Federal house (c. 1800) in Yarmouth, Massachusetts (fig. 1.7).[82] More often, however, established historical and archaeological dogma gave way at the Cambridge School to modern pedagogy. Consequently, the faculty's stance progressed from initial skepticism—when Modernism was simply viewed as a "phase similar to the Gothic or the Tudor"—to an embrace of its programmatic underpinning.[83]

Despite the polarized attitudes regarding traditional and contemporary design, the Cambridge School constituency felt a responsibility to engage with Modernism. One architecture graduate, Anita Rathbun (Bucknell; 1902–83), then working for Cross and Cross (1909–42), a New York firm recognized for its Colonial Revival work, advised readers of the *Bulletin*, "Whether one likes the Modern style or not … we must be attune[d] to all new phases both here and abroad." She explained that at first she had found it hard to believe that Modernism was prophetic of future domestic architecture, but ever since Buckminster Fuller's Dymaxion House had been brought to Harvard (in 1929, by the Harvard Society of Contemporary Art), she had become more open to modern experiments—even collapsible houses whose positions were to be controlled by radio.[84] Her naive but enthusiastic impression was echoed by the nine students who, at Bogner's prodding, entered a *Pencil Points* competition in 1930. For five weeks, each was engrossed in designing a modern eight-room house, and though none of their submissions placed, the one by Marion Spelman Walker (Bailey; 1908–82) was published (fig. 1.8).[85] Consisting of stiff, unadorned volumetric masses inspired by European models, the tallest with a roof terrace, the design illustrates a widespread ambiguity at the time about how best to articulate Modernism in small house design.

The wide range of student work by Katharine "Kay" Frances Wilson (Rahn; 1915–92) into the 1940s documents her understanding of Modernism, exemplified by her drawings for a school, civic buildings, houses, and community developments as well as parks, gardens, and even a badminton court.[86] As a "rare" and "brilliant" student with a remarkably fine capacity for design and construction, she was considered "especially good professional material." After Wilson attained a master's degree in landscape architecture on scholarship, she received (encouraged by the faculty) a bachelor's degree in architecture. During that time, she also did site planning for both permanent and demountable defense housing in the office of the landscape architect H. (Harry) Clay Primrose in Baltimore.[87] Though Wilson settled in landscape design in Rochester, New York, and eventually was named a fellow of the American Society of Landscape Architects, her design ability in modern architecture is evident in her numerous landscape plans, which often featured exquisite small buildings or colorful building elevations (fig. 1.9; see fig. 7.1).

The Cambridge School's engagement with Modernism is further evidenced by the projects submitted by both students and alumnae to a promotional booklet produced in 1936.[88] One of the boldest interpretations of early modern design is a drawing for a boat club on the Charles River by Martha Louise Meyer (Gates; 1914–2004; fig. 1.10), a student who also did an exchange at the Architectural Association School of Architecture in London between 1935 and 1936, where she was likely exposed to the inspirational work of such modernists as Berthold Lubetkin.[89] Like his zoo designs, her building articulates its purpose in that the severe two-story horizontal span with portholes, outdoor decks, a deckhouse, and a curved bow resembles a modern ship. Another notable design in the booklet is the five-bedroom house by Elizabeth Wiley Dunlap (1894–1985) in Knoxville (fig. 1.11). Although she described her "very livable" house as only "mildly modernistic," the exterior exudes the influence of European Modernism in its severe rectangularity, flat roof, stark-white stucco walls, and dramatic siting.[90] Wiley Dunlap studied landscape architecture at the Cambridge School in the early 1920s, well before Modernism was established there, but because of her comprehensive training, as she explained, she was able to work her way into the architecture field and open herself up to contemporary trends.[91]

Such women architects had been taught to be versatile so they could accommodate the stylistic predilections of their clients, recognizing that they would rarely, if ever, have the opportunity to develop a specific aesthetic with a readily identifiable modern signature. Take Victorine du Pont Homsey, for example, who established a successful joint practice in 1935 with her husband, Samuel in Wilmington, Delaware (fig. 1.12). The subjects of her two Cambridge School theses are frankly traditional—"Restoration of Nomini Hall: An Old Virginia Manor" (1925) for her certificate in architecture, and "A Southern Colonial Estate" (1935) for her master's in architecture.[92] That she was also accomplished at modern design was affirmed in 1945 by Howard Myers, editor of *Architectural Forum*, who wrote that they were among the few Americans capable of producing modern architecture.[93] Their modern designs, such as the Henry Belin Roberston house (1936) in Centreville, Delaware, staunchly adhering to the austere, functional European aesthetic, were widely published (fig. 1.13).[94] But because their architecture firm was located in Delaware, where du Pont Homsey had deep-seated connections through her family, they were required to be equally proficient in historical design, demonstrated by the two alternative schemes for a branch library: while similar in form and dimension, one is decidedly modern, with unadorned walls and a flat roof and the other is Colonial Revival, with red brick walls, a gabled roof, and a pilastered entrance (fig. 1.14).

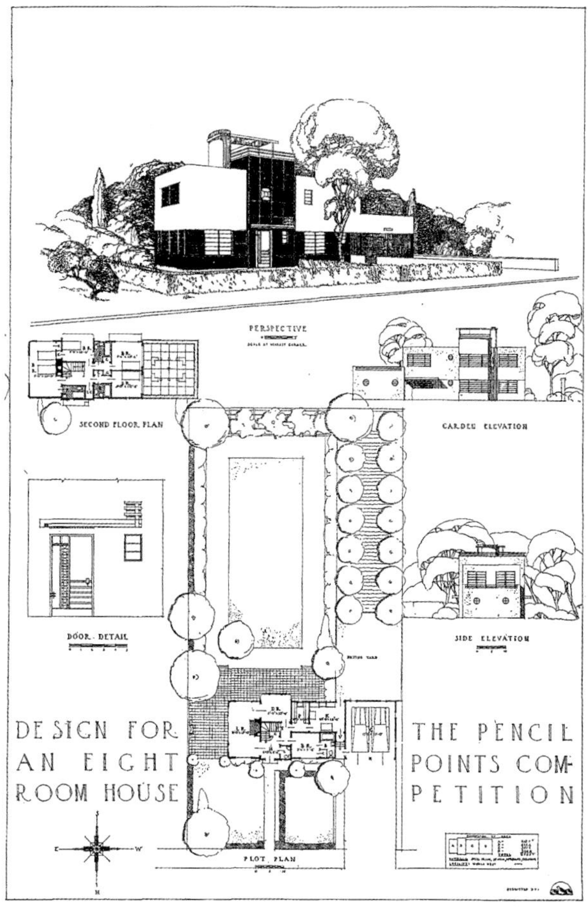

1.8. Marion Spelman Walker, "Design for an Eight-Room House," *Pencil Points* 11, no. 9 (September 1930): 731.

1.9. Katharine Wilson, student drawing, c. 1939. *Katharine Wilson Rahn Papers, Division of Rare and Manuscript Collections, Cornell University Library.*

The Cambridge School's modern agenda was buttressed by numerous co- or extracurricular events for its entire constituency, demonstrated in 1935 by a summer study tour of modern architecture in Western Europe—an idea that, remarkably, the school had considered since 1931.[95] The tour gave some fourteen students the opportunity to observe how the new architecture, especially of reinforced concrete, effectively articulated the social, political, and economic changes of the period. "The whole point of the trip," Elizabeth "Betsy" Pillsbury Pringle (1912–97) emphatically recalled, "was to see the International School, the actual buildings."[96] Even though not all appreciated Le Corbusier's functionalism, the group of neophyte modernists did make an impression—at least in Sweden, where the *Svenska Dagbladet* observed that "these girls were not ordinary pleasure-seeking 'Misses.'"[97]

One of the most public displays of the Cambridge School's commitment to modern architecture and its intended role in resolving social issues was the presentation at its twenty-fifth anniversary in 1940 of the circulating exhibition *Houses and Housing*, a smaller, traveling version of the housing section that the houser Catherine "Casey" Krouse Bauer (Wurster; 1905–64) organized for the exhibition *Art in Our Time* at MoMA, in 1939.[98] The celebration also presented an opportunity to boast about the faculty's newly completed modern projects. Recent houses by Bogner and Perkins were shown in photographs along with Perkins's drawings of his submission to the acclaimed Smithsonian Gallery of Art competition (1939). Also featured were drawings by the Harvard-trained architect Marc Peter Jr., the school's instructor of interior architecture, and his professional partner Hugh Asher Stubbins Jr., a visiting critic at the Cambridge School who had not yet joined Harvard's faculty. Other examples included a model and plan of the *Gardens on Parade* horticultural exhibition at the 1939

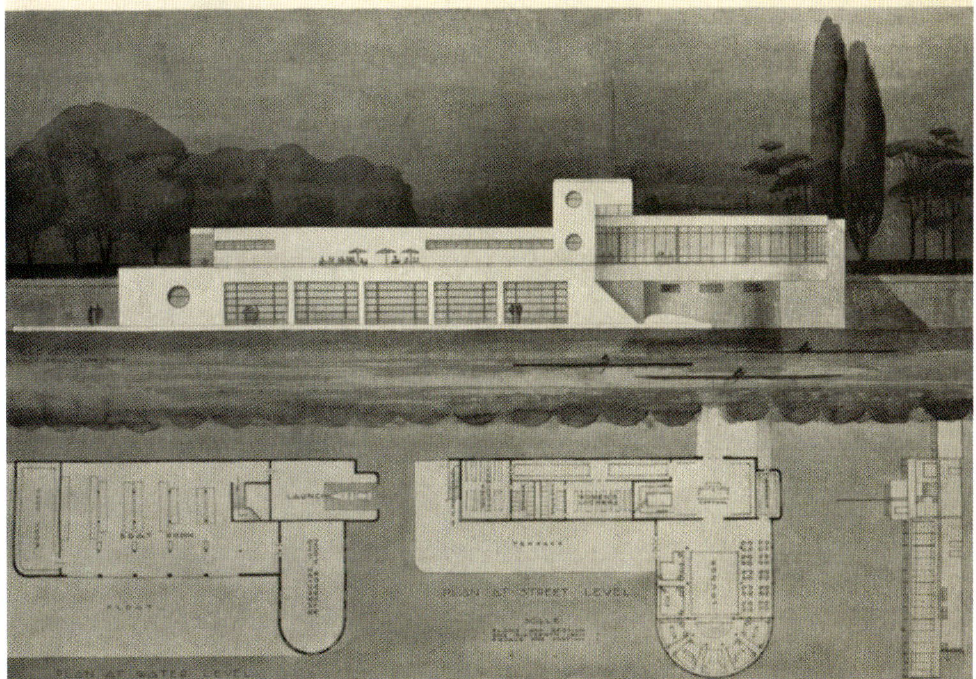

1.10. Martha Louise Meyer, drawing of a boat club, pictured in a Cambridge School booklet, 1937. *Cambridge School Records.*

1.11. House designed by Elizabeth Wiley Dunlap for her family, 1079 Scenic Drive, Knoxville, Tennessee, 1933. *Calvin M. McClung Historical Collection, Knox County Public Library.*

1.12. Samuel Eldon Homsey (1904–94) and Victorine du Pont Homsey, 1940.

1.13. Homsey Architects, House of Henry Belin Robertson (now demolished), Centreville, Delaware, 1936.

New York World's Fair by J. Carol Fulkerson, an instructor of landscape history and design at the school since 1932.[99] Of the two lectures presented, one was by the second wife of Gropius, Ilse "Ise" Frank Gropius (1897–1983), perhaps at the prompting of Eleanor Raymond and Ethel Power, who had met her in Berlin in 1930 (fig. 1.15). Such opportunities were rare for Frank Gropius who, although now viewed by some as her husband's "creative partner," is better known for scaffolding him—as archivist, interpreter, editor, and promoter, as well as manager of his home office and hostess to a great many visitors.[100]

Another avenue that allowed the Cambridge School to advance Modernism was through social and educational events. Committed to informing alumnae about current trends and developments, the school hosted a conference week in 1941, consisting of lectures, tours, and a sketch problem in Lincoln, a town that by 1942 was recognized as a "Focal Point for the Invasion of N.E. by Modern Architecture."[101] The biggest draw for alumnae, however, were the annual weekends, each with an exhibition of student and / or alumnae work, a regional study tour, challenging study problems (with awards), and, best of all, an animated dinner—a tradition since 1921, replete with speeches and toasts by alumnae, faculty, and a who's who of the architecture community. Correlating with the interest in Modernism, the 1937 weekend was organized around the schedule of Gropius, who had recently arrived from England and was soon to be recognized as the "architectural coup" at Harvard.[102] A student named Deborah Champion Gilbert (1914–2003) was so taken by the Gropiuses at the tea in their honor that she wrote a twelve-verse poem titled "A Light 'Snark' for Gropius," modeled on "The Hunting of the Snark" by Lewis Carroll (1876). The fifth and tenth verses illuminate the obvious veneration for the senior architect:

The honored guests they all praised to the skies—
Such carriage, such ease, and such grace!
Such dignity too! One could see He was wise,
And could gaze all the day at Her face! [...]
Then the guests all confessed, with affectionate looks
More eloquent even than tears,
They had learned in ten minutes far more than all books
Would have taught them in seventy years.[103]

The author's emphasis on Gropius as a lone heroic male figure of Modernism at once shows how the Cambridge School students and alumnae recognized his international importance and anticipated his American legacy.

Though Gropius did not become a design critic at the Cambridge School, as Frost had hoped, the following year he did give a talk at the annual alumnae dinner, making it "the best ever," according to Elizabeth-Ann Campbell.[104] His citation from *Walden, or, Life in the Woods* (1854) by Henry David Thoreau—if one builds from within, an unconscious truthfulness follows—was all the more

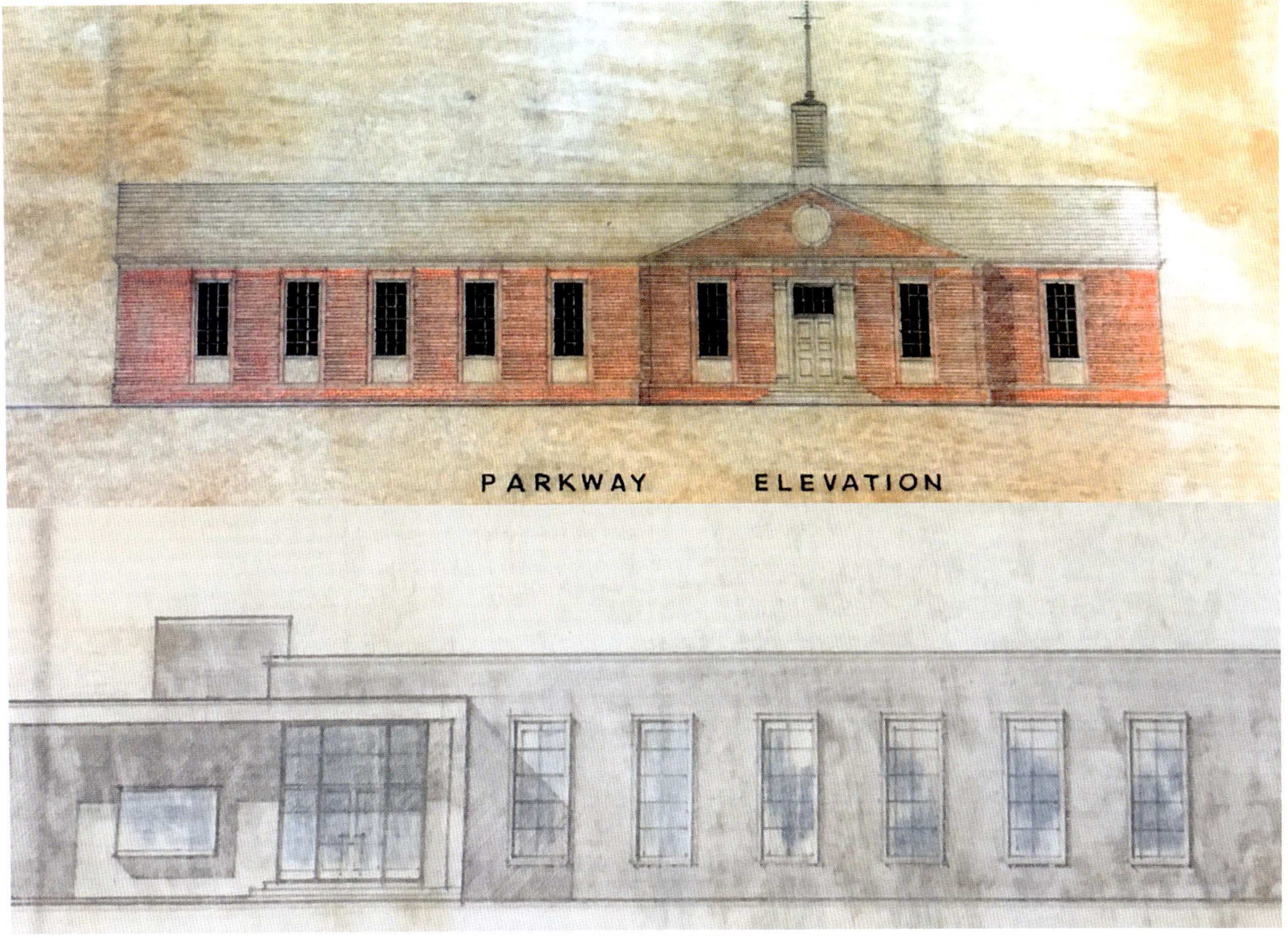

1.14. Alternative projects by the Homseys for a branch library in Wilmington, Delaware, c. 1950. *Homsey Architects Collection, Hagley Library.*

moving because the Transcendentalist's famous retreat was not far from the school and quite close to where Gropius would settle.[105] The women were gratified that Gropius appreciated the ability of women architects to give form to new ways of living while also satisfying economic demands. They failed, however, to observe that his comment, as reported in the *Boston Globe* the next day—that more women were needed to solve architecture's "blackest spot," meaning the improperly designed house—reinforced their professional relegation to the domestic sphere.[106]

The 1937 and 1938 study tours were equally focused on Modernism and included a visit to a house on a small lot in Cambridge, which would soon garner extensive publicity for its reconciliation of Modernism with vernacular traditions. The architect Edward Durell Stone, in association with the owner's architect son Albert "Carl" Koch Jr., achieved privacy without diminishing a sense of spaciousness by extending the rooms through walls of glass into a garden entirely enclosed by a rubble wall, anticipating the house and garden plan that Johnson would build for himself nearby as his Harvard thesis project.[107]

The women also toured two equally significant commissions by Eleanor Raymond. The Theodore Miller house (1936) at 105 Juniper Road in Belmont, a stripped neoclassical volume oriented toward a fine, distant city view (as Raymond was fond of doing), is conventional in plan and elevation but modern in compactness and efficiency. At Amelia Peabody's forty-acre Mill Farm in Dover they saw a group of functional wood structures with an almost abstract flatness that Raymond loosely derived from Federal Neoclassicism. They also observed her ambitiously modern sculpture studio consisting of austere geometric cinder-cement block forms covered with stucco and penetrated by steel casement windows

1.15. Walter and Ise Frank Gropius in their Lincoln home, c. 1942. *Historic New England.*

and glass blocks (see figs. 1.6, 2.2). The overall industrial feeling was assuaged inside by the dramatically curved staircase leading to the second-floor apartment with an Art Deco overmantel with hunting scenes made of copper and aluminum (see fig. 3.10).[108]

Providing access to these two sites was one of many ways Raymond backed the school. In her own practice, Raymond offered both long- and short-term opportunities to at least eight students and graduates; more than once she signed off on plans by Sarah Pillsbury.[109] As a student and under Raymond's direction, Pillsbury designed a redwood-clad summer house for her parents. Modern in its functionalism but inspired by New England barns, the house conformed to Raymond's aesthetic interests. The collaboration left a lasting mark on Pillsbury, who recalled years later, "It was when Modernism was still new, fresh thought, and Raymond stood for everything I respected, and continue to." Raymond shared the sentiment, informing Pillsbury in 1984 that the house testified to the kind of relationship they had while producing the plans.[110]

Other architects associated with the Cambridge School followed Raymond's example and helped to launch women students in professional practice. Perkins, for instance, took students or recent graduates into his office, including Ann Halle, who in 1939 worked on a design for a two-story, open-plan house (unbuilt) in Cleveland for her sister Jane Murphy Halle Crile and her husband Dr. George Crile Jr. (fig. 1.16). Given that Gropius and Breuer completed their adjacent houses in Lincoln in 1938 and 1939, respectively, Halle's effort was cutting edge. She composed the house of flat-roofed rectangular blocks on which windows are run to the corners to emphasize that the structure was to be of thin, most likely steel, elements, rather than traditional masonry or stick construction. Also notable in 1938 was Frances Whitmore Hartwell's (Burgess; 1910–97) partnership with Perkins on an architectural entry for the art center at Wheaton College, for which they received an honorable mention in the competition of 254 entries; Hartwell was one of only five women to participate.[111]

The architect Walter Harrington Kilham Jr., a long-term trustee of the school, also gave work opportunities to women in his partnership with Ides Van der Gracht in New York, between 1937 and 1942. Stockard made models there for three years before she entered (at their encouragement) the Cambridge School. Her unsurpassed academic record is demonstrated by a school project for a housing development (completed in collaboration with two other students) at Fresh Pond in Belmont, which is organized with several cul-de-sacs branching off a main artery (figs. 1.17, 1.18).[112] Situated for privacy and access to the surrounding green space, the houses exhibit such modern features as slanted cantilevered roofs, upper-level terraces, thin lally columns, and non-supporting walls punctuated by horizontal corner windows. Alice Morgan Carson (Hiscock; 1908–2001) also worked in the office, designing a modern house for a client at the prestigious Jupiter Island Club in Hobe Sound, Florida. Dominated outside by cypress-latticework to deflect the sun (a feature Gropius used on his own house), the house was featured in *Architectural Record* in 1941 (fig. 1.19).[113]

In addition to her other roles at the school, Raymond was its sole representative on the board of trustees at Smith College. In 1942, reflecting the overall attitude of the alumnae, she protested the decision to terminate the Cambridge School after Harvard gave up its single-sex policy and allowed women into the GSD on the same terms as men. Given that Harvard made the commitment to women *only* as a wartime emergency measure, Raymond was "loath" to see the school completely shut

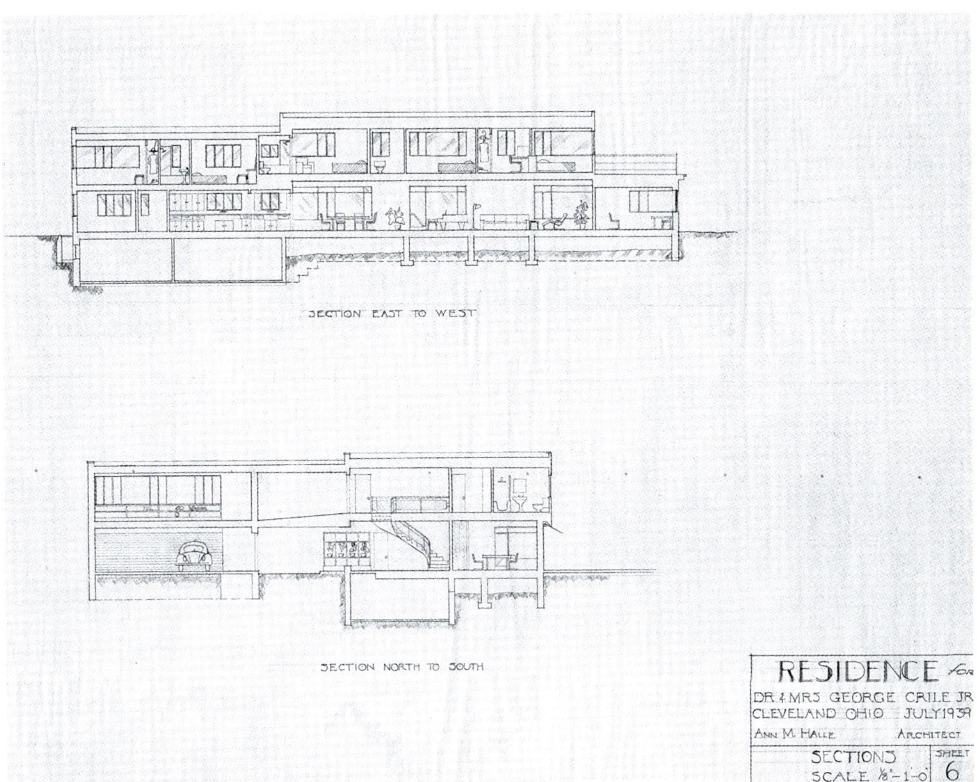

1.16. Ann Halle, designs for a Cleveland house (unbuilt) for Jane Halle Crile and Dr. George Crile Jr., July 1939. *Private collection.*

down. She was concerned about postwar opportunities for the architectural training of women who were "just coming into their own."[114]

A Milestone at Harvard

It has been assumed that few women chose to continue their studies at Harvard's GSD after the Cambridge School closed in the spring of 1942. Yet, fifteen of the twenty-three women (out of fifty students) enrolled in Harvard's summer school that year were from the Cambridge School.[115] That fall, a third of the sixty-two enrollees at Harvard's GSD had transferred from the Cambridge School.[116] Seven of the women were offered scholarships, as reported in the papers, which announced women would be allowed to study design at Harvard.[117] Even more, in the summer and fall design studios, eight women exceeded expectations by receiving commendations.[118]

Several factors led to the fluid transition of women from the Cambridge School (as well as from other schools) to Harvard. First, through the years, Harvard kept a sharp eye on academic developments at the Cambridge School. In fact, in 1935, Frost had counseled the president, James Bryant Conant, on how to establish a collaborative, interdisciplinary approach like the one at the Cambridge School. The exchange may have influenced Hudnut's formulation a year later of the graduate school as a single school with three departments (architecture, landscape architecture, and regional planning) under one dean.[119] The section in Harvard's course catalog of 1944–45 entitled "Professional Collaboration in the Design School" is reminiscent of the long-standing traditions of the Cambridge School in that all GSD students participated in a first-year program based on shared processes and objectives.[120] Second, Harvard had entertained the idea of admitting women since at least 1938, but the existence of the Cambridge School made it possible to defer a decision and continue single-sex education.[121] When coeducation was put back on the table due to the sagging wartime enrollment (by December 1942, the GSD reportedly was losing about one man a week), Hudnut gave his full support. He recognized the ongoing prejudice against professional women but nonetheless believed that there were no reasons other than "convention and custom" that women could not work in architecture—especially because he had observed that the practical difficulties that presented "so grievous a handicap upon women as practitioners" were being removed.[122] Hudnut's advocacy never ceased: in 1951, he penned a two-part article about "The Architectress" for the *Journal of the American Institute of Architects* in which

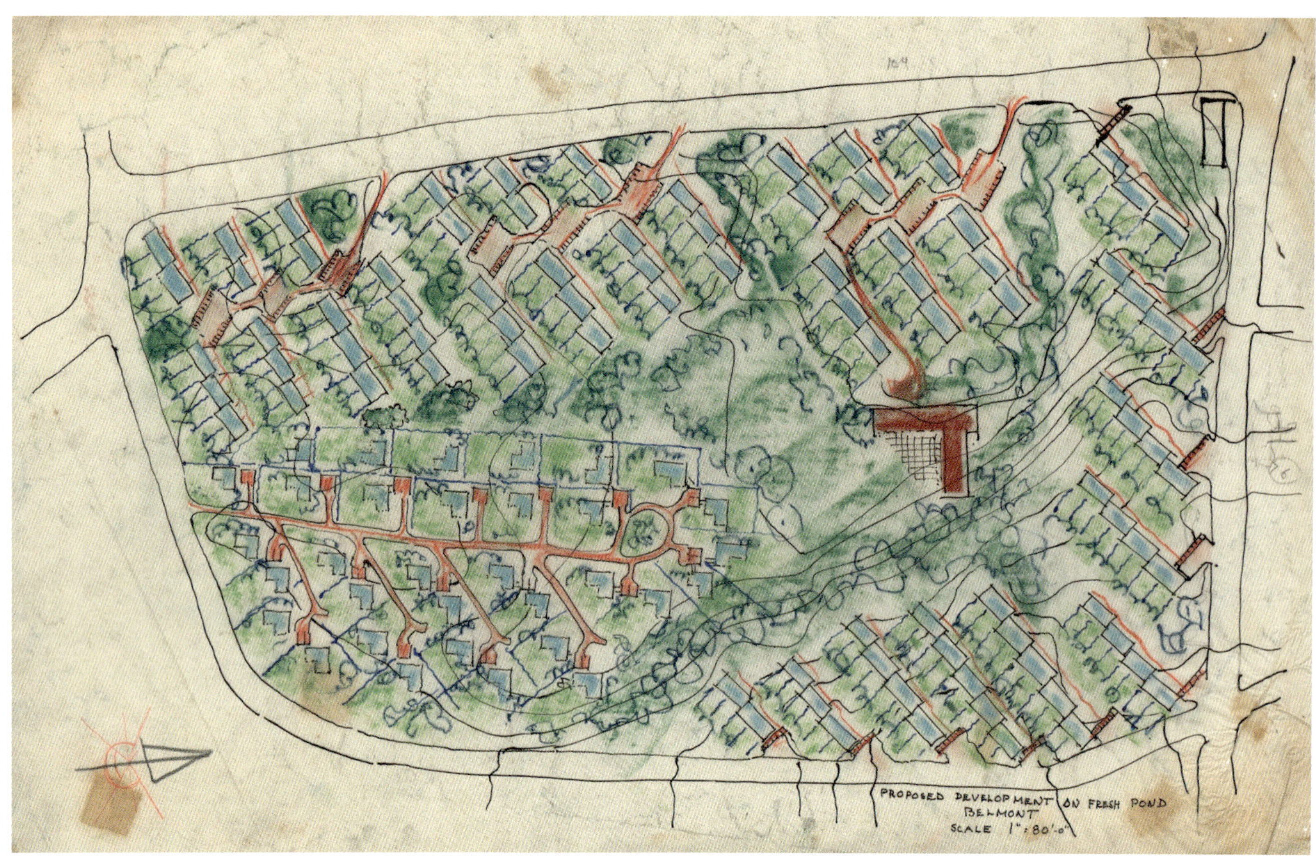

1.17. Suzanne Stockard with Marjorie Elizabeth Robbers (Elmquist; 1919–2008) and Jeannie "Patty" Patrie Allinson (1918–2006), collaborative student drawing of a development at Fresh Pond in Belmont, Massachusetts, 1942. *Private collection.*

1.18. Suzanne Stockard with Marjorie Robbers and Jeannie Allinson, collaborative student drawing for a development at Fresh Pond, February 17, 1942. *Private collection.*

1.19. Alice Morgan Carson with Van der Gracht and Kilham (associate architects), house (now demolished) for S. (Samuel) Robert Glassford (1874–1946), Jupiter Island Club, Hobe Sound, Florida, 1940. *Gottscho-Schleisner Collection, Prints and Photographs Division, Library of Congress.*

he described the characteristics that not only "qualify" but "entitle" women to join the profession.[123]

In addition, the students at both schools had already participated together in social and academic pursuits. In 1939, for example, the women codesigned the setting for that year's Fête Charette, Harvard's annual costume ball modeled on the Fête d'École in Paris. More importantly, some women engaged that year in the discussion group organized by students at Harvard and MIT to contemplate issues primarily related to housing, but also to employment, curricula, and societal roles of architects. The conversations led to the liberal-minded, quarterly publication *Task: A Magazine of the Younger Generation of Architecture*. One of the two women on the initial editorial board in 1941 attended the Cambridge School—Eunice Engle Hull (Campbell; Purdy; 1917–2007), someone whom Frost considered thoroughly intelligent and progressive, though sometimes radical in her point of view.[124]

More significantly, the two schools had already begun to integrate academically. In the summer of 1938,

1.20. Party at the Graduate School of Design, Harvard University, c. 1942. *Center front*: Anne Tyng dancing; *back left*: Walter Gropius (in white pants); *back center*: Jean League (with dancing partner near column). *Jean League Newton Personal Archive, Harvard University Archives, Pusey Library.*

landscape architecture students at the Cambridge School were required to take an eight-week course of "inestimable value" on plant materials at Harvard under Stephen Francis Hamblin, an assistant professor of horticulture.[125] Subsequently, in 1940 and 1941, the two schools jointly orchestrated a six-week summer session at Harvard, under Bogner's direction, in which eight to ten courses in planning, design, mathematics, history, horticulture, and statics were taught by ten to twelve faculty members (including Josef Albers in 1941 as a guest instructor of the Theory and Practice of Design). Of the seventy-eight summer school students in 1940, twenty-seven (or 35 percent) were women, half from the Cambridge School; of the ninety-one students in 1941, forty-two (or 46 percent) were women, about twenty from the Cambridge School.[126] The summer schools, then, were instrumental in earning women the right to participate equally with men at Harvard by providing an opportunity for them to demonstrate their talent and their eagerness to collaborate; at the same time, the educators were able to evaluate the women's academic performance and experience coeducation in architecture.

The amusing sketch in figure 1.5 by Franziska Porges, a Cambridge School architecture student who transitioned to Harvard, captures the elation on the part of the women as well as the resistance of their male counterparts. Retrospectively, Anne Tyng concurred, writing, "I like to think the influx of women raised the standards, although we were frequently and rather ominously told we would lower them."[127] Drawings for a postwar housing problem in Breuer's studio, completed in 1943 by Jean Bodman and Margaret "Peggy" Chase Greene (Watson; 1920–92), suggest that the women stuck together when collaboration was required. Similarly, a letter from Jean League (Newton; 1919–2000) describes how she and Jean McMullen (Coolidge; May; 1919–2008) got bogged down for a weekend "charetting" on a sketch for a restaurant and nightclub for a hotel problem—the most complicated she had ever seen.[128] Socially, it was different; during the "lively period of the Bauhaus renaissance" as Anne Tyng referred to the Harvard years of 1942–44, the two sexes comingled with fervor in the homes of Gropius, Breuer, and Johnson, as well as at parties at Harvard (fig. 1.20). Many weddings followed.

Academically, the women at Harvard 's GSD were on a par with their male peers; their withdrawal rate was low and their enthusiasm palpable. After the war, however, the representation of women in architecture at Harvard diminished: whereas in 1944 they accounted for 55 percent of the architecture students, from 1947 to 1949 women only represented between 9 and 14 percent in the entire graduate school.[129] Fortunately, Harvard did not renege on its commitment to women, as some feared it would. Despite diminished attendance levels, equal education for women in architecture was firmly entrenched.

The postgraduation accomplishments of the women who attended Harvard are comparable to those of women who only attended the Cambridge School. The obituaries of those from the first generation of women architects at Harvard, however, typically reference their education, indicating that regardless of their professional success, their greatest legacy is their role at Harvard—where they broke down gender barriers and demonstrated their capability. The admission of women into Harvard's GSD was a signal event in the ongoing movement for them to achieve parity with men in architectural education. However, as Raymond presciently noted, the resultant integration of men and women came at a cost that numerous Cambridge School women regretted: the loss of an institution dedicated exclusively to them. Nonetheless, the progressive single-sex school not only created an environment in which Modernism could be enthusiastically proposed and rigorously interrogated, but it also fostered the resilience and perseverance that its students—along with their female peers in coeducational schools—would need to call on as they confronted the sexist barriers in the profession.

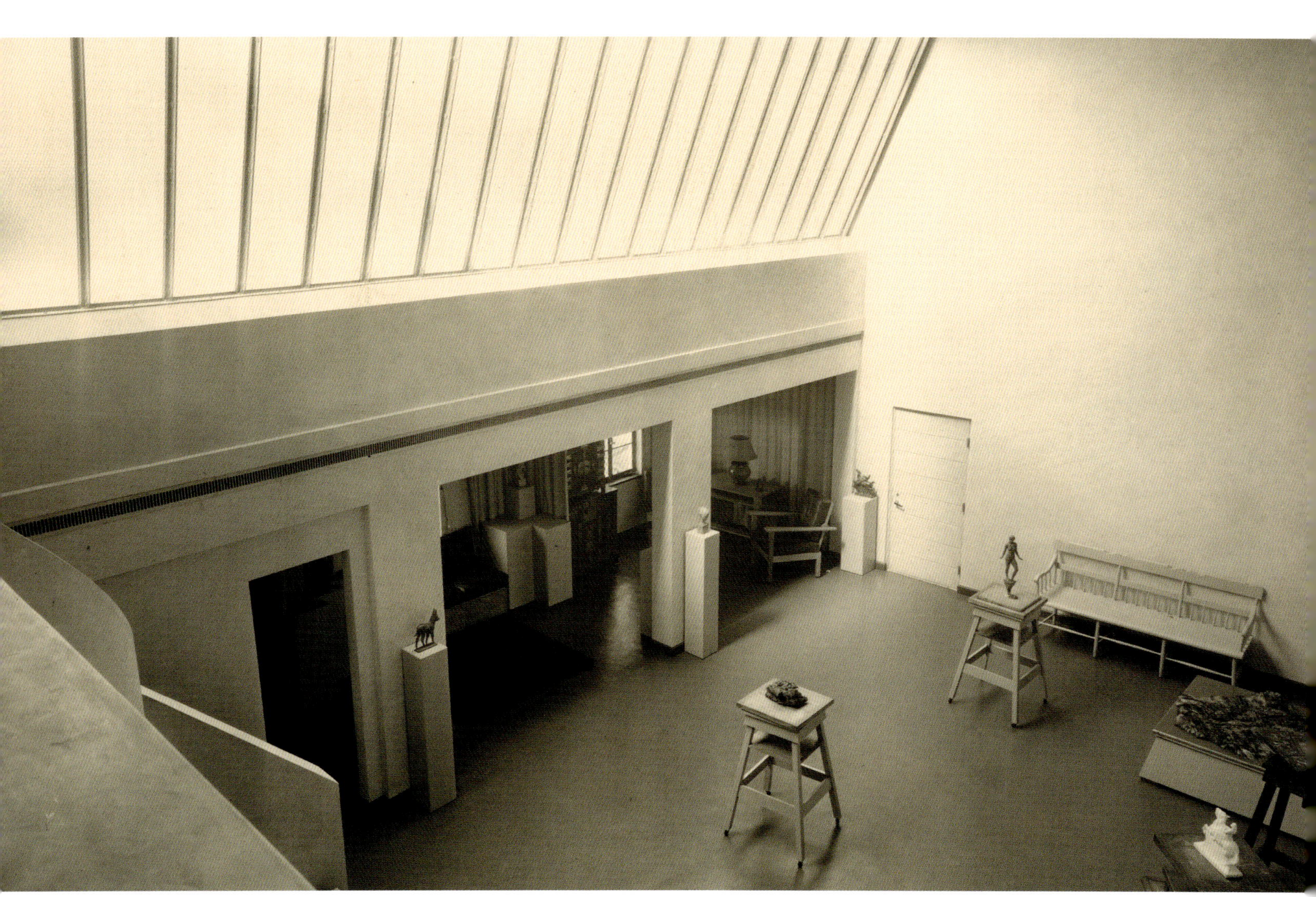

CHAPTER II

International Exchanges

INTERNATIONAL INFLUENCES WERE VITAL TO THE transformation of modern architecture in the United States, and in the 1930s such European émigré architects as Ludwig Mies van der Rohe, Walter Gropius, and Marcel Breuer inculcated young architects and patrons with their knowledge of European avant-garde architecture and displaced Beaux-Arts classicism in the school curricula. But as Jill Pearlman establishes in *Inventing American Modernism*, these former Bauhaus instructors were not alone in making some American architecture programs into purveyors of Modernism, since Joseph Hudnut too had a leading role in the formulation of a new humanistic Modernism in his role at Harvard.[1]

The evolving version of Modernism promulgated at Harvard bore some similarities to the one that women had already begun developing at the Cambridge School of Architecture and Landscape Architecture by the mid-1930s. Like their male counterparts, these women were conversant with contemporary developments in Europe and adapted them to the American context. They saw connections between Modernism and vernacular architecture in the United States—notably, in New England, the Mid-Atlantic, and the Southwest. They also took leading roles in popularizing this new American approach to design, and in addition to demonstrating the applicability of European models, advocated for both traditional and contemporary Mexican design.

The women's ideas about Modernism were brought to bear on many aspects of visual and material culture as they entered the architecture field in the United States in greater numbers between the 1930s and 1950s. As professionals, both foreign- and American-born women excelled at visualizing designs that responded to the requirements of the whole family, promoted regional cultural variations, and relied on sources from other parts of the world gleaned through travel, study, or work.

European and Vernacular Inspirations

Many women believed that architects of the modern movement shared with vernacular builders a commitment to such tenets as the use of simple geometric forms, avoidance of gratuitous decoration, direct expression of materials, and functional planning, even though the comparisons ignored the profound historical, cultural, and geographic differences between modernists and traditional makers. As Faith Bemis wrote in 1931 of the local vernaculars in Santa Fe, New Mexico: "The adobe houses have a unique style. Of course, the architecture has been influenced strongly by Mexico, but I believe it is much

Detail of figure 2.2. Eleanor Raymond's sculpture studio for Amelia Peabody, 1933.

simpler here and more primitive, and of course the Indian pueblo architecture is the real beginning of it all. It is a style as truly American as the Colonial and I think it is too bad it is not more widely realized. I think, however, that it soon will be, as there is a lot in it for the 'moderns.'"[2] As much as her characterization of the adobe architecture of the Southwest now seems patronizing, her statement illustrates several concepts that were common: a connection between Mexico and the American Southwest, a comparison of the architecture of the Anglo-European colonies of the Northeast with that of the indigenous peoples of the Southwest, and most important, the influence that vernacular inspirations would have on modern architecture.

The house that Eleanor Raymond designed in the early 1930s for her sister Rachel perfectly embodies the inspiration women derived from both traditional buildings and international Modernism, the latter showing the impact of her various sojourns in Europe, documented in the letters and diaries of Ethel Power (see figs. 1.1, 1.2, 3.6, 3.7).[3] Considered by many as the first modern house in New England, the Belmont house's startling geometric austerity calls to mind the work in France of Le Corbusier, Robert Mallet-Stevens, and André Lurçat, whose houses Raymond and Power visited in 1928 along with Rachel Raymond and her professional (and probably personal) partner Edith Maud Kingsbury (Tucker; 1884–1971). Together, the two couples interpreted what they saw abroad and then promoted their variation of Modernism in built form, well before Henry-Russell Hitchcock and Philip Johnson presented their ideas in 1932 at the International Style exhibition at the Museum of Modern Art (MoMA).

Raymond and Power's interest in European Modernism began in the winter of 1928 when they read aloud to each other Le Corbusier's manifesto *Vers une architecture* (1923) in translation.[4] Though they were somewhat wary, their interest was piqued by the "plain unadorned box-like concrete masses" illustrated in the book, and they organized a two-month tour later that spring to France, Germany, and the Netherlands with the objective of viewing "the best manifestation of the modern" instead of the historic architecture they had seen on previous trips abroad. Understandably, then, while they were enthusiastic about the contemporary work they viewed in the Pressa exhibition in Cologne, they did not warm to the "hard" and "ugly" yellow brick of Hendrik Petrus Berlage and the Amsterdam School, an earlier aesthetic derived from Expressionism, nor to the decorative arts referencing the Art Nouveau. They had a similar response to the art moderne, or Art Deco, which they had observed in 1925 at the Exposition internationale des arts décoratifs et industriels modernes in Paris. In 1928, they were more intent on assessing whether modern houses really were direct expressions of their plans and if, in turn, the plans articulated the specific needs of the inhabitants. That is, they were evaluating the vaunted functionalism of the modern home as it was pioneered in western Europe and promoted by Le Corbusier and others.

Near Paris, where they hunted down what seemed like every modern house, they were armed with a list of buildings and architects provided by Hitchcock, whose article "Six Modern European Houses" Power would publish the following September in *House Beautiful*.[5] They also carried with them a recent *New York Times* clipping about steel and concrete houses in France titled "Machine-Age for Ultra-Moderns" written by the young Vassar graduate Catherine Bauer before she established herself as an international housing expert.[6] According to one of Power's letters, the illustrations enabled the women to locate the house of Edmond Bomsel, completed in 1925 by André Lurçat (1894–1970) in Versailles. Though surprised by the bright blue exterior stucco walls, juxtaposed with a lone white bay at the top of the front facade, they were held rapt by the plan, especially the series of rooms above the garage and servants' rooms on the *premier étage* (fig. 2.1). The enfilade of three rooms—from east to west, the main bedroom, living room, and dining room—could be "thrown into one" by opening two sets of doors, while the dining room led further to a curved terrace on pilotis overlooking an asymmetrical garden. Such a house, they decided, resembled an industrially designed airplane or steamship. At the same time, however, it lacked the amenities to which they were accustomed in the United States.

In October 1930, Raymond and Power returned to Europe for six weeks to continue their survey of modern design. The couple was especially enthusiastic about the design of the Stockholmsutställningen (Stockholm Exhibition), headed by Erik Gunnar Asplund (whose office they also visited), consisting of modern buildings with facades of faded red or bright blue, making them "gorgeously gay." The curved Paradiset (Paradise) restaurant (now demolished) was "too jolly for words" with red, green, yellow, and blue awnings. Power repeatedly recorded the polychromy they observed, presaging its significance in Raymond's architecture. Other innovative buildings they visited, some not yet finished, included the department store De Bijenkorf (1930; now demolished) by Willem Marinus Dudok and the now iconic Van Nelle Factory (1925–31) by Brinkman and Van der Vlugt, both in Rotterdam, as well as Grundtvig's Church (1927–40) by Peder Vilhelm Jensen-Klint in Copenhagen.

In Germany, they dedicated an entire day to circling Berlin by car to look at block after block of contemporary *siedlungen*—apartments built by the city for working people. About the interiors, Power noted soaring ceilings, an abundance of glass, cheerful and colorful tiles, and wood walls, all immaculately kept, as well as exterior gardens, playgrounds, and porches or balconies, always with flowers. "We got a wonderful idea of the new building here … and there is so much of it," Power exclaimed.[7] Their tour may have been spurred by Elisabeth von Knobelsdorff von Tippelskirch, the tenacious *diplom-ingenieur* whose responsibility for designing large-scale housing during World War I was unprecedented for women.[8] Raymond and Power struck up a friendship with the German architect during the time she lived in Boston, between 1927 and 1938, when her husband served as the German consul general there, and she twice visited their summer home.[9]

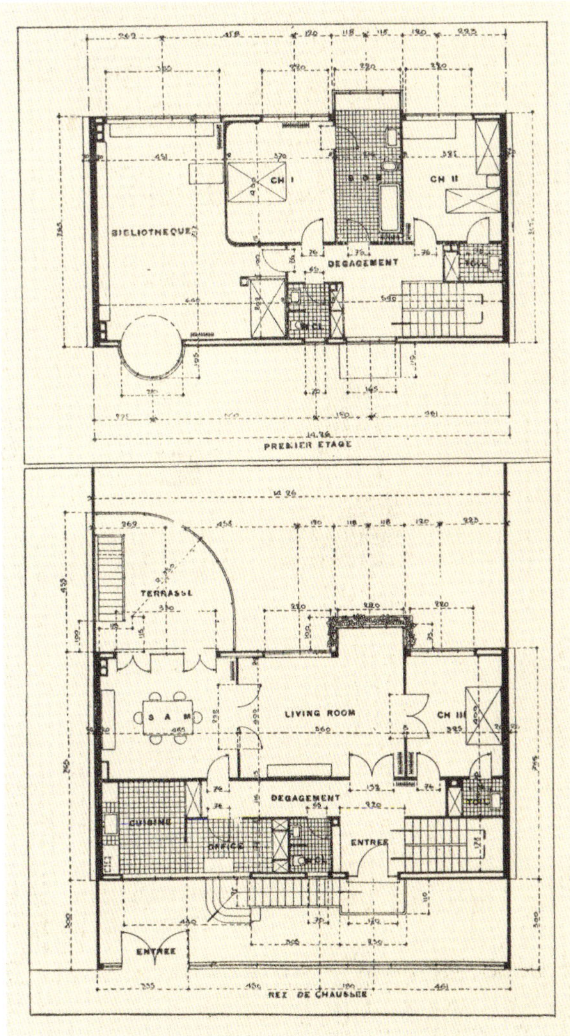

2.1. André Lurçat (1894–1970), plan of the *premier étage* of the Edmond Bomsel house, Versailles, France, 1925. *Architecture & Design—Image Archive, Architecture & Design Study Center Department, Museum of Modern Art.*

Internationalism in the United States

The impact of Raymond's study of modern architectural concepts formulated in Europe in the 1920s combined with her knowledge of traditional regional styles in the Northeast is demonstrated in the Rachel Raymond house (see figs. 1.1, 3.6).[10] Its exterior was of rough-sawn cedar board siding stained the soft gray-green color of the adjacent cedar trees, while the front door and railings echoed the vibrant red of the abundant barberry shrubs, thereby satisfying Raymond's predilection for "a touch of red" in her designs.[11] Along with these references to the local environment, Raymond added expansive windows, industrial steel-pipe railings, and voided spaces for terraces and porches, which were modeled on European examples. She relished her experiment in fusing these inspirations because it challenged Romantic period ideas about design: "Here, for the architect is the thrill of exploring new fields, and creating from scratch, which makes a high adventure instead of a Cook's Tour," she informed fellow Wellesley College alumnae.[12] Her in-depth "adventure" in American Modernism has attracted critical and scholarly attention for its successful integration of stylistic sources.[13]

The Rachel Raymond house illustrated the architect's ideas about Modernism some six years before Walter Gropius built his own house in Lincoln, Massachusetts, for which he has been erroneously credited with having single-handedly introduced Modernism to New England (see fig. 1.7). Financed by Helen Osborne Storrow (1864–1944), one of the very few female philanthropists to sponsor an avant-garde development, his house is acclaimed for its modern elements, some recalling his earlier buildings in Dessau. While recognizing the Gropius house for its steel-framed ribbon windows, glass block, cantilevered slabs on lally columns, and a metal spiral staircase, critics also have caricatured it as a "sugar cube," a metaphor referencing its geometric simplicity.[14] At the same time, the structure evidences his fascination with the New England vernacular,

Fig 2.2. Interior gallery in the Amelia Peabody sculpture studio, Dover, Massachusetts, 1933. *Raymond Collection, Historic New England.*

derived from the local climate, landscape, and culture.[15] The tongue-and-groove vertical boards of white-painted wood on the exterior had been a characteristic of Northeast architecture since the seventeenth century; the screened porch was also popular with New Englanders.[16] As Gropius once explained, he would never have built such a house in Europe, where conditions were radically different.[17]

The Rachel Raymond house was described in similar terms as a modern house adapted to its local context. In an article about the house that Edith Kingsbury wrote for *House Beautiful*, she explains that the architecture was experimental because it evolved from the requirement of a residence "with all possible beauty, comfort, and convenience for simple living, but as little as might be walling us in from the out-of-doors. The solution was a 'contemporary' house, with flat roofs for porches, large glass areas to let in sunlight, and views of the ever-changing trees and sky and birds." Accordingly, she says, the house grew out of its functional requirements—namely, comfort and convenience, features consistent with what European modernists emphasized in their house designs. Kingsbury, however, avoided the polemics advanced by Le Corbusier, whose argument that the house is a *machine à habiter* (machine for living) had compelled Raymond to look at modern architecture in France. Although Kingsbury acknowledged the house as a derivation of European models, she did not view it as a statement in opposition to traditional or historical designs, as European modernists did.[18] Kingsbury also did not see the house as the vision of Eleanor Raymond, its maker, but rather as "our experiment," referring principally to Rachel Raymond and herself, and assumedly, their coupling. Thus, the design decisions, she contends, responded only to their pragmatic requirements, including an attached stable for the horse (see figs. 1.1, 3.6).

In her romanticized conclusion, Kingsbury makes clear that the third partner in the "experiment" was the design itself, as she rhapsodizes, "And all the while, forming the background of our lives, there is our little house, so comfortable, so adequate to our desires, so much a partner in our experiment in the country."[19] Unlike male modernist architects, whose names are firmly attached to their work, Raymond's signature on the building, erased by another woman designer no less, anticipated the eclipse of the house as the first example of Modernism in New England.

The studio that Raymond built for Amelia Peabody on her farm in Dover reveals a more rewarding collaboration (fig. 2.2; see figs. 1.6, 3.10). The relationship between architect and client could have begun at the Cambridge School, where Peabody was reportedly a student sometime before 1929, after which she became a trustee alongside Raymond. By the time her studio was completed in 1933, Peabody had already been showing her sculpture in public, for instance in the exhibition at the Guild of Boston Artists in 1932 on Newbury Street.[20] Most of her work was conservative, consisting of figural groups and representations of animals; when shown in 1938 alongside that of Isamu Noguchi and other modernists in New York, Peabody said of her own work, "Mine looked trite."[21]

In the "Alumnae Notes" in the *Bulletin* the studio is extolled as the "most modern of the moderns."[22] The ground floor, comprised of a workshop, a double-height gallery to accommodate large sculptures, and a sitting area in an alcove, is connected by a partially curved staircase to a second-floor guest room with full bath. Raymond relied on her posse of designers to complete it: Rachel Raymond and Kingsbury for the interiors and Mary P. Cunningham (1888–1934), a Cambridge School landscape architect alumna and instructor.[23]

Similar to the Rachel Raymond house, European influence in the Peabody studio is everywhere, for example, in the glass block windows, an iconic feature of Modernism, as well as in the stucco facade, originally painted blue (reminiscent of Lurçat's Bomsel house) with jade green railings and doors.[24] Inside, greenish-gray walls provided a neutral backdrop to the bright-blue linoleum flooring

2.3. Henry John Stahlhut (1908–after 1949), cover of *House Beautiful* 72, no. 3 (September 1932).

and accents of pomegranate-red on the light fixtures, steel window framing, and a sitting room door. The steel beam at the center of the gallery ceiling, which supports the block and tackle, was also red, reminiscent of the red structural column in the library of the Bomsel house. Also recalling the Versailles house is the sitting area that could be divided into three spaces by curtains.

Whereas Raymond did not hesitate to imbue her work with her knowledge of European Modernism, Power, by contrast, cautiously instilled her magazine with its concepts and examples. Even though she was aware of the advantages of modern design, Power knew that the readers of *House Beautiful* (numbering as many as 106,000) were less inclined to experiment with progressive ideas. She acknowledged their apprehension, reassuring them in 1928 that Modernism was "not going to displace the delight of the old."[25] Consequently, when the German-born émigré Alfred "Seppel" Clauss approached her in 1931 to publish photographs of his small apartment in Sunnyside, Queens, which he furnished with the tubular steel furniture he had designed, Power responded that the pictures would be "labelled as extreme" by her average reader, and she could only publish such material "very infrequently."[26] Nonetheless, as she intermittently covered Modernism in *House Beautiful*, Power identified its principles, shared opposing viewpoints, and illustrated a wide variety of designs.[27] Even though she thought the discussion over Modernism was fledgling and confusion about the meaning of the word was rampant, in December 1928, the magazine's Home Builders' Service Bureau—managed by Esther Lucile Kilton (1896–1983) a Cambridge School alumna—offered for sale house plans that fused European and American details, and in September 1932, an award-winning cover of the magazine illustrated a hybrid modern house (fig. 2.3).[28] Her interest in educating her readers intensified so that by 1934 Power was presenting them with "Talking Points On

Modernism"; she understood that widespread acceptance would be a gradual process and she coaxed her readers with finesse and patience.[29]

Discovering Modernism

While Raymond and Power discovered European Modernism as professionals in their prime, younger generations of women undergraduates embraced it but developed their own ideas about the movement based on their firsthand experiences or evaluations of the work of its acknowledged leaders. In many cases, their education in elite women's colleges made them informed viewers of contemporary art and architecture. An example is Elizabeth Bauer, whose letters to her older sister, Catherine, document her early interest in modern architecture. During the spring semester of her senior year (1931–32) at Vassar College and under the attentive eye of Agnes Marion Rindge (Claflin; 1900–1977), an art professor with robust MoMA connections, Elizabeth Bauer agitated for a new calisthenium, or gymnasium, derived from a modern functional plan with light, air, and large, open spaces instead of the proposed historical scheme by the firm of Frederick R. Allen and Charles Collens. As the school's architecture consultant, the Allen and Collens firm had already erected twelve buildings on campus, some reminiscent of the English homestead of the founder, Matthew Vassar.[30] In one of three pieces submitted to the school newspaper, she criticized the proposed "pretty, picturesque, or 'cute'" group of structures with the "sham rustic coating of 'an English farm manor'" and instead proposed a flat-roofed, steel-framed structure with large panes of glass and a light-colored brick wall to complement nearby buildings.[31] Perhaps with the aid of her sister, who also protested the proposed building in *Arts Weekly*, Elizabeth Bauer won the confidence of 72 percent of the students, who voted for the architects to submit plans using modern principles.[32] The campus activism propelled her interest not only in modern architecture but also in educating others about its benefits, which presaged her curatorial role at MoMA.

At the time, Elizabeth Bauer was already exploring ways to pursue a career in modern architecture. Her initial plan was to spend her junior year studying in Berlin under Mies van der Rohe, director of the Bauhaus between 1930 and 1933. She was working through a connection with her Yale-trained architect friend Julian Hill Whittlesey, and he offered to introduce her to Knud Lönberg-Holm, a Danish émigré who was in touch with other European architects familiar with the school.[33] Owing to her father's financial losses from buying stocks on margin, however, she could not afford to go to Europe as her sister did in 1926–27. Instead, after she graduated, Elizabeth Bauer signed on as a charter apprentice in the newly formed fellowship of Frank Lloyd Wright at Taliesin, his home and studio in Spring Green, Wisconsin. During her four-month residency, beginning in October 1932, she gained practical knowledge from a learn-by-doing approach, but complained that the on-site "ceaseless ditchdigging" made her hands calloused, feet permanently frozen, back bent, and head bowed. She enjoyed learning about Wright's technically exciting wood and stone constructions, but it was "painful," she said, not to have much opportunity to draw with a pencil.[34] In hindsight, she would better appreciate her experience at Taliesin and, in fact, would convalesce there when in 1948 she separated from her Swiss architect husband, Rudolf Jacob Mock.[35]

Though the couple had fled to Mexico for three months in early 1933, Bauer Mock's dream of living in Europe had apparently not subsided and after marrying later that year they relocated to Basel, Switzerland, where they resided until 1937. The newlyweds settled on Tüllingerstrasse, in the city's only modern flat-roofed apartment building (fig. 2.4). Their dedication to modern design is referenced in her description of the space as "a chaste little orgy in natural wood, steel pipes, and Jenaer Glas" with neutral-colored raw-silk curtains, six Thonet chairs with black frames and natural cane seating, a linoleum-covered wood buffet, and a low tri-footed table in black and chromium with a round wooden top.[36] The other place they lived, in 1935–37, was what she called "the handsome and rather famous" apartment house at Zossenweg 3, designed by her husband with Otto Heinrich Seen. Its two-story glass-walled living room opening onto a terrace was so uncompromisingly modern that it was featured in MoMA's exhibition and catalog *Art in Our Time* (1939).[37]

While in Basel, Bauer Mock studied between 1933 and 1936 at the Gewerbeschul, where she had a "swell time" learning about construction from the architect and city planner Hans Benno Bernoulli. Finally able to satisfy her longing to draft, she informed her sister that she learned more in two weeks from Bernoulli than in the four months with Wright.[38] She also reported on her stimulating but nerve-racking art history courses with Georg

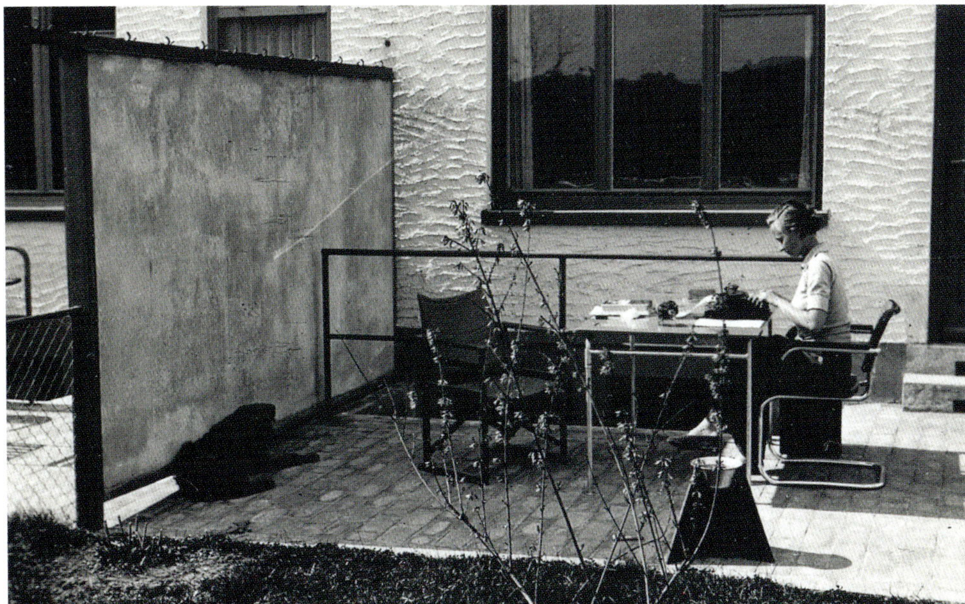

2.4. Photograph of Elizabeth Bauer Mock working at her apartment in Basel, Switzerland, c. 1935. *Private collection.*

Schmidt, an art critic and historian who at the time was also assistant to the director at the Gewerbemuseum. He opened her eyes to exhibition design in his lectures about and visit to *Das Kastenmöbel: Von der Einbaumtruhe bis zum Typenschran* (Cabinet Furniture: From the Built-in Chest to the Cabinet; 1934); she was intrigued by the artfully arranged progression of tools—their development, use, and influence on furniture design. Through Schmidt, she observed how efficiently art exhibitions can put across ideas and information.[39] Her blossoming interest in exhibition design was triggered again in 1936, when she visited the Triennale di Milano at which large photographs of Italian farmhouses were arranged to show the evolution of regional forms from climate conditions, materials, and purpose.[40] She had an understanding of art forms as manifestations of a cyclical series of overlapping economic and social conditions rather than as a succession of styles, an understanding that would have prepared her to appreciate the variations of modern architecture then being developed in the United States.[41]

All the while, Bauer Mock was able to travel throughout Western Europe to survey new developments in architecture. In Paris and its environs, she observed "a swelter of mangled modernism," the exceptions being those buildings by the obvious architects—Perret, Le Corbusier, and Lurçat. She recognized how influenced she was by Wright's principles but nonetheless appreciated Lurçat's work: she saw his Karl Marx School (1932) in Villejuif as "a triumph of functional architecture" because of its ideal hygienic and environmental conditions, and she also admired his Villa Seurat (1926).[42]

Having seen the buildings of Le Corbusier, whose office she also visited, Bauer Mock cited in her letters his Cité de Refuge (1933) for its exciting combinations of forms and his Pavilion Suisse (1931) at the Cité Internationale Universitaire de Paris as a "perfect example" of the pure "*creation de l'esprit*." In her opinion, it was vastly superior to the Collège Néerlandais (1938) nearby, the only building in France by Willem Dudok, a Dutch modernist.[43] These exposures prompted Bauer Mock to try her hand at writing reviews, and, with her sister's guidance, she wrote a feature on Le Corbusier's pavilion in the *American Magazine of Art* in January 1934, the first of many articles she would produce for this and other publications.[44]

Though she did not fulfill her initial aspiration to become an architect, Bauer Mock's international experience put her in a favorable position to obtain a job in the architecture department at MoMA upon her return to the United States. Her part-time work for John McAndrew led to a curatorial assignment there between 1943 and 1946. In that position, she made a significant contribution to the presentation and interpretation of European Modernism.

Progressive International Influence

Whereas Elizabeth Bauer abandoned her initial plan to study at the Bauhaus and instead found a place in Wright's new fellowship, just the opposite happened to her Vassar friend Nathalie Swan.[45] Though the two women had considered attending Taliesin at the same time, Swan's blue-blooded father, a banker, viewed the apprenticeship as "ridiculous radicalism" and promised to financially cut her off if she followed through with her intention.[46] The social connections of her prosperous New York family, however, enabled her to find her way to the Bauhaus. Though her practical experience in design was limited to only a stone garden at the Connecticut estate of her parents, she was determined to study under a modernist. Her cousin, James Hampden Robb, an architect trained at Columbia University, sent an inquiry on her behalf to a colleague in Berlin, who, in his reply, recommended Hans Poelzig at the Technische Hochschule as well as the studios of Walter Gropius and of Erich Mendelsohn. He also named Mies van der Rohe, the "extremely capable" director of the "big modern school in a famous building," which he had heard was "very inspiring."[47]

In the fall of 1932, Swan attended the Bauhaus in Dessau, but after the National Socialist government forced it to close, Mies van der Rohe moved the operations to Berlin, where more women studied architecture than previously.[48] Though she was only able to spend one semester at the Bauhaus (operating in Berlin as a private school), as one of twenty students, three of them Americans, she passed the first stage of training and assessment (based on Gropius's former six-month preliminary course) by developing a sense of material and space through mathematics, descriptive geometry, drawing, material science, color theory, and workshop participation.[49] In March 1933, Swan was invited to progress to the second of three stages, for which she chose construction and expansion over four other subjects (advertising, photography, weaving, and fine arts). She abruptly abandoned the program, however, and on April 25 boarded a ship in Bremen bound for New York, most likely because two weeks earlier the Bauhaus had been sacked and students temporarily detained by police. Nonetheless, Swan claimed to have "profited greatly" from being connected to what she considered "the best European culture," and she never lost sight of her Bauhaus training.[50]

While the Bauhaus was more technical under Mies van der Rohe's leadership, the school's longstanding multidisciplinary approach to art and design would have complemented Swan's educational background.[51] Between 1918 and 1926, she had attended the Lincoln School (1917–40), a Rockefeller-funded laboratory school under the aegis of Columbia's Teachers College in New York; the interactive curriculum was structured to relate classroom materials to everyday life, so in addition to core subjects she was also able to study drawing, painting, ceramics, woodworking, and carpentry. Her ensuing three years at the Chapin School in New York were less satisfying because there she did not feel she could exercise her artistic proclivity. Then, at Vassar, beginning in 1929, where her botany teacher noted how "distinctively clever and creative" she was, Swan was at least able to study sculpture and model making. Even so, she left after three years, convinced there was nothing more for her at the college.[52]

Despite her unsatisfactory collegiate experience, after she returned to the United States in the fall of 1933, Swan studied architecture at Columbia University, where she was awarded a bachelor's degree four years later.[53] Three years into the program, she enrolled in a new course called Laboratory of Design Correlation conceived by Frederick Kiesler, an Austro-Hungarian émigré and multidisciplinary artist, who was interested in integrating ideas and theories about emerging concepts and developments—from Constructivism to De Stijl, to Surrealism—in architecture, design, and theatrical staging. Writing in his *Architectural Record* monthly column, Kiesler explains his purpose in combining "such strange parts as painting, sculpture, industrial furnishings, and building structure into a heterogenous unity."[54] Kiesler undoubtedly relied on his prior experience in Berlin, between 1921 and 1926, when he came to appreciate theater as a place of dynamic interaction between object, environment, and human experience. He designed his course to give students the opportunity to contribute to "stage totality" in the student-performed operas at the Juilliard School in New York.[55] Swan's extant sketches for three operas include settings and costumes for *Joseph and His Brethren* (1936), the act 2 setting for *The Poisoned Kiss* (1937), and the setting and costumes for *The Abduction from the Seraglio* (1938).[56] Though the drawings are insipid, the photographs of the sparse, patently abstract setting in her first production, featured in *Architectural Record*, show ability at interpreting the assignment: to synthesize set and costume designs using simple, inexpensive materials; effective lighting projections; and harmonious, cohesive schemes (fig. 2.5). Visions of Joseph are projected onto a triangular-shaped flat, juxtaposed by a low, curved horizontal wall while groups of simple wooden posts sprouted from secondary forms. The experience must have been formative for Swan, as she entertained Kiesler and his wife, Stefanie Frischer, until at least 1955, both in New York and at her Millbrook retreat in upstate New York.

Swan nurtured relationships with such cultural elites, sometimes inside but more often outside her profession. She kept up with the famous textile artist and printmaker Annelise "Anni" Fleischmann Albers (1899–1994) whom she probably met at the Bauhaus before the artist and her husband Josef (whose work Swan owned) fled to Black Mountain College in North Carolina. Others included the pioneering modern artist Marcel Duchamp; Julien Levy, an influential dealer in avant-garde art; the Bauhaus artist Xanti Schawinsky; and another Columbia architecture graduate, Graham Erskin.[57] In a chronicle of an evening spent at Swan's home, Jean Stafford (1915–79), an established author (and a former wife of the poet Robert Lowell) named the guests: John Malcolm Brinnin, a poet; William Read, a critic and photographer as well as an authority on Gertrude Stein; and a young architect whose name she did not catch but who she quickly realized would soon be among the nation's most famous.[58]

Despite these notable connections, Swan never formally set up her own professional practice, instead preferring to work in firms managed by others.[59] She began in 1937 in the office of Harry P. Jaenike, an architect and engineer in New York, and two years later joined the firm founded in 1934 by John Barney Rodgers and William Turk Priestley, the latter of whom she knew at the Bauhaus in both Dessau and Berlin and then at Columbia. Her regard for Rodgers and Priestley is logical since they were full-blown modernists; by the time she joined them, their work had been hung in two MoMA exhibitions and Priestley had produced models, drawings, and photographs of the Stanley and Helen Resor house (1939; unbuilt) for Mies van der Rohe.[60] Swan followed Priestley to Chicago with her new (or soon-to-be) husband, Philip Rahv, the essayist, critic, and founding coeditor of the *Partisan Review* (1934–2008), an influential left-wing literary magazine.[61]

Living with the powerful New York intellectual came with its challenges: while Rahv was said to be gentle, humorous, and vulnerable, he was also "a massive, overpowering personality," according to Mary McCarthy, his ex-lover and one of Swan's former Vassar classmates.[62] Though an avowed modernist, Rahv lacked the aesthetic sensibility of some of his peers, among them Dwight Macdonald and Clement Greenberg, and so Swan Rahv was able to fortify him by drawing on her European experience—in addition to providing financial support, or at least an affluent lifestyle. The period of their marriage between 1941 and 1959 was his most effective professionally, but it ended in divorce. From time to time, he asked

STAGE DESIGN:
"JOSEPH AND HIS BRETHREN"
FREDERICK J. KIESLER, Architect

Ballet with music by Werner Josten. Produced for the first time February 1936, at the Juilliard School of Music, New York City.
Settings and costumes by students of the Department of Stagecraft of the Juilliard Foundation for architectural students of Columbia University, under the direction of Frederick J. Kiesler. (Designer: Miss N. Swan.)

2.5. Performance of *Joseph and His Brethren* at the Juilliard School, New York, showing costumes and sets designed by Nathalie Swan in "Stage Settings," *Architectural Record* 80, no. 3 (September 1936): 96.

Swan Rahv to remarry, but she refused, alleging that he would interfere with her architectural projects.[63] Despite his girlfriends and subsequent wives, she paid for his burial in 1973.[64]

During their marriage, there was not much of a divide between work and pleasure: friends tended to be *Partisan Review* authors, which included Kiesler, who contributed two essays.[65] Swan Rahv too benefited professionally from the literary relationships: she did work on the apartment of Lionel and Diana Trilling in the Morningside Heights neighborhood of New York and on Allen Tate's Princeton home, which earned her his deep admiration.[66] Though she made a few lasting friends, among them the poet Elizabeth Bishop, Swan Rahv remained outside the inner circle whose members used their literary success to belittle her, in their correspondence, memoirs, biographies, and even novels.[67] A letter from Lowell to Bishop in 1958 demonstrates one of many biting quips: "I have two mean verbs for an evening with the Rahvs: One *blows* and the other *sags*."[68] Unfortunately, Swan Rahv was remembered by them as a failed first wife, rather than as a modern architect with a prosperous professional career.

Her descendants have little knowledge of her production, though a résumé in the family's collection does document her work. When she was employed in 1956–57 at Shreve, Lamb & Harmon in New York (architects of the Empire State Building), she was promoted from a senior draftsperson to job captain, contributing to a small medical clinic; a church in Yonkers, New York; and the College Center at Crozier-Williams (1959) at Connecticut College in New London.[69] More can be gleaned from her independent work. Her most substantial client was the famed restaurateur Patricia Murphy (1905–79), whose chain of Candlelight restaurants in New York was well regarded for moderate prices and plain, good food. Swan Rahv may have met Murphy through her husband, a former ship's hull superintendent at what is now the Brooklyn Navy Yard, since during the war she had been a senior tracer in the hull division of Gibbs and Cox.[70] Between 1949 and 1954, she designed three restaurants for Murphy, with construction costs amounting to the equivalent in 2024 of nearly $9,000,000.[71] For the first, at 35 East 60th Street, a restaurant targeted to working-class women, she simply altered an existing interior; for the second, in Manhasset, she did a massive makeover of a golf clubhouse; and finally, in Yonkers, she designed an entirely new complex, capable of feeding eight hundred guests at once.

Unlike Swan Rahv, Murphy adored antique-looking things, especially French, but the two somehow managed to meld their disparate tastes. In the garden room, the most ambitious space in the Manhasset restaurant, Swan Rahv covered the walls, ceiling, and former stage in US Plywood Corporation's "wonderwood" panels made from thin sheets, or piles, of wood veneer glued together with the grain of each piece running perpendicular to the next (fig. 2.6). Plywood had been around for some time, but it was not until after World War II, when its lightness and strength had made it a choice material for airplanes, that it received wide interior application. Swan Rahv anchored the square and rectangular panels of gray-colored plywood with yellow battens—the color also used for the plastic chair upholstery and inside the polished-brass hoods over the lamps custom designed by Robert Kelly.[72]

It was in the Yonkers restaurant, however, that Swan Rahv most effectively revealed her modern sensibility and a fascination with new materials, both of which would have been encouraged at the Bauhaus. The rectilinear-shaped pavilion consisted of two floors of expansive windows set behind a wrought-iron railing in the style of New Orleans townhouses, and thin structural columns that emphasized its strict symmetrical order. Set on ten acres, the restaurant was fronted by a large reflecting pool and embellished with a profusion of gardens and parking for five hundred cars.[73] This composition reveals her competence at adapting to an established, or in this case emergent, aesthetic (called New Formalism by some), made popular by such second-generation modernists as Edward Durell Stone. It also displayed an element of kitsch—in its excessiveness, pretension, exoticism, historicism, and artifice.[74] Said to be a "glittering invitation" at night, the building functioned as a billboard, anticipating the Postmodern analysis of midcentury commercial architecture by Robert Venturi and Denise Scott Brown.[75] Though, as her later work shows, Swan Rahv remained indebted to the Bauhaus, her experience there also encouraged her openness to experimenting with new design concepts.

The Atelier of Le Corbusier

Jane Beach West (Clauss; 1907–2003) was equally inspired during her sojourn in Europe, where between 1931 and 1932 she worked in Le Corbusier's Paris atelier and explored the city's cultural riches with a group of international friends. Throughout her career, she attempted, with

2.6. Nathalie Swan Rahv, Garden Room, Candlelight Restaurant, Yonkers, New York, 1949–54. *Gottscho-Schleisner Collection.*

modest success, to build a practice based on European Modernism, even in regions where it was unknown. After obtaining a Bachelor of Science in interior decoration in 1929 at the University of Minnesota, West took a job designing simple room elevations and perspectives in the established decorating firm of the W. P. Nelson Company in Chicago. About a year later, West announced she had had enough of eclectic historicism (thereby showing an interest in Modernism) and that she was headed to Europe, whereupon the president of the company offered to connect her to his architect son, Paul Daniel Nelson, in Paris.[76] She recalled how anxious she felt when she introduced herself to the son, who had studied for six years at the École des Beaux-Arts and apprenticed in the architecture ateliers of Emmanuel Pontrémoli and of Auguste Perret. Though he had not been out of school for long, the young Nelson had already constructed a reinforced concrete framed house, following Le Corbusier's principles, for the American writer Alden Brooks at 80 Boulevard Arago and designed modern sets for the film *What a Widow!* (1930) starring Gloria Swanson.[77]

Through Nelson, West met Le Corbusier and, in an outcome that was beyond her wildest dreams, she landed in his famed atelier on an upper floor of a former Jesuit seminary at 35 rue de Sèvres. The long whitewashed gallery was lit by high windows and heated by coal; toward the back, it contained about a dozen drafting tables for unpaid assistants, not far from which was a small bay where the principal and his talented cousin and collaborator, the engineer Pierre Jeanneret, were situated. As West Clauss recalls in an unpublished autobiography, she initially familiarized herself with the Jeanneret drawing and photograph files she was required to organize, after which time she was more challenged by the foreign metric scale and making notes on drawings, one assumes in French.[78] In addition to working on the Armée du Salut (Salvation Army) Cité de Refuge (1933), she succeeded, in Le Corbusier's opinion, in her work on "*la totalité de détails*" for the Pavillon Suisse (1931–33).[79]

The mood of the firm was relaxed yet hardworking, with Le Corbusier generating design ideas and solutions at great speed.[80] West Clauss remembered being there when he famously sketched his proposed plan for the city of Algiers in North Africa, using coal soot from the dirty windows. She also participated in a two-day charette, making models for the Palace of the Soviets competition—the project on which Le Corbusier later said she proved herself as an architect. At the Champagne after-party, West made "real good friends" with some office colleagues, among them, Junzo "Saka" Sakakura of Tokyo, Japan; Gordon "Robert" Stephenson of Liverpool, England; and François (or František) Sammer of what was then Czechoslovakia.[81] Together with her women artist friends—Anne Heyneman (Kappel; 1909–68) of San Francisco and Agnessa "Sisi" Elizabeth Larsen (Sammer; Frazier; Sedgwick; 1910–2002) of Honolulu—she cooked "splendid meals" in her Montparnasse studio, danced at the *boîtes de nuit*, strolled along the Seine, and drank coffee on the Boulevard St. Michel on the Left Bank. These were enduring friendships, as demonstrated by the Christmas card she later sent to Sammer (fig. 2.14).[82]

Though her stint in Le Corbusier's atelier was, as she improvised to him in French, *là comme le plus excitant de ma vie* (the most exciting of my life), in August 1932 the Depression forced West back to the United States where, as she quickly realized, the drafting rooms were empty.[83] Despite six "kind" letters of recommendation from Le Corbusier—including one to Oskar Gregory Stonorov, who apparently offered her an unpaid position—she knew there was no chance of finding a paying job in her field.[84] Still, she pursued introductions to the cluster of modernists in the United States. A. Lawrence Kocher, who with Albert Frey had completed the Aluminaire house in 1931 (originally on Long Island but now in the Palm Springs Art Museum in California) sent her to the small, bare

2.7. Jane West looking at a brochure for the summer tour in Europe she had been asked to lead in 1933. *Private collection.*

office of Alfred Clauss, whom she would marry a little more than two years later.[85] Just as had happened in Paris, Clauss invited her to work in the evenings on competition charettes and to meet his architect colleagues, including Frey and Norman Nathanial Rice (both of whom also trained with Le Corbusier). She must have fit in comfortably with young modernists, given that in 1933 Catherine Bauer recruited her to take her place leading a summer tour of modern architecture in Europe sponsored by what is now the Association for Women in Architecture + Design, a national sorority for women architecture students (fig. 2.7). Even though the tour was canceled, her involvement foretold her interest in educating and promoting professional women.

While both Clausses worked for leading protagonists of the modern movement—she for Le Corbusier in Paris, 1931–32; he for George Schneider in Hamburg, 1926–28, and for Mies van der Rohe in Berlin, 1928–29—a comparison of their early careers illuminates the disparity in opportunity between the two sexes, even when they both came with recommendations from highly regarded mentors. In New York, West could only find part-time work drawing graphs for the American Institute of Physics and selling unpainted contemporary furniture at Macy's; Clauss, on the other hand, arrived with a job, overseeing the installation of the apartment Mies van der Rohe designed for Philip Johnson at 424 East 52nd Street. Through a network of modernists, Clauss also managed in 1930 to land a designer position in the New York office of William Edmond Lescaze, whose variety of projects include the groundbreaking Philadelphia Saving Fund Society bank and office building (1932) designed in collaboration with George Howe. There, Clauss met the architect George Daub, with whom he partnered in 1932–33 (with Johnson's support) and again in 1945–50.[86]

Even though a number of his projects never got off the drawing board, Clauss created a name for himself as the "guiding spirit" of the group of nine *Rejected Architects*, as their contemporary version of the Salon des Refusés exhibition was called, whose modern designs had been excluded by the Architectural League of New York from the "sluggish and smug" annual Architectural and Allied Arts Exposition.[87] Extensive favorable press coverage of the *Rejected Architects* show—in which Clauss, partnering with Daub, exhibited five designs—led to other exhibitions: the *Modern Architecture: International Exhibition* (1932) at MoMA and *Modern Architecture* (1933) at the New School for Social Research. The increasing divergence of the husband and wife's careers is vividly illustrated in their subsequent jobs in Chicago, where he was an associate designer responsible for making scale models of exhibition buildings under Louis Skidmore, chief of design in the Department of Works for the Century of Progress exhibition (1933), while she returned to her pre-Europe vocation as a designer of interiors for Mandel Brothers, a large department store then focused on producing bar, lounge, and nightclub interiors in anticipation of the repeal of Prohibition in December 1933. Though it is not known if she ever met Richard H. Mandel, a store partner, he would have been impressed with her experience in France, since at the time he was building a house for himself designed by Edward Durell Stone in Westchester County, with details quoted from Le Corbusier.[88]

In 1934, the couple married and settled briefly in Chattanooga, Tennessee, so that Clauss could begin an eleven-year tenure as head model maker of exhibits for the newly created Tennessee Valley Authority (TVA). His bride, deemed a "charming young intellectual," allegedly worked for the Electric Home and Farm Authority (1933–42), a New Deal agency charged with promoting and enhancing sales of large electrical appliances, which was located in the same building as the TVA.[89] After the couple relocated in 1935 to a more remote location in Knoxville, her career options further diminished.[90] Consequently, she volunteered at the National Park Service and supervised the fitting of vacation cabins erected in the Big Ridge and Norris recreational parks near the TVA reservoirs (figs. 2.8, 2.9). Her drawings of diverse types of bed frames, some with complex perspectives, suggest how frustrated West Clauss felt at only being able use her training for something as mundane as cabin beds to be constructed by unskilled workers.

Although the Depression and then the war sidetracked them, the two remained unswerving in their allegiance to Modernism, despite how unfamiliar it was in Tennessee. The article "Simple Changes by Expert Hands Make Old House Modern" in the *Knoxville News-Sentinel* focuses on their innovative interiors in an otherwise ordinary wood-framed house. They modernized the interior by stripping the wallpaper and painting the brick fireplace surround, the woodwork, and the floors black to set off the tubular steel furniture that Clauss had previously made for his apartment in New York.

Though West Clauss shared a drafting board with her husband at least from the time of their marriage, she was not acknowledged as his collaborator until 1940, when *Architectural Forum* featured the modern split-level house they had built for themselves on the wooded lot they purchased a year earlier.[91] Located in Little Switzerland—as the subdivision was named after its mountainous setting some six miles outside of Knoxville—the house was the first of five designed and built by the Clausses between 1939 and 1945 on a tract they developed and restricted to modern architecture (fig. 2.10).[92] The venture was unparalleled in the South and by 1955 was already "almost an 'avant-garde' legend in Knoxville architecture."[93]

The "crazy idea" for the development, as noted in the local newspaper, began when Clauss and three other TVA employees, along with a professor of French at the University of Tennessee, decided to build cooperatively to save on expenses.[94] The initial concept was for five or six families each to purchase lots (120 feet wide by 240 feet deep) on which their respective houses would be set back from the road at the top of a narrow ridge so as not to block views or intrude on the privacy of neighbors. Significantly, the group agreed that every house be of a certain quality, cost (no less than $5,000, about a quarter of the median value of a home in Tennessee at the time), and style ("modern" as opposed to "traditional" English, Georgian, Grecian, or Colonial).[95] While the restrictions prevailed, the group commitment did not, and three (of five) backed out, including David Stone Martin (later nationally recognized for his album covers) who was supposed to design the landscape as well.[96]

Consequently, only two houses, each a mirror image of the other, were initially erected—for the Clausses and

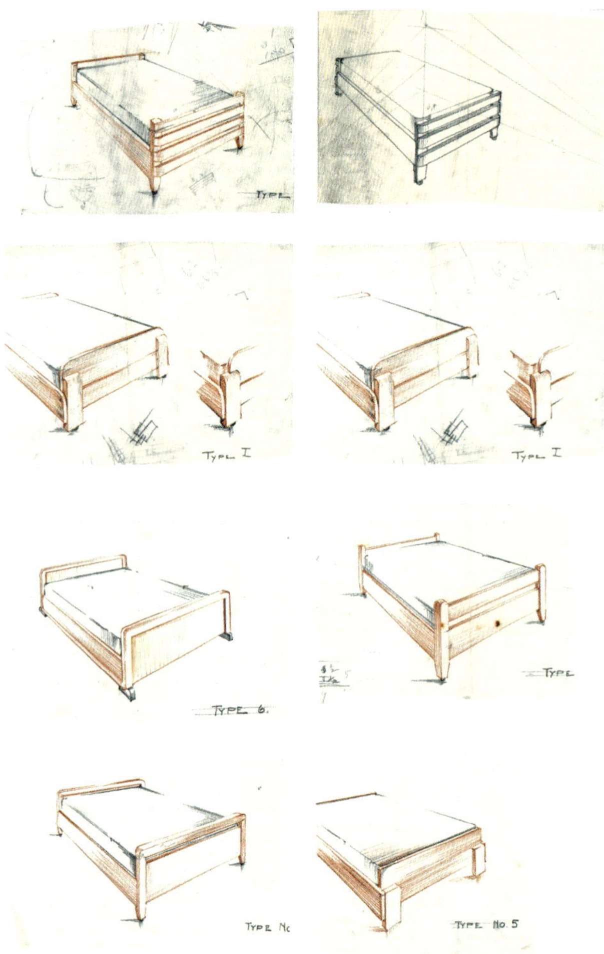

for Walton and Katherine Deniston Seymour, who lived there only until 1941. Located on the northern side of the road, the houses were tucked neatly into the slope. Supported on a concrete foundation, the rigid, flat-roofed, geometrical structures are faced with hollow clay tiles intersected with steel-framed, sliding, plate-glass windows to take advantage of the views of the Great Smoky Mountains on one side and the Cumberlands on the other. To the side of each front door is a panel of glass blocks, perhaps inspired by those on the house that William Lescaze built for himself in New York in 1933.[97] Inside, an entrance vestibule is midway between an upper level (with a living room opening onto a raised terrace as well as two bedrooms and a bath) and the lower, more functional level (with a kitchen opening onto a screened porch with a terrace above, utilities, and a dining / play area as well as one or two bedrooms and a bath).[98] The couple's intention to introduce modern design to Back Country inhabitants is apparent in the publicity they sought and obtained, as was their desire to cultivate a market for their work. In addition to receiving seventy-five friends and colleagues at an open house, an article appeared in the local paper, appropriately titled "Clausses Build Modern Home, Not as Their 'Dream House' But as Functionalism Proof and to Get Folks Used to It."[99] The house also attracted national attention: photographs and a model were included in the exhibition *Forty*

2.8. Jane West Clauss, sketches of bed frames for vacation cabins in a recreational park for the National Parks Service in Tennessee, 1935. *Jane West and Alfred Clauss Papers, Athenaeum of Philadelphia.*

2.9. Interior of a vacation cabin by Jane West Clauss, 1936. *Clauss Papers.*

2.10. House of Jane West Clauss and Alfred Clauss (1906–98), 429 Little Switzerland Drive, Knoxville, Tennessee, 1939. *Clauss Papers.*

Under Forty (1941), organized by the Architectural League of New York.[100] Given the publicity, the house was intended both as a calling card for the architects and as a means of establishing a reputation.

For the third structure the Clausses built in Little Switzerland, they gave up the "ultra-modern" look in favor of a rustic one—essentially a small log cabin—in keeping with regional traditions; still the couple thought of it as a "modern mountain cottage" that despite retaining the "far-up-in-the-mountains atmosphere" had "the comfort of city conveniences" (fig. 2.11). While the couple had considered using it as a garage and workroom, the structure may also have been built on speculation since it was offered for sale in May 1941.[101] Its distinguishing interior and exterior features are walls of interlocking hand-hewn logs between thick courses of cement plaster and a pronounced chimney and fireplace of rough fieldstone.[102] Nonetheless, it is patently modern in that the rear is of light-gray-painted redwood siding intersected with sliding plate-glass windows wrapping around the corners, and inside is an L-shaped open plan originally with a curtain that could separate the sleeping area from the living room. Moreover, it stands on six concrete piers to cantilever dramatically over the northern slope, recalling Clara Fargo Thomas's summer house in Maine, designed in 1937–39 by George Howe, with whom Clauss previously worked.[103] The entire composition is situated on the slope so as not to disrupt the expansive view from their first house across the road.

In 1943, the Clausses moved into a fourth house they designed and built, which was just west of the log cabin to accommodate their expanding family (figs. 2.12, 2.13). Still known as the Redwood House, the structure was named after its primary material: a soft, lightweight wood whose stable and durable qualities made it a favorite of the California Bay Area architects earlier in the century. As a nonpriority war material, redwood must have been readily available since the exterior, which stands on local

2.11. Log cabin designed by Alfred and Jane West Clauss, 428 Little Switzerland Drive, Knoxville, Tennessee, 1941. *Clauss Papers.*

fieldstone, is entirely covered in horizontal boards.[104] The house design expands on the plan of the first two houses in that the upper level is an open space, long and narrow, with a living and shared work area separated by a curtain from the main bedroom; the lower level contains a dining room opening to a kitchen, with an outdoor porch to one side as well as three bedrooms and a bath. The house is more flexible than the others in that it has removable, full-height closets as well as sliding panels and curtains. A roof trellis extends on the rear over two levels of expansive windows to provide shade and mitigate the planar surfaces.[105]

The Redwood House succeeded as a refinement of their ideas about functional, affordable family living, and it integrated European-inspired concepts with a warmer, softer, and more natural vernacular aesthetic. Despite their bold example, the architects had only limited success introducing Tennesseans to a more humanistic Modernism that had been gaining popularity elsewhere, and correspondence reveals their interest in moving further east. William Wilson Wurster, then dean of the architecture school at MIT, empathized with their frustration, replying to Clauss in 1945, that "possibly Knoxville is like New England in its lack of ability to really use modern design."[106] In fact, by the end of World War II, Modernism was more accepted in New England than in Tennessee.

When the Clausses did relocate in 1940, to Wallingford, Pennsylvania, it was only Alfred Clauss who teamed up as an associate under George Daub to design another community called Avondale Knolls. Presented as "a development of new homes planned by well-known architect in the style of tomorrow," the community of half-acre lots was to be situated on a former golf course, according to promotional material.[107] The cedar-covered house the Clausses built for themselves there does not mimic any of the three types of houses proposed for the development ("modern," "ranch," and "solar"), but it does utilize the horizontal split-level conception of their former homes, albeit with a rearrangement of rooms so that sleeping and formal living areas are on the upper level while dining and recreation are below. Further, instead of stairs at the midlevel entrance, there is a ramp, broken into two runs—perhaps after those of Le Corbusier or because of the back pain West Clauss experienced after years of laying bricks, shoveling cement, and other strenuous physical efforts put into building their homes.[108] Focused on attracting others to their aesthetic, the couple

2.12. Redwood House designed by Alfred and Jane West Clauss, 424 Little Switzerland Drive, Knoxville, Tennessee, 1943. *Clauss Papers.*

2.13. Redwood House interior, 1943. *Clauss Papers.*

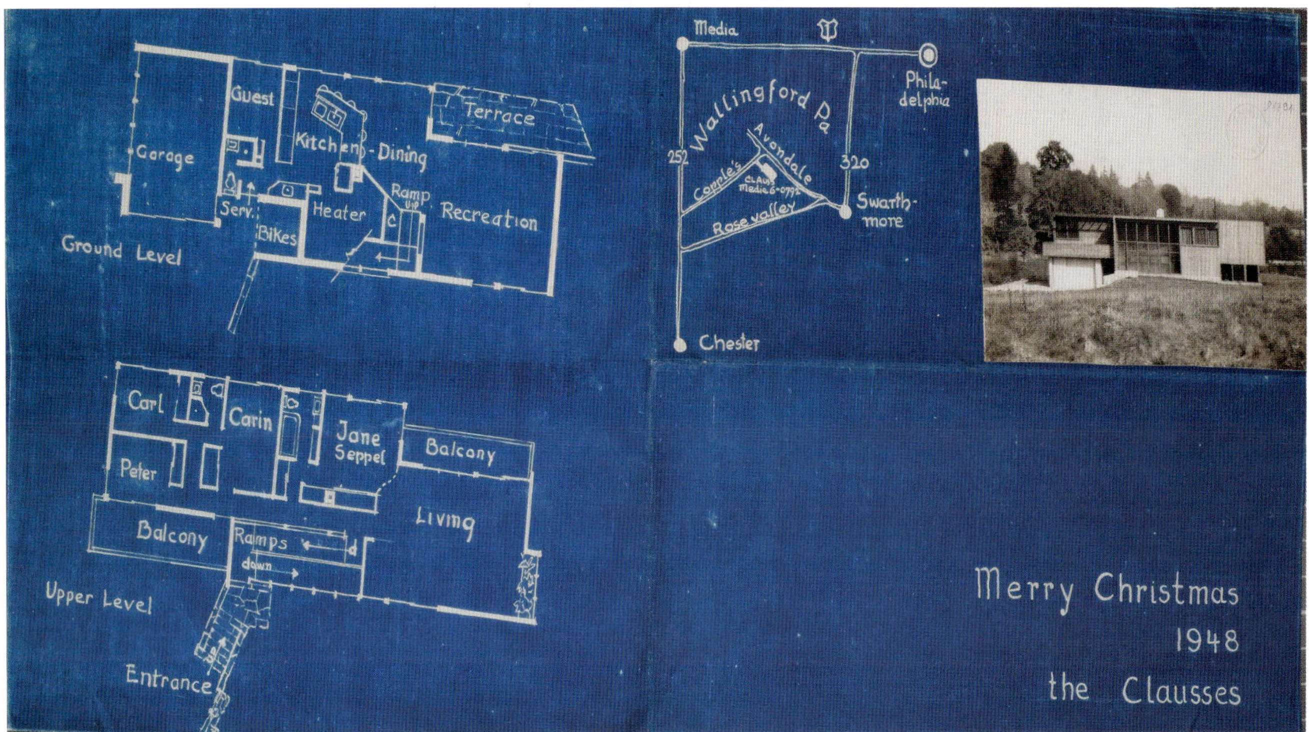

2.14. Christmas card illustrating the Alfred and Jane West Clauss house, 314 Copples Lane, Wallingford, Pennsylvania, 1940. *František Sammer Collection, Archiv města Plzeň.*

2.15. Peter Clauss house, designed by Alfred and Jane West Clauss, 316 Copples Lane, Wallingford, Pennsylvania, 1952. *Clauss Papers.*

promoted the design on their Christmas card with a photograph, house plan, and map showing its proximity to Philadelphia, Chester, and Swarthmore (fig. 2.14). After they built a second house nearby, in 1952, for their son Peter Otto Clauss, it was apparent that the modern agenda had failed to appeal to clients, and thus a traditional builder developed the rest of the lots (fig. 2.15).[109]

Despite West Clauss being "happiest" when dreaming up novel schemes with her husband or, in other words, living architecture together every day, she was no longer thought of as his professional partner when they moved to Wallingford.[110] In fact, one feature article about their house described her as an interior designer who actually did her own planning and labor![111] Though West Clauss demonstrated interest in cultivating women two decades earlier when she had organized the (canceled) European tour, she does not appear to have maintained a professional network of her own, much less one with women. An exception is the relationship she maintained with Anne Tyng, who introduced West Clauss to Beaver College (now Arcadia

University) about ten miles outside of Philadelphia. In 1950, she replaced Tyng there as a part-time instructor in interior design, a job she maintained until 1963. As educators, both architects had a degree of autonomy not present in their own design work since each collaborated professionally with a male figure with whom they were intimately involved. While the women may have considered the arrangement professionally advantageous, each sacrificed her individuality. Even though West Clauss supported her husband's ongoing practice by making models, renderings, material selections, and interior layouts, the genius was always considered his; her signature as a designer is an enigma even to the most discerning eye. While her own involvement, both personally and financially, in the creation of Little Switzerland (ironically, the country in which Le Corbusier was born) may well have exceeded other projects, she never exercised independently those lessons she took away from the architect who first inspired her.

Modernism in Great Britain

Upon her return from London in 1937, Mary Elizabeth Coss Cooke (Barnes; 1911–2008) leveraged her international experience more successfully than others by demonstrating a grasp of modern architecture on which her future architect husband, Edward Larrabee Barnes, a successful second-generation modernist, came to rely. Her career path typifies women who navigated through a variety of professions, but her background in European Modernism remained central.

In 1928, Mary Coss had followed family tradition by enrolling at Bryn Mawr College in Pennsylvania, where as an unconventional student she wore pajamas to class and painted her room flat black; still, she was discontented. Thus, in 1930, Mary Coss followed her sister, Margaret (later Flower) to England. She enrolled in Newnham College at the University of Cambridge, where she had a romantic relationship with Michael Redgrave (before he became an actor).[112] Once called a "girl of unusual beauty," she evidently possessed other qualities that attracted intellectual aristocrats such as Richard Llewelyn-Davies, soon to become an eminent architect and city planner, as well as Julian Heward Bell, son of the painter Vanessa Stephen Bell and her husband, Clive, the prominent art critic and nephew of Virginia Woolf.[113] By association, she knew members of the Bloomsbury Group, as is substantiated by the 1931 oil portrait of her by Duncan Grant (fig. 2.16).[114]

2.16. Duncan Grant (1885–1978), *Miss Mary Coss*, oil on canvas, 1931. *© Fitzwilliam Museum, University of Cambridge, gift of Frank Hindley Smith.*

Her marriage from 1931 to 1936 to the barrister Arthur Francis Benn Cooke of Oxton, Cheshire, is incidental to her more productive architecture study and work in England. Between 1932 and 1936, Coss Cooke attended the Architectural Association School of Architecture (AA), the prestigious London institution that admitted women, beginning in 1917, but still had a quota for them.[115] For two years, she worked for Berthold Lubetkin and his six male partners in the Tecton Group (1932–39), at the time involved in one of the firm's zoo installations as well as a Highpoint apartment block in Highgate, projects that largely ushered Modernism into the country. The latter project aroused her "greatest desire" to learn more about housing and town planning.[116] While at Tecton, she also won first place in a competition for working-class domestic flats of reinforced concrete, and she designed a luxurious bathroom in the London apartment of Francis David Langhorne Astor. Her design, which juxtaposes white, blue, and red tiled surfaces, appeared in *Architectural Review* in 1936.[117] She also assisted the

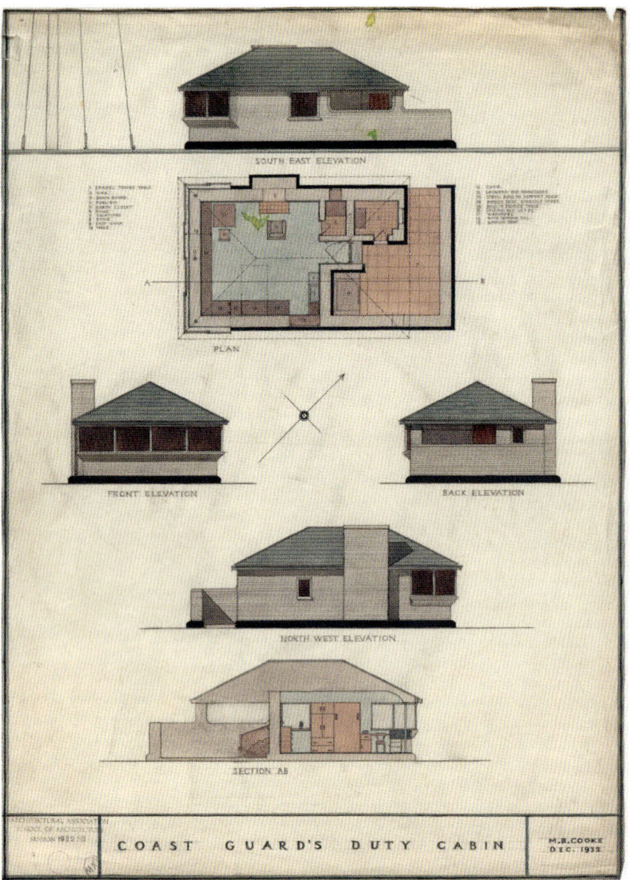

2.17. Mary Elizabeth Coss Cooke, *Coast Guard Duty Cabin*, drawing made as a student at the Architectural Association School of Architecture, London, England, December 1932. *Edward Larrabee Barnes Papers, Loeb Library.*

Tecton architect Anthony Chitty on a wooden bungalow (1935) on the grounds of Bron-y-der, the estate of former prime minister David Lloyd George in Churt Village, Surrey. A long room with views through French windows to the courtyard and gardens dominates the five-bedroom house called Avalon, designed for his lover and then secretary, Frances Stevenson.[118] Though Coss Cooke had an enriching experience and benefitted from working for modernist architects, it is surprising that her only archived work is a Beaux Arts-inspired drawing of a coast guard's duty cabin, completed in her first year at the AA (fig. 2.17).

When in 1937 Coss Cooke relocated to New York, she benefited from the relationships she formed with the Bauer sisters. Just as Catherine Bauer and her friend and colleague Frederick "Fritz" Albert Gutheim were about to head out for lunch with the modernist Oskar Stonorov, Coss Cooke appeared in her office with a letter of introduction from Lubetkin, praising her considerable graphic ability, reliability and conscientiousness, social skills, conversance in architectural principles, and relationships with European architects.[119] Her timing could not have been better since Bauer had recently contributed an essay on housing to MoMA's exhibition catalog *Modern Architecture in England* (1937), in which the Tecton Group figured prominently. Bauer may also have met Lubetkin and his wife, Margaret Louise Church Lubetkin (1916–78), when they attended the opening of the exhibition as sponsors. Church Lubetkin, incidentally, had been in the same class as Coss Cooke at the AA.

As a member of the architecture committee at MoMA, Bauer was able to support Coss Cooke in finding work at the museum, where she committed herself to an intermittent career between 1937 and 1945.[120] After assisting with the exhibition *The Making of a Contemporary Film* (1937), Coss Cooke designed *Subway Art* (1938) and assembled and installed the momentous exhibition *Aalto: Architecture and Furniture* (1938). Along with Elizabeth Bauer Mock, she assisted John McAndrew that year with the architecture section of the exhibition *Trois Siècles d'Art aux États-Unis* (1938) for the Jeu de Paume in Paris. Coss Cooke also published a review of MoMA's exhibition *Bauhaus: 1919–1928* (1938) in the *American Magazine of Art*, perhaps at the suggestion of Catherine Bauer, who had recognized early in her own career that journalism was a field widely open to women.[121]

Though during the war Coss Cooke took a job with the United States Housing Authority in Washington, DC, in 1943 she was also on the advisory committee of the architecture section that Bauer Mock was curating for MoMA's *Art in Progress* exhibition (1944). She also designed and directed *US Housing in War and Peace*, with Catherine Bauer (now Wurster) as the consultant. In Bauer Mock's opinion, Coss Cooke did "a fine and fancy job" on the exhibition, which the US Office of War Information (1942–45) circulated to England, Germany, Russia, South Africa, and Australia before it was shown at MoMA as *The Lesson of War Housing* (1945).[122] Coss Cooke's connection with the Bauer sisters remained strong enough that she also worked on a traveling exhibition corresponding to the museum's publication *The Architecture of Bridges* (1949) authored by Bauer Mock. Even so, she was anxious to finish so that she could "get the house in order" and begin work with her second husband, Edward Larrabee Barnes, whom she had married in March 1944.[123]

She met Barnes in Washington, DC, when he was a candidate for a bachelor's degree at Harvard and was studying defense housing and prefabrication under a fellowship (1940–42). The articles they produced for *Task* show their parallel interest: "Defense Housing—March 1941" by Barnes and "War-Time Advances in Housing" (1944) by Coss Cooke.[124] In the same period, Barnes immersed himself in the circle of Gropius and Breuer, for whom he was an occasional draftsperson on housing projects.[125] In fact, according to Barnes, he courted his future wife in the living room of the Breuer house in Lincoln.[126] The couple developed a lasting friendship with Breuer, who depended on them both: in one letter, for example, he asked Coss Cooke to lend a "friendly hand" in introducing him to connected people in Washington, DC—not just in housing but hospitals, recreation centers, and office buildings.[127]

After their marriage, Coss Barnes struggled to balance the complex litany of tasks required of the postwar wife with her professional life, candidly noting in a diary in 1943: "It's impossible to work on marriage and collect recipes, investigate gardenias, observe behaviors of pregnant women, think about the education of children, the managing of a house, gardening, holidays and everything that I've been doing with half my mind and all my heart—and at the same time to work just hard enough to be paid."[128] Importantly, her husband did not waver from supporting her professional interests. In a letter concerning his discussion with Breuer about the idle talent of his second wife (and former secretary) Constance "Connie" Crocker Leighton Breuer (1914–2002), Barnes conveys his attitude toward the professional development of women: "I went very exhaustively into the subject of Connie's talent in drawing and I'm sorry to say that Lajos's replies to my statements were not at all what you or I would like them to be—at one point he said, 'one talent in a family is enough.' I'm afraid his whole point of view—and particularly re women and children (having them) is downright selfish."[129] Breuer's sentiment that a couple could only accommodate one (male) artist was unfortunately pervasive, but it was not one that Barnes shared. Given that his own mother, Margaret Ayer Barnes (1886–1967), was a Pulitzer Prize–winning author as well as a progressive education activist, it is no surprise that his wife's architectural experiences appealed to Barnes.[130]

It was most likely after she joined Barnes in California, where he was stationed during the war as a Navy architect, that he became fully aware of his wife's "exquisite taste—modern, pure, classical, unerring," as one employee of the Barnes firm succinctly remembers.[131] Apparently, the couple collaborated in 1946 with Henry Dreyfuss in South Pasadena, though her role in the collaboration is unknown. After they relocated to New York in 1948, where they set up a modern apartment, she contributed to his private practice in endless ways, including making important social connections. Among those in her MoMA network were Elodie Courter Osborn (1911–94), director of the museum's circulating exhibitions, 1939–47, and her artist husband Robert Osborn. In 1949, Barnes designed one of his first platform houses for the couple in Salisbury, Connecticut—a structure situated with an outdoor living space on a podium to distinguish it from the surrounding landscape.[132]

Coss Barnes sporadically recorded in her diary the stimulating company the couple kept between 1947 and 1950 with such architects as Josep Lluís Sert, William Wurster, Gerhard Kallman, and Robert Rosenberg. She

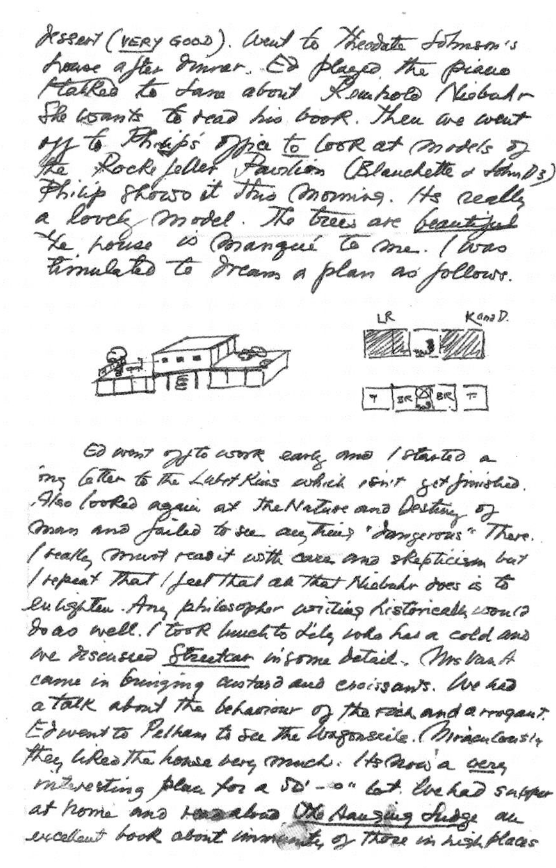
dessert (VERY GOOD). Went to Theodate Johnson's house after dinner. Ed played the piano I talked to Jane about Reinhold Niebuhr. She wants to read his book. Then we went off to Philip's office to look at models of the Rockefeller Pavilion (Blanchette & John D 3) Philip shows it this morning. Its really a lovely model. The trees are beautiful the house is manqué to me. I was stimulated to dream a plan as follows.

Ed went off to work early and I started a long letter to the Lubetkins which didn't get finished. Also looked again at The Nature and Destiny of Man and failed to see anything "dangerous" there. I really must read it with care and skepticism but I repeat that I feel that all that Niebuhr does is to enlighten. Any philosopher writing historically would do as well. I took lunch to Lily who has a cold and we discussed Streetcar in some detail. Mrs Van A came in bringing custard and croissants. We had a talk about the behaviour of the rich and arrogant. Ed went to Pelham to see the Wagonseile. Miraculously they liked the house very much. Its now a very interesting place for a 50'-0" lot. We had supper at home and [illegible] about The Hanging Judge an excellent book about [illegible] of those in high places

2.18. Letter from Mary Coss Barnes to Edward Larrabee Barnes (1915–2004), 1948. *Private collection.*

also describes an evening in 1948 at the home of Theodate Johnson (1907–2002) who, though named after her aunt, the architect Theodate Pope Riddle, was instead an opera and concert singer. When Barnes finished playing the piano after dinner, the group proceeded to the office of Johnson's brother, Philip, to view the model of the pavilion he was designing for Blanchette and John D. Rockefeller at their Kykuit estate in Mount Pleasant, New York.[133] Coss Barnes found the model "lovely" but thought the design was "manqué." She decided "to dream a plan" of her own for the building and made a small sketch (fig. 2.18). Whereas the Johnson model shows a modern pool house with two bathrooms—like the Edith Farnsworth House (1951) by Mies van der Rohe in Plano, Illinois, and Johnson's Glass House (1949) in New Canaan, Connecticut—her revision expands both the pavilion program and its square footage; Coss Barnes added a second story with two bedrooms and broke the simple rectangular plan of the first story into two parts with a living room on one side and a kitchen and dining room on the other. Coss Barnes's sketch has the same modern elements as the Johnson model, but she extended the quality of openness by putting an outdoor terrace at the center of the plan.

After the couple moved in 1952 to their own platform house in Westchester County, New York, Coss Barnes became involved with the newly created Katonah Gallery. As with Anne Tyng and Jane West Clauss, her volunteerism, especially in the gallery's exhibitions, gave her an independence she did not have elsewhere. Nonetheless, according to the architect and critic Peter Blake in his introduction to the only monograph on the work of Edward Barnes, she was her husband's "most important collaborator": her "sure eye, color sense, understanding of people, architectural sensitivity, and total unselfishness" underpinned all his work, as Barnes himself confirmed.[134] However, none of her contributions to the firm, or elsewhere, are documented in his private archive even though, as with other husband-wife collaborations, she had a fluid, hands-on role. In time, her responsibilities became more defined; she managed all color and material selections as well as interior spaces. The boardroom in the forty-three-story IBM Building (1978–83) at 590 Madison Avenue in New York was all hers, as was the Indiana limestone on the Dallas Museum of Art (1984).[135] With few extant records, however, her design thinking, particularly in her later years, is hard to specify, other than to cite her husband's enduring respect for her aesthetic sensitivity. Though it is not possible to identify her unique signature, the work that went out of the Barnes office was inevitably the outcome of a collaborative effort inspired by international Modernism.

International Women Architects in the United States

While Coss Barnes obviously benefited from her introduction to Modernism in London, travel abroad was not the only means for the exchange and circulation of ideas. As with the male émigré architects who shared their proficiency in modern architecture in their buildings and writings, women architect émigrés also arrived in the United States with comprehensive experience. The Latvian-born architect Elsa Mandelstamm Gidoni (Gluckmann; 1901–78) and the Polish-born architect Marie Frommer (1890–1976) were two of the three foreign-trained architects among the eighteen featured in the two-part article, "A Thousand Women in Architecture" in *Architectural Record* in 1948.[136] The images of their European work in the journal implies that Frommer and Mandelstamm Gidoni had greater opportunities abroad compared to those working at the same time in the United States, where women seemed "less sophisticated" due to prevailing educational and professional obstacles, as Mary Otis Stevens contended in her 1977 essay "Struggle for Place: Women in Architecture, 1920–1960."[137] Mandelstamm Gidoni herself observed that it never occurred to her that she would *not* find employment in an architecture firm, and she was surprised to discover upon immigrating to the United States, in May 1938, that it was "a man's haven and refuge not to be invaded by women."[138] The Europeans were nevertheless at an advantage in that Modernism had evolved in Europe just after World War I, while few examples had been built in the United States.

Mandelstamm Gidoni had studied architecture, in 1916–17, at the Imperial Academy of Art and Architecture in Saint Petersburg, Russia, and then at the Technische Universität Berlin. She never completed her degree but did work in the office of the leading German modernist Leo Nachtlicht. While on an extended visit to the United States beginning in 1922, she married Aleksandr Iosifovich Gidoni, a Russian lawyer, critic, and writer then on a lecture tour in Chicago.[139] After she divorced him, in about 1926, she briefly returned to Nachtlicht's office before setting up her own practice in Berlin, primarily working on renovations and expansions of villas and apartments.[140]

In 1933, she sought asylum from the Nazis in Tel Aviv with her widowed mother and a younger sister. She initially joined the office of the Levant Fair (1934), working on five buildings, the best known being the Café Galina on which she collaborated with the Ukrainian-born architect Genia Averbuch (1909–77) and her husband, Shlomo Ginsburg.[141] She then built up a "considerable office," reputed to be one of the best in the city, and became recognized for housing projects, among them the Beit Hehalutzot (Women Pioneers' House).[142]

The Depression as well as male bigotry in the profession were challenges to Mandelstamm Gidoni when in 1938 the thirty-seven-year-old divorcée had to recreate herself again, this time in the United States. The plans, renderings, and photographs of modern buildings in her sizable portfolio, however, convinced Norman Bel Geddes that her contemporary approach, honed in Europe and Tel Aviv, was what he needed for the General Motors Futurama diorama he was creating for the New York World's Fair (1939).[143] Subsequently, Mandelstamm Gidoni consistently found work, albeit not on the scale she had in Germany or Palestine; she started with the New York firm of Mayer and Whittlesey, for whom she participated in the Fort Greene Houses (now the Walt Whitman Houses) for the New York Housing Authority (NYHA) in 1941. She also apprenticed for the "New Hope Experiment" on the Pennsylvania farm of the Bohemian architect Antonin Raymond and his designer wife Noémi Pernessin (1889–1980).[144] Though nothing is known about her responsibilities there, the couple had been inspired by Wright's Taliesin, where they had worked before Raymond assisted Wright on the Imperial Hotel in Japan. Equally influenced by Le Corbusier, Raymond and his wife embodied an international perspective on modern architecture that would have appealed to Mandelstamm Gidoni.

For three years, beginning in 1942, Mandelstamm Gidoni was a senior designer and draftsperson in the firm of Alfred Fellheimer and Steward Wagner, working on buildings for Hoffman LaRoche in New Jersey; the firm also sponsored her application to the American Institute of Architects (AIA) for membership in 1943.[145] In about 1944, she joined the large New York firm of Kahn and Jacobs (1941–72). Ely Jacques Kahn had shown his partiality toward women architects back in 1926, when he mentored the London-educated architect Doris Adeney Lewis (Lady Robertson; 1899–1981) after she won a traveling scholarship from the Royal Institute of British Architects for her social housing scheme to accommodate 350 people.[146] Understandably, then, Kahn was amenable to naming Mandelstamm Gidoni as an associate in 1957, during a period in which his firm of at least fifty-five employees (four of them partners) was responding to a "violent" and "vigorous" demand for skyscraper architecture.[147]

Despite the proclamation she made in 1960—"If a woman is able to prove her merit and ability there is absolutely no difference in attitude toward her"—Mandelstamm Gidoni remained anonymous during her twenty-three-year tenure with Kahn.[148] Still, as one of the first women to break into a major firm, her production was far-reaching, with projects ranging from skyscrapers, office buildings, and department stores to schools, housing, and exhibition spaces. The buildings Mandelstamm Gidoni designed for the Hecht Company department store (1956) in Ballston, Virginia, and the Connecticut Light and Power Company (1953) on Manresa Island were widely published, but there are also extant drawings of lesser-known projects in her archive at the Library of Congress, which equally indicate her ability.[149] Among them are her preliminary (and unrealized) schemes for the Travelers pavilion at the New York World's Fair (1963), in which a main wing of metal and glass is covered with thirty-six plastic domes and connected by a second-story bridge to a horizontal glass lounge standing on pilotis (fig. 2.19). Imaginative, colorful, and spirited, the design demonstrates her understanding that temporary fair architecture must be eye-catching and adventurous. Her familiarity with European Modernism is also vivid in an intriguing design for a border checkpoint in which she juxtaposes an unyielding horizontal metal roof on conspicuous piers with vertical chain-linked gates and a Miesian agent's station (fig. 2.20).

Indeed, even the young progressives appreciated her work, as evidenced by her role as an editor of the fourth issue of Harvard's *Task* magazine. She also maintained connections with international modernist architects in the United States, demonstrated by the illustration she contributed in 1947 to an article about the panel system developed by Gropius and a fellow German émigré architect, Konrad Wachsmann, whom she had known since 1920. Her design of a two-bedroom house comprised of two rectangular blocks with the upper one supported on pilotis was featured in *Architectural Forum* alongside illustrations by Gropius, the Dutch architect and modern furniture designer Paul Bromberg, and the Austrian

2.19. Elsa Mandelstamm Gidoni, preliminary design for the Travelers Pavilion at the New York World's Fair, 1961. *Elsa Gidoni Collection, Prints and Photographs Division, Library of Congress, gift of Gunter Arndt.*

2.20. Elsa Mandelstamm Gidoni, design for a border checkpoint. *Gidoni Collection, Arndt gift.*

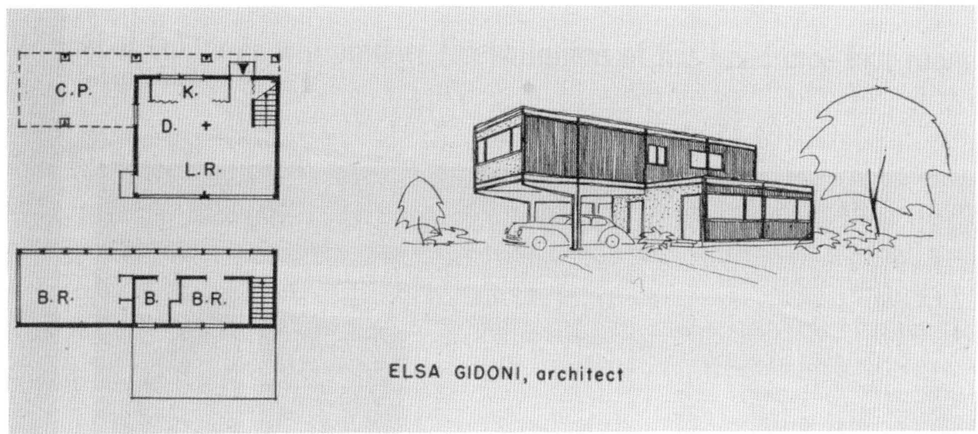

2.21. Elsa Mandelstamm Gidoni, "The Industrialized House," *Architectural Forum* 86, no. 2 (February 1947): 120.

architect Richard Neutra (fig. 2.21).[150] Mandelstamm Gidoni also collaborated with the Russian-born construction engineer Alexis Lazar Gluckmann (whom she married by 1952) on a demountable moving picture theater, which they applied to copyright in 1947.[151]

Mandelstamm Gidoni kept up with Marie Frommer and, in fact, supported her application to the AIA in 1952.[152] Unlike Mandelstamm Gidoni, however, Frommer does not have an archive, and there are few published images of her work in the United States, even though she maintained an independent practice in New York from 1946 to at least 1970. Frommer graduated in 1919 from the Technische Hochschule in Dresden, Germany, where she was allegedly the first woman to receive a doctorate in architecture, and she apprenticed on a reconstruction project in Angerburg (then in East Prussia) and as a planner for the city of Dresden. She opened a practice in Berlin in 1926 and remained there for a decade. As as a member of the Bund Deutscher Architektinnen (Association of German Architects) Frommer was well-versed in residential architecture, demonstrated in her housing advice column and consultancy introduced in the January 1930 issue of *Die Schaffende Frau* (The Creative Woman). She is best known, however, for her commerical projects—hotels, shops, and stores, most of them conversions.[153] Built in the city's heyday after World War I, such commmissions were meant to portray cultural and economic prosperity using a technologically oriented aesthetic. The two storefronts she designed for Seidenhauses Leiser, a large retailer in Berlin-Charlottenburg (1926; now demolished) and in Berlin-Mitte (1927; now demolished), placed her among such seminal modern architects as Paul Zucker and Erich Mendelsohn.[154] The facade of the remodeled Berlin-Mitte store, defined by its rounded corner entrance, featured not only prominent, recurring geometries but smooth, polished travertine surfaces, rich bronze window framing, and boldly projecting signage that took on its own architectural character—all echoing contemporary stylistic trends observed elsewhere on the Continent.[155]

Frommer is also known for her conversion of the Villa Majestic (1929; rebuilt into a residence hotel for single women) in Berlin-Wilmersdorf, for which she preserved the neighborhood character and at the same time introduced modern concepts—for example, by raising the original two-story villa to three stories and topping it with a flat roof with a terrace. Her five-story hotel addition had a smooth, unadorned facade with rows of identical windows as well as a hipped roof to resemble nearby apartment buildings. The bold lines of the barrel-vaulted bar, customized with riveted-copper panels and hand-hammered copper fixtures, juxtaposed rectilinear strips in contrasting colors on both the seating and the floor, imparting a sense of theatricality.[156]

Interestingly, in the section on Frommer in the "A Thousand Women in Architecture" feature, she did not provide images of these two commissions. Instead, she showed an expressionistic staircase in the Swiss Life Insurance building (1938) in Berlin, marking Mendelsohn's direct influence; she also showed a classically restrained Greco shoe store in Paris-Deauville (whereabouts unknown), recalling the Tristan Tzara house (1926) by Adolf Loos in Paris, and a penthouse (1930; now demolished) for Carl Frankl in Berlin-Steglitz, inspired by the pronounced cantilevered roofs of Mies van der Rohe. The latter two works especially align with the conception of the International Style promoted by Hitchcock and Johnson.[157]

2.22. Marie Frommer with Paul Bry (1899–1953), Radio Frank's Knight Club, 70 East 55th Street, New York, c. 1944. *Kim Hoffman Photograph Collection, Department of prints, Photographs, and Architectural Collections, New-York Historical Society.*

Before she emigrated to the United States in December 1939, Frommer sought asylum between 1937 and 1939 in London, where she launched an office but most likely had difficulty finding work since she would have had to partner with a British architect; there is no known record of her work there. When she arrived in New York, Frommer set herself up as an architecture consultant living in the American Woman's Association Clubhouse (1929) on West 57th Street, and may have worked for the established architect Walter Harrington Kilham Jr., based on her AIA membership application, which he sponsored and where he stated he had known her for twelve years. Of Frommer's handful of documented American commissions, ranging from residences and shops to a hotel lobby, nightclub, and law office, the earliest is an extensive makeover of Radio Frank's Knight Club in New York, published in *Pencil Points* in 1944 (fig. 2.22).[158] As the "Architect, Collaborator," Frommer worked alongside the German émigré Paul Bry, a designer and interior decorator who had arrived in New York about the same time as Frommer. Maybe they had known each other in Berlin before Bry moved to Paris, where he worked for five years mostly designing commercial interiors as well as furniture and lighting, some in the Art Deco style.[159] Based on his published designs, Bry's professional experience and evolving aesthetic complemented Frommer's. Even so, the nightclub is markedly like her Majestic hotel barroom in its expressionistic exuberance: sumptuous materials, curved forms, sensational colors and lighting, and boldly articulated geometries predominate. Admired by one Broadway gossip columnist for its "ebony walls, sunken dance floor, gold-leaf bar and snug hideaway loges," the festive but functional interior also had a fuchsia-colored bar wall and leatherette sofa, as well as large mirrors and forty-four wall sconces mounted on diagonal strips.[160]

After Frommer received her architecture license in 1946, she established her own practice in New York, consisting primarily of interior alterations to stores and offices.[161] Even when producing an "inexpensive design" for the Regina specialty shop of jewelry, bags, and luggage in New Rochelle, Frommer enlivened the small space with a midnight-blue ceiling and black linoleum floor with yellow joints to set off the simple gray-finished oak cases.[162] The sleek, slim lettering of the signage at the rear entrance, pictured in *Progressive Architecture* in 1946, was a far cry from her previous signage at Leiser in Berlin and demonstrates her effort to adapt her aesthetic to the American market. Her professional letterhead, a copy of which is in the Cooper-Hewitt, Smithsonian Design Museum, gives the same sophisticated impression.[163] The law office interior for Mansbach and Paley at 52 Broadway shows similar restraint. This "convenient, efficient, cheerful and very impressive establishment," which was pictured in *Interiors* in 1948, was organized around a core reception room with furniture designed by Frommer, including a semicircular wood reception desk (recalling Bry's work) as well as a wood tripod table with a glass top.[164] Significantly, the room was her only American commission illustrated in the article "A Thousand Women in Architecture."

Since both Mandelstamm Gidoni and Frommer had worked independently before moving to the United States, they arrived with the understanding of how to set up a practice for themselves. Two other women architect émigrés of note—Stanisława "Siasia" Sandecka Nowicki (1912–2018) of Pultusk, Poland, and Susanne Katherina Raedermacher Wasson-Tucker (earlier Kraus; 1911–2008) of Vienna, Austria—initially relied on or collaborated with their architect husbands for some of their work. Significantly, however, their careers evolved in ways neither could have anticipated and both had to continually reinvent themselves professionally.

By the time Sandecka Nowicki, herself the daughter of an architect, arrived in the United States with her four-year-old son Pawel "Paul" in January 1946, she had already shown talent, resourcefulness, and versatility in her production, ranging from designs for buildings and interiors to textiles and graphics—books, magazines, leaflets, and posters. As an architecture student at the Politechnika Warszawska between 1930 and 1936, she had learned how to depict the geometries of architecture in simple, two-dimensional formats using architectural lettering reflecting such contemporary movements as Cubism and Constructivism; along with other architects of her generation, she participated in graphic art commissions and competitions. Sandecka Nowicki supplemented her education by apprenticing in Paris in 1934, when she worked on the Art Deco Normandie cinema by Adrianna Gurwik-Górska (1899–1969), a French-trained Polish architect, and her husband, Pierre de Montaut. She was also employed in Bucharest on a railroad station. Following graduation, she worked briefly for Le Corbusier on a photomontage for his Temps Nouveaux pavilion for the Exposition Internationale des Arts et Techniques dans la Vie Moderne (1937). She was also a senior assistant to Lech Niemojewski, an influential professor at her university.[165]

In about 1930, Sandecka Nowicki started to collaborate professionally with fellow student Maciej "Matthew" Nowicki, which led to their joint graphic studio as well as their marriage in 1936. Together, the Nowickis engaged in various sorts of commercial work—especially posters, a popular form of propaganda that architects could take on with success owing to their familiarity with modern design.[166] Well into the 1940s, the couple used the composite name "Nowicki Sandecka" (or "M. S. Nowicki"), signaling their insistence on collaboration and equal recognition. They won numerous awards in local competitions for their graphic designs and were also recognized internationally: their posters and decorative panels in the Polish Pavilion at the Paris exposition in 1937 won a grand prize, and the cartograms on which they collaborated with the artist Tadeusz Pruszkowski illustrating Poland's recent economic development are pictured in an official catalog of the Polish Pavilion at the New York World's Fair (1939).[167] Other types of graphic work include multiple vignettes and illustrations for the Polish journal *Arkady,* as well as items for the ocean liner *MS Piłsudski* (1935).[168]

The Nowickis also participated in architecture competitions: they received a first and third prize, respectively, for a spa (1938; with Jerzy Sołtan) in Druskininkai and a mosque (1936; unbuilt) in Warsaw.[169] Among other types of commissions are a tourist house (1938; with Władysław Stokowski) in Augustów (now in Lithuania) and a center for physical education (1939; with Zbigniew Karpinski) at Podskarbińska 11 in Warsaw.[170] Along with her husband, Sandecka Nowicki also collaborated on the reconstruction of Warsaw for the Capital Rebuilding Bureau after the city was destroyed by the Nazis, no small task.

Unable to withstand the repressive totalitarianism after Russian communists took over, the couple emigrated to Chicago in 1945 using Nowicki's diplomatic passport, where he allegedly took on the role of cultural attaché to promote the rebuilding of Poland.[171] In 1947, Nowicki joined the prestigious fifteen-member board of architects designing the United Nations Headquarters (1947–52) in midtown New York. Meanwhile, Sandecka Nowicki seemingly worked on her own, producing graphic designs for the Container Corporation, Abbott Laboratories, R. R. Donnelley and Sons, and Marshall Field & Company in Chicago, probably under the auspices of the Vogue-Wright Studio.[172]

At first, it might appear as if they dropped their established collaboration with one another in the United States. Closer examination reveals, however, that it remained intact. The book *Made in Poland* (1949) features illustrations signed by "M. S. Nowicki" (fig. 2.23). Similarly, in May 1949, the North Carolina State Art Gallery in Raleigh hosted a "Nowicki man-and-wife show" composed of modern textiles, book illustrations, advertising art, and architecture designs.[173]

It had been Lewis Mumford, her husband's advocate, who urged them to move a year earlier to Raleigh, where Nowicki was named a visiting professor and acting head of architecture at the newly conceived School of Architecture and Landscape Design at North Carolina State University. At their introductory meeting, Sandecka Nowicki also showed her portfolio to the dean, Henry Leveke Kamphoefner; he immediately grasped the "quality and elegance" of her work and asked her to teach as well. Though apprehensive, she agreed to an assistant professorship and was responsible for the required Elements of Design course.[174] The couple's academic appointments were compatible as were their continued interests in design, exemplified by the school's catalog for which he produced the text and she the visuals.[175]

Outside the university, they completed the interior decoration of the Carolina Country Club (1947–49; now demolished) in Raleigh.[176] Her name is not attached to the State Fair Arena (1952; now the J. S. Dorton Arena),

2.23. Stanisława Sandecka Nowicki and Maciej "Matthew" Nowicki (1910–50), cover of Louise Llewellyn Jarecka, *Made in Poland: Living Traditions of the Land* (New York: Alfred A. Knopf, 1949).

also in Raleigh, for which her husband innovated an influential steel-cable structural system to span large areas. But according to a biographical sketch by the Canadian architect Blanche Lemco van Ginkel (1933–2022), a longtime colleague of Sandecka Nowicki, she also participated in that important project.[177]

After her husband died in a plane crash in 1950, Sandecka Nowicki relocated to the School of Fine Arts (now the Stuart Weitzman School of Design) at the University of Pennsylvania at the behest of its new dean, G. Holmes Perkins. During her quarter-century tenure, Sandecka Nowicki taught Basic Design; Architecture, City Planning, and Landscape Architecture; and a design seminar.[178] She apparently also intended, at least initially, to open a contemporary interiors store and decorating firm in Chestnut Hill with the dean's wife, Georgia Gray Hencken Perkins (1909–94), a Cambridge School alumna (fig. 2.24). Though she did not ultimately commit to the enterprise, the announcement for the business in the hand of Sandecka Nowicki is a testament to the frequency with which women architects turned to retailing modern furnishings as an alternative to professional practice. It also indicates the esteem in which Perkins and his wife held her; in 1958, he named Sandecka Nowicki the first female full professor in architecture at the university (fig. 2.25).[179] Twenty years later, when honored by the AIA with the Medal of Education, she was credited by Perkins with having been second in influence as a teacher only to László Moholy-Nagy (Bauhaus and the forerunner of the Illinois School of Technology) and Josef Albers (Bauhaus, Black Mountain College, and Yale University).[180]

Sandecka Nowicki wanted to integrate herself seamlessly into the American system rather than call attention to herself. Hence, few know her history, particularly that she was the one who received the prizes in Poland and who professors predicted would become an architect of distinction. Instead, Lewis Mumford emphasized Nowicki's primacy; in his memoirs he labels Sandecka Nowicki a "sympathetic critic," "catalyst," and even "reagent," but not a collaborator.[181] Nonetheless, toward the end of her life, she was recognized with two prestigious awards: Distinguished Professor Award (1987) from the Association of Collegiate Schools of Architecture, and the Gloria Artis gold medal for Merit to Culture (2016) from Poland's Ministry of Culture and Heritage.[182] Particularly as a respected teacher, Sandecka Nowicki made an important contribution to modern architecture

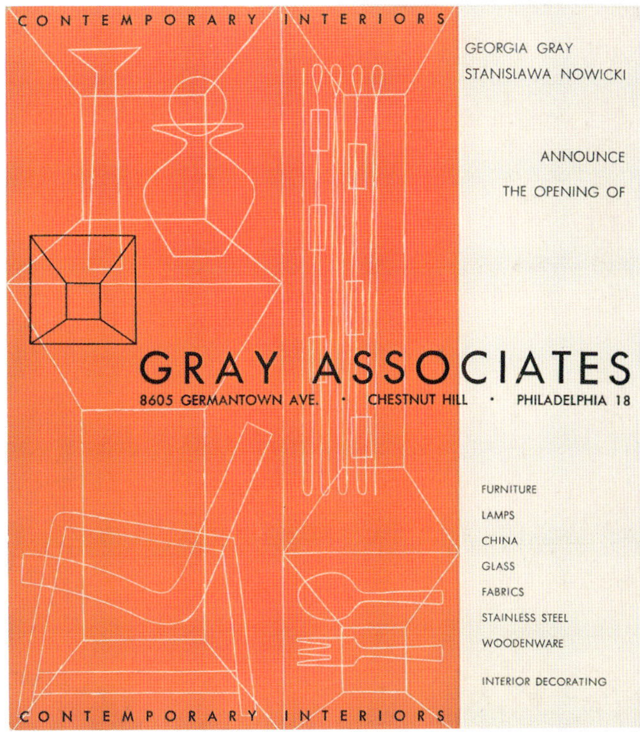

2.24. Stanisława Sandecka Nowicki, announcement of the opening of Gray Associates (1952–63). *G. Holmes Perkins Papers and Architectural Records, Architectural Archives, Stuart Weitzman School of Design, University of Pennsylvania.*

2.25. Stanisława Sandecka Nowicki with students in the School of Fine Arts at the University of Pennsylvania, Philadelphia, 1960–70. *George Pohl Collection, Architectural Archives, Stuart Weitzman School of Design.*

and ranks among the European émigré educators who had a significant impact on the transformation of the architectural culture in the United States.

Susanne Raedermacher Wasson-Tucker also immigrated to the United States with her husband, Arnold Wasson-Tucker, just about a month after marrying him in Sweden. After earning his degree in 1934 at the University of Manitoba in Winnipeg, Canada, he had spent three years in England followed by three more in Sweden.[183] Raedermacher Wasson-Tucker was able to adjust to the variable work situations she encountered in the United States undoubtedly because of her transient life in Europe. Though she grew up in an intellectual milieu in which her parents were friendly with Adolf Loos and Oskar Kokoschka, her early life was interrupted by political unrest; she was forced into exile in Denmark and later in Sweden, where by 1939 she was able to utilize the architecture degree she obtained in 1935 at the Vienna Techniche Hochschule in the offices of Sune Lindström, as well as of Ivar Stähl.[184]

After they arrived in New York, the young couple had an initial stroke of luck. Having read in a newspaper that Alvar Aalto and his architect wife Aino Marsio-Aalto (1894–1949), also a first-generation modernist architect, recently had come to the city, the Wasson-Tuckers called their hotel, and (even to their surprise) the Aaltos promptly invited them over.[185] As a result of their visit, Raedermacher Wasson-Tucker assisted Marsio-Aalto in updating the award-winning Finnish Pavilion at the New York World's Fair to show the impact of the Winter War (1939–40) while her husband pursued recommendations and funding to support his professorship and housing research at MIT in Cambridge.[186] Just days into the fall semester of 1940, the Aaltos abruptly returned to Finland, but Wasson-Tucker carried on as far as he could with Alto's studies on postwar reconstruction in Finland, which compelled the Wasson-Tuckers to remain in Cambridge.[187] Raedermacher Wasson-Tucker confessed in a letter to Breuer, a fellow central-European émigré, to feeling "lost and dull" without the inspiring couple, but nonetheless continued to busy herself by lecturing on furniture at MIT and working at the Peabody Museum of Archaeology and Ethnology at Harvard, where the exhibition rooms were being reorganized. She also worked with Carl Koch and, through Breuer, with architect Marc Peter Jr.[188]

2.26. View of the "Design for Use" section of the *Art in Progress: 15th Anniversary Exhibition*, Museum of Modern Art, 1944, showing the chair designed by Arnold Wasson-Tucker (1910–96) and Susanne Katherina Raedermacher Wasson-Tucker. *Photographic Archive, Museum of Modern Art Archives.*

It could have been Peter who introduced Raedermacher Wasson-Tucker to Sarah Pillsbury (who also worked for Peter at one point) or perhaps even Marsio-Aalto herself since the Aaltos' Artek designs for furniture and other items were being marketed in the Boston distributorship founded in 1940 by Pillsbury and another Cambridge School architect alumna, Louisa Loring Vaughan (Conrad; 1913–2003). It was not long before Raedermacher Wasson-Tucker took over for Pillsbury, in 1942, and the name of the firm was changed to Artek in Boston. Though that unprofitable enterprise only lasted to 1943, the collaboration of the Aalto couple made an impression on the Wasson-Tuckers.[189] Together, the couple designed a plywood chair (reminiscent of those by the Aaltos), illustrated in the *Art in Progress: 15th Anniversary Exhibition* (1944) at MoMA, and they entered a competition for a postwar worker's house, for which they won an honorable mention in *California Arts and Architecture* (figs. 2.26, 2.27). The two-story house was modern in both its simple, austere presentation and in its conception: the facilities for laundry, food deliveries, and a central garage were to be shared with others in a semi-urban community. These two collaborations, however, seem to be the only ones the couple took on; he entered the Canadian armed service and disappeared from the picture; she moved to the East Village and continued, both independently and successfully, with the support of her émigré connections.[190]

The Russian-born architect Serge Ivan Chermayeff proved to be especially influential in her career. In 1943, she assisted him in the "Design for Use" section of the *Art in Progress* exhibition for which she was responsible for the installation layout as well as the exhibition stands and screens.[191] Deemed one of the most "important," "timely," and "urgent" components of the exhibition, the installation built on the museum's precedent of revealing relationships between art and manufacturing, particularly in the area of plastics.[192] Following its three-month run, in November 1944, Raedermacher Wasson-Tucker was named acting curator of the industrial design department during the wartime absence of Eliot Fette Noyes (see fig. 1.3). She again worked with Chermayeff on another exhibition called *Tomorrow's Small House* (1945).[193] Although its content—eight house models (scaled one inch to the foot)—had been previously commissioned from modernist architects to illustrate articles in *Ladies' Home Journal*, the two collaborated with Vernon DeMars to situate them in a community development consisting of apartment blocks and rowhouses as well as parks and schools, along with such popular contemporary structures as a shopping center, filing station, tennis pavilion, library, and recreation hall.[194] With the endorsement of Chermayeff and another émigré, Bernard Rudolfsky, who was also active at MoMA, in the summer of 1947 Raedermacher Wasson-Tucker studied woodworking at Black Mountain College in North Carolina.[195] Through Rudolfsky, she also received a commission to design a cover for *Interiors*, a publication of which he was the architectural editor; the image—rows of traditional brownstones interrupted by a severe modern structure—is strikingly akin to the neighborhood context of the MoMA building (1939) at 11 West 53rd Street, the place where she had had her strongest connections (fig. 2.28).

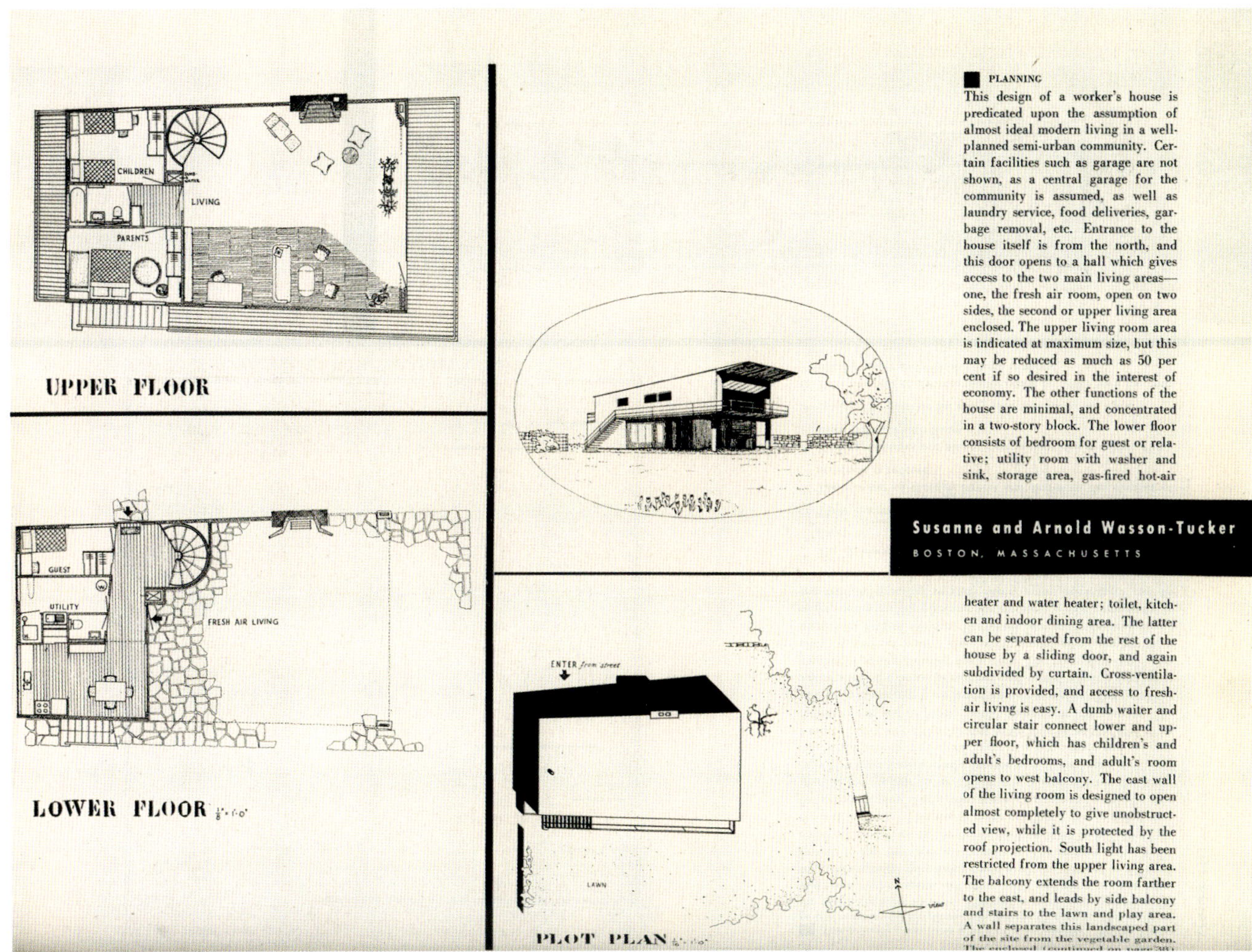

■ PLANNING

This design of a worker's house is predicated upon the assumption of almost ideal modern living in a well-planned semi-urban community. Certain facilities such as garage are not shown, as a central garage for the community is assumed, as well as laundry service, food deliveries, garbage removal, etc. Entrance to the house itself is from the north, and this door opens to a hall which gives access to the two main living areas—one, the fresh air room, open on two sides, the second or upper living area enclosed. The upper living room area is indicated at maximum size, but this may be reduced as much as 50 per cent if so desired in the interest of economy. The other functions of the house are minimal, and concentrated in a two-story block. The lower floor consists of bedroom for guest or relative; utility room with washer and sink, storage area, gas-fired hot-air

Susanne and Arnold Wasson-Tucker

BOSTON, MASSACHUSETTS

heater and water heater; toilet, kitchen and indoor dining area. The latter can be separated from the rest of the house by a sliding door, and again subdivided by curtain. Cross-ventilation is provided, and access to fresh-air living is easy. A dumb waiter and circular stair connect lower and upper floor, which has children's and adult's bedrooms, and adult's room opens to west balcony. The east wall of the living room is designed to open almost completely to give unobstructed view, while it is protected by the roof projection. South light has been restricted from the upper living area. The balcony extends the room farther to the east, and leads by side balcony and stairs to the lawn and play area. A wall separates this landscaped part of the site from the vegetable garden.

2.27. Designs for a worker's house by the Wasson-Tuckers in the "designs for post war living" competition, *California Arts and Architecture* 60, no. 9 (September 1943): 26–27.

Raedermacher Wasson-Tucker was resourceful in finding other forms of employment throughout the city that related to her interests and expertise. She worked in the department of layout and typography for *Architectural Forum* in 1946–47. She also did some teaching: a course in 1945–47 on wood and fiber design in the industrial design department at Pratt Institute in Brooklyn and in 1951 in interior design at the New School for Social Research, as well as a class in 1952 for homemakers on how to solve their design problems.[196] Her job at Knoll Associates, beginning in the fall of 1947, had a large influence on her career, however. As a designer in the planning unit managed by Florence Schust Knoll (1917–2019) to coordinate spatial plans, furnishings, and color programs, her interior projects ranged from the thirty-story Aluminum Company of America Building (1953) by Max Abramovitz in Pittsburgh to a women's dormitory at Howard University in Washington, DC. She also worked on the interiors at the American embassy in Havana, Cuba (1953), designed by Harrison and Abromovitz; she capitalized on that experience to supervise the interiors at the American embassies in Stockholm (1953) and Copenhagen (1954), both designed by Ralph Earl Rapson and John van der Meulen.

In June 1952, Raedermacher Wasson-Tucker went to Stockholm, intending to stay for six weeks to determine the furnishing programs for the latter two embassies and to research manufacturers to produce the furniture in them designed, or licensed, by Knoll International (established in 1951). A year later, she was still there, serving as a liaison between the State Department's Foreign Building Operations (FBO), Knoll, and Nyköping

Kompaniet (1904–73), the wholesale workroom that ended up making much of the Knoll-designed furniture using parts sourced from Europe and the United States.[197] The FBO then hired Raedermacher Wasson-Tucker directly to plan the interiors of the American Embassy designed by Eero Saarinen in Oslo, Norway (1959; now owned by Fredensborg), using Knoll-designed furniture made locally by Tannum Møbler.[198]

It was then that Raedermacher Wasson-Tucker chose to remain and work in Sweden—only as a freelance designer—but she maintained her presence in the United States through her exhibition and interior work at least through 1981.[199] Her talent is palpable in the literature: rarely do editors pay attention to an installation process, but in *Interiors*, in 1958, the influential editor Olga Gueft (1915–2015) devoted two pages to her flexible, demountable installation of natural wood for the traveling exhibition *Swedish Textiles Today*, sponsored by Sweden's Ambassador to the United States and circulated by the Smithsonian Institution.[200] Like Sandecka Nowicki, her career evolved from a life with unexpected turns, but there was a certain continuity—in her areas of focus, openness to new opportunities, network of expatriates, and international exchanges. In the end, it all made for a productive and fulfilling life.

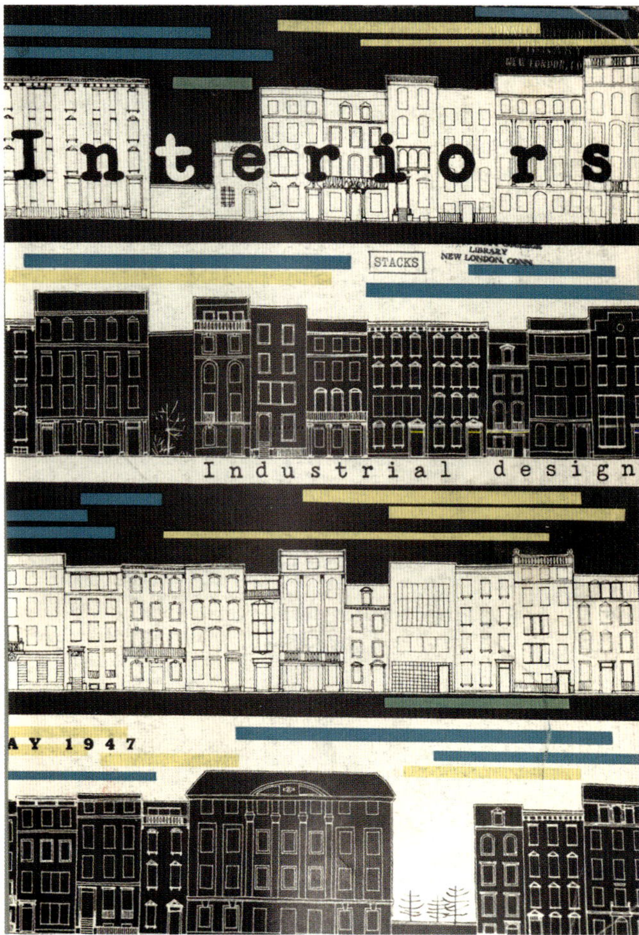

2.28. Susanne Raedermacher Wasson-Tucker, cover of *Interiors* 106, no. 10 (May 1947).

Mexican Design—Modern and Vernacular

Raedermacher Wasson-Tucker's career underscores how the international interchange of modern architects and designers led to the integration of Modernism into American culture. It also shows how adept women can (or need to) be in creating professional opportunities for themselves. In March 1949, she produced a feature for *Architectural Record* titled "So You're Going to Mexico," comprised of thirty-four photographs of modern buildings, an illustrated map she drew to locate them, and a list of twenty-one architects and their new buildings.[201] Intended as a companion piece to "Modern Mexico," an article written two years earlier by the modernist architect Ann Binkley Horn (formerly Rand; 1918–2012), the piece by Raedermacher Wasson-Tucker convincingly reveals her familiarity with Mexico (she owned a house in Cuernavaca), where in 1946 her husband transported from Canada to Mexico a prefabricated pavilion of plywood and laminated wooden panels to exhibit at the Feria del Libro.[202] Her focus on Mexico could not have been timelier, given that *House Beautiful* reported in 1949 that Mexico was the subject "of more books, more guides, more literature than any land in North America."[203]

The outpouring of American interest and investment in Mexico that started around the end of that country's revolution was endorsed by emerging publications that promoted Mexico as a viable and rewarding destination. Among them was Stuart Chase's *Mexico: A Study of Two Americas* (1931), a "swell" book with a heated and sensuous tone that made it irresistible, in the opinion of Elizabeth Bauer, who read it in preparation for her extended stay in Mexico.[204] Some of the most popular publications were written by women, among them Anita Brenner's influential *Idols behind Altars: Modern Mexican Art and Its Cultural Roots* (1929) and *Your Mexican Holiday: A Modern Guide* (1932), as well as Alice Leone-Moats's *Off to Mexico* (1931) and *Frances Toor's Guide to Mexico* (1933).[205]

For American writers, Mexico embodied two ostensibly antithetical sources of modern inspiration:

contemporary design and vernacular tradition. In his memoir *Exile's Return* (1934), Malcolm Cowley recognizes this dual perspective by observing, according to art historian Mary Panzer, "that bohemian Americans embraced a distinctive, if paradoxical aesthetic: a devotion to the most modern art and a keen interest in 'the primitive,' as found in archaeological excavations, ancient sculpture and artifacts, folk art, and craft, and commitment to an American or New World culture independent of European tradition. In Mexico, the two combined."[206] The simultaneous attention to both traditional and contemporary aspects of Mexican culture may not have been paradoxical after all, as the architectural historian Luis Esteban Carranza argues, since the two were promoted as crucial elements of a hybrid culture that hoped to unify Mexicans in the postrevolutionary period.[207] Appreciating the distinct though ostensibly compatible qualities of contemporary and traditional design, it is not surprising then that women versed in American Modernism, a synthesis of European Modernism with regional vernaculars, embraced and would be influenced by Mexican culture.[208]

American interest in Mexico was fostered by exhibitions and installations: *Mexican Arts*, for example, organized by René d'Harnoncourt (the future director of MoMA), premiered in October 1930 at the Metropolitan Museum of Art in New York before it traveled to seven other venues. While MoMA's *Twenty Centuries of Mexican Art* in 1940 was staged as the world's "largest and most comprehensive" exhibition about the country's art and culture, the museum had already hosted a five-week, attendance-breaking retrospective on Diego Rivera in 1931–32, which contended that the quality of his fresco paintings was virtually unrivaled.[209] His work was also exhibited in a survey of Mexico's architectural history at the Architectural and Allied Arts Exposition at New York's Grand Central Palace in 1931.[210] Along with Edward Weston and Tina Modotti, Rivera also provided illustrations for publications bound for the American market, indicating the central role he had in disseminating imagery of Mexico, well before he was famously dismissed by the Rockefeller family in 1933 for his image of Vladimir Lenin on the mural in the RCA Building at Rockefeller Center.[211]

Extant logs and correspondence by women travelers to Mexico, including the twelve who studied at the Cambridge School, usually included accounts of visits to large-scale public murals with social and political content, a post-revolutionary genre established by Rivera along with José Clemente Orozco and David Alfaro Siqueiros.[212] The Cambridge School landscape architect Dorothea K. Harrison (1897–1978), for example, recognized Rivera's intention to integrate his murals with the architecture itself. Writing in 1938 about the chapel (1927) at the Universidad Autónoma de Chapingo in Texcoco, she informed likeminded alumnae, "He has such a sense of composition and of appropriateness to the architectural surroundings that one feels the painting [is] one with the building."[213] Elizabeth Bauer also reported home about Rivera's murals, explaining that those on the walls of the government schools in Mexico City seemed to display "much more feeling for the suffering of the Indians and their essential character" than those by Orozco.[214]

Her comment, somewhat surprisingly, was part of her larger exposition about Mexican architecture that compelled her to query her sister, Catherine Bauer, "Did you know that there is a modern architecture in Mexico?"[215] The leader of the movement, she explained, was Juan O'Gorman—"a nice guy, young, communist, and functionalist"—who headed the government school, the Escuela Superior de Construction (1931–36). She compared it to the Bauhaus, observing that the student-made models she viewed in an exhibition were "honest and fresh" with "emphasis laid on constructions as opposed to architecture." Of the more than twenty elementary schools O'Gorman built for the Ministry of Education, all were similarly "bare" and "functional," generally of two stories with open-air corridors and partially enclosed courts juxtaposed with an official wing, in a contrasting color. Unlike the modern architecture to which she was accustomed, "the use of color," she claimed, was "more exciting than anything else—never white. Always combinations of five or six giddy colors." Not only were facades inherently connected to the brightly painted vernacular houses, but to her they were also "a great relief after the dicta of Hitchcock and Johnson."[216] In spite of her jibe at the organizers of MoMA's International Style exhibition, Bauer could not help but compare the two houses O'Gorman built in 1931 in San Angel—a white and deep pink house and studio for Rivera joined at the top floor by a bridge to the roof of a smaller, dark-blue house for Frida Kahlo—to the house Le Corbusier completed in 1922 for the cubist painter Amédée Ozenfant in Paris.[217] Nonetheless, Bauer's impassioned response to the fusion of established color traditions and modern forms and construction anticipated

2.29. Elisabeth Coit, watercolor of Mexican buildings, 1930s. *Elisabeth Coit Papers, Schlesinger Library.*

the formation of a type of Modernism in the United States that eschewed what Bauer, as well as Raymond and Power, saw as the austerity of the approach favored by Hitchcock and Johnson.

In the exhibition catalog *South of the Border: Mexico in the American Imagination, 1914–1947* (1993), James Oles conjectures that artists "found images of modernity and urban life in Mexico of little aesthetic interest," but the experience of Power and Raymond was just the opposite.[218] According to a travel diary Power kept during the third (of four) trips she and Raymond made to Mexico between 1939 and 1965, their favorite way to tour was by car with a knowledgeable driver who would take them to anything new. They saw the Unidad Independencia (1960), for example, a "most magnificent" housing development for social security workers that included abundant gardens, playgrounds, shops, markets, and differently sized pools. In their opinion, this development (along with their German counterparts) put American housing projects "to shame." The Museo de Historia Natural (1964) in the second section of Chapultepec Park, a series of pastel-colored concrete domes, each housing a different branch of science, also made the equivalent at home seem "puny and very inadequate." Their favorite building, which they visited twice, was the Museo Nacional de Antropología (1964) by Ramírez Vázquez, whose overwhelming scale, outstanding ground plan, and jointless stone walls in muted colors complement lower-level fountains with water cascading down a large central column.

Like Victorine du Pont Homsey and Elisabeth Coit, whose watercolors documented the rural and sometimes still undiscovered (by Americans) qualities of small villages in valleys rimmed by mountains of varied hues, Power and Raymond did not limit themselves to recent developments (fig. 2.29; see fig. 1.9). On their drive south along the Pan-American Highway, Power noted the agrarian vista: "Mountains, always, on [the] horizon; ploughed fields with oxcarts, sugar and alfalfa growing and brilliant green, and always the ubiquitous burro; typical Mexican landscape and typical bright blue sky with cumulous clouds casting shadows."[219]

On their fourth trip to Mexico, Power and Raymond were excited to encounter Verna Cook Shipway (formerly Salomonsky; 1890–1978), an architect with a similar viewpoint.[220] In the second of five illustrated books on house interiors and details in Mexico that she and her second husband, Warren Shipway, an engineer, compiled between 1960 and 1970 (she made the selections and detailed drawings; he took the photographs), Cook Shipway explained how at first they were moved solely by "the massive public buildings with their provocative murals." After a few years of research, however, they emerged from their preoccupation with monumental images to embrace a broad sensitivity to "the charm and the not-by-rule conceptions" of vernacular interiors.[221] Like other visitors from the United States, the Shipways publicized both modern and traditional architecture for the American market. In so doing, they implicitly supported the argument that these disparate architectural expressions shared basic characteristics.

Victorine du Pont Homsey was more enthusiastic about the unfamiliar indigenous villages than about their month in Mexico City. In 1932, she and her husband drove a Ford roadster on the "perilous" Pan-American Highway, which was still unfinished and made for miles of "rough going," including a collapsing bamboo bridge, narrow roads, and terrifying blasts. After settling southwest of Mexico City in Taxco, an enclave of artists and craftspeople, they spent two months sketching the small mining town's pastel-colored houses with tiled roofs nestled in the "fantastically warped and twisted mountains." They befriended two young pupils of Diego Rivera and Roberto Montenegro and learned how to grind their own colors from earth pigments for oil, tempera, and watercolor paints, as well as how to use their "section of gold" (golden ratio). Their artwork records their appreciation for indigenous methods, regional forms and materials, and colorful, lively settings, and it anticipates the influence Mexico would have on their architecture. In Wilmington, for example, when they completed their own modern office building in 1962, they demarcated facade details in red and blue (fig. 2.30). Du Pont Homsey had traveled extensively throughout Europe, but she attested that Mexico was the most exciting country she ever visited.[222] Bauer Mock would have agreed; about a year after her extended visit she confided, "I have an aching nostalgia for Mexico. … I should rather live there than any other place on earth."[223]

Esther Frances Baum Born (1902–87) took herself to Mexico for about ten months in 1936 to photograph primarily contemporary buildings (figs. 2.31, 2.32). Her unprecedented concept was to survey and document the country's modern concrete architecture, and she sold it to *Architectural Record*, which, in turn, devoted its April 1937 issue to the project and co-published the material in book format with William Morrow under the same title, *The New Architecture in Mexico* (1937; republished in 2021). The plans and illustrations in the publications, most of which Baum Born herself photographed, concentrate on the countless cement structures (many still standing), which she arranged in the publications by type and then by architect. As historian and critic Beach Riley explains in an accompanying essay, the new architecture was "essentially a native Mexican affair" generated by the government to accommodate the social reform effort after the Mexican Revolution.[224]

Baum Born's photographs of Mexico, today housed in three different archives, are credited "with directing the attention of the world to the rise of modern architecture in Mexico." She considered contemporary Mexican architecture as rooted in its own culture, and consequently, she also examined vernacular settings and cultural traditions, ranging from ceremonial dress and plume dances to open markets and bullfights.[225] In fact, the architect and historian Ernestina Osorio notes that Baum Born explored the "traditional / modern dialectic" that was visible in the forms of modern Mexican architecture by, for instance, juxtaposing an image of the pyramid of Cuicuilco near Tlalpan with the stepped outline of a building by Le Corbusier.[226]

Baum Born had taken up photography after moving to New York in 1929 with her husband, Ernest Alexander Born, an architect also recognized for his graphic work. She had married the fellow Californian in 1926 after receiving her Bachelor of Arts in architecture (1924) from the University of California, Berkeley. Her impetus for studying photography was that she was so "mad" at the quality of the photographs she shot on their European

2.30. Office building and apartment of Homsey Architects, 2003 North Scott Street, Wilmington, Delaware, 1962. *Joseph W. Molitor architectural photograph collection, Department of Drawings and Archives, Avery Architectural and Fine Arts Library, Columbia University.*

tour in 1927–28 that she enrolled in a studio school of art photography on West 56th Street organized by Ben Magid Rabinovitch in 1933.[227] There, her pursuit of photography was rewarded by the inclusion of her images in group shows, as well as in two solo exhibitions, in 1933 and 1934, of fifty and sixty photographs, respectively. Rabinovitch also planned a series of thematic exhibitions featuring her Mexican images, beginning in November 1936 with *Picturesque Mexico: Its Life, Landscape and Architecture in Photographs by Esther Born*. Although only photographs of "Old Mexico" were shown, still, as Rabinovitch explained on the invitation, Baum Born's approach was "entirely architectural," no matter what the subject.[228]

The couple's personal and professional network paved the way for the Mexican project, and to a certain extent it was a collaboration, since her husband designed the layout of the book. It may be that Baum Born's interest in Mexico was piqued when Rivera and Kahlo resided for a time in their apartment building at 176 Bleecker Street in Greenwich Village; Baum Born's photographs of the famous pair testify to this connection.[229] Concurrently, however, her husband publicly endorsed Rivera in *Architectural Forum* after the "Rockefeller Center experience."[230] He also could have introduced his wife to the staff at *Architectural Record*, given that between 1932 and 1936 he produced its cover designs and was on the editorial staff.[231] During the same period, he was a consultant for the H. E. Fletcher Company in West Chelmsford, Massachusetts, which may have had a professional relationship with Federico Sánchez Fogarty at Cementos Tolteca, the largest producer of cement in Mexico.[232] This "smart, imaginative, advertising man," as one Texas newspaper reported, was responsible for promoting new concrete architecture in Mexico, and he "swamped the country with so much propaganda" that "'functional' building soon became the official style of the land."[233] Fogarty was crucial to Baum Born's project since he was able to make important introductions; consequently, the publications include a photograph of him at Cementos Tolteca and his essay about modern architecture in Mexico.[234]

The New Architecture in MEXICO

Modern architecture, painting and sculpture in Mexico, collected and arranged with photographs, by Esther Born.

Mexico, the land of mañana and siestas, has suddenly waked up and found itself in the midst of a wave of modern construction, a new kind of revolution, carrying with it a renaissance of the creative talent of the Aztecs and the Spanish Americans.

The new architecture in Mexico includes outstanding examples in practically every important class of building—office buildings, store groups, factories, hospitals, schools, apartments, workers' houses, town and country houses. In their own setting, the new structures with their straight lines and unornamented flat surfaces present a dramatic contrast with neighboring buildings heavily ornamented in the Spanish Colonial tradition; yet the new architecture has been perfectly acclimated to its background.

This new volume is a reference source for building designers everywhere, and contains a complete assemblage of the progressive thought of architects and engineers below the Rio Grande.

The New Architecture in Mexico, by Esther Born, in text, photographs and colored diagrams, including supplementary text on mural painting, sculpture, and pottery $3.50

THE ARCHITECTURAL RECORD
119 W. 40th St., New York

Enclosed is $3.50 for which please send me a copy of THE NEW ARCHITECTURE IN MEXICO.

Name ....

Address ....

A.R. 6-37

....

2.31. Advertisement for *The New Architecture in Mexico* (New York: Architectural Record and William Morrow, 1937) in *Architectural Record* 81, no. 6 (June 1937): 102.

Baum Born likewise played a key role in promoting a vision of the country's contemporary architecture that emphasized its monumentality, its composition with flat masonry walls and strip windows, and its use of concrete to create dramatic forms and spaces. One striking photograph shows the facade of the Tuberculosis Sanatorium (1929) outside Mexico City by José Villagrán García. Baum Born photographed the classically symmetrical front of the building from dead center so that the lines of the formal plantings in the foreground draw the viewer's eye to the entrance pavilion marked by a tower; for other images, she dramatized the buildings through oblique views (fig. 2.32). As different as her approach sometimes was, Baum Born was sophisticated in her use of imagery to construct a conception of Modernism that was both stable and dynamic. Historian Nicholas Olsberg argues that Baum Born "pioneered observations of the new architecture" in her photographs and that time in Mexico exerted a decisive impact on their own production and the creative means they used to represent it. Mexican influence, for instance, is evident in the experimental urban house on which they collaborated with landscape architect Thomas Dolliver Church that was shown in 1937 in a group of highly creative images at the San Francisco Museum of Art.[235]

2.32. Esther Baum Born, photograph of Sanatorio para Tuberc (Tuberculosis Sanatorium; 1929) by José Villigrán García (1901–82), Huipulco, Tlalpam, Mexico, 1936. *Esther Born Collection, Center for Creative Photography, University of Arizona.*

The international circulation of architectural ideas—transmitted through photographs and publications as well as through immigration and travel—is a well-documented characteristic of the interwar period. Typically, the male émigré architects are the only ones credited with transferring avant-garde sensibilities to a retardataire American design culture. That story is too simplistic. First, it minimizes Mexico's place in the imagination of contemporary United States architects; second, it erases the significant roles of women in the "transnational discourse on Mexican architecture," as Osorio describes it.[236]

Women located the sources of modern architecture in both traditional buildings and contemporary examples in Europe and Mexico; the latter had a unique appeal because women considered its traditional architecture fully compatible with Modernism, especially the humanistic variation, which many embraced. This alternative idiom was arguably more international in both its sources and expressions than the Modernism that MoMA was advocating at the time: the sources of women modernists were expansive and they made use of them in varied ways in their American careers, which, by necessity, were wide ranging.

CHAPTER III

Forging Networks

NETWORKS, OR CONTACTS, WERE SO UBIQUITOUS AND central to architectural practice in the mid-twentieth century that they have scarcely warranted comment in discussions of the profession. Though women needed networks to advance, they were largely excluded from the conventional male-dominated networks—clubs, societies, competitions, and scholarships, as well as social, recreational, and leisure activities—among them, the proverbial golf game.[1] Still, women architects succeeded in creating their own, largely outside of the existing structures, through which they promoted modern architecture and sometimes found patrons for their most ambitious ideas.

Although the American Institute of Architects was organized in 1857 to "unite in fellowship the architects of the United States," the field lacked a system into which women could readily integrate.[2] Further, there was no defined path for them to make the critical transition from school into the workplace. The Russian-born American architect Morris Lapidus looks back on his forty-year career in the United States in his book *Architecture: A Profession and a Business* (1967), observing, "All architects must start somewhere. We work for others. Unlike the medical profession, there is no residency or internship required, although most states require three years of employment with a registered architect before taking the state examination."[3] The Kentucky architect C. (Clarence) Julian Oberwarth made a similar comparison of architecture to medicine in 1945: "No practical means have yet been found to bridge the gap between college and architectural practice with opportunities for the normal expansion of skill such as that available to the medical internee in the hospital."[4]

Newly graduated architects had to rely on established firms to obtain the practical experience necessary for registration and certification. During this crucial period of training, young practitioners, typically working as draftspersons, gained knowledge of the business, accumulated cash, and, importantly, focused on establishing "some contacts," as Lapidus said, for whom they could create designs.[5] An unwillingness of male architects to employ women graduates at this key juncture could interrupt, if not suspend, their professional ambitions. "In a field in which apprenticeship was the norm and professional contacts a necessity," Alice Friedman explains, the lack of learning opportunities for women could create insurmountable obstacles in the initial stages of their careers.[6] The formation of networks that typically contribute to professional success was not as straightforward for women

3.1. Photograph of Norma Merrick Sklarek, 1988. *National Portrait Gallery, Smithsonian Institution, partial gift of Lynda Lanker and a museum purchase made possible with generous support from Robert E. Meyerhoff and Rheda Becker, Agnes Gund, Kate Kelly and George Schweitzer, Lyndon J. Barrois Sr. and Janine Sherman Barrois, and Mark and Cindy Aron.*

architects as it was for men. Even so, women could be adept at using nontraditional means to secure education and employment. Marion Mahony, for example, whose father died when she was young, relied on the contacts of her mother, Clara Hamilton Perkins Mahony (1841–1927), a longtime school principal, to connect her with others who could support her education and career: her MIT education was paid for by Anna Hawes Wilmarth Ikes (1873–1935), the daughter of a wealthy suffragist colleague of Mahony's mother; afterward, she worked for her first cousin on her mother's side, the Prairie School architect Dwight Heald Perkins in Chicago.[7] It was again through her mother that she was introduced to a Mrs. Davis from the Hubbard Woods neighborhood of Winnetka, Illinois, who evidently connected her to Frank Lloyd Wright, leading to her employment with him in 1895.[8] Though her mother's network provided decisive opportunities for Mahony, her own network did not bring her clients.[9] Instead, her career was overshadowed by Wright and by Walter Burley Griffin, whom Mahony married in 1911.

Mahony's failure to set up the networks that lead to commissions and notoriety was not unusual for women. Architectural historian Lynn Walker discusses a similar phenomenon in the career of Eileen Gray (1878–1976), one of the best-known early modernist architects in Europe. As Walker explains: Gray "did not set up on her own an architectural office or work within an architectural practice, nor was she part of the professional networks of architectural culture. These social networks were, and are, a site for the production of architectural identity, profile and recognition, and they are crucial to getting commissions and having work published, the track which leads ultimately to incorporation in the canon of architectural history."[10] Despite her high-quality work and the publication of her designs during the 1920s and 1930s, Gray, like Mahony, was left out of most histories of the modern movement until recently. She was even, as Walker details, deprived of authorship for her most prominent design: E. 1027 (1926–29), a house by the sea at Roquebrune in the South of France that she shared with her architect lover Jean Badovici, the editor of *L'Architecture Vivante*.[11] Gray's concentration on the design of domestic interiors and furnishings contributed to her association with the putatively feminine aspects of architecture and therefore to her omission from the histories that privilege large-scale public and commercial commissions.

When women entered the architecture field, their abilities to network in ways that set them up to work independently or in partnership were often circumscribed not only by gender-based stereotypes and expectations but by class identities. As Lapidus explains: "Some of us are fortunate in our friends and social contacts. We move in a milieu of potential builders, and we use our contacts to sell, or should I be more circumspect and say 'persuade' our friends and potential clients that we have the background, the skill, the talent and the ability to design that home, that school, that church, or that fine office building which they are about to build. Even this type of selling ... requires skill and refinement."[12] The words *skill* and *refinement* were code for aristocratic or at least bourgeois attributes that enabled architects to hobnob successfully with potential employers.

It is easy to imagine that if architects lacked the middle- to upper-class backgrounds of their clients, then they would be less prepared to "sell" their talent. Since men managed most businesses or professions, they would have responded more positively to male than female architects. Racial and ethnic identities similarly affected patronage, given that those in positions to hire architects—executives, municipal officials, and institutional leaders, among them—were typically white Protestants and would have gravitated to others from the same demographics. In her study of Black American architects, the sociologist Victoria Kaplan argues that systemic racism has blocked Black architects from important and lucrative areas of practice, especially public and corporate buildings.[13] One exception is Norma Merrick Sklarek (1926–2012), a Harlem-born Black woman who graduated in 1950 in architecture from Columbia University (fig. 3.1). Though she faced substantial obstacles, in 1960 she nevertheless became director of architecture at (Victor) Gruen Associates (founded in 1946) in Los Angeles. An article in *Preservation* magazine describes the complexity and richness of her life: Merrick Sklarek married multiple times and raised two children; she was an avid golfer and a bridge player, as well as a host of legendary garden parties at her home in Pacific Palisades, a predominantly white, affluent suburb of Los Angeles from which she would have been barred as a resident on the basis of her race prior to 1948.[14] By excelling in social and recreational activities tied to elite white culture, Merrick Sklarek was able to transition friends into clients and vice versa.

Merrick Sklarek figured out that socializing with clients was "a must for any architect," as Lapidus advised, and that an architect should be prepared to receive informal calls in their office or home.[15] In keeping with the general acceptance of the role of women as homemakers, much of the wining and dining was carried out by wives even when they too were architects.[16] Typical of the postwar period, women who undertook professional employment in architecture and related fields still retained primary responsibility for domestic labor.[17] Their burden was not particularly lightened by the modern houses in which they lived and, in many cases, also envisioned. As architectural historian Kristina Wilson observes, "Modernism may have been a rational, efficient servant for White men, in particular, but it set onerous standards of physical domestic labor for both White women and women of color."[18] An architect's home had to be visually cohesive, attractive, and functional, which meant for the wife and any domestic worker she employed cleaning, shopping, and cooking. The type of home entertaining Lapidus recommends, which presumes a married architect with a private house, would have been challenging for a woman with multiple roles as a homemaker, mother, and professional.

Entertaining clients in the way Lapidus or other male architects did would also have been difficult for unmarried women who lived with other women. Nonetheless, the New York architect Elisabeth Coit did not discount the possibility that as a single woman she could network in the ways Lapidus advocated or otherwise. In her article "Architecture as a Profession for Women," published in 1936 in the *Radcliffe Quarterly*, she describes an essential component in the daily life of an architect—"a chat with a fellow townsman on the commuters' train; dinner with a prospective client."[19] She was circumspect about what might come of such discussions businesswise: "New jobs may result from those train and other contacts. On the other hand, the immediate happy result may simply be better human, civic, and professional relationships."[20] At the time, Coit was no longer taking the train to a downtown Manhattan office from her retreat in Croton Heights, but instead was living full time with her partner in a rented apartment in midtown. Her inability to engage in the sort of networking Coit herself saw as part of the daily grind of an architect may help explain why her listing in the federal census changed from "architect" in 1930 to "freelance painter" ten years later.

Academic Networking

For most male architects, their educational institutions regularly provided entry into the established offices of fellow alumni. The initial foothold of that job, usually as a draftsperson, typically led to further advancement through networking, as Lapidus advised. Women architects likewise used their alumnae connections to further themselves professionally. While their networks neither had the same reach nor the direct results of men, they still functioned effectively.

When students or alumnae volunteered at the Cambridge School of Architecture and Landscape Architecture, for example, in fundraising, administration, critiques, or exhibitions, they bolstered their networks and established collaborations. The pages of *House Beautiful* during Ethel Power's editorship, between 1923 and 1933, are filled with writings by or about the work of at least twenty-five Cambridge School alumnae and faculty, especially the inner circle of friends she shared with Eleanor Raymond.[21] The magazine featured their varied collaborations: when one woman was the architect and another the landscape architect or interior decorator for a particular project, as well as when a nascent, unlicensed architect worked with an associated architect who stamped the drawings. Another activity that provided connections included activism in the women's rights movement. Florence Luscomb found her way in 1912 to the firm of Ida Annah Ryan (1873–1950), the first woman to graduate with a master's degree in architecture at MIT. Also a committed suffragist, Ryan allowed Luscomb to take a leave of absence from her job in Waltham, Massachusetts, to campaign for votes. Later, in the 1930s, the League of Women Voters, which had been organized to promote suffrage rights, invited the Viennese émigré Elizabeth "Lisl" Scheu Close (1912–2011) to lecture on "Modern European Housing," thus enabling her to connect as an architect with its female audience.[22]

Networks of women architects existed in the United States during the early decades of the twentieth century, but they were rarely identified as such. Thus, historians have been led to believe, as Gwendolyn Wright did in 1977, that "to appear successful, each woman architect had to stand apart from other women, both from her few peers and from the many beneath her in the hierarchy. To band together with others facing similar difficulties would be to acknowledge that women, generally, were subordinate, and that the system was discriminatory."[23] Female networks, however, have been recorded in sources ranging from the publication of built projects in shelter magazines and journals to personal and professional correspondence, to school communications. The mentions in each issue of the *Cambridge*

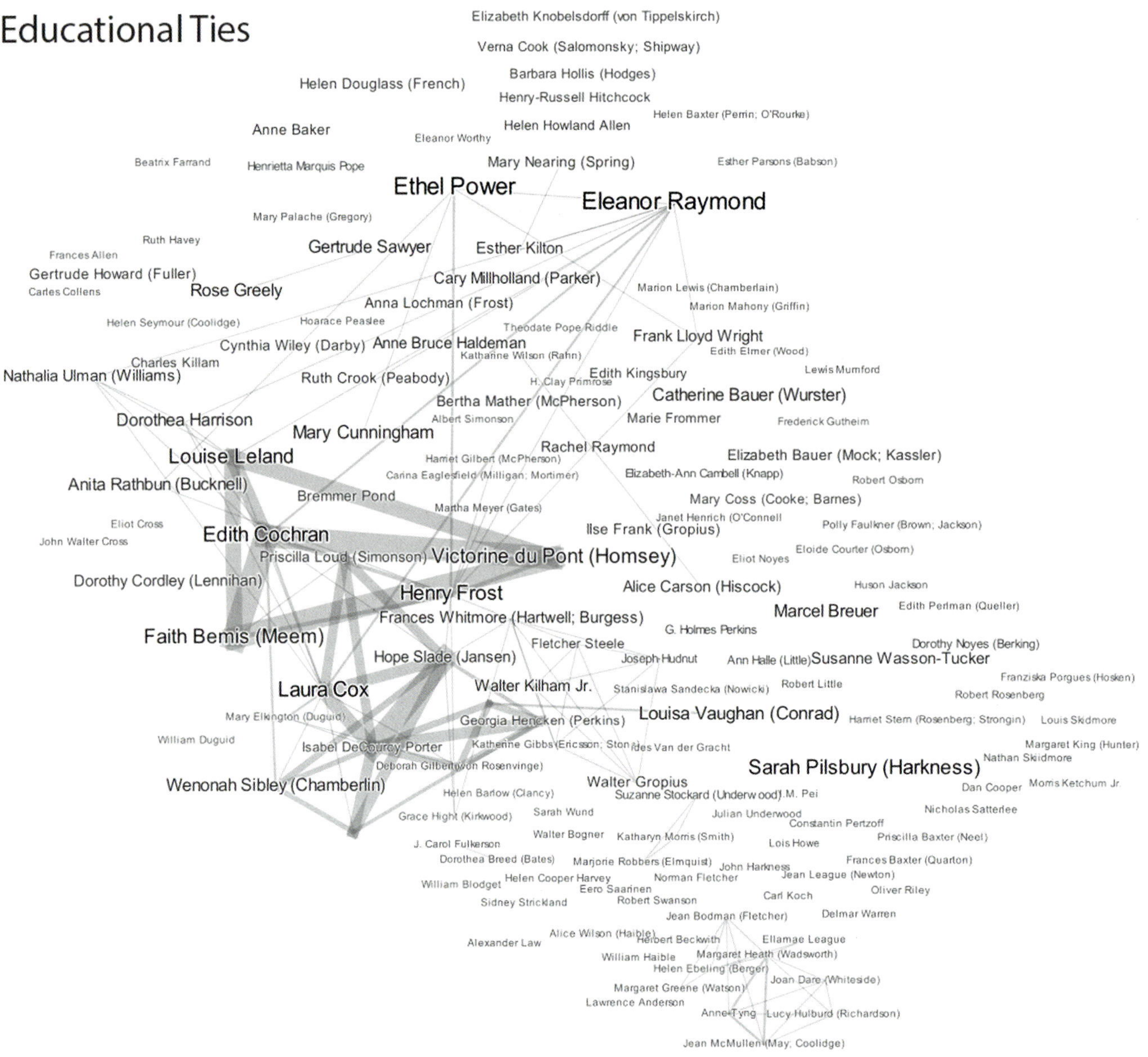

3.2. Visualization of the educational networks of women architects.
Design by Scott Weingart.

School Alumnae Bulletin—of architects studying, working, traveling, fundraising, or socializing together—document a strong underlying web of associations. As important as their connections were to them, until recently, it has not been possible to categorize and enumerate, much less envision, the networks women in architecture formed.

A Network Analysis of Women Architects

The recent introduction of computer-aided network analysis in the discipline of art history has made it possible to see more clearly the infinite webs of the communication and interdependence of women architects—with each other as well as with faculty and even clients. The network analysis conducted for this book commenced with names of Cambridge School architects (some of whom subsequently studied at Harvard's Graduate School of Design [GSD]) along with their life dates, and education histories. Also listed are men and women outside the school who had important roles in their educational or professional development. Eventually, women who received their architecture degrees at other institutions were also added. The database generated from their documented interactions was organized according to

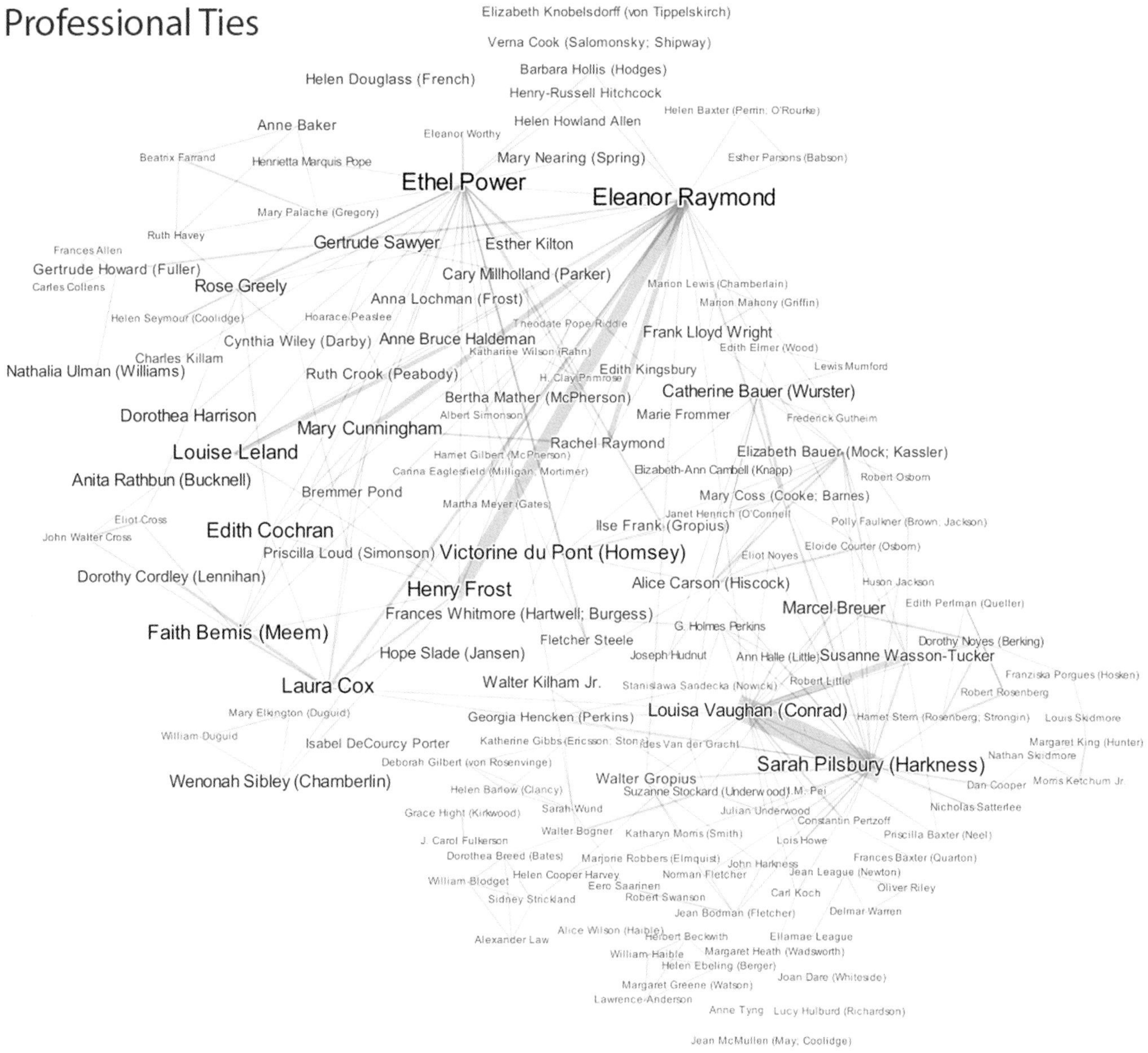

3.3. Visualization of the professional networks of women architects. *Design by Scott Weingart.*

the types of relationships the women kept: educational, professional, and social (figs. 3.2, 3.3, 3.4). The data made possible several visualizations in which the centrality of a name is a function of the number of relationships a woman had (indicated by the lines connecting a particular name to others), while the type size of the names themselves identifies the degree to which a woman was integrated into her community.

Given the absence of written descriptions of the practices of Cambridge School architects, these network visualizations are compelling in that they reveal the types of relationships as well as the degree of participation of each woman. While the networks of the alumnae and faculty are strong in the educational visualization, they are even more so in the social visualization. At the same time, they show that the three women who trained at MIT—Florence Luscomb, Annah Ryan, and Eleanor Manning O'Connor—similarly gave their female peers mutual support. At the same time, the clustering of Anne Tyng and Jean League demonstrates that the women who attended the GSD connected with one another around educational endeavors, perhaps because they often collaborated with one another on joint school projects, for example, in Marcel Breuer's studio.[24] Networks for women who

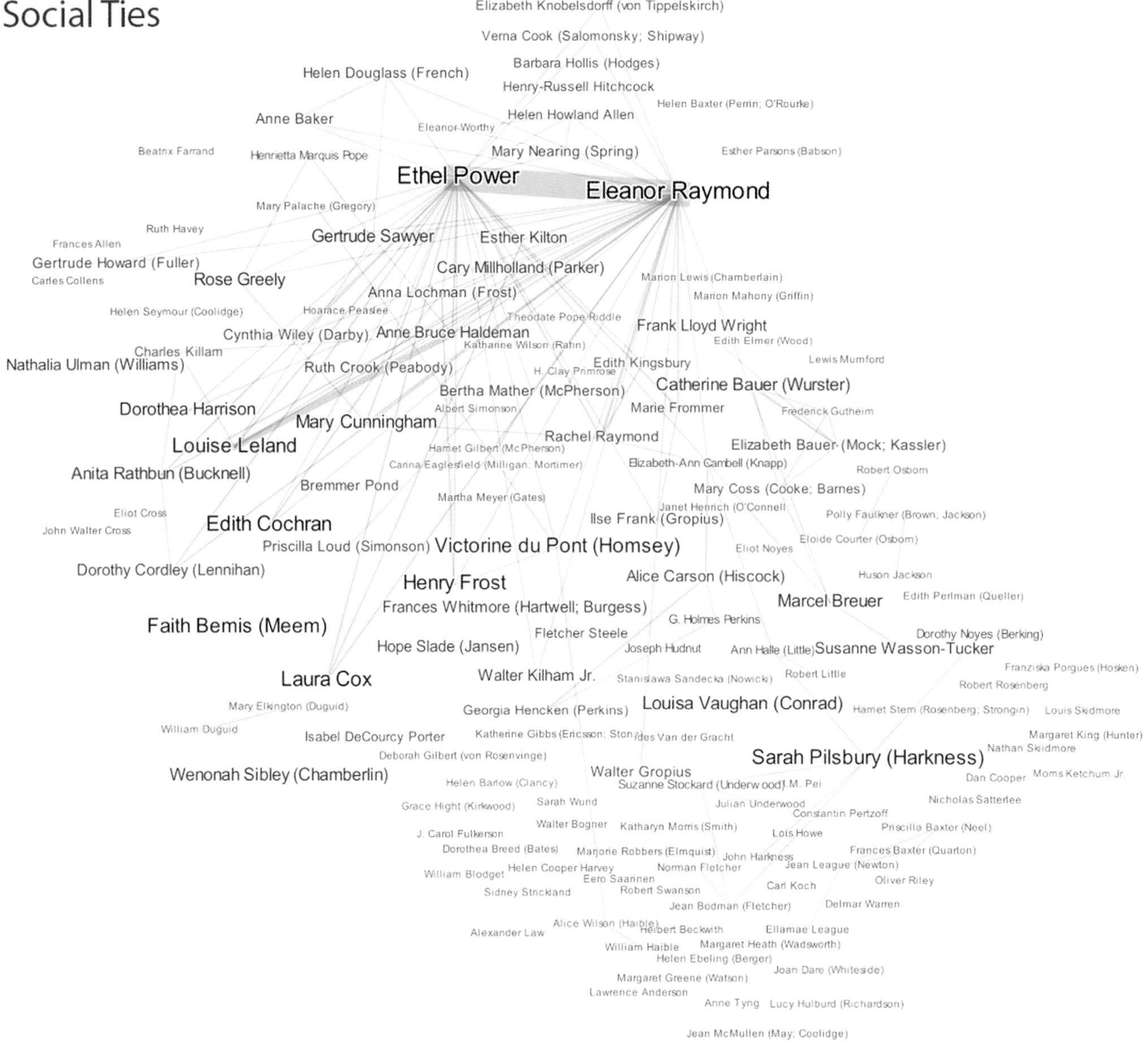

3.4. Visualization of the social networks of women architects.
Design by Scott Weingart.

trained at the same institution, the visualizations confirm, were essential to their professional success.

The most active women in the social and professional network visualizations were predictable since they are well known through the publication and exhibition of their work; other women, however, show unexpected prominence. Wenonah "Winnie" Sibley Chamberlin (1911–2000), for example, a 1934 architecture graduate of the Cambridge School, lived in New York between the time of her marriage in 1937 and divorce in 1959, when she moved to Louisville, Kentucky, and practiced in the architecture firm of Jasper Dudley Ward III. The visualizations place Sibley Chamberlin in proximity to Elizabeth Wiley Dunlap, who lived in Chattanooga, Tennessee, not far from where Chamberlin resided.

While the names of a few of the women, such as Anne Tyng, who attended Harvard's GSD in the formative years of coeducation, are widely familiar, others in the visualizations are not. Margaret "Meg" Heath Wadsworth (1920–2008), for instance, was a Wheaton College (Massachusetts) graduate who, after attending the Cambridge School and then Harvard, went on to work for modernist Carl Koch before earning her MFA in ceramics from Pratt, where her husband, Christopher Wadsworth, taught architecture.[25] Although she branched out into pottery, the clay bas reliefs and sculptures she derived from her sketches of Venetian facades merged her two passions.[26]

Among the women *not* from the Cambridge School, the strongest interconnections were forged by the sisters Catherine Bauer and Elizabeth Bauer Mock with such colleagues as Susanne Raedermacher Wasson-Tucker and Mary Coss Barnes (formerly Cooke), all of whom were connected to MoMA (as can be seen on the timeline in figure 1.19). The personal ties between these women also existed with the men with whom they were in relationships. For instance, before her marriage in 1940, Catherine Bauer and Lewis Mumford maintained an intimate relationship while Coss Barnes was married to the modernist architect Edward Larrabee Barnes. Two characteristics of this network stand out: the visualizations show, first, the intensiveness with which these women interacted with one another, primarily at the museum, and second, the group of male architects and critics circling around them (Barnes and Mumford, as well as Bertold Lubetkin, Frederick Gutheim, and Frank Lloyd Wright). The picture that emerges of a core of collaborative women surrounded by males with whom they were likewise professionally involved is fundamentally different from the image of Cambridge School women networking among themselves. It is true that Cambridge School women partnered with or worked for male architects, but in the visualizations, their interconnections with each other predominate.

The Centrality of Eleanor Raymond and Ethel Power

The most telling insight gleaned from the visualizations is the importance of Eleanor Raymond and Ethel Power in their homosocial communities. To some extent, the prominence of Raymond is the consequence of the data: she was one of the most active alumnae at the Cambridge School; her output was widely reported on in *House Beautiful* (with at least thirty-four citations to her work in an eleven-year span; see Appendix II); and she was one of the few women architects to create her own archive before her death, ensuring the survival of a lot more information than there is for most women architects. The visualizations also demonstrate the crucial role of Power, undoubtedly because she regularly published the work of Cambridge School alumnae and faculty. Until now, scholars have not been able to assess her influence as editor of *House Beautiful* and, moreover, the dominance the two women wielded as a couple.

Modern spaces were crucial for encouraging their social interactions. Raymond inveighed against the "stagey, stuffy" Victorian interiors of her youth that forced inhabitants to "act a part" and instead advocated for simple, clean spaces to promote "friendly congeniality."[27] The (homo) sociability she often facilitated through architecture is visible in the residences Raymond designed for herself, family members, and friends. Their townhouse in Boston, and summer complex in Gloucester, Massachusetts, as well as her sister Rachel Raymond's house in Belmont, Massachusetts, enhanced all three of their networks.

The residential community they created in 1922 in the Boston townhouse Raymond owned with her sister exemplifies a purpose-built space for alternative living (fig. 3.5). Situated on the "flat" between Beacon Hill and the Charles River, Raymond reconfigured the nineteenth-century townhouse to accommodate an accomplished group of women so that each could benefit from both personal and communal spaces. The choice of location on Charles Street was not incidental to the program, since at the time the neighborhood was being revived with progressive, artistic, and, in some cases, bohemian residents, like themselves.[28]

As the plans show, each of the three independent suites in the house contained a bedroom (the first floor had two), a kitchenette, and a living room, while the basement area (other than a studio for Rachel) and adjoining outdoor garden were shared.[29] On the first floor lived landscape architect Mary Cunningham and her twin sister Florence C. Cunningham (1888–1980), both of whom had connections to the arts: after graduating in 1910 from Vassar College, Mary Cunningham attended the Lowthorpe School of Landscape Architecture in Groton, Massachusetts, and, between 1916 and 1918, the Cambridge School, where she eventually taught a course in plant materials. After she died unexpectedly in 1934, Florence Cunningham continued to live in the house while teaching diction and drama at private schools until 1950. She also directed the Gloucester Little Theatre on Cape Ann, which would have been an important locus for the community building of Raymond and Power. While the second floor was given to the widowed mother of the Raymond sisters, the third and fourth floors were dedicated to the Raymond sisters, along with Power. Besides the living and cooking spaces on the third floor, a loggia was at the rear with a view toward the river, which was also visible from above, where a sleeping porch

A Beacon Hill Restoration

A Very Modern House from an Almost Hopeless Wreck

BY ETHEL B. POWER

BEACON HILL, that historic part of Boston that will long be associated with such names in American literature as Thomas Bailey Aldrich, Dr. Oliver Wendell Holmes, James T. Fields, Francis Parkman, and others, has recently seen many strange and interesting restorations, but none perhaps that has started from so unpromising a beginning as did this one shown here.

Of the two owners of the house, one is an architect, and this owner and architect is a woman. This fact is not necessarily in all cases an important one, but it is in this instance because to appreciate and understand the house it is necessary to take into account its household which is entirely a non-masculine one. It is also necessary to know that the eager desire for a house in the Beacon Hill district with a view of the Charles River Basin determined the architect not to yield in her search until such a view was found and without doubt instilled in her the faith that there were possibilities for restoration in the wreck shown in the accompanying photograph. This wreck, which owed its being to the yielding of a ten-foot slice of its façade to the exigencies of street widening, had one supreme merit. At its rear was an unimpeded view of the river basin, a view that was not only unobstructed but was considerably enhanced by a foreground of a large, well-kept garden.

The neighbors were, then, one morning later considerably amused and more than mildly curious to see two women enter the wreck by means of a ladder procured from a near-by Chinese laundry, a ladder being under the circumstance a much more important piece of equipment than a latchkey. Armed with tape, detail paper, and pencil they proceeded to the arduous and extremely dirty task of measuring the house, or that part of it left which, al-

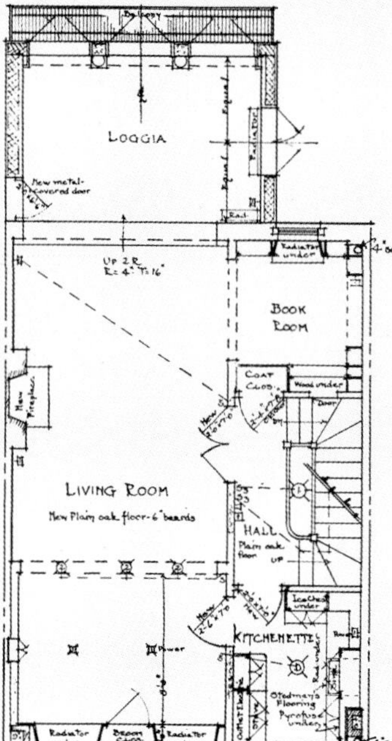

THE PLAN AT THE LEFT SHOWS THE THIRD FLOOR, AND THE ONE BELOW THE SECOND FLOOR WHICH IS ALSO TYPICAL OF THE FIRST AND FOURTH FLOORS. ON THE FIRST FLOOR THE HALL REPLACES THE BATH, AND A BATH THE KITCHENETTE. ON THE FOURTH FLOOR A BATH REPLACES THE KITCHENETTE, A DRESSING-ROOM GOES ACROSS THE ENTIRE FRONT, AND A SLEEPING-PORCH OCCUPIES THE SPACE OVER THE LOGGIA

Photographs by Paul J. Weber

ONLY FAITH AND A PRACTISED EYE COULD HAVE FORESEEN ANY POSSIBILITIES OF RESTORATION IN THIS WRECK

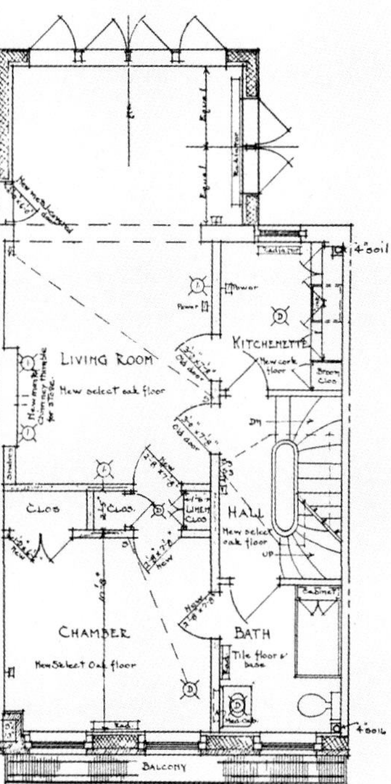

Architect, Eleanor Raymond of Frost & Raymond

THE WRECK RESTORED TO THE DIGNITY OF A GEORGIAN EXTERIOR OF OLD BRICK, LIMESTONE TRIM, AND GOOD FENESTRATION

462

3.5. Townhouse of Eleanor Raymond and Rachel Raymond, 112 Charles Street, Boston, in *House Beautiful* 56, no. 5 (November 1924), 462.

with three beds was located. The fourth floor contained two dressing rooms and a bathroom. Architectural historian Nancy Beth Gruskin compares the program of the house to that of a Progressive-era settlement house in which women could live autonomously but also with opportunities to share cooking and household chores and to create intentional communities.[30]

In a substantial story about the restoration of their "Very Modern House from an Almost Hopeless Wreck" in *House Beautiful*, Power presents the project as an architectural response to an unconventional program intended to accommodate the group: "To appreciate and understand the house it is necessary to take into account its household which is entirely a non-masculine one."[31] The unusual floor layout, however, was concealed by the conventional facade, designed by Raymond to replace the original that was removed when the street was widened and the house lost ten feet on the front. Described as Georgian, and not "modern," the facade corresponds to the formula developed in the previous century for Boston townhouses: "a protective coloration," in Friedman's words, that did not disclose the unusual interior arrangement.[32]

As Power explains, the project was motivated by both aesthetic and practical considerations: "These floors must be planned for the convenience of three women, business women who therefore demanded not only a comfortable and attractive house but one that would be as far as possible, self-running."[33] Her functionalist approach eschews overwrought domestic interiors of the previous century in favor of homes suited to such modern requirements as being maintained without servants. The phrase *self-running* also recalls the nearly contemporary and polemical text *Vers une architecture*, in which Le Corbusier argues that "Une maison est une machine à habiter."[34] Although Power would later express enthusiasm for Le Corbusier, there is no indication that she was then thinking of his work. However, she did describe the kitchenette on the third floor as a "tiny but compactly arranged room ... electrically operated. An electric motor makes ice and an incinerator burns refuse, so that no iceman nor garbage man need defile its black tile floor."[35] In conception then, the house was modern, even though the exterior was traditional to fit into its setting.

While Power considered the house plan suitably adapted to the needs of its occupants, she also argues that the furnishings expressed the "taste and of the life of the owners" as well as their "individuality." Conceding that the living room, decorated by Rachel Raymond, would "offend the lover of period rooms as it has nothing of the element of period consistency," Power describes the interior spaces, including some antique furnishings collected abroad, as fluid arrangements reflecting the changing preferences of the residents.[36]

Rachel Raymond's eclectic decorating style developed after graduating from Wellesley College in 1916, when she attended the School of the Museum of Fine Arts (SMFA) in Boston, operated by the architect Charles Howard Walker, a founding member of the Boston Society of Arts and Crafts.[37] Her educational experience led to employment in New York at Herter Looms, a tapestry and textile firm founded in 1908 by Albert Marsh Herter, from where she encouraged "visits from all the married 1916-ers [her Wellesley classmates] who are having new lamp shades [made] or rearranging curtains, to say nothing of interior decorating new homes." Though she then worked independently designing daybeds "with regal canopies, real lace and chic puffy pillows," she balanced her service to the "modern moneyed bourgeoisie" by attending lectures presented by the socialist economist Scott Nearing.[38]

When Eleanor Raymond designed Rachel's house in Belmont, about a decade after the Boston townhouse, her approach was entirely different in that she created an austere construction inspired by examples she and her fellow travelers had seen on their European tours. Like the Boston house, it was also an "experiment" in domestic life that accommodated a group of friends and family: Rachel and her professional (and likely personal) partner Edith Kingsbury, along with her mother, Lucy Jones Kingsbury (figs. 3.6, 3.7; see figs. 1.1, 1.2). In her article in *House Beautiful* entitled "Spring Pasture—Our Experiment in the Country" (October 1932), Kingsbury explains that after a "long trial in the city," she and Rachel "wanted a house that would make the most of the opportunities this land was giving us—that is, a house with all possible beauty, comfort, and convenience for simple living, but as little as might be walling us in from the out-of-doors." Their solution, she said, "was a 'contemporary' house, with flat roofs for porches, large glass areas to let in sunlight, and views of the ever-changing trees and sky and birds."[39]

As Kingsbury reports, the Belmont house provided a space that could enhance both their personal and professional lives. The interiors were as eclectic as those in Boston, based on photographs that show an unremarkable mixture of Asian and early American furnishings (see fig. 1.2). Nevertheless, the finishes and details were significantly more

3.6. Eleanor Raymond, Rachel Raymond house, Belmont, Massachusetts, c. 1932. *Private collection.*

progressive than those in Boston.[40] Since Kingsbury had not lived with Rachel Raymond in that house, their cohabitation added a dimension to their personal and professional collaboration that would span more than fifteen years.

In its original configuration, the Belmont house contained two bedrooms with no hierarchy between them. Labeled simply as "1" and "2" on the plan, the rooms are essentially the same size and shared a hall bathroom. Raymond apparently wanted a degree of privacy that she did not have earlier in Boston, and the furnishings in her bedroom suggest a creative person in need of a "room of one's own," as Virginia Woolf succinctly labeled essential private spaces. Judging by the photograph of her bedroom, it was a sanctum, even though not sumptuously outfitted and, in fact, rather austere (fig. 3.7). Below the expansive horizontal windows providing a view to contemplate nature was a cloth-draped table with a multi-drawer jewelry box flanked by small urns that together look like an altar. The curtained sleeping alcove, nearly filled by a metal-frame single bed, was her place for complete privacy. And yet, the portrait by Margarett Williams Sargent (McKean; 1892–1978) above the bed is the (only) indication of the larger social network of which the Raymonds and their small coterie were a part.

Described as an "out-and-out modernist," Sargent had trained in Europe as well as in New York with George Luks, an artist who immortalized her in a portrait titled "The White Blackbird" (1919).[41] Though in 1920 she married a Boston aristocrat, Sargent was also reputed to have had a romantic bohemian life with both men and women.[42] At about the time the Raymond sisters were planning the Belmont house, she was engaged in a spate of exhibitions: a review of her second solo exhibition at the Arts Club of Chicago, to which Rachel Raymond loaned her painting *Speakeasy*, describes Sargent as a "leading 'Modernist' of Boston."[43] Certainly, the Raymonds encountered her work either in Cambridge or in Gloucester, where in 1931, Sargent exhibited her paintings at the F. C. Poole Shops, only a mile and a half from Raymond and Power's summer home.[44] By hanging the portrait in her sleeping alcove, Rachel Raymond gave visual expression to

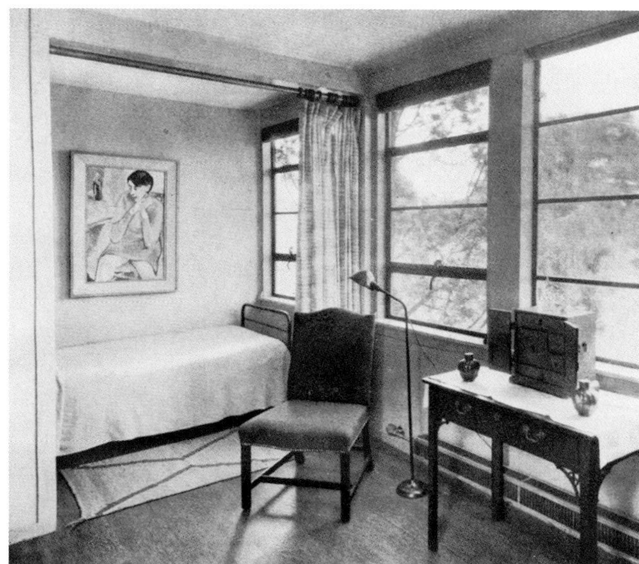

3.7. Bedroom of Rachel Raymond pictured in Edith Kingsbury, "Spring Pasture—Our Experiment in the Country," *House Beautiful* 72, no. 4 (October 1932), 202.

the network of artistically sophisticated women to which they belonged.

This intellectual network, extending from Boston and Cambridge to Gloucester, may well have inspired Eleanor Raymond to purchase a shingled house for Power and herself in Gloucester on Old House Cove.[45] Perhaps it was Florence Cunningham, a native of Gloucester, who led them to the area or, at least, introduced them to the local culture, which included the likes of May Sarton (1912–95), then a novice actress but later a lesbian poet, novelist, and memoirist, who was deeply attached to Cunningham, whom she described as "so tiny and slight, between a star and a flower, exquisite."[46] Another resident with whom Raymond would have been familiar was the wealthy businessman and mining expert John Hays Hammond, whose daughter Natalie Hays Hammond (1904–85), an artist and theatrical designer, commissioned Raymond to design a group of houses on a neighboring property, in 1942.[47] The program was similar to Raymond's Boston home: Hammond built her compound for "single women [to] live their lives surrounded by other professional women."[48]

Power and Raymond acquired their coveted waterfront retreat from a neighboring estate that had existed since at least 1913.[49] In her writing about the property in *House Beautiful*, Power ignores the main house (since Raymond did not build it) and instead emphasizes their transformation of a ramshackle garage, perhaps using the remnants of other outbuildings, into a garden house with a bath and guest room, which was "never without occupant or applicant," according to Power's summer diary.[50] "To a coolly appraising eye," Power comments, there was not much architectural merit other than its "unassuming simplicity."[51] Though they painted it a deep blue to match the ocean, the structure was, according to Power, an "unsophisticated bit of functionalism."[52] Her statement is given visual expression in their attractive arrangement of garden tools hanging on an interior wall, capturing the modern ethic that pervaded the place (fig. 3.8).

3.8. Garden tools artistically arranged on the garden shed wall of Eleanor Raymond and Ethel Power in Gloucester, Massachusetts. *Private collection.*

They enhanced their "small paradise" with a fenced-in garden containing boxed beds and a gravel terrace (fig. 3.9).[53] Guests were reportedly "charmed by the unique atmosphere" that was central to their intimate homosocial community and to maintaining their network of personal and professional associations, including multiple visits from Henry Frost and Walter Kilham.[54] After a couple of women visited one day, Power notes in her diary, "It is strange how much we seek the garden in preference to the terrace [of the main house]; a garden is like the sky; it veils the infinite and so by reducing its scale makes it bearable."[55]

Viewed collectively, the Gloucester, Boston, and Belmont dwellings demonstrate their inhabitants' diverse interpretations of Modernism, and, more importantly, the significance that they attached to the spaces that nourished their professional and social wellbeing, as the two were profoundly intertwined. Their success and satisfaction relied on the networks they used to publicize their ideas and images, to find employment, and to construct buildings that demonstrated their concepts of Modernism.

Networks and Patronage

Informal networking likely produced the notable architect-client relationships between Raymond and Amelia Peabody. Both were from elite Boston backgrounds: the Raymond family was in railroads; the Peabody family, in finance, and so it would not be surprising if they knew one another in Boston society. The convenience of Raymond's

3.9. Eleanor Raymond (*left*) and Ethel Brown Power (*right*) in the garden of their summer home, 9 Doliver Road, Gloucester, Massachusetts, on the cover of *The American Home* 38, no. 1 (June 1942).

office at 126 Newbury Street, just one block from the family home periodically occupied by Peabody, also could have benefited the architect-client collaboration over several decades at Peabody's farm in Dover, Massachusetts.[56]

In addition to a farm group, Raymond designed various houses and garages as well as a greenhouse on the property.[57] However, the sculpture studio, most likely the first project Raymond completed for Peabody, in 1933, is the most noteworthy modern building she designed for her dedicated patron (see figs. 1.6, 2.2). In addition to this work, Peabody consented to other experimental projects by Raymond: a plywood house (1941), a Masonite house (1946), and a solar house (1949)—the latter a widely reported early effort at passive solar heating, designed in collaboration with the Hungarian-born scientist Mária Telkes (1900–1995) of MIT. Peabody also hired Raymond to manage the construction of a prefabricated Deck house (1968) in southern New Hampshire.[58]

Since Peabody gave Raymond complete artistic freedom, she acquired a group of buildings that far

3.10. Gladys Treeby Calthrop, stage set for Noël Coward's *Design for Living*, Ethel Barrymore Theater, New York, 1933. *Vandamm Theatrical Photographs, Billy Rose Theater Division, New York Public Library.*

3.11. Curved staircase in the Amelia Peabody studio by Eleanor Raymond. *Raymond Collection, Historic New England, Robinson gift.*

exceeded her personal requirements: the Colonial Revival house was appropriate for the large property, as were the handsome stables; in contrast, the sleek, modern studio, said to be fireproof, was more sophisticated than Peabody's lifestyle.[59] Though she produced some large-scale sculpture groups, they were not particularly monumental, but her studio could easily have accommodated both production and exhibition on that scale.

Peabody's extensive archive at the Massachusetts Historical Society scarcely hints at a patron who would have demanded an interior as *luxe* as the one Raymond provided in the studio. The dramatic staircase that spirals to richly appointed guest quarters on the second floor completely eschews traditional forms and recalls the Manhattan penthouse in the contemporaneous play *Design for Living* (1933) by Noël Coward (figs. 3.10, 3.11). Pivoting on a ménage à trois formed by a woman and her two rival male suitors, the comedy's risqué theme was matched by its setting, inspired by the 1920s domestic architecture of Le Corbusier and other modernists, as interpreted by Coward's frequent collaborator on sets and costumes, Gladys Treeby Calthrop (1894–1980). The British critic Stephen Patience commented about the penthouse set, explaining that it was "dominated by the sweeping arc of a staircase with low, metal-frame armchairs" and that it had an "austere chic that is closer to a cinema lobby or a West End nightclub than a home."[60] Its striking similarity to Peabody's stylish studio interior suggests that Raymond was attuned to high architecture fashion, which she could only achieve through the support of the type of patron who moved in the same circles as she did. Patronage was just one outcome of networking. As the network analyses demonstrate, the extent to which women connected with one another varied by the type of relationship. Starting in the drafting rooms of the schools themselves, where women were thrown together on architecture projects, they inevitably formed essential social and professional networks with peers and faculty as well. The centrality of Raymond and Power in the networks reflects both their dedication to encouraging professional women and their ability to create spaces where their connections prospered.

CHAPTER IV

Collaboration as a Primary Strategy

CULTURAL AND ARCHITECTURAL CRITICS CLAIM THAT women in architecture have an innate sensibility for domestic architecture, a perception that evolved from the gendering of the home as female in the nineteenth century. Among the women who resisted this essentialist arguments was architect Marcia Mead (1879–1967), who observed in 1931 that although some male architects design houses, generally, they "are idealists and dreamers and will be more abstract in their work: they will choose to do imposing public buildings, triumphal arches, churches, music halls that is—monuments to ideas." At the same time, Mead maintained, "I cannot agree that a woman is a natural born housekeeper or house planner." Nonetheless, she allowed, "Women might be said to be fundamentally conservationists and would naturally be interested in the humanities—buildings that have to do with living conditions such as hospitals, the Young Women's Christian Association buildings, Young Men's Christian Association buildings, city planning and dwellings!"[1]

Shortly after graduating from Columbia University in 1913, Mead formed a partnership with Anna Schenck (1874–1915), thereby establishing one of the earliest architecture firms in the country consisting solely of women architects.[2] Before Schenck's premature death, they designed country houses, low-income housing, and community centers—"housekeeping on a large scale," as she referred to their work. Though the two architects professed to be interested in housing as a specialization, they flatly refused to work as interior decorators: "We'll starve first," they declared in an interview for an article about them in 1914 in the *New York Times*, where it was surmised that the partnership "must be a most enjoyable circumstance."[3] Their model of collaboration would ground many more women in their professional training and practice.

Entrenched in the Cambridge School of Architecture and Landscape Architecture from the moment it was established in 1915, the concept of collaboration in education spread to other schools as well, including the Graduate School of Design (GSD) at Harvard, where students were also encouraged to look holistically at projects based on genuine situations. In their subsequent practices, collaboration took a variety of forms: some were brief and others long-lasting; some were linked to landscape architecture and others to interior architecture (or decoration). While there were those who only worked

4.1. Founding partners of the Architects Collaborative (1945–95), 1950. *Front row, left to right*: Jean Bodman Fletcher, Walter Gropius (1883–1969), and Sarah Pillsbury Harkness; *back row, left to right*: Robert Senseman McMillan (1916–2001), Norman Collings Fletcher (1917–2007), Benjamin Casper Thompson (1918–2002), Louis Albert McMillen (1916–98), and John Chessman Harkness (1916–2016). *Harvard Law School.*

with women, others partnered with men, often as married couples, and sometimes parents collaborated with their children. These arrangements produced a wide range of results, although those women who partnered with men tended to be professionally overshadowed, even if they had equal, if not larger, roles in the design process.

Architecture production has always been largely collaborative, but rarely has it been acknowledged as such. Accordingly, when The Architects Collaborative (TAC) was organized in Cambridge in 1945, the firm's unprecedented proclamation of equal collaboration among its eight architect partners was called out not only in the name of the firm but also in the widely published photographs of the partners (fig. 4.1). The collaborators insisted that everyone had a voice at requisite weekly reviews of current commissions, each managed by a team leader, whose name was publicized along with that of the firm. Despite the participation of Gropius, or "Grope," as the TAC partners called the eldest and most prominent partner, the intention was for there to be no hierarchy among the partners, nor for any one of them to specialize in anything but architecture.[4]

This radical experiment demonstrating the significance of collaboration in modern architecture provides an important starting point for discussing the role of women in collaborative practices. Collaboration in the arts is hardly unprecedented since it was emphasized by the turn-of-the-century Arts and Crafts and Aesthetic movements as well as by the Bauhaus design school. After World War II, Le Corbusier and others called for a renewed "synthesis of the major arts," and, as the influential modernist critic Reyner Banham observed, it became "a consecrated theme of the Modern Movement."[5] Scholars continue to associate Gropius with artistic synthesis as well as with an egalitarian concept of practice due to his affiliation with the Bauhaus and its advocacy of the German concept of the *Gesamtkunstwerk* (total work of art).[6] As an acknowledged master of the movement and the chair of Harvard's architecture department from 1938 to 1952, Gropius was renowned for his teamwork approach to design, and thus has been credited with disseminating collaboration in architecture in the United States.

It is also said that Gropius brought about the implementation of collaboration as the primary methodology at TAC, even though his partners there also had a voice in forming the practice. Giving credit to Gropius for the innovative approach at TAC, rather than to the team, indicates how invested historians are in the concept of the lone modernist master. Individual production, rather than creative exchange within a partnership, has long been a central premise in art history.[7] Ever since Giorgio Vasari established the canon of Renaissance artists in *Le vite de' più eccellenti pittori, scultori, ed architettori* (Lives of the Most Excellent Painters, Sculptors, and Architects), the fixation on the singularity of makers has persisted, as noted by architectural historian Beatriz Colomina: "The phallic myth of the solo architect, the isolated genius, is one of the most regressive and reactionary understandings of architecture—but unfortunately still one of the most pervasive."[8]

The Development of Collaborative Architectural Practices

From at least the second half of the nineteenth century, the lone practitioner was the dominant model for architecture firms. The firm of Henry Hobson Richardson is an excellent example of a practice organized like a Beaux-Arts studio with draftspersons and associates executing the concepts of the lead architect.[9] As architecture grew in scale and complexity due to advancements in industrialization, urbanization, and new building types, an alternative model of practice emerged in which participants took on specialized roles. An example of this phenomenon was in the firm comprised of Charles Follen McKim, William Rutherford Mead, and Stanford White, each of whom had a distinct responsibly: chief architect of public buildings, managing partner, and artistic leader in residential design, respectively. Their Boston contemporaries, Robert Swain Peabody and John Goddard Stearns Jr., formed a similar partnership after the Civil War in which Peabody was responsible for design and Stearns the management. By the mid-twentieth century, when large corporate operations relied on specialists—epitomized by the prolific firm of Skidmore, Owings & Merrill (SOM), established in Chicago in 1936—collaboration became the norm among practitioners working in teams of specialists under a firm partner whose name was the only one attached to the project.

In contrast, there were few prevailing models of established women architects practicing independently or running an office with multiple draftspersons in the way of Richardson. Short of Julia Morgan, who led her own practice in San Francisco only after partnering with Ira Wilson Hoover between 1907 and 1910, it was unimaginable that a woman architect could run her own multifaceted firm, particularly because most potential clients considered the female sex suited only to domestic design.[10]

Discovering Collaboration: The Case of Sarah Pillsbury Harkness

The extensive private archive of Sarah Pillsbury Harkness provides much insight into what it took for such women to devise careers in architecture. As her story reveals, her mainstay was collaboration, which eventually led her to the formation of TAC. Like many other women, she initially followed a circuitous path, one that moved from architecture to retail, to furniture design, and to museum work. Her first tangible project was a summer house for her parents in Duxbury, Massachusetts, which she completed in 1938 as a student at the Cambridge School. She benefited from the supervision of Eleanor Raymond, who was inspired by historic New England barns but modern in her approaches to functional planning, siting, and design.[11] The house articulated Raymond's interest in "fitting form to function" and showed how she infused modern concepts with vernacular expressions.[12] Pillsbury also consulted with Raymond on the renovation of a carriage house for her grammar-school friend Susan Binney at 9 Byron Street in Boston, for which she designed functional, built-in furniture as well as an innovative skylight, while also utilizing vibrant colors—a Raymond signature.[13]

Raymond helped Pillsbury launch her career as a modernist by providing her with an opportunity for collaboration, for which Pillsbury would forever be grateful. But finding a job after graduating in 1940 was a terrific challenge. In letters to her soon-to-be-husband John Chessman Harkness, she expressed her envy of him getting to spend that summer in Frank Lloyd Wright's Taliesin studio in Spring Green, Wisconsin. Already recognizing that by "being a girl" she was vulnerable to biases, at Taliesin, she conjectured, she would too easily be "confined to the kitchen."[14] Instead, and without pay, she assisted Marc Peter Jr., her former instructor of interior architecture, in the design of a prize-winning members room at the Institute of Modern Art (now the Institute of Contemporary Art / Boston).[15]

When there were no further job prospects in his office, Pillsbury vacillated about her next move: she could try the architecture firm of Walter Bogner, an instructor at both the Cambridge School and Harvard's GSD who might consider taking her in after the "Harvard boys" went back to school in the fall; or perhaps she could work, again without pay, for Carl Koch, a modernist architect open to hiring women. In addition, she considered industrial design, housing development, and construction, all reasonable alternatives but mostly unavailable to women.[16] Finally, she settled on opening a display room to market modern furniture and accessories. She sensed, however, that she would be better off with a partnership, as she had with Raymond (and before that, as Raymond had with Henry Frost when she embarked on her career). Pillsbury convinced fellow Cambridge School alumna Louisa Vaughan of her "wild" idea to collaborate with her in the business, to be called Pillsbury and Vaughan, which would primarily offer Artek products designed by Aino Marsio-Aalto and Alvar Alto, but interior design as well.[17]

Pillsbury confessed that she was concerned that, by venturing into interiors work, she might end up doing nothing more consequential than "peddling flowery chintz and putting unnecessary decoration on clean rooms."[18] But her take on the Artek furniture, reflecting her understanding of the qualities of modern design—functionalism, technology, natural materials, and organicism—helped her evade the stereotypical role of women as mere decorators of historical styles. Though personally involved for only a year in the Boston-based distributorship, Pillsbury profited from being able to engage with the architecture community, get some experience, make a little money, and learn how to promote and manage a business. Even more, it gave Pillsbury an opportunity to observe collaboration in a way she had never done.

It was not just the day-to-day operations with Vaughan that were so instructive, but also her introduction to Marsio-Aalto, an architect who, although not well-known in the United States, had prospered in her working partnership with her more prominent architect husband. Marsio-Aalto was equally capable, demonstrated by the drawings she submitted in 1938 to Finland's open competition for the design of the pavilion to be erected at the New York World's Fair (1939); her design came in third, next to her husband's first and second prizes.[19] Pillsbury immediately understood her multifaceted artistic abilities and took it upon herself to draft a feature (eventually published in the *Christian Science Monitor* under the byline of her successor, Raedermacher Wasson-Tucker) that focused on Marsio-Aalto and her

4.2. John and Sarah Pillsbury Harkness, *Hypothetical Project for a Bank in Syracuse, NY* in "New Buildings for 194X," *Architectural Forum* 78, no. 5 (May 1943): 86.

collaboration with her husband: "When a woman does such an amazingly brilliant and complete a job," she wrote in a draft, "we feel we should like to tell about her."[20] She explains, admiringly, that in addition to being the mother of two and the Aalto partner most responsible for the execution of interiors and exhibitions, Marsio-Aalto had an equally important responsibility in both overseeing and interpreting her husband's incessant outpouring of ideas. In so doing, Pillsbury noted, Marsio-Aalto showed tremendous patience and perseverance; her practicality and thoroughness in detail enabled her to resolve every problem she tackled: "She works like an engine with such concentration that she cannot be stopped," she wrote.[21]

While Pillsbury respected Marsio-Aalto for the projects she completed in her own name, such as the wooden house she designed in just two days for a Finnish masseuse in New York, it was the husband-wife collaboration that most captivated her. When she asked Marsio-Aalto what furniture pieces she personally designed, the Finnish architect could not say because the couple's thoughts were so blended. So deep was their understanding and confidence in one another that each could anticipate and carry out the other's ideas, as Marsio-Aalto did in 1940 with the update of the Finnish Pavilion at the World's Fair. As "the rock" of the family enterprise, she arguably modeled for Pillsbury how to achieve a many-faceted life as proprietor and designer, wife and mother, and, of course, architect too.[22] It did not seem to matter to Pillsbury that Marsio-Aalto played second fiddle to her husband, who remains the better-known architect of the pair.

After Pillsbury terminated her involvement in the distributorship and married in 1941, she found employment, but only in fits and starts. Louis Skidmore would not employ her in his firm allegedly because she was female, but he did introduce her to Dan Cooper, for whom she worked for two years, in 1941–43, designing Pakto furniture, consisting of interchangeable plywood components for war housing and starter homes. Subsequently, she made her way to the Museum of Modern Art (MoMA), where she was more content working under Elodie Courter in the circulating exhibition department, preparing such traveling exhibitions as *Brazil Builds: Architecture New and Old, 1652–1942* (see fig. 1.3).[23]

Likely inspired by Marsio-Aalto, the Harkness couple began to seek professional opportunities in which they could collaborate. Having already assisted him on a first-prize design for a student competition at the Boston Society of Architects in May 1943, Pillsbury Harkness worked with her husband on a design for a hypothetical bank in Syracuse, New York, for *Architectural Forum*'s "New Buildings for 194x" issue (fig. 4.2). Their proclivity for practical, functional design is present in the drawing of a severe rectangular glass and metal building standing on pilotis, bluntly contrasted to the traditional buildings on either side of it. The large, open space under the structure at street level houses a teller's cage so that it could be immediately accessible to the public—like a ticket booth at a movie theater. Conspicuously refuting the typical monumental bank with an austere, templelike quality, theirs was meant to appeal to a public immersed in popular culture.[24]

The couple's collaborative interest continued even when Harkness was in the American Field Service in 1944 in Italy. He asked for her support in developing a reconstruction plan for a war-torn Italian village that *Architectural Forum* agreed to publish: "It may also mean another charrette when I do get home, but I think that would be fun if you do. Again, I have to call on you for help," he unabashedly wrote to her.[25] They obviously found a way to communicate long-distance; after he reviewed the layout, Harkness lamented that hers had been more striking because it emphasized the town's destruction.[26]

4.3. Benjamin Thompson in collaboration with Norman and Jean Bodman Fletcher, winning design (unbuilt) for the Smith College dormitories competition, in *Progressive Architecture*, 27, no. 4 (April 1946): 54.

When Harkness returned to wartime service in 1945 with the army, his letters reference the professional business they intended to open together. Reading the December issue of *Architectural Forum*—reporting on the worst housing famine in history—he suggested they collaborate on converting existing buildings to residential use until more permanent reconstruction could begin.[27]

Soon after the couple reunited, they entered a competition to design a group of three dormitories at Smith College, sponsored by MoMA and *Progressive Architecture / Pencil Points*.[28] Out of ninety-one entries by such notable architects as Marcel Breuer, Carl Koch, and I.M. Pei, the Harknesses won second place and a $1,000 prize. First place, with twice the money, went to Benjamin Casper Thompson in collaboration with Norman Collings Fletcher and his wife, Jean Bodman Fletcher, for their scheme of three rectangular dormitories, each connected by a glass bridge to a more loosely organized wing with dining, living, and service functions (fig. 4.3).[29] The Fletcher couple was also experienced in collaborative design, having won just a year earlier a house competition organized by *Progressive Architecture / Pencil Points* and the Pittsburgh Plate Glass Company.[30]

The Smith dormitories competition was modeled on a series of other high-profile architectural competitions—a campus plan and library at Goucher College (1938), an art center at Wheaton College in Massachusetts (1939), a festival theater and fine arts center at the College of William and Mary (1938–39), and an art gallery at the Smithsonian Institution (1940), each sponsored by an established architecture journal and (except for Goucher) by MoMA. In the opinion of architectural historian James D. Kornwolf, these competitions produced the largest body of modern work in the United States. Collectively, they were significant because they endorsed Modernism to an unprecedented degree.[31] The Smith dormitories competition was an important moment for the five "young people," as the press materials described the awardees. Not only did they receive publicity, but the prize money gave them the ability to bankroll their own firm, which became known as TAC.

Creating an Iconic Collaborative Practice

In the extended discussion about TAC in *Architect: Chapters in the History of the Profession*, the architect and educator Bernard Boyle describes the formation of the firm as a group of young architects who decided to create a partnership and invited Gropius to join them in a practice run according to his principles of teamwork.[32] He never mentions that four of the eight members were married, nor that two were women. Despite this and other (erroneous) variations of the origin story published elsewhere, only the male architects are ever cited as the instigators of the firm, even when the partners themselves tell the story. Thompson recalled that when trying to organize an office with other recent architecture graduates from Yale—Robert Senseman McMillan and Louis Albert McMillen, as well as Norman Fletcher—it was John Harkness who proposed they congregate in Cambridge to talk with Gropius about forming an office, and "from that meeting," Thompson recalled, "came the beginning of The Architects Collaborative." Pillsbury Harkness, on the other hand, thought that Fletcher was the "leader" and "spirit" of the firm, though he never received the credit he deserved, while her husband remembered that just after becoming an assistant in the design studio led by

Gropius for master's degree students, in November 1945, he received a letter from Fletcher suggesting they form an office, possibly with Gropius: "I suggested the idea to Grope the next day, and he agreed," Harkness wrote, and "that is how TAC started."[33] Consistent with the field's preference for singular geniuses, the inspiration of TAC has also been solely attributed to Gropius.

Regardless of how the firm unfolded, the connections between and within the two couples also readied them for the collaboration in the firm that would have long-lasting implications for its partners. The Fletchers had already worked with John Harkness in 1943–44 in a branch office of Saarinen, Swanson & Saarinen in Washington, DC, where they designed Lincoln Heights, a 325-unit low-cost housing development for the Alley Dwelling Authority; they also had worked briefly together at the firm's home office in Bloomfield Hills, Michigan.[34] By then, the two architect wives would have not only known each other but recognized that they shared the Cambridge School experience: Pillsbury Harkness in 1934–39 and Bodman Fletcher in 1941–42, before she transferred to Harvard's GSD. Both would have learned from the influential curriculum to view collaboration as a strategy more efficient than individual competition, and both would have experienced the modern movement as a liberation from staid ways of living—professionally and personally.[35] When in her "Remembering Gropius" statement of 1994 Pillsbury Harkness exclaimed, "We 'girls' at the Cambridge School of Architecture and Landscape Architecture agreed that the approach to architecture that we were learning applied to all aspects of life," she undoubtedly was also speaking for Bodman Fletcher, who had long since died.[36] As a result of the participation of Pillsbury Harkness and Bodman Fletcher in TAC, the Cambridge School, at least partly, is responsible for the firm's emphasis on collaboration.

The collaborative model adopted by TAC was not based exclusively on a design philosophy. In fact, it was part of a larger approach that entailed fusing their professional and private lives, a tactic especially important to the younger partners. The Harkness couple had already shared with each other their interest in collective family living arrangements: while stationed in Denver, Harkness had proposed that he and his wife cohabitate with a major and his family in a large building for officers.[37] Thus, as TAC was being organized, they were comfortable with the notion of cohabitation. In correspondence, the two wives contemplated living arrangements: finding adjacent houses or apartments—or even one large house in which they could have a common room where their children could play while the women took turns working in the firm's office.[38] They also discussed such practical domestic issues as sharing childcare, a diaper service, storage, and even temporary housing until they could find a permanent place.[39] Eventually, they established a cooperative arrangement in a rented house in which the Fletcher family lived on the top floor and the Harkness family on the bottom. In addition to alternating morning and afternoon shifts at work and at home, they shared a washing machine and a telephone as well as a maid and babysitters (the Harkness and Fletcher couples each had two children at the time, though they ultimately had seven and six, respectively). Their exemplary arrangement drew attention in the newspapers: "Two Girls Share as Equal Partners in Modern Architecture" and "No Woman Should Stay Home: Two Cambridge Wives Solve Career Problem," read two headlines.[40]

What is especially significant about the Harkness–Fletcher collaboration is that it led to the creation between 1948 and 1950 of a community of about thirty families called Six Moon Hill in Lexington, Massachusetts (see figs. 7.6, 7.7; cover). In addition to five houses designed and occupied by seven TAC founding partners (Gropius was already settled in Lincoln), three other houses were designed by architects for their families: Richard Southwick Morehouse, a Harvard-trained architect who had joined TAC as a draftsperson in 1948; the Harvard-trained architect Leonard James Currie and his wife Virginia M. Herz Currie (1913–2006), a graduate in interior architecture from the University of Minnesota; and the MIT-trained architect William E. Haible and his wife Alice du Pont Wilson (1913–69), a Cambridge School and Harvard architecture alumna.[41] All the homes, grouped together along a primary artery, were emblematic of the collaborative process at TAC: they were individualistic, but nonetheless consistent in their modern details.[42] Though TAC moved on to larger public commissions, Six Moon Hill still stands as a definitive example of collaboration—in its conception, design, operation, and proprietorship.

Bodman Fletcher and Pillsbury Harkness were able to build profitable careers by collaborating first with their respective husbands, second with the firm they helped organize, and third with each other by innovating flexible, alternative choices for managing their domestic lives. Their situation did not become a widespread model for others, although some tried to emulate it, at least professionally. In 1947, for example, the *New Haven Register* featured an "architecture quartet" of two couples attempting to collaborate: Jean McMullan Coolidge, who had attended the Cambridge School and Harvard's GSD at the same time as Bodman Fletcher, and her Harvard-trained architect husband Robert Tilton Coolidge, who assisted with the introductory course at the Cambridge School in 1941. They were joined by the Yale-trained architect Edwin Carleton Granbery Jr. and his wife Diana Allyn Granbery (1920–2000), a Bennington College graduate who also studied architecture at Harvard in 1944. Though the four reportedly designed houses in Connecticut, Rhode Island, Massachusetts, and New York, as well as a store and a state hospital alteration, there is no indication that the loosely organized collaboration lasted.

The Smith College Dormitories: An Ill-Fated Collaboration

Though the Smith dormitories competition facilitated the launch of TAC, the collaborative approach was already firmly ingrained in the production of the Fletcher and Harkness couples, both of whom had a say in the new firm's statement of aims. Motivated by its guiding principle that "a team can raise its integrated work to higher potentials than the sum of the work of just so many individuals," and recognizing that they did not desire "authoritative direction by a boss" but rather "freedom of initiative," it is surprising then that, in a final attempt to realize the Smith plan, the firm resorted to positioning Gropius as that solitary figure of authority.[43]

While the competition jury of professionals was reportedly "very happy" with the "beautiful" modern scheme by Thompson and the Fletchers, Lucia Garrison Norton Valentine (1902–92), chair of the building committee, was not.[44] Before studying architecture at Columbia University between 1924 and 1928 (without graduating), she had attended the École des Beaux-Arts; her predisposition to classicism had come by way of her great-uncle, the architect Charles Follen McKim, founder of the American Academy in Rome, as well as her father, Charles Dyer Norton, a benefactor and trustee of the academy.[45] Though she had the support of other influential Smith alumnae, a campus-wide debate ensued about whether to preserve the sedate red-brick Georgian quadrangle concept with comparable designs or to enhance its harmony with diversity—buildings with large glass areas, free planning, and an absence of ornament, as Philip Lippincott Goodwin, the president of MoMA, encouraged the school to do.[46] MoMA may well have exacerbated the situation when, in a Smith College lecture, Elizabeth Bauer Mock maintained that Modernism was "caviar to experts—fish eggs to the uninitiated."[47]

The project was repeatedly postponed until 1949, when Bodman Fletcher, herself a Smith alumna, heard that it was on the table again and doggedly pursued anyone who would listen: Smith administrators and alumnae, the editor of *Progressive Architecture / Pencil Points*, and even the wife of the Smith president.[48] What she did not realize was that the decision not to utilize the plan had been made (at least informally) three years earlier, after Norton Valentine had visited TAC to restudy the plans. She recounted in a letter to the Smith president that as she tried to explain to the partners—Thompson, the Fletchers, and, significantly, Gropius—why the pajamaed young women at Smith would not care a bit if there were venetian blinds for privacy over the expansive windows, Gropius looked at her as if she was "slightly mad." She continued: they only reluctantly accepted her request for exterior brick facing and only gave up on the use of tile after a battle, while her suggestion of a pitched roof over the living and dining areas filled them all with revulsion. She elucidated that Gropius

> *is a kind of fanatic with all the limitations and even ignorance that that implies. He simply never caught on to our point of view, our need for help to bring acceptable modern architecture to Smith. He sat there dominating the situation, defending the plans of his ewe lambs against philistine attack and generally keeping … me on the other side of the fence without a flicker of humor, or comprehension of our problem, or even apparent respect for our point of view. … He is a giant in many ways, but a dead hand also and I longed to get the others out into the fresh air where we could work things out together. Any modifications of the drawings became a betrayal of his tenets, and in his presence, for the young ones to yield an inch would have been heresy.*

Doubting that they were capable of escaping "modern clichés and Bauhaus mannerisms," she said that it was not just the design itself but also the firm and, even more, Gropius, "the maître himself," with whom she could not work.[49] By privileging modern design over the founding

4.4. Natalie L'Hommedieu Griffin de Blois, design for the General Assembly room of the United Nations in the New York City Building (1939; now the Queens Museum), Flushing Meadows Corona Park, 1946. *Natalie de Blois Architectural Collection, Ms2007-017, Special Collections and University Archives, University Libraries, Virginia Polytechnic Institute and State University.*

principles of the firm, the partners not only failed to convince but antagonized the client. Had they stuck to the collaborative model in which each had an equal voice instead of one smug genius posturing for control, the age-old approach, they perhaps could have won back the commission that Bodman Fletcher had so desperately wanted from her alma mater.

A New Type of Collaboration in a Modern Firm

Though the collaborative model at TAC was strikingly different than that at Skidmore, Owings & Merrill (SOM), the latter firm did employ Natalie Griffin de Blois between 1944 and 1974—in New York, Chicago, and, for a brief time, in Bonn, Germany. At SOM, the concept of team-based cooperative practice was applied to small, restricted groups of practitioners headed by a partner.[50] The inconsistent way in which Griffin de Blois was recognized for her contributions to SOM underscores how susceptible women were to being eclipsed in collaborative practice.

Descended from a line of engineers, she was encouraged to enter architecture by her father, who, as Griffin de Blois recalled, talked at home about his work on the French Pavilion by Roger-Henri Expert and Pierre Patout at the New York World's Fair (1939).[51] After attending the Western College for Women (now the Western Campus of Miami University) on scholarship for a year, she transferred to Columbia University, where she was one of five women in a class of eighteen. Griffin de Blois worked her way through school by both drafting and teaching drafting to those in war-related jobs. Like Nathalie Swan earlier, her appreciation for modern design grew from her work for Frederick Kiesler in his course Laboratory of Design Correlation. She documented both the display fixtures and biomorphic "universal," or multiuse, chair he designed for Peggy Guggenheim's gallery, Art of This Century (1942) in New York.[52]

After graduating in 1944, Griffin de Blois began her career at Ketchum, Gina & Sharp (1941–58) in the way of most men but few women: "I didn't have to look for a job. The architect Morris Ketchum was a graduate of Columbia, and he wanted to hire someone from my class, so I was chosen," she recalled.[53] Already focused on modern architecture, she was "delighted" with the offer since she had no interest in "eclectic" design. Hence, one of the first projects on which she tirelessly worked was a line of interchangeable window wall components for Kawneer, a manufacturer of building envelope solutions. After just nine months, however, her job came to a stunning halt when pervasive sexism canceled her performance as an "industrious, capable, and sincere" employee.[54] As she later explained:

> *There was a fellow architect [Joseph Nowlin Boaz] who joined the office. He used to take me out dancing to hear Benny Goodman and Tommy Dorsey. I went out with him quite often. He was very fond of me, but he was not encouraged. So, he went to Mr. [Morris] Ketchum [Jr.] and told him that he just couldn't work with me there. Mr. Ketchum called me over to his desk. We were all in one room. He said he was sorry. I'd have to leave. Just like that. Of course, I hadn't experienced a shock like that before.*[55]

After that, Ketchum arranged for Griffin to work at SOM (then located in the same building), likely because wartime attrition had left an opening in the ranks of junior architects. Although her departure was instigated by an unjustified firing, it was fortuitous since it brought her a thirty-year association with SOM.

Of the numerous civic and residential buildings for which Griffin de Blois (she married in 1945) was responsible, her earliest include comfort stations and beach facilities at Jones Beach State Park on Long Island, the redevelopment of the New York City Building from the World's Fair (1939) to accommodate the General Assembly of the newly formed United Nations (1946), and the Abraham Lincoln houses (1948) in East Harlem (fig. 4.4). Her first widely proclaimed project was the Terrace Plaza Hotel building (1948) in Cincinnati, Ohio, an eighteen-story steel-frame structure sheathed in oversized bricks. Situated on top of a seven-story base (containing the J. C. Penney and Bond stores), the setback "penthouse hotel" with some 324 rooms and 12 apartments was noted for its technical advances, integrated functions, and interior art program (figs. 4.5, 4.6).[56] Though Griffin de Blois was the project (or senior) designer, because she was a woman she never visited the actual site, nor did she meet the client in person, instead participating only by telephone in on-site meetings attended solely by men.[57] When Griffin de Blois was creating her collection for the International Archive of Women in Architecture (IAWA) at Virginia Tech, she wrote at the top of an article about skyscraper design, "What if I had visited Cincinnati and knew [the] site?"[58] Correspondingly, Donna Dunay, a professor of architecture at the university, made a note in 2008 at the top of the "Penthouse Hotel" article in *Architectural Forum* (December 1946), "She says she is the designer of the building—it has been attributed to someone else."[59] These comments underscore how even successful women architects received ambiguous or no credit for their work.

It was not until the 1960s that Griffin de Blois became recognized as a "masterbuilder," as the *New York Times* called her in a review of the Pepsi-Cola headquarters building (1960; now demolished) at 500 Park Avenue, for which she was the senior designer. As one of her favorite projects (along with the Connecticut General building of 1957 in Bloomfield), its tightly organized geometric block was grounded on concrete columns behind a thin curtain wall of gray-green glass between aluminum spandrels.[60] While she did not claim to have a mentor (but found satisfaction in mentoring other women), the architect most closely fulfilling that role was the SOM partner Gordon Bunshaft, under whom she also worked on the lobby, plaza, cafeteria, and first three floors of the iconic glass-clad Lever House (1952) at 390 Park Avenue as well as the black-paneled Union Carbide headquarters (1960; now demolished), which was also on Park Avenue (fig. 4.7).[61]

4.5. Skidmore, Owings & Merrill, Terrace Plaza Hotel, 15 West Sixth Street, Cincinnati, Ohio, 1948.

4.6. Skidmore, Owings & Merrill, Gourmet Restaurant with a mural by Joan Miró (1893–1983), Terrace Plaza Hotel, 1948.

4.7. Skidmore, Owings & Merrill, Union Carbide headquarters (now demolished), 270 Park Avenue, New York, 1960. *Molitor collection.*

4.8. Natalie Griffin de Blois in "We Name for Glamour," *Glamour* 22, no. 4 (February 1950), 117.

Despite her eventual recognition for cracking the glass ceiling and establishing a precedent for women in corporate architecture, Griffin de Blois knew that her gender prohibited her from rising above the level of associate—a title she did not get until after about twenty years of employment. Although she later claimed not to be concerned about "upward mobility" or "climbing a ladder," it was meaningful to her that *she* was one of the eleven "Architects from 'Skid's Row' " listed in *Fortune* (January 1958)—even if she was the last to be named.[62] Her view of her own professional image is conflicted: in an interview, at age eighty-one, Griffin de Blois said she did not "become an architect to be recognized," but at the same time she lamented her relative obscurity. For example, when MoMA exhibited the thirty-two-foot-long mural by the Catalan artist Joan Miró soon to be installed in the circular Gourmet Restaurant on top of the Terrace Plaza Hotel, Griffin de Blois regretted that she was not credited for her architectural drawing of the proposed installation, which was also exhibited (fig. 4.6).[63]

By accepting a position in a patriarchal culture that emphasized the roles of firm principals, or partners, and mostly ignored the teams of specialists who created the buildings, Griffin de Blois was precluded from having a public image, which is why the small archive about her at IAWA that she helped organize is so informative. For instance, the collection includes a 1950 tribute published in *Glamour* magazine, in which she is complimented for successfully side-stepping the conventional "feminine path" of interior design and landing a coveted assignment at a large architectural firm (fig. 4.8). She is also noted for maintaining a sideline of designing houses and making her own clothes, as well as decorating her own apartment—aspects of her life not generally known and certainly not remembered.[64] *Glamour*'s accolades acknowledge Griffin de Blois's ability simultaneously to engage in pursuits that were gendered female (like fashion and decorating) while also working for a leading architecture firm—a balance few women achieved.

Complementary Backgrounds and Skills Enhance Collaborations

Women architects more often found positions among smaller circles of practitioners, often in pairs, in which they could more fully present themselves. Working with family members may well have seemed practical, although many

4.9. House (now demolished) designed by Frances Baxter Quarton for her family, 135 Weston Road, Lincoln, Massachusetts.

collaborated with a peer, mentor, or educator instead—either male or female; even women who eventually led firms mostly or entirely comprised of women sometimes started out in partnerships with men.

Frances Baxter Quarton partnered between 1961 and 1970 with the Russian-born architect Constantin Alexander Pertzoff in Lincoln.[65] Though today he is thought of as a notable modernist, in fact Pertzoff graduated from Harvard in 1924, well before Modernism was established there. Baxter Quarton, on the other hand, had been a scholarship student both at the Cambridge School and at Harvard's GSD, where she studied under Breuer and Gropius and attained a master's degree in 1943. Her modern training most likely appealed to Pertzoff, with whom she partnered as "Pertzoff and Quarton, Architects."[66] Extant drawings of the houses they designed in the neighborhoods on Woodcock Road or Twin Pond Lane are initialed by either one or the other; however, Pertzoff is the only recognized designer (see fig. 7.8).

The collaboration with Pertzoff did not preclude Baxter Quarton from designing her own house in 1949 on Weston Road in Lincoln, nor from collaborating in 1951 with her twin sister, Priscilla Baxter Neel (1918–2012) on her house at 2235 Belmont Road in Ann Arbor, Michigan (fig. 4.9). Baxter Neel had also attended Radcliffe College and the Cambridge School but had declined the scholarship offer at Harvard and so with her education incomplete, she probably relied on input from her sister.[67] Nevertheless, the designs of the "architect-turned-housewife," as a local newspaper described Baxter Neel, showed her awareness of postwar trends in domestic planning, materials, and construction. In fact, the houses of both sisters were open-plan, single-story structures that emphasized connections to their sites through expansive windows and outdoor spaces—a patio for Baxter Neel and a screen porch for Baxter Quarton.

A better-known family collaboration is the wide-ranging practice of Ellamae Ellis League and her daughter, Jean League Newton, who operated out of a one-story brick office building in downtown Macon, Georgia (fig. 4.10). Like Griffin de Blois, Ellis League was a pioneering architect preceded by six generations of male architects, including her uncle, Charles Edward Choate of Atlanta, who encouraged her to pursue architecture.[68] She married after her first year at Wesleyan College in Macon; the relationship only lasted four years but produced two children, Jean and her brother, Joseph Choate League. According to Ellis League, because it was almost impossible to get a license to practice architecture without a diploma from the Georgia Institute of Technology in Atlanta, where women were not allowed to study architecture until 1952, she apprenticed in Macon in the firms of William Elliott Dunwody IV and William F. Oliphant, 1922–28; Claude W. Shelverton, 1928–30; and Oliphant, 1930–33.[69] In addition, in 1924–26 she took correspondence courses with the Beaux-Arts Institute of Design in New York, and in 1928 she attended the Institute's three-month summer school of classical training at the École

4.10. Office building of Ellamae Ellis League, 670 Mulberry Street, Macon, Georgia, 1948. *Middle Georgia Archives, Washington Memorial Library.*

des Beaux-Arts at Fontainebleau (1923–39) in France.[70] She opened her own firm in 1934, which lasted forty-one years. In contrast to other women architects, Ellis League did not restrict her practice to residences; she designed educational and municipal buildings as well as low-cost housing for the Macon Housing Authority.[71] Similar to Griffin de Blois, her ambition resulted at least in part from having to support herself and her family: "With me, I had an incentive you can't beat; I had two children that I wanted to educate and it was up to me to make a living for them and raise them and just do it."[72]

Ellis League's exposure to historical French architecture through study and travel led her to take a traditionalist approach. It was challenged by her daughter, however, when in 1944 she returned from her graduate studies in the Northeast to join her mother's firm—then League, Warren, & Riley. Jean League parlayed her contemporary training into a career in which she familiarized her home territory with modern planning and design. After studying at the Choate School for young women in Brookline, Massachusetts, she earned an undergraduate degree at Radcliffe College, where League said she "got side-tracked" by "a few minor courses" at the Cambridge School during her senior year. She later explained she had no intention of studying architecture, but the Baxter twins, also at Radcliffe, convinced her to do so.[73] She attended the Cambridge School with a tuition scholarship and like Frances Baxter transferred to Harvard's GSD in the fall of 1942, when the Cambridge School closed.[74]

It long has been thought, as a local newspaper reported in 1945, that "Jean belongs to the Modern school [of] architecture, her mother to [the] Beaux Arts," which led Ellis League to comment wryly, "But I'm being converted."[75] In fact, before her daughter returned home from school, Ellis League had already expressed an interest in modern architecture in the design of her own house (1940) in the Shirley Hills neighborhood, a residential enclave with single-family houses predominantly in historical revival styles (fig. 4.11).[76] While the house fits in with its neighbors by incorporating such period details as small-paned, double-hung wood sash windows and a pitched roof, its entire concept was new for Macon: the split-level plan consists of a one-story section containing the main living area and a two-story section with two bedrooms (and one bathroom) over the garage; sided with wide redwood clapboards, it recalled contemporary Bay Area architecture, a movement in which her daughter was greatly interested. Since Ellis League built it during the period her daughter was away at school, the house suited the needs of the single professional woman: the spacious, light-filled living room, with a mirrored fireplace wall, opens onto a patio, from where a ladder provides access to a partly covered roof deck off one of the bedrooms—a modern feature that League hid from the street. Significantly, between the conception and construction phases, she made the house more modern by installing additional doors to integrate the house with its rear landscape, by simplifying the muntin pattern in the large living room window to provide more expansive panes of glass, and by adding the ladder and partial roof deck.

After Jean League joined her mother's firm, she made an "immediate impact" by expanding the corporate portfolio with forthright modern designs, such as their own modern office building (fig. 4.10).[77] Located on one of the oldest streets in Macon, the low, one-story building with a projecting roof over walls and doors of glass contrasts with the adjacent Victorian commercial buildings and churches.[78] Ellis League's private office on the front right and the drafting room overlooked the courtyard in an arrangement that recalls the Cambridge School plan (see fig. 1.4). The signature building, which announced the firm's interest in Modernism, suited Ellis League, for she remained in it for the duration of her career.

Successful Husband-Wife Collaborations

Joseph Hudnut recognized, after seventeen years of deanship at Harvard, that given the fixed "patterns of prejudice" against women in architecture, the most viable

4.11. Rear facade of the house Ellamae Ellis League designed for herself, 1790 Waverland Drive, Macon, Georgia, 1940.

career strategy for professional women was the age-old husband-and-wife-partnership.[79] Since the 1880s, explains architect and historian Kate Reggev, women architects primarily practiced with their husbands to evade the usual proscription against married women working. Louise Blanchard Bethune formed a partnership between 1881 and 1890 in Buffalo, New York, with her Canadian-born architect husband Robert Armour Bethune under the firm name of R. and L. Bethune. (They suppressed their first names to disguise the involvement of a woman.) Early husband-and-wife partnerships, Reggev contends, provided a model for subsequent collaborating architect couples as well as for the greater presence of women in the field. Although the wives in architect couples also had to fulfill household duties conventionally assigned to them, partnering with their husbands often provided the only opportunity to which they could aspire.[80] It was not until late in the twentieth century, however, that scholars gave attention to collaborating couples in modern design— Aino Marsio-Aalto and Alvar Aalto, as well as Margaret Macdonald (1864–1922) and Charles Rennie Mackintosh; Lilly Reich (1885–1947) and Ludwig Mies van der Rohe; and Alison Margaret Gill Smithson (1928–93) and Peter Smithson.

Surprisingly, there is little documentation about the way women architects functioned in joint practices with their husbands. Not only is it difficult to pinpoint day-to-day responsibilities, but the creativity that emerged from the interaction of couples—during work and leisure—is invisible, or nearly so, to everyone but them. When, in 1995, historian Pat Kirkham described the process of her decade-long study of the design practice of Charles Eames and his wife, Rae Kaiser Eames (1912–98), she confessed how "painfully aware" she was that her study was only one of a few to expose the "rich, complex, mutually respective and supportive" working partnerships between husband and wife.[81] Though Kaiser Eames was an artist, Kirkham's research provides useful insight that can also be applied to women architects. The collaborations between husbands and wives, she discovered, raise a variety of issues that require understanding from the perspectives of multiple academic disciplines, from art and design history to women's and gender studies and communications, to material culture and social sciences. As Kirkham established, joint male / female authorship has been subject to claims that the important design ideas flow from the man, a conjecture that Gill Smithson bitterly observed about her forty-plus-year architecture collaboration with her husband, Peter.[82] Kirkham contends that the structuralist binary oppositions that have been applied to collaborating couples misrepresent their practices and minimize the contributions of women. The terms commonly used in art history to contrast the differences between females and males, respectively—such

4.12. Photograph of Ruth Millicent Reynolds Freeman with *(left)* William Wallstone Freeman (1908–2004) and *(right)* John Charles French Jr. (1903–89), c. 1948. *Vermont Division for Historic Preservation.*

as talent versus genius, traditionalism versus modernism, decoration versus functionalism, amateur versus professional, handwork versus machine, and craftmanship versus industrialization—are not only misleading, but inappropriate.[83] The supposition that women principally worked in private spaces and men in public ones does not necessarily characterize their work responsibilities either. Although the mid-twentieth century was a time when gender roles were widely promoted in the media and staunchly defended by social, political, educational, and religious institutions, it is not possible to speculate or generalize about how the responsibilities were divided between married professional partners.

Even though the career outcomes of husbands and wives in collaboration were unpredictable, the strategy was practical, at least initially, for young, aspiring couples. Given the deep-seated common interests of the partners as well as their long hours of study, many marriages inevitably took shape at graduate schools. Architect couples surely recognized that a collaboration between them could afford the woman a practice that was otherwise difficult to attain and perhaps also allow them to balance work and family. These partnerships tended to work for wives when they had equal standing with their husbands and received credit for their contributions. For instance, the professional partnership established by Victorine du Pont and Samuel Homsey in 1935 received national critical attention early in their careers. In 1941, architect Henry Hodgman Saylor commented in *Architectural Record* that "the bringing together of two such qualified practitioners in a professional partnership is phenomenon enough; their collaboration in marriage and bringing up a family is rather piling it on." Describing how the couple merged their work and home life, Saylor explains that once they establish the parameters of a project, an evening finds the two developing tentative schemes, sometimes Homsey doing the drafting, sometimes his wife, "with the other partner kibitzing from across the board."[84]

Throughout the 1930s and 1940s, the Homseys completed a wide range of buildings, from houses to clubs to schools, in a variety of styles. Despite taking the leading design role in many projects, du Pont Homsey mostly depended on collaboration: when her husband was a commander in the United States Naval Reserve, she teamed up with the architect Eugene Henry Klaber in the second-wave development of the Greenbelt community in Prince George's County in Maryland (see fig. 6.6).[85] The areas of expertise of each architect complemented one another: he was experienced in housing economics and community planning, she in modern design.[86]

After the war, she resumed her collaboration with her husband, designing houses, which included low-slung ranches with expanses of glass as well as institutional buildings, for instance, a branch library in Wilmington for which they devised both neoclassical and modern solutions (see fig. 1.14). Although their extensive professional archive in the Hagley Library in Wilmington illustrates the pressure exerted on them by their aesthetically conservative patrons, the Homseys never stopped promoting modern concepts and designs.

Like the Homseys, Ruth Millicent Reynolds Freeman (1913–69) and her architect husband William Wallstone Freeman—who both trained at Cornell University—as well as John Charles French Jr., practiced in a geographic region distant from a center of architectural production and discourse (fig. 4.12). Though it worked against their ability to develop a broader reputation, the firm has been acknowledged for bringing Modernism to Vermont.[87] The credit likely belongs to Reynolds Freeman, the firm's principal designer, as an article in *Progressive Architecture*—(ironically) titled "The Architect and His Community"—attests, saying, "Mrs. Freeman is responsible for most of the design and makes most of the

4.13. Freeman French Freeman, "Two-Apartment Building," 217 Church Street, Burlington, Vermont, 1946. *Upper*: Church Street entrance; *lower*: second-floor entrance on the west side of the house. *Freeman French Freeman archive.*

presentation drawings," while Freeman is described as the resident "design critic," a role more commonly ascribed to women in professional married partnerships.[88] The "two-apartment building" constructed in 1946, which was recognized in the *Burlington Free Press* as "California in style," typifies their approach as functionalists intolerant of an impractical use of material or space. The Church Street entrance accesses a ground-floor one-bedroom apartment that could be converted to business use, if required, while the second-floor entrance on the west side of the house opened to the other one-bedroom apartment (fig. 4.13).[89] The resolute rectilinearity of the structure, emphasized by a cantilevered roof bisected by a bold chimney, is patently Miesian, while the vertical board and batten covering the facade are reminiscent of the barns that dot the agricultural landscape of Vermont.

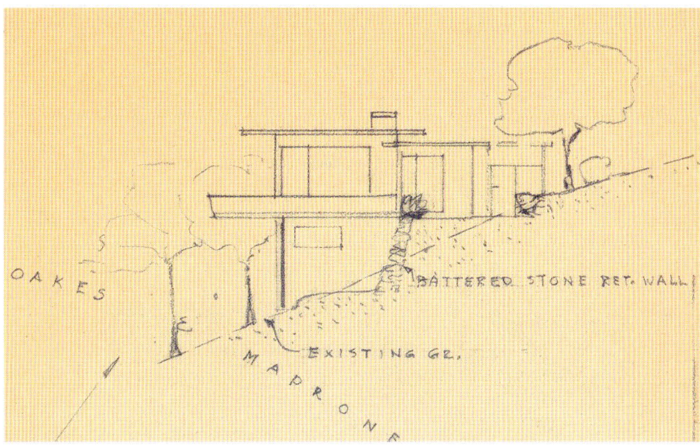

4.14. Helen Louise Douglass French, detail on a plot plan for her house in Kent Woodlands, California, 1950. *Records of Helen D. and Prentiss French, Environmental Design Archives.*

Whereas the Freeman and Homsey firms capitalized on active postwar building in their communities, Helen Louise Douglass French (1901–94) became recognized for her practice in expanding urban and suburban areas in Northern California. She built a substantial career, in part through a professional partnership with her husband, Prentiss French, a landscape architect with a master's degree from Harvard. Her interest in architecture stemmed from visiting job sites with her father, Walter Bailey Douglass, president of the New England Structural Steel Company.[90] In fact, he allegedly applied to the Cambridge School on his daughter's behalf; she graduated in 1922. Subsequently, Douglass worked as a draftsperson for various firms and in 1927 attended the Fontainebleau school. After her return from Europe, she married and set up a joint practice with her husband in Boston and in Stockbridge, Massachusetts, where they worked for more than a decade until 1942. The couple then moved to Florida's west coast, collaborating with architect Clarence Augustine Martin, a former dean of the architecture department at Cornell.[91] They were active with house designs on Bay Island, off the north end of Siesta Key, where they built their own residence in 1936 in the so-called Monterey style.[92] When they permanently settled in California after World War II, the couple shared an office in San Francisco through the 1960s. The two collaborated on numerous residential commissions, although during the 1950s he also independently undertook larger institutional projects.[93]

Douglass French rarely ventured beyond house design, but when she did, it primarily resulted from her association with her husband's family—he was a nephew of Daniel Chester French, the sculptor of the monumental figure of Abraham Lincoln (1920) in the Lincoln Memorial in Washington, DC. Douglass French was first invited to Chesterwood, the artist's country home and studio in Stockbridge, Massachusetts, just before her trip to Europe, and henceforth her connection to the estate was lifelong.[94] In 1932, she and her husband converted the Little Studio, which had been built in 1905 and later rechristened the Meadowlark, as a summer residence; in 1954, Douglass French renovated the Hawkins house and painted it yellow, causing it to be renamed The Canary.[95] Her final project at Chesterwood was in 1962, when she reconfigured a barn as an exhibition building, which opened to the public under the auspices of the National Trust for Historic Preservation.[96] For Douglass French, this was a rare foray into institutional building, albeit on a modest scale.

For the most part, her single-family houses are comparable to those of the better-known practitioners of the Bay Area style. The designs of Douglass French are modern but include traditional forms and materials, especially redwood siding, a staple of midcentury Modernism. According to extant drawings, she built many striking examples with open plans and expansive windows to capture views of the vivid landscape, but the standout is the split-level house she designed for her own family, in 1950, in Kent Woodlands in the East Bay.[97] It may have been her most intentional modern expression, judging by a small sketch at a corner of one of the plans (fig. 4.14).

Adept at building on the famously steep sites with (maintenance-free) natural growth in and around San Francisco, the French couple chose for their own house a spectacular piece of property with an unobstructed view of Mount Tamalpais. Yet it was also daring, given that the site was nearly vertical.[98] Because of the downward slope from the road, the entrance to the house is on the upper level, screened by her husband with dense plantings. Living and dining room areas, as well as a study, merge at the back of the house, where they open onto a deck (fig. 4.15). The main bedroom suite and kitchen completed the upper level, while the lower one contained living and sleeping areas for their daughter, as well as a guest room. Although the early plan shows a low, flat-roofed mass, Douglass French also experimented with a pitched roof, typical for the California ranch house, but the flat one prevailed. Evidently thinking of her own house design, Douglass French conveyed her "definite ideas about home planning" to a newspaper reporter in 1952, saying that "a

4.15. View of the house designed by Helen Douglass French and landscaped by Prentiss French (1894–1989) for their family, 54 Rancheria Road, Kent Woodlands, California, 1956. *French Records, Environmental Design Archives.*

contemporary house of modern lines, on a hillside, still can be built so the interior will prove a perfect background for an owner's antiques."[99] Her statement signaled to potential clients that she would be more accommodating than male modernist architects, who were notorious for evicting traditional furnishings. Douglass French tacitly criticized (male) architects when she said: "No architect has the right to force spectacular design on a client." Instead, "the needs and life of a client should be considered first and a home planned with those things in mind."[100]

In addition to building a thriving practice in residential design with her husband often supplying the complementary landscapes, Douglass French became a leader in the architectural profession in her region. In the early 1950s, she was one of four women members of the San Francisco chapter of the American Institute of Architects (AIA), and she was the first woman elected treasurer.[101] Unlike Julia Morgan, another female AIA member who produced a wide range of building types, Douglass French remained squarely in the field of residential design, perhaps because she held to traditional notions of women's roles and their association with domestic architecture. While in an interview in 1960 she said that the average female student of architecture compared

4.16. *McCall's* magazine advertisement, *Architectural Forum* 80, no. 4 (April 1944). The painting of the woman is by John Koch (1909–78).

favorably with her male counterparts, she thought "no woman student ever measures up to the very best man student. And that's just the way I want it." When pressed for further explanation, Douglass French went on, "Why? Because women need to admire and respect men: we're just built that way. And because men want to feel superior."[102] Even though Douglass French espoused the widely held views concerning the inferiority of professional women before the second wave of the feminist movement, the self-assurance that evolved from her collaboration with her husband, it can be argued, enabled her to build a successful practice as well as take on leadership roles in professional associations.

Challenges of Married Collaborators

Nearly always, professional couples were confronted with challenges beyond their control. After the Depression sand then the war years, the profession supported men in taking over the workplace while women were encouraged to fulfill their traditional domestic responsibilities. An advertisement for *McCall's* magazine in *Architectural Forum* in 1944 illustrates the partition between the man, holding blueprints as the "builder of houses," as opposed to the woman arranging flowers as "the maker of homes" (fig. 4.16). *Life* magazine similarly tied women architects to the domestic realm. Two features, in 1953 and 1956, similarly show architect wives at leisure in the living room but within earshot of the kitchen, rather than in an office (figs. 4.17, 4.18). The first, "A House with Reasons," does not mention that Ann Halle Little, pictured stoking the fire in her house in a Cleveland suburb, is an architect with a master's degree from the Cambridge School. Rather, the magazine credits the authorship of the house only to her husband, Robert Andrews Little. A diagram in the article does not illustrate her role as an architect. Instead, she is shown preening at a dressing table, sleeping in bed, singing at a piano, and working at a photo enlarging stand; in contrast, he stands alone at a drafting table.[103] In reality, Halle Little had an open office cleverly positioned in a corner alcove above the living room.

The second *Life* article shows Margaret King Hunter tranquilly reading a book in the living room mock-up she designed for the magazine's special issue about American women. Even though in the title of the article King Hunter is identified as the designer, her primary role in that illustration is as a housewife.[104] The irony is that her life did not revolve around domesticity but rather the architecture firm of E. H. and M. K. Hunter, where she and her husband Edgar "Ted" Hayes Hunter Jr. were copartners for fifty years, first in Hanover, New Hampshire, and then in Raleigh, North Carolina.

The pictures of the two capable women architects in *Life* corroborate the observation made by Beatriz Colomina: "Couplings raise an enormous level of nervousness and resentment from all camps (including women)."[105] Entrenched gender stereotypes made it easier for society to accept the more familiar ancillary roles of wives who supported, or inspired, the output of their architect husbands as publicists, chroniclers, and hostesses and then, after their deaths, as agents of their legacies.[106]

Wives who managed the secondary interests of their architect husbands by selling modern furnishings and design services were also not on equal footing since running a retail operation was not considered by some

4.17. Ann Halle Little in the living room of her home, 5 Pepper Ridge Road, Pepper Pike, Ohio, in "A House with Reasons," *Life* 34, no. 24, June 15, 1953, 113.

4.18. Margaret King Hunter in the living room mock-up she designed for "Housewife's House: Designed by a Woman, It Puts Kitchen in the Center," in the special issue, "The American Woman: Her Achievements and Troubles," *Life* 41, no. 26, December 24, 1956, 136.

4.19. Aerial view of the house Ernest Born (1898–1992) and Esther Baum Born designed for themselves, 2020 Great Highway, San Francisco, California, 1949.

as prestigious as practicing architecture. A case in point is Design Research (D/R; 1953–79) in Boston, a modern lifestyle retailer founded by TAC architect Benjamin Thompson.[107] According to his second wife, Jane Fiske Thompson (1927–2016), an eventual co-owner of D/R as well as his ongoing collaborator on such projects as the re-creation of Faneuil Hall Marketplace (1976) in Boston, he was belittled by his colleagues for extending his practice beyond conventional parameters and "tangling with 'commercialism.'"[108] Understandably then, Mary Christine Dolan Rapson (1920–2000) and Kitty Baldwin Weese (1918–2005) were designated as managers of the adjunct retailing projects of their architect husbands who provided the professional validation but avoided direct participation.

Sometimes the architect, often the male, would perpetuate separate or even unequal roles among partners. Esther Baum Born rarely has been acknowledged for her contributions to the "joint practice" with her architect husband Ernest Born in San Francisco.[109] As was the case in their work arrangement, he was the public figure of the firm that was formed in 1937—in his name only—and he received the honors. Even though she is the documented author of *The New Architecture of Mexico* (1937), recognized by historian Nicholas Olsberg as "the primary record of the first years of the Functionalist revolution in Mexican architecture," Born listed himself as coauthor in his nomination form for the AIA fellowship he received in 1955 (see fig. 2.31).[110] Similarly, for their own modern house of 1949 in San Francisco, he is listed as "architect" and she "associate" in a feature in *House and Home*.[111] Locally known as "Born's barn" because of its unadorned cubic form and vertical redwood siding, the twenty-five-foot-wide house contained on the first floor both a darkroom and a multistory living space with a wall of glass oriented to a courtyard at the rear, facing away from the ocean (fig. 4.19).[112] The stark exterior and the open, light-filled interior recalled the modern architecture that Baum Born had photographed in Mexico. The formal similarities between the Born house and the house and studio of architect Luis Barragán, completed in Mexico City just a year earlier, suggest that Mexican architecture remained a point of departure for the Born couple.[113] A photograph of the Barragán residence by Elizabeth Timberman (1908–88), a near contemporary of Baum Born, shows the similarities between the two residences: both feature double-height living rooms, glass walls that open to rear courtyards, and largely blank walls facing the street (fig. 4.20).[114]

Baum Born was allegedly the glue of the Born firm as interior designer, project manager, photographer, research director, and more. And yet, the Born monograph by Olsberg does not discuss her design ability or specific contributions. But when in the 1970s the firm was involved in the conceptualization and design of the Bay Area Rapid Transit (BART) system, Baum Born informed a friend that she was more deeply engaged than ever and immensely enjoying her work, including her extensive research photography of both American and European metro stations.[115] Her husband's master's thesis, "The Relation of Painting to Architecture" (1922), offers a clue as to why she was not recognized in the office. Describing the challenges faced by artists, especially those inclined to improvisation, Born recommended that they work under "a captain or dictator … and obey him. This is very essential—otherwise two men will waste a stroke at the same time."[116]

Working Architect Couples at Home

Though the divisions of labor are particular to each married couple in collaborative practice, their shared workspaces could meld the public and private realms. The office the Homseys maintained on the second floor of a

4.20. Elizabeth Timberman, photograph of the interior of La Casa Luis Barragán (1902–88), General Francisco Ramírez 12, Colonia Ampliación Daniel Garza, Mexico City, 1947–48. *Esther McCoy Papers, Archives of American Art.*

building on Market Street in 1941 was smaller (at twelve by fourteen feet) and less important than their studio, or workshop, in the house they built for themselves in 1940 in Hockessin, Delaware (fig. 4.21). The Homsey residence served as an advertisement for their design approach, which blended modern planning with materials and forms that referred to the local vernacular, a design strategy to which du Pont Homsey undoubtedly was exposed at the Cambridge School.

Sometimes a home was where architect couples collaborated most closely and where their manner of working is best documented. Following a fleeting courtship during the 1942 summer school at Harvard, in September, Suzanne Stockard married William Julian Underwood, a fellow modernist who, as she informed her parents, preferred "the simple life" of plain white plates and big deep bowls instead of flowered china or fancy linen tablecloths.[117] Together, they socialized with a coterie of trailblazers at Harvard, including Philip Johnson, an usher at their wedding.[118]

Her trajectory in modern architecture is evidenced by the drawings of modern buildings and interiors she completed in art class at Bennington College, under the tutelage of Edwin Avery Park, an architect who would have required her to complete practical and realistic design problems (fig 4.22; see fig. 1.2).[119] His praise meant everything to her: when he complimented Stockard on a house model, she noted in her diary, "That Thrilled me terrifically."[120] She continued to learn about contemporary design issues when she worked on a housing project as an intern in January 1936 in the Detroit architecture office of J. Robert F. Swanson, to whom her father, an investment banker, introduced her. Though her father was initially concerned that higher education could dampen "any simple domestic happiness" for his daughter, and her mother was opposed to the idea of an apprenticeship in an architect's office, they apparently came around after she realized that "architecture is more difficult and more fun than I imagined."[121]

Though as an undergraduate Stockard was not ready to pay "due homage to the 'modernist,'" as she explained to her parents, the diary she kept at Bennington documents her interest in Gropius and in prefabricated modern design.[122] She thought about applying to the Cranbrook Academy of Art perhaps because it was near Grosse Point, Michigan, where she was raised, but after graduating she took a job in New York making architecture models in the office of Van der Gracht and Kilham.

4.21. Home workspace of Samuel Eldon and Victorine du Pont Homsey, Lancaster Pike, Hockessin, Delaware, 1940.

4.22. Suzanne Stockard Underwood at work, c. 1943. *Private collection.*

Between 1941 and 1942, she attended the Cambridge School, where she was so "exceptional in her work and excellently fitted" for architecture that she obtained a bachelor's degree in just one year, a record unequaled at the school.[123] Her first commission was the house she designed for her parents at Disheroon Farm in Tyron, North Carolina; although required to conform to the traditional setting, the project allowed her to experiment with various ideas. She had more of an opportunity to learn about modern design in the office of Walter Bogner in the summer before she entered Harvard's GSD, where she was "very excited" to be in complete charge of working drawings for $30 a week for an addition to the industrial plant of H. K. Porter in Somerville, Massachusetts.[124] This experience amply prepared her to collaborate with other notable modern architects after she obtained her master's degree in 1943: she was one of a team of six (that included her husband) working with Carl Koch on an entry to the Jefferson National Expansion Memorial competition (1947) and in 1944 she did residential design for Marcel Breuer.[125]

The correspondence between the Underwood couple during his wartime absences (delaying the completion of his bachelor's degree at Harvard until 1948) divulges that their mutual attraction was entwined with a shared commitment to Modernism. While Underwood considered himself an utter functionalist, she was more willing to compromise, by employing traditional stonework on residential exteriors, for instance, so that people would stop saying, "But I have never seen a modern house I liked."[126] The drawings and critiques shared in their letters illustrated their melded positions. The bathhouses they designed for their favorite summer retreat in Nonquitt, Massachusetts, underwent a transition: the first attempt featured structures on pilotis, with prefabricated parts that could be dismounted every winter, but a later iteration featured buildings constructed of concrete block with flat roofs and skylights (fig. 4.23). These elements distinguished the bathhouses as modern, particularly in contrast to the vernacular shingle-style examples along the New England shore from the last quarter of the nineteenth century onward.

However, it was on their small house in Nonquitt that the couple collaborated most closely (figs. 4.24, 4.25). Their exchange of alternative sketches and ideas, including a version with a circular plan and glass walls, ultimately resulted in an H-planned house raised on pilotis ten feet off the ground to capitalize on the view of Buzzards Bay—a concept with which Stockard had experimented for a house made from prefabricated units devised by Walter Gropius and Konrad Wachsman for General Panel and illustrated in *New Pencil Points* (December 1943).[127] Though the Underwood house also featured expanses of plate glass and shallow-pitched roofs, when *Architectural Forum* featured the house in 1951 it was called "modern

4.23. William Julian Underwood (1919–96) and Suzanne Stockard Underwood, bathhouses (now demolished), Nonquitt, Massachusetts, c. 1950. *Private collection.*

colonial"—a stylistic moniker referencing the wood shingle cladding and fieldstone foundations and chimney.[128]

A desire for professional independence may have diverted Stockard Underwood to garden design for a time, a logical transition given that a fundamental tenet at the Cambridge School was the dual consideration of architecture and landscape architecture. It began with a planting program for her own house that probably was created when she and her husband expanded and winterized their home in the 1950s. After completing a course at Harvard's Arnold Arboretum, Stockard Underwood was especially keen on the propagation of woody plants, conifers, and broad-leafed evergreens.[129]

While the Underwood collaboration initially produced architectural innovations, particularly a blend of Modernism with the vernacular, Stockard Underwood's dream—that *together* they would "make a couple of good architects"—remained unfulfilled. Inherited wealth relieved the couple of the need to work full-time, although Underwood was a partner in a New Bedford firm between about 1959 and 1965. Nonetheless, in 1964, the two worked together again when he took on two new jobs—a ski lodge and a large house, both of which he planned to design in their shared home studio. Stockard Underwood wrote her parents, somewhat tentatively, "Jules is letting me do the drafting—so you might say that we are sort of opening a home office."[130] Other residential projects followed, judging by extant drawings.[131] Even so, after her husband died in 1997, Stockard Underwood lamented, "They didn't want women in the office," and confessed she was "crushed" that she never had a full-blown partnership.[132]

Career Choices by Architect Wives

As Stockard Underwood understood, marriage to an architect could provide a path to rewarding architectural practice, but women could fall short in equality or in legacy. Cambridge School alumna Mary Weed Noyes noted with pride to other high school alumnae in 1983 that she was "in charge of interiors" in the renowned firm of her husband, Eliot Noyes (one of the so-called Harvard Five), beginning in 1961; she was responsible for corporate interiors (and fine art acquisitions) for Cummins, General Fireproofing, IBM, Mobil Oil, Pan Am, Westinghouse, and Xerox as well as libraries, schools, and houses.[133] Her role in the firm, however, is largely elusive today, exemplified by the documentary *Modernism, Inc.: The Eliot Noyes Design Story* (2023) in which she makes only a fleeting appearance. Although a photograph of her impressive workspace is pictured in the only monograph about her husband's production, it is eerily empty, reflecting the difficulty even her own children have in identifying her

4.24. House designed by Julian and Suzanne Stockard Underwood for their family, 1 Old Wharf Road, South Dartmouth, Massachusetts, 1949.

4.25. Underwood house interior, 1949.

professional contributions.[134] They remember the ongoing, animated architectural discussions that extended to home, and they know that their father—the iconic figure of the family—relied on their mother's influential, incisive eye.[135] Perhaps their lack of understanding is because they primarily think of her as "mom" or because her important job of entertaining clients at home to promote not just modern architecture but an entire lifestyle prevails in their memory. Although Weed Noyes functioned differently in her professional coupling than her friends Rae Kaiser Eames and Sarah Pillsbury Harkness, she was also essential to her husband's widespread success.

Faith Bemis perhaps was even more dedicated to architecture than many of her peers after graduating from the Cambridge School in 1928, as demonstrated by her role in acquiring the Federal-period house to accommodate the school and in designing and supervising the construction of the drafting room wing (see fig. 1.4). She slowly drifted away from architecture, however, after marrying the architect John Gaw Meem.[136] From Cambridge, she had found her way to his small, informal office in Santa Fe, where her appreciation for the Southwest adobe tradition—in which she found much for "the moderns" to admire—had undoubtedly been shaped by the attitude toward the vernacular in Cambridge.[137] Although the parallels she saw between the New Mexico vernacular and modern architecture are vivid in their Santa Fe house of 1937, she and her husband never extensively practiced together—other than the unexecuted library scheme for Colorado College that took her to the Meem office in the first place. Despite her report that she occasionally worked in the firm, her path is more typical of women in architecture who availed themselves of new educational opportunities in the profession before and during World War II but were subsequently swept up into conventional domestic roles.[138]

In the same vein, the Littles never set up a joint practice, although their initial years of collaboration showed promise when they won an honorable mention in the Smith dormitories competition. Later, in the 1950s, the couple joined with the artist couple Algesa D'Agostino O'Sickey (1917–2006) and Joseph O'Sickey, whom they knew from volunteering at the Ten-Thirty Gallery in Cleveland. Together, they initiated a business called Design Service that pledged "service wherever design counts" (fig. 4.26).[139] Perhaps modeling themselves on the Harkness couple at TAC, whom they knew well from the Cambridge School and from Harvard, they portrayed themselves as a tightly knit group collaborating in an office, according to the marketing booklet. In 1956, the two couples again collaborated on a hypothetical project for *Life* magazine for which they constructed two large-scale models comparing the "before-and-after" redevelopment of Kingsbury Run, "a shabby, dump-ridden" post-industrial tract east of the more prominent Shaker Heights neighborhood.[140]

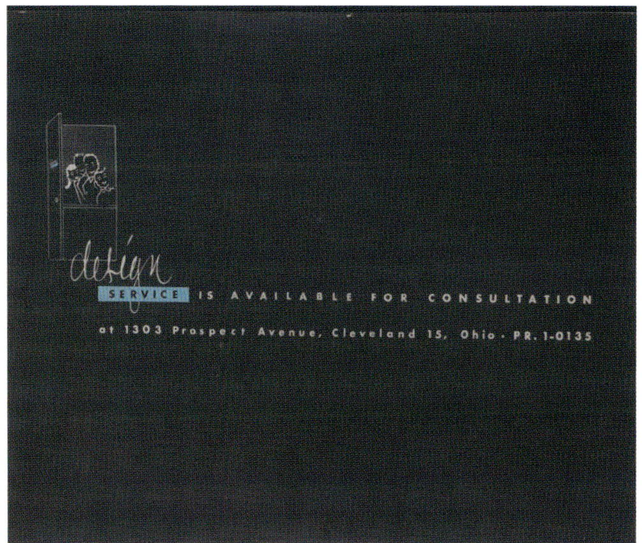

4.26. Design Service booklet promoting the collaboration of Robert Andrews Little (1923–2011) and Ann Halle Little with Joseph Benjamin O'Sickey (1918–2013) and Algesa D'Agostino O'Sickey. *Cleveland Architecture Foundation Collection.*

The pattern of women architects whose production was limited or overwhelmed by their more recognized spouses leads to the question of whether they accepted domestic responsibilities at the expense of architecture or if their personal and professional lives were so intertwined that it is impossible to demarcate them. Understandably, the production by and recognition of women architects in collaboration is complex. What is clear, however, is that regardless of how successful they were, women architects gravitated toward collaborative work arrangements. As the case of Pillsbury Harkness demonstrates especially well, partnerships for women were a crucial but largely unrecognized agent for the development of Modernism.

CHAPTER V

The Enterprising Spirit

A PAIR OF EVENING SHOES WRAPPED IN NEEDLEPOINT dating to 1939 serves as evidence that women were adept at innovating careers for themselves in which they could utilize their architectural training, if not their full talent, in unconventional ways (fig. 5.1). The shoes were designed by Alice Morgan Carson (the name she wanted to be professionally known by, even after her marriage, in 1943) and finished by Saks Fifth Avenue.[1] Carson herself thought of them as an "art deco, a Chrysler Building sort of thing."[2] Indeed, the band of pale blue triangles against the pink background near the center of the pattern echoes the windows on the upper stories of the famed New York building designed by William Van Alen and completed in 1930. Her donation of the shoes in 1983 to the Metropolitan Museum of Art in New York (after they went unsold for $10 in a yard sale) implies that Carson considered them as exemplary of her design career. Produced when she was completing her professional education at the Cambridge School of Architecture and Landscape Architecture as an architect (1940), as well as a landscape architect (1939), the shoes eventually stood in for the work in fields that ultimately eluded her.

Carson's shoes show how the vibrancy associated with modern art and architecture could infuse other media and, conversely, how work in the more putatively minor media could also broadly inform Modernism. The Ukrainian artist Sonia Terk Delaunay (1885–1979), a fixture of the Parisian avant-garde, had already made that point in her abstract needlework, fashion design, and even automobile decoration.[3] Terk Delaunay's influential abstract forms also demonstrate how the decorative, or applied, arts could make important contributions to the objectives of modern painting.[4] Her friend, the Swiss-born artist Sophie Henriette Gertrud Taeuber-Arp (1889–1943), likewise created abstract needlework designs.[5] In time, Taeuber-Arp shifted from traditionally female-gendered crafts to the fine arts, including architecture, in which her earlier exploration of abstraction in needlework informed her work. Though Carson did just the opposite by transitioning to needlework from garden and building design, both women prospered through their ability to adapt their aesthetic inclinations to varied types of media. Male architects were less likely to make a similar move, in part because textile design historically was gendered feminine.[6]

Women across multiple design fields in the mid-twentieth century realized that their professional practices would not be as straightforward as those of men due to prejudice or to a dearth of opportunity and, by necessity, could lead to an alternate destination. Thus, women trained in architecture found their ways, at various

5.1. Alice Morgan Carson, pair of evening shoes, silk petit point on canvas with leather, 1939. *Metropolitan Museum of Art, gift of Alice Morgan Carson.*

points in their careers, to other types of design, including furniture, toys, jewelry, graphics, photographs, models, works on paper, and textiles. By also taking on diverse professional roles, ranging from journalist, critic, and curator to gallerist, educator, and merchandiser, they were able to promote American Modernism, perhaps to a greater degree than they could have done in architecture.[7] Especially in their later years, many parlayed their experience into city planning, historic preservation, real estate sales and development, or environmental conservation. Although ancillary to architecture per se, such activities were compatible with Modernism in that they were often aimed at resolving social issues, especially those concerned with housing and community development. By broadening the perspective on Modernism to include not just buildings but a wide variety of objects and practices, women's production can be appreciated more fully.

The employment potential that design fields other than architecture offered to women is demonstrated by the trajectory of Irene "Inka" Janina Aronson-Sanna Benton (1918–2015). Born in Poland, she studied architecture at the Stanislas Noakowski School of Architecture for Women (1926–72) before fleeing to New York in 1940. As she immersed herself in American culture, she married Hale Powers Benton, whom she had met some years earlier on a trip to Italy (where his father was the business manager of the American Academy in Rome). Aronson-Sanna Benton also earned an undergraduate architecture degree at the Cambridge School (and later, in 1946, a master's degree at Harvard's Graduate School of Design [GSD]).[8] When in 1942 she could not find work in architecture, Henry Frost arranged for her to interview at Steuben Glass in New York, where she was offered an opportunity to train (without pay) in production. She asked Frost for his advice, confessing, "The only thing that bothers me is that it is not architecture." Still, she reasoned, "it is *creative* design—That was always one of my main interests since childhood. Be[ing] able to develop new ideas, create new lines, new forms—that certainly is a wonderful satisfaction!"[9] Frost agreed, responding that "while it may not be architecture, it is, as you say, creative work, and it would give you excellent experience in handling materials, which, after all, is part of architecture."[10]

Though the shift into related fields was a strategic way of locating professional opportunity, those in which they engaged were often associated with domestic design, which since the nineteenth century were gendered feminine. Le Corbusier pathologized the feminized domestic realm by setting it in opposition to Modernism: in *Vers une architecture*, he "inveighed against the 'sentimental hysteria' surrounding 'the cult of the house,' and proclaimed his determination to create instead 'a machine for living,'" argues art historian Christopher Reed.[11] Implicit in such statements, particularly in Le Corbusier's choice of the word *hysteria* (one that Sigmund Freud used to describe a mental illness that only afflicted women), is a deep misogyny that sprang from a fear of the potentially demasculinizing feminine realm. Among modernists, it was the abstract expressionist painters who especially inflated this anti-domestic rhetoric—for instance, Mark Rothko and Adolph Gottlieb, who proclaimed with pride that their work "must insult anyone who is spiritually attuned to interior decoration."[12] This polemicized and emphatically gendered discourse about the antagonistic relationship of Modernism to domesticity provided the intellectual backdrop for the transition of women architects into related areas of employment.

Historians have argued that, despite a misogynistic discourse around design and pervasive institutionalized sexism, women were instrumental in developing and publicizing modern design in the United States, Europe, Great Britain, and beyond. Accordingly, the varied background and production of pioneering women modernists Eileen Gray, Lilly Reich, Charlotte Perriand, Aino Marsio-Aalto, and Ray Kaiser Eames have all received increased academic and market interest.[13] In fact, it was within the disciplines most accessible to women that they used their social and professional networks to communicate about opportunities and exchange ideas. As the design author and critic Alice Rawsthorn observes, "Historically women have thrived on new turf where there are no male custodians, and they are free to invent their own ways of working."[14]

From Architecture to Craft

Alice Morgan Carson had not been short of formative experiences or social connections, and her early work was promising.[15] Beginning in 1921, the young Mayflower descendant allegedly made thirteen trips to Europe, most with her widowed mother, Jennie Madge Sugg Carson (1869–1952), who introduced her to business methods as they shopped for English and French antique furniture for her gallery in Greenwich, Connecticut. Carson also studied for two years at the Sorbonne Université in Paris before earning a Bachelor of Arts cum laude at Smith College in 1930. These varied interests prepared Carson to be adaptable and opportunistic, as Renaissance women tend to be. In 1931–33, she learned to catalog rare books under the tutelage of Henrietta Collins Bartlett, a noted bibliographer who likely supported her work in the aeronautical library of William A. M. Burden, a well-known financier and philanthropist.[16] In the mid-1930s, Carson also wrote and lectured up and down the Eastern Seaboard about flower arranging.[17] Her proclivity for modern design inevitably deepened between 1937 and 1940 at the Cambridge School, where her performance was "brilliant" (see fig. 1.3).[18]

Even before Carson completed her education, in 1938 she was given a shot at landscape architecture by Joseph Verner Reed Sr. and his wife Permelia Pryer Reed (1906–94), both from socially prominent, wealthy families. They commissioned her to design, with the assistance of Katharine Wilson, another Cambridge School student, terraces for Denbigh Farm, their Greenwich estate.[19] Their confidence in Carson led her two years later to do some landscaping as well as two vacation houses at the Jupiter Island Club in Hobe Sound, Florida, which the Reeds were instrumental in developing into an elite enclave. One of the houses, completed while Carson was working in the New York office of Van der Gracht and Kilham, was designed for S. (Samuel) Robert Glassford (see fig. 1.19), a retired cotton goods merchant as well as a founding trustee of the club.[20] The house consisted of two separate units: one with the living area and master bedroom (a kitchen was not necessary since meals were served at the clubhouse); the other had four wood-paneled guest rooms, each tightly organized with built-in furniture. A breezeway, also serving as an entrance porch, joined the two sections. Outside was an "ingenious" cypress lattice, like those that deflected the sun over lathhouses and reminiscent of the one Walter Gropius built over his roof deck at his own house (see fig. 1.7).

The other house Carson designed, called Pieces of Eight (1941), was a two-story frame structure owned by and adjacent to the clubhouse. Though that house also no longer stands, Arthur Hays Sulzberger, a club member and publisher of the *New York Times*, memorialized Carson's project in verse:

Just a cottage by the sea,
That was all it meant to me,
'Til along came Alice Carson
With an air much like a parson
Said, a name must quick be found
For this little spot of ground
And the building that she'd furnished
Shiny, bright and freshly burnished.[21]

In both structures, Carson proclaimed herself an architect dedicated to synthesizing geographical and cultural contexts in the way she had learned to do at the Cambridge School.[22] Although her career was far from established, the Glassford house, illustrated in *Architectural Record* (July 1941), enabled Carson to stake a place for herself in the modern movement. Not long after, she took a job at the Museum of Modern Art (MoMA) as an assistant to Eliot Noyes, then the director of industrial design.[23] Among her responsibilities was the exhibition design of *New Rugs by American Artists* (1942).[24] Carson compared the rugs to a group shown at the museum in an earlier exhibition, in 1937, called *Rugs Designed by American Artists*, in which one of the eleven exhibitors was Marguerite Zorach (1887–1968), a painter and textile artist. Zorach was recognized for her ability to break down boundaries between modern art and craft, and she would have provided an example for Carson in her own practice in which she too demonstrated that Modernism was adaptable to many media.[25] When Noyes took leave in May 1942 to join the glider division of the Army Air Force, Carson assumed the position of acting director of industrial design as well as acting curator of the architecture department, one of several instances in which women achieved greater responsibility when the "male custodians" (to borrow a phrase from Rawsthorn) left for war-related work. Of the seven or so exhibitions Carson organized at MoMA, the fifth annual *Useful Objects* (1942) exhibition consisting of 282 wartime items most prepared Carson subsequently to mount an exhibition of 4,500 examples of emergency rescue equipment for the Office of Strategic Services (OSS), the government intelligence agency in Washington, DC.[26] Though promoted at the OSS as chief of the exhibit section, she maintained her connection to MoMA by serving on the special advisory committee alongside (mostly male) architects, editors, and critics for "Built in U.S.A., 1932–44," the architecture section of the museum's fifteenth anniversary exhibition *Art in Progress* (1944).[27]

5.2. Alice Morgan Carson and her husband, Earle Francis Hiscock (1903–80) in her home studio in Chatham, Massachusetts, c. 1960. *Private collection.*

After the war, she either could not find employment or avoided taking a job away from a man, as the mainstream media urged women to do, and instead did an about-face by designing needlepoint canvas patterns. Her transition to what was considered traditional women's work is logical, given that she had already designed furniture upholstery patterns for her mother's customers. But this time, Carson elevated her woman's work by developing a hugely productive mail-order business (she was known at the post office as "five-o'clock Alice") from her home studio, located first in Arlington, Virginia, and then in Chatham, Massachusetts (fig. 5.2). Her production ultimately surpassed 2,500 needlepoint canvas designs—ranging from shoes and handbags to upholstery and rugs—each accompanied by meticulous directions and specialized materials.[28]

Carson developed a culturally sophisticated clientele, exemplified by her most consistent patron, Pernelia Pryer Reed. In 1945, the two women corresponded about the design of a twelve-foot-round rug she planned to needlepoint with her husband for the circular study in their Connecticut home. After much back-and-forth about the composition and layout—comprising thirteen medallions, each representing a distinct aspect of their Greenwich estate—the final order, delivered in early 1946, included twenty-three pieces of painted canvas, eight cartons containing skeins of wool, and a detailed blueprint.[29] The rug took six years to complete. Over time, Carson produced other patterns for Pryer Reed, whose individual needlepoint items fetched as much as $10,000 at a charity bazaar for the Palm Beach Garden Club.[30]

Another influential client of Carson, Marcia Davenport (1903–96), the American biographer of Wolfgang Amadeus Mozart, experienced "pervasive and lasting" satisfaction with needlepoint as a hobby, according to the *New York Times*. Davenport recalled that between 1945 and 1948, when living in Prague, she began a five-year needlepoint upholstery project for a pair of armchairs with scenes from stories by the Brothers Grimm set against backdrops of Prague architectural landmarks.[31] Davenport emphasized how the custom kit supplied by Carson was markedly different from commercially produced retail kits:

Months went into assembling the pictorial material for the project. Books, drawings (not by me, I can't draw a line), photographs, illustrations, color ideas and personal descriptions went, together with the upholsterer's muslin patterns to my designer, Alice Morgan Carson, in Massachusetts. She required more months to make the designs, consult with me, revise the pictures, draw and paint them on 14-count mono canvas and select and supply the hundreds of shades of wool and silk necessary for the work. I will not state what this cost; it was expensive then and it would be vastly more so today.[32]

Davenport collaborated with Carson the way patrons do with other artists or architects, by engaging in a protracted discussion of the forms her work could take, as well the professional fee.

While Carson's patterns typically contain recognizable motifs such as plants, flowers, animals, and zodiac signs—probably in response to customer requests—she also designed more abstract patterns for herself.[33] An example is the needlepoint telephone book cover, which remained in her personal collection, passed down to a descendent (fig. 5.3). The composition—of telephone equipment and a switchboard operator unified by a wire that unspools and loops through the image—recalls the arabesque ropes deployed by Fernand Léger in work from the early to mid 1930s, as well as by Le Corbusier in his paintings of the same period.

5.3. Alice Morgan Carson, needlepoint telephone book cover and its corresponding paper pattern inspired by Fernand Léger (1881–1955), c. 1936. *(top) Private collection; (bottom) Embroiders' Guild of America.*

Architecture of a Toy

While Carson was able to combine her artistic interests with her architecture training by diverting her energy into needlepoint pattern design, Anne Tyng had a more linear professional trajectory, somewhat more like a man's. Each episode of her life work built on her experience and contributed to the next phase, moving from product design to architecture. The furniture and "construction toy" for children that she invented in 1947, and patented in 1951, not only shows her influences but anticipates her preoccupation with the space-frame architecture of interlocking geometries for which she would be best known.

Her training in architecture (at Radcliffe, the Cambridge School, and Harvard's GSD) enabled Tyng to find informative, entry-level jobs: making perspectives of the prefabricated General Panel House for Konrad Wachsmann as well as working for the industrial design firms of (Harold) Van Doren, (Roger) Nowland & (Peter) Schladermundt, and of H. (Hans) G. Knoll Associates. Combined with her work in the short-lived partnership of Oskar Stonorov and Louis I. Kahn, these exposures coalesced to spark her interest in instructing children, in 1947–48, in the Saturday morning art program at the Philadelphia Museum of Art and in teaching architecture and furniture design in 1949 at Beaver College, outside Philadelphia.[34] Although Tyng followed Kahn to his own firm in 1947, where she became a critical member of the design team, the construction toy was, significantly, her first independent venture.

The initial idea for the Tyng Toy—as she named it—is illustrated on three sheets of drawings showing five flat pieces of varied shapes and sizes of plywood, each with notches and / or holes in which the other pieces can be attached to make seven life-size, weight-bearing toys or

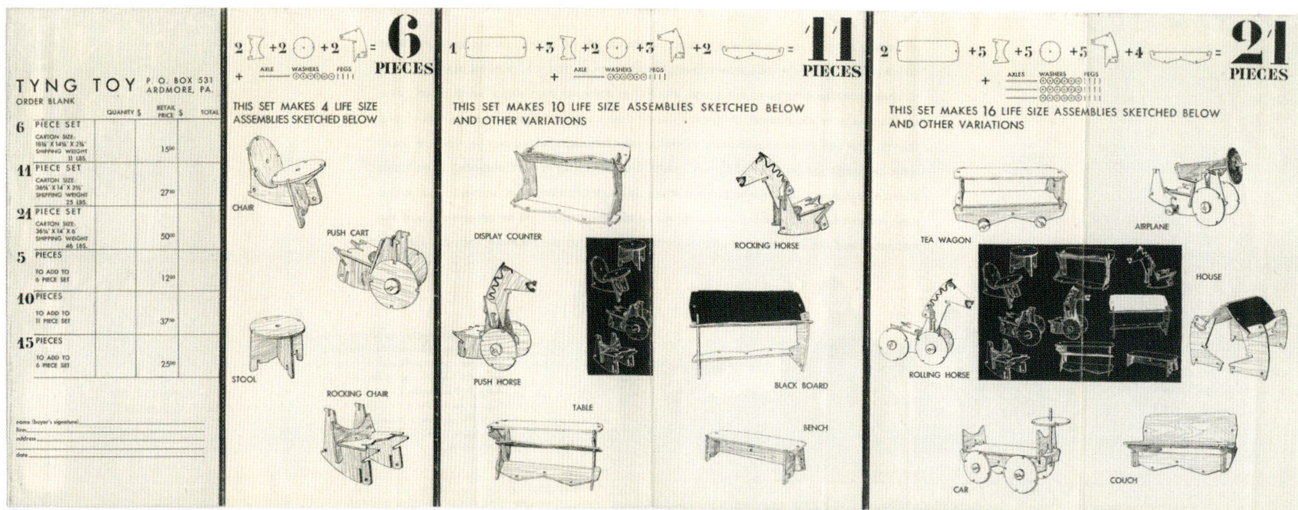

5.4. Anne Griswold Tyng, instructions for the Tyng Toy (pushcart and rocking horse), 1950. *Anne Griswold Tyng Collection, Architectural Archives, Stuart Weitzman School of Design.*

pieces of furniture—both fixed (stool, table, bench, display counter, and chair) and mobile (pushcart and rocking horse; fig. 5.4).[35] When the toy went to market in 1950, the concept was expanded to include three differently sized kits, beginning at $15, of six, eleven, or twenty-one pieces, each five-eighth inches thick. The "sturdy," "simple," and "neat" features—made of naturally finished shapes along with pegs (the upper half of each painted bright red to prevent slippage when inserted in a hole), washers, and an axle—were modern in their ingenuity, flexibility, and material.[36] Some of the pieces also call to mind the organic shapes in the contemporary abstract paintings of Joan Miró and Jean Arp.[37]

The highly regarded toy was featured in five exhibitions across the country, including the *Children's Fair* (1948) organized by Hilda Reiss at the Walker Art Center in Minneapolis.[38] In 1951, it was displayed at the San Francisco Museum of Art, in an exhibition also curated by Reiss, and organized by the American Federation of Arts so that it could be circulated (secretly) by the State Department to the *Amerika Häuser* institutions throughout Germany, for citizens to learn about American culture and politics.[39] Although only a toy, it exemplified the essential characteristics of Modernism.

Though the Tyng Toy predates the better-known Toy (1951) and House of Cards (1952) of Charles and Ray Kaiser Eames, construction (or demountable) objects had already penetrated the market.[40] In a review of the Tyng Toy, the home editor of the *New York Times* referenced its connection with popular contemporary knock-down furniture forms, commenting, "Small fry who have recently been interested by the sight of their elders struggling to construct a table, a chair or a chest may now have a try at it themselves."[41] Conceptually, it did not veer far from the Pakto furniture that Sarah Pillsbury had helped design

5.5. Promotional photograph of Anne Griswold Tyng with her toy components, c. 1950. *Tyng Collection.*

for Dan Cooper. Just like that furniture, which was being promoted even in news magazines, the Tyng Toy could be assembled quickly and efficiently.[42] The essence of the Tyng Toy—the organization of simple geometric forms into more complex ones—would be vivid in Tyng's work going forward. In fact, a photograph of the beautiful young Tyng sitting among the plywood pieces is still one of her most prominent images; it is a metaphor for her approach to design, which, regardless of the medium, had geometry at its core (fig. 5.5).

Multifaceted Production

A photograph of Franziska Porges Hosken, one of Tyng's contemporaries at the Cambridge School and at Harvard's GSD, is similarly iconic in that she is ornamented in the jewelry she made from brass or copper coiled wire, sometimes plated in gold or nickel (fig. 5.6).[43] Between 1948 and 1951, Porges Hosken also immersed herself in the design of the furniture she produced and marketed in collaboration with her engineer husband James. Her Austrian background as well as her education in important centers of Modernism prepared her for a diverse and successful practice. Like other pioneering women architecture graduates, her professional career gravitated to fields adjacent to building design, including jewelry, in which she was able to expand the impact of Modernism.

She had fled Vienna as a university student in 1938, just five days after Adolf Hitler's forces entered the city, where her Jewish father was a prominent professor of medicine.[44] Nonetheless, she thrived in the United States, entering Smith College in the spring of that year and graduating in 1940 with recognition for her outstanding work in creative art.[45] Porges worked briefly in interior display at Marshall Field and at the Display Factory in Chicago, where her parents had settled. She would have learned about the Cambridge School at Smith, and though she admitted to not knowing much about architecture, she was accepted and began in the summer of 1941. With the others, she transferred in the fall of 1942 to Harvard's GSD and graduated with a bachelor's degree in architecture in 1944.[46]

After working in the United States Coast Guard Women's Reserve during the war, Porges Hosken obtained a job as a draftsperson, between 1946 and 1947, in the established architecture firm of Skidmore, Owings & Merrill in Chicago, as Natalie Griffin de Blois did in New York at the time. Though her career in architecture was

5.6. Photograph of Franziska Porges Hosken wearing the metal coil jewelry she designed, c. 1949. *Private collection.*

on track, she had to abandon it when her husband, whom she married in 1947, took a job with the management consulting firm Arthur D. Little; the couple moved to the Jamaica Plain neighborhood in Boston. Realizing that they could not afford to buy the commercially produced modern furniture they desired—by Knoll, Herman Miller, and such Scandinavian imports as Artek—they invested in tools to make their own, mostly from hollow-flush or cupboard-door stock. Using "taste, time, talent, instead of dollars," according to *House and Garden* in 1949, the couple made themselves six types of tables or desks, various shelves, two service carts, a sideboard, and a lighting fixture.[47] Encouraged by two colleagues—"architectural editor" Katherine Morrow Ford (1906–59) and Cambridge School alumna Dorothy "Dotty" Quincy Noyes (Berkling; 1914–62)—she embraced the idea of shifting her focus from architecture to commercial furniture design.[48]

She modeled many of the furniture forms—tables, carts, stands, trays, racks, stacking stools, shelves, and case pieces—on what already was on the market.[49] What differentiated the Hosken furniture from others, however, was its target market of young postwar couples requiring small-scale, inexpensive, adjustable, and portable pieces. Though certain parts were made of solid wood, most were of popular or new materials such as plywood (in

5.7. Franziska Porges, sketch for a living / dining area, c. 1942. *Porges Hosken Papers.*

natural, stained, or painted finishes), fiberboard, lacquered hardboard (Masonite or Duron), tubular steel, sheet metal, and plastic (primarily Formica). Initially distributed by Raymor Manufacturing in New York, the furniture was also sold in department stores (Macy's and Bloomingdale's) and in such retail establishments as Paine Furniture Company in Boston, Baldwin Kingrey (1947–57) in Chicago, and New Design (1947–52) in New York, the latter cofounded by her friend Dorothy Noyes.[50]

Though the timing was right, as Porges Hosken recalled, the couple lacked capital, business acumen, and marketing experience. Nonetheless, the Hosken furniture had favorable reviews and placement in exhibitions.[51] The tea / service cart available in tubular steel or colored plastic pipe—a popular form in the early 1920s that the Aaltos reinvigorated for Artek—was in the exhibition *For Modern Living* (1949) at the Detroit Institute of Arts. A more popular item (but also problematic since it was easy to copy at a reduced cost) was the stack of four square-topped stool-tables of solid birch that was shown in the second "Good Design" installation jointly organized by MoMA and the Merchandise Mart in Chicago in 1951–52 "to reward excellent examples of new modern design."[52]

Even before creating the Hosken furniture line, Porges Hosken had shown an inclination toward interior design. As a student, she made herself a dining set that consisted of a tabletop (a repurposed door) that could be stored on a wall above a horizontal cabinet (also made by her) or could be laid over the cabinet and stabilized on one side by an end panel cutout with an abstract pattern.[53] Her extant Cambridge School drawings (of a dormitory, design shop, and house) as well as her drawings from Harvard's GSD (of a nursery school, hotel, and ski lodge) feature stunningly detailed interiors. Of note are the elevations, dated August 1941 (likely made at the Cambridge School / Harvard collaborative summer school), of a house on Ash Street—the same street where Philip Johnson was building his infamous modern house, completed in 1942. She must have been intrigued with the Johnson house, as it is illustrated in her cartoon reviewing the academic year of 1942–43, when women were first allowed to study at Harvard's GSD. She wrote, "The chief attraction of Friday afternoon is a certain house on ASH STREET. Outside you see nothing but a fence. But inside is the ARCHITECTS PARADISE [with] unlimited drinks till 7 PM!" (see fig. 1.5).[54]

The ideas Porges Hosken applied in concepts for a house for a family with children obviously deviate from Johnson's bachelor's salon. Nonetheless, her (undated) sketches of the interior relay a similar commitment to Modernism in such details as a lally column, a sundeck, continuous indirect ceiling lighting, a space-dividing curtain, and ample windows, including the awning type (fig. 5.7). Her appreciation for functional design is also apparent in such space-saving features as extensive built-in cabinetry and shelving as well as pull-out beds; her knowledge of popular contemporary materials is evident in her choice of plywood for the sliding doors, cork tiles for flooring, and corrugated glass for partitions.

While the artistic joinery of the Bauhaus is absent from her furniture, the straightforward forms and clearcut construction correspond to the school's design precepts, as do the juxtaposed neutral and primary colors—for example, on a chest of drawers, echoing the de Stijl aesthetic that took hold there (fig. 5.8).[55] Such objects are at once "decorative and austere, optimistic, and naïve," as Larry Weinberg, a dealer in mid-twentieth-century design, observed in his 2001 exhibition of Hosken designs.[56] Porges Hosken claimed that her interest in the Bauhaus was piqued when she attended the Cambridge School, and it led her to believe that "the Bauhaus was and is first of all an idea—and important ideas never die."[57]

Porges Hosken never deviated from the progressive Bauhaus commitment to making objects that were meant to improve living conditions, nor from her deference to Gropius, its founder and her Harvard professor. She saved her student drawings of the Aluminum City Terrace for defense workers during World War II by Gropius and Breuer, as well as a photograph of her visiting one of the prefabricated houses by General Panel (conceived by Gropius and Wachsmann).[58] Porges Hosken and Gropius maintained a personal and professional relationship for years: he reviewed and wrote a back-cover blurb for her book *The Language of Cities* (1968), and she translated from German his Bauhaus diaries and notes for the acclaimed two-volume biography by Reginald Isaacs.[59]

Porges Hosken was adept at working in media other than architecture—photography, lighting, apparel, and graphics, as well as commercial interiors—which enabled her to segue her architecture training into other fields.[60] She began a photograph collection of architecture and urbanism in 1946, when with Dorothy Noyes she traveled cross-country for more than a year surveying architecture. She then set up a leasing business, first at MoMA and then independently (the collection of more than 66,800 images is at Texas A&M University). As a journalist, Porges Hosken wrote articles, columns, reviews, and stories in magazines, books, newspapers, and newsletters, and as an instructor she lectured on various related subjects at three Massachusetts institutions.[61] As one Boston newspaper recognized in 1949—when she was only a third of the way through her life—Porges Hosken was "tossing off more ideas than Paul Revere hammered out in a lifetime."[62] Though she was not a member of a specific movement, guild, circle, or bee, as women historically were, and was perhaps singular in her strategy to partake in unusually diverse projects outside her areas of expertise, the common thread in her production is an adherence to cutting-edge ideas and design, which even included, later in life, feminist advocacy.[63] She never did erect the "strictly modern" building she once envisioned for herself, but her

5.8. Prototype chest of drawers, no. 210, birch plywood and fiberboard, by Hosken Inc., founded by Franziska Porges Hosken with her husband, James Cuthbert Hosken (1909–93), 10 Roanoke Avenue, Boston. *Private collection.*

diverse contributions not only disseminated Modernism, but enhanced modern living for the many who benefited from her ingenuity.[64]

Modernism in Photographs

Porges Hosken's photographic practice demonstrates the increasing importance of the medium to the field of architecture during the twentieth century. Indeed, the strategies adopted by architectural photographers were essential to establishing the modern movement in the United States. Discussing what she terms the "photographic architecture" of the early twentieth-century modern movement in Europe, historian Claire Zimmerman writes, "The visual practices that were part of photography entered into the design procedures of architects, resulting in new architectural concepts that were manifested in constructed projects, even if these were not always immediately evident to the public."[65] Later in the century, the modern qualities of the work of such women architects as Eleanor Raymond, Victorine du Pont Homsey, and Natalie Griffin de Blois were dramatized in published photographs that made modern architecture better known and more compelling.

The architect Esther Baum Born, who used photography to promote Modernism as dynamic and innovative in its use of novel forms in new materials, is an example. Still widely recognized for her photographs that culminated in the book *The New Architecture of Mexico* (1937), Baum Born applied her photography skills to a variety of other projects, such as documenting the Golden Gate International Exposition in San Francisco (1939) and the designs produced in her husband's architecture firm.[66] Less known are her photographic commissions from regional architects, among them Michael Arthur Goodman, William Clement Ambrose, John Savage Bolles, and George Patton Simonds. For Bernard Maybeck, with whom she studied architecture at the University of California, Berkeley, she photographed the Orin Kip McMurray house (1924), the Wallen Maybeck house no. 2 (1937), the First Church of Christ, Scientist (1910), and the Mobilized Women of Berkeley building (1937; now demolished).[67]

The significance of her photography to the careers of American architects is also demonstrated by her California work for Frank Lloyd Wright: the Paul R. and Jean S. Hanna house at Stanford University in Palo Alto, and the Sidney Bizette house in Hillsborough, both shown at MoMA in *Frank Lloyd Wright: American Architect* (1940), the first comprehensive presentation of his work.[68] In October 1940, *Architectural Forum* named Baum Born in its salute to professional photographers (the nine others were male) alongside such well-known names as Ezra Stoller, Samuel H. Gottscho, and Robert M. Damora (all of whose work is shown throughout this book).[69] This early tribute recognizes Baum Born's important role in popularizing Modernism. Unlike her peers, however, she faded from view, leading the critic Kenneth Caldwell to wonder why Baum Born and her husband have languished in relative obscurity.[70]

Given the extensive publication of Baum Born's photographs of contemporary architecture, particularly in Mexico, it is surprising that she has not received greater recognition, especially considering that other female architecture photographers, notably Margaret Bourke-White (1904–71) and Berenice Abbott (1898–1991), have achieved canonical status. Still, these prominent women photographers were exceptional; many, like Baum Born, made "unique yet underrecognized contributions to American modernism" and have only received belated historical consideration.[71] For instance, Rosalie "Rollie" Thorne McKenna (1918–2003), a 1940 graduate of Vassar College, enjoyed a career as an architectural photographer, which included a long-term professional relationship with MoMA and an important commission to photograph the newly completed Seagram Building in New York City in 1958. Yet she did not receive her first career survey until a 2024 exhibition at her alma mater.[72]

Retailing Modern Furnishings

Another promising allied field for women architects was the promotion and advancement of modern design through retailing. Among the earliest ventures of this kind undertaken by Cambridge School alumnae was the small display room established in 1940 by Sarah Pillsbury and Louisa Vaughan. Located in what they considered "the worst looking building" at 687 Boylston Street in Boston's Back Bay neighborhood, Pillsbury and Vaughan, as their business was called, was conceived primarily to sell the Artek furniture designed by Aino Marsio-Aalto and Alvar Aalto.[73]

Pillsbury would have been familiar with the furniture through publications, especially after MoMA disseminated the furniture through its retrospective exhibition on Aalto in 1938. She knew Artek would appeal at least to her network of students and alumnae, who typically furnished their models with two or three small replicas of the furniture.[74] When she first met Clifford Pascoe, the entrepreneur who had contracted with the Aaltos to produce and distribute their furniture designs in the United States, she was overwhelmed: "As for me I'm going absolutely bats," she wrote John Harkness in August 1940, "I saw the Pascoe kid … and his ideas of how we would sell the furniture are colossal."[75] Not only was he determined to maintain the high standard of Scandinavian production, but he had ambitious goals for the regional distributors he intended to sign on.[76] Cautioning her not to begin with too small a storefront in the Boston area, Pascoe insisted she display twenty-five pieces in addition to retaining duplicates to be stocked or stacked together.[77] He also advised her to develop a strong publicity campaign, a sensational grand opening, and aggressive marketing directed to both the wholesale and more profitable retail trades, as he had done in his display room at 640 Madison Avenue in New York, where he allegedly brought in $8,000 in sales during the first six weeks.[78]

Pillsbury was not sure if she wanted to be a businessperson, much less a proprietor, but she knew she wanted to prove she could make money with her professional training. Perhaps she was aware of two other Cambridge School alumnae, Helen Rosenbaum Linard (Baldwin; 1905–89) and Martha McGervey (Patrick; 1906–98), who reported in 1937 that they were maintaining a Shop for Modern Interiors in Washington, DC, in which they "did everything from furniture and pillows to church interiors."[79] With no eminent role model, however, Pillsbury was on her own, contemplating the various scenarios for setting up a distributorship. She considered showing the furniture in the office of Marc Peter Jr., for whom she had recently worked, or in an independent showroom at the Institute of Modern Art (now the Institute of Contemporary Art / Boston), where her friend Ann Tredick (Dickey; 1917–2009), who would later work at MoMA like Pillsbury, was employed and could take orders (see fig. 1.3). Instead, she strategically decided on a collaboration with Vaughan, a prudent choice, as she was considered at the Cambridge School to be unusually intelligent and thoroughly dependable, with the highest integrity and charm, and a strong business sense.[80]

The women admired Artek because it corresponded with the trend in architecture then transitioning from a Bauhaus-inspired aesthetic to one that privileged vernacular American details and materials. They were convinced that those interested in modern living would respond to its functionality (light, movable, stackable, easy to clean), technological advancements (laminated wood that was bent and glued in one process and assembled without blocks, dowels, or multiple screws), natural materials (primarily birch and maple), organicism (graceful, sinuous lines, scaled and contoured to the body), human-centered design (warm, comfortable, and friendly), and affordability. As architects, they believed they were positioned to guide clients in their choices of furniture as well as the design of their homes, as they would do as "interior consultants" for the Pertzoffs in Lincoln.[81] Thus, in September 1940, the two signed a year's agreement with Pascoe, each committing $600 (equivalent in 2022 to nearly $20,000) for their space and stock, which was available to them at 40 percent off the list price.[82] In addition to nearly forty pieces of Artek furniture (the stacking dining chair at $14.50 being the bestseller), they offered examples by the Swedish designer Bruno Mathsson (also made by Pascoe), Carl Koch, and Jorge Ferrari-Hardoy, among others, as well as textiles, screens, lighting, glassware, ceramics, and woodenware.[83]

Following Pascoe's lead, Pillsbury penned a press announcement two months after the opening noting the range of guests—from architects and curators to academics and alumnae from Harvard, MIT, and Smith.[84] She also turned to her social and professional networks to generate publicity, for instance by writing a feature for the *Cambridge School Alumnae Bulletin*, where a photograph of the sparingly decorated Pillsbury and Vaughan display room was shown, along with one of the Artek-furnished living rooms in the Albert Koch Sr. house (1936) in Cambridge, which had been featured on the alumnae tour in 1938.[85] She also advertised in the *Harvard Crimson*—with her husband, then a GSD student, listed as the contact.[86] Perhaps the cards she sent to the "engaged girls" did not pan out, but the architects (or their wives) responded. Among those who bought furniture were Breuer, Gropius, Johnson, Koch, Little, Pei, Perkins, Pertzoff, Raymond, Satterlee, and Underwood, as well as Elliot and Dorothy Noyes. In addition to taking on the role of "design consultant" for Pertzoff, the entrepreneurial women supplied Perkins with various types of textiles for the John P. Monks house in Lincoln and the Karl Terzaghi house in Winchester, Massachusetts.[87]

Though Pillsbury fully immersed herself in the partnership, which in the first nine months netted the equivalent (in 2022) of $14,688, she had lingering doubts about business ownership, as opposed to design, and was disappointed that the interior work they had anticipated failed to materialize.[88] In January 1942, Raedermacher Wasson-Tucker formally took over for Pillsbury, and the distributorship was renamed Artek in Boston. The new partnership only lasted to late 1943, undoubtedly because of the wartime hiatus in homebuilding and consumption, as well as the novelty of the furniture itself, especially in Boston, where the conservative Yankee mentality so prevailed that even after the war, one of the more established furniture companies hosted a "Colonial Month" for its clientele.[89]

Nonetheless, in 1947 the distributorship was resuscitated by Christina Kimball Nute (Simmons; 1921–88) as an "unpretentious little shop" in a Beacon Hill townhouse—with the approbation of Raedermacher Wasson-Tucker (the only attendant at Nute's wedding in 1951).[90] Nute may have been introduced to the Artek business as one of the "five little attendants" that Pillsbury had signed on from the Modern School of Applied Art (founded in 1934), located in the same building as Pillsbury and Vaughan.[91] Nute had also worked, at least in 1945, in Pascoe's New York showroom. Her Artek distributorship lasted only about two years, after which she became associated with Knoll, perhaps through Raedermacher Wasson-Tucker, who at the time was employed by Knoll in New York.[92] Conservative New Englanders, however, also did not "trample" Nute to revolutionize their stately drawing rooms and Colonial Revival family rooms with Knoll either, and she only remained in business until 1952.[93] Nute did not enter into the business with the same architecture background as the others, but rather she was the product of a progressive new college (Goddard, in Plainville, Vermont) and had studied with the African American sculptor Meta Vaux Warrick Fuller (1877–1968). While her interior decoration studies at the Modern School were more conventional, she too could not succeed as a retailer.[94]

Elizabeth "Betty" Louise Vonderlieth Shotwell (Olson; 1918–2013) also was not an architect but instead studied pictorial illustration at Pratt before opening her Artek distributorship, called America House, on K Street in Washington, DC. Her situation was different from Nute's, in that her husband Henry Titus Shotwell was an architect and presumably participated in the business.[95] More is known about Elizabeth "Betsy" Montagu Roberts Church (1903–97), the wife of the Harvard-educated landscape architect Thomas Dolliver Church. In a letter to Aalto in February 1941, she wrote, "I have meant long since to thank you for letting me handle your beautiful stuff. … [I]t is a daily pleasure to work among these fine things."[96] While initially Roberts Church appears to have been the one selling the Artek furniture in a small space at Cargoes, a retail store in San Francisco, by 1947 she was collaborating with her husband on a distributorship spanning the West Coast; that Church was also vested in the business is illustrated by his letterhead, which announced: "Thomas D. Church / Importer of Artek Products."[97]

A comparable arrangement transpired in Chicago, where the architect Harry Mohr Weese and his wife Kitty Baldwin Weese joined in 1947 with Jody Kingrey (Albergo; 1918–2003) to create Baldwin Kingrey, a retail store that flourished until 1957.[98] Though the two women managed the day-to-day operations, the initial idea came from Weese, who maintained the correspondence with Aalto. It was probably not a coincidence that Ralph Rapson, who knew Weese as a student at Cranbrook, also opened a retail store in Cambridge in 1950, co-managed with his second wife, Mary Christine Dolan Rapson, a Smith College graduate and former secretary who became his "life-long partner running his office for almost fifty years." She helped market furniture designed by Rapson and others as well as lighting, textiles, and accessories.[99]

Given the short duration of the Boston enterprises, the women retailers may appear to have failed. Their investments in themselves—as professionals in female business partnerships—is worth noting, however, especially because they achieved some career success. After her stint at Knoll, both in the United States and in Sweden, Raedermacher Wasson-Tucker chose to work independently in exhibition and commercial interior design. Both Pillsbury and Vaughan, on the other hand, relied on collaboration to establish themselves as architects: Pillsbury with her husband at The Architects Collaborative (TAC), Vaughan with the Lincoln-based architect Constantin Pertzoff, to whom she was related through his wife.[100] With Pertzoff, Vaughan Conrad (she married in 1945) applied her retail experience to the alteration of the front of E. A. Conrad Company, a boys' clothing store operated by her husband at 299 Cabot Street in Beverly, Massachusetts. The exterior is distinguished by inward-slanting display windows consistent

5.9. Louisa Loring Vaughan Conrad, rear facade of the house she designed for Elbert A. Conrad and herself, 454 Hale Street, Prides Crossing, Massachusetts, 1950. *Private collection.*

with midcentury updates to traditional commercial streetscapes.[101] Vaughan Conrad also designed a house for her husband and herself at Prides Crossing, close to the shore in Beverly (fig. 5.9). She divided the house into two rectangular blocks, one for bedrooms and the other for living areas, which were joined by a glass-walled entryway with a cast-iron spiral stair down to the daylit basement. Perched dramatically on a rock ledge, the house exterior incorporated granite walls and rough-sawn boards; the design recalls Raymond's earlier work and Breuer's domestic commissions in its synthesis of modern forms and traditional, organic materials.[102]

The New York furnishing business called New Design departed from most others in the way it came about in 1947. Dorothy Noyes initially joined up with the architect Robert Hays Rosenberg, whom she probably met while studying at Harvard, to create a retail business with design services and high quality contemporary furnishings by name designers to convey a better understanding of "new design" in architecture, housing, and planning. Her vision may have evolved from her Cambridge School days when, in 1941, she won an interschool competition with her design for a shop with modern furniture.[103] Though Noyes transferred to Harvard after the Cambridge School closed in 1942, she left (without finishing) to do more urgent wartime work in Washington, DC, as a draftsperson in the cartographic section and then as an illustrator of special exhibits at the OSS and as a visual information assistant in the National Housing Agency. During her photography tour with Franziska Porges, Noyes became convinced of a pent-up demand for modern furnishings in every price range. Shops were springing up everywhere, she observed, but none were displaying the best contemporary design.[104]

Both Noyes and Rosenberg are listed in the annual retrospective of important work by leading designers in *Interiors* magazine in 1949.[105] However, according to a New Design fact sheet, Rosenberg's wife Harriet Amy Stern Rosenberg (Strongin; 1915–91) was also a founding partner. Although she studied music at Bennington College, from which she graduated in 1937, Stern Rosenberg was able to parlay her architecture exposure in a way that the others could not. During her youth, she had been introduced to Wright's pioneering work through her mother's sister Sophie Amberg and her husband Meyer May, who in 1908 commissioned a house and interiors by Frank Lloyd Wright in Grand Rapids.[106] About two years later, her grandparents built the Amberg house just a few blocks away, designed by Marion Mahony while Wright was in Europe (see fig. 1.8).[107] Though Stern Rosenberg's grandfather established himself as a liquor wholesaler, he could have piqued her interest in furniture design since he was also a director for Imperial Furniture (1903–54) and for Grand Rapids Chair (1872–1973).[108]

Noyes (director) and Stern Rosenberg (assistant director) were joined at New Design by a third woman, Edith G. Perlman (Queller; 1917–92), whose more diverse experience would have been a boon. Perlman

5.10. New Design showroom (1947–52), 33 East 75th Street, New York.

had studied industrial design in 1934–37 at Pratt and in 1937–40 attended the Design Laboratory, a WPA project in New York directed by Gilbert Rohde.[109] Between 1937 and 1944, she worked for a ceramicist, an architect, and a lighting company.[110] It was her art teaching job at Newcomb College in New Orleans, 1944–47, however, that was relevant to New Design, since part of the mission there was to educate the public about Modernism and planning through displays, lectures, films, and publications. An advertising leaflet emphatically endorses this effort: "IF YOU / *believe in* / *hate* / *don't understand* / *are confused by* / *come and see the* [*hand*]*picked collection of* FURNITURE AND ACCESSORIES FOR CONTEMPORARY LIVING / *handsomely displayed* at / NEW DESIGN INC." Not only did this educational piece distinguish New Design from competitors but so did its setting. Located in a brownstone with "speakeasy-like doors," the ground floor was set up as a living room, dining room, and study, separated by a mesh curtain; on the second floor was a bedroom setting (fig. 5.10).[111]

Though Rosenberg eventually took an ancillary role, as husbands tended to do in their wives' retail stores, he brought commissions to New Design through his own practice. He also maintained a presence as a consultant, along with Raedermacher Wasson-Tucker, Eliot Noyes (no relation to Dorothy Noyes), and the architect and designer Benjamin Baldwin.[112] The publicity materials were thoughtfully designed, most likely with the input of Max Brombacher Berking, an advertising executive whom Noyes married in 1951. The promotional activities in which the firm engaged were also specifically targeted at audiences who would welcome modern design. In 1948, Noyes and Perlman designed an "All-Purpose Family Room" for the *Tomorrow's World* exhibition, sponsored by the New York Chapter of the American Institute of Architects (AIA), and in 1950 Noyes furnished the model house designed by the Harvard-trained modernist Huson Jackson on Long Island.[113] New Design's most worthwhile promotional project was the more than two hundred furnishings it provided to the six-room demonstration house that Marcel Breuer designed in 1949 for in the garden at MoMA (fig. 5.11). Consequently, in the wake of the exhibition, New Design's revenue increased dramatically.[114]

New Design closed in 1952, but Noyes Berking continued to work in her home in Rye, New York. Though her customers could no longer drop by a metropolitan showroom, they could benefit from seeing her modern furnishings in the split-level, open-plan house she designed with Edward Larrabee Barnes.[115] Photographs of the living room with its dramatic pitched ceiling demonstrate that she lived the modern lifestyle she sold to others (fig. 5.12).

The studied presentation of the modern furnishings sold by Georgia Hencken Perkins in her shop in Chestnut Hill, Pennsylvania, was central to her business model.[116] A Cambridge School landscape architect by training, Hencken Perkins initiated the enterprise with Stanisława Sandecka Nowicki, who in 1951 had been recruited to teach architecture in the School of Fine Arts at the University of Pennsylvania by her husband, G. Holmes Perkins (see fig. 2.24). She apparently reconsidered, however, and Hencken Perkins was the sole proprietor of what became known as Gray Associates.

5.11. Interior of *The House in the Museum Garden* by Marcel Lajos Breuer (1902–81), with furnishings provided by New Design, 1949. *Museum of Modern Art.*

5.12. Interior of the house (now demolished) designed by Edward Larrabee Barnes with Dorothy Quincy Noyes Berking, 10 Drake-Smith Lane, Rye, New York, 1955. *Private collection.*

5.13. G. Holmes Perkins, rear facade of Gray Associates, 8605 Germantown Avenue, Chestnut Hill, Pennsylvania, 1955. *Chestnut Hill Historical Society.*

As the story goes, when the Perkinses relocated to Philadelphia in 1950, the couple took with them the furnishings from their Brookline house, which Perkins had designed in 1938 to demonstrate his ideas about Modernism, just as other Harvard instructors did.[117] So many of their new associates and friends in the Philadelphia area expressed interest in their modern furnishings that Hencken Perkins hatched the idea to open up a business. Even though the locals reportedly laughed at, or were befuddled by, the modern objects she displayed—furniture, glassware and metalware, ceramics, textiles, and lamps—Hencken Perkins viewed herself as a disciple of Modernism, determined to prove that modern interiors could be beautiful.[118]

Despite her enthusiasm, she was careful to keep her husband outside of the business, likely because the discipline of house interiors was still gendered female.[119] Consequently, the only contribution Perkins is known to have made was the showroom design itself (fig. 5.13). He adapted a little stone building, formerly a pastry shop, by adding a wing to the back and by designing an open, white, metal staircase inside to unite three levels of showroom space, including a balcony four feet above the main showroom floor, which allowed for eye-level viewing.[120] The gray, wood-plank walls, together with the black vinyl floor, provided a neutral background for the "relatively unfamiliar" merchandise.[121] On the front of the "old pitched-roof house" was a window with nine large, square panes—reminiscent of the larger window on the storefront of Artek New York, designed by Morris Ketchum and Francis X. Gina.[122] The patently modern treatment of the vernacular building in which Gray Associates was located announced the arrival of contemporary furnishings in a traditional city, where she challenged local expectations concerning architecture and design, just as her husband did in his teaching.

Model Making for Architects

As retailers, women demonstrated their awareness of the new opportunities that specialization in the design fields could offer, and they became more successful in presenting contemporary design to the public. In her study of model-making, Teresa Fankhänel observes, "If the early 1920s were all about [architectural] rendering, the following decades were largely about model-making and photography."[123] Whereas other women did contribute to modern architecture through rendering or photography, such architects as Helen Baxter Perrin were also able to shape a vision of Modernism through model making (C.1). A native of Brooklyn, New York, Baxter Perrin earned her degree in architecture in 1924 from MIT and then worked in New York for a year on designs for Sutton Place apartments before moving to Massachusetts. She began her "little model business" in 1926, at first with another MIT-trained architect, Elizabeth Frances Cope Aub (1898–1977). She was "very proud" of the first model, a house at the Kittansett Club in Marion, Massachusetts, designed by (James Lovell) Little and (Benjamin F. W.) Russell, which was exhibited at the architecture school at MIT.[124] Another project she prized was the exhibition of eleven quarter-inch-scale models showing the development of house forms—from Neolithic to modern times—based on research by Albert Bemis and John Burchard II for *The Evolving House: A History of the Home* (1936), an MIT publication.[125]

Even as she was developing her model-making business, Baxter Perrin continued to practice architecture, albeit at a modest level. It is likely that the support of Eleanor Raymond, who lived a block away from her in Boston, was instrumental to her practices. As graduates of Wellesley College, in 1909 and 1923, respectively, Raymond and Baxter Perrin together designed a building for the Tau Zeta Epsilon arts and music society at their alma mater, which they completed in 1929.[126] They were required to replace an earlier Colonial Revival building with a clubhouse inspired by vernacular architecture of the Mediterranean region with whitewashed walls, massive chimneys, and a slate roof.

In 1934, her architect husband Hugh Perrin, whom she probably met at MIT and then married in 1925, joined Baxter Perrin in her business, which saved them financially during the Depression. Theirs is a common story, according to Fankhänel, who writes that "the profession of the architectural model maker emerged out of the disastrous collapse of the architectural trades during the years of the Depression."[127] The firm of Perrin and Perrin, however, subsequently flourished as "one of the foremost architectural model-makers in the country" of buildings, dioramas, and stage sets for study, promotion, and display.[128] Models were an increasingly popular means of representing complex architectural and spatial concepts; by producing them, the Perrins remained engaged in architecture despite the economic crisis.

During World War II, after they completed a model for the Army Air Force of an information filter center in an armory in Chelsea, Massachusetts, Perrin was swept away to New York to take charge of $150 million worth of filter centers across the nation. Their model-making business, Baxter Perrin later lamented, "quietly died—at its peak."[129] Unfortunately, she never returned to the business that she was responsible for creating, even though extant records reveal how proud she was of it.

Architecture from a Different Vantage Point

Even if women architects were open to alternative work, finding a suitable path could be as challenging as it was for those who remained in the profession. Despite financial, cultural, and social connections, Margaret "Margo" Fisher (1898–1990) struggled to find fulfillment and to identify a way to express her commitment to Modernism. Though the fifth of seven (living) children, Fisher was as the first daughter in the high-achieving Chicago family led by her father, a prominent lawyer and secretary of the interior from 1911. Fisher obtained a degree in economics from the University of Wisconsin in 1921, and then studied art in various media: at the School of the Art Institute of Chicago; at the Gloucester art colony; and at the Art Students League of New York. Her decision to study architecture at the Cambridge School between 1926 and 1928 must have appeased her family for two reasons: first, rather than bouncing between artist colonies and studios, she could participate in a stable educational environment and in an established discipline related to the arts; second, since the first four sons graduated from Harvard College between 1913 and 1919, and the youngest son, Howard Taylor Fisher, was an architecture student there at the time, the Cambridge School's connection to Harvard satisfied the family tradition. In addition, since her mother had grown up in Boston and preferred it to Chicago, she was able to move into the apartment that Margaret Fisher rented for them on Memorial Drive in Cambridge along with her youngest sister Ruth (Rhetts; 1910–90), who was enrolled at the Winsor School in Boston (where several Cambridge School women had also been students).[130]

Following her time at the Cambridge School, Margaret Fisher traveled the world before settling into a job in 1930, at the prestigious firm of Holabird and Root in Chicago. While she did work on tracings for one of the firm's most notable Art Deco buildings, the Racine County Courthouse (1931) in Wisconsin, she found herself unemployed during the Depression, despite her efforts to find an apprenticeship.[131] Consequently, she assisted her brother Howard, by then an established architect and vice president of General Houses (1931–47), in constructing a prefabricated steel house installed on the family's property in Hubbard Woods for her sister-in-law, the ballerina and choreographer Ruth Marian Page (1899–1991).[132] Photographs of the Page house were exhibited at MoMA in the exhibition *Work of Young Architects in the Middle West* (1933); according to a press release, Europeans already considered General Houses "the 'General Motors' of the industry" (fig. 5.14).[133] Despite being prodded by Henry Frost to keep looking for "the right job" so that her brother would not run off with all the architecture honors, Fisher was conflicted about what field to work in, but painting won out.[134]

Fisher never became a widely exhibited or collected artist, but, even so, she did apply what she had learned about architecture at the Cambridge School to her painting, which she first exhibited in 1936, under

5.14. Prefabricated house (now demolished) of Ruth Marian Page (1899–1991), Hubbard Woods, Illinois, designed by Howard Taylor Fisher (1903–79) for General Houses, c. 1930. *Historic Architecture and Landscape Image Collection, Ryerson and Burnham Art and Architecture Archives, Art Institute of Chicago, digital file #55629.*

the auspices of the Chicago Public School Art Society (founded 1894), in a small show of women artists.[135] She subsequently sought placement in the New York galleries, and although she did not secure long-term representation, by early 1938 her doggedness paid off.[136] When Alfred Stieglitz reviewed her paintings, he did not take any for his gallery, An American Place, but he did provide an introduction to Duncan Clinch Phillips, who established the Phillips Memorial Gallery (later the Phillips Collection) in Washington, DC.[137] In 1939, the nascent gallery agreed to a solo exhibition, *Watercolors by Margaret Fisher*, consisting of sixteen works, among them landscapes, still lifes, and figures; three of them—"Red Barns," "Farm Group," and "Barn and Blue Silo"—were conspicuously architectural.[138] The *Washington Post* commented that her architecture training was a source for the "neat and compact form of her work," as did the *Chicago Tribune* art editor, Eleanor Jewett, who said about a solo exhibition at the Quest Art Galleries: "Miss Fisher, we learned, trained for a time as an architect and this, we guess, is the reason for her amazingly fine drawing. With her ability as a draftsman goes an excellent sense of composition and a sensitive flair for color. She seems also to have a quick and vigorous imagination and to be able to create uncommon things out of a common beginning" (fig. 5.15).[139]

Fisher thought she had finally found her purpose, given her jotting on an invitation to her exhibition at the Quest Gallery that she sent to Frost: "This is just to let you know what one of your 'old girls' is up to. I wonder what you would think of this? Not a T □ or a Δ in the lot. As for a shade and a shadow I am not at all sure you would approve. I have done my best to try and forget all that you taught me on that score. I feel like a debutante all framed up and hanging on the wall."[140] Fisher may have felt as if she had abandoned architecture, but her connection to architecture did not escape the critics, even after 1941, when her paintings became increasingly abstract.[141]

Women Architects as Volunteers

For generations, volunteerism has been a primary means for women, especially those of higher education or income levels, to establish themselves in society or to be active in fields that interested them while avoiding the barriers to women in the professions.[142] Departing from past conventions in which women offered their services but not expertise, professional women's volunteerism provided a means by which they could use their skills and experiences and at the same time build on their social and professional networks.

Ann Halle Little, the daughter of the founding family of the legendary Halle Brothers department store (1891–1982), applied her professional experience by volunteering at the Ten-Thirty Gallery in Cleveland, an exhibition space dedicated to paintings, sculptures, and crafts by regional artists. After attending Smith College, Halle proceeded to the Cambridge School, where she obtained a master's degree in architecture in 1940. Before she graduated, she worked in the office of G. Holmes Perkins, where she impressed Robert Little with her plans for a modern flat-roofed boxy house with ribbon windows and plate glass that she was designing for her sister (see fig. 1.16). Already a staunch modernist, he called it "direct, rational, consistent, and resolved."[143] When the two young architects moved to her hometown after their marriage in late 1940, they were determined to disseminate Modernism to their conservative community. Since she worked only sporadically in the office headed by her husband, Halle Little became involved with the Ten-Thirty Gallery when it reorganized as a cooperative in 1945. Along with others, Halle Little and her husband pitched in with "brawn, brain and purse" to design a new space, which opened to

5.15. Margaret Fisher, untitled painting, c. 1940. *Margaret Fisher Archive.*

hundreds of guests in September 1946 (fig. 5.16).[144] They designed the gallery "from an artistic as well as a practical point of view" so that several exhibits could be shown at once by means of inexpensive movable wall panels and plug-in lights.[145] In addition to joining in on the community painting, scrubbing, and mounting, they also made possible the display of work by Ten-Thirty Gallery artists in the storefront windows at Halle's. The gallery gained a national reputation as a collective center for art exhibitions and experimental classes as well as lectures and discussions. It was a place where community members could share in the inspiration of the creative arts with such artists as Roy Lichtenstein, who began showing his work there in 1948. It was there that Lichtenstein met his first wife, Isabel Wilson Sarisky (1921–80), the assistant director of the gallery.[146]

Like Halle Little, the professionally trained architect Mary Coss Barnes (formerly Cooke) was married to a prominent modern architect in whose firm, Edward Larrabee Barnes, she was employed. After moving in 1952 to northern Westchester County, Coss Barnes became involved in a volunteer venture called the Katonah Gallery, conceived by a committee of women to make the visual arts readily available to the community.[147] Its ten-to-twelve annual loan exhibitions were comprised of contemporary works selected by an advisory committee, of which Coss Barnes was a member. Her professional connections helped to procure loans, and she applied her curatorial experience (at MoMA between 1937 and 1948) to the exhibitions focused, for example, on Charles Demuth, Winslow Homer, Jacques Lipchitz, and Joseph Stella. The ambitious exhibition schedule required hours of labor from Coss Barnes, whose sure eye for proportion, scale, and spatial order made her hangings stand out, from 1955 to at least 1972, as her son John Barnes recalls. He remembers how she intuitively knew how to arrange the mobiles and lighting in the *Alexander Calder* (1961) exhibition so that the shadows would play off the walls; for *Josef Albers* (1962), she hung the paintings lower than was typical, forcing the viewer to stand further back.[148]

While the exhibitions were initially hung in a small, unpretentious upstairs room in the local library, in 1969 Coss Barnes and her husband oversaw an expansion at the library, three times the size of the original.[149] Subsequently, in 1990 her husband designed a completely new building for what became the Katonah Museum of Art, a non-collecting institution centered on presenting three major

5.16. Volunteers at the Ten-Thirty Gallery (1943–1950), 1030 Euclid Avenue, Cleveland, Ohio, c. 1946. Robert Little is holding the broom; Ann Halle Little is likely sitting on the table in the rear; Algesa D'Agostino O'Sickey is front right and on the left may be Isabel Wilson Sarisky (Lichtenstein). *Algesa D'Agostino O'Sickey Papers, Special Collections and Archives, Kent State University.*

exhibitions annually to approximately sixteen thousand visitors. Though George Gordon King, the founding director of the museum between 1988 and 1998, fondly remembers her many contributions—in particular, the unforgettable "Mary Barnes blue" exhibition wall color—it was not she whom the museum saluted during its fiftieth anniversary celebration (2004) but her husband.[150] Thus, what was initially *her* project became *theirs* and then, surprisingly, only *his*. Like other women architects who were married to prominent male architects, her own artistic identity was subsumed under that of her husband, although it was initially through her talent that the small, unknown, suburban venue was able to mount exhibitions of recognized modern artists.

While the two worked collaboratively as volunteers, Coss Barnes did not pursue a formal arrangement in her husband's firm. Nevertheless, she and other women like her made use of the problem-solving skills as well as the visual awareness developed in their professional education in the art exhibition realm where they made crucial contributions to the dissemination of Modernism.

Women in Architecture at MoMA: The Early Years

As with suburban or regional art galleries, small museums were dependent on volunteer labor. Though MoMA became one of the most influential institutions to promote European Modernism in the United States, it too needed volunteer, or low-paid workers, oftentimes women. While the male leaders of the institution—Alfred Barr, Henry-Russell Hitchcock, Philip Johnson, Anson Conger Goodyear, René d'Harnoncourt, and James Johnson Sweeney, among them—have been the subjects of individual biographies or have figured prominently in institutional histories, the cohort of women who made the institution run, especially during the war years when the men were absent, have been the subjects of only scattered recognition.[151] Some began as volunteers; others had to subsidize their scant pay with outside jobs. As female employees, they struggled with the masculinist biases of Modernism and barriers to professional work that typically relegated them to the decorative arts or design. As a timeline in figure 1.19 shows, women achieved their most influential positions during World War II, but after the men returned, women lost their influence or their position, or both.

Conceived, backed, and patronized by women and fostered by a circle of largely homosexual men dedicated to legitimizing avant-garde design and ideologies, at its inception, MoMA was on the fringe of the art world and thus provided a setting where women could be employed and to some extent accepted. By way of contrast, at such long-established institutions as the Metropolitan Museum of Art, which was organized, managed, and funded by a coterie of professional men, women historically had only marginal jobs.[152] According to Kathleen D. McCarthy in *Women's Culture: American Philanthropy and Art, 1830–1930*, the moment women, including the fieriest of feminists, passed through the portals of that museum, they became docile and deferential.[153]

The women in the architecture and industrial departments at MoMA (from 1935 to 1940, the two departments were combined) were different in that the senior staff quickly came to recognize that the best of them were endowed with abilities at organization, communication, and socialization, not to mention connoisseurship—qualities that were developed in architecture school. They were also hardworking, adventuresome, and less expensive than their male peers. While Carson, Pillsbury, Coss Cooke, and Raedermacher Wasson-Tucker possessed professional degrees in architecture, other women had not much more than an interest in art history, albeit typically from one of the elite women's liberal arts colleges or from a European institution. Since the small museum was young, the women were given a variety of responsibilities, some of them quite rewarding. Though nearly always acknowledged in the press releases and catalogs, the women tended to be described only by their tasks—arranger, organizer, installer, designer, selector, editor, or (occasionally) director—rather than by a job title that, at least initially, rarely surpassed the word *assistant*. If their work eventually merited a title change, it did not happen instantaneously but, instead, gradually—from assistant to assistant in charge, to acting curator, and finally to curator, as an example. The women generally were not hired as curators, apart from during the war years, and they typically did not rise to that professional level. Despite being open to women, MoMA favored men in hiring and promotion.

The story about MoMA has tended to overlook the role of women, other than those who served as trustees. In 2010, however, the museum made a corrective gesture by mounting the exhibition *Women Artists and the Museum of Modern Art*, and, even more, by producing a 528-page catalog. In her contribution to "The Missing Future: MoMA and Modern Women," feminist art historian Griselda Pollock argues that the museum "created a vision of modern art that effectively excluded the new, and importantly, modern participation of women."[154] Although women did not make much of the art that was hung in the museum, they did produce the exhibitions—and the publications too. Juliet Kinchen recognized as much in her essay in which she acknowledges, somewhat fleetingly, Susanne Raedermacher Wasson-Tucker, Alice Morgan Carson, and Elizabeth Bauer Mock as well as Greta Daniel (1909–62) in architecture/industrial arts. Kinchen maintains that their brief but intensely productive tenures are often overlooked but nonetheless significant because they brought the needs and perspectives of women to the fore and influenced the next generation of curators.[155]

Interestingly, neither the essay nor the "partial history" in *Women Artists* (both in the back matter and online) mentions Ernestine Marie Fantl (Carter; 1906–83). Her thirteen-year tenure that led to her curatorship in what is now the Department of Architecture and Industrial Design, was initiated by an apprenticeship of sorts under two pioneers: Alfred Barr, the knowledgeable and visionary museum director, and Philip Johnson, whose eye for emerging artists and passion for new ideas informed his chairmanship of the architecture department.[156]

Fantl proved her intellectual ability and understanding of modern art before she entered the museum. A native of Savannah, Georgia, Fantl had been among the handful of women at Wellesley College in 1926 who participated in Barr's eye-opening Tradition and Revolt in Modern Painting seminar. They developed a deep mutual respect: she considered Barr, her gentle, witty, and scholarly instructor, to be a loyal friend; he thought of her as "possibly the most mature [of students] in the understanding of modern art."[157] After she graduated in 1927, through Barr, Fantl was hired by the Austrian-born art dealer Jsrael B(er) Neumann, after which she moved on to a more interesting job in the New York office of William Lescaze (then designing the Philadelphia Saving Fund Society building).[158] There, she would have met the young maverick Alfred Clauss, a nucleus of the notorious *Rejected Architects* (1931) exhibition of models and drawings, which Fantl helped mount. Along with others, she donned a sandwich board to picket the Architectural League of New York for refusing to show modern architecture at its exhibition at the Grand Central Palace.[159] Having demonstrated her affinity for Modernism, as well as a willingness to flout aesthetic tradition, Fantl was asked, again by Barr, to assist Johnson (on his personal payroll) with MoMA's first architecture exhibition, *Modern Architecture: International Exhibition* (1932). It was probably during the lead-up to the exhibition that she came to know Johnson as "intransigent, intolerant, [and] brilliantly intelligent."[160] When the exhibition was completed, Barr asked her to organize a summer show of paintings and sculptures from the collections of trustees; not only was it the "most awesome pinch-hitting" experience she had ever had, but her success led to a full-time, paid position assisting Johnson in his newly created chairmanship of the architecture department. Of the four exhibitions on which she worked alongside Johnson, *Machine Art* (1934) was the most memorable for her because of the presentation of utilitarian objects displayed as art, confronting the public with "the shock value of the unfamiliar."[161]

In addition to the ten or so exhibitions she produced as curator between 1935 and 1937, Fantl made her first trip to Europe and to Great Britain at the suggestion of Abby Aldrich Rockefeller (1874–1948), the influential founder and vice president of the museum, to study modern architecture using surefire introductions provided by Hitchcock. Shortly thereafter, she succeeded in convincing her superiors to send her back to Europe as an American representative at the *Congrès internationaux d'architecture moderne* (CIAM; 1928–59), an international union of architects focused on modern design concepts and ideologies.[162] Hélène de Mandrot (1867–1948), an artist and Le Corbusier's patron, would not allow Fantl to stay at her château, La Sarraz, outside Geneva, Switzerland, where the conference was held. Nonetheless, Fantl dined with Gropius, whom she described as the "handsome, serious and unassumingly friendly" architect who soon would relocate from London to Cambridge, Massachusetts.[163]

When Fantl returned to Britain after the conference to research MoMA's upcoming exhibition *Modern Architecture in England* (1937), she was part of the conversation about how still photographs could not adequately capture the "usual ludicrously, pompous, self-important manner" of the penguins in the brilliant pool design by the Tecton Group at the London Zoo.[164] Consequently, László Moholy-Nagy made a film, *The New Architecture for the London Zoo*, which was the first of its kind to be shown at a museum exhibition. Fantl also collaborated on the exhibition itself with Catherine Bauer, her "particular favourite," who contributed the essay "Elements of English Housing Practice" to the catalog.[165]

Bauer and Fantl had known each other since 1932, when both worked on the International Style exhibition at MoMA; in 1936, they also collaborated, as essayist and curator, respectively, on the exhibition *Architecture in Government Housing*, showcasing modern examples. Though never a museum employee, Bauer was a long-standing contributor on issues of housing, and she was an active member of the architecture committee (until Johnson dissolved it in 1946) on which Fantl relied during her curatorship. In 1937, Fantl gave up the museum job to marry an Englishman and move to London, where she evolved into a fashion journalist. Nonetheless, she helped to establish a precedent for women at MoMA and in her position played a significant role in introducing contemporary architecture to the American public.

Not long after Fantl began working at MoMA, another Wellesley graduate, Elodie Courter, joined the museum, initially as a volunteer to label the two thousand slides that Johnson and "Eddie" Warburg (soon to become a trustee) had taken in Europe. She quickly found her way to the position of secretary, overseeing traveling exhibitions, a new and as yet unproven enterprise, for the museum.[166] Though Barr was no longer teaching modern art at Wellesley, Courter also held him in esteem as "the most prescient scholar of twentieth-century arts," and her admiration no doubt contributed to her fourteen-year tenure at MoMA.[167] Early on, Courter had academic intentions, attending the Sorbonne on a Carnegie fellowship in the summer of 1935 and subsequently the graduate fine arts program at New York University while also working at MoMA, but it was too much for her, given the demands of museum work. In 1937 she was named director of circulating exhibitions—a department positioned to fulfill the museum's crucial educational mandate as well as to promote Modernism. Over the next three years alone, she organized more than 110 exhibitions—some developed only for circulation, others stemming from those presented at the museum—each with an average of twelve showings over a two-year period.[168] Understandably, then, she has been recognized for introducing modern art to more people than anyone else at the museum.[169] In 1944 she married the artist and cartoonist Robert Osborn and after her two children were born, in 1946 and 1949, Courter devoted herself to the local cultural scene in Simsbury, Connecticut, where she brought about the appointment of Eliot Noyes as the architect of an elementary school and started the Simsbury Film Society in 1951.[170]

It was not until the male employees left during World War II that MoMA granted women curatorial positions in the architecture and industrial design departments, albeit mostly in "acting" capacities. Janet MacNair Henrich (O'Connell; 1913–88) was the first acting curator in the Department of Architecture, followed by Alice Carson and then Elizabeth Bauer Mock. In 1942, Carson described her situation to a colleague as she tried to hold down the desks of the architecture and industrial design departments as well as that of the chief administrator: "At times," she confessed, "I feel it is all useless, but again there seem to be important things to be done."[171] Indeed, the museum was immersed in preparing wartime exhibitions, exemplified by the twenty-eight that were circulating. Carson's argument in the *Useful Objects in Wartime* (1942) exhibition—that shortages in metals were inspiring more functional, better-looking, and less expensive items of glass, paper, and plastics—received national media attention.[172]

During the tenure of Raedermacher Wasson-Tucker as acting curator in industrial design, she too presented an exhibition of *Useful Objects* (1945), in which she highlighted objects on asymmetrically hung wooden shelves. The practical display of the limited number of new items in the stores dismissed "adjectives like glamorous and exotic [that] have no business about the place," according to the *New York Times*.[173] Her aptitude for simple, bold presentations would become a mainstay of her career.

Following the war, Greta Daniel and Mildred "Connie" Constantine (1913–2008) enjoyed substantial responsibility in the Department of Architecture and Design for some nineteen and twenty-six years, respectively, though neither earned a title above associate curator.[174] Daniel was a tenacious, energetic, German-born exile who did not complete university but had four years of administrative experience at the Museum Folkwang in Essen (founded 1906), whose focus on new and innovative art made the museum a target for Nazi destruction. Curiously, it is not known how Daniel found her way to MoMA, where she is best remembered for her constant sourcing of industrially designed objects for the permanent collection.[175] The culmination of her effort came in 1958, when she cocreated with Arthur Justin Drexler, director of the Department of Architecture and Design between 1956 and 1987, *Twentieth-Century Design from the Museum Collection*, an exhibition (with a corresponding catalog) that was touted as the first in MoMA's history to be devoted entirely to its own holdings.[176] Daniel was recognized in the industry for being especially conversant with contemporary designers and craftspeople whom she knew as a buyer, critic, panelist, and juror. Everyone relied on her encyclopedic knowledge, and when she died in 1962, her absence left a void, if not pandemonium, in the museum to which she had been passionately devoted.[177]

Whereas Daniel was a specialist in utilitarian objects, Constantine's focus was graphic design, and of the more than thirty exhibitions in which she was involved, at least nine focused on posters. She never felt "closeted" by her specialization, however, and, in fact, participated in a variety of museum projects, including architecture exhibitions under Johnson. Mesmerized by his sharp, critical point of view and ability to teach at the same time, she became one of his "great admirers" while working on *Skidmore, Owings & Merrill: Architects U.S.A.* (1950), the museum's first monographic architecture exhibition to concentrate on a firm as opposed to an individual.[178] Even though Johnson was bent on forwarding his thesis concerning the pervasive influence of first-generation European modernists on the firm, he left Constantine on her own to research and structure the exhibition and also to oversee its short catalog.[179] Of the ten building designs displayed in the exhibition, Lever House on Park Avenue and 53rd Street was the most noteworthy. Still under construction, and certainly not yet iconic, the curtain-walled building was being supervised by the firm's rising star, Gordon Bunshaft, and was touted as a civic monument in the making—akin to Rockefeller Center. Even Natalie Griffin de Blois, who worked on the project, remembered how impressed she was when she saw, for the first time, the "spectacular" model in the exhibition.[180] Though not from an architecture background, Constantine had earned Johnson's respect, since he asked her to update and edit the second edition (1960) of another one of his pet projects: his publication *Mies van der Rohe* (1947).[181]

Constantine admired Arthur Drexler even more than Johnson. At the beginning of Drexler's curatorship in 1951, they immediately set to work on the small but trying exhibition *Le Corbusier: Architecture, Painting, Design*. During the making of this "first, modest, concise and beautiful" show, she became aware of Drexler's diverse talents and genius, as she recalled in a memoriam.[182] In her opinion, the department was at its most creative under his leadership—and so was she—because Drexler managed to unite his staff members as if they were one big family, squabbles and all.[183] The many years Constantine spent with Drexler "working, talking, agreeing, arguing, each winning some and losing some" led to her making a lasting and satisfying contribution to Modernism.[184]

Whereas Constantine relied on Johnson and Drexler at MoMA, Elizabeth Bauer Mock (Kassler, after she married the architect Kennith Kassler in 1951) relied on her older sister, Catherine Bauer Wurster, who had been engaged at the museum by 1932 as an authority on housing, through Lewis Mumford's intercession. In 1937, Bauer Mock began as a part-time assistant at MoMA, where she discovered a "system of amateurish enthusiasm and divided responsibility."[185] Among her earliest exhibitions during her nine-year tenure was *Stockholm Builds* (1940), in which she relied on her sister's knowledge, explaining that she had never written so extensively about anything of which she knew so painfully little.[186] Nonetheless, Bauer Mock managed to earn the respect of Barr, who by 1941 both "admired" and was "really devoted to her."[187] In the same year, she was made a full-time assistant to John McAndrew, then the curator of architecture, and in 1943, she took on his role for three years as "acting curator."[188]

Letters between the Bauer sisters—neither with an architecture degree but both devoted to the built environment—show Bauer Wurster's influence on the formation of the advisory committee and the building selections for "Built in U.S.A., 1932–1944," the architecture section that Bauer Mock organized for the *Art in Progress* exhibition.[189] Upon reading the accompanying book (eventually published in three editions, totaling 16,700 copies, making it a best-selling architecture publication by the museum), Bauer Wurster "drop[ped] everything" to inform her sister: "I haven't read a piece of architectural criticism of yours that can touch it ... Your piece isn't written solely for a tiny group of smut-knowing intellectuals. ... It simplifies and clarifies the involved history of recent modern architecture more successfully than I would have thought could have been done."[190] Bauer Mock's strength was neither as a designer nor as a connoisseur but rather as a writer capable of explaining modern design to the nonspecialist.[191]

It was also her staying power. Though Bauer Mock moved to Knoxville in 1946, where her husband, Rudolf Mock, was employed by the TVA, few women exceeded her in sustaining a long-term relationship with the museum. MoMA published her books *The Architecture of Bridges* in 1949 (and organized a corresponding traveling exhibition) and *Modern Gardens and the Landscape* in 1964. Then in 1967, thirty-five years after arriving at the museum, she contributed an essay to the museum's exhibition catalog *The New City: Architecture and Urban Renewal.* Ultimately, Elizabeth Bauer (now Kassler) produced more than fifteen exhibitions for MoMA in roles ranging from assistant and designer to director and curator, and she authored eight publications. Nonetheless, the first line of her curriculum vitae (c. 1990) states "1911 b. Elizabeth L. Bauer in Elizabeth, NJ; sister of Catherine Bauer (Wurster) (1905–64)," implying that she never came out from under the shadow of her more famous older sibling.[192] Bauer Mock typifies women who worked at MoMA in the early years of its existence in that she had important responsibilities but was eclipsed by colleagues, many of

5.17. Elizabeth-Ann Campbell, cardboard model of the house (now demolished) she designed for her father, Thomas D. (Donald) Campbell Jr. (1881–1966), Albuquerque, New Mexico, c. 1946. *Private collection.*

them men, although in her case, her own sister's reputation also overshadowed her.

Working in MoMA's male-dominated culture, women like Bauer Mock (Kassler) nonetheless achieved a modicum of professional success and benefited from personal connections with peers who inspired their engagement with artistic innovation and shared their interest in contemporary culture. What they could not obtain, however, was a job title that reflected their ability or seniority, nor did they achieve the fame of its male principals: the coveted roles of tastemaker or tastebreaker (someone who reveals a chain of groundbreaking works by visionary artists) were exclusively reserved for men.[193]

Women Architects Beyond Design Disciplines

Though numerous women architects turned to allied fields, others applied their professional skills to unrelated entrepreneurial undertakings, which tend to be unknown. Elizabeth-Ann Campbell Knapp's training in architecture provided skills that led to wide success in other fields. Born in Pasadena, California, Campbell graduated from Vassar College in 1936 before receiving her architecture degree from the Cambridge School in 1941.[194] She then spent two years in Washington, DC employed by the camouflage department of the Navy before working as a draftsperson in Santa Fe, in about 1942, for John Gaw Meem (by then married to Cambridge School alumna Faith Bemis). In 1946, Campbell designed a modern house for her parents in Albuquerque, New Mexico, not far from the Rio Grande, for which a model and plans (but not the

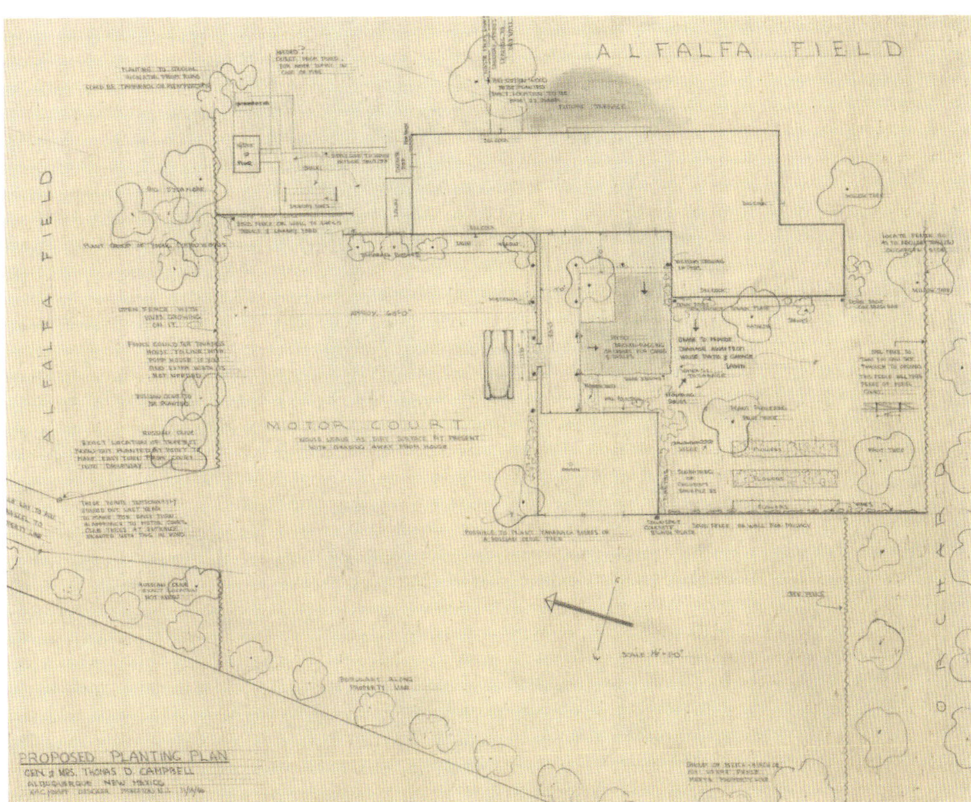

5.18. Elizabeth-Ann Campbell Knapp, proposed landscape plan for her father's Albuquerque house, November 14, 1946. *Private collection.*

house) survive (figs. 5.17, 5.18). Her landscape plan shows the surroundings planted with alfalfa, an unusual ground cover to specify in such an arid climate. However, her father, Thomas D. Campbell Jr., was a pioneer in industrial farming methods, some of which he innovated and patented himself. In a 1952 interview, he boasted, "On my farm in Montana, no handwork whatever is involved."[195]

After settling in Princeton, New Jersey, with her husband John Merrill Knapp, a musicologist on the Princeton University faculty until 1982, she practiced architecture less frequently. Still, Campbell Knapp did work in the 1950s for architect Martin Luther Beck, and in addition to a few houses for friends, she designed her own family home in Princeton in 1951, the drawings for which are stamped by the Albuquerque architect Louis Gilbert Hesselden, suggesting that she relied professionally on her New Mexico network (figs 5.19, 5.20). The entryways of her house, however, return to those Gropius designed in the late 1930s: for Josephine M. Haggerty in Cohasset, Massachusetts, as well as his own, both of which Campbell visited and photographed as a student (see fig. 1.7).[196] Campbell Knapp's life took a decisive turn in 1966 with the death of her father, who by then was recognized as the "World's Wheat King" and "the Henry Ford of Agriculture."[197] Until 1982, she headed his large, complex holdings, including businesses and lands totaling 500,000 acres in New Mexico and Montana. Despite the immense responsibilities Campbell Knapp took on, she continued to spend the academic year in Princeton, and then in the late spring she took the train to Harden, Montana, where she assumed on-site supervision. In addition, she presided over the Campbell Family Foundation.[198] Campbell Knapp's work as a businessperson might first appear to have little to do with her study of architecture. However, the skills of organization, conceptualization, problem-solving, and self-discipline she developed at the Cambridge School served her as she addressed the challenges of running farms and ranches. Campbell Knapp's decisions regarding the legacy of her father's estate were different in that she had to evaluate the distributions and long-term implications for the communities where the employees were located. Both her professional training and the networks she maintained—including her lifelong friendship with architect Ann Halle Little, also an heiress whom she met at the Cambridge School—contributed to her propensity for historic preservation and land conservation (see fig. 1.3). In 1973, she oversaw the conveyance of some 230,000 acres of land to the federal government, a swath that spanned an area

5.19. Elizabeth-Ann Campbell Knapp (designer) and Louis Gilbert Hesselden (architect; 1895–1978), elevation for the house she designed for her family, 108 Rosedale Lane, Princeton, New Jersey, June 30, 1951. *Louis G. Hesselden architectural drawings and plans collection, Center for Southwest Research and Special Collections, University of New Mexico Libraries.*

5.20. Entrance of the John and Elizabeth-Ann Campbell Knapp house in Princeton. *Private collection.*

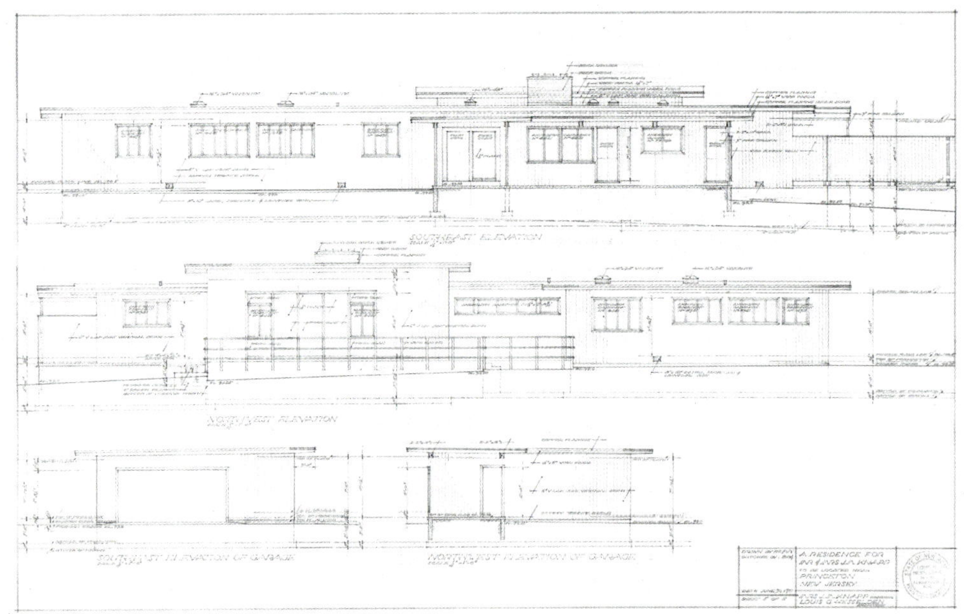

from the Los Piños mountains to the Sierra Ladrones near Socorro, New Mexico. Her formation of the Sevilleta National Wildlife Refuge, as it is known, was to her "like collecting a great painting."[199]

Campbell Knapp undertook other historic preservation projects: in 1971, she financed the preservation of her father's homestead in North Forks, North Dakota, a late nineteenth-century wood-framed Gothic Revival house fused with an earlier log cabin from about 1879.[200] According to her daughter Phoebe Knapp, another one of Campbell Knapp's dreams was to preserve Camp Four, one of the two permanent camps for workers built around 1920 on an open plain above the Big Horn River. As a historical site, the camp still contains about a dozen white wood-framed structures—bunkhouses as well as a commissary workshop, a cowboy house, an outhouse, and an oil house, along with a root cellar and a water tank—to project the "wholesome" and sanitary lifestyle of the laborers that Campbell insisted be maintained.[201] In addition to the camp, the Big Horn County Historical Museum in Billings, Montana, maintains four other structures from Camp Four.[202] They were part of the vernacular built environment that, as such, corresponded to the functional, unpretentious architecture that inspired many Cambridge School students. Campbell Knapp's commitment to historic preservation also continued in her personal collection: she kept an archive of her drawings, photographs, and architecture books from her student days in Cambridge and even the Ford V8 convertible (with rumble seat) that she drove at school.

Women in Historic Preservation

The contributions of Campbell Knapp were just a few of the many made by women architects to historic preservation, starting in at least 1853, when Anne Panela Cunningham (1816–75) established the Mount Vernon Ladies' Association in Virginia to preserve the home of the first president. Women with access to a formal education in architecture have brought their professional skills, for instance in drawing and photography, to the task. Dorinda Hinckley (Jarest; 1919–2002), after studying architecture in the School of Agriculture and the Mechanical Arts at the University of New Hampshire in Durham, worked for the Historic American Buildings Survey (HABS). She produced measured drawings of at least half a dozen historic houses between 1935 and 1939 in New Hampshire, a rarity in a period when women at HABS were typically secretaries or stenographers (fig. 5.21).[203]

5.21. Dorinda Hinckley, north and south elevations (after 1933) of the Weeks family house, built in the early eighteenth century in Greenland, New Hampshire. *HABS.*

Similarly, in 1950, Cambridge School alumna Felicia Doughty Kingsbury (1898–1982) was curator of properties for the Society for the Preservation of New England Antiquities (now Historic New England) in Boston and editor of its journal *Old-Time New England.*[204] Alice Morgan Carson also applied her architectural training to historic preservation in Cape Cod, Massachusetts, where she developed a reputation as an advocate for the built environment. At seventy-nine years old, Alice Morgan Carson was said to be effective in part due to her "discriminating eye for her environment [developed] during her training, as a student in architecture and landscape architecture ... and as an acting director of industrial design at the Museum of Modern Art."[205] In their studies, Carson as well as Campbell Knapp, Hinckley Jarest, and others learned how to examine and critique emerging ideas about modern architecture while they also gained an appreciation for buildings, particularly the utilitarian structures (and their landscapes) of the preindustrial period.

As these women demonstrated, the talents and habits forged in their progressive educations could be successfully extended to related fields as well as to work within their communities or in the larger society and economy. Whereas women maneuvered around professional barriers by innovating new ways to utilize their modern sensibilities in various forms of paid work, they could also apply their interest or expertise to volunteer efforts, as women had done since the suffrage movement at the turn of the century.

As curators, they intervened in institutions that were significant promoters of Modernism; as preservationists, they maintained valuable parts of the natural and historic built environments; as entrepreneurs, they discovered arenas in which they could independently promote modern design; as writers or educators, they perhaps had the most widespread influence. The list goes on. Doing so, they contributed to the fundamental transformation of American culture that was constituted by the modern movement.

CHAPTER VI

Houses and Housing

DURING THE WINTER HOLIDAYS IN 1936, ELISABETH COIT accepted an invitation from the pilot Wolfgang Langewiesche to fly in his Taylor Cub from New York to Key West, Florida.[1] The ambitious architect fitted the cockpit with an "air-going studio" consisting of pouches for watercolor brushes and pencils hung from structural members of the plane, as well as a water flask strapped onto her so that from a thousand feet above ground she could pioneer a "whole new technique of seeing," as she explained (fig. 6.1).[2] As the pilot recalled, when forced to make an emergency landing in a small, rural town on the return trip, he was figuring out how to get the plane up in the air while Coit "was talking to some women. … about different types of kitchen ranges, of all things."[3] Despite his bemused tone, Langewiesche sheds light on just how absorbed Coit was with housing conditions. In fact, the broad perspectives evident in her watercolor landscapes anticipate the expansive view she would develop about the larger social issues connected with the built environment, especially low-income housing.

The activist Jane Addams (1860–1935) had already played a vital role in the Progressive Era effort to improve urban conditions—particularly as they pertained to the housing and education of immigrant communities—through the settlement house movement. Subsequent generations of women focused on relieving housing shortages as well as improving the substandard accommodations frequently occupied by working-class dwellers in such crowded centers as Chicago and New York. Coit and her contemporaries deemed an adequate supply of safe, functional, and affordable housing to be essential, and they specifically sought to bring the foresight of their predecessors to their projects in urban, suburban, and even resort environments.

Coit's trajectory took her from designing traditional small houses to cultivating communities, to advocating for functional low-cost housing. It parallels the paths followed by other women who found a niche in the expanding field of housing advocacy and design. In 1914, when Anna Schenck and Marcia Mead announced the establishment of their architecture partnership in New York, they insisted, "We are interested … in [creating] whole neighborhoods—parks and community houses, streets, and homes, and stores."[4] They drew national attention in 1915 with their collaborative prize-winning design for a mile-long redevelopment in the Bronx between the George Washington Bridge and Macomb Dam Park as well as for the Ellen Wilson Memorial Homes (now demolished), a model tenement for 250 families in Washington, DC.[5]

Since housing was still without established experts, as noted by Lewis Mumford, the field was wide open to neophytes willing to challenge accepted practices and

6.1. Elisabeth Coit, watercolor made on an airplane, 1936. *Coit Papers.*

innovate new concepts, from theorists, teachers, and writers to advocates, bureaucrats, and architects.[6] In 1934, architect Eleanor Manning O'Connor reported that women architects were achieving distinction at every level of housing, not just for low-wage earners but for those in all economic strata.[7] Her opinion, offered to prospective women architects, stemmed from her participation in the Boston Housing Association and as chair of the housing committee for the Massachusetts Civic League. She was also one of the Seventeen Associated Architects engaged in planning the Old Harbor Village (1935–40; later the Mary Ellen McCormack Development), one of the nation's first low-cost public housing projects designed to meet the needs of its predominantly Irish American constituency. In contrast to the superblocks of later housing projects, the development consists of small-scale, two-story residences that are traditional in form, echoing Boston's residential architecture of the Federal period, organized around courtyards and doorways.[8]

Coit similarly used a variety of methods to promote her views on housing as a lecturer, educator, and occasional writer, for example in the *National Altrusan*, a journal that promoted new fields for women.[9] As the role of women in housing evolved, two tendencies became evident: first, that women relied on their female networks to advance as professionals and second, that they promoted the modern approach to improving housing in the United States. This is not to say that men were not involved as critics or designers. However, women had a unique position in the field given their traditional association with domesticity and the fact that they were more accepted in this area of architectural practice than in others. Some of them evolved a particular view of housing that started with the needs of the users rather than with preconceptions on the parts of architects and planners, as male professionals often did.

Early Housing Projects by Woman Architects

After Coit graduated from MIT in 1919, she was encouraged by Manning, an MIT alumna, to apply for a drafting position with Grosvenor Atterbury, since his New York firm was known to hire women architects (such as Anna Schenck). Accordingly, Coit "sailed right into a job without a day's searching"—an unusual scenario for a woman.[10] In Atterbury's office, Coit observed women taking on responsibilities, sometimes stereotypical, that contributed to her conviction that no other profession could compare with "the extent and variety of the satisfaction" that came with architecture.[11] Under the supervision of John Almy Tompkins II, the chief designer who was charged with translating preliminary sketches into drawings of alternative approaches, Coit was in the company of two other women who, as she recalled, ranked higher than the few capable draftspersons in the firm.[12] One of the women was probably Marcia Mead; the other, "a rather dour, somewhat unattractive middle-aged woman," Coit remembered, who followed the more typical pattern of being assigned to architectural errands and interior residential jobs.[13] Coit, on the other hand, benefited from a more diverse experience with Atterbury, who even allowed her to take a year-long leave beginning in 1923 so that she could travel and study in Western Europe, a requisite experience for ambitious American architects. Upon her return, he hired her back as a part-time designer, although with full-time pay, an arrangement that enabled her to study for her architecture license and drum up work for her own practice, established in 1931.[14]

Coit's avowed "zeal for housing" was not only kindled in Europe, but also during her decade of employment in the Atterbury office, where she was exposed to his pioneering prefabrication processes at Forest Hills Gardens (1909–22) in Queens, New York.[15] Conceived by the Russell Sage Foundation, the community was predicated on the early twentieth-century British garden city movement in which collective planning and top-down control were meant to bring about healthy, economical, and picturesque settings within reach of urban centers. Situated on 142 acres landscaped by Frederick Law Olmstead Jr., the buildings by Atterbury widely employed traditional vernacular models, and for some public buildings, *Jugendstil* elements.[16] When Coit joined the Atterbury firm, the Forest Hills commission was near completion, but she was required to give "special attention" to the "group housing and experiments by Mr. Atterbury in [the] prefabrication of building units."[17] Coit would have been familiar with the concrete precast hollow-panel system (produced in a makeshift, on-site factory) that he used for the semidetached houses in Group 48, dating to around 1917 (fig. 6.2).[18] While the development fell short of providing affordable housing to working-class families, it still exposed Coit to the complexities of building economical housing, including the challenges of prefabrication and of adapting British and European planning and architectural models to American settings.[19]

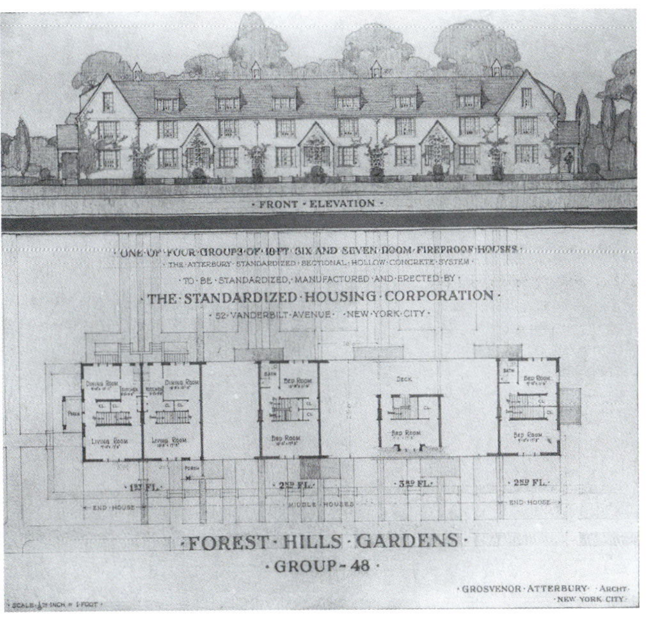

6.2. Grosvenor Atterbury (1869–1956), rendering of prefabricated concrete houses in Group 48, Forest Hills Gardens, Queens, New York, 1917, in *The Manufacture of Standardized Houses: A New Industry* (New York: Standardized Housing Corporation, 1918), 30. *Museum of the City of New York.*

Undoubtedly, Coit also would have known that Margaret Olivia Slocum Sage (1828–1918) had spearheaded the Forest Hills development using her husband's fortune from railroads. Among other women patrons of model communities was Mary Hopkins Emery (1844–1927). She applied the inheritance from her husband, an industrialist and real estate developer, to a new town called Mariemont (1920–26) about ten miles outside of Cincinnati, Ohio. This "woman's project," the *Women's Journal* insisted, exemplified the responsibility women "*must*" take in town planning. Instead of being pigeonholed as home designers, it argues, the ability of women to appreciate beauty and comfort, organize the home, and focus on family had amply prepared them for the profession.[20] The role of women in planning was paradoxical: on the one hand, they experienced barriers to participation as a result of their limited access to education and employment that could have led to major positions; on the other, they received encouragement to be involved in town and city planning because of what was perceived as their ability as wives and mothers to assess the shortcomings of urban and suburban plans.[21]

Despite the positive endorsement from the *Women's Journal*, only one of the twenty-six architecture firms invited to design residences in Mariemont was composed of women. It was landscape architect John Nolen, the author of the master plan (and at one time a trustee of the Cambridge School), who invited Manning and her partner Lois Howe to participate. In 1923, they presented their homogenous grouping of three "more or less conventional" variations of small speculative houses to demonstrate the standards to which future property buyers would be beholden.[22] A year later, they had completed seven single-family and two double houses there for professional people with moderate salaries in what Manning deemed to be one of the most artistic communities in the country (fig. 6.3).[23] Compactly organized around a small green on Denny Place, some of the structures were planned with combined living and dining spaces to create an open floor plan, a central feature of modern domestic design. The exteriors, however, conform to traditional Georgian-revival models in that their walls are of warm-colored native fieldstone or stucco, originally offset with green doors, some also with green shutters around the sash windows, and topped with brown-shingled hip or gable roofs. Coit would have been familiar with the Mariemont development because Atterbury produced ten half-timbered houses there while she was in his employ.[24]

User-Centered Public Housing

International developments were of immense importance to women active in housing, some of whom were captivated by the contemporary innovations in architecture and urban design they observed on their European tours. During her second trip to Europe in 1934, Coit was taken by the advancement in low-cost housing—both the city planning strategies and the structures themselves.[25] She explained in the *Radcliffe Quarterly* that her visits to the Plessis-Robinson development outside Paris, the Karl Marx-Hof in Vienna, and a Tannenhof settlement in Düsseldorf incited a range of emotions—from awe to jealousy to shame—which made her determined to advocate for equivalents in the United States. Armed with the "quantities of important material" and "sermons in brick and concrete" that she gathered abroad, Coit applied for and received (at age forty-five) an Edward Langley Scholarship from the American Institute of Architects (AIA) to survey pragmatically, in 1938 and again in 1939, the economic practices of 150 low-income residential dwellings in the East and Midwest.[26] Published in 1941 as two comprehensive reports in the *Octagon* (the organ of the AIA), her

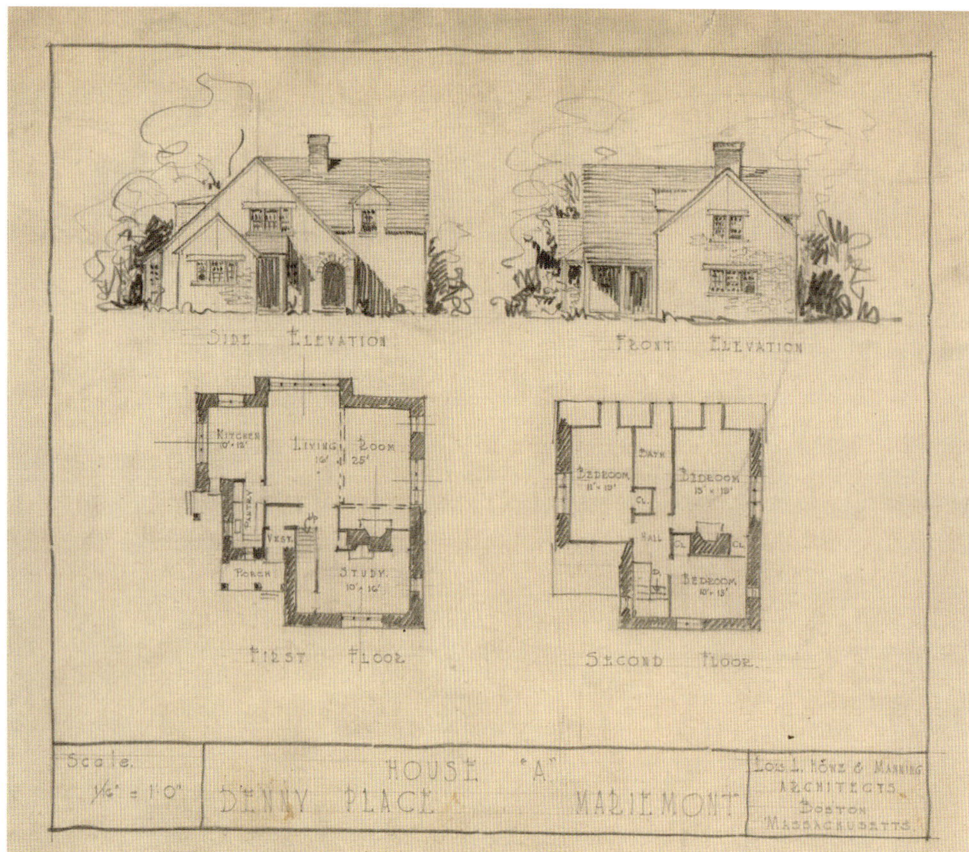

6.3. Lois Lilley Howe and Eleanor Manning, one of a few house designs for Denny Place in the Mariemont (Ohio) development, 1923. *Howe, Manning, and Almy records, Institute Archives, Distinctive Collections,* MIT *Libraries.*

painstaking study marked a decisive turn in her career as an advocate for changes in living conditions.[27]

Coit's concern with housing for lower-income city dwellers retrospectively put her at risk of being "lumped with what was termed in those days 'N.Y. housers,'" according to Susana Torre in *Women in American Architecture*. However, Coit's career is distinct in that well before the approach became mainstream, she encouraged designers to start with the needs of tenants rather than with assumptions made by professionals.[28] In the *Octagon* articles, she was not "criticizing" but rather "collating and comparing" the opinions of the occupants as well as the architects and planners of the low-income housing projects she visited. Nonetheless, by comparing what the tenants thought they needed or would like to have with what the professionals thought they ought to or could have, Coit at least implicitly questioned the authority of architects and planners in housing design.[29] Unlike other professionals who believed the occupants did not understand the aesthetics of their housing, as evidenced in their failure to respect outdoor plantings, Coit was moved by the occupants' visual sensitivity, which often manifested in unexpected ways: "Even the very 'disorder' of the forbidden fire-escape gardens," she wrote, "are a strong bid for beauty, as are the tenant-maintained gardens frequently seen."[30] Correspondingly, she recognized the high level of skill that homemakers demonstrated in their "cozy and coquettish interiors with dainty curtains, colored kitchen and table ware, all requiring time, thought, and money to maintain."[31] Such amenities, she said, were desirable because they could be cared for by the tenants themselves.

Coit saw beauty in the lower-class urban domesticity that elites frequently criticized. For instance, rather than decry crowded fire escapes as evidence of urban decay, Coit commented that "the intensive use of some of the little metal slat balconies, with a bit of linoleum or oilcloth for flooring, in Manhattan's Yorkville, with their morning-glories and petunias, and a safe place for children, give anything but a slum appearance to these unimproved properties tenanted chiefly by people of various central European origins."[32] Coit's appreciation for the visual qualities of the working-class enclaves on the Upper East Side countered ethnic stereotypes as well as the pervasive elitist perspective on dense urban neighborhoods. Rather than viewing their housing simply as overcrowded and ugly, Coit recognized the small ways in which occupants imbued them with beauty and individuality.

Although Coit claimed she was not a critic, she nonetheless offered a thoroughgoing demographic analysis of the American family and its need for accommodations. A major finding was that although most family units, especially in urban centers, were comprised of four or fewer members, accommodations typically were built for larger families. Advocating for housing complexes that served families of varied sizes, Coit subtly argued against the imposition of a bourgeois notion of the American family home on tenants of low-cost housing.[33]

Her analysis of ethnic working-class neighborhoods anticipated some of the observations later made by Jane Jacobs in *Death and Life of Great American Cities* (1961). Like Jacobs, Coit pointed to the informal ways in which communities shared childcare responsibilities and used different public spaces for recreation. She observed that elaborate play equipment often went unused by children while sand or unpaved ground was more popular for digging. If planners insisted on playgrounds, she advised, they should be located where parents could supervise from the windows of their homes.[34]

This research on low-income housing led to a substantive career for Coit in housing between about 1940 and 1962, first in the technical division of the Federal Public Housing Authority (FPHA; 1942–47) to subsidize low-cost construction, and then in the New York City Housing Authority (NYCHA). She also worked in 1947 and 1948 for the urban planner Clarence Samuel Stein, interviewing residents in the communities he designed to assess their future needs.[35] Despite the attention her writings received, Coit had a relatively minor impact on housing policy, Torre laments. Instead, she sees Coit as an exemplar of a particular career path for women: "Perhaps her greatest contribution to women architects of the present and future is that she pointed the way toward turning an ordinary job into a creative process."[36] The letters written by peers in support of Coit's nomination for the prestigious AIA fellowship (awarded to her in 1955) tell a different story: her research so profoundly influenced the advancement of housing that, years later, it was still considered a standard reference.[37] Her variety of skills—from technical and legal to academic, administrative, and communicative—enabled Coit not only to bring about vast improvements in living conditions but, according to Eero Saarinen, to uphold the long-forgotten human side of housing.[38] Coit was able, then, to exploit the traditional perspective on the home that she, and every woman, was required to develop, in order to bring about widespread awareness.

Public Housing in New York

The trajectory of Ida Brown Adelberg Webster (1899–1983) echoes the path Coit followed, in that she transitioned from single-family house design in order to dedicate her career to housing policy and eventually to large-scale development. After graduating in 1920 with a Bachelor of Arts in mathematics from Adelphi College (then in Brooklyn), Adelberg Webster attended MIT, where she obtained a Master of Architecture and won the Francis Ward Chandler Prize for achievement in architectural design. After graduation and travel in western Europe for a year, she settled in New York and in 1924 found drafting work—allegedly after seventy-five interviews that came to nothing—in the office of the École des Beaux-Arts-trained architect Richard Henry Dana Jr.[39] Adelberg Webster was likely exposed to modern architecture between 1926 and 1930, when she worked for one of Dana's former employees, architect Almus Pratt Evans, who gave a radio talk in 1930 called "Building for Modern Living" and designed for himself a green-painted cinder-block house that *Pencil Points* illustrated in 1941.[40]

Adelberg Webster achieved professional independence in 1933 when she was made a partner in the expanded firm of Evans, Moore & Woodbridge; however, after the firm closed at the start of World War II, she was forced to find interim work at the United Service Organizations as regional director of building services.[41] It was not until about 1947 that Adelberg Webster formed a professional partnership with Saul Edelbaum.[42] In 1950, the two partners designed a modern house in Katonah, New York, for stockbroker Joseph L. Gitterman Jr. (fig. 6.4). Located on a large, rural property, it was designed to take advantage of the surroundings with long views through expansive windows, and it successfully combined organic materials like fieldstone and rough-sawn board siding with more modern features.

At the same time, Adelberg Webster was involved in a variety of ways in housing; she was on housing committees of both the Women's City Club of New York and the New York chapter of the AIA, for example, and she directed the Citizens Housing and Planning Council

6.4. Saul Edelbaum (1908–2003) and Ida Brown Adelberg Webster, house of Joseph L. Gitterman Jr., 72 Old Cross River Road, Katonah, New York, 1951.

(founded 1937), dedicated to research and education on housing and planning policies. Her firm also designed public housing in New York, including the E. Roberts Moore Houses (1963) on East 149th Street in the Bronx, and the 131 St. Nicholas Avenue house (1965) in Harlem, both NYCHA projects. The firm also designed the nearly block-long RNA House (1967) developed by the Riverside Neighborhood Assembly on West 96th Street. This middle-class, urban renewal complex between Amsterdam and Columbus avenues is recognized for its distinctive concrete beehive facade, which reportedly won an Excellence in Design Award from the city (fig. 6.5).[43]

Adelberg Webster used her location in New York to obtain commissions for modern single-family houses, while also taking a leading role in organizations that attempted to resolve the acute need for safe, affordable, and appropriate accommodations for the city's expanding population.

Housing in Higher Education Curricula

Women who became active in the housing field brought expertise that they gained in a variety of ways—through education, independent study, and more. While some were fortunate enough to observe modern housing in

6.5. Saul Edelbaum and Ida Adelberg Webster, RNA House developed by the Riverside Neighborhood Assembly on West 96th Street, New York, c. 1967.

Europe in the 1920s, it was not until about the mid-1930s that American architecture school curricula focused on housing. In 1935, for example, Columbia University offered a town-planning studio led by Henry Wright, a pioneering architecture-trained planner who advanced the garden city movement. Since neither MIT nor Harvard added housing to the architecture curricula until 1939 and 1940, respectively, architecture students tended to study housing issues in city or regional planning departments (or earlier, in social economics). At the Cambridge School, there was no course specific to housing, although extant projects demonstrate the degree to which, by the early 1930s, students had already moved beyond the limitations of the simple house to design suburban neighborhoods, mass-produced housing, and model tenements.[44]

During the Depression, Henry Frost recognized housing as a central concern and must have seen it as an unprecedented opportunity for women students. Expressing a characteristic viewpoint on the social responsibility of modern architecture, in 1935 he elaborated on how his school met the challenge of rectifying the prevailing crowded living conditions and scarcity of affordable housing: "That we were the first school to give serious thought to the problem [of housing, individually and collectively] was chance, that we have continued in this direction has been due to conviction, that we are in a favorable position for what has become a matter of general and intense interest is due largely to our organization."[45] Given the small student body and nimble administration, the school realized that it was possible to incorporate the critical issue of housing into existing studio work. Moreover, the uniquely integrated curriculum of architecture and landscape architecture positioned the Cambridge School favorably to address issues around housing.[46]

Housing New Communities

Even though low-income housing was not yet a central issue when Victorine du Pont Homsey attended the Cambridge School between 1924 and 1926, as a trustee and the president of the alumnae association in the early 1930s she would have been cognizant of the attention the school was giving to housing. The role of her architect husband Samuel as design critic at the school in 1931 would also have engaged him in discussions of housing, as did their trip to Europe in 1931–32. Though du Pont Homsey was from the Kentucky branch of the family of industrialists and grew up in the Midwest, in 1935 the couple moved to the family seat in Delaware, where commissions from relatives kept their architecture partnership afloat. Between 1931 and 1939, they completed at least eight projects for family members in the region, including Mt. Cuba, a Colonial Revival estate in Hockessin, Delaware.[47] While the Homseys had already shown a disposition toward the International Style, the work she did for the family was traditional, albeit with elements of Modernism in planning and detail (see fig. 1.13).

In 1939, E. I. du Pont de Nemours and Company (of which the president was du Pont Homsey's uncle) commissioned the couple to design thirty houses (with the possibility of future expansion) on 153 acres in Seaford, Delaware, for the supervisors and foremen of the plant it had recently opened to manufacture low-cost women's nylon hosiery. Since the mid-nineteenth century, industrialists had frequently erected housing and sometimes even "company towns" with community functions for employees. For instance, when the United States entered World War I, the government contracted with du Pont de Nemours to build the world's largest gunpowder factory at Old Hickory Village, outside Nashville, Tennessee. In short order, the company constructed housing for 35,000 people, which the company expanded even after the war. The houses at Old Hickory Village followed a handful of stock plans built on conventional city blocks. At Seaford, on the other hand, the Homseys organized the residences around a circular roadway as well as along the road that ran down its center. Still known as the Martin Farms houses, they are staggered on their respective 100-by-150-foot lots to provide a sense of openness. While every house is a two-story Colonial, the six different plans, derived from a Nationwide House Plan Services pattern book by Harry Marshak, are varied in color and detail.[48]

When during the war du Pont Homsey partnered with Eugene Henry Klaber in Washington, DC on the New Deal's Greenbelt town program under the FPHA, they were required to expand the infrastructure for the occupants of the 1,000 new dwellings recently added in Maryland's Prince George's County.[49] Their three projects

6.6. Victorine du Pont Homsey and Eugene Henry Klaber (1883–1971), addition to the Rural High School, Greenbelt, Maryland, 1936. *Greenbelt Museum.*

included a maintenance building complex; a two-story elementary school called North Side (now demolished); and a nine-room addition to the Rural High School (1936; fig. 6.6). The unadorned, flat-roofed geometries of each building, interrupted only by steel-framed windows, recall the previous work of the Homseys inspired by European Modernism.[50] As described in *Pencil Points*, the maintenance complex, consisting of three buildings (for offices, storage, and workshops) and two garages, went beyond mere practical considerations. The white-painted brick structures were arranged in a pentagon-shaped plan surrounded by a wall, making the project both economical and functional as well as in keeping with the modern aesthetic of the original on-site buildings.[51]

Housing Development in Philadelphia

Not far from the locus of the Homsey practice in Delaware, Elizabeth Hirsh Fleisher devoted her energy to housing in Philadelphia, where she sometimes partnered professionally with her landscape architect husband, Horace Teller Fleisher. Before graduating in 1914 from Wellesley College, Hirsh Fleisher had spent the academic year of 1912–13 in Berlin, where she would have been exposed to the beginnings of European Modernism. She did not find her way into architecture, however, until

1926, when she and their three children accompanied her husband to Cambridge so that he could study at Harvard. She became interested in landscape architecture, too, and when she attempted to enroll she was advised to consider the Cambridge School. She followed the recommendation, as others had done before her, and though she initially studied landscape architecture, she switched to architecture. The year before graduating in 1929, both Fleishers joined the Cambridge School's summer session in Oxford, England, where they learned about garden city planning under the direction of Edward Unwin, the architect son of the distinguished English town planner Sir Raymond Unwin. As the students collaborated on their assigned problem of a satellite town, they visited the garden cities of Letchworth (1903) and Welwyn (1920), both influential models for town planning. Their project was critiqued, informally, by the elder Unwin, who also accompanied them to Kelmscott Manor, the summer home of the late William Morris, for a memorable visit with his artisan daughter, Mary "May" Morris (1862–1938).[52]

After the couple moved to Philadelphia, Hirsh Fleisher worked for the architect Edward P. Simon as well as for John Craig Janney, A. (Albert) M. (Miles) Davis, and D. Owen Stephens, with whom she conducted research on housing. As only the fourth woman licensed to practice architecture in the state of Pennsylvania, in 1941 Hirsh Fleisher entered a long-term professional partnership with Gabriel Blum Roth. Their collaboration produced designs for a variety of building types, from housing to a Buick showroom. Although she was satisfied with their success, Hirsh Fleisher recalled in 1954 that her early years in practice were a struggle against prevailing gender stereotypes for women architects, even more than against the economic downturn: "The fall of 1929 was hardly the best time to launch any kind of a career, but the idea of a woman [architect] doing anything more demanding than providing enough closets and seeing that the kitchen sink was at the right height was just ridiculous. Friends and relatives threw me a few additions and alteration jobs and as the Depression wore on, the commissions grew big enough to view with the naked eye."[53]

Their English study tour most likely sparked the interest of the Fleishers in cost-effective community housing, and in 1935 they partnered with Stephens to design a group of sixteen three-bedroom rowhouses on Howland Street in Philadelphia. While the two-story brick facades conform to the traditional designs preferred by the Federal Housing Administration, the planning recalls garden cities with their ample outdoor spaces and interiors with light and circulation. Each house departed from the local precedent: it was two rooms deep (instead of three) and thirty feet wide (instead of fifteen), and the footprint covered only 30 percent of each lot. In addition, the exterior designs did away with "the usual array of fake gables and imitation eaves" associated with nineteenth-century rowhouses in revival styles, and instead featured facades that critics considered "simple" and "honest"—watchwords for Modernism.[54] The trade praised their effort at "modern planning," possibly leading Hirsh Fleisher to the assignment as secretary of the Mayor's Housing Committee, which focused on addressing Philadelphia's housing problem of some 25,000 dwellings considered unfit for habitation. There was only one other architect on the committee, Georgina Pope Yeatman (1902–82), an MIT-trained architect alumna recently named director of the department of city architecture.[55] Their work was part of what John F. Bauman, the historian of housing policy in Philadelphia, called a "full-scale assault on urban blight," for which numerous civic organizations were advocating.[56]

During the war, Hirsh Fleisher did little work other than defense housing. By the early 1950s, however, she had more assignments, among them the Queen Lane Housing project (1954) in Germantown, the sixth low-rent development commissioned by the Philadelphia Housing Authority (PHA) since first organized in 1937 (fig. 6.7). The sixteen-story rectangular concrete building contained 120 units of one to three bedrooms, each with a screened balcony; set-back columns allowed for large areas of glass.[57] It overlooked the Wissahickon Playground, designed by Fleisher, who explained that he "humored" the square composition, informed by the original city plan of William Penn—with curved patterns to form "tot lots."[58]

The radically modern approach taken by the Fleishers echoed public housing in other cities but was unusual in Philadelphia. Indeed, as Bauman documents, there were ten public housing projects built in Philadelphia between 1949 and 1955, and only one of them, Queen Lane, eschewed the low-rise rowhouses for which the city was known.[59] Not long after its completion, disillusionment with public housing based on modern precepts took hold. "The idea that row housing—especially 'used row housing'—could provide good, affordable accommodations for low-income, working-class families," writes

6.7. Elizabeth Hirsh Fleisher and Gabriel Blum Roth (1893–1960), Queen Lane Housing (now demolished), 301 West Queen Lane, Germantown, Pennsylvania, 1955.

Bauman, "gained ascendancy among Philadelphia housing reformers."[60] At the same time, both modern superblocks and the open spaces around them began to be viewed as detrimental, if not downright dangerous. As a result of physical decay and decreasing confidence in the viability of high-rise public housing, many projects were demolished, including Queen Lane, which was imploded in 2014 and replaced by lower-scale structures.[61]

The firm's standout project, however, in which even Roth chose to live, is the Parkway House (1951–53), a luxury apartment building on Pennsylvania Avenue; it faced the Benjamin Franklin Parkway (1918), a prominent roadway that boldly disrupts the city's grid plan and connects its important cultural institutions (fig. 6.8). The fourteen-story building of more than 230 multi-bedroom units, developed by E. J. Frankel (1936), has a shallow U-shaped plan. From its center, the building steps down to reach eight stories at the flared ends of the U, from which cantilevered terraces provide distinctive park views. The flat facades are broken up with dramatic curved bays, each with five floor-to-ceiling windows organized in vertical rows; contrasting geometric forms in red brick and cantilevered elements recall northern European Expressionist architecture from the first decades of the twentieth-century, examples of which Hirsh Fleisher could have seen as a student in Germany.

Approaching Housing from Allied Fields

While a career in architecture was a logical way for women to enter the field of housing, other avenues—in sociology, city development, politics, and economics—were also options, though eventually professionals in these related fields wound up collaborating with the architects. Before becoming a prominent housing reformer, Edith Elmer Wood (1871–1945) had shown an interest in the home environment as the author, in 1899, of a long-forgotten but award-winning *Cosmopolitan* magazine article entitled "The Ideal and Practical Organization of a Home."[62] Elmer Wood had previously only written genteel fiction and travel literature, but while living in Puerto Rico in 1906, she became aware of the inadequacy of the public health system when she discovered that her tuberculosis-stricken cook had nowhere to convalesce. Her advocacy for public health facilities there led to a broader interest in the problems of low-income housing, particularly slum clearance and subsidized housing in the United States. Determined to eliminate the dark-roomed tenements that she believed were the source of immorality, social unrest, and disease, from 1910 on she engaged in legislation, activism, and education. She won respect from a broad spectrum of people as an authority with a sociological perspective whose effort contributed to the ideological foundations of United States housing policies.[63]

Although Elmer Wood held a bachelor's degree from Smith College, her professional path was unusual in that, some twenty-five years after that first degree, she resumed her education at Columbia University to study social economy. After receiving a Master of Arts—which included two years of coursework at the New York

6.8. View of the Parkway House, designed by Roth and Fleisher, 2201 Pennsylvania Avenue, Philadelphia, 1952.

School of Philanthropy (now Columbia's School of Social Work)—she was awarded a Doctor of Philosophy in 1919, at age forty-eight.[64]

As other professional women often did, she used her proven writing ability to produce a succession of books, complemented by copious reports and articles on housing. She began in 1918 with a feature based on her master's thesis in the *Journal of the American Institute of Architects* in which she argued that poor housing could not be eradicated only by the enforcement of minimum standards—light, air, sanitation, and safety—and that "constructive housing legislation" and public loans were also necessary.[65] Her broader dissertation, *The Housing of the Unskilled Earner: America's Next Problem* (1919) reported on historical housing efforts, defined current problems, and outlined new policies. Soon after its completion,

Elmer Wood produced *Housing Progress in Western Europe* (1923) to demonstrate how inferior American low-income housing was in relation to that in Europe: "I have nowhere [in Europe] seen houses even remotely comparable to the ten thousand old-law tenements of lower Manhattan, built before 1879, with their hundreds of thousands of inhabited rooms devoid of any opening to the outer air. Nor have I seen any surviving layout as bad as that of the North End of Boston, with its four- to seven-foot streets between five-story buildings and labyrinths of rear tenements filling the interior of its blocks."[66]

All the while, Elmer Wood advocated for her ideas through lecturing and consulting. In the summer of 1925, she returned to Columbia to teach Housing and Town Planning in Relation to Family Welfare, and for more than ten years thereafter taught a variety of housing courses in University Extension (adult education). Her experience was esteemed by others at the university, especially Carol Aronovici, a widely published authority on social welfare who sought her guidance in 1934 for a new course on urbanism, and again in 1935 for one on housing. Significantly, these were under the auspices of the department of architecture rather than social economics, where housing courses were historically offered.[67] Elmer Wood's conviction—that students in city planning, engineering, and architecture must unite with those in the social sciences—was realized by 1939 when University Extension experimented with a course on housing "not heretofore covered by university training," organized jointly by the architecture school and the social science department.[68] The new concentration on the social and economic problems underlying architecture reflects the groundwork laid by Joseph Hudnut as dean of Columbia's faculty of architecture between 1934 and 1935, prior to his move to Harvard.[69]

Elmer Wood was also involved in reforming inadequate housing through a host of enterprising organizations and governmental agencies. She leveraged relationships with women, recognizing that when they did the organizing, they effectively solved the problem.[70] When she founded and chaired, for twelve years, the national housing committee for the American Association of University Women (formerly the Association of Collegiate Alumnae), she established its housing policy; she then mobilized some fifty regional committees into branches not only to promote its agenda but to cooperate with local agencies, as she explained to Elisabeth Coit, who was the committee secretary some ten years later.[71] Elmer Wood was initially the only female member of the Regional Planning Association of America (RPAA; 1923–33), an organization that fostered urban reform, until the younger houser Catherine Bauer Wurster joined in 1931 and became executive secretary.[72] The two women predictably converged—for example, both contributed essays to the MoMA exhibition catalog *America Can't Have Housing* (1934), which focused on the far-ranging factors that could generate radical changes in housing conditions.[73] They came to admire each other's capability to the extent that they corresponded about coauthoring a book on housing in international cities, though it never materialized.[74]

The Preeminent Houser

Much has been published about the formidable role of Catherine Bauer Wurster in advocating for functional, affordable low-income housing; influencing public policy; and inspiring public interest and support through her writing, activism, and teaching. She was said to have possessed a gift for clear, abstract thinking and systematic research.[75] Her output is remarkable: by age thirty-two (just ten years after graduating from Vassar College), she had been awarded three grants for international travel, research, and writing; placed reviews and editorials (increasingly about housing and urban planning) in at least fifteen publications; and authored the authoritative book *Modern Housing* (1934)—a comprehensive survey of social policy and government-sponsored housing, said to be "as Timely as This Morning's Newspaper."[76] Though the publication drew national attention to the significant issues of housing in Europe and the United States, she was humble: "I've done hundreds of things that I personally consider more important and useful than that exceedingly youthful and uneven tome I wrote almost ten years ago," Bauer Wurster later confessed. Even so, she attributed 95 percent of her prestige and influence as a houser to that one book.[77]

It was only her first act in her too-short but nevertheless packed career. Among her achievements is the fundamental role she played in the passage of the Housing Act of 1937, the first national legislation to assist financially in clearing and then constructing low-rent housing on former "slum" property; the new housing was reserved for families who could not adequately be served by private enterprise.[78] Although in the 1960s the practice of slum clearance and replacement with mid- and high-rise public housing was controversial, in the 1930s there was enormous enthusiasm for the practice in such cities as Philadelphia, New York, and Boston. Bauer, as others did, adopted comprehensive approaches to provide housing for low-income people, which resulted in the loss of existing urban fabric and possibly the destruction of communities, not to mention the modest expressions of individuality that Coit had singled out for comment. Bauer was subjected to criticism for embracing urban renewal, just as her male counterparts were.

Catherine Bauer found her way into housing reform by means of her writing ability. Her engaging communications won respect from the likes of the pioneering Dutch modernist architect J.J.P. Oud, who responded to her in 1931, "We seldom get letters so vividly and interestingly written as yours. Do cultivate this [writing] talent and bring it into the world."[79] The biographies of Bauer Wurster do not differentiate between her career path and those of other reformers—although her interest in housing was kindled by an early attraction to architecture, and particularly Modernism, for its functionality, honesty, simplicity, directness, fitness, and purpose.[80] Although Bauer had transferred in her junior year to the College of Architecture at Cornell (with a lot of math but only one art course under her belt), she returned to Vassar to graduate in English. The decision may well have paid off: the following September, when she traveled for a year in Western Europe, she was able to subsidize her expenses through freelance journalism, a path, unlike architecture, that was amenable to women. Cavorting with fellow architects and meeting such members of the avant-garde as the Austrian architect Adolf Loos, Bauer wrote letters home that made mention of her budding appreciation for Modernism, and in her diary of 1926–27, she contemplated topics for possible articles: "Modern French Arch. / Lack of modernism in Am[erica] / Theories of Urbanism etc. / Le Corbusier / Loos / Debt to Germany & Austria / Houses & Apartments / General tendencies / Large glass spaces, [large] plain [spaces] / Right angles / Flat roofs / Geometric plans."[81]

Bauer began to develop some of her ideas after she returned to the East Coast in the article "Machine-Age Mansions for Ultra-Moderns," published in the *New York Times* on April 15, 1928. As she succinctly conveyed her understanding of the work of French modernists Robert Mallet-Stevens, Le Corbusier, and André Lurçat, she expressed her cognizance of the schism between contemporary European and American architecture. She held firm to her opinion, explaining later that American Modernism "got shoved on a very unexpectant and tired world as an exotic tour de force, smelling faintly like a stale gin-fizz."[82] Her viewpoint intensified on her next two trips abroad: in 1930 to survey more purposefully the aesthetics of modern architecture, and in 1932 to research modern housing specifically for a series of articles in *Fortune*, which she intended to produce with Lewis Mumford (with whom she was also romantically involved).[83] Mumford shepherded her career in the early 1930s by making introductions and initiating professional pathways. Obviously, he also impressed on her his essential argument about "the regional construction of the modern world."[84] The culmination of these formative years was her appreciation of modern architecture as an expression of the social order of its inhabitants and their communities and her belief that affordable, functional housing could only evolve from a national commitment to social and civic improvement, as in Europe.[85]

Her prize-winning essay "Art in Industry" (*Fortune*, May 1931) on the Römerstadt development by Ernst May in Frankfurt, Germany, is typically cited as the inception of her international reputation as a houser. Even she agreed that "that piece of luck made me a 'housing expert' whether I wanted to be or not."[86] Less often remembered are the many essays she wrote for a variety of publications, from the *Nation* and the *New Republic* to *Collier's* and *Arts Weekly*. The range of her subject matter was broad: she reviewed works by Kem Weber, Gilbert Rohde, Fritz-Cross, and Deskey-Vollmer, not to mention photographs by Man Ray and Paul Strand.[87] She also engaged in the popular trend of championing the celebrity male architect (the *starchitect*, in today's parlance), and for her, in 1931, Frank Lloyd Wright was a "lyric genius" whose *Modern Architecture* (1931) was "the very best book on modern architecture."[88] Even so, her progressive ideas increasingly penetrated her writings, regardless of the topic. In her review "Who Cares about Architecture?"—one of three essays she published in 1931 in the *New Republic* (where Mumford was a contributing editor)—she reiterates her perspective: "I mean by architecture, real architecture, the clear and consistent expression of a social order that people can make out of their physical environment, for their own satisfaction."[89] She maintained a similar stance in her review of MoMA's *Modern Architecture: International Exhibition* (1932), in which she writes, "If buildings do not express an integrated society, they merely state the fact that society is discordant—and little more."[90] She never faltered in her view of architecture as an integral element of a larger social system; more significantly, she believed that a national housing movement could present "the one great opportunity for a real modern architecture."[91] For Bauer, then, the modern movement was inextricably linked to housing.

Bauer's ability to express herself with clarity and persuasiveness enabled her to forge a relationship with the vanguard at MoMA during the period in which the department of architecture—reputedly the first of its kind in the world—was being launched.[92] In the 1930s, she participated in six museum projects, earning her a place on MoMA's Committee on Architecture and Industrial Arts (1936–46); in the 1940s, she contributed to three exhibitions and was a juror of two design competitions (see fig. 1.3).[93] While her focus broadened with time, her earliest solo contributions had to do with housing reform in an effort to educate the public about the need for a national housing policy. In her essay for the *Architecture in Government Housing* exhibition in 1936, for example, she affirmed her point of view that low-income housing is a complex problem that cuts across "almost as many fields as there are special interests and viewpoints in our society"—economics, industry, sociology, technology, and culture.[94]

Bauer's involvement at MoMA not only provided her with an opportunity to promote her own principles but to form an important and lasting personal and professional network. She was introduced to the museum by Mumford when she, along with two other RPAA members, Clarence Stein and Henry Wright, assisted him on the housing section of the *Modern Architecture: International Exhibition* (and its catalog).[95] She garnered the respect of the community to the extent that, only a month after the show's opening, she joined Henry-Russell Hitchcock and Philip Johnson on the masthead of the inaugural issue of *Arts Weekly* (successor to *The Arts*). During the journal's short run of nine issues, Bauer and Hitchcock both contributed to the architecture column; the disparity in the perspectives of their respective contributions—sociological for her and formalistic for him—reflected the larger disagreement over the significance of style between Hitchcock and Mumford.[96] Despite their differences, she maintained her professional relationship with Hitchcock, evidenced by the fact that they were the only essayists in the catalog of the notable exhibition *Modern Architecture in England* (1937). Other MoMA projects include her talk on the modern city for a series of radio broadcasts hosted by the museum as well as an essay published concurrently in *Art in America in Modern Times* (1934).[97] As director of the division of research and information of the United States Housing Authority (USHA; 1937–42), an agency created by the Housing Act of 1937, Bauer collaborated with MoMA on the housing section of the exhibition *Art in Our Time* (1939). In fact, her assistant, Frederick Gutheim, coauthored the catalog essay with John McAndrew, then the museum's curator of architecture and industrial design.

While the MoMA opportunities facilitated Bauer's quest to educate the public about large-scale housing and community planning, she, in turn, helped to expand the focus of the museum's architecture department beyond aesthetic considerations. In 1941, she acknowledged that the museum had succeeded in expanding the meaning of architecture beyond a limited appreciation for the facades of individual buildings to a recognition of its impact on the total environment. Although not an architect herself, Bauer brought to MoMA a broad perspective on the social implications of Modernism that had a decisive impact on the institution.[98]

In the postwar years, Bauer Wurster's contributions at MoMA leveled off. She relocated in 1943 to Cambridge so that her architect husband, William Wurster (whom she married in 1940) could participate in courses at what is now the Department of Urban Planning and Design at Harvard's Graduate School of Design (GSD). In 1944, fate played a part when the Wursters extended their stay in Cambridge so he could take over the deanship of architecture and planning at MIT. This move made it possible for her to accept an offer from Hudnut in 1945 to take on the role of "lecturer in housing" at Harvard, where historically women had not been allowed to teach. Initially, she was determined to limit the assignment to "a strictly temporary one-term basis," but from the spring of 1946 until they permanently relocated to the Bay Area, Bauer Wurster organized and taught a comprehensive seminar called Housing 7. Topics of discussion ranged from consumption to production to financing, as well as to social and political sciences, so that each student could argue from the perspective of his or her discipline.[99] Ever since they had sat together on the architecture committee at MoMA, Hudnut had been "deeply impressed" with her understanding of housing. In fact, in 1940, he had lamented to her, "If it were not for the quaint restriction of Harvard University, which prohibits a woman from serving as a professor, I know quite definitely the person to whom I should offer the first vacancy."[100] Clearly, he got his way.

Correspondence between Hudnut and Bauer Wurster describes the depth of respect they had for one another: when the Wursters were in California, perhaps for the summer, Hudnut wrote to them, "I must say that Robinson Hall [where the GSD was housed] has a distinctly let-down feeling since your departure. It is very much as if an orchestra had stopped playing, leaving everybody in the middle of the dance floor wondering what to do next."[101] Hudnut valued the invigorating presence of the Wursters, but, even more, he respected professional women and relied on Bauer Wurster's judgment—not just in matters of housing but also in staff appointments, lecture content, and writing assessments.[102] Not surprisingly, when he organized the American Society of Architects and Planners (ASAP; 1944–48), Bauer Wurster was a founding member.[103]

On the surface at least, Bauer Wurster appears to have escaped from the barriers that most women faced in their careers, perhaps because her role as a houser was without much precedent. Nonetheless, she could not avoid traditional gender labels. Despite her professional renown, in the MoMA press release for the international competition for low-cost furniture design in 1948, she is listed under the jury as "Housewife, Housing Expert," an incompatible description at best.[104] Similarly, though showcased in the article "Housing's White Knight," edited by Jane Jacobs in 1946 for *Architectural Forum*, she was attached to the familial concerns of housework, cooking, marriage, and motherhood. Building on a *Chicago Tribune* piece in which Bauer Wurster was labeled a "handsome blonde with brunette economic ideas," the *Forum* offered its own take on her as a "tweedy woman" with a "masculine stride" and a "boyish bob."[105] The insistent association of her with domesticity and the (mis)characterization of her as masculine shows an uneasiness on the part of the critics regarding women who were confident in their professional standing. Nor does it fit with Bauer Wurster's gender identification, at least in the eyes of her sister: Elizabeth Bauer Kassler (formerly Mock) said she was "an extremely complex woman, dedicated to the idea that she was Woman as well as everything else."[106]

In no way did Bauer Wurster acquiesce to the archetype of the midcentury woman, including the professionals who concluded the only way to practice their trade was to partner with their husbands. Bauer Wurster outwardly expressed a disdain for "that husband-and-wife machine" of which neither she nor her husband wanted any part, and she refused to make a life out of promoting his oeuvre as did the wives of other architects.[107] Though both Wursters agitated against professional teamwork, academic or otherwise, their individual outlooks inevitably blended; after joining the faculty at the University of California, Berkeley in 1950, Bauer Wurster eventually became professor of city and regional planning and associate dean of the College of Environmental Design, where her husband was the founding dean. Though the building in which it was housed was initially named after her husband, in late 2020 the school changed it to Bauer Wurster Hall to reaffirm her influential role.[108]

Bauer Wurster's interventions in the field of housing were visible through her career as a writer, curator, and educator. While she was one among many housers, she nonetheless challenged the perception that male professionals fundamentally shape housing policy in the United States. Bauer Wurster was part of a larger cohort of women who turned the potential liability of being tagged with an affinity for the domestic realm into an asset that could be used in their professional practices.

Women in early housing reform have received varying degrees of attention from scholars, ranging from the near complete neglect of Coit to the wider acknowledgement of Bauer Wurster. However, by considering them collectively, the pervasiveness of women in the field is apparent. Moreover, their innovative perspectives—for instance, their emphasis on the needs of residents—challenged the orthodoxies of government housing policy and had a long-term impact on the field.

CHAPTER VII

Creating Community

ELISABETH COIT, IDA ADELBERG WEBSTER, AND ELIZABETH Hirsh Fleisher—all of whom completed their professional educations in architecture between the wars—were deeply engaged in housing, one of the period's most pressing issues. Those who studied a decade or two later also demonstrated a keen interest in housing, with the addition of the related issue of planning suburban communities, a building activity that grew after World War II as veterans used the GI Bill to finance their homes. In comparison to male architects, city planners, or real estate developers, women professionals had a relatively small role in such projects. Yet their contributions are important evidence of progressive thinking about how communities could be organized physically and articulated architecturally.

The focus on community design at the Cambridge School is exemplified by the student projects beginning in the late 1930s. Among them are two subdivisions by Katharine Wilson: one in Mount Kisco in Westchester County, organized around a circular road with an arm ending in a cul-de-sac, and another on Brattle Street in Cambridge, in which eight modern houses are arranged around an elliptical shaped road (fig. 7.1). The provision of outdoor space was one objective that architecture students were taught to incorporate into their projects, and despite pervasive stereotypes of postwar suburban and resort planning as racially, socially, and economically divisive, as well as environmentally destructive, community plans by women display tendencies toward social inclusiveness and respect for natural surroundings.

Women architects engaged in planning a wide range of communities, from full-blown towns to housing developments to neighboring houses, some of which are obviously modern because they incorporate such accepted forms and materials as large spans of glass and flat cantilevered roofs. At the same time, their buildings frequently invoke local vernaculars and regional quotations. Some works are self-consciously traditional, often to fit into an existing neighborhood. Nonetheless, they too can be understood as modern since they were intended as progressive forms of domestic life. Designing a community entailed more than simply laying out roads and house lots: it meant creating a physical environment in which social relations could thrive in ways that often failed in other kinds of developments. Their planning facilitated the sorts of interactions that the theorist and critic Raymond Williams describes in *Keywords: A Vocabulary of Culture and Society* (1976). He contends that since the nineteenth century, the word *community* has been used as a "warmly persuasive word" to imply the "more direct, more total and therefore more significant relationships" that occur on the local level as opposed to larger contexts of "state, nation, society, etc."[1] Accordingly, *community*

Closeup of figure 7.6. Norman and Jean Bodman Fletcher house, Six Moon Hill, Lexington, Massachusetts, 1949.

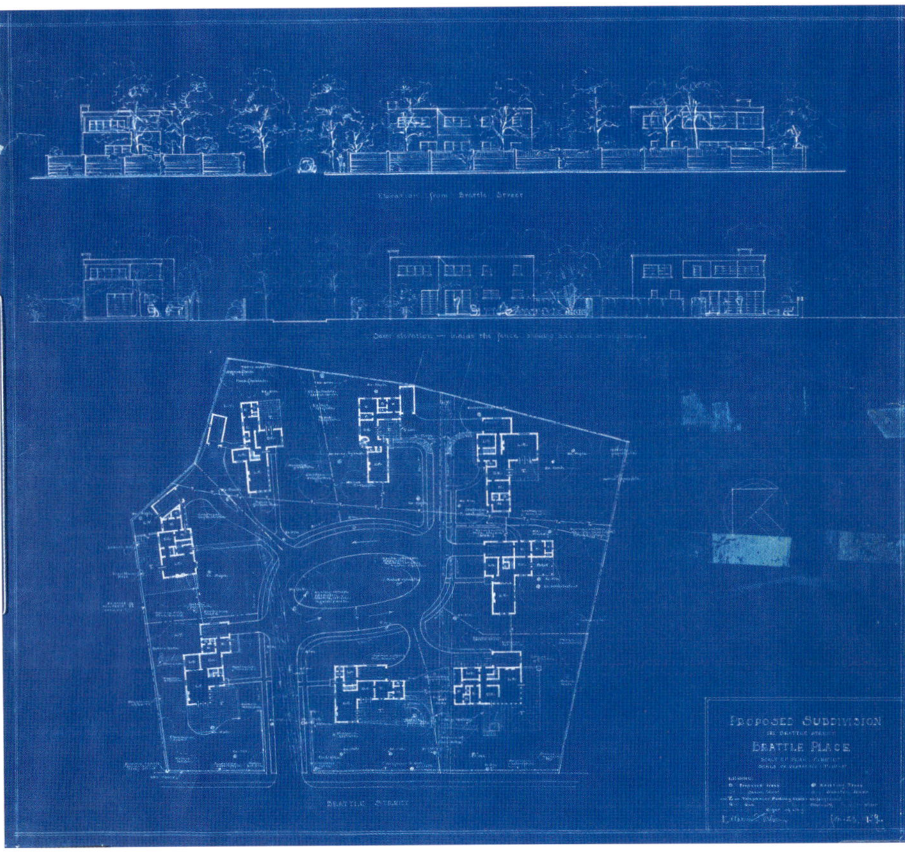

7.1. Katharine Wilson, blueprint for a hypothetical subdivision, 121 Brattle Street, Cambridge, January 28, 1939. *Wilson Rahn Papers.*

can describe "an existing set of relationships," for example, families living adjacent to one another, or "an alternative set of relationships" that foster those who otherwise were not sufficiently accommodated in prevailing places of work or living. What is most significant, Williams says, is that unlike other terms of social organization, *community* "seems never to be used unfavourably."[2]

The communities designed by women were largely conceived as spaces for those whose needs for social interaction had not yet been met. One of their most positive contributions to community planning were their interior spaces: a group of rooms or even smaller spaces to accommodate unconventional living arrangements or, as Williams explains, as "experiments in an alternative kind of group living."[3]

Elisabeth Coit in Croton Heights, New York

As Elisabeth Coit branched out to design "economical and modern dwellings," she may have had in mind the suburban developments of Forest Hills and Mariemont, both inspired by the British garden city concept in which individual houses were united in a community through shared open spaces and aesthetics. One of her first projects, five buildings for a "colony of professional people" in Holderness, New Hampshire, prepared her for the sixteen houses she would build between about 1926 and 1941 in the nascent community of Croton Heights, located in Yorktown, about thirty-five miles north of New York City.[4] From a programmatic point of view, Croton Heights was different from the other communities because it was a residential enclave designed primarily for women, some with long-term women companions.

Between 1924 and 1925, Halsey William Wilson, founder of the renowned reference publishing house H. W. Wilson, purchased about 240 acres on what once was part of the Van Cortlandt land grant. Not only did he plan to spend summer weekends there in a mid-eighteenth-century house (the backdrop of a memorable Revolutionary War skirmish), but he wanted to join the

7.2. Elisabeth Coit house, 250 Colonel Greene Road, Croton Heights, New York, c. 1926. *Coit Papers.*

suburban development movement pushing northward in Westchester County.[5] To realize his concept for a low-density development of single-family houses, Wilson founded the Croton Heights Realty Company (1924–59) to market wooded plots, from half an acre on up to professionals who wanted a remote retreat.[6] In order both to entice buyers and ensure a cohesive community of intellectuals, in 1926 Wilson and his wife converted a structure into the Croton Heights Inn (subsequently renamed Peter Pratt's Inn) to house, feed, and entertain visitors. Though hit economically in the Depression, by 1941 the development consisted of some forty-six homeowners, twenty-one of whom were year-round residents.[7]

Though Wilson considered his project an investment, he was also remembered for his "baronial gesture" of first offering parcels of land to "worthy employees" and their colleagues—especially female librarians. In 1926, Coit and her partner Eleanor F. F. Duncan, editor of the *Library Journal*, were among the first to arrive.[8] The simple "camp" Coit designed for the two of them and occupied for ten years featured a covered porch running the length of the rectangular structure that contained only a living area and small bunk room (fig. 7.2).

Among the dwellings Coit designed for at least fourteen others in Croton Heights are a primitive woodland lodge called Stonecrop for Marion A. Knight, editor of Wilson's *Book Review Digest*, and a summer cottage (with the potential to be converted for year-round living) in 1927 for Mary Burnham, editor of Wilson's *Cumulative Book Index*.[9] Other "strong-minded women" with whom Coit collaborated include Isadore Gilbert Mudge, a revered reference librarian at Columbia University for thirty years, and her partner Minnie Earl Sears, a Wilson employee recognized for her *List of Subject Headings for Small Libraries* (1923). Coit also converted an outbuilding that Isadore Mudge had relocated to a wooded slope into a two-story cottage. Called Hayslope, it featured a large living room with salvaged wood paneling and a wall of windows capturing the dramatic views of the valley below.[10] Coit designed more sophisticated year-round dwellings there following the installation of electricity, gas, water, telephones, and additional roads. Her plan with "domesticity and real charm" for the two-story colonial house called Four Acres for Anna B. Van Nort and her companion Charlotte F. Savage won honorable mention in a 1932 competition sponsored by Better Homes in America (1922–35), a national not-for-profit organization mandated to educate the public about home improvement.[11]

Amaza Lee Meredith and African American Communities

Coit's Westchester development was part of the interwar expansion of rural and suburban communities. In the postwar years, recently completed highways led to new resort communities on the Atlantic Coast, around inland lakes, and in the mountains. Yet these middle-class developments were often segregated, excluding African American, Jewish, or ethnic minority buyers. In this context of systemic racial and ethnic prejudice, as documented by the racist and xenophobic language in property deeds, it became necessary to create communities where barred groups could live or vacation without being subject to hostility. Consequently, early in the twentieth century, resort areas for Black people sprouted near population centers and fulfilled an important role until the Civil Rights Movement of the mid-1960s provided greater openness to majority white enclaves.[12]

Such communities already existed in the late nineteenth century—for instance, in the village of Oak Bluffs on the island of Martha's Vineyard in Massachusetts.[13] Founded in 1866 as a Methodist summer camp meeting, Oak Bluffs evolved into a resort town that welcomed Black visitors, and by the end of World War II was recognized as a beachfront haven for them.[14] Another resort community, Idlewild, located in a rural wooded section of western Michigan, was developed between the wars by four white couples as the Idlewild Resort Company for African Americans. The Black Eden of Michigan, as it was called, thrived as a major center for entertainment, "as good as any you would see in Las Vegas"; the Four Tops, Jackie Wilson, Bill Doggett, Sarah Vaughan, and others performed in the nightclubs that opened there with such names as the Flamingo and Paradise.[15]

Another haven for Black summer residents is the influential postwar development Azurest North, a vacation destination in Sag Harbor, which was an incorporated village on eastern Long Island.[16] It had evolved from Eastville, a nearby community of free Black people and Native Americans who worked in the whaling industry, the area's commercial mainstay from the American Revolution to the end of the Civil War.[17] Azurest North took shape when "Miss Amaza," as Amaza Lee Meredith was known by neighbors, followed the lead of her older sister Maude Kenney Meredith Terry (1887–1968) in the development of the waterfront community.

The Meredith sisters were the daughters of Samuel Peter Meredith, a white carpenter from Lynchburg, Virginia, and Emma Pink Kenney, an African American seamstress. The mixed-race couple could not marry in Virginia, but did so in 1902 in Washington, DC, after which time they lived in the Queen Anne–style house he built in Lynchburg. Although Meredith taught his daughter Amaza how to read architectural plans and make building models from cardboard, he reportedly discouraged her professional interest in architecture, perhaps realizing that racist and sexist attitudes could severely limit her potential success.[18] He was well regarded as a builder but fell into debt, the reason given for his suicide in 1915.[19] His wife was well educated and wanted the same for her children, so in the summer of 1915, Amaza Lee Meredith took courses at the historically Black Virginia Normal and Industrial Institute in Petersburg, Virginia (now Virginia State University), to prepare for a teaching career. She developed an intimate relationship with Edna Meade Colson, who, though only a few years older, was already an established college instructor. A graduate of Fisk University, a private Black institution in Nashville, Colson had followed the tradition of education in her extended family. She was a political activist and committed to educating African Americans.[20] Meredith and Colson stayed together as a couple throughout their adult lives, despite extended periods apart.

After studying in Petersburg and teaching for six years at a high school in Lynchburg, Meredith continued her education at Teachers College at Columbia University, where she received her bachelor's and master's degrees in art education in 1930 and 1935, respectively. Between these two stints in New York, Meredith returned to the Virginia Normal and Industrial Institute, where she taught art and, in 1935, became head of the art department, which she also founded (and where she remained until her retirement in 1958). Even though she had been discouraged from pursuing architectural training, Meredith nonetheless had a small practice that began with Azurest South (1939), a house she designed for Colson and herself on the property they jointly purchased in 1938 adjacent to the campus (see figs. 8.2, 8.3, C.3).[21]

However sporadic Meredith's architectural work was, she maintained her interest into the postwar years as she and Colson, along with their family and friends—doctors, lawyers, city workers, undertakers, and teachers—became deeply immersed in the Azurest North project (fig. 7.3). The Pulitzer Prize–winning author Colson Whitehead—whose great-grandmother, Mary Colson Woody (1874–1966), was among the first generation of residents—described his summers of "pure pinned joy" at Azurest North in his most personal novel *Sag Harbor* (2009).[22] "Black boys with beach houses. It could mess with your head sometimes. … Or you could embrace the contradiction," as everyone ostensibly did.[23] He explained that "forced social-interaction" was unavoidable at Azurest North, where, especially on the beach, "middle-aged ladies camped out in front of someone's house each afternoon" and neighbors from the two nearby African American

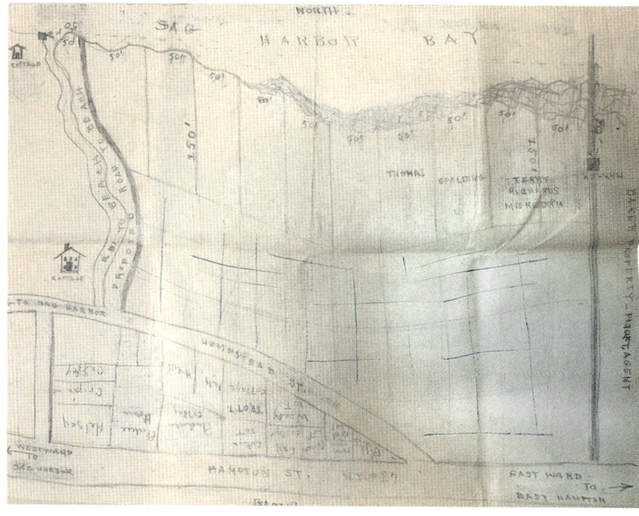

7.3. Plan for the first phase of Azurest North, Sag Harbor, New York, 1947. *Amaza Lee Meredith Papers, Special Collections and Archives, Virginia State University.*

communities (Sag Harbor Hills and Ninevah Beach) "promenaded by, making the rounds, leaving footprints that were physical traces to a dozen conversations."[24]

The close-knit community of the 1970s that Whitehead portrays had been established several decades earlier when Meredith Terry—a schoolteacher educated at Teachers College who was living in the Jamaica section of Queens—began spending summers in Sag Harbor. For some nine years, Meredith Terry apparently kept an eye out for a suitable property where she could plant her own stake until, in 1947, she was offered the sandy, wooded land from Havens Beach to Hampton Street. The family's excitement was uncontainable: "The unbelievable has taken place," Meredith exclaimed in a letter to Colson, "The 'Azurest' bluff is being offered for sale to colored." As she explained, the 580-foot property was to be parceled into ten or eleven waterfront lots, each 50 by 150 feet, at $20 a foot, and the remaining property would move down in price to $300 a lot, based on location. An early plan reveals their initial vision: Meredith and Colson would reside on the two easternmost lots along with Meredith's sister Maude and her husband, Hunter Hereford Terry, a post office clerk, and their daughter, Iris Meredith Terry Richards (1910–80) and her husband, Dr. Frederick Forrest Richards, both New York physicians (fig. 7.4). As Meredith explained, they wanted "to get only the most desirable persons for neighbors, for security, standards, etc. so that the spirit of the residential area will remain as perfect as the setting." Her niece was already contacting some twenty of her friends who might be interested in their "ideals." Meredith thought that there were surely enough African Americans who could afford this once-in-a-lifetime opportunity, and in a letter urged Colson to get there as fast as she could—with her ideas.[25]

The Meredith family was at the forefront of what became a two-phase development, along with Dorothy "Dot" M. Coleman Spaulding, a Brooklyn attorney, who had attended Hunter College with Iris Terry Richards, and James P. "Smitty" Smith, a civil engineer and an employee of the NYCHA. Each contributed his or her own expertise to the development.[26] For Meredith, it meant designing the family house at 63 Terry Drive, which, according to the deed, she owned with her nephew. Her original concept may have been to build a modern house incorporating the Art Deco elements of Azurest South—smooth white walls, flat roofs, and curved lines, as documented in an extant drawing, the "HIHIL-Residence" for the Richards (fig. 7.5; see figs. 8.5, 8.6, C.3). Given the location on Sag Harbor Bay, the forms of the house would have easily recalled the ocean liners of the earlier decades. Though the "HIHIL" design is not radical, it remained unbuilt, and instead the house that was constructed is more sympathetic with the conservative tract houses being constructed in large numbers on Long Island. It is covered with traditional red cedar siding and topped with a shallow gable roof, but it also utilizes the more contemporary wide spans of glass to enjoy the sweeping water view. When it was nearly finished, Meredith wrote to Colson, "Oh, Edna, it's too beautiful for words. I'm actually humble!!"[27] She also designed the house next door at 59 Terry Drive, called Edendot, for Coleman Spaulding and her husband, James Edward Spaulding, and she may have designed a few others, though the plans she drew up for the long, narrow lots of Vinie Scott and of Mary Colson Woody (an aunt

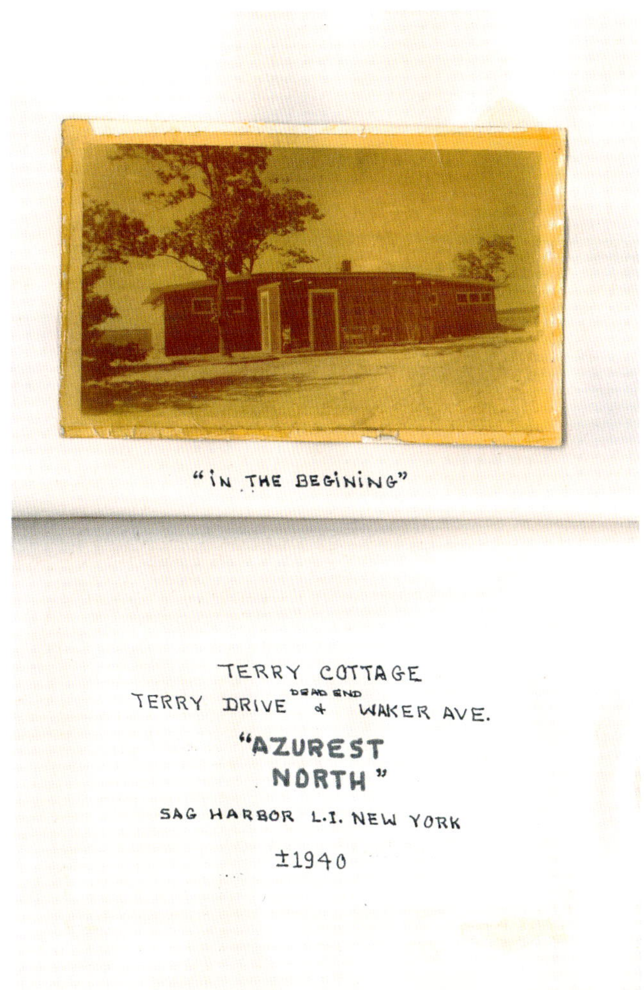

7.4. Amaza Lee Meredith, scrapbook pages documenting the house she designed at 63 Terry Drive, Sag Harbor, c. 1950. *Meredith Papers.*

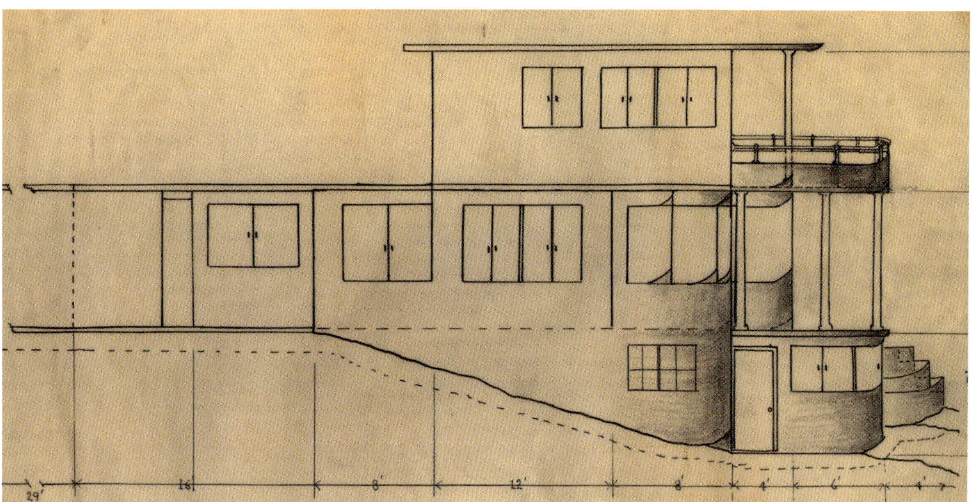

7.5. Amaza Lee Meredith, unexecuted design for the "HIHIL-Residence" in Azurest North. c. 1950. *Meredith Papers.*

of Edna Colson) are not known to have been realized. Eventually, the Woody family did build a house at 51 Terry Drive, where it stands near the others Meredith designed, "bunched up all over one another … in a close-knit beach culture … moored behind the dunes like battleships."[28] The development's modest bungalows, however, were not distinguished by a formal consistency as they sometimes were in other planned communities.

During the second phase of development, beginning in about 1953, the group set up the Azurest Syndicate to enable lot sales, to offer small mortgages to buyers who otherwise did not have access, and to facilitate the payment of the original mortgage, which was held by the previous property owner, Elsie Birks Gale (1893–1970), a white realtor based in nearby Huntington. Also in the business was her son, Daniel Kent Gale, who had been stationed at Schofield Barracks (Oahu) during the Pearl Harbor attack and had commanded a multiracial unit. His non-racist perspective, influenced, if not inspired, the sale of the property to African Americans, despite scattered local resistance.[29] The Syndicate depended upon the financial investment of Meredith, Colson, and the Richardses, all of whom continued to acquire lots (in lieu of payments for loans) well into the 1960s.[30] Meredith's architectural expertise was also valued, since at one point the Syndicate considered offering lots, each with one- or two-room expandable houses designed by Meredith.[31] Though there is no record that the speculative houses were built, Meredith's interest in design at Azurest North did not waver, since at the age of eighty she was engaged in creating "suggestive house plans [and] ideas" for a potential buyer.[32] The vision of Meredith and her family members is still firmly imprinted on the names of the roads themselves: Terry Drive, Meredith Avenue, and Richards Drive.

Family Communities in the Boston Suburb

The Meredith sisters and their cohort of friends and family at Azurest North inverted the usual pattern of postwar residential development that prioritized profitability over respect for the land and for the composition of the community. The architect developers of the twenty-acre neighborhood in Lexington, Massachusetts—dubbed Six Moon Hill by its creators—had the same intention. In 1947, seven partners in The Architects Collaborative (TAC) purchased property on which to build a community of well-designed modern houses for professionals. The steeply sloped site was convenient to Cambridge and Boston, as well as to local amenities, such as shops and schools. The architects made sure that the designs of the houses were directly controlled by a planning board, which stemmed from a larger corporation that they created to oversee the land subdivision and infrastructure. Each property owner was entitled to two voting shares—so that spouses could vote separately but equally. Like Azurest North, the Six Moon Hill houses—almost exclusively populated by servantless families with children—were guided by the needs of the owners, rather than by financial gain.[33] At Six Moon Hill, the relationship of the houses to their respective landscapes and to other structures was of vital importance. The initial plan called for twenty-nine half-acre lots, as well as four acres of common land for recreation, including a swimming pool and tennis court.[34] Unlike the postwar developers of American suburbia, the architects of Six Moon Hill resented the rise of automobile culture and only reluctantly integrated the use of cars into the plan. "We thought cars were the enemy," recalled Sarah Pillsbury Harkness in the mid-1990s. As an unfortunate necessity, a single street runs through the center of the property to provide access to all the lots but dead ends in a cul-de-sac to avoid through traffic. The street also served as a play area for children and a place where the adults could interact spontaneously and informally. As Pillsbury Harkness remembered, the street was "the social center of the community," which at its height included ninety-six children.[35]

By 1950, nineteen houses had been erected at Six Moon Hill at a cost of between $10,000 and $22,000 each, ranging in size from 1,100 to 2,200 square feet. By comparison, the average new American single-family house in 1950 was 1,065 square feet and cost on average $11,000. The year 1950 was extraordinarily active for single-family home construction, which totaled 1.7 million units (out of 1.9 million housing starts, a number that was unequaled in the next twenty years).[36] Thus, the Six Moon Hill houses ranged from the average size and price of new suburban residences to nearly double by both measures. At the smaller end, the Six Moon Hill houses were the same size as the mass-produced, inexpensive houses in the postwar Levittown development on Long Island, which were built at a time when they were needed but were later well known for their poor siting and banal architecture.[37]

Although the Six Moon Hill houses exhibit character and diversity, they also share common features, as *Architectural Forum* observed in 1950: flexible plans, flat or shed roofs, steel casement windows with large spans of glass for "space flow" from indoors to outdoors, and Plexiglas skylights to maximize daylight.[38] At the same time, they employed such natural materials as cedar siding, typically painted gray with white trim.[39] The integration of modern elements with traditional, vernacular materials and colors typifies the humanistic Modernism many women practiced.[40] While some historians have attributed the Six Moon Hill aesthetic to Walter Gropius, since he was the most recognized partner of TAC, in fact, both Gropius and Eleanor Raymond were close associates of Pillsbury Harkness, a founding partner of TAC who, unlike Gropius, resided at Six Moon Hill.[41] Pillsbury Harkness later reflected, "I was exceptionally lucky in knowing and being influenced by [these] two remarkable people." Even though he was worldly and public, and she was domestic and private, Gropius and Raymond, as Pillsbury Harkness recognized in hindsight, were alike in their ability to solve social and living problems using new methods and materials while also being attentive to the surrounding environments of the buildings they designed.[42]

Before TAC was even founded, Pillsbury Harkness and Jean Bodman Fletcher had been corresponding about living near one another, or perhaps sharing a residence, to balance work and child-rearing, so it is not surprising that their families built adjacent houses at Six Moon Hill.[43] Close to the cul-de-sac, where social interaction occurred, the two houses are both flat-roofed with ribbon windows and expanses of glass. The house Bodman Fletcher designed with her husband capitalized on its steep site to create a half-basement for the three-level building. Its open, light-filled interior displayed materials commonly found in modern houses—natural-finished plywood, cinder block, and plastic (fig. 7.6). The one by the Harknesses was similarly adapted to the needs of their family as well as to New England's climate. At its core was a playroom, easily visible from the dining room and kitchen, with glazed overhead doors that could be raised in the summer to create an open breezeway and lowered and covered with wooden shades in the winter for warmth (fig. 7.7; cover).[44] Six Moon Hill's cooperative approach to planning and design is still highly regarded, but as a model the community did not alter the general course of suburban development. However, the success of the plan did inspire other projects—for example, the larger development of sixty-eight houses in Lexington called Five Fields, which TAC began designing in 1951. Not all the houses there were as distinctive as those at Six Moon Hill, in part because the architects were not designing for themselves but for economy. The three standardized plans the firm created at first proved too expensive for buyers to customize, and the architects eventually turned to more individualized plans based on a twelve-by-twelve-foot module. As at Six Moon Hill, a corporation was formed at Five Fields, called Site and Shelter, to develop and sell the property, which also included common recreation land. The project's success can be gauged by the fact that all the lots sold by 1957.[45]

The relatively brisk sales can be attributed to the fact that the Five Fields development coincided with a period of rapid suburbanization outside of Boston and a corresponding depopulation of the historic core: during the 1940s and 1950s, the number of residents in greater Boston grew by more than 17 percent while the city itself lost 13 percent, many of them white residents. Investment

7.6. Rear view of the house Norman and Jean Bodman Fletcher designed for their family, 36 Moon Hill Road, Lexington, 1949.

in the regional highway system and especially in the construction of the ring road to the west of Boston, Route 128, made it more feasible to commute between the city center and the suburbs, where new business facilities were being spawned on former farmland. Originally conceived to ease travel from the north and south of the city, Route 128 eventually earned the epithet "America's Technology Highway" for the kind of developments it facilitated; it was also called the "Road to Segregation" because it drew white professionals to outlying areas.[46]

Women as Community Architects and Developers in Lincoln, Massachusetts

As residential developments sprouted to serve the employees of corporations along Route 128, bordering towns adopted zoning regulations, such as minimum lot sizes, to ensure they remained rural in feeling and to discourage tract housing. Like the TAC developments that were part of a larger, but nevertheless limited, resistance to mainstream suburbanization, the town of Lincoln adopted zoning to avoid what residents feared would be an onslaught of developers hastily throwing up identical, cheap, and poorly designed houses—sometimes referred to derisively as *snob zoning*.

In partnership with Constantin Pertzoff, the Cambridge School- and Harvard-educated architect Frances Baxter Quarton contributed to the environmentally conscious growth of two small neighborhoods in Lincoln, where, by the postwar period, a second-growth forest had taken over. The financial backing for the Lincoln developments came from Pertzoff's wife Olga Monks Pertzoff (1911–80), a grandniece of the renowned Boston art collector and patron Isabella Stewart Gardner (1840–24).[47] Soon after their elaborate wedding in 1937 in her palazzo (and eventual museum, named after her), the Pertzoffs purchased fifty acres in Lincoln, where they built a large house with dramatic modern features—flat roofs, white walls, glass block, and ribbon windows. At the same time, it paid tribute to local vernacular architecture in a very particular way, as Pertzoff explained in 1944, by quoting the characteristically New England "geometry" of the regional crisscrossed stone walls in his designs for the patios and walls adjacent to the house. Pertzoff did not claim that the house fit neatly into the landscape, but instead maintained that its relationship with the setting was identical to that established long ago by simple, white geometric farmhouses with "an ungroomed but mellowed landscape."[48] The setting Pertzoff created, essentially a relationship of contrasts, is like those established by Walter Gropius in Lincoln, Eleanor Raymond in Belmont, and Le Corbusier in France.

Whereas the Pertzoffs conceived of their home as a place to graciously entertain Boston's social and cultural elite, Baxter Quarton tailored her house in Lincoln to the needs of her family by employing a modern open plan and expanses of glass overlooking a large yard (see fig. 4.9). Pertzoff and Quarton clients recalled meeting with "Franie" in her kitchen and intimately discussing details of their own modern houses as she tended intermittently to her children. The functionality of her house allowed her simultaneously to work and look after her children, demonstrating the kind of modern house design conducive to a contemporary lifestyle for which the Pertzoff and Quarton firm became locally recognized.

The developments on which the partners collaborated resemble the communities TAC laid out but are smaller in scale and lack the formalized mechanisms to ensure consistent design and rehabilitation of the houses. Of the two neighborhoods on Woodcock Road and Twin Pond Lane, the latter is the better preserved. Culminating in a cul-de-sac, it weaves through a wooded property divided into some ten lots of at least several acres each. Though the landscapes around some houses slope steeply, all the

7.7. Lower-level playroom in the house John and Sarah Pillsbury Harkness designed for their family, 34 Moon Hill Road, Lexington, 1949.

lots were disturbed as little as possible to preserve existing vegetation. This respect for the natural environment was part of the larger organic approach to planning for which Pertzoff advocated in *Architectural Record* in 1944, in an article he coauthored with the Viennese émigré architect and planner Hermann Herrey and his wife, Erna M. J. Herrey (1904–80), a physicist at Queens College in New York.[49] The three argued for urban planning to accommodate both automobile transportation and social life, modeled on such traditional New England centers as Portsmouth and Marblehead, where narrow streets and densely built townhouses encouraged social interaction. The authors were convinced that contemporary cities were too large, overwhelming, and alienating, and that only by remembering that "*an urban community is a living organism*" could planners fix them.[50]

In Lincoln, property buyers were not required to employ the Pertzoff and Quarton firm to design their houses, but in practice it usually happened. As with the TAC developments, the integration of landscape and architecture set the development apart from others, as did the modern concepts applied to the house designs, each customized to the needs and budgets of its owners. The house built in 1963 for Florence Scott Hollingsworth (1896–2006) and Lowell M. Hollingsworth took advantage of its steep site, so that the back of the house, which was approximately 2,500 square feet overall, was three (instead of two) stories high to provide for a four-hundred-square-foot studio in the daylit basement as well as a large, spacious screened porch on the top floor overlooking the wooded property (fig. 7.8).[51] Highly educated and culturally informed, the Hollingsworths exemplified modern house owners in Boston's suburbs after World War II. After they met at Oregon State University, and after he completed his advanced degrees in electrical engineering at Stanford University, the couple relocated to New England in 1946, where he took a job at the Air Force Cambridge Research Center and she began a career as a silversmith and also taught for more than fifty years at the deCordova Museum School in Lincoln.[52] Like other young progressives, the Hollingsworths eschewed tract houses in favor of a larger lot, preserved open space, and more distinctive architecture.

A Modern Community in Pepper Pike, Ohio

As in suburban Boston, the postwar Pepper Ridge development outside of Cleveland in Pepper Pike attracted young, educated, and cultured buyers who sought solutions to the environmental degradation and social isolation that suburbs often brought about. The number-one criterion for joining the community was the fit of the

7.8. Frances Baxter Quarton and Constantin Alexander Pertzoff (1899–1970), house for Lowell M. and Florence Scott Hollingsworth, 18 Twin Pond Lane, Lincoln, Massachusetts, 1963.

family, regardless of race or religion. It makes sense that the community drew the same kind of progressive owners as those at Six Moon Hill, since the two instigators, Robert and Ann Halle Little, had studied architecture, respectively, at Harvard and the Cambridge School, the same institutions attended by the Harkness couple.[53] In fact, it was Little's associations with Gropius and Breuer that reportedly led to a gainful introduction to the Cleveland architect J. Byers Hays. Recognizing their challenge in obtaining approval to build modern houses in a region where the chief developer, the Van Sweringen family, insisted on revival styles, the Cleveland architect was able to lead them to Seth and Frances "Franny" Prindle Taft (1921–2017), a lawyer and art historian who had the wherewithal to support their idea and share in their interest. Together, they were determined to provide "the things that seem desirable for a small community just beyond the noise, smell, and congestion of the city.[54]

By controlling the entire tract and subdividing the land into twelve lots, ranging in size from one to seven acres, they gained a degree of freedom not just in their choice of residents but in the plan and much of the architecture.[55] Each lot was sized and sited to its topographical and environmental disposition, with particular attention given to seasonal sunlight and breezes. Of the eleven original houses, Little designed eight between 1951 and 1957, which gave them a stylistic consistency. The houses designed by others were required to be reviewed by an architecture committee, on which the Littles no doubt were engaged.[56] While the location of each house maximized individual privacy, common land provided for neighborhood recreation, including a swimming pool and tennis court. The "unstuffy" community with nearly thirty children cherished such annual traditions as Christmas caroling, Memorial Day water fights, and Labor Day Olympics. As one "Ridger" recalled, it seemed that "every dog was your dog, every back yard was yours and everybody was your aunt or uncle."[57] It was like living in a "suburban Shangri-la," according to Little.[58]

The five-bedroom house that Little—with the input of his talented wife—designed for the family of four is tucked neatly into a hill under preexisting trees on four acres.[59] The use of stone, wood, and Roman brick—salvaged from a church—made it possible for the front facade and its unassuming entrance to disappear into the landscape. The drama is in the rear of the split-level house, where the two-story living room is visible through sprawling glass panes, said to be the largest available at the time (fig. 7.9). The interior rafters extend outside to support the roof overhangs, calculated to let in winter light and keep out summer sun. The integration of the in- and outside continues with the exterior "wiggle wall" of Roman brick that runs into the living room; in turn, the living room's flagstone flooring is repeated outside on the contoured terraces, reminiscent of the natural features in the living room of Frank Lloyd Wright's Falling Water (1937) house. The materials themselves emphasize the connection between the house and its site, one of the main advantages of suburban planning.

A Community for Dartmouth College Professionals

Another architect couple, Edgar Hayes Hunter Jr. and Margaret King Hunter, envisaged a much smaller community of professionals, though no less inspirational. Unlike the Littles, the Hunters had formally established a professional partnership three years earlier, in 1945, in Hanover, New Hampshire, where he had attended Dartmouth College and had been on the ski team as an undergraduate. Though they found a "lovely" thirty-three-acre site on Hemlock Hill with a panoramic mountain view, neither could afford it, and so the ambitious couple convinced his older brother, Dr. Ralph William Hunter, and his wife to purchase the property in February 1948.[60] The architects then proceeded to lay out roads, identify building sites, and locate neighbors—all of whom would be associated with Dartmouth.[61] The community design shared principles with the projects of the Harknesses and the Littles (the men would have known each other at Harvard): private, wooded lots along with a communal area for socialization. In July 1949 they divided the property into five parcels, each of which was only permitted to have one structure, costing no less than $5,000, and contain no professional office.[62]

They did not stipulate that the houses be modern or that the Hunters design them, although the architect couple did design the first four.[63] An article in *Architectural Record* in November 1953, showing the earliest houses and their plans, illustrates how the Hunters thoughtfully took into consideration the rugged siting and cold climate.[64] Each home was thoroughly modern in its functionality, open plans, materials (both natural and industrial), and integration with the exterior through large windows, and each distinctly responded to the needs of its owners and was constructed with the materials available at that time: fieldstone for the Ralph Hunter house at 17 Hemlock Road; concrete block for the two-story L-shaped house of Dr. O. (Oscar) and Mable H. Staple Sherwin at 14 Hemlock Road; and wood for the house of Dr. Walter Charles Lobitz and Caroline Rockwell Lobitz at 25 Hemlock Road.[65]

The house that the architects built for themselves was probably the first (fig. 7.10). Consisting of two rectangular blocks joined by a narrow hall with stairs, it was erected in two stages: the first block (1950) contained an open-plan space with a step-down study and living room with fireplace, the southern end of which was dramatically cantilevered outside on pilotis; a dining area, enclosed kitchen, and bath. The second block (1953) contained three bedrooms and two baths, with the master bedroom leading out to an eastern terrace. Though they satisfied their objective of developing residential properties that merged natural surroundings with houses using modern

7.9. Rear facade of the Robert and Ann Halle Little house (1950) in the Pepper Ridge development in Pepper Pike, Ohio.

7.10. House designed by Margaret King Hunter and Edgar Hayes Hunter (1914–95) for themselves, 15 Hemlock Road, Lebanon, New Hampshire, 1949. *Molitor collection.*

and traditional elements, the couple could not find enough clients willing to embrace their aesthetic. As King Hunter opined to the *New Hampshire Architect* in March 1953, "Can it possibly be true that New Hampshire is so backward that there is any question about the suitability of contemporary architecture for our times?" For her, the proliferation of ranch houses across the state indicated the lukewarm reception of modern architecture: "It could be called the house type of the timid who want to advance but don't quite dare."[66] Although their house designs had patently contemporary features like flat roofs, expanses of glass, exposed concrete walls, and corrugated metal siding, King Hunter did not see them as foreign to their New Hampshire context: "We are trying to develop an indigenous American architecture. I love genuine old homes, but I think it's a travesty to copy them. We can and must satisfy the needs of today's families with today's architecture."[67] King Hunter rejected copyism, as did other women, but still appreciated historic architecture, while advocating for modern domestic architecture to accommodate contemporary life.

The Design of Crockett Cove in Deer Isle, Maine

Similar ideas were more widely received in resort developments elsewhere in New England, where Route 128 and other highways made it possible for metropolitan residents to reach farther north. Second homes became increasingly common along the seacoast, even in such remote locations as Deer Isle, Maine, where the village of Stonington had once prospered through fishing and granite quarrying. After a bridge was constructed from the mainland in 1939, Deer Isle attracted many more visitors, and among the visual artists to whom it especially appealed was the painter Emily Stewart Lansingh Muir (1904–2003).[68] Lansingh Muir had studied at Vassar College (from where she evidently was encouraged to leave after attending graduation exercises dressed partly in men's clothes) and at the Art Students League of New York. Like Meredith, who also lacked formal training, Lansingh Muir embarked on a small-scale practice designing houses and developments after she relocated there. She began with the home of her parents on the Deer Isle Thoroughfare, followed by a house and studio she shared with her sculptor husband William H. Muir and inhabited for the rest of her life.[69]

Eventually, Lansingh Muir designed some forty-six houses on Deer Isle, thirteen of which were part of a development she laid out on a wooded parcel around Crockett Cove, which she purchased in 1959.[70] Explaining her intention, she said that the houses "turned out contemporary, but they're not copies of anything I ever saw. They're meant to fit the needs of the landscape." Because they were frequently situated in wooded settings—as opposed to open fields, where the original farmhouses

stood—Lansingh Muir adopted a specific tactic of putting "the drama" on the Penobscot Bay side.[71] Thus, soaring walls of glass face the water, while wood siding and other "friendly" materials are on the land sides, echoing the simple vernacular dwellings she admired (figs. 7.11, 7.12). Lansingh Muir's buildings respond to local building traditions, for example, through the prominent use of locally quarried granite for foundations and massive fireplaces, while also mirroring the modern houses in progressive suburban developments.

Her aesthetic complemented her interest in local environmental conservation, and in 1975 she donated one hundred acres to the Nature Conservancy (now the Crockett Cove Woods Preserve). Not only was the land an amenity for the owners of adjacent houses, but it also provided a buffer between the houses she had designed and any future development.[72] The conserved land (including several small islands nearby) is now used for recreation and contributes to Lansingh Muir's legacy as an architect who blended modern design concepts with environmental preservation.[73] Her approach to modern architecture, as well as her respect for nature, places Lansingh Muir in a tradition of women designers of communities for both full-time residence and leisure.

7.11. Emily Stewart Lansingh Muir, house for Robert J. and Dorothy H. Ralston, 129 Barbour Farm Road, Stonington, Maine, 1968.

7.12. Robert J. and Dorothy H. Ralston house interior.

CHAPTER VIII

Singular Statements

A DREAM FOR MANY NEOPHYTE ARCHITECTS IS TO FIND a patron who can fund a pivotal building that will lead to further commissions and the creation of a signature aesthetic. London architect Alison Brooks (b. 1962) underscored this ambition when she wrote, in 2011, "I believe producing one seminal house project is the best preparation for a lifetime's body of work."[1] For women architects, that "one" early and definitive commission often came from families or friends who provided opportunities for them to explore their approach to Modernism. Both Sarah Pillsbury and Suzanne Stockard, for example, designed vacation homes for their parents in Duxbury, Massachusetts, and Tyron, North Carolina, respectively, when still in (or barely out of) the Cambridge School—but such commissions were rare for women.

For male architects, commissions tended to come more easily. An exceptional first project that impressed just about everyone is the four-bedroom bachelor house (now owned by Harvard) that Philip Johnson designed and funded for himself at 9 Ash Street, the likes of which Cambridge had not seen before its completion in 1942.[2] Though its standardized plywood components went no further in his future work, the Miesian discipline of regulated, formal perfection in which nothing was "casual" or "accidental," according to *Architectural Forum*, was the germ of his masterpiece, the Glass House (1949), in New Canaan, Connecticut, completed seven years later.[3]

Women architects fortunate enough to design a noteworthy building during their formative professional years rarely had the follow-up opportunities of their male counterparts. Thus, the number of "singular statements" of women, especially for secondary homes, seems disproportionate to those of men. Nonetheless, in these one-offs, women could express how they saw themselves as designers, how they could use modern design to solve contemporary problems, and how they could employ its concepts to facilitate more open-ended social roles, in contrast to the previous century, when interiors seemed staged and forced a person to play a certain part, as Eleanor Raymond observed.[4]

For many women, making modern architecture that fulfilled their needs, or those of their clients, was more important than meeting a set of formal criteria. The hanging garden tools in figure 3.8 epitomize this perspective in that their purposeful arrangement not only shows Raymond and Power's esteem for beauty but also utility. As a functional aesthetic, the groupings are reminiscent of MoMA's annual *Useful Objects* exhibitions (1938–49), where " 'ordinary' consumer products were given pride of place."[5] Many women architects were unpersuaded by Henry-Russell Hitchcock and Philip Johnson's formalist

Detail of figure 8.2. House designed by Barbara Webb Rockwell, Upper Jaffrey Road, Dublin, New Hampshire.

recipe for International Style architecture, because it appeared to them cold and unwelcoming. Instead, and as their designs and arrangements reveal, Modernism was an all-encompassing ethos that guided every aspect of how to engage with the material world.

Though the singular works presented in this chapter vary in size, purpose, style, and patronage, they are alike in that they are at once autobiographies and assessments of Modernism. Together, they do not add up to a distinct variant of Modernism, nor are they entry points for discussing full-blown careers in the way of Johnson's work. Still, they belong in the history of Modernism because they provide crucial glimpses into the philosophies, priorities, and influences of women architects—even when they were unable to build upon that *one* project to produce a lifetime's body of work.

Rural Vernacular Retreats

The democratization of leisure along with increased disposable income and time in the early twentieth century presented unprecedented building opportunities for women, even if only for simple one-room structures. Mary Linder Putnam (1905–37) and her husband Patrick Tracy Lowell Putnam, for example, anticipated that venturesome travelers would be drawn to the "camp" they built in the early 1930s on a rise overlooking the Epulu River in the macrolobium forest in the Belgian Congo.[6] Linder Putnam had attended Smith College before studying at the Cambridge School, in 1928, where she proved herself capable in landscape design.[7] She then worked for the established modernist landscape architect Fletcher Steele, a trustee of the school, before marrying Putnam in 1933 and moving shortly thereafter to Central Africa. Because of her premature death, Linder Putnum did not make a significant professional contribution, but, nevertheless, their "Camp on the Epulu" as it was called, demonstrates her appreciation for certain aspects of Modernism—functionalism, an honest use of organic materials, and a fusion with nature.[8]

Her husband initially had traveled to Africa in 1927 as part of a Harvard College expedition to the source of the Niger River. Due to a yellow-fever quarantine, the group diverted to the Ituri forest, where Putnam was nearly killed by an elephant. Because of the care he received from indigenous inhabitants, he was inspired to establish a settlement to facilitate their medical care.[9] With his new wife,

8.1. Mary Farlow Linder Putnam, map in the pamphlet *Our Camp on the Epulu in the Belgian Congo*, c. 1935. *Special Collections, Field Museum of Natural History.*

he also wanted to create a place for travelers with "several small sleeping bungalows, each with a bathroom and a large living room-veranda."[10] The pamphlet they designed assured potential visitors it was not a "Grand Hotel" or "tourist resort," but rather a comfortable accommodation (fig. 8.1).[11]

They constructed their buildings "exactly as the American pioneers" did, by using logs—tied, instead of nailed together, as Linder Putnam proudly reported to Cambridge School alumnae.[12] The main building contained a living room "of excellent proportions" with a raised hearth at its center, from which the smoke wafted through the thatched roof. Their "comfortable armchairs" and "antelope skins or beautifully designed fibre mats," as well as ethnographic objects embellished their unassuming but attractive space. Period photographs and descriptions comment on how their regional decor, including vases with flowers, evidenced "Mrs. Putnam's taste." The adjoining guest rooms and bathrooms were also said to be appealing.[13] Although Linder Putnam saw only the main

8.2. Alice Dodge Osborn Brown standing at her house designed by Barbara Webb Rockwell, Upper Jaffrey Road, Dublin, New Hampshire, 1953. *Private collection.*

building completed before she died from pneumonia on a return trip to Massachusetts, their effort was celebrated, widely discussed, and written about in the American press. While not modern in the sense of Machine Age materials and forms, the visual emphasis on straightforward vernacular construction, an approach grounded in nineteenth-century architecture practice and theory, would have appealed to those familiar with modern design.[14]

Another unassuming resort project, this one by Barbara Webb Rockwell (1916–91), also a Cambridge School alumna, demonstrates that even the smallest commission could allow an architect to be creative. The house she designed for "her dear cousin" in Jaffrey, a White Mountains resort area in New Hampshire, is notable not so much for the overall composition, but rather for its two guileless elements—large picture windows and a massive fireplace cutting across the front corner of the living and dining area (fig. 8.2). Designed in 1952–53, the project met the requirements of the owner, Alice Dodge Osborn Brown and her husband Newell, for "part camp, part a summer house," with only two bedrooms to accommodate themselves and their five children.[15] The two essential features of the house outwardly proclaim their intentions: to congregate the family around the hearth while relishing extensive mountain views. While Webb Rockwell went on to develop a modest New England practice to the late 1970s, this house is the project most esteemed by her descendants.

Faith Bemis also designed a building for her family. In fact, as labeled on the blueprint title blocks, it was a "STUDIO AT S^o TAMWORTH / FOR / MR. A. F. BEMIS," her father, who had encouraged all seven of his children to build a structure on their property in New Hampshire (fig. 8.3). Dubbed "Ski-High" for its location atop a "good" slope for skiing, the building was composed of old lumber from two vernacular barns, whose steep roofs and board siding would have been an inspiration. Dominated by a large room with "big tables," the interior also had an alcove with a massive brick hearth on the western end that could be closed off by an Indian cotton curtain. French doors on the northern side opened onto an "always cool porch" with a "magnificent view," and prominent sash windows were on the southern side. As a retreat shared by father and daughter, the venture was the only one Faith Bemis could call her own, even though the following year she would design the drafting room addition at the Cambridge School under the eyes of Eleanor Raymond and Henry Frost.[16]

Two other vacation retreats by Cambridge School alumnae reiterate the desire of women architects to construct their own recreational spaces. Louisa Vaughan Conrad, for example, shared with her husband the resourceful one-room haven that she built on a hill on the island of San Lucia in the West Indies (fig. 8.4). Primarily composed of traditional natural materials—uncut stone and wood shingles—the graceful conical tented roof not only augmented air flow and provided shade, but governed the aesthetic itself. No less innovative is the functional aesthetic that Sarah Pillsbury Harkness constructed on Squam Lake in New Hampshire. The "gazebo," as the family called it, consisted of a hip roof over canvas walls that could be rolled up in good weather. A woodburning stove and kerosene lamps allowed Pillsbury Harkness to gather with her seven children while also painting the beautiful landscape. While none of these dwellings are outwardly modern, they facilitated an uninterrupted experience with nature and, with their functionality, maximized recreation time with families and friends.

Conspicuous Modernism

Amaza Lee Meredith and her partner Edna Meade Colson obviously intended their home, called Azurest South, to stand out against the adjacent traditional brick-fronted buildings at Virginia State University in Blacksburg, where both women were faculty (figs. 8.5, 8.6; see fig. c.3). Completed in 1939, the house's forthright interpretation of the International Style—evident in the flat roof, unadorned white walls, metal-sash windows, and glass blocks—is

8.3. Faith Gregg Bemis, Ski-High, South Tamworth, New Hampshire, c. 1926.

even more pioneering for having been produced by Meredith, who was self-taught. Its rejection of the traditional architecture that predominated at the historically Black institution created an educational tool for Meredith to use in art class.

In many respects, Azurest South is comparable to the house of Walter Gropius, completed a year earlier in Lincoln, Massachusetts—as a modern showcase, as a place to entertain students and colleagues, and as a studio for artistic production (see fig. 1.7).[17] But whereas the Gropius house and its land was funded by Helen Osborne Storrow so that Americans could "see what the German émigré might do," Meredith and Colson lacked patronage.[18] Frankly, their approach was too unfamiliar to most Virginians, whose residential architecture generally engaged the historic Colonial or Tudor styles. Consequently, Meredith never built another house like Azurest South.

The house Elizabeth Wiley Dunlap completed in 1933 in Knoxville, Tennessee, was also vanguard in an architecturally conservative region (see fig. 1.11).[19] The project demanded that Wiley Dunlap venture outside of her formal education—at Smith College, where she received a degree in horticulture in 1918, and at the Cambridge School, where she studied landscape architecture.[20] She continued her education informally when, in 1922, she made an extended trip to Europe with the artist Augusta St. Gaudens to survey landscape architecture, which, at least in her hometown, was considered noteworthy since it was one of the "new fields of the profession for women."[21] Following the tour, where she made a special study of parks and cemeteries, and where she met landscape architect Hobart Delancy Dunlap, whom she married in 1923, Wiley Dunlap practiced landscape architecture and was "busy drawing plans" for a Tudor-style house at 934 Scenic Drive in the prestigious Sequoyah Hills neighborhood, which she occupied with her family beginning in 1927.[22] However, it was the second house Wiley Dunlap built for her family on the same street that locally established her newfound identity as an architect "in the modern manner."[23] Obviously pleased with the result, she exhibited photographs of it in a 1938 art exhibition for Smith College alumnae and in a Cambridge School brochure.[24]

The house bears similarity to the Stran-Steel house by Detroit architects H. (Henry) Augustus O'Dell and Wirt C. (Clinton) Roland that Wiley Dunlap observed in the *Homes of Tomorrow* exhibition at the Century of Progress in Chicago (1933).[25] A local newspaper reported that she had been "encouraged in her desire for a modern home after seeing how lovely [were] some of those at the Fair, which were built with liveableness as their first consideration."[26] During the Depression, these so-called miracle houses generated excitement for their ability to accommodate the relaxed form of family life then taking shape in developing suburbs.[27] Most dreams of homebuilding were deferred until after World War II, but the Dunlaps' financial resources facilitated their project. In Knoxville, where historic styles predominated, Wiley Dunlap's stripped-down design inspired by the Art Deco style was daring. Like the Stran-Steel house, its white facade pays homage to traditional architecture with rigorous symmetry and organization into three parts, although a projecting center entrance bay gives the composition the spirit of eighteenth-century Neoclassicism. In contrast, on the more private rear side, Wiley Dunlap was free to place window and door openings in locations that functioned best, rather than conforming to a symmetrical pattern (fig. 8.7).[28] The family adored their avant-garde house, but it did not lead to future commissions.

Carina Eaglesfield Mortimer (Milligan; 1890–1978) similarly introduced modern concepts into a conventional culture in New Haven, Connecticut. Though her own house (1925) at 300 Odgen Street indulged historicist idioms, as much of her work did, the stand-out house by Eaglesfield Mortimer was for Richard Foster Flint, a

8.4. Louisa Vaughan Conrad, vacation house, St. Lucia, West Indies, c. 1960. *Private collection.*

8.5. Amaza Lee Meredith, Azurest South (now the Virginia State University Alumni House, 87 Boissean Street, Petersburg, Virginia, 1939.

Yale professor and pioneer in the field of glaciation and Quaternary-period geology, and his wife Margaret Cecil Haggott Flint (1899–1977), active in interior design and historic preservation.[29] When Eaglesfield Mortimer designed this non-traditional two-story house in 1936, the Flints were in their thirties and evidently open to Modernism, as they built the first modern house in the area (fig. 8.8).[30] The year after its completion, *Architectural Forum* characterized the Flint house as a combination of "traditional and modern forms" that "leans more toward the modern."[31] The nearly square plan and austere exterior enhances its rectangularity, relieved only by the semicircular roof over the front entrance and the curved dining room bay on the side. Four courses of projecting bricks between the first and second stories give a streamlined moderne quality. Although the overall mass of the restrained design is complemented by a conventional hipped roof, relating to New England Federal-style architecture, the house was a bold move for Eaglesfield Mortimer.

She had been in her early thirties when she attended the Cambridge School, in 1921–22, so it is not surprising that she left without graduating to marry and settle in New Haven.[32] First working out of her home and later sharing a professional office with the Canadian-born architect Louis Eugene Jallade, she received her membership in the American Institute of Architects (AIA) in 1930.[33] She also studied architecture at Yale, again without obtaining a degree. The recommendation by Frost in 1937, in which he stated, "It is hard to judge a person whose training has been so irregular," adding that she had "developed a practice rather earlier than we would consider wise," is understandable.[34]

She was one of the fortunate ones to have had first-hand knowledge of European Modernism from yearly trips in the 1920s to Paris, where she once visited Le Corbusier. He provided introductions to Leo Stein, whose house at Garches was designed by Le Corbusier between 1926 and 1928, the first she had ever seen "set up on stilts,"

8.6. Detail of the glass-block construction in Azurest South, 1939.

8.7. Rear facade of the Hobart Delancy and Elizabeth Wiley Dunlap house, 1079 Scenic Drive, Knoxville, 1935. *Private collection.*

8.8. Carina Eaglesfield Mortimer, Richard and Margaret Haggott Flint house, 265 Bradley Street, New Haven, Connecticut, 1936. *New Haven Preservation Trust.*

8.9. Carina Eaglesfield Mortimer, rear facade of Windy Hill, the house of Van Wyck and Eleanor Stimson Brooks, 16 Old Weston Road, Weston, Connecticut, c. 1940.

as she recounted.[35] While she considered Le Corbusier "a gifted engineer" (he was not trained as such), she did not believe him to be a "real" architect. Still, Eaglesfield Mortimer conceded that "a beauty showed in the very honest[y] and clarity" of his designs, an image she took home and incorporated into her own residential vocabulary.[36]

The Flint house led to one other modern house commission by Eaglesfield Mortimer for Van Wyck Brooks, a renowned literary historian and critic, and his wife, Eleanor Stimson Brooks, a translator of books by French authors (fig. 8.9).[37] The couple decided to relocate from their modest wood-frame house in Westport, Connecticut, to the adjacent town of Weston, following the publication of his highly-awarded book *The Flowering of New England, 1815–1865* (1936). Their new house followed the approach of the Flint house, except that it was larger, starker, and patently cubic. The main block is a two-story rectangular mass with a hipped roof, but there is just one projecting brick course (instead of two) between the stories, making the walls look more planar than those of the Flint house. While it too has elements recalling the Federal period, they are simpler, exemplified by the three Palladian-style windows above the center entrance and by the sidelights flanking the front door, in the manner of the New England vernacular of the early National period (1789–1837).

As one of only seventeen women (and one of four Cambridge School alumnae) whose work was illustrated in the feature "A Thousand Women in Architecture" in *Architectural Record* (part II, June 1948), Eaglesfield Mortimer epitomized successful women architects, underscored by the Gallery of Fine Arts at Yale, which in 1938 showed her Connecticut work (along with that of Theodate Pope Riddle and Cambridge School alumna Bertha Mather McPherson). Nonetheless, Eaglesfield Mortimer maintained it was "a Man's world," writing, "The dedication the profession [of architecture] requires is more suited to a man—I have never put it first as a man does and should [do]."[38] Given her outlook on gender as well as the prevalent discrimination in the profession and societal expectations for women at the time, it would have been impossible for Eaglesfield Mortimer to parlay her career on a par with her architect neighbors in New Canaan, where she later built a "one-story contemporary retirement home."[39] She put herself in a hotbed of Modernism, populated by the likes of Philip Johnson, Marcel Breuer, and

Eliot Noyes, but she refused to present herself solely as a modernist.[40] Instead, she took enormous pride in maintaining cordial relationships with a wide variety of clients who appreciated her eclectic approach to architecture, and as a result, she had a steady stream of commissions.

Jean League Newton was more dedicated than Eaglesfield Mortimer to integrating Modernism into the buildings she designed in Macon, Georgia, with her mother, Ellamae Ellis League. The house they conceived for her brother Joseph and his wife Mary Jane League in about 1950 announced their unconventional and innovative approach (fig. 8.10). Though topped with a shallow-pitched gabled roof to match the local context of traditional houses, it was more contemporary than its neighbors since it is set back from the street on an ample lot. Moreso, it is an early adaptation of the low-slung, one-story ranch house, a type already familiar in Georgia, usually covered in a local red brick to correspond with earlier houses. The mother-daughter team departed from the vernacular by cladding the League house in the redwood siding associated with contemporary California ranch houses.[41] This novel approach likely came from League Newton who had written to her mother from Cambridge in 1942: "I finally got to see that grouping of houses out in Lincoln that Gropius and Breuer and Bogner built for themselves. You know who I like though? That man out in California—William Wurster—Some of his houses look like they'd be such fun to live in."[42] Undoubtedly, League Newton was attracted to Wurster's aesthetic for its ability to incorporate local conditions and respond to contemporary concepts of domestic life.

The League house further departs from local conventions in its innovative H-shaped plan, consisting of two long masses paralleling the street. After being published in *Progressive Architecture* in 1953, it was praised by Katherine Morrow Ford and Thomas H. Creighton in *Quality Budget Houses* (1954) for its open and flexible configuration: "Note how the living room, dining room and terrace … are all comparatively small spaces, but they are planned so that all three can be opened and used together for entertaining a large group."[43] In addition, the expansive windows and glass doors could be opened to the terraces and to the landscape beyond, as in the California houses.[44]

The house Elisabeth Coit built in 1937 in Pound Ridge, New York, also conspicuously breaks from local design traditions. Its idiosyncrasy may result from the objectives of the owner, Clara Delafield Sturges Johnson (1877–1969), a middle-aged divorcee.[45] Her former husband, William Templeton Johnson, was an architect whose San Diego practice included houses that complied with the Spanish-inspired eclectic style in California, denoted by red-tiled roofs and warm-toned stucco walls.[46] Sturges Johnson's house was far different from those produced by him—and perhaps that was the point.

Described by one critic as the "most interesting design" among Coit's residential projects, the house is made of concrete block that give its stark geometry a

8.10. Ellamae Ellis League and Jean League Newton, Joseph and Mary Jane League house, 1849 Waverland Drive, Macon, Georgia, 1950.

8.11. Elisabeth Coit, front facade of the Clara Delafield Sturges Johnson house, South Salem Road, Pound Ridge, New York, 1937. *Coit Papers.*

forlorn appearance (figs. 8.11, 8.12).[47] Its location on a rock outcropping explains some of its eccentricities inside, but certainly not all. The first-floor plan radically departs from those typical of large New England houses, in that the most central space, traditionally given to the hall, is taken up by a bedroom and bath; the staircase is pushed to the rear; and the kitchen, usually at the back of the house, is on the front. There is no dining room or any dedicated space for eating. In fact, the main entrance leads directly into what looks like a pantry, connecting to the kitchen. Formal entertainment, or even the reception of guests, could not have been a consideration in the plan, given the perplexing pattern of circulation.

Coit was able to give the patron the functional plan she wanted, but she did not build anything like it again. In fact, the house is so unusual that the town still does not recognize it for what it is: a pathbreaking work that was several years in advance of what have been identified (erroneously) as the "first modern houses" in Pound Ridge.[48]

An Expressionist's Home

Elizabeth Hirsh Fleisher and her landscape architect husband, Horace Fleisher built themselves a house they called "Tulipwood" in Philadelphia that was unique in the way it reveals their modern sensibility. Described in 1956 as "distinguished" in the Pittsburgh Architectural Club's journal, the house hugs the landscape beneath its flat roof and, typical of the period, features expansive windows as well as a patio for outdoor living. As modern as the house is, it also incorporates scattered stone walls to connect it with local building traditions.[49]

The most distinctive interior space is the living room, where an amoebic sofa by Vladimir Kagan, a German-born émigré who launched his signature furniture collection in Manhattan in 1949, is offset by an expressionistic sculpted wood fireplace wall by Wharton Esherick, a renowned Philadelphia artist and a leader of the studio craft movement (fig. 8.13). The room was the subject of careful consideration, beginning in 1953, when Hirsh Fleisher wrote to Esherick explaining that she and her husband were "much taken" with the random pattern in the wall boards and that the work would "be a source of deep and abiding satisfaction" in their home.[50] Esherick made a model of the wall before commencing on the actual construction, presumably for approval by the Fleishers. The final product differs in one important aspect from the model in that instead of being perfectly horizontal, the top edge of the firebox slopes dramatically downward to the right, a change that enhances its dynamic quality.

Just as the dynamic, stepped profile and protruding bays added liveliness to the Parkway House, which Hirsh Fleisher had recently completed with her partner Gabriel

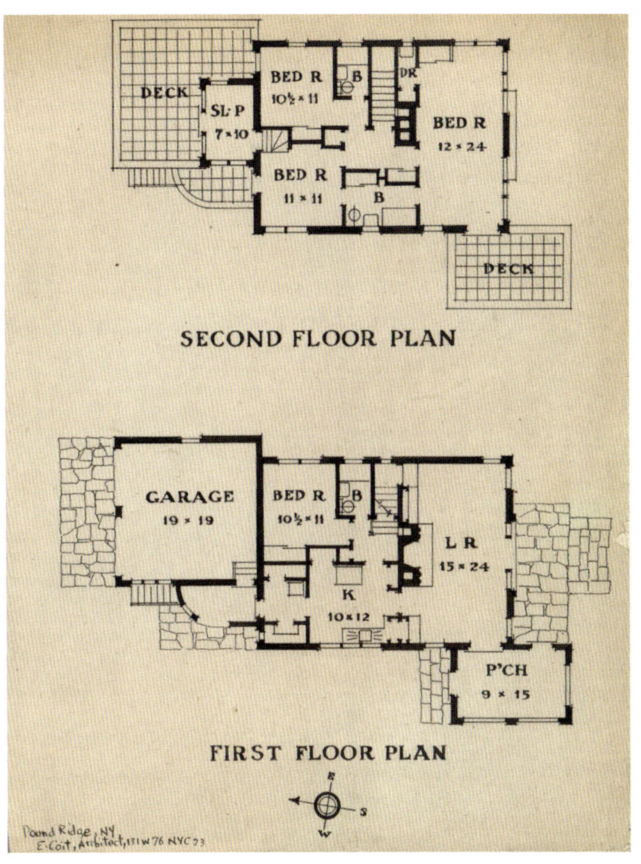

Roth, the Expressionist quality of the fireplace wall and curved sofa also offset the boxlike shape of the living room. Hirsh Fleisher was pleased with the outcome of the room, though she and Esherick locked horns over its expense of $1,400 (nearly double the original estimate). The living room would have been an enormous investment: combined with the price of the Kagan sofa, at $1,300, the two decorative features cost almost as much as a car or about a third of the average house at the time. Nonetheless, in this one room, Hirsh Fleisher privately demonstrated the Expressionist approach she adopted in more public work.

The brick rowhouse Anne Tyng redesigned for herself in the Filter Square neighborhood of Philadelphia was also a magnum opus (fig. 8.14). Before she began her decade-long project in 1960, however, Tyng had experimented with her ideas about space frame construction in the renovation of the house of her parents in Cambridge, Maryland, which received an honorable mention from the Philadelphia chapter of the AIA. The original farmhouse, typical of vernacular architecture in the Northeast, is one-and-a-half-stories in height with a steeply pitched gable roof with dormers. In her renovation (1949–51),

8.12. Elisabeth Coit, floorplan of the Clara Delafield Sturges Johnson house, 1937. *Coit Papers.*

8.13. Living room fireplace wall by Wharton Esherick (1887–1970) in the house designed by Elizabeth Hirsh Fleisher and landscaped by Horace Teller Fleisher (1887–1964) for themselves, 4030 Apalogen Road, Philadelphia, c. 1953. *Wharton Esherick Museum.*

8.14. Anne Tyng house, 2511 Waverly Street, Philadelphia, c. 1970. *Tyng Collection.*

8.15. Anne Tyng house interior, 2511 Waverly Street, Philadelphia, c. 1970. *Tyng Collection.*

Tyng extended the geometric structural frame to the exterior, where it announces the underlying concept. As Tyng herself described the project, "The Walworth Tyng house was built as a total space-frame structure, a consistent geometry that harbors living space within itself and extends in apparently random asymmetry to form dormer windows, trellises and entrance balcony. It demonstrates that the space frame lends itself to a domestic building with structural economy, flexibility and hierarchy of scale."[51]

The integration of the local vernacular with sophisticated architectural design is also dramatized in her Philadelphia home. The rowhouse itself typifies others in the city, though hers was among the smaller ones, at about 1,300 square feet, and it only had a few small rooms on each of the two stories. Her addition of a third story to the house increased its size, functionality, and distinctiveness, while at the same time it essentially remained within the scale and spirit of the neighborhood, since the new boxy mansard roof disguises the space within the geometric frame. Concerned with functionality, inside Tyng minimized the sizes of the kitchen appliances, for example, and maximized light and storage, both notoriously in short supply in historic buildings (fig. 8.15).

As functional as Tyng's house was for her, it must have been satisfying to see her spatial concepts take shape and then to live within them. Tyng worked on the design just when she began Jungian analysis, a process that she believed brought her greater consciousness and made her "feel less a victim of circumstances."[52] She understood the inherent conflict in attempting to convey her own ideas while serving as a muse to Louis Kahn: "I find that in addition to the role of mother, the physical vessel for creating new life traditionally named for the father, and the role of muse, the symbolic vessel for inspiring creations identified as the man's, there is the even more difficult role of individuation, of creativity toward self-identity."[53] Her own house stands as a nearly unique example in built form of the artistic identity Tyng struggled to express.

Singular Reinventions

In the silo house (so named for its form) in Charlottesville, Virginia, Mary Palache Gregory (1902–96) similarly articulated her interest in both modern and vernacular architecture, though she did not have an opportunity to create this one outstanding work until some twenty-five years after she attended the Cambridge School (figs. 8.16, 8.17).[54] Like her modernist contemporaries, Palache Gregory professed inspiration from Frank Lloyd Wright and Le Corbusier. She was probably amenable to their work in part because of her undergraduate experience at Bryn

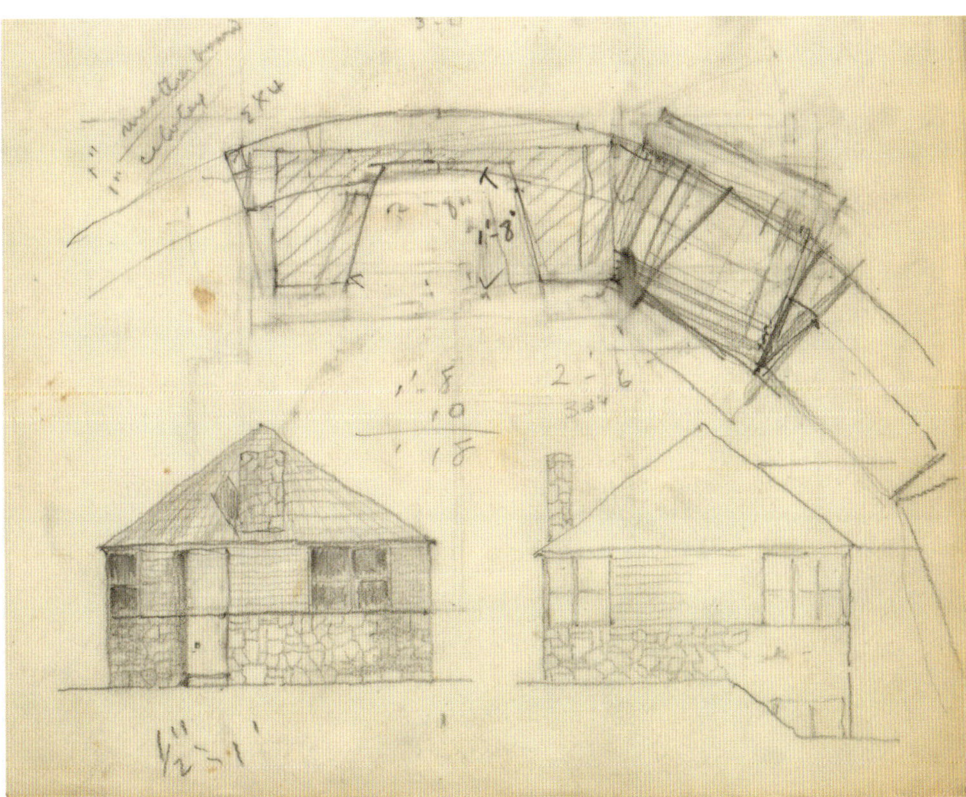

8.16. Mary Palache Gregory, silo house, 5 Orchard Road, Charlottesville, Virginia, c. 1950.

8.17. Mary Palache Gregory, drawing of the silo house, c. 1950. *Palache Gregory files, Papers of the Palache Family, Schlesinger Library.*

Mawr, where in 1913 Georgiana Goddard King (1871–1939) founded the art history department. King was renowned for her scholarship on medieval Spanish architecture, but she was also an enthusiast of modern art, teaching courses on Cubism and Fauvism as early as 1912, the year she confided to Gertrude Stein (1874–1946)—whose literary work she taught at Bryn Mawr—that she was struggling to comprehend the transition of Pablo Picasso to Cubism.[55] King was familiar with the exemplary modern art collection of the Steins and even tried to convince Leo Stein to teach a course on modern art at Bryn Mawr in 1919, without success.[56] As a pioneering modernist, King influenced Palache Gregory, as she recalled in a talk during an alumnae weekend, a quarter century after graduating. She vividly described King's "exacting" art appreciation course: "Of course the real stimulus was the remarkable and unpredictable personality of Miss King, her wide and diverse background of knowledge and her enigmatic way of throwing out hints and clues."[57]

In her early career, Palache Gregory worked in the Washington, DC offices of Cambridge School alumnae Rose Greely and Gertrude Sawyer. While nothing is known about her production at that time, in 1927–28 she had a six-month stint in the New York firm of Harrie Thomas Lindeberg, best known for his opulent houses in historic styles.[58] Her employment came to a "sudden" end after she asked for a modest pay increase.[59] Leaving the office was "no disappointment," however, although she was left scrambling for a job "without having made provisions." As she was leaving, "Bill the office boy" wished her "good luck—get a *good* job next time."[60] She did just that and in 1928–29 returned to landscape architecture in the more prominent firm led by a woman, Beatrix Cadwalader Farrand (1872–1959).

Palache Gregory's professional work, however, was interrupted by her husband's blossoming career as a legal scholar: he taught for a brief period at the University of Wisconsin; then between 1930 and 1948 at the University of Chicago; and beginning in 1949, at the University of Virginia, where he was known as "Mr. Torts" until his retirement in 1967.[61] While also devoted to raising their two children, Palache Gregory never lost her affinity for architecture: one of the highlights of their time in Wisconsin was their proximity to Taliesin, Wright's house and studio.[62]

An article about her landscape painting, published when Palache Gregory was in her seventies, reported that she "did not take up architecture professionally."[63] This assessment, however, contradicts an earlier description in the 1950s that said she renovated a nineteenth-century cottage called the Deanery (now demolished) for Bryn Mawr alumnae: as the chair of long-range planning explained, Palache Gregory had "wide architectural experience" and had "done much independent architectural work in the designing of new houses and the altering of old ones."[64] Other than the Thorndike Club in Jaffrey, where the family summered and where she "ingeniously" used "materials from the old clubhouse to stay within the budget," little is known of her work in the 1950s.[65] The drawings and correspondence that do survive in the Palache family papers have a gap between her early and late years, most likely reflecting the period in the 1930s when she was raising children.[66]

Nonetheless, when Palache Gregory accompanied her husband on a trip to Australia in 1953, she spoke on a radio program about the superiority of women in residential design, stating that "every big architecture firm should have a woman on its staff." Another newspaper reported that her ambition was to "to advise people before they build."[67] At about the same time, Palache Gregory gave a talk to the American Association of University Women chapter in Charlottesville in which she touched on some similar themes, advising them to pay close attention to the house-planning phase.[68]

Significantly, in her autobiographical notes, Palache Gregory referred to only one built project: the farmhouse she redesigned for her husband and herself in Charlottesville.[69] When looking for a house, reported Palache Gregory, real estate brokers took her to "big clumsy oldfashioned [*sic*] houses within the city limits" as well as to "very innocent looking but still—to me—unattractive suburban developments." She shunned pretentious historic estates but "fell in love with" an old farmhouse, which she later described as "a neglected frame building set amid a grove of large oak trees."[70] The Gregorys purchased the property in 1949, and she renovated the farmhouse for her family's use during their eighteen-year residency.

Among the outbuildings was the grain silo that Palache Gregory decided to convert into a residence for her elderly father-in-law. Its sensibility parallels earlier projects by modernists that show a fascination with masonry silos, recalling Le Corbusier's praises of "American grain elevators and factories" as the "FIRST-FRUITS of the new age" in *Vers une architecture*.[71] His comment was not

8.18. Apartment of Natalie Swan Rahv, 23 Fayette Street, Boston, c. 1960. *Richard Kelly Papers, Manuscripts and Archives, Yale University.*

about the more traditional, smaller-scale silos like the one Palache Gregory turned into a house but rather about the massive concrete structures that served industrialized agricultural production. Still, Le Corbusier's praise of grain elevators as simplified geometric forms (cylinders) apparently informed Palache Gregory's point of view, given her comment that when a house is adapted to the needs of its inhabitants it provides the "means of attaining a way of life, as Le Corbusier argued it should."[72]

Although her silo house was original for Virginia, where the Colonial style predominated, it did not further the career of Palache Gregory. It is impossible to know what her professional ambition was at that point, but she undoubtedly encountered the same obstacles other women did when they attempted reentry after a hiatus. Thus, the silo house stands as her singular reinvention of vernacular traditions for modern living.

In another revitalization project, the Bauhaus-influenced architect Nathalie Swan Rahv adapted that modern idiom to her own Boston apartment (fig. 8.18).[73] Located in an 1840s row house in the Bay Village neighborhood, her home was a "delightful shock," according to the *Boston Globe* in 1962, because of its contrasting interior: a traditional mellow-red brick wall running the length of the skylighted sixteen-foot-high living room provided a dramatic backdrop for such modern furnishings as two Austrian linen-fold shades, curved at the top. The few other essentials in the "luxury of spaciousness" were low, narrow, and rectangular, including a diamond chair by Harry Bertoia and a "Homage to the Square" print by Josef Albers, a former Bauhaus instructor, positioned with "great restraint" along with items by Michael Thonet and Hans Wegner. The space articulated the philosophy that Swan Rahv described in an earlier editorial in the *New York Times*, where she argues that the Bauhaus was not a style but rather "a conglomeration of the principles and methods of various art cliques in Europe, groups who were working and influencing European art education before the Bauhaus was conceived and whose work continued during and after the Bauhaus."[74]

Swan Rahv's earlier exposure to German art when she attended the Bauhaus in 1933 undoubtedly inspired her space, in which the furnishings were both visual and stylistic expressions of Modernism. At the same time, the exposed brick wall in her living room was a common feature of renovated nineteenth-century houses and apartments throughout the gentrified historic districts of American cities. Even old brick expresses modern preferences in that it reveals the underlying structure that earlier finishes obscured. Swan Rahv's apartment was far from her only architectural project, but she preferred to work under the guise of male-led firms, where her own name was relatively anonymous.[75] Thus, the Boston apartment is the one known example of her own approach to design. Moreover, it is singular as a portrait of its owner—a travelogue of sorts—since Swan Rahv furnished it with canonical objects that spoke to her experience with European avant-garde culture.

A Brutalist Home

Well into the postwar period, women continued to adapt Modernism to reinvent the American home, and, in the case of one (now lost) example, to reconceive domesticity entirely. In 1965, the architect Mary Otis Stevens (b. 1928) and her husband and professional partner, Thomas Frederick McNulty, built for themselves a residence called the Lincoln House—named after the Massachusetts town in which it was located (fig. 8.19). Likely the earliest house in the country constructed of exposed concrete and glass, the house is a pioneering translation of the Brutalist style that more often was applied in institutional contexts.[76]

Stevens received her undergraduate degree in 1949 from Smith College and, following a short stint in New York, where she studied drafting, she was accepted to MIT. She delayed her matriculation in architecture there until 1953, due to her first, short-lived marriage, but when she

8.19. Julius Shulman (1910–2009), photograph of Lincoln House (now demolished), designed in 1965 by Mary Otis Stevens and Thomas Frederick McNulty (1919–85) for themselves, 71 Weston Road, Lincoln, Massachusetts, 1970. *Julius Shulman Photography Archive.*

finally arrived, she reconnected with her childhood mentor and friend, the architect-inventor Buckminster Fuller, as well as with the renowned Harvard historian Samuel Eliot Morison, to whom she was distantly related. Her network was expanded by McNulty, who was teaching at MIT and whom Stevens married in 1958.[77] Stevens subsequently developed a radical proposal for reinventing what she perceived as the obsolete model of American domestic architecture. Her "critical domesticity," as she called her approach, took shape in the Lincoln House, which Stevens described decades after its construction as a manifesto for the reform of domestic life and family relations:

> *I was against ordinary American domesticity. I didn't want my children to grow up in the conventional restrictive environment I had been brought up in. This was the '60s. I wanted my sons to be part of the flow of life. Before the industrial revolution, children and adults had shared a common life, and I wanted my children to be able to leave the child world and enter adult life when they wanted. The children's quarters and the parents' quarters were always open. There was no difference in the living standard. Here was democracy. There was freedom and individuality, but also community. The individual and the community should be nourishing each other and be held in balance.*[78]

The openness to which Stevens alludes resulted from the avoidance of interior walls, a characteristic that occasionally stunned visitors. Although open plans are celebrated in modern houses, the integrated spaces in the Lincoln House suggested, as Susana Torre observed, "a life-style lacking in propriety, where the conventional meaning of privacy was profoundly contradicted."[79] Stevens intended to overturn traditional norms of privacy in domestic space, which she believed isolated its inhabitants.[80] Thus, the Lincoln House was composed of curved walls and glass shapes to frame the exterior rather than enclose the interior; it seems more like a piece of minimalist sculpture than a dwelling. Outside, the simplified, massive concrete forms change the quality of the environment as they swirl outward like a work of contemporary land art.

When in 1970 Julius Shulman photographed the house for a front-page article in the *Los Angeles Times*, it was recognized as an iconic expression of a countercultural reinvention of the American home.[81] Even though it was the architect couple's most celebrated creation, its notoriety was relatively short-lived; the house disappeared from the canon of American modern houses and Stevens was omitted from discussions of Modernism and even of Brutalism. The Lincoln House met the fate of other singular statements and was demolished in 1999.

The Lincoln House exemplifies how women architects employed their individual interpretations of Modernism to fashion spaces intended to reshape domestic life. Not all women left explicit statements about the social role of architecture, or articulated a manifesto for modern domestic life, as Stevens did, but many held progressive views about how the house (or housing) was intended to improve the lives of its residents. The projects ran the gamut from traditional to avant-garde. Even Florence Luscomb's compact and conventional log cabin in the New Hampshire woods was fitted with the sorts of conveniences a feminist woman, and an inveterate hostess, required of a retreat intended to enhance a circle of friends (see fig. 1.7). The loss of some of these singular efforts erases from the record significant experiments in Modernism. In other instances, what is lost is the sole expression of a career in which professional challenges prevented the achievement of a large body of work. The personal interpretations of Modernism in a single project show that as women achieved unprecedented standing in the profession, they used their architectural skills to respond to a period of enormous changes and challenges in American culture.

Conclusion

THIS GROUP PORTRAIT OF EARLY TO MID-TWENTIETH-century women architects, many educated at the Cambridge School of Architecture and Landscape Architecture goes beyond previous studies by considering the diverse ways in which they contributed to and advocated for American Modernism. The productions of Eleanor Raymond, Victorine du Pont Homsey, Natalie Griffin de Blois, and Ruth Reynolds Freeman were published extensively in their time. Other women wrote about the intentions behind their designs, as Mary Otis Stevens did, or had partners who spoke for them, in the way of Ethel Power for Eleanor Raymond in *House Beautiful*. Women architects were often authoritative communicators of modern aesthetics: the photographer Esther Baum Born provided commanding images of contemporary Mexican architecture; Ethel Power promoted a hybrid version of Modernism responding to local conventions and customs in her magazine; and, through their own houses, Elizabeth Wiley Dunlap and Jane West Clauss introduced their Southern communities to aspects of modern design.

Yet, none of these women had staying power in the history of Modernism. The story of how the movement was adapted to craftsmanship has also been lost, despite Alice Morgan Carson's successful needlework business and patronage by prominent artists and cultural leaders. The roles of women like Elisabeth Coit and Elizabeth Hirsh Fleisher in the debate on housing reform and the production of large-scale housing developments has also been marginalized—although the important voices of other housers, especially Catherine Bauer Wurster, have been recognized.[1] Women educators such as Stanisława Sandecka Nowicki and Amaza Lee Meredith, promoters of modern design across artistic media, are mostly forgotten, even as the scholarly and popular literature has recognized the role played by émigré male architects in making Modernism the orthodoxy within educational institutions.

Systemic sexism, and, in some cases, racism and classism, obviously contributed to the occlusion of women in the narratives of Modernism. On a more subtle level, the preferences of scholars for certain kinds of life stories and careers are equally to blame: scholarly interpretations are preoccupied with artistic genius as well as with practitioners whose prolific output demonstrates a familiar pattern from early development to resolution, to a mature style, to late mannerism. This arc is seldom visible in the lifetime work of women architects, who typically lacked the patrons and hence the opportunities to design a string of buildings until they arrived at a signature style. Most female graduates had difficulty finding a drafting job in an architecture firm, let alone identifying clients able to

C.1. Robert Tilton Coolidge (1915–55), photograph of women students making a model, perhaps at the Cambridge School of Architecture and Landscape Architecture, where he was an assistant in 1941. *Private collection.*

support their aesthetic journeys through multiple commissions. Elizabeth Pillsbury Pringle recalled that on her first job in 1940 in a small San Francisco office of Henry Temple Howard, she "had seen the light," meaning that with little opportunity for advancement, women "could be draftsmen for the rest of their lives."[2]

The types of modern design in which women often engaged could also undermine their recognition, since they were inclined to plan buildings that complemented an existing built environment rather than standing apart with bold, even arrogant architectural statements. Through diverse means, they shaped neighborhoods with respect for the human-made and natural environments, and they sought to enhance their communities rather than improve them by fiat. By doing so, women architects sometimes made their own aesthetic concepts less visible than did male architects. Still, those examined in this study promoted approaches to design that they perceived to be aesthetically and socially progressive, as well as informed by first-generation European modernists.

A comprehensive understanding of the careers of women in architecture is uneven because of lost documentation. Without an organized archive—public or private—it is nearly impossible to follow the progression of any one person's ideas. Some chose to collaborate with well-known male architects, as Mary Weed Noyes did with her husband Eliot Noyes. Although at least two of their children recognize that she played a vital role, they are unaware of records that can illustrate her specific involvement. Conversely, numerous drawings by Helen Douglass French are archived in the College of Environmental Design at the University of California, Berkeley, and substantial correspondence with family members on her husband's side, including the sculptor Daniel Chester French, are at Williams College. Still, those materials have received little attention from scholars. Many families have been conscientious stewards of the archives of their architect forbears; for example, a daughter of Elizabeth Campbell Knapp not only kept her mother's student drawings but the large cardboard model of the house she designed for her parents in Albuquerque, New Mexico.

As for the buildings themselves, they have fared abysmally. The house Eleanor Raymond designed for her sister Rachel Raymond is among the most important examples of early modern architecture by women, yet it fell to the wrecking ball in 2006. The community of historians and enthusiasts recognized it as a groundbreaking example of the impact of the International Style in New England, but their arguments had no effect on the outcome. Frances Baxter Quarton's house in Lincoln was demolished by its new owners in 2018 to make way for a larger home, despite the Lincoln Historical Commission expressing regret at the loss.[3] Similarly, the Lincoln House by Mary Otis Stevens and Thomas McNulty was torn down, even though it was recognized as the first house made entirely of concrete and glass in the United States.[4] By way of contrast, the preservation organization Historic New England maintains the Walter Gropius house, also in Lincoln, as an icon of American Modernism. Thankfully, the startlingly modern split-level house that Ellamae Ellis League designed for herself has had an uncharacteristic fate in that it was acquired and restored in 2022 by the Historic Macon Foundation in Georgia.[5]

The history of Modernism suffers from the loss of built records of women along with the narratives that went with them. Rarely, if ever, has a husband / partner, child, or sibling posthumously authored a book, produced a documentary film, or mounted an exhibition about the production of the woman architect to whom they were attached. By comparison, their male contemporaries have been given tremendous attention due to efforts by their descendants who are vested in their legacies. Fortunately, however, women architects had a propensity to document their production in scrapbooks. The practice of compiling them, a popular activity across all classes and vocations since the nineteenth century, represents a construction of identity outside formal and institutional records.[6] Unlike a diary, which records private feelings or experiences, scrapbooks not only reveal someone's memory or impression of a particular moment, but how that person wants to be remembered. The way they are organized, pieced together, and displayed is as telling as the content itself. The deliberate arrangements are at once a narrative, an archive, an exhibition, a piece of art, and sometimes a trophy.[7] Elizabeth Bauer Kassler explained her process of creating a scrapbook to her sister, Catherine Bauer Wurster: "I immersed myself completely, but drowned, I did, in the concoction of a scrapbook of odds and ends of my life. Looking over it this way, it seems the most wonderful exciting full kind of life. … News clippings, photographs, children's drawings, anything I'd happened to keep that reminded me of something pleasant or important."[8] Bauer Kassler created her scrapbook for her own enjoyment and her family's, and they have

C.2. Helen Frances Baxter Perrin and Hugh Perrin (1899–1973) making a model, c. 1934. *Private collection.*

kept it. Helen Baxter Perrin, on the other hand, bought a scrapbook to document the architecture model-making business she began in the 1920s; it holds photographs, articles, descriptions, and even a letter to her children describing the enterprise she shared with her husband (fig. C.1). Amaza Lee Meredith was an indefatigable scrapbooker: she compiled more than a dozen, spanning her adult life (figs. C.2, C.3, C.4; see fig. 7.4). Some of them contain material related to milestones such as her teaching career and retirement, while others document her legacy, including those filled with memories of Azurest North and Azurest South.[9]

Women architects also created scrapbooks for clients to peruse. Elizabeth Hirsh Fleisher and her partner Gabriel Roth archived articles about their Philadelphia partnership between 1941 and 1958 in a formal gold-embossed black leather scrapbook. Elsa Mandelstamm Gidoni also archived photographs and articles about her work between 1933 and 1972. She cut her initials out of cardboard and glued them onto the covers of two spiral scrapbooks, thus giving them a homemade, practical quality. As the primary record of her production, they are now in the Library of Congress. Another example of a handcrafted record is the series of presentation boards on which Margaret Hunter King and her husband Edgar pasted articles about their joint work, which are now in their archive at North Carolina State University. Alice Morgan Carson was a "meticulous recordkeeper," but her scrapbooks did not fare as well: the Embroiders' Guild of America accepted them as a donation, but, as one member explained in 2003, they were so "tattered, very worn, and water damaged" that she took them apart for conservation. The material is now missing.[10] These vulnerable, homespun objects represent an attempt by women to construct and preserve their legacy. Though often the only source of information about their careers, scrapbooks and other ephemera typically are stored in attics or basements, where adverse conditions or mishaps can hasten decomposition.

The loss of archives contributes to the notion that women architects were "rare" or "unusual," an idea propagated in the 1988 traveling exhibition *That Exceptional One: Women in American Architecture 1888–1988*. The accompanying catalog explains the derivation of the title from the striking statement made in 1955 (in a life insurance brochure, of all places) by the modernist Pietro Belluschi: "I cannot, in whole conscience, recommend architecture as a profession for girls. I know some women who have done well at it, but the obstacles are so great that it takes an exceptional girl to make a go of it. If she insisted on becoming an architect, I would try to dissuade

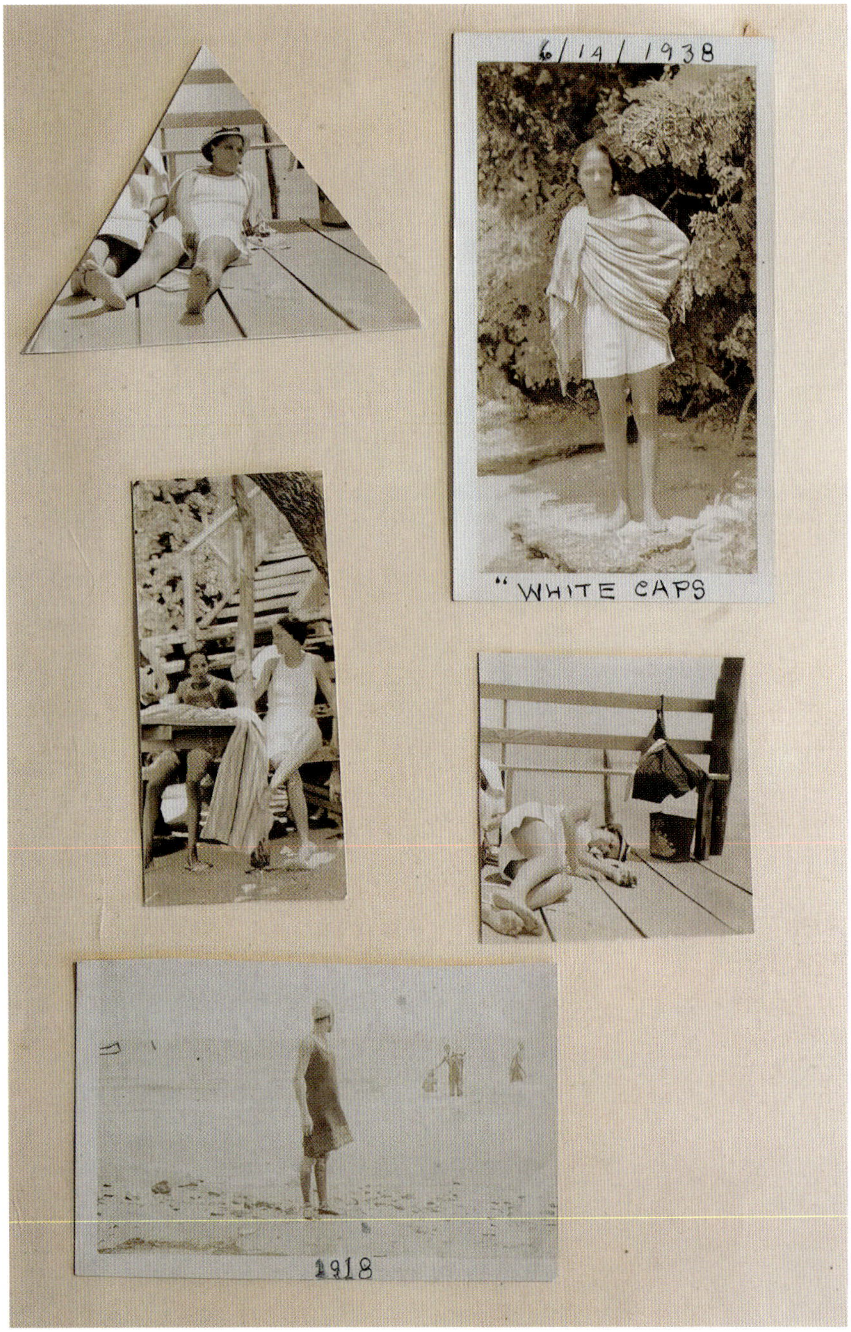

C.3. Amaza Lee Meredith, page of photographs in one of her scrapbooks, 1918–38. *Meredith Papers.*

her. If then, she was still determined, I would give her my blessing—she could be that exceptional one."[11] At the time, Belluschi was dean of the architecture school at MIT, a place where women students had historically not felt encouraged. Though his outlook may say more about the school's attitude to coeducation than about the field of architecture, the label *exceptional* stuck and is still applied with regularity. Unfortunately, Belluschi's words—paradoxically employed to frame an examination of the contributions of women architects on the centennial of the first woman being admitted to the American Institute of Architects—continue to exert an undue influence.

As architects, women were not "exceptional." But as trailblazers they were, deviating from the bourgeois social norms of exclusive focus on marriage, child-rearing, and homemaking.[12] For some women, doing so meant partnering with another woman or remaining single. Some of the architects who felt compelled to comply with societal expectations developed innovative ways of being wives and mothers, such as by creating cooperative parenting or

C.4. Amaza Lee Meredith, photograph in her Azurest South scrapbook, c. 1940. *Meredith Papers.*

work-sharing arrangements that made it possible for them to function professionally. Others, like Baxter Quarton, practiced at home, where they strategically balanced children and work. Many women sought out or designed communities in which their children could participate in group activities under the shared supervision of parents.

Despite cultural or familial expectations, somehow these women were driven to break free from conventions and find professional identities for themselves beyond the home. Each has her own narrative, including her individual career path and form of practice, but all were part of a movement for more inclusive representation in architecture and design, harking back to women's suffrage, in which some of the older women architects had participated. Not all women architects espoused a feminist point of view, however: Carina Eaglesfield Mortimer and Helen Douglass French both defended the superiority of men in architecture, even if they worked hard to establish themselves professionally and achieve recognition.

The success of women architects is especially apparent when measures different than those used to evaluate their male peers are applied. Few women found positions in large firms executing designs for diverse types of buildings; instead, they mostly practiced in smaller partnerships or alone. Their personal and professional circumstances demanded that they continually re-create themselves by being open to opportunities that differed from those traditionally pursued by men. Consequently, the wide-ranging productions of women in different media—made possible by reliable networks of colleagues—enabled them to disperse Modernism to larger audiences than they could have done as sole practitioners.

Many women contributed to modern design in varied ways and created a wide array of exhibitions, publications, and works of art, not to mention the architecture and communities they developed under the rubric of Modernism. Their near invisibility in the history of Modernism, however, has resulted in a canon of architects and designers that overwhelmingly consists of white males. Without the inclusion of women in the narrative of Modernism, our comprehension of this dynamic movement is impoverished.

Acknowledgments

We extend our sincerest gratitude to all who supported our research journey, beginning with our editor, Michelle Komie and her assistant Annie Miller, who unfailingly believed in our project from the moment we presented it. We are equally grateful to the dedicated and enthusiastic descendants of the women architects, especially Joan Harkness Hantz, Phoebe Knapp, Jessica Raymond, and Joan Underwood, all of whom offered not only their personal stories and primary sources but their hospitality. From the East to West Coasts, others generously shared their records, sometimes long forgotten in basements, attics or outbuildings, including Mary Applegate, John Barnes, Jonathan and Patti Berger, Peter Berking, Caril Clauss, Carol Clauss, Peter Clauss, Winthrop B. Conrad Jr., Robert Coolidge, Kate Corkum, Joe Gitterman, Geoff Goldberg, Richard C. Hiscock, Tristen Holmberg, Elizabeth Homsey, Ellen Howe, Mark Isaacs, Angus H. and Joseph Swan Junkin, Alice Lissarrague, Gael Minton, Fritz Mock, Suzy Newton, Peter L. Nowicki, Frederick and Derry Noyes, Gail Perrin, Arthur Perry, Shannon T. Richards, Beatrice Roberts, Virginia G. Searl, Robert and Nancy Smith, Alice Spencer, Anne-Seymour St. John, Kate Thompson, Trina K. Waters, Edith Wilson, and Nancy Meem Wirth.

We further benefited from the input of such scholars as Alice Friedman, Nancy Beth Gruskin, Eliana Perotti, Despina Stratigakos, and Marta A. Urbańska, in addition to the instrumental suggestions from the two anonymous readers of the manuscript for Princeton University Press. Numerous archivists helped to access materials essential to the study, including Nanci Young at Smith College, Nancy Hadley at the American Institute of Architects, Ines Zalduendo at Harvard's Graduate School of Design, Dana Pilson at Williams College, Heather Isbell-Schumacher at the University of Pennsylvania's Stuart Weitzman School of Design, Lorna Condon at Historic New England, and Frida Milen at the Swedish Centre for Architecture and Design (ArkDes). Among the many who contributed to the book, we would like to call out Fred Albert, Marie-Rose Andriadi, Margaux Augier, Chris Barker, Anita Bassie, Ellie Bemis, Dorothy Blakeley, Edward Bottoms, Marc Brodsky, Cynthia Carris, Devin A. Colman, Marisa Cortright, David Ellison, Hedvig Hedqvist, Kurt Helfrich, Margaret Laster, John Monkovic, John Murphey, Tom Nimen, Dean Rogers, Heather Shannon, Brian Sirman, Jacqueline Taylor, and Margaret Warren. Several made important introductions, including George King, Mary McLeod, Gordon Bruce, and Nicholas Olsberg. We also appreciate the families who opened their women-designed homes to us: Mei-Lin Browne in Philadelphia, Pennsylvania; Michael Fowler and Tyler Jo Smith in Charlottesville, Virginia; Robert and Nancy Smith as well as Alexandra Kern, Rachel Drew, Zachary and Debra Woods, Deborah Weisgall, and Throop Wilder in Lincoln, Massachusetts; Mark and Laura Heinz in Knoxville, Tennessee; Peter and Lisa Simpson in Prides Crossing, Massachusetts; and QuanQui Wang in Pepper Pike, Ohio. The FAIA architect John Lynch Sanders graciously hosted us for a weekend at Little Switzerland, outside of Knoxville. The Hagley Library gave us a research grant to study the Victorine du Pont and Samuel Homsey Papers. A Mellon Digital Humanities Fellowship from the Digital Humanities Center at Vanderbilt University supported the creation of network visualizations with the consultation of Scott B. Weingart. Vice Dean Bonnie Dow in the College of Arts and Science at Vanderbilt provided a subvention that supported the acquisition of several key illustrations.

We are also thankful for the opportunities to present papers on our subject at the "Modernism in New England" symposium at Wellesley College (November 2015); the annual international conference of the Society of Architectural Historians in the session "Life to Architecture: Uncovering Women's Narratives" (April 2018); the conference "Expanding the 'Archive.' Latent Connections: Evidence and Speculation" at Virginia Tech (March 2019); and "Minding her Business: Women, Architecture, and Design" in Dublin, Ireland (June 2024). We are pleased that our proposal for "The Forgotten Art of Florence Hope Luscomb" was published in *The Routledge Companion to Women in Architecture*, ed. Anna Sokolina (New York: Routledge, 2021) and that our review of three documentaries about New England Modernism is in the *Journal of the Society of Architectural Historians* (January 2024).

APPENDIX I

Women who studied architecture at the Cambridge School of Architecture and Landscape Architecture

Names mostly from the *Cambridge School Alumnae Bulletin* (1928–42)

Name first/maiden/ (married)	Life dates	Location before Cambridge School	Undergraduate institutions (attendance or graduation dates)	Cambridge School (attendance or graduation dates)	Other education
Elizabeth True Abbott (Pierce) (Fries)	1899–1987	New Bedford, MA	Vassar 1921 Brown 1923 NYU 1924	1927–31	
Charlotte Clara Aldes (Isaacs)	1912–96	Saint Paul, MN	University of Minnesota ex1940	b/4 1940	School of the Art Institute of Chicago
Helen Howland Allen	1878–1964	New Bedford, MA	Bryn Mawr; University of North Carolina 1937	1937 MArch	
Jeanne "Patty" Patrie Allinson	1918–2006	West Chester, PA	Radcliffe 1939	1942 BArch	
Dorothy Anne Durfee (Nickerson) (Cilley)	1916–2004	Newton Center, MA	Mt. Holyoake; Trinity	1940 certificate	
Geneva Angelia Bacon	1899–1983	Quebec, CA	University of Michigan 1932	1927 certificate *1934 MArch	
Margaret Bannerman (Betts)	1911–2007	Elizabeth, NJ	Wells 1933	1937 MArch	
Helen Woodberry Barlow (Clancy)	1910–2000	Amherst, MA	Smith 1933	1938 MArch	
Priscilla Baxter (Neel)	1918–2012	Wollaston, MA	Radcliffe 1940	1942 BArch	
Frances "Franie" Baxter (Quarton)	1918–2017	Wollaston, MA	Radcliffe 1940	1942 BArch	Harvard GSD 1942–43 MArch (scholarship)
Faith Gregg Bemis (Meem)	1902–89	Newton, MA	Vassar ex1924	1928 certificate	
Irene "Inka" Aronson-Sanna (Benton)	1918–2015	Warsaw, Poland	Stanislas Noakowski School of Architecture for Women 1935	1941–42 BArch	Harvard GSD 1946 MArch
Clarice Theodora Melinat Berg (Norton)	1910–2001	St. Paul, MN	University of Minnesota 1932	1934 MArch	

Jean Bodman (Fletcher)	1915–65	Boston, MA	Smith 1937	1941–42	Harvard GSD 1942ss–44 BArch (scholarship)
Dorothea Breed (Bates)	1905–1943	Lynn, MA	Smith 1927	1931 certificate *1934 MArch	
Ruth Bemis Burke (Ungar)	1899–1986	Boston, MA	Smith 1922	1934 MArch	
Elizabeth-Ann “Libby” Campbell (Knapp)	1913–90	Pasadena, CA	Vassar 1936	1940 MArch	
Alice Morgan Carson (Hiscock)	1908–2001	Clinton, IA	Smith 1930	1939 BLA 1940 BArch	Sorbonne c. 1927
Alice Kelsey Chase (Gibson)	1916–71	Toledo, OH	Bryn Mawr 1938	1941 BArch 1942 MArch	
Alice Muriel Childs (Whitney)	1899–1939	Milton, MA	Vassar 1922	1928–32ss *1934 MArch	Lowthorpe School
Abby Winch “Winnie” Christensen	1887–1969	Beaufort, SC	Radcliffe 1910	1915–17	MIT 1914–15
Dorothy Cordley (Lennihan)	1892–1976	Orange, NJ	Mount Holyoke 1914	1920–22	
Laura May Cox	1896–1986	Lynn, MA		1920 certificate	
Mary Elizabeth Craver	1898–1986	Youngstown, OH	Wellesley 1921	1930 certificate *1934 MArch	
Ruth Margaretta Crook (Peabody)	1891–1968	Kenosha, WI		b/4 1929	
Margaret Mary Davidge (Lewis)	1912–2015	Etham, UK	AA School of Architecture 1931–36 (diploma)	1937 BArch (exchange student)	
Louise Dees-Porch	1910–2002	Reading, MA	Wellesley; Antioch; University of Washington	1930ss	Taliesin Fellowship 1932–33
Alice S. Dodge	1901–	Washington, DC		1929	
Margaret Felicia Doughty (Kingsbury)	1898–1982	Winsted, CT		1922 certificate	
Helen Louise Douglass (French)	1900–1994	Arlington, MA		1922 certificate	École des Beaux-Arts 1927
Victorine “Vicki” du Pont (Homsey)	1900–1998	Grosse Point, MI	Wellesley 1923	1926 certificate 1935 MArch	
Carina Eaglesfield (Mortimer) (Milligan)	1890–1978	Indianapolis, IN	Sweet Briar 1909	1921–22	Yale 1923
Helen Louise Ebeling (Berger)	1920–2001	Morristown, NJ	Vassar 1941	1941–42	Harvard GSD 1942ss–44 BArch
Mary Cope Elkinton (Duguid)	1888–1975	Philadelphia, PA	Wellesley 1911	1929–30ss	
Helen Chittenden Elliot	1920–		Vassar c. 1937–39	1939–42	Harvard GSD 1942–43
Constance Wilson Emerick (Bromley)	1900–1972	Oswego, NY		1927 certificate	
Polly Evarts Faulkner (Brown) (Jackson)	1921–2020	Boston, MA		1942	Harvard GSD 1942ss–43
Margaret “Margo” Fisher	1898–1990	Winnetka, IL	University of Wisconsin 1928	1926–28	

Mary Elizabeth Forsberg	1906–71	VA	Radcliffe 1926	1926–27	MIT 1927–30
Katherine "Katy" Charlotte Gibbs (Ericsson)	1907–91			1938 certificate LA certificate Arch (scholarship)	
Harriet Henderson Gilbert (McPherson)	1906–74	Harrisburg, PA	Vassar 1928	1931 certificate *1934 MArch	
Deborah Champion Gilbert (von Rosenvinge)	1914–2003	Winchester, MA	Smith 1934	1938 MArch	
Priscilla Congdon Gladding (Moore)	1916–59	Hopewell City, VA	Radcliffe 1937	1940 MArch	
Anne Laurie Westbrook Gould (Hauberg)	1917–2016	Seattle, WA	University of Washington 1935–36 Vassar 1937–38	1938	
Rose Ishbel Greely	1887–1967	Washington, DC		1919 certificate	
Margaret "Peggy" Chase Greene (Watson)	1920–92	Groton, MA	Vassar 1941	1941–42	Harvard GSD 1942ss–44 BArch
Ann Murphy Halle (Little)	1914–2012	Cleveland, OH	Smith 1935	1940 MArch	
Eleanor Joslyn Ham	1912–78	Cambridge, MA	Scripps 1937	1941 certificate	
Elizabeth M. Harding	1907–	England		1930 certificate	
Helen Cooper Harvey (Sachs)	1915–64	Columbus, OH	Smith 1938	1941 MArch	
Ruth Mildred Havey	1899–1980	Boston, MA	Smith 1920	1923 certificate *1934 MArch	
Eleanor Gawthrop Hayes (Livengood)	1907–2008	Swarthmore, PA	Swarthmore 1927 PA Museum School of Industrial Arts	1940 certificate	
Margaret "Meg" Draper Heath (Wadsworth)	1920–2008	Winchester, MA	Wheaton 1941	1941–42	Harvard GSD 1942ss–44 BArch (scholarship); Pratt Institute
Georgia Gray Hencken (Perkins)	1909–94	New York, NY	Mt. Vernon Seminary	1931–32	
Linda Smith Hires	1878–1967	Philadelphia, PA	Wellesley 1903	1921 certificate *1934 MArch	
Elizabeth "Bess" R. Hirsch (Fleisher)	1892–1975	Philadelphia, PA	Wellesley 1914	1929 certificate *1934 MArch	University of Berlin 1912–13
Sarah "Sally" Meacham Hitchcock (Satterlee) (Yerkes)	1918–	Cleveland, OH	School of the Museum of Fine Arts 1936–38	1941–42	Harvard GSD 1942–45 BArch
Barbara Mary Hollis (Hodges)	1906–95	Randolph, VT	Boston University	1928–34	
Gertrude Whitwell Howard (Fuller)	1910–84	San Mateo, CA		1936 certificate	
Lucy Wheelock Hulburd (Richardson)	1919–2010	Exeter, NH	Vassar 1941	1941–42	Harvard GSD 1942ss–45 BArch (scholarship)
Eunice Engle Hull (Campbell) (Purdy)	1917–2007	Rochester, NY	Smith 1939	1940ss	Columbia 1934 MIT 1941

Marie Victoire Iasigi (Taveau)	1883–1962	Boston, MA		1916	
Frances Halton Jackson	1895–1986	Providence, RI	Smith 1918	1919 *1934 MArch	
Alice Woodmansie Jones	1911–98	Brooklyn, NY	Manhattanville College of the Sacred Heart 1933	1940 MArch	Columbia 1934
Dorothy Kalbfleisch				1942	Harvard 1942
Margaret Burnham Kelly (Geddes)	1907–95	Evanston, IL	Vassar 1929	1936ss	MIT 1933 BSA
Eleanor Taft Kew (Przybylska or Prybot)	1911–1974	Keene, NH		1932 certificate	
Esther Lucile Kilton	1896–1983	Worcester, MA		1920 certificate	
Margaret Greenough King (Hunter)	1919–97	Baltimore, MD	Wheaton 1941	1941–42	Harvard GSD 1942–45
Eleanor Cassandra Kinsman (Dexter) (Coburn)	1915–2002	Salem, MA	Smith 1938	1941 BArch	
Jean League (Newton)	1919–2000	Macon, GA	Radcliffe 1941	1941–42	Harvard GSD 1942–44 BArch (scholarship) 1970 MArch
Louise Leland	1902–56	Springfield, IL	Smith 1923	1929–32 certificate *1934 MArch	
Mary Farlow Linder (Putnam)	1905–37	Canton, MA	Smith 1927	1928–29	
Florence Hope Luscomb	1887–1985	Lowell, MA	MIT 1900 BSA	1916	
Bertha Floy Mather (McPherson)	1906–93	Chicago, IL	Vassar 1928	1931 certificate *1934 MArch	
Jean McMullen (May) (Coolidge)	1919–2008	Kenosha, WI	Swarthmore 1941	1941–42	Harvard GSD 1942–45 BArch
Martha Louise Meyer (Gates)	1914–2004	St. Paul, MN		1937 certificate	AA School of Architecture 1936 (diploma; scholarship)
Katharyn "Tat" Elizabeth Morris (Smith)	1918–96	Plainfield, NJ	Vassar 1939	1942 BArch	
Constance "Connie" Mumford (Warren)	1903–87	Merion, PA	Radcliffe ex1925	1926–27	MIT 1923–25
Dorothy "Dottie" Quincy Noyes (Berking)	1914–62	White Bear Township, MN	Sarah Lawrence ex1936	1940–42	Harvard GSA 1942
Mary Palache (Gregory)	1902–96	Cambridge, MA	Bryn Mawr 1924	1925–27	
Harriette Wilder Patey (Long)	1905–99	Boston, MA	Mount Holyoke 1927	1933 *1934 MArch	
Jane Mumford Pearson (Hansen)	1919–2009	High Falls, NY		1942 certificate	
Ruth Markham Pearson (Eakin)	1916–2003	Ames, IA	Smith 1938	1939	Harvard GSD 1942–43

Barbara Pierce (Clement)	1920–2011	Milton, MA		1941–42	1942ss–43
Elizabeth "Betsy" Eldredge Pillsbury (Pringle)	1912–97	Boston, MA	Bryn Mawr ex1936	1940 certificate	
Sarah "Sally" Pillsbury (Harkness)	1912–97	Swampscott, MA		1940 MArch	
Franziska "Fran" Maria Alma Porges (Hosken)	1919–2006	Vienna, AT	Smith 1940	1941–42	Harvard GSD 1942ss–44 MArch
Ethel Brown Power	1881–1969	Marblehead, MA	Boston Normal School of Gymnastics 1902–4	1920 certificate *1934 MArch	
Anita Reed Rathbun (Bucknell)	1902–83	Woonsocket, RI	Mills 1924	1929 certificate *1934 MArch	
Eleanor Agnes Raymond	1887–1989	Cambridge, MA	Wellesley 1909	1919 certificate *1934 MArch	
Cornelia Reck (Billard) (Meiklejohn)	1916–2004	Bridgeport, CT	Smith 1938	1942 BArch	
Hester Lansing Reed (Eggert)	1917–80	Cold Spring Harbor, NY	Vassar 1939	1942	Harvard GSD 1942ss–43
Marjorie Elizabeth Robbers (Elmquist)	1919–2008	Stearns, MN	University of Minnesota 1941 (BIntArch)	1942 BArch	
Mildred A. Rutherford	1898–1962	East Cleveland, OH		1921 certificate	
Frances Sandler (Borofsky)	1913–2003	Boston, MA	Simmons	1937 certificate	
Gertrude Elizabeth Sawyer	1895–1996	Tuscola, IL	University of Illinois 1918	1920 certificate *1934 MArch	Harvard (special study in town planning)
Esther Schwinck	1896–1969	Saginaw, MI	University of Michigan 1932	1926 certificate *1934 MArch	
Elizabeth C Shaw (Milton)	1904–71	Teaneck, NJ	Columbia	1934 MArch	
Wenonah "Winnie" Edna Sibley (Chamberlin)	1911–2000	Somerville, MA		1934 MArch	
Barbara Crawford Smith (Depenbrock)	1912–2001	Utica, NY	George Washington 1938	1931–34, 1939 MArch	University of Perugia
Florence "Flossie" R. Smith	1910–	Milwaukee, WI	Milwaukee-Downer	1930–35	
Lucy Freelove Smith (Wigginton)	1913–42	Poughkeepsie, NY	Smith 1934	1938–39	Columbia 1934–35
Pauline "Polly" Spencer (Groves)	1912–2007	Bronxville, NY		1934	
Suzanne Marjorie Stockard (Underwood)	1917–2001	Detroit, MI	Bennington 1938	1942 BArch	Harvard GSD 1942–43 MArch
Elizabeth Dutch Swan (Ladd)	1905–84	Providence, RI	Wellesley	1929	
Elizabeth "Boots" Taylor (Gauger)	1900–1992	Greenville, MS	Wellesley 1923	1931 certificate *1934 MArch	
Ida Holt Touchstone (Matthews)	1912–2001	Griffin, GA	University of Georgia 1937	1937–40	

Juliet Mabel Triggs (Wallace)	1911–68	Liphook, UK	AA School of Architecture 1929–34	1932–33 (exchange student)	
Anne Griswold Tyng	1920–2011	Lushan, China	Radcliffe 1942	1941–42	Harvard GSD 1942–45 BArch (scholarship)
Nathalia Ulman (Williams)	1910–95	Boston, MA	School of the Museum of Fine Arts 1928–29	1933–34	
Evelyn White Underhill				1942 certificate	
Louisa Loring Vaughan (Conrad)	1913–2003	Prides Crossing, MA		1936–39	
Elizabeth "Betty" Webster Wales (MacGregor)	1904–89	Indianapolis, IN		1925–28ss	
Marion Spelman Walker (Bailey)	1908–82	Short Hills, NJ	University of Wisconsin 1925–27	1930 certificate	
Mary Duncan Walker (Weed)	1826–1957	Brookline, MA		1935–39 (no credit)	
Charlotte "Lottie" K. Wallum	1884–1960	Brooklyn, NY	NY School of Fine and Applied Arts 1919	1922 certificate	
Joan Warland (Leslie)	1921–2014	Boston, MA		1940ss–42	Harvard GSD 1942–43
Barbara Webb (Rockwell)	1916–91	Shelburne, VT	Bennington 1938	1938–40	
Mary "Molly" Duncan Weed (Noyes)	1915–2010	Brookline, MA		1939 certificate	
Virginia Wells (Turner)	1912–95	Boston, MA	Smith 1934	1934 MArch	
Joan Dare Whiteside	1919–2015	New York, NY		1942	Harvard GSD 1942ss–44; 1945–46
Frances "Fran" Pearce Whitmore (Hartwell) (Burgess)	1910–97	West Hartford, CT	Vassar 1930	1930–34 *1934 MArch	
Elizabeth Wiley (Dunlap)	1894–85	Knoxville, TN	Smith 1918	b/4 1922 certificate (BLA)	
Elizabeth R. Willcox (Robinson)	1911–2000	Englewood, NJ	Smith 1933	1937 MArch	
Alice du Pont Wilson (Haible)	1916–69	Wilmington, DE	Smith 1938	1941–42	Harvard GSD 1942ss–46 BArch
Katharine "Kay" Frances Wilson (Rahn)	1915–92	Stamford, CT	Smith 1937	1940 MLA 1942 BArch	
Sarah "Sally" Owen Wund	1905–83	New York, NY	Vassar 1927	1932 certificate *1934 MArch	Cranbrook Academy of Art 1933–34; American Fine Arts School, 1929; Harvard ss1930; American University 1935

ss: summer school
*1934: women with a "certificate" who also received a degree *after* the Cambridge School affiliated with Smith College in 1934.

APPENDIX II

Writings by or Work of Eleanor Raymond in *House Beautiful*

1922 "The First of Our New Houses for 1922" [unidentified house by Frost and Raymond], 51, no. 2 (February), 104–7; "A House for James H. Cleaves, Esq." [by Frost and Raymond], 51, no. 3 (March), 218; Rose Greely, "A Small House of Distinction" [Cleaves house], 52, no. 5 (November) 420–23; 468–69.

1923 "Specifications: What Does the Owner Need to Know About Them?" [Cleaves house], 53, no. 2 (February), 130–31; 171–72; "The House in Good Taste" [unidentified interiors], 54, no. 4 (October), 349–51; Mary Elkins, "A Lilliputian Kitchen" [drawings by Raymond], 54, no. 5 (November), 470–71.

1924 Ethel Power, "A Beacon Hill Restoration," 56, no. 5 (November), 462–64, 514, 516, 518; "The House in Good Taste" [Beacon Hill house], 56, no. 5 (November), 465–68; Robert L. Ames,"Camouflaging the Radiator," 56, no. 6 (December), 589, 634.

1926 Rose Greely, "An Architect's Garden in the City" [Beacon Hill house], 60, no. 5 (November), 556–59, 612–14; "The Garden in Good Taste," 60, no. 5 (November), 573–76.

1927 The House of William K. Jackson, Esq." [by Frost and Raymond], 62, no. 1 (January), 58–59; "The House of Miss Ruth W. Wellman" [by Linda Hires with Frost and Raymond], 61, no. 5 (May), 644.

1928 The House in Good Taste" [Richard H. Lennihan house by Frost and Raymond], 62, no. 4 (April), 437; "The House of Mr. and Mrs. Richard H. Lennihan," Portfolio of Small Houses [insert], 63, no. 5 (May), 11; Mary Byers Smith, "Two Houses From One," and "The House in Good Taste" [Byers Smith house restored by Frost and Raymond], 64, no. 3 (September), 240–45, 310–12, 257; "Two Houses from One II," 64, no. 4 (October), 383–87.

1929 Houses That Can Be Expanded" [Claude B. Ross house by Frost and Raymond], 66, no. 2 (August), 143–45.

1931 "Color Schemes for Four Bathrooms," 69, no. 5 (May), 486–87; "Design in the City Garden" [Mrs. John Briggs Potter and Beacon Hill house], 70, no. 1 (July), 70–72, 82, 84.

1932 Ethel Power, "High Spruces I" [Dorothy Raymond Ellis house], 71, no. 3 (March), 171–79; Ethel Power, "High Spruces II," 71, no. 4 (April) 280–85, 311–12; "Built-in Beds for the Summer Cottage" [on the estate of F. Robins Mitchell], 72, no. 1 (July), 26; editorial by Power about their summer house in Gloucester, Massachusetts, 72, no. 3 (September); Edith Kingsbury, "Spring Pasture: Our Experiment in the Country" [Rachel Raymond house], 72, no. 4 (October), 200–207, 263–64.

1933 Ethel Power, "The Experimental House" [Raymond / Power summer complex], 73, no. 4 (May), 213, 226–28; "A Model Kitchen" [design by Raymond], 73, no. 5 (June), 269–71, 289; "The House of To-morrow" [design by Raymond], 74, no. 1 (July), 18–19, 33–34; Table of Contents and "Giving Character to a Nondescript House" [Frank E. Barnes house], 74, no. 2 (August), 41–44; "An Artist's Retreat" [Marguarite Mitchel studio], 74, no. 3 (September), frontispiece.

1934 Ethel Power, "Talking Points on Modernism" [Rachel Raymond house], 75, no. 6 (June), 60; Ethel Power, "Modern in New England" [Amelia Peabody studio], 76, no. 2 (August), 32–35, 66.

1935 "Money for New Houses" [Raymond design] (January), 49 and 67; Gove Hambidge, "Part-Time Squire" [Peabody farm] (December), 39.

Notes

Abbreviations

Publications

AR *Architectural Record*
CSAB *Cambridge School Alumnae Bulletin*
HB *House Beautiful*
JAIA *Journal of the American Institute of Architects*
JSAH *Journal of the Society of Architectural Historians*
PP *Pencil Points* or *Progressive Architecture.*
SAQ *Smith Alumnae Quarterly*

Collections

CSR Cambridge School Records, Smith College Archives
CBW Catherine Bauer Wurster Papers, University Archives, Bancroft Library, University of California, Berkley
GSD Graduate School of Design, Loeb Library, Harvard University

Preface

1. Mary Anne Hunting, "Through the Eye of the Editor: Ethel Brown Power" (CUNY Graduate Center, Spring 2000); Kevin D. Murphy, "The Vernacular Moment: Eleanor Raymond, Walter Gropius, and New England Modernism between the Wars," *JSAH* 70, no. 3 (September 2011): 308–29.
2. Doris Cole, *Eleanor Raymond: Architect* (Philadelphia: Art Alliance Press, 1981); Nancy Beth Gruskin, "Building Context: The Personal and Professional Life of Eleanor Raymond, Architect (1887–1989)" (PhD diss., Boston University Graduate School of Arts and Sciences, 1998).
3. The *Cambridge School Alumnae Bulletins* had various titles between 1928 and 1942. They are archived in the CSR.
4. For descriptions of network analysis projects in art history, see the list of Teams in the NA+DAH Workshop, supported by the Getty Foundation, 2019–21, https://sites.haa.pitt.edu/na-dah/; see also Pamela Fletcher and Anne Helmreich with David Israel and Seth Erickson, "Local / Global: Mapping Nineteenth-Century London's Art Market," *Nineteenth-Century Art Worldwide* 11, no. 3 (Autumn 2012), http://www.19th-artworldwide.org/autumn12/fletcher-helmreich-mapping-the-london-art-market. See also Scott B. Weingart, "Demystifying Networks," *Scottbot* (blog), December 14, 2010, http://www.scottbot.net/HIAL/index.html@p=6279.html.
5. See the database Pioneering Women of American Architecture, edited by Mary McLeod and Victoria Rosner, supported by the Beverly Willis Architecture Foundation, accessed October 9, 2022, https://pioneeringwomen.bwaf.org/. See also Jan Digliano Hartman, *The Women Who Changed Architecture* (New York: Beverly Willis Architecture Foundation and Princeton Architectural Press, 2022).
6. See the Virginia Tech Libraries website: "International Archive of Women in Architecture,", accessed November 29, 2022, https://spec.lib.vt.edu/iawa/.
7. Hermione Lee, *Virginia Woolf* (New York: Vintage Books, 1999), 13. See also Caroline G. Heilbrun, *Writing a Woman's Life* (New York and London: W. W. Norton, 1988).
8. See the website of the SAH Women in Architecture Affiliate Group, accessed January 1, 2023, https://sahwomeninarchitectureaffiliategroup.sah.hcommons.org/.

Introduction

1. William H. Jordy, "The International Style in the 1930s," *JSAH* 24, no. 1 (March 1965): 10–14, quote at 12. On the larger debate about humanized Modernism, see Jordy, "Humanism in Contemporary Architecture: Tough- and Tender-Minded," *Journal of Architectural Education* 15, no. 2 (Summer 1960): 3–10. At "An Evening with Ise [Frank] Gropius" at Harvard University, April 5, 1978, she criticized the definition of the International Style by Henry-Russell Hitchcock and Philip Johnson for its simplification and misunderstanding of the publication *Internationale Architektur: Bauhaus Bücher* (Munich: Albert Langen Verlag, 1925), edited by her husband. See "Ise Gropius," *Bauhaus Bookshelf*, March 10, 2024, https://www.bauhaus-bookshelf.org/ise-gropius-lecture-harvard-1978.html.
2. Edith Kingsbury, "Spring Pasture: Our Experiment in the Country," *HB* 72, no. 4 (October 1932), 205–6.
3. Daniel P. Gregory, "An Indigenous Thing: The Story of William Wurster and the Gregory Farmhouse," *Places Journal* 7, no. 1 (1990): 80, https://placesjournal.org/assets/legacy/pdfs/an-indigenous-thing-william-wurster-and-the-gregory-farmhouse.pdf.
4. Eleanor Raymond, undated writing formerly in the private collection of Jessica Raymond.
5. The Seven Sister colleges are Bryn Mawr, Mount Holyoke, Pembroke

(subsequently absorbed into Brown University), Radcliffe, Smith, Vassar, and Wellesley.

6. A member of the Harvard College class of 1905, Henry Atherton Frost also received a master's degree in 1918 from Harvard, where he studied under Herbert Langford Warren. According to George T. LeBoutillier, "Henry Atherton Frost," *Harvard University Gazette* 48, no. 14 (December 27, 1952), Frost was named a teaching assistant at Harvard in 1909; an instructor in 1910; acting dean of the Faculty of Architecture in 1928; associate professor in 1938; professor in 1940; and chairman of the Department of Architectural Sciences (Harvard College) in 1941.

7. Henry Frost, "A New Curriculum," *CSAB* VII, no. 3 (May 1935): 1–2.

8. Henry Frost "The Cambridge School of Architecture and Landscape Architecture—Reminiscences," n.d., 23, CSR.

9. Frost, "Reminiscences," 8.

10. Linda Nochlin, "Why Have There Been No Great Women Artists?," *ARTNews* 69, no. 1 (January 1971): 22–39 and 67–71, and Despina Stratigakos, *Where Are the Women Architects?* (Princeton, NJ: Princeton University Press, 2016).

11. See Doris Cole, "Education of Women Architects: The Cambridge School," in *From Tipi to Skyscraper: A History of Women in Architecture* (Boston: i press, 1973), 78–105; Mary Otis Stevens, "Struggle for Place: Women in Architecture," in *Women in American Architecture: A Historic and Contemporary Perspective*, ed. Susana Torre (New York: Architectural League of New York and Whitney Library of Design, 1977), 91.

12. Dorothy May Anderson, *Women, Design, and the Cambridge School* (West Lafayette, IN: PDA Publishers, 1987); Dorothy May Anderson, "The Cambridge School: An Extraordinary Professional Education," in *Architecture: A Place for Women*, ed. Ellen Perry Berkeley and Matilda McQuaid (Washington, DC: Smithsonian Institution Press, 1989), 91–98. See also Mary Pope Furr, "'The Purpose … Is to Train Women': The Academic Program of the Cambridge School of Architecture and Landscape Architecture, 1915–1942" (MA thesis, School of Architecture, University of Virginia, 1995).

13. Gwendolyn Wright, "On the Fringe of the Profession: Women in American Architecture," in *The Architect: Chapters in the History of the Profession*, ed. Spiro Kostof (New York: Oxford University Press, 1977), 280–308.

14. Dolores Hayden, *The Grand Domestic Revolution: A History of Feminist Designs for American Homes, Neighborhoods, and Cities* (Cambridge, MA: MIT Press, 1981).

15. See *Proceedings of the West Coast Women's Design Conference, April 18–20, 1974* (Eugene: University of Oregon, 1975).

16. "Women in Architecture: A Symposium," School of Architecture, Washington University, March 29–31, 1974, https://openscholarship.wustl.edu/wia/1974/Program/.

17. Pietro Belluschi, "Should You Be an Architect?," New York Life Insurance Company brochure, 1955, quoted in Wright, "On the Fringe," 285. The emphasis was added by Wright.

18. Among the articles is Gwendolyn Wright, "The Women's Commonwealth: A Nineteenth-Century Experiment," *Heresies: A Feminist Publication on Art and Politics* 3, no. 3 (1980): 24–27.

19. See, for example, Gabrielle Esperdy, "Natalie Griffin de Blois," Pioneering Women, accessed October 9, 2022; https://pioneeringwomen.bwaf.org/natalie-griffin-de-blois; Doris Cole, "Eleanor Raymond," Pioneering Women, accessed October 9, 202, https://pioneeringwomen.bwaf.org/eleanor-raymond.

20. Finn Enke, "Cis," in *Keywords for Gender and Sexuality Studies*, ed. The Keywords Feminist Editorial Collective (New York: New York University Press, 2021), 47–54.

21. Ellamae Ellis League, *Macon Telegraph and News* [GA], 1975, quoted in Debbie Piland, "Mrs. League Is Honored by Architects," *Macon Telegraph and News*, October 17, 1982, and in Cheri Dennis, *Dear Mr. Ellamae* (Austin: MaCauley Publishers, 2021), 112.

22. Barbara Barnes, "Plans for Nurses' Home Show Woman's Touch," *Evening Bulletin* [PA], April 19, 1950; Barbara Barnes, "Beauty, Utility Blend in Woman's Medical Nurses Home," *Evening Bulletin*, January 31, 1952.

23. See the Berkeley City Club website: https://www.berkeleycityclub.com/history.htm; Molly McClain, "ZLAC Rowing Club, 1892–2007," *Journal of San Diego History* (June 2007): 89–116.

24. James F. O'Gorman, "Theodate Pope Riddle," Pioneering Women, accessed December 6, 2022, https://pioneeringwomen.bwaf.org/theodate-pope-riddle.

25. Kelly Hayes McAlonie, "Louise Blanchard Bethune," Pioneering Women, accessed December 4, 2022, https://pioneeringwomen.bwaf.org/louise-blanchard-bethune/.

26. Faith Bemis, questionnaire, May 1942, student file, CSR.

27. Monica Penick, *Tastemaker: Elizabeth Gordon, House Beautiful, and the Postwar American Home* (New Haven, CT: Yale University Press, 2017), 11.

28. Julie V. Iovine, "Elizabeth Gordon, 94, Dies; Was House Beautiful Editor," *New York Times*, September 17, 2000.

29. Ethel Power, "I've Got My Own Ideas," *HB* 79, no. 9 (September 1937), 52–53, 110–14; Frank Luther Mott, *A History of American Magazines, 1741–1930*, vol. 5 (Cambridge, MA: Harvard University Press, 1958), 162–63.

30. Ethel Power, untitled poem, June 1967, private collection.

31. Doris Cole, "An Interview with Eleanor Raymond," in *Eleanor Raymond, Architectural Projects, 1919–1973*, exhibition catalog (Boston: Institute of Contemporary Art, 1981).

32. See "Edna Colson Dies; Pioneer at VSU," *Richmond Times-Dispatch*, January 18, 1985.

33. For the relationship between Amaza Lee Meredith and Edna Colson see Jessica Lynne, "That Which We Are Still Learning to Name," *Southern Cultures*, 26, no. 2 (Summer 2020), https://www.southerncultures.org/article/that-which-we-are-still-learning-to-name/.

34. Rachel Hope Cleves, "'What? Another Female Husband?': The Prehistory of Same-Sex Marriage in America," *Journal of American History* 101, no. 4 (March 2015): 1078; John D'Emilio and Estelle Freedman, *Intimate Matters: A History of Sexuality in America*, 3rd ed. (Chicago: University of Chicago Press, 2012), xv.

35. Mary Anne Hunting and Kevin D. Murphy, "The Forgotten Art of Florence Hope Luscomb," in *The Routledge Companion to Women in Architecture*, ed. Anna Sokolina, 70–82 (New York: Routledge, 2021).

36. Virginia Brookings, "A Few Words About a Memorable Friend," [1989], private collection.

37. James F. O'Gorman, "The Modernism of Theodate Pope," *Connecticut Explored* 8, no. 1 (Winter 2009 / 10): 31.

38. Doris Cole and Karen Cord Taylor, *The Lady Architects: Lois Lilley Howe, Eleanor Manning and Mary Almy, 1893–1937* (New York: Midmarch Arts Press, 1990), 13–14.

39. O'Gorman, "Modernism of Theodate Pope," 31.

40. On Hazel Wood Waterman, see Catherine W. Zipf, *Professional Pursuits: Women and the American Arts and Crafts Movement* (Knoxville: University of Tennessee Press, 2007), 30–50; for Katharine Cotheal Budd, see her article, "The Hostess House in the Army Cantonment," *Architecture* 38, no. 4 (October 1918): 264–68.

41. Karen McNeill, "Julia Morgan: Gender, Architecture, and Professional Style," *Pacific Historical Review* 76, no. 2 (May 2007): 248–49; Wendy Bertrand, "If I Knew Then What I Know Now … ," in *Enamored with Place: As Woman + As Architect* (San Francisco: eyeonplace press, 2012), 363. Bertrand generalizes from the research of Inge Horton, *Early Women Architects in the San Francisco Bay Area: The Lives and Works of Fifty Professionals, 1890–1951* (Jefferson, NC: McFarland and Co., 2010).

42. McNeill, "Julia Morgan," 248–49.

43. "Houses and Gardens Designed by Women," *CSAB* 4, no. 1 (December 1931): 8–9.

44. Eleanor Manning, quoted in *CSAB* 3, no. 3 (July 1931): 4.

45. James F. O'Gorman, "Hill-Stead and Its Architect," in *Hill-Stead: The Country Place of Theodate Pope Riddle* (New York: Princeton Architectural Press, 2010), 79.

46. Theodate Pope Riddle to Lunette Brooks Pope, March 11, 1915, quoted in O'Gorman, "Hill-Stead and its Architect," 78.

47. The postcard is in the Eleanor Raymond Collection in the GSD. See also "Avon, Old Farms: A School for Boys at Avon, Conn.," *American Architect* 128, no. 2484 (November 5, 1925): 391–94; "Avon Old Farms, Avon, Connecticut: A Junior College and Preparatory School for Boys, Founded by Theodate Pope, Its Architect," *Architect* 7, no. 3 (December 1926): 309; *Architect* 10, no. 3 (June 1928): 319–53.
48. In Sandra L. Katz, *Dearest of Geniuses, A Life of Theodate Pope Riddle* (Windsor, CT: Tide-Mark Press, 2003), 248, Katz states that the dollar figure is in her will.
49. Katz, *Dearest of Geniuses*, 44–46.
50. Sarah Holmes Boutelle, *Julia Morgan, Architect*, revised ed. (New York: Abbeville, 1995), 23.
51. Lois Lilley Howe, "An Alumna's Architectural Career," *MIT Technology Review* 66, no 2 (December 1963): 21. A typescript version, "MIT Fiftieth Reunion Notes Written in 1940 for the MIT Fiftieth Reunion of the Class of 1890," in the Cambridge Historical Society, predates the published article by more than twenty years.
52. Andrea Jeanne Merrett, "Lois Lilley Howe," Pioneering Women, accessed November 12, 2023, https://pioneeringwomen.bwaf.org/lois-lilley-howe.
53. Howe, "An Alumna's Architectural Career," 21–22.
54. Howe, "An Alumna's Architectural Career," 21–22.
55. S[arah] A[llaback], "Lois Lilley Howe," in *The Women Who Changed Architecture*, ed. Jan Cigliano Hartman (Hudson, NY: Princeton Architectural Press, 2022), 22.
56. John Lloyd Wright, *My Father Frank Lloyd Wright* (Mineola, NY: Dover, 1992), 35, initially published as *My Father Who Is on Earth* (1946). John Wright attributes a greater architecture role to Isabel Roberts than did his father, who referred to her variously as a "secretary," "bookkeeper," and "factotum." Thomas A. Heinz, *The Vision of Frank Lloyd Wright: A Complete Guide to the Designs of an Architectural Genius* (New York: Chartwell Books, 2014), 140–41 contends she was a talented architect with a position in the office that has been underestimated or ignored.
57. Wright, *My Father Frank Lloyd Wright*, 35.
58. Marion Mahony Griffin, "The Magic of America: Electronic Edition," August 2007, section 4, no. 6, 125–28, https://archive.artic.edu/magicofamerica/link/moa_1.html.
59. The official title of the *Wasmuth Portfolio* is *Ausgeführte Bauten und Entwürfe von Frank Lloyd Wright*. H. Allen Brooks, "Frank Lloyd Wright and the Wasmuth Drawings," *Art Bulletin* 48, no. 2 (June 1966): 195–97, explains that even though staff members contributed to the drawings, the only ones in the *Wasmuth Portfolio* that can be attributed with certainty are those by Marion Mahony in about 1906, in part because she affixed her monogram to some of them. Brendan Gill, *Many Masks: A Life of Frank Lloyd Wright* (New York: Putnam, 1987), 11–12, maintains that Isabel Roberts and John van Bergen were left to complete Wright's commissions when he departed for Europe in 1909. See also David Rifkind, "Isabel Roberts," Pioneering Women, accessed November 14, 2023, https://pioneeringwomen.bwaf.org/isabel-roberts.
60. Alice Friedman, "Girl Talk: Marion Mahony Griffin, Frank Lloyd Wright and the Oak Park Studio," *Places Journal*, June 2011, https://placesjournal.org/article/marion-mahony-griffin/?cn-reloaded=1#0.
61. Anna Rubbo, "Marion Mahony and Walter Burley Griffin: A Creative Partnership," *Architectural Theory Review* 1, no. 1 (1996): 86. See also James Weirick, "Marion Mahony at MIT," *Transition* 25 (Winter 1988): 49–54.
62. Thomas S. Hines, "Portrait: Marion Mahony Griffin Drafting a Role for Women in Architecture," *Architectural Digest* 52, no. 3 (March 1995): 38, 40.
63. Elizabeth Birmingham, "The Case of Marion Mahony Griffin and the Gendered Nature of Discourse in Architectural History," *Women's Studies* 35, no. 2 (2006): 87–123.
64. Elizabeth Bauer Kassler to Frederick Gutheim, box 138, folder 12, Frederick Albert Gutheim Papers, American Heritage Center, University of Wyoming.
65. Hines, "Portrait," 40. Hines also reports that "friends and relatives close to the couple insisted that at least two of Walter Burley Griffin's major projects in Melbourne were, in fact, largely his wife's: the Australia Cafe (1914) and the Capitol Theatre (1922–24). The Castlecrag Community ... also owed much to her input."
66. See Helen Lefkowitz Horowitz, *Alma Mater: Design and Experience in the Women's Colleges from Their Nineteenth Century Beginnings to the 1930s*, 2nd ed. (Amherst: University of Massachusetts Press, 1993).
67. See, for example, Ann [Elizabeth] Binkley Horn, "Modern Mexico: Personal Observations, Impressions and Appraisals of Current Architecture," *AR* 102, no. 1 (July 1947): 70–83; Margaret Olthof Goldsmith, "A Garden of Four Rooms," *AR* 89, no. 1 (January 1939): 40–41, 73. Keith Eggener, "Toward an Organic Architecture in Mexico," in *Frank Lloyd Wright: Europe and Beyond*, ed. Anthony Alofsin (Berkeley: University of California Press, 1999), 166–83, at 180.
68. See Ethel Power, "Prefabricated—No Waiting," *HB* 77, no. 3 (March 1935), 50–53. Solar houses by Victorine du Pont Homsey and Samuel Homsey and by Ruth Reynolds Freeman are in Maron J. Simon, *Your Solar House: A Book of Practical Homes for All Parts of the Country* (New York: Simon and Schuster, 1947), 32–33, 46–47; the one designed by Eleanor Raymond with Maria Telkes for Amelia Peabody is in Daniel Barber, "The World Solar Energy Project, c. 1954," *Grey Room* 51 (Spring 2013): 63, 68–69. Raymond also designed for Peabody a house made of plywood and another of Masonite; see "A Thousand Women in Architecture: Part I," *AR* 103, no. 3 (March 1948): 111. Designs for an asbestos house by the Homseys are in their archive in the Hagley Library.
69. Henry Frost to Herbert Davis, June 20, 1941, CSR.
70. "A Thousand Women in Architecture: Part I," *AR* 103, no. 3 (March 1948), 105–13 and "A Thousand Women in Architecture: Part II," *AR* 103, no. 5 (June 1948): 108–15. The women discussed in this book who are featured are in "Part I": Elsa Mandelstamm Gidoni (p. 106), Ruth Reynolds Freeman (p. 107), Marie Frommer (p. 110), and Eleanor Raymond (p. 111); in "Part I": Victorine du Pont Homsey (p. 109), Gertrude Sawyer (p. 110), Carina Eaglesfield Mortimer (p. 113), and Elisabeth Coit (p. 114).

I: Early Experience and Education

1. Suzanne Marjorie Stockard was one of four from Bennington College to attend Harvard's Graduate School of Design after it opened to women in 1942. The others were Janet MacColl Taylor (1921–2005), Katharine Wyman (Roll; 1921–2008), and Margaret Quincy Young (Myhrum; 1921–2011).
2. Arthur Drexler, ed., *The Architecture of the Ecole des Beaux-Arts* (New York: Museum of Modern Art and MIT Press, 1977); Joseph Hudnut, "Graduate School of Design," *Official Register of Harvard University* 41, no. 25 (1942–43): 199.
3. For example, Cole, *From Tipi to Skyscraper*, 75, states that most women "had to wait another forty years" after the close of the nineteenth century to obtain architecture degrees because "it was a constant struggle for women to gain admittance."
4. Henry Frost, "Professional Training in General," March 28, 1938, CSR.
5. Quoted in Theodor Karl Rohdenburg, *A History of the School of Architecture: Columbia University* (New York: Columbia University Press, 1954), 22. The spatial exclusion of women architects continued well into the twentieth century. Christopher Domin, "Early Practice," in Christopher Domin and Kathryn McGuire, *Powerhouse: The Life and work of Judith Chafee* (New York: Princeton Architectural Press, 2019), 35, states about Judith Chafee (1932–98) that when she went to work in 1960 for her former teacher at Yale, Paul Rudolph: "As the only woman in her graduating class and one of the few in the professional office setting, it is not surprising that she would often work from her New Haven apartment away from the male-dominated culture of the studio."
6. Marilynn A. Bever, "The Women of M.I.T., 1871 to 1941: Who They Were, What They Achieved" I, June 1976, Institute Archives, Distinctive Collections, MIT Libraries.
7. Caroline Shillaber, *Massachusetts Institute of Technology School of*

Architecture and Planning, 1861–1961: A Hundred Year Chronicle (Cambridge: MIT, 1963), 81.
8. See the Student Thesis Drawings Collection, MIT Museum: https://mitmuseum.mit.edu.
9. See Nathalie Henderson Swan to Robert Leigh, January 10 and 22, 1934, Edwin Avery Park Collection, Bennington College Archive, https://crossettlibrary.dspacedirect.org/bitstream/handle/11209/12174/Leigh%2c%20Nathalie%20Swan%20Series%20re.%20Josef% 20Albers%201934.pdf?sequence=1&isAllowed=y.
10. Before the Bauhaus, Lila Fairbairn Ulrich studied industrial design at the Chicago Art Institute under Margaret Artingstall (1883–1951) and Emil Zettler. At the Bauhaus in Dessau and Berlin, she studied under Ludwig Mies van der Rohe, Josef Albers, Lilly Reich, and Walter Peterhans. See Corinna Isabel Bauer, "Architekturstudentinnen in der Weimarer Republik: Bauhaus und Tessenow Schülerinnen" [Architecture students of the Weimar Republic: Bauhaus and Tessenow students], ([PhD diss.], Universität Kassel, Germany, 2003), 217 and 403–04, https://kobra.uni-kassel.de/bitstream/handle/123456789/2010090234467/DissertationCorinnaIsabelBauer.pdf;jsessionid=863DC0A7083DC8B48951E0F28C5BA181?sequence=7.
11. Hannah Benoit, "Beyond Bricks and Ivy: The Making of a Modern Campus," *Wheaton Quarterly* 98, no. 3 (Summer 2009): 25–26.
12. Marni Epstien-Mervis, "How Three Colleges Brought Modernist Design to the US," *Curbed*, September 24, 2014, https://www.archdaily.com/552257/how-three-colleges-brought-modernist-design-to-the-us#. See also Judith Keller, "The Wheaton College Commission," in *Walker Evans: The Getty Museum Collection* (Malibu, CA: J. Paul Getty Museum, 1995), 241–56.
13. The telegram is quoted and discussed in Thomas J. McCormick, "Wheaton College: Competition for an Art Center, February 1938–June 1938," in *Modernism in America, 1937–1941*, ed., James D. Kornwolf (Williamsburg, VA: Joseph and Margaret Muscarelle Museum of Art, 1985), 36–37.
14. "Bauhaus at Dessau Is Vital Experiment," *Wellesley College News*, May 23, 1929.
15. See Richard Meyer, "Young Professor Barr (1927)," in *What Was Contemporary Art?* (Cambridge, MA: MIT Press, 2013), 37–114; Christopher Shea, "The Young Wellesley Professor Who Invented Contemporary Art," *Boston Globe*, July 28, 2013.
16. See Alfred Hamilton Barr Jr., "The Necco Factory," *Arts* 13, no. 5 (May 1928): 292–95; Douglass Shand-Tucci, *The Crimson Letter: Harvard, Homosexuality, and the Shaping of American Culture* (New York: St. Martin's Griffin, 2003), 331.
17. Conference on Modern Architecture, *Radcliffe Quarterly* 17, no. 2 (April 1933): 77–84.
18. "Alumnae News Items," *CSAB* 5, no. 3 (March 1933): 7.
19. Frances Baxter Quarton, interview with Mary Anne Hunting and Kevin D. Murphy, January 8, 2016.
20. "Graduate School is Added at Smith," *New York Times*, October 2, 1935; "A Report Submitted by the Executive Committee to the Board of Trustees of the Cambridge School," June 9, 1939, CSR; Henry Frost to President William Allen Neilson, January 7, 1938, CSR.
21. "The Cambridge School," *SAQ* 33, no. 3 (May 1942): 150–51; Joseph Hudnut, "Graduate School of Design," *Official Register* 41, no. 23 (1941–42): 292.
22. Karrie Jacobs, "Anne Tyng and Her Remarkable House," *Architect* 107, no. 2 (February 2008): 82.
23. Anne Griswold Tyng, "Finding Identity in Time and Space," in *Louis Kahn to Anne Tyng: The Rome Letters, 1953–1954*, ed. Anne Griswold Tyng (New York: Rizzoli, 1997), 24.
24. According to her Radcliffe student file in the Schlesinger Library, Anne Tyng took Architecture Science 10a in the summer school and a half year each of Architecture 3 (graphics), Architecture 5a (elementary design), and Architecture 5b (second-year design) at the Cambridge School.
25. See Hunting and Murphy, "The Forgotten Art of Florence Hope Luscomb."
26. Winnie Christenson to Abbie Holmes Christensen, March 3 and 11, April 2 and November 5, 1916; January 25, 1917, Christenson Family Papers, South Caroliniana Library, University of South Carolina. A third woman at the Cambridge School from MIT was Marie Victoire Iasigi (Taveau; 1883–1962) of Brookline, Massachusetts.
27. Herbert Langford Warren, "Architectural Education at Harvard University," *Harvard Engineering Journal* 1, no 2 (June 1902): 84.
28. Henry Frost, [editorial], *CSAB* 1, no. 1 (December 1928): 1.
29. Frost "Reminiscences," 38.
30. "Let Women Plan Houses for Women: Mere Man Doesn't Know Where to Put the Closets or Arrange for the Furniture," *Boston Daily Globe*, February 24, 1918. See also "Women Taught Architecture," *Cambridge Tribune*, March 2, 1918.
31. "Girls are Taught Domestic and Landscape Architecture," *Christian Science Monitor*, December 15, 1922; "Architecture and Landscape School Will Move into Abbot Building in September," *Cambridge Tribune*, August 26, 1922; Frost, [editorial], *CSAB* 1, no. 1, 1–2.
32. Nancy Beth Gruskin, "Designing Woman: Writing about Eleanor Raymond," in *Singular Women: Writing the Artist*, ed. Kristen Frederickson and Sarah E. Webb (Berkeley: University of California Press, 2003), 151–52, says that Raymond worked as a draftsperson for Henry Frost while still a student (the two became associates in September 1919, according to an announcement in the Raymond Collection) and remained in partnership until Raymond went out on her own in 1935. However, the *Boston Directory* of 1935 lists her at 126 Newbury Street with Frost, Edith V. Cochran (landscape architect), and Laura Cox (architect).
33. Mary E. Duguid, "TVA," *CSAB* 7, no. 3 (May 1935): 5.
34. Albert Farwell Bemis, an MIT-trained engineer, succeeded his father at the Bemis Brothers Bag Company and became president in 1929. His primary interest, however, was mass-produced housing: in 1918, he created the Housing Company in Boston and beginning in 1929 he partnered with the architect John (Johannes) F. (Frederick) G. (George) Gunther—whose wife, Elizabeth White Clark Gunther (1901–2002) studied landscape architecture at the Cambridge School in 1924–26. He was also coauthor of the three-volume publication, *The Evolving House* (1933–36) and a founder of the industrial town of Bemis, TN. See John Burchard II, "Research Findings of Bemis Industries, Inc.," *AR* 75, no. 1 (January 1934): 3–8; "Bemis Leaves Public Fund," *Daily Boston Globe*, May 6, 1936.
35. Faith Gregg Bemis, "The Development of a Fifty Suburban House Including Several Community Features Such as a Garage, Heating Plant, Tennis Courts, Gardens, etc.," student file, CSR.
36. Tyng, *Louis Kahn to Anne Tyng*, 20.
37. Anne Griswold Tyng, "Architecture Is My Touchstone," *Radcliffe Quarterly* 70, no. 3 (September 1984): 5; "Petite Blonde Succeeds as an Architect in Phila., Designing Woman, *Philadelphia Inquirer*, May 19, 1950.
38. Obituary of Margaret Burnham Kelly Geddes, *Providence Journal*, March 12, 1995.
39. Henry Frost, note about Mrs. Charles [Mary Duncan Walker] Weed, December 28, 1949, student file, CSR.
40. Catrina Hill, "The Harvard Society for Contemporary Art," in *The Routledge Encyclopedia of Modernism* (2016), accessed July 11, 2022, doi:10.4324/9781135000356-REM1572-1.
41. Shand-Tucci, *The Crimson Letter*, 110.
42. Gertrude Elizabeth Sawyer, student file, CSR.
43. See Annie Allen, "Our History, Our Heritage," Maryland Historical Trust Blog, accessed June 8, 2021, https://mdhistoricaltrust.wordpress.com/2020/05/26/gertrude-sawyer-pioneer-and-architect/; Jefferson Patterson Park and Museum, accessed June 8, 2021, https://jefpat.maryland.gov/Documents/education/the-pattersons/point-farm.pdf.
44. "Society Honors Miss Rose Greely," *Washington Star*, January 21, 1937; Joanne Seale Lawson, "*Remarkable Foundations: Rose Ishbel Greely, Landscape Architect*," *Washington History* 10, no. 1 (Spring/Summer, 1998): 46–46; AIA Historical Directory of American Architects, s.v. "Sawyer,

Gertrude," application for membership, May 29, 1939, https://aiahistorical directory.atlassian.net/wiki/spaces/AHDAA/pages/37881779/ahd1039279?preview=/37881779/2195950199/SawyerGertrude.pdf.

45. Henry Frost, "A Report to the Trustees of the Cambridge School," October 25, 1928, CSR; Henry Frost, "Professional Training in General," March 28, 1938, CSR.

46. Henry Frost to James Bryant Conant, May 2, 1935, President's Records, Harvard University Archives.

47. Henry Frost, [editorial], *CSAB* 6, no. 1 (October 1933): 1–3; Henry Frost, "An End and a Beginning," *CSAB* 14, no. 2 (July 1942): 6, 8. The Middlesex Village project won a gold medal in 1935 from the Massachusetts Horticultural Society.

48. Albert E. Simonson, "An Imaginary Village Model: With Notes on How It Was Made," *PP* 16, no. 11 (November 1935): 579–82.

49. Ann Bruce Haldeman and Louise Leland, "'Never A Dull Moment': Sidelights on a Collaborative Adventure," *CSAB* 13, no. 1 (March 1941): 14–19.

50. Katherine Gibbs, "By Their Scales Shall Ye Know Them (A Landscape Architect Studies Architecture)," *CSAB* 10, no. 3 (April 1938): 11–12.

51. Henry Frost, "Report of the Graduate School of Architecture and Landscape Architecture," 1938–39, 2, CSR.

52. Frost, "Reminiscences," 13.

53. "General Information," *Cambridge Graduate School Bulletin of Smith College Architecture and Landscape Architecture*, no. 34 (1938): 4, CSR.

54. "University of Minnesota, Board of Regents Meeting and Committee Meetings," March 14, 1928, and "The President's Report," 1924–25, University of Minnesota Archives. Although a curriculum in interior decoration had existed for several years in the College of Science, Literature, and the Arts, a professional degree was established in 1924 at the College of Engineering and Architecture (in 1928, the name was changed to Interior Architecture). The curriculum at the Cambridge School departed from the University of Minnesota in that students were required to take more color theory and historic research. See "A New Curriculum," *CSAB* 7, no. 3 (May 1935): 1–2.

55. Interior Architecture, survey, June 15, 1937. The other universities at the time offering bachelor's degrees in interior decoration were University of Pennsylvania, University of Michigan, University of Cincinnati, and Washington University.

56. See "Houses and Gardens Designed by Women," *CSAB* 4, no. 1 (December 8, 1931): 8–9; *CSAB* 3, no. 3 (July 1931): 3–4; "Alumnae Dinner at Rockport," *CSAB* 4, no. 3 (June 1932): 3.

57. Frost, "Reminiscences," 7, 23–24; Henry Frost, [editorial], *CSAB* 2, no. 2 (April 1930): 1; Cambridge School *Bulletin* (March 1932), CSR.

58. Judith S. Baughman, Victor Bondi, Richard Laymon, et al., "Working Women in the 1930s," *American Decades* 4 (2001).

59. Jill Pearlman, "Joseph Hudnut's Other Modernism at the 'Harvard Bauhaus,'" *JSAH* 56, no. 4 (December 1997): 460.

60. The Harvard instructors engaged at the Cambridge School include Walter Francis Bogner, Walter Louis Chambers, Kenneth John Conant, George Harold Edgell, J. Carol Fulkerson, Charles Edward Greene, Jean Jacques Haffner, Stephen Francis Hamblin, Samuel Franklin Hershey, Joseph Hudnut, John Sanford Humphreys, Byron S. Hurlbut, Charles Wilson Killam, Martin Mower, G. (George) Holmes Perkins, J. (Jean) Georges Peter, Bremer Whidden Pond, Arthur Pope, James Sturgis Pray, Paul J. Sachs, Hugh Asher Stubbins Jr., Christopher Tunnard, Harold Broadfield Warren, Herbert Langford Warren, Richard K. Webel, Charles Augustus Whittemore, and Morley Jeffers Williams.

61. John McAndrew, interview with Russell Lynes, October 1971, Russell Lynes Papers, Archives of American Art / Smithsonian; Arthur Clason Weatherhead, *The History of Collegiate Education in Architecture in the United States* (Charlottesville: University of Virginia, 1941), 108; Anthony Alofsin, *The Struggle for Modernism: Architecture, Landscape Architecture and City Planning at Harvard* (New York: W. W. Norton, 2002), 32–33.

62. Joseph Hudnut to Catherine Bauer Wurster, June 30, 1950, carton 15, CBW.

63. "New Appointments Made by President and Fellows," *Harvard Crimson*, May 22, 1923; Alofsin, *Struggle for Modernism*, 28 n. 19.

64. Jill Pearlman, *Inventing American Modernism: Joseph Hudnut, Walter Gropius, and the Bauhaus Legacy at Harvard* (Charlottesville: University of Virginia Press, 2007), 86–87. The theses involving housing were by Faith Gregg Bemis and Sarah Owen Wund (see their student files, CSR) and by Alice Muriel Childs (see her 1938 biographical register questionnaire in the alumnae records at Vassar College).

65. MIT, *Catalogue … Academic Year, 1934–35* (Cambridge, MA: Technology Press, June 1934), 25.

66. Henry Frost, "The Twenty First Year," *CSAB* 8, no. 1 (November 1935): 4; LeBoutillier, "Henry Atherton Frost." See also Pearlman, *Inventing American Modernism*, 159.

67. "Albert Farwell Bemis," *CSAB* 8, no. 3 (May 1936): 1.

68. Frost, [editorial], *CSAB* 1, no. 1, 2.

69. See Murphy, "The Vernacular Moment," 313–18; "Nomination Form," 2003, Cambridge Preservation Awards, Cambridge Historical Commission. In 1992, neither the Harvard University Planning Group nor the Cambridge Historical Commission considered the addition historically significant but rather a "neutral feature at best." See Charles M. Sullivan to Edwin C. Bearss, January 31, 1992, and Kathy A. Spiegelman to Edwin C. Bearss, February 2, 1992, Cambridge School Records, Cambridge Historical Commission.

70. Anne Stearns Molloy and Wayne Davis, "Higher Education for Women in Architecture and Landscape Architecture," *SAQ* 29, no. 2 (February 1938): 147–48.

71. Henry Frost, [editorial] and "Alumnae News Journal," *CSAB* 3, no. 1 (November 1930): 1–7.

72. Frost, [editorial], *CSAB* 1, no. 1, 4.

73. Henry Frost, [editorial], *CSAB* 1, no. 4 (September 1929): 3.

74. Henry Frost, "Outside the School," *CSAB* 2, no. 1 (November 1929): 4–5. See also "Decorations of Modern Homes Express Period, Educator Says," *Christian Science Monitor*, January 20, 1930.

75. Anita Rathbun, "Lectures 1929–1930," *CSAB* 2, no. 2 (April 1930): 6; "Extracts from Professor Haffner's Lectures on Modern Architecture Given in Boston, Chicago, Washington," *CSAB* 2, no. 2 (April 1930): 9–10.

76. *CSAB* 2, no. 2 (April 1930): 10.

77. "The Following Students Are on Thesis," *CSAB* 3, no. 2 (February 1931): 5–6. The theses were respectively by Elizabeth True Abbott, an architect, and Cynthia Ensign Wiley (Darby; 1898–1992), a landscape architect.

78. Henry Frost to Paul J. Sachs, February 24, 1931, Harvard Art Museums Archives.

79. Tom Long, "Henry A. Frost, Jr, Architectural Designer," *Boston Globe*, September 15, 2004, http://archive.boston.com/news/globe/obituaries/articles/2004/09/15/henry_a_frost_jr_84_architectural_designer/.

80. Joseph Hudnut to Walter Gropius, December 23, 1936, quoted in Pearlman, *Inventing American Modernism*, 116.

81. Marjory Gane Harkness, "The Alumnae College: Fourth Session," *SAQ* 27, no. 4 (August 1936): 335, http://saqonline.smith.edu/publication/?m=45764&i=432800&p=16.

82. See "Woods End Road Historic District," National Register of Historic Places continuation sheet, section 7, p. 2; "Northside [MA] Historic District," National Register of Historic Places registration form, August 24, 1987, file:///C:/Users/hunti/Downloads/87001777.pdf.

83. "The History of Western Civilization," *CSAB* 4, no. 1 (December 1931): 9.

84. Rathbun, "Lectures 1929–1930," 6.

85. See Henry Frost, [editorial], *CSAB* 2, no. 3 (May 1930): 1–2; "The Alumnae News Journal," *CSAB* 3, no. 1 (November 1930): 10. See also "Additional Pencil Points Competition Designs," *PP* 11, no. 9 (September 1930): 731. Pearlman, *Inventing American Modernism*, 117, states that Walter Bogner did not embrace modern architecture until after the arrival of Walter Gropius, but his interest was earlier based on this project. Katharine Wilson

also submitted a drawing—"A House for Cheerful Living in the Northeast States"—to the *Pencil Points* competition, carton 148, Katharine Wilson Rahn Papers, collection #4810, Division of Rare and Manuscript Collections, Cornell University Library.

86. "Katharine W. Rahn, Landscape Architect," *Buffalo News* [NY], September 23, 1992.

87. Albert Evans Simonson to the Students' Aide Society, February 11, 1939; Henry Frost to the Students' Aid Society, February 11, 1939; Henry Frost to Marjory P. Nield, February 15, 1939; alumnae questionnaire, Katharine Wilson student file, CSR.

88. Henry Frost, "The Middle of the Year," *CSAB* 8, no. 2 (February 1936): 1; Henry Frost, "Goings on About School," *CSAB* 8, no. 3 (May 1936): 1.

89. "Alumnae Notes," *CSAB* 8, no. 1 (November 1935): 20.

90. "Alumnae News Notes," *CSAB* 6, no. 2 (January 1934): 10; "Alumnae Notes," *SAQ* 26, no. 2 (February 1935): 207.

91. Elizabeth Wiley Dunlap, student file, CSR.

92. The two theses by Victorine du Pont Homsey are in a private collection.

93. Howard Myers, memorandum to Wesley Bailey, August 31, 1945, box 98, Henry R. Luce Papers, Library of Congress.

94. See, for example, "House for Henry B. Robertson," *Architectural Forum* 68, no. 2 (February 1938): 125–32; "A Portfolio of Recent Work by Victorine & Samuel Homsey of Wilmington, Delaware," *Architectural Forum* 73, no. 3 (September 1940): 159–72.

95. "Summer Plans," *CSAB* 3, no. 2 (February 1931): 8; Frost, "Middle of the Year," 2.

96. Penny Pringle Knowles, ed., *Our Beloved Betsy: Elizabeth Eldredge Pillsbury Pringle, 1912–1997* (privately printed, 2015), 31. Elizabeth Pillsbury's thesis took a traditional setting—a clubhouse on the first tee of a golf course on Martha's Vineyard—and gave it a modern twist—"a great big circular dining room that stuck out with terraces around it"—in the International Style (44–45).

97. A translation of "Kvinnliga arkitekter på visit från U.S.A.," *Svenska Dagbladet* [Stockholm], July 1, 1936, is in "European Trip," *CSAB* 8, no. 4 (August 1936): 1–3, along with another translated article, "Corbusier's Functionalism Does Not Appeal to Americans," from *Dagens Nyheter* [Stockholm], July 1, 1936.

98. See Dorothea L. MacMillan, "Houses and Housing Exhibition," *CSAB* 12, no. 2 (April 1940): 4–8; "Houses and Housing Exhibition to Open March 1 at Somerset," *Boston Herald*, February 23, 1940.

99. The houses by Walter Bogner and G. Holmes Perkins are pictured, respectively, in James Ford and Katherine Morrow Ford, *Classic Modern Homes of the Thirties* (New York: Dover Publications, 1989 [1940]), 22–23, 97–99. For work by Marc Peter Jr. and Hugh Stubbins, see "Small House Competition Sponsored by *Ladies Home Journal*," *Architectural Forum* 69, no. 4 (October 1938): 285–86; for the garden by J. Carol Fulkerson, see *Gardens on Parade: The Horticultural Exhibition at the World's Fair of 1940 in New York* (privately printed, 1940), 27.

100. Bauhaus Kooperation. "Ise Gropius, 1923–1928: Initiator of the 'Friends of the Bauhaus' and Editor," Bauhaus Kooperation, 2022, https://www.bauhauskooperation.com/knowledge/the-bauhaus/people/biography/413/. Katy Kelleher, "The Forgotten Story of 'Mrs. Bauhaus,'" *Artsy*, September 7, 2018, https://www.artsy.net/article/artsy-editorial-forgotten-story-mrs-bauhaus, argues that the Gropiuses "were true creative partners" and that "had she lived today, we might view Ise as Walter's equal."

101. Eleanor Garfield, "Alumnae Conference Week," *CSAB* 14, no. 1 (December 1941): 7–9; Ruth M. Havey, "An Alumnae Session at The Cambridge School," *SAQ* 33, no. 1 (November 1941): 25; "Town of Lincoln Focal Point for the Invasion of N.E. by Modern Architecture," *Christian Science Monitor*, November 27, 1942.

102. Hope Slade Jansen, "Alumnae Day," *CSAB* 9, no. 3 (April 1937): 1; "Architectural Coup," *Harvard Crimson*, January 25, 1937.

103. "Mr. and Mrs. Frost's Tea," *CSAB* 9, no. 4 (June 1937): 5–7.

104. "Cambridge School Minutes," June 3, 1937; Gropius, "Architecture at Harvard University," *AR* 81, no. 5 (May 1937): 9–10.

105. Elizabeth-Ann Campbell, "School Dinner, 1938," *CSAB* 11, no. 1 (November 1938): 6–7.

106. "Gropius Tells Lack of Properly Built Homes," *Daily Boston Globe*, May 22, 1938.

107. Rhoda Nichols Martin, "Alumnae Day Trip," *CSAB* 11, no. 1 (November 1938): 5–6. For the Albert "Carl" Koch house, see Mary Anne Hunting, *Edward Durell Stone: Modernism's Populist Architect* (New York: W. W. Norton, 2013), 35–36; for the Philip Johnson house, see "Houses," *Architectural Forum* 79, no. 6 (December 1942): 89–92.

108. Martin, "Alumnae Day Trip," 5–6; Hope Slade Jansen, "Alumnae Weekend," *CSAB* 9, no. 4 (June 1937): 2.

109. "Alumnae Notes," *CSAB* 8, no. 1 (November 1935): 20; "Alumnae Notes," *CSAB* 14, no. 1 (December 1941): 26. In addition to Sarah Pillsbury, the following worked with Eleanor Raymond: Laura Cox, Frances Whitmore Hartwell, Linda Smith Hires, Barbara M. Hollis, Gertrude Whitwell Howard (Fuller; 1919–84), Louise Leland, and Wenonah Edna Sibley.

110. "Pillsbury Summer House, Duxbury (Plymouth), MA," National Register of Historic Places continuation sheet, November 27, 2004, 2–3; "Sarah Pillsbury Harkness: Homemade Modernism," *PP* 77, no. 7 (July 1995): 77; Eleanor Raymond to Sarah Pillsbury Harkness, October 13, 1984, private collection.

111. See McCormick, "Wheaton College," 61, 251; "Prizewinning Designs," *Architectural Forum* 69, no. 2 (August 1938): 145, 156. The other female participants in the competition were Gertrud E. Ebbeson (1909–88), Irma Franzen-Heinrichsdorff (1892–1983), Ms. Sobotka (probably Ruth; 1925–67), Taina Tellervo Waisman (Katz; 1912–90), and Sylvia Wilde (1906–54).

112. Marjorie Stockard Underwood, "Bennington '38," private collection; Henry Frost to Mark C. Stevens, June 10, 1942, Stockard student file, CSR.

113. "Vacation Houses," *AR* 90, no. 7 (July 1941): 62–65. See also "Alumnae Notes," *CSAB* 12, no. 3 (August 1940): 15; "Alumnae Notes," *CSAB* 13, no. 1 (March 1941): 24; "Other Alumnae News," *CSAB* 14, no. 2 (July 1942): 28. The interior of the house by Alice Morgan Carson is illustrated in George Nelson and Henry Wright, *Tomorrow's House: A Complete Guide for the Home-Builder* (New York: Simon and Schuster, 1945), figs. 135–36.

114. Eleanor Raymond to President Herbert Davis, February 14, 1942, CSR; "Our New Trustee," *SAQ* 30, no. 4 (August 1939): 414.

115. Alofsin, *Struggle for Modernism*, 176.

116. See Henry Frost, "The Cambridge School at Harvard II," June 7, 1943, CSR. The Cambridge School women (including those who participated in the summer schools co-organized with Harvard in 1940 and 1941) who transferred to Harvard's Graduate School of Design in 1942 were Frances Baxter, Jean Bodman, Ruth Pearson Eakin, Helen Louise Ebeling, Helen Chittenden Elliot, Polly Evarts Faulkner, Margaret Chase Greene, Lucy Wheelock Hulburd, Margaret Greenough King, Jean League, Jean McMullen, Dorothy Noyes, Barbara Pierce, Franziska Porges, Hester Reed, Sarah Hitchcock Satterlee, Suzanne Stockard, Anne Tyng, Margaret Heath Wadsworth, Joan Warland, Joan Whiteside, and Alice Wilson Haible.

117. "Twins Given Scholarships: Harvard Award to Wollaston Girls," *Boston Herald*, July 9, 1942; "Women Will Enter School of Designing," *Harvard Crimson*, February 7, 1942. Frances Baxter, Jean Bodman, Lucy Hulburd, and Jean League accepted the scholarships; Priscilla Baxter, Katharyn Elizabeth Morris, and Marjorie Elizabeth Robbers did not.

118. Frost, "The Cambridge School at Harvard II," describes the commendations received by Jean Bodman, Margaret Greene, Helen Ebeling, Margaret Heath Wadsworth, Lucy Hulburd, Jean League, Jean McMullen, and Dorothy Noyes in the design studios led by Walter Bogner, Hugh Stubbins, and Marcel Breuer.

119. Henry Frost to James Conant, May 3, 1935, CSR; Henry Frost, "Suggestions for Changes in the Curriculum of the School of Architecture," April 10, 1935, President's Records, Harvard University Archives; Frost,

"A Report to the Trustees of the Cambridge School"; Pearlman, *Inventing American Modernism*, 4, 96.
120. *The Graduate School of Design: Description of the Courses in Architecture, Landscape Architecture and City Planning* (Cambridge, MA: Harvard University, 1944–45), 11–12.
121. Frost to President Neilson, January 7, 1938.
122. Hudnut, "Graduate School of Design," 292.
123. Joseph Hudnut, "The Architectress—Part I," *JAIA* 15, no. 3 (March 1951): 111. See also Joseph Hudnut, "The Architectress—Part II," *JAIA* 15 no. 4 (April 1951): 181–87.
124. See "School and Faculty Notes," *CSAB* 12, no. 1 (November 1939): 23; "School and Faculty Notes," *CSAB* 12, no. 2 (April 1940): 24; "School Notes," *CSAB* 4, no. 1 (December 1941): 15; Eunice Engle Hull student file, CSR. See also "Discussion Group," *TASK* 1 (Summer 1941): 7–8; Peter Blake, *No Place Like Utopia: Modern Architecture and the Company We Kept* (New York: Alfred A. Knopf, 1993), 59–60.
125. Joseph Hudnut, "Graduate School of Design," *Official Register* 35, no. 4 (1936–37): 248.
126. Joseph Hudnut, "Graduate School of Design," *Official Register* 38, no. 20 (1939–40): 265; Henry Frost, "A Note to the Alumnae," *CSAB* 14, no. 1 (December 1941): 3; Frost, "An End and a Beginning," 14.
127. Anne Griswold Tyng, "Records of the Radcliffe College Alumnae Association," 1894 2004, RG IX, series 2, carton 567, Schlesinger Library, Radcliffe Harvard Institute.
128. Jean League Newton to Ellamae Ellis League, September 14, 1943, private collection.
129. According to the annual reports of Joseph Hudnut in the *Official Register*, the department of architecture in 1938–39 enrolled seventy-nine students; in 1939–40, seventy-eight students; in 1940–41, seventy-eight students; in 1941–42, sixty students, twenty-nine of them women; in 1942–43, sixty-eight students; in 1943–44, fifty-one students (that diminished to less than forty), twenty-eight of them women; in 1944–45, eighty-two students, twenty-eight of them women; in 1945–46, 138 students; in 1946–47, 206 students (148 in architecture), nineteen of them women; in 1947–48, 235 students (167 in architecture) thirty-one of them women; and in 1948–49, 212 students (147 in architecture), thirty of them women.

II: International Exchanges

1. Pearlman, *Inventing American Modernism*, 2–5. Lewis Mumford used the word *humanistic* to describe what he dubbed the "Bay Region Style" in a controversial Skyline column in the *New Yorker*, October 11, 1947. Stanford Anderson connects it to a larger postwar debate about Modernism in "The 'New Empiricism—Bay Region Axis': Kay Fisker and Postwar Debates on Functionalism, Regionalism, and Monumentality," *Journal of Architectural Education* 50, no. 3 (February 1997): 197–207.
2. "Alumni Notes," *CSAB* 4, no. 1 (December 1931): 3.
3. The travel diaries by Ethel Power are in the Eleanor Raymond Collection. Nancy Beth Gruskin shared with us her research notes on the letters Power wrote when abroad that were in a private collection and are now missing. Unless stated otherwise, all references to the travels of Power and Raymond are taken from these notes.
4. Le Corbusier, *Towards a New Architecture*, trans. Frederick Etchells (London: John Rodker, 1927).
5. Henry-Russell Hitchcock, "Six Modern European Houses: That Represent Current Tendencies in France and Germany" *HB* 64, no. 3 (September 1928), 253–55.
6. Catherine Bauer, "Machine-Age for Ultra-Moderns," *New York Times*, April 15, 1928. André Lurçat's house for Edmond Bomsel was also featured in the *Machine Age* (1927) exhibition at the Museum of Modern Art (MoMA) in New York, and its rear facade is pictured in "French Designs for Small Homes," *New York Times*, May 22, 1927.
7. Ethel Power to Dorothy [Dorothy Raymond Ellis or Dorothy Power Hutchinson], October 5, 1930.
8. Despina Stratigakos, "The Professional Spoils of War: German Women Architects and World War I," *JSAH* 66, no. 4 (December 2007): 465; Despina Stratigakos, " 'I Myself Want to Build': Women, Architectural Education and the Integration of Germany's Technical Colleges," *Paedagogica Historica* 43, no. 6 (December 2007): 743–48.
9. Eleanor Raymond and Ethel Power likely arranged for the lecture on German housing by Elisabeth von Knobelsdorff von Tippelskirch at the Cambridge School. See "Lecture and Exhibition at the School," *CSAB* 5, no. 4 (June 1933): 10.
10. See the "Raymond-Kingsbury House," in Murphy, "The Vernacular Moment," 318–19.
11. At the annual school dinner in 1940, Eleanor Raymond confessed her weakness for red accents, which she attributed to the influence of Bremer Whidden Pond; Sally Hitchcock, "25th Anniversary School Dinner," *CSAB* 12, no. 2 (April 1940): 11.
12. Quoted in Wellesley Collage Alumnae Association, *Record Book of the Class of 1909* (1934), 84, Wellesley College Archives.
13. According to the assessor's office, before it was demolished by the Belmont Hill School, the Rachel Raymond house had three previous owners, beginning in 1951.
14. After the death of Helen Osborne Storrow, Walter Gropius and his wife purchased their house from her son and heir. Storrow also financed the construction of a house for Marcel Breuer in Lincoln, Massachusetts. See: "Gropius House (1938)," Historic New England, accessed June 19, 2022, https://www.historicnewengland.org/property/gropius-house/; Shantel Blakely, "Solid Vision, or Mr. Gropius Builds His Dream House," *AA Files* 75, no. 75 (2017): 88, 91.
15. From as early as 1922, Walter Gropius also used the metaphor of *stacked sugar cubes* to describe the arrangement of spaces in modern buildings. See Charles Jencks, *The New Paradigm in Architecture: The Language of Post-Modernism* (New Haven, CT: Yale University Press, 2002), 26.
16. "Gropius House," National Historic Landmark Nomination form, January 13, 2000, https://npgallery.nps.gov/GetAsset/25c952d1-64d8-4143-a4b0-c486dd51b940/.
17. Walter Gropius, "Introduction," *Scope of Total Architecture: A New Way of Life* (New York: Harper and Row, 1943), xx–xxi.
18. Edith Kingsbury, "Spring Pasture: Our Experiment in the Country," *HB* 72, no. 4 (October 1932), 205.
19. Kingsbury, "Spring Pasture," 264.
20. The brochure for the exhibition is in box 1 of the Amelia Peabody Papers, Massachusetts Historical Society.
21. Amelia Peabody, diary entry, October 20, 1938, box 6, Peabody Papers.
22. "Alumnae News Notes," *CSAB* 5, no. 4 (June 1933): 12.
23. Linda Smith Rhoads, *Amelia Peabody* (Boston: Amelia Peabody Charitable Fund, 1998), 2.
24. Eleanor Raymond, "Job Book, Color, Mileage Etc.," Raymond Collection.
25. [Ethel Power], [editorial on Contents page], *HB* 64, no. 2 (August 1928), 131.
26. Ethel Power to Alfred Clauss, November 18, 1931, Alfred Clauss records, Ubu Gallery. The apartment by Clauss is pictured in "Modernism for Economy," *House and Garden* 62, no. 4 (October 1932), 8d; "Domestic Architecture and Decoration in 1932–33," in *Decorative Art: Year Book of the Studio*, ed. C. G. Holme (London: Studio Limited, 1933), 98; "TVA Architect Pictures Home of Future," *Knoxville News-Sentinel*, May 3, 1936. The chrome chairs and chaise lounge by Clauss are in storage at the Philadelphia Museum of Art.
27. See for example, "Will This Modernism Last?," *HB* 65, no. 1 (January 1929), 44–45 in which the architects Ralph Adams Cram and Thomas E. Tallmadge take opposing positions.
28. "Our Modern House," *HB* 64, no. 6 (December 1928), 724; cover of *HB* 72, no. 3 (September 1932). "Prize-Winners in *HB*'s 10th Annual Cover

Competition," *HB* 72, no. 2 (August 1932), 65, announced that Henry John Stahlhut won honorable mention for his modern house cover design of *House Beautiful* in September 1932. Stahlhut graduated in 1930 with a degree in advertising design from Pratt Institute in Brooklyn, where he was also on the faculty in 1937–38 while at the same time a commercial artist and designer.

29. [Ethel Power], "Next Month," *HB* 72, no. 5 (November 1932), 281; Ethel Power, "Talking Points on Modernism," *HB* 75, no. 6 (June 1934), 60–62 and 74.

30. Elizabeth Bauer Mock to Alfred Barr Jr., private collection; Elizabeth Bauer to Catherine Bauer, box 1, CBW. Most of the letters between the two sisters, many of which are undated, are in box 1.

31. Elizabeth Bauer, "Vassar Buildings," *Vassar Miscellany News* 16, no. 39 (April 27, 1932). See also Elizabeth Bauer, "Public Opinion," *Vassar Miscellany News* 16, no. 42 (May 7, 1932); Elizabeth Bauer, "Vassar Buildings: A Modern Gymnasium," *Vassar Miscellany News* 16, no. 44 (May 14, 1932). The article by Catherine Bauer, "New Calisthenium for Vassar Female College," is in the architecture column (to which she was a consistent contributor) of *Arts Weekly* 1, no. 9 (May 7, 1932): 192–93.

32. Elizabeth Bauer Mock to Alfred Barr Jr., private collection.

33. Elizabeth Bauer to Catherine Bauer, July 4, 1932, CBW. See also the Ubu Gallery exhibition, "Knud Lonberg-Holm: The Invisible Architect," *Art Blart*, July 26 and 31, 2014, https://artblart.com/2014/07/26/exhibition-knud-lonberg-holm-the-invisible-architect-at-ubu-gallery-new-york-part-1/.

34. Elizabeth Bauer Mock to Catherine Bauer, CBW; Elizabeth Bauer Mock to Alfred Barr, carton 2, CBW.

35. The correspondence of 1947 between Elizabeth Bauer Mock and Olgivanna and Frank Lloyd Wright is in the Frank Lloyd Wright Archives, Avery Architectural and Fine Arts Library, Columbia University (henceforth Avery Library).

36. Elizabeth Bauer Mock to Catherine Bauer, August 22, CBW.

37. *Art in Our Time* (New York: Museum of Modern Art, 1939), 310. See also G. E. Kidder Smith, *Switzerland Builds—Its Native and Modern Architecture* (New York: Albert Bonnier, 1950), 102–3.

38. Elizabeth Bauer Mock to Catherine Bauer, CBW.

39. Elizabeth Bauer Mock to Alfred Barr, private collection.

40. Elizabeth Bauer Mock to Catherine Bauer, October 7, 1936, CBW.

41. Elizabeth Bauer Mock to Catherine Bauer, private collection.

42. Elizabeth Bauer Mock to Catherine Bauer, June 6, 1933, CBW.

43. Elizabeth Bauer Mock to Catherine Bauer, June 6, 1933, CBW; Elizabeth Bauer Mock to Olgivanna and Frank Lloyd Wright, June 21, 1933, M038D06, Wright Archives.

44. Elizabeth Bauer Mock, "Le Corbusier's Swiss Pavilion," *American Magazine of Art* 27, no. 1 (January 1934): 18–20. Two other articles she wrote for *American Magazine* are about the Paris Exposition (May 1937) and industrial arts (June 1940).

45. In a letter to Catherine Bauer, Elizabeth Bauer wrote, "Nat Swan, a very good person, may skip out on her senior year at Vassar and come with me—which would help," CBW. See also Frank Lloyd Wright to Nathalie Swan, January 1, 1932, SO26A06, Wright Archives.

46. Elizabeth Bauer to Frank Lloyd Wright, September 27, 1932, fiche id B017C08, Wright Archives.

47. James Hamden Robb to Nathalie Swan, private collection.

48. Bauer, "Architekturstudentinnen in der Weimarer Republik," 75.

49. The other two Americans were Bertrand Goldbert and William Turk Priestley. Under Walter Gropius, Bauhaus students were required to take the preliminary course so that they could discover their natural talent. See Walter Gropius, "Bauhaus Training: Preliminary Course," in *Scope of Total Architecture*, 12–13.

50. Nathalie Swan to the art editor, *New York Times*, December 18, 1938. See also Elizabeth Otto and Patrick Rössler, *Bauhaus Women: A Global Perspective* (London: Bloomsbury Publishing, 2019), 9; Elizabeth Otto, *Haunted Bauhaus: Occult Spirituality Gender Fluidity, Queer Identities, and Radical Politics* (Cambridge, MA: MIT Press, 2019), 100–101.

51. Nathalie Swan, "Lebenslauf" [resume], private collection.

52. Edith A. Roberts, letter of recommendation, October 22, 1932, private collection; Swan, "Lebenslauf."

53. Ludwig Mies van der Rohe to Nathalie Swan, August 30, 1933, private collection.

54. Frederick Kiesler, "The Architect in Search of Design Correlation: A Column on Exhibits, the Theater and the Cinema," *AR* 82, no. 1 (February 1937): 11.

55. Peter Bogner and Gerd Zillner, eds., *Frederick Kiesler: Face to Face with the Avant-Garde; Essays on Network and Impact* (Basel: Birkhäuser, 2019): 54.

56. The sketches by Nathalie Swan are in "Ten Years of American Opera Design [graphic], 1931–1941," Archives and Manuscripts, New York Public Library.

57. Diaries of Frederick J. and Stefi Kiesler, 1930 to 1955; letter from Nathalie Swan Rahv to Stefi Kiesler, June 10, 1941, Frederick Kiesler Foundation, Vienna, Austria.

58. Jean Stafford to the president of Con Edison, July 20, 1968, private collection.

59. According to her resume and letters, Nathalie Swan Rahv worked for Harry P. Jaenike in New York, 1937–39, and for Rodgers and Priestley in New York and Chicago, 1939–42. In New York, she also worked for Gibbs and Cox, 1942–45; Peter Copeland, 1945–46; Knoll Associates, 1947–49; and Shreve, Lamb & Harmon, 1956–57. Sometime in the 1940s, she worked in the Architect's Office in the New York State Department of Public Works. After moving in 1957 to Massachusetts, where she worked for Anderson Beckwith and Haible in Cambridge and, at least by 1970, until retirement, for Jung-Brannen Associates in Boston.

60. Perhaps Nathalie Swan saw MoMA's exhibited designs for a house in North Carolina, by William Priestley in the summer of 1933 and the G. H. Smith house (1933) by Rodgers and Priestley in Jericho, New York, in *Three Centuries of American Architecture* (1939). MoMA also holds a collage of the Stanley Resor house by William Priestley and George Danforth.

61. Margret Kentgens-Craig, *The Bauhaus and America: First Contacts, 1919–1936*, (Cambridge, MA: MIT Press, 1999), 92–93, identifies the other American women at the Bauhaus as Elsa Hempl Hill (1892–1974), whose father had been a German professor at Stanford; Virginia Tooker Weisshaus (Bredendiect; 1904–88), whose husband Imre led the musical program at the Bauhaus; and Leila Ulrich, who had studied at the Art Institute in Chicago. Of these, only Ulrich was in Berlin.

62. Mary McCarthy, "Philip Rahv, 1908–1973," *New York Times*, February 17, 1974.

63. See Andrew James Dvosin, "Literature in a Political World: The Career and Writings of Philip Rahv" (PhD diss., New York University, 1977); Philip Rahv to Nathalie Swan Rahv, August 25, 1960 and January 25, 1961.

64. Irving Karg to Nathalie Swan Rahv, January 9, 1974, private collection.

65. The articles by Frederick Kiesler are "Notes on the Spiral Theme in Architecture" *Partisan Review* 13, no. 1 (Winter 1946): 98–103; "Pseudo-Functionalism in Modern Architecture," *Partisan Review* 16, no. 7 (July 1949): 733–42.

66. In a letter of May 23, 1945, private collection, Allen Tate confessed, "I take my recent visit to NY as an occasion to tell you what I have long owed myself to say: that there are no people I enjoy more than you and Philip, that of the two of you I enjoy you more … the kindness and graciousness of your reception of me adds to the sum of the enduring things."

67. Mary McCarthy caricatured Nathalie Swan Rahv as Lakey in *The Group* (1963) and as Eva, the wife of Will Taub, a character based on Philip Rahv, in *The Oasis* (1949).

68. Robert Lowell to Elizabeth Bishop, October 16, 1958, in Thomas Travisano, with Saskia Hamilton, eds., *Words in Air: The Complete Correspondence Between Elizabeth Bishop and Robert Lowell* (New York: Farrar, Straus and Giroux, 2008), 271. Marcia Biederman consolidated the criticisms in *Popovers and Candlelight: Patricia Murphy and the Rise and Fall of a Restaurant Empire* (Albany, NY: SUNY Press, 2018), 106–7.

69. Office of Shreve Lamb to Herbert L. Beckwith, June 20, 1957; Nathalie Swan Rahv, resume.
70. Rebekah T. Dallas to the State Education Department, SUNY, May 3, 1946, private collection.
71. Inflation Calculator, https://www.usinflationcalculator.com/.
72. "The Candlelight Restaurant: Manhasset, L.I.," *Magazine of Light* 22, no. 1 (February 1953): 12, 23; "Patricia Murphy Candlelight Restaurant," b.45, Robert Kelly Papers, MS 1838, Manuscripts and Archives, Yale University Library. Nathalie Swan Rahv had used plywood on the exterior of a speculation house she and her realtor sister, Lois Swan (Junkin; 1916–96), designed and built for $30,000 on property in Westchester County's Bedford Village. A photograph of the house is in a private collection.
73. For images of the Candlelight Restaurant in Yonkers, NY, see "Remember When?" *Westchester*, April 6, 2005, https://westchestermagazine.com/life-style/remember-when/.
74. See Hunting, *Edward Durell Stone*, 18–19.
75. "Candlelight Restaurant: Luminous Pavilion Touched by the Orient," *Interiors* 114, no. 12 (July 1955): 76. See also "Decorating with Lighted Plants!," *Magazine of Light* 24, no. 1 (January–February 1955): 11–13.
76. Marion Petri, "Who Says We Can't Get Jobs?," *Minnesota Technology* 10 (May 1930): 253. See also "W. P. Nelson Company," in *Manufacturing and Wholesale Industries of Chicago* (Chicago: Thomas B. Pool, 1918), 289–92.
77. AIA Historical Directory, s.v. "Nelson, Paul [Daniel]," application for membership, November 8, 1957, https://aiahistoricaldirectory.atlassian.net/wiki/spaces/AHDAA/pages/35296724/ahd1032327?preview=/35296724/2201747663/NelsonPaul.pdf.
78. See the unpublished autobiography "Jane West Clauss," private collection. See also Avigail Sachs, "Jane West Clauss," accessed March 23, 2024, Pioneering Women, https://pioneeringwomen.bwaf.org/jane-west-clauss.
79. Le Corbusier to Oskar Stonorov, June 28, 1932, private collection.
80. Gordon Stephenson, "Le Corbusier," November 1979, Papers of Professor Gorden Stephenson, Special Collections and Archives, University of Liverpool, UK.
81. "Jane West Clauss"; Gordon Stephenson and Christina DeMarco, eds., *On a Human Scale: A Life in City Design* (Fremantle, Australia: Fremantle Arts Centre Press, 1992), 43. Unless otherwise noted, information about the Clausses is from the undated autobiography as well as another by West Clauss in the Clauss Papers, Athenaeum of Philadelphia.
82. See Gordon Stephenson, "Two Years in Paris (1930–32)," Stephenson Papers; Agnessa Larsen, *Graffiti on My Heart: An Autobiography, 1926–1937* (Seattle: Peanut Butter Publishing, 1994), 142; "Galaxy Le Corbusier: New Book [by Martina Hrabová] Tells Fascinating Story of Czech Architect František Sammer," Radio Prague International, June 11, 2022, https://english.radio.cz/galaxy-le-corbusier-new-book-tells-fascinating-story-czech-architect-frantisek-8752897. Anne Heyneman became an award-winning author and illustrator of children's books; Agnes Larsen married and divorced František Sammer while living in Russia between 1933 and 1937.
83. Jane West Clauss to Le Corbusier, June 14, 1962, Fondation Le Corbusier.
84. Agnessa Larsen to her mother, July 2, 1932, in Larsen, *Graffiti on My Heart*, 149. The letter from Le Corbusier is in a private collection.
85. Jane West Clauss to Lawrence Woodhouse, September 9, 1982, cited in Lawrence Woodhouse, "Houses by Alfred and Jane Clauss in Knoxville, Tennessee," *Arris* 1 (1989): 52 n. 12.
86. Alfred Clauss and George Daub produced a prototype for a standardized gas station for Standard Oil of Ohio (1932) and a few modern houses, including one for Louise Pope Johnson in Pinehurst, North Carolina (1931; unbuilt) and for the Cleveland curator Charlotte Young Bates (1931; built).
87. See "Young Architects Stage Rival Show," *New York Times*, April 21, 1931; "Architectural Show Will Aid Building," *New York Times*, March 8, 1931; Douglas Haskell, "The Architectural League and the Rejected Architects," *Parnassus* 3, no. 2 (May 1931): 12–13.
88. See Hunting, *Edward Durell Stone*, 26–30; Mary Anne Hunting, "The Richard H. Mandel House in Bedford Hills, New York," *The Magazine Antiques* 160, no. 1 (July 2001), 72–83.
89. "Unrestrained Gayety, Informality Marks Clauss-West Wedding Rites," *Chattanooga Daily Times*, December 23, 1934.
90. "TVA Display Staff Will Go to Knoxville," *Chattanooga Daily Times*, March 27, 1935.
91. "Houses in Knoxville, Tennessee," *Architectural Forum* 72, no. 4 (April 1940): 276–77. For more recent articles about Little Switzerland, see Cheryl Weber, "Modernizing the Moderns," *Residential Design Magazine* 2 (2023), 32–38; Anthony Paletta, "A Tennessee Subdivision Became a Model for Modern Living: Now It's Getting a Second Act," *Wall Street Journal*, June 15, 2023.
92. In 1944, the Clausses sold their first house, after which it was occupied by six different owners until John Lynch Sanders purchased it in 2017. Its twin at 417 Little Switzerland Drive was only owned by Walton and Katherine Deniston Seymour until 1943; after three more owners, it was purchased by Sanders in 2013. The Redwood House was lived in by the Clausses until 1946 and then passed on to four other families before Sanders bought it in 2015. The Clausses owned the log cabin until 1946 and the house at 432 Little Switzerland Drive until 1945. Two other Knoxville homes designed by the Clausses are the Joseph T. and Susan Mengel house at 6308 Westland Drive and the Virginia Baily and Henry Cowles Hart house at 4215 Holston Hills Road. See "Two Houses in Knoxville, Tennessee," *Architectural Review* 96, no. 571 (July 1944): 5–7; "In Knoxville, Tennessee," *PP* 26, no. 2 (February 1945): 60–62.
93. Sarah Booth Conroy, "View Ever Changing in Little Switzerland," *Knoxville-News-Sentinel*, January 9, 1955.
94. Bob Cunningham, "Knoxville's First Group Home Building Project Planned," *Knoxville News-Sentinel*, April 16, 1939. See also "Development Restricted to Houses of Contemporary Design," *PP* 27, no. 2 (February 1946): 66. The initial group of organizers included David Stone Martin, TVA graphic arts division; John M. Franz, TVA office service division; Walton Seymour, TVA director of power utilization; and Stratton Buck, a professor at the University of Tennessee.
95. Knox County Register of Deeds, Knoxville, TN, Deed Book 596, April 1939, 404. The median value of a house (land included) in Tennessee in 1940 was $19,000; see Wyoming Economic Analysis Division, "Historical Census of Housing Tables—Home Values," March 12, 2024, http://eadiv.state.wy.us/housing/Home_Value_ST.htm.
96. Cunningham, "Knoxville's First Group Home Building Project Planned."
97. See Daniel Williamson, "William Lescaze House and Offices," in the SAH Archipedia, ed. Gabrielle Esperdy and Karen Kingsley, accessed March 23, 2024, https://sah-archipedia.org/buildings/NY-01-061-0017.
98. Plans for the Clauss house are illustrated in "Development Restricted to Houses of Contemporary Design," 77.
99. "New Home Opened by Clauss Family," *Knoxville Journal*, January 23, 1940; "Clausses Build Modern Home, Not as a 'Dream House' but as Functionalism Proof and to Get Folks Used to It," *Knoxville Sentinel*, January 27, 1940.
100. "Alfred Clauss Home in Subdivision Here Is Praised by N.Y. Architectural League," *Knoxville News-Sentinel*, March 23, 1941.
101. See the want ads for "Little Switzerland," *Knoxville Journal*, December 2, 1945; "Mountain Homes," *Knoxville News-Sentinel*, May 4, 1941.
102. For the log cabin, see "Two Hillside Camps," *HB* 83, no. 8 (July–August 1941), 20; "Development Restricted to Houses of Contemporary Design," 67, 78; "Four Houses at Knoxville," *Architectural Review* 96, no. 576 (December 1944): 164–65, 168.
103. See "Summer House for Mrs. Clara Fargo Thomas, George Howe, Architect," *Architectural Forum* 71, no. 6 (December 1939): 446–54; John McAndrew, ed. *Guide to Modern Architecture: Northeast States* (New York: Museum of Modern Art, 1940), 27.
104. See Esther McCoy, *Five California Architects* (Los Angeles: Hennessey + Ingalls, 1975).
105. Floor plans of the Redwood House are in "Development Restricted to Houses of Contemporary Design," 69.

106. William Wurster to Alfred Clauss, July 10, 1945, Clauss Papers.
107. The Avondale Knolls promotional materials are in the Clauss Papers.
108. Carol Gabler, "The Clausses Drew a Blueprint for a Happy, Working Marriage," *Sunday Bulletin*, October 20, 1960.
109. The Peter Otto Clauss house is shown in Katherine Morrow Ford and Thomas H. Creighton, *Quality Budget Houses: A Treasury of 100 Architect-Designed Houses from $5,000 to $20,000* (New York: Reinhold Publishing, 1954), 186–87.
110. See "The Clausses Drew a Blueprint."
111. Doris E. Wiley, "Ramps Feature This Home," *Times of Delaware County* [Pennsylvania], May 4, 1957; A. H. Alexander, "Modern Functional House," *Philadelphia Inquirer*, February 13, 1949.
112. See Corin Redgrave, *Michael Redgrave: My Father* (London: Fourth Estate, 1996), 69; letters from Mary Coss to Corin Redgrave, 1930–1931, GB 71 THM / 31 / 3 / 5 / 3 / 1–15, Sir Michael Redgrave Archive, V&A Theatre and Performance Collections.
113. Sibilla Skidelsky, "Young America Builds," *Mademoiselle* 13, no. 4 (August 1941), 239.
114. Another striking portrait of Mary Coss Barnes by Herbert Matters is in the Stanford University Library.
115. Elizabeth Darling and Lynn Walker, eds., *AA Women in Architecture 1917–2017* (London: AA Publications, 2017), 6.
116. Skidelsky, "Young America Builds," 239.
117. The working-class domestic flats competition is described in John Allen, *Berthold Lubetkin: Architecture and the Tradition of Progress*, 2nd ed. (London: Artiface, 2012), 281–85; the David Astor bathroom is in the "Decoration," supplement, *Architectural Review*, no. 20 (November 1936): 226. A photograph of Mary Coss Cooke with Lindsay Drake, Berthold Lubetkin, William Tatton-Brown, Francis Skinner, Ove Arup and his wife, Ruth "Li" Sorensen, and Margaret Church boarding an airplane for a weekend in Paris is in "Notes and Topics," *Architect's Journal* 81 (March 1935): 397.
118. The David Lloyd George house is illustrated in Michael Page, "Winning the War in Walton on the Hill and Claiming the Credit in Churt: Lloyd George in Surrey," Surrey in the Great War (A County Remembers), A Surrey [County Council] Heritage Project, May 9, 2016, https://www.surreyinthegreatwar.org.uk//story/winning-the-war-in-walton-on-the-hill-and-claiming-the-credit-in-churt-lloyd-george-in-surrey/.
119. Berthold Lubetkin, letter of recommendation, May 25, 1937, private collection.
120. Frederick Gutheim, "Memoirs," box 1, Frederick Gutheim Papers, Department of Drawings and Archives, Avery Library.
121. Mary [Coss] Cooke, "Bauhaus Post Mortem," *Magazine of Art* 32, no. 5 (January 1, 1939): 37–40. Catherine Bauer published "Exhibition of Modern Architecture: Museum of Modern Art" in *Creative Arts* 10, no. 3 (March 1932): 201–6.
122. "The Museum Goes Abroad," *Bulletin of the Museum of Modern Art* 12, no 2 (1944): 2–4; Elizabeth Bauer Mock to Catherine Bauer Wurster, November 10, 1943, box 2, CBW.
123. Mary Coss Barnes, "Diary," 1947–50, August 3, 1948, private collection.
124. The two articles in *Task* are Edward L. Barnes, "Defense Housing—March 1941," *Task*, no. 1 (Summer 1941): 20–24; Mary Cooke, "War-Time Advances in Housing," *Task*, no. 5 (Spring 1944): 37–38. Catherine Bauer also contributed "Outline of War Housing," *Task*, no. 4 (1943): 5–8.
125. According to a resume, 1938–42 (private collection), at various times between June 1941 and March 1942 Edward Larrabee Barnes was a draftsman for Walter Gropius and / or Marcel Breuer, working on Federal Works Agency housing General Houses, and Yankee Portable prefabricated housing units.
126. Edward Barnes letter, n.d., Marcel Breuer Digital Archive, Syracuse University, https://breuer.syr.edu/xtf/view?docId=mets/3770.mets.xml;query=edward%20larrabee%20barnes;brand=breuer.
127. Marcel Breuer to Mary Coss Cooke, August 23, 1940, Marcel Breuer Digital Archive, https://breuer.syr.edu/xtf/view?docId=mets/2815.mets.xml;query=mary%20cooke;brand=breuer; Marcel Breuer to Mary Coss Cooke, October 7, 1941, Breuer Digital Archive, https://breuer.syr.edu/xtf/view?docId=mets/2357.mets.xml;query=mary%20cooke;brand=breuer.
128. Mary Coss Barnes, "Diary," December 14, 1943, private collection.
129. Edward Barnes to Mary Coss Cooke, April 19, 1942, private collection. For a description of Constance Crocker Leighton Breuer, see Natalie Gordon, "Our Gracious Ladies," *American Magazine of Art* 35, no. 9 (September 1942): 25, Marcel Breuer Digital Archives, https://breuer.syr.edu/Documents/Detail/our-gracious-ladies/156381.u.
130. Tatyana Likhonin, "Margaret Ayer Barnes," Literary and Cultural History Maps of PA, Pennsylvania Center for the Book, 2018, https://pabook.libraries.psu.edu/literary-cultural-heritage-map-pa/bios/Barnes__Margaret_Ayer.
131. Amelie Rives Rennolds, "Mary Coss Barnes 1910–2008," *Amelie Rives Rennolds* (blog), November 15, 2010, http://www.arrennolds.com/blog/?p=85.
132. For more about the Robert and Elodie Osborn house, see Christian Bjone, *First House: The Grid, the Figure, and the Void* (New York: Wiley, 2002): 55; "Platform Houses: Edward L. Barnes, Architect," *AR* 120, no. 4 (October 1956): 208–13.
133. Images of the Rockefeller pavilion model are in box 8 of the Philip Johnson Papers, 1908–2002, Getty Research Collections. According to Sybil Gordon Kantor, *Alfred H. Barr, Jr. and the Intellectual Origins of the Museum of Modern Art* (Cambridge, MA: MIT Press, 2002), 279, Theodate Johnson took creditor introducing her brother Philip Johnson to Alfred Barr at her performance of "Antony and Cleopatra" at Wellesley College, where Barr was teaching at the time.
134. Edward Barnes, *Edward Larrabee Barnes, Architect* (New York: Rizzoli, 1995), 9, 12.
135. John Barnes, interview with Mary Anne Hunting, March 4, 2022.
136. "A Thousand Women in Architecture: Part II," 108.
137. Stevens, "Struggle for Place," 98.
138. Elsa Mandelstamm Gidoni, "So Now They Are Sending Me Female Architects!," Elsa Mandelstamm Gidoni Papers, Prints and Photographs Division, Library of Congress.
139. Elsa Mandelstamm Gidoni, "Declaration of Intention," August 30, 1938, Mandelstamm Gidoni Papers.
140. Konrad Wachsmann, "Eidesstattliche Versicherung" [affidavit], March 1957, Konrad-Wachsmann-Sammlung, Akademie der Künste.
141. "Shelter for Girls: New Institution in Tel Aviv," *Palestine Post* [Jerusalem], February 18, 1935; Despina Stratigakos, "Elsa Mandelstamm Gidoni," Pioneering Women, March 9, 2024, https://pioneeringwomen.bwaf.org/elsa-mandelstamm-gidoni/; "Café Galina at Levant Fair, Tel Aviv, Designed by Elsa Gidoni and Genia Averbuch," Prints and Photographs Division, Library of Congress, https://www.loc.gov/item/2014646273/.
142. "Shelter for Girls"; Naama Riba, "The Forgotten Female Architects Who Changed the Face of Pre-state Israel," *Haaretz*, January 19, 2021, https://www.haaretz.com/israel-news/.premium.MAGAZINE-the-pioneering-1930s-female-architect-forgotten-in-tel-aviv-immortalized-in-nyc-1.9461174.
143. "Shelter for Girls."
144. See Sara Gdula, "The New Hope Experiment: An Investigation and Conservation Plan for the Antonin and Noémi Raymond Farm" (MA thesis, University of Pennsylvania, 2018), https://repository.upenn.edu/cgi/viewcontent.cgi?article=1656&context=hp_theses; Kurt Helfrich and William Whitaker, *Crafting a Modern World: The Architecture and Design of Antonin and Noémi Raymond* (New York: Princeton Architectural Press, 2006).
145. AIA Historical Directory, s.v. "Gidoni, Elsa," application for membership, January 27, 1943, https://aiahistoricaldirectory.atlassian.net/wiki/spaces/AHDAA/pages/35541486/ahd1015844?preview=/35541486/2217378239/Gidoni_Elsa.pdf.
146. Ely Jacques Kahn, "American Office Practice," *Journal of the Royal Institute of British Architects* 64, no. 11 (September 1957): 447; *Oxford Dictionary of National Biography*, s.v. "Robertson, Doris Adeney, Lady Robertson (1899–1931)," July 11, 2019, https://www.oxforddnb.com

/browse?gender=Female&t_0=OccupationsAndRealmsOfRenown%3A121&t_1=OccupationsAndRealmsOfRenown%3A1893. For more about Lady Robertson, see "Australian Girl's Success: Miss Doris Lewis," *Argus* [Melbourne, Australia], April 23, 1926, 14.

147. Kahn, "American Office Practice," 443; Marilyn Hoffman, "Key Skills Linked," *Christian Science Monitor*, April 27, 1960; AIA Historical Directory, s.v. "Kahn and Jacobs," architects' roster questionnaire, January 30, 1953, https://aiahistoricaldirectory.atlassian.net/wiki/spaces/AHDAA/pages/35780669/ahd4002927?preview=/35780669/2193097107/KahnJacobs_roster.pdf.

148. Mary King, "There's a Quiet Woman's Quiet Touch in the Travelers Insurance Building," *Boston Globe*, April 3, 1960.

149. See King, "There's a Quiet Woman's Touch"; Thomas W. Ennis, "Women Gain Role in Architecture," *New York Times*, March 16, 1960.

150. "The Industrialized House," *Architectural Forum* 86, no. 2 (February 1947): 120.

151. *Catalog of Copyright Entries*, 3rd ser., 2, parts 7–11A, no. 1 (Washington, DC: US Government Publishing Office, January–June 1948), 34, https://archive.org/search.php?query=gidoni&and[]=collection:%22copyright records%22&sin=TXT.

152. AIA Historical Directory, s.v. "Frommer, Marie," application for membership, August 28, 1952, https://aiahistoricaldirectory.atlassian.net/wiki/spaces/AHDAA/pages/36938819/ahd1014890?preview=/36938819/2216330208/FrommerMarie.pdf. See also her biography in Ines Sonder, Mary Pepchinski, Christina Budde, Wolfgang Voight, et al, eds., *Frau Architekt: Over 100 Years of Women in Architecture* (Tübingen: Wasmuth Ernst Verlag, 2017), 141–45, and Tanja Poppelreuter, "Sustaining Independence: Marie Frommer's Networks and Architectural Practices in Berlin and in New York," in *Designing Transformation: Jews and Cultural Identity in Central European Modernism,* ed. Elana Shapira, 221-36 (Bloomsbury Publishing, 2021).

153. Ennis, "Women Gain Role in Architecture."

154. Tina Ciesolik, *Marie Frommer: Architektin; Emigrantin* (Zürich: Eidgenössische Technische Hochschule, 2008), 20. Paul Zucker was the editor of *New Architecture and City Planning: A Symposium* (New York: Philosophical Library, 1944), in which he published the important essay by Siegfried Giedion, "The Need for a New Monumentality," 549–68. See also "Dr. Paul Zucker Is Dead at 82: Many Years at Cooper Union," *New York Times*, February 16, 1971.

155. See Kathleen James-Chakraborty, *Erich Mendelsohn and the Architecture of German Modernism* (New York: Cambridge University Press, 1997).

156. See Marie Frommer, "Umbau der Villa Majestic in Berlin-Wilmersdorf zum Hotel," *Bauwelt* 21, no. 14 (April 1930): 9–12. According to the travel diaries of Ethel Power, on October 10, 1930, Frommer escorted Eleanor Raymond and her to various building sites, including the Majestic, which they thought showed no sense of color.

157. "A Thousand Women in Architecture: Part I," 110.

158. Other than what is discussed in the text, Marie Frommer's work is identified in the following: "Novel House Plan," *AR* 104, no. 1 (July 1948): 164, 166; "Showroom and Building for Creative Looms, Inc.," *AR* 106, no. 4 (October 1949): 124–25; 19 West 31st Street alteration in "Building Plans Filed," *New York Times*, November 8, 1946; Manhattan Towers Hotel alteration (1949) in "Building Plans Filed," *New York Times*, December 21, 1946; a penthouse (1952) at 525 Park Avenue in American Architects Directory, s.v. "Frommer, Marie," March 9, 2024, http://content.aia.org/sites/default/files/2018-09/Bowker_1962_F.pdf; a townhouse (1958) at 75 East 52nd Street in American Architects Directory, s.v. "Frommer, Marie," March 9, 2024, http://content.aia.org/sites/default/files/2018-09/Bowker_1970_F.pdf.

159. "Radio Frank's Knight Club, New York City," *PP* 25, no. 7 (July 1944): 60–61. According to the In the Forum column in *Architectural Forum* 88, no. 5 (May 1948): 52, while in Germany, Paul Bry obtained a doctorate in "economy" from Breslau University (now in Wrocław, Poland), and attended a craftsmen school in Berlin and a decorative arts school in Charlottenburg.

160. Louis Sobol, "New York Broadway Cavalcade," *Press Democrat* [Santa Rosa, CA], May 28, 1944.

161. American Architects Directory, s.v. "Frommer, Marie," 1962 and 1970.

162. "Inexpensive Design for Specialty Shop," *PP* 27, no. 8 (August 1946): 73–76.

163. The letterhead of Marie Frommer is in the Drawings, Prints and Graphic Design Department, Cooper-Hewitt, National Design Museum, https://collection.cooperhewitt.org/objects/18650807/.

164. "New Light on Forensic Interiors," *Interiors* 108, no. 10 (May 1948): 96–98. For examples of furniture by Paul Bry see Boris J. Lacroix, "Un Décorateur Europeen aux États-Unis: Paul Bry," *Art and Décoration*, no. 8 (1948): 32–34.

165. Marta A. Urbańska, "Maciej Nowicki: Architekt, urbanista, wizjoner osobowość twórcza na tle epoki," paper presented at the Faculty of Architecture, Cracow University of Technology, Cracow, Poland, 2000; Marta A. Urbańska, "Kalendarium życia I twórczości Macieja Nowickiego: Wizjonera I humanistry architektury," *Załacznik*, no. 1 (2014).

166. Andrea Austoni, "The Legacy of Polish Poster," *Smashing Magazine*, January 17, 2010, https://www.smashingmagazine.com/2010/01/the-legacy-of-polish-poster-design/; Danuta A. Boczar, "The Polish Poster," *Art Journal* 44, no. 1 (Spring 1984): 18, 26 n. 12; Przeclaw Smolik, "Pracownia Graficzna M. Nowickiego i S. Sandeckiej," *Arkady* 1, no. 5 (September 1935): 287–93. Twenty-two illustrations by both Nowickis are in *Album Młodej Architektury, 1935* (Warsaw: Związek Słuchaczów Architektury Politechniki Warszawskiej, 1935), http://bcpw.bg.pw.edu.pl/Content/7839/PDF/ama35.pdf. The Muzeum Plakatu in Warsaw contains graphic designs by the Nowickis.

167. *Official Catalogue of the Polish Pavilion at the World's Fair in New York* (Warsaw: printed by Drukarnia Polska, 1939), A111, viii.

168. See, for example, *Arkady* 3, no. 11–12 (December 1937): 633–40, 555, and frontispiece, https://kpbc.umk.pl/dlibra/publication/17453/edition/26576/content.

169. The designs for the spa are in "Dom Zdrojowy w Druskienikach," *Arkady* 5, no. 7–8 (July–August 1939): 313–18, https://kpbc.umk.pl/dlibra/publication/17532/edition/26648/content.

170. Designs for the mosque are illustrated in "Konkurs na Meczet w Warszawie," *Architektura i Budownictwo* 12 (June 1936): 190–93. The tourist house is illustrated at "Tourist House," Zabytek, accessed October 22, 2020, https://zabytek.pl/en/obiekty/augustow-dom-turysty/; "Augustów: Dom Turysty," Polska Niezwykla, accessed October 22, 2020, http://polskaniezwykla.pl/web/gallery/photo,159161.html; and "Podskarbińska 11—Budynek Klubu Sportowego 'Orzeł,'" Twoja-Praga, accessed October 22, 2020, https://www.twoja-praga.pl/praga/ulice/2491.html.

171. In the 1920s, Maciej Nowicki's father Zygmunt Nowicki was a Polish consul general in Chicago. See "Konsul Polski Zygmunt Nowicki w Chicago," *Dziennik Chicagoski* [Poland], June 28, 1920.

172. A color newspaper advertisement for Marshall Field designed by Stanisława Sandecka Nowicki with Hal Reif, Dorothy Christy, and the Vogue-Wright Studio was exhibited as #154 in the *Art Directors Club of Chicago's Annual Exhibition at the Art Institute of Chicago*, May 20–June 2, 1947, https://www.artic.edu/assets/cc034f3f-8c06-47bf-658e-cfe93e78d6ca. A logo by Sandecka Nowicki for Lakeside Press, an imprint of R. R. Donnelley and Sons, is in the company's archives, box 465, Special Collections Research Center, University of Chicago.

173. "Architects to Speak at Art Gallery Show," *News and Observer* [Raleigh, NC], June 5, 1949. The invitation to the exhibition is in the Ryerson and Burnham Libraries at the Art Institution of Chicago and in the North Carolina Museum of Art.

174. Henry L. Kamphoefner to the AIA board of directors, October 31, 1977, Stanisława Stanislawa Nowicki medal nomination file, AIA Archives.

175. A copy of the School of Design catalog is in folder 460-3,"Matthew Nowicki 1910–1950, exhibition file, MoMA Archives.

176. "Country Club: Raleigh, North Carolina," *PP* 32, no. 10 (October 1951): 84–88. See also "New Carolina Country Club Opens Today," *News and Observer* [Raleigh, NC], December 21, 1949; "New Country Club: Members Delight in Glass House That Can't Burn Down," *Life*, July 31, 1950.

177. The biographical sketch of Stanisława Sandecka Nowicki by Blanche Lemco van Ginkel is in a private collection.
178. "Unsung Women Pioneers at Penn Who Paved the Way for the Future," *University of Pennsylvania Almanac* 63, no. 28 (March 2017): 7, https://almanac.upenn.edu/uploads/media/032817-issue.pdf.
179. See "Modern on Chestnut Hill: New Shop Incorporates an Old Pitched-Roof House," *Interiors* 115, no. 3 (October 1955): 126–29; "Fenced In, a Little Store Designs for Space," *Architectural Forum* 104, no. 6 (June 1956): 153. See also Barbara J. Richberg "Georgia H. Perkins, Decorator," *Philadelphia Inquirer*, November 26, 1994.
180. G. Holmes Perkins to the AIA board of directors, November 2, 1977, Nowicki medal nomination file, AIA Archives.
181. Lewis Mumford, "In Memoriam," *New Yorker*, November 18, 1950.
182. See "Distinguished Professor Award, 1986–87," ACSA, March 9, 2024, https://www.acsa-arch.org/awards/awards-archive/#dp.
183. University of Manitoba alumni journal in *University Bulletin* 6, no. 1 (October 21, 1941).
184. Gedvug Gedqvustm, "Susanne Wasson-Tucker," Svenskt Kvinnobiografiskt Lexikon, June 23, 2020, https://www.skbl.se/en/article/SusanneWassonTuckero.
185. "Möbler intresserar inte inredaren Susanne Tuhcker," *Svenska Dagbladet*, December 23, 2000.
186. "Finns to Rebuild, Architect Asserts," *New York Times*, March 20, 1940; Arnold Tucker to Alvar Aalto, July 6, 1940, Alvar Aalto Foundation and John E. Burchard, "President's Report Issue," special issue, *Massachusetts Institute of Technology Bulletin* 76, no. 1 (October 1940): 72–73. See also "Aalto's American Town in Finland," *Yale Books* (blog), July 13, 2012, http://blog.yalebooks.com/2012/07/13/aaltos-american-town-in-finland/.
187. Alvar Aalto Foundation and John E. Burchard, "President's Report Issue," special issue, *Massachusetts Institute of Technology Bulletin* 77, no. 1 (October 1941): 72. For the role of Aalto at MIT, see Göran Schildt, "An American Town in Finland," in *Alvar Aalto: The Mature Years* (New York: Rizzoli, 1989), 28–40.
188. Susanne Raedermacher Wasson-Tucker to Marcel Breuer, October 23, 1940, Marcel Breuer Digital Archive, https://breuer.syr.edu/xtf/view?docId=mets/3068.mets.xml;query=wasson-tucker;brand=breuer.
189. The Commonwealth of Massachusetts, "Contract," January 22, 1942, Louisa Vaughan Conrad Collection, GSD. The "Profit and Loss Statement of Artek in Boston," August 1 to November 30, 1943 (in the same collection) shows that, in that period, each partner only profited $36.71 (equivalent to $616.05 in 2022).
190. "Arnold Tucker," June 6, 1957, Library at the National Gallery of Canada, University of Manitoba; "Erwin Hauer's Continua," Knoll, https://www.knoll.com/knollnewsdetail/hauer.
191. Raedermacher Wasson-Tucker's blueprint of the installation layout of the "Design for Use" section is in the Serge Ivan Chermayeff Architectural Records and Papers, Avery Library.
192. See "Designed for Use," *Architectural Forum* 81, no. 7 (July 1944): 4; John Hartell, "Fifteen Years New," *Art News* 43, no. 8 (June 1944): 9, frontispiece. See also Serge Ivan Chermayeff and Rene d'Harnoncourt, "Design for Use," in *Art in Progress: A Survey Prepared for the Fifteenth Anniversary of the Museum of Modern Art, New York* (New York: Museum of Modern Art, 1944), 191–201. Three earlier exhibitions focused on product design: *Machine Art* (1934), *Bauhaus, 1919–1928* (1938), and *Organic Design in Home Furnishings* (1941).
193. "Museum of Modern Art Opens Small Permanent Gallery of Architecture and Industrial Design," 1944, press release 441113–39, MoMA Archives, https://www.moma.org/momaorg/shared/pdfs/docs/press_archives/961/releases/MOMA_1944_0047_1944-11-13_441113-39.pdf.
194. See Elizabeth [Bauer] Mock, ed., "The House in Its Neighborhood," in *Tomorrow's Small House* (New York: Museum of Modern Art, 1945), 18–20; "Exhibit: Tomorrow's Small House," *Architectural Forum* 82, no. 7 (July 1945): 68, 72.
195. The recommendations for Susanne Raedermacher Wasson-Tucker are in the Black Mountain College Collection at the Western Regional Archives, States Archives of North Carolina.
196. "Susanne Wasson-Tucker," *Interiors* 111, no. 5 (December 1951), 166; Amy Rollinson, "If Your Interior Decorating Stumps You, Blame Architect," *Boston Globe*, April 2, 1952.
197. "Amerikanska ambassaden," *NK-Rullan*, 1954, Wasson-Tucker Papers, 10–14; Paul Makovsky, "Knoll Before Knoll Textiles, 1940–46," Bard Graduate Center Research Forum, 2011, https://www.bgc.bard.edu/research-forum/articles/203/knoll-before-knoll-textiles-1940.
198. The Cuban, Swedish, and Danish embassies were featured in the exhibition *Architecture for the State Department* (1953) at MoMA.
199. Between 1964 and 1969, Susanne Raedermacher Wasson-Tucker organized four exhibitions in San Francisco, Chicago, and Minneapolis in addition to a corporate showroom. In 1981, she also redesigned the interiors of the American-Scandinavian Foundation in New York.
200. Olga Gueft, "Swedish Carpentry Supports Swedish Textiles," *Interiors* 117, no. 11 (1958): 110–11.
201. Susanne [Raedermacher] Wasson-Tucker, "So You're Going to Mexico," *AR* 105, no. 3 (March 1949): 100–105.
202. Binkley Horn, "Modern Mexico," *AR* 102, no. 1 (July 1947): 70–83. Walter Horn, her second husband, collaborated with Ernest Born on a three-volume book on medieval architecture, *The Plan of St. Gall: A Study of the Architecture and Economy of, and Life in a Paradigmatic Carolingian Monastery* (Berkeley: University of California Press, 1979), suggesting that their wives, both interested in Mexico, would have known each other. For Arnold Wasson-Tucker, see "El Pabellón Canadiense: Proyecto y realización del Arq. Arnold Wasson Tucker," *Arquitectura y lo demás* 2, no. 9 (April–August 1946): 46–52.
203. Marva P. Shearer, "A Vacation in Another World," *HB* 91, no. 12 (December 1949), 158, 207–9, 211–14.
204. Mary Panzer, "The American Love Affair with Mexico, 1920–1970," *Archives of American Art Journal* 49, nos. 3–4 (Fall 2010): 17; Elizabeth Bauer to Catherine Bauer, CBW.
205. The modern apartment house and studio of Frances Toor (now demolished) was designed by Juan O'Gorman and featured in Esther Born, *The New Architecture in Mexico* (New York: Architectural Record and William Morrow, 1937), 66–67 as well as in the article of the same title in *AR* 81, no. 4 (April 1937): 67.
206. Panzer, "The American Love Affair with Mexico, 1920–1970," 16.
207. Luis E. Carranza, "Race and Miscegenation in Early Twentieth-Century Mexican Architecture," in *Race and Modern Architecture: A Critical History from the Enlightenment to the Present*, ed. Irene Cheng, Charles L. Davis, and Mabel O. Wilson, 155–71 (Pittsburgh: University of Pittsburgh Press, 2020).
208. See Eleanor Raymond, *Early Domestic Architecture of Pennsylvania* (New York: William Helburn, 1931).
209. "Twenty Centuries of Mexican Art Opens at the Museum of Modern Art," press release 40511–34, May 15, 1940, MoMA Archives, https://www.moma.org/momaorg/shared/pdfs/docs/press_archives/608/releases/MOMA_1940_0039_1940-05-11_40511,-34.pdf; Rene d'Harnoncourt, "The Loan Exhibition of Mexican Arts," *Bulletin of the Metropolitan Museum of Art* 25, no. 10 (October 1930): 210–16; Jere Abbott, "Notes on the Style of Diego Rivera," in *Diego Rivera* (New York: Museum of Modern Art, 1931), 39.
210. Douglas Haskell, "The Architectural League and the Rejected Architects," *Parnassus* 3, no. 2 (May 1931): 13.
211. See, for example, "Rockefellers Ban Lenin in RCA Mural and Dismiss Rivera," *New York Times*, May 10, 1933. For Diego Rivera's book illustrations, see Carleton Beals, *Mexican Maze* (Philadelphia: J. B. Lippincott, 1931); Stuart Chase, *Mexico: A Study of Two Americas* (New York: Macmillan, 1931).
212. See Matthew Affron, Mark A. Castro, Dafne Cruz Porchini, and Renato González Mello, eds., *Paint the Revolution: Mexican Modernism, 1910–1950* (New Haven, CT: Yale University Press and Philadelphia Museum of Art,

2016). The Cambridge School women who traveled to Mexico, according to the *CSAB*, were Margaret Fisher, Mary Palache Gregory, Ann Bruce Haldeman, Dorothea K. Harrison, Victorine du Pont Homsey, Dorothy Lannihan, Louise Leland, Elizabeth Abbot Pierce, Ethel Power, Eleanor Raymond, Sarah Hitchcock Satterlee, and Anna Stearns.
213. Dorothea K. Harrison, "A Trip to Mexico," *CSAB* 10, no. 3 (April 1938): 7–11.
214. Elizabeth Bauer to Catherine Bauer, 1933, CBW.
215. See, for example, Diego Rivera with Gladys March, *My Art, My Life: An Autobiography* (New York: Dover Publications, 1991 [1960]), 125.
216. Elizabeth Bauer to Catherine Bauer, 1933.
217. Interestingly, the colors Elizabeth Bauer noted are different from those observed by Kathryn E. O'Rourke in *Modern Architecture in Mexico City: History, Representation, and the Shaping of a Capital* (Pittsburgh: University of Pittsburgh Press, 2016), 182.
218. James Oles, ed., *South of the Border: Mexico in the American Imagination, 1914–1947* (Washington, DC: Smithsonian Institution Press, 1993), 171.
219. Ethel Power, "Mexico, 1965 & 1968," January 20, 1965, Raymond Collection.
220. Power, "Mexico, 1965 & 1968."
221. Verna Cook Shipway and Warren Shipway, *Mexican Interiors* (Santa Monica, CA: Hennessey and Ingalls, 2007 [1962]), 7.
222. Victorine Du Pont Homsey, "Our Trip to Mexico," *CSAB* 6, no. 1 (October 1933): 5–6. See also "Alumnae News," *CSAB* 5, no. 4 (June 1933): 13; *CSAB* 5, no. 3 (March 1933): 8; Guillermo Rivas, "The Water Colors of Samuel Homsey," *Mexican Life* 9, no. 4 (April 1933): 22–23.
223. Elizabeth Bauer Mock to Catherine Bauer, CBW.
224. Beach Riley, "Social Progress and the New Architecture," in Esther Born, *The New Architecture of Mexico* (New York: The Architectural Record, W. Morrow & Company, 1937), 19.
225. Ernest and Esther [Baum] Born collection, Environmental Design Archives, University of California, Berkeley, https://ced.berkeley.edu/collections/born-ernest-esther. The other two archives are in the Center for Creative Photograph at the University of Arizona and in the Canadian Centre for Architecture.
226. Ernestina Osorio, "Interdependence and the Construction of Mexican Modernist Discourse," *LA Metro*, Zoom webinar, May 13, 2021; Ernestina Osorio, "Intersections of Architecture, Photography, and Personhood: Case Studies in Mexican Modernity" (PhD diss., Princeton University, 2006), 322–90.
227. An advertisement for the school is in the *Brooklyn Daily Eagle*, August 22, 1929.
228. Invitation to *Its Life, Landscape and Architecture in Photographs by Esther Born*, November 10, 1936, box 1, Esther [Baum] Born Collection, CCP.
229. The photographs are in the Esther [Baum] Born Collection at the CCP.
230. Ernest Born, "Diego Rivera," *Architectural Forum* 60, no. 1 (January 1934): 1–2. Photographs by Esther Baum Born of Diego Rivera and Frida Kahlo are pictured in Nicholas Olsberg, *Architects and Artists: The Work of Ernest and Esther Born* (San Francisco: The Book Club of California, 2015), 106–7.
231. AIA Historical Directory, s.v. "Born, Ernest," application for membership, January 24, 1944, https://aiahistoricaldirectory.atlassian.net/wiki/spaces/AHDAA/pages/35844559/ahd1004387?preview=/35844559/2195948881/Born_Ernest.pdf.
232. Letter from Nicholas Olsberg to the author, August 5, 2020. Photographs by Esther Baum Born of the Fletcher quarry are in "Pictures of Granite," *Federal Architect* 6 (January 1936): 14–21. A photograph by Baum Born of the president of the company, Harold Ellery Fletcher, is in box 4 of the [Baum] Born Collection at the CCP.
233. "Public Relations Confuses Even the PR Executives," *Lorado Times* [TX] September 1, 1960. For more on Federico Sánchez Fogarty, see James Oles, "Industrial Landscapes in Modern Mexican Art," *Journal of Decorative and Propaganda Arts* 26 (2010): 142–57. The photograph of Fogarty by Esther Baum Born is in Olsberg, *Architects and Artists*, 108.
234. Federico Sánchez Fogarty, "Architect as Contractor," *AR* 81, no. 4 (April 1937): 10–13. Twelve lithographs by Ernest Born produced for Harold Fletcher are in the Westford [Massachusetts] Historical Society, https://museum.westford.org/collections-database/.
235. Nicholas Olsberg, "The Work of Ernest and Esther Born: Models for the City House," Drawing Matter, November 18, 2022, https://drawingmatter.org/the-work-of-ernest-and-esther-born-models-for-the-city-house/.
236. Osorio, "Interdependence and the Construction of Mexican Modernist Discourse."

III: Forging Networks

1. For the importance of leisure activities to professional advancement, see Jennifer Grandis, "Fishing, Strip Clubs and Golf: How Male-Focused Networking in Medicine Blocks Female Colleagues from Top Jobs," *The Conversation*, April 8, 2022, https://theconversation.com/fishing-strip-clubs-and-golf-how-male-focused-networking-in-medicine-blocks-female-colleagues-from-top-jobs-179931.
2. "The Role of the AIA," in *The Architect at Mid-Century: Evolution and Achievement*, ed. Turpin C. Bannister (New York: Reinhold Publishing, 1954), 451. Architectural registration was established on a state-by-state basis, beginning at the end of the nineteenth century.
3. Morris Lapidus, *Architecture: A Profession and a Business* (New York: Van Nostrand Reinhold, 1967), w"Candidate Training for the Practice of Architecture," in *Architect at Mid-Century*, ed. Turpin C. Bannister (New York: Reinhold Publishing, 1954), 331–49.
4. C[larence] Julian Oberwarth, "Apprenticeship and Early Professional Experience," in *Architecture: A Profession and a Career* (Washington, DC: AIA, 1945), 30. A comparison of the professional paths in medicine and architecture is also made in Dana Cuff, *Architecture: The Story of Practice* (Cambridge, MA: MIT Press, 1991).
5. Lapidus, *Architecture: A Profession and a Business*, 5.
6. Friedman, "Girl Talk."
7. For more on Marion Lincoln Lewis Chamberlain, see Lisa D. Schrenk, *The Oak Park Studio of Frank Lloyd Wright* (Chicago: University of Chicago Press, 2021), 91–92.
8. Stuart Cohen, *Frank Lloyd Wright and the Architects of Steinway Hall: A Study in Collaboration* (Novato, CA: Oro Editions, 2021), 8–11. Wright had an office in Steinway Hall between 1900 and 1908.
9. James Weirich, "Marion Mahony at MIT," *Transition* 25 (Winter 1988): 49, 51–54, quote at 52.
10. Lynne Walker, "Architecture and Reputation: Eileen Gray, Gender and Modernism," in *Women's Places: Architecture and Design, 1860–1960*, ed. Brenda Martin and Penny Sparke, (London: Routledge, 2003), 96.
11. Walker, "Architecture and Reputation," 97–100, quote at 100.
12. Lapidus, *Architecture: A Profession and a Business*, 54.
13. Victoria Kaplan, *Structural Inequality: Black Architects in the United States* (Lanham, MD: Rowman and Littlefield, 2006), 149–82, quote at 166.
14. Meghan Drueding, "Blazing a Trail: Three Designers Who Helped Light the Way for Women in Architecture," *Preservation* 73, no. 1 (2021): 34.
15. Drueding, "Blazing a Trail," 34.
16. Wright, "On the Fringe," 296.
17. Joanne Meyerowitz, "Beyond the Feminine Mystique," *Journal of American History* 79, no. 4 (March 1993): 1455–82.
18. Kristina Wilson, *Mid-Century Modernism and the American Body: Race, Gender, and the Politics of Power in Design* (Princeton, NJ: Princeton University Press, 2021), 27.
19. Elisabeth Coit, "Architecture as a Profession for Women," *Radcliffe Quarterly* 20, no. 2 (May 1936): 16.
20. Coit, "Architecture as a Profession," 16.
21. James-Chakraborty observed this phenomenon in her talk, "Expanding Agency: Women and Modern Architecture and Design" at the Center for

Advanced Study in the Visual Arts, National Gallery of Art, December 2, 2021. Earlier, in 2000, Mary Anne Hunting addressed Ethel Power's role in promoting modern architecture by women in her paper, "Through the Eye of the Editor," written for the Domesticity and Architecture seminar at the CUNY Graduate Center.

22. Jane King Hession, *Elizabeth Scheu Close: A Life in Modern Architecture* (Minneapolis: University of Minnesota Press, 2020), 13, 190 n. 21.

23. Wright, "On the Fringe," 283.

24. See the architecture student problems in the GSD History Collection: Student Affairs (student work), folder CA100, GSD.

25. See the obituary of Margaret Heath Wadsworth, *Legacy*, October 19, 2008, https://www.legacy.com/us/obituaries/theday/name/margaret-wadsworth-obituary?id=23513512.

26. "Illusion of Space to be Exhibit Theme," *New London Daily* [CT], January 16, 1989.

27. Eleanor Raymond, "The House of To-morrow," *HB* 74, no. 1 (July 1933), 18.

28. Shand-Tucci, *The Crimson Letter*, 164–67, 232–34; Kevin D. Murphy, "Welcome to the Gayborhood: Beacon Hill Between the Wars," *Art Bulletin* 106, no. 1 (March 2024): 28–33.

29. Alice T. Friedman, *Women and the Making of the Modern House: A Social and Architectural History* (New York: Abrams, 1998), 18.

30. Gruskin, "Building Context," 78–81.

31. Ethel Power, "A Beacon Hill Restoration," *HB* 56, no. 5 (November 1924), 462.

32. Alice T. Friedman, "Hiding in Plain Sight: Love, Life and the Queering of Domesticity in Early Twentieth-Century New England," *Home Cultures: Journal of Architecture, Design and Domestic Space* 12, no. 2 (2015): 143.

33. Power, "A Beacon Hill Restoration," 463.

34. Le Corbusier, *Vers une architecture*, 2nd ed. (Paris: Éditions G. Crès et Cie, 1925 [1923]), ix.

35. Power, "A Beacon Hill Restoration," 463.

36. Power, "A Beacon Hill Restoration," 464.

37. William Emerson, "Charles Howard Walker (1857–1936)," *Proceedings of the American Academy of Arts and Sciences* 72, no. 10 (May 1938): 396–97; "Items of Interest," *American Magazine of Art* 13, no. 6 (June 1922): 197.

38. Clippings of alumnae news, 1920, 1921, and 1939, Rachel Raymond alumna file, Wellesley College Archives.

39. Kingsbury, "Spring Pasture," 204. The house is also illustrated in Power, "Talking Points on Modernism," 60.

40. Kingsbury, "Spring Pasture," 205–6.

41. "Margarett Sargent Paints Our Times," *Boston Evening Transcript*, February 12, 1930.

42. Honor Moore, *The White Blackbird: A Life of the Painter Margarett Sargent by her Granddaughter* (New York: W. W. Norton, 2009). Shand-Tucci, *The Crimson Letter*, 330, refers to the artist as "the still shamefully neglected Margaret [sic] Sargent."

43. "Paintings by Margarett Sargent," November 28–December 13, 1930, boxes 11 and 3, scrapbook 6, Arts Club of Chicago Papers, Newberry Library. A "Speak-easy" painting by Sargent was also shown in 1932 in an exhibition at Doll and Richards in Boston.

44. See Anne Higonnet, *Margarett Sargent: A Modern Temperament* (Wellesley, MA: Davis Museum and Cultural Center, 1996). F. C. Poole offered antiques and reproduction furniture, decorative objects, reupholstery, and restoration services; see the advertisement in *Cape Ann Shore* [MA], August 8, 1914.

45. For photographs of the property, see Cole, *Eleanor Raymond*, 148–52; "Visiting the Cottage of Eleanor Raymond and Ethel Power," Cape Ann Museum, Vimeo video, May 20, 2021, https://vimeo.com/552981061.

46. Diary entry by May Sarton for July 30, 1930, quoted in Margot Peters, *May Sarton: A Biography* (New York: Ballantine Publishing Group, 1977), 59. For Florence Cunningham, see Gloucester Historical Commission, "Rocky Neck [Gloucester, MA] Historic District," National Register of Historic Places registration form, August 2016, https://www.gloucester-ma.gov.

47. Gruskin, "Designing Woman," 156; Nancy Beth Gruskin, "Raymond, Eleanor 1887–1989," in *Encyclopedia of 20th-Century Architecture*, ed. R. Stephen Sennott, vol. 3 (New York: Fitzroy Dearborn, 2004), 1086; and Cole, *Eleanor Raymond*, 47.

48. Quotation from an unspecified source in Neil Baldwin, *Martha Graham, A Life: When Dance Became Modern* (New York: Alfred A. Knopf, 2022), 273.

49. Massachusetts land records and maps show the house standing at least by 1913. See "Plan of Land in Gloucester," April 12, 1913, 1922 subdivision plan (cert. of title no. 1544), and Deed no. 24103 from Francis W. Kimball to Eleanor Raymond, November 14, 1930, (cert. of title no. 6342), Secretary of the Commonwealth of Massachusetts, Massachusetts Land Records, https://masslandrecords.com.

50. Ethel Power, Gloucester summer diaries, Raymond Collection.

51. Ethel Power, "The Experimental House," *HB* 58, no. 4 (May 1933), 213, 226–28.

52. Power, "The Experimental House," 213.

53. Ethel Power, "A Garden Sun Trap Described by Ethel B. Power," *Woman's Home Companion*, June 1937, 68–69. See also Christine Ferry, "Backyard Vacationing," *American Home*, June 1942, 21–23; Margaret Olthof Goldsmith, *Designs for Outdoor Living* (New York: George W. Stewart, 1941), 247–48.

54. Scrapbook made for Eleanor Raymond, March 23, 1976, Raymond Collection; Robert Campbell, "The Ethic of Eleanor Raymond," *Boston Globe*, October 2, 1981; Power, "A Garden Sun Trap," 68–69.

55. See Ethel Power's diary entries especially for April 23, May 27, and August 15, 1933, and July 31, 1950.

56. Rhoads, *Amelia Peabody*, 18–19.

57. For illustrations of the farm group by Eleanor Raymond see *HB* 77, no. 12 (December 1935), 39, and the Raymond Collection.

58. Press release about Eleanor Raymond, Wellesley College, February 15, 1953, Wellesley College Archives. For the plywood and Masonite houses by Raymond, see "A Thousand Women in Architecture: Part I," 111. Among the numerous publications about her solar house, see Morgan Sherburn, "The House of the Day after Tomorrow: A 1948 Solar House Designed by (Gasp) Women," *MIT Technology Review*, October 27, 2016.

59. Cole, "An Interview with Eleanor Raymond."

60. Stephen Patience, "Surface Tension: The Glamorous World of Noël Coward," *Apollo*, March 1, 2021, https://www.pressreader.com/uk/apollo-magazine-9lam/20210301/281522228798076. See also John Potvin, *Bachelors of a Different Sort: Queer Aesthetics and the Modern Interior in Britain* (Manchester, UK: Manchester University Press, 2014), 234–35. Photographs of the original production are in the New York Public Library for the Performing Arts.

IV: Collaboration as a Primary Strategy

1. Marcia Mead, "Women's Versatility in Arts Enriches Field of Architecture," *Christian Science Monitor*, November 27, 1931.

2. "Girl Architects Organize a Firm," *New York Times*, March 8, 1914.

3. "Girl Architects Organize a Firm."

4. See "The Architects Collaborative," in *The Architects Collaborative, 1945–1965*, ed. Walter Gropius and Sarah P[illsbury] Harkness (Teufen AR, Switzerland: Arthur Niggli, 1966), 12; Walter Gropius, "My Conception of the Bauhaus Idea," in *Scope of Total Architecture: A New Way of Life* (New York: Harper and Row, 1943), 6–19; "The Architects Collaborative," *Architectuul*, accessed June 23, 2022, http://architectuul.com/architect/the-architects-collaborative.

5. Reyner Banham, review of "This Is Tomorrow," *Architectural Review* 120, no. 716 (September 1956): 186–88, quoted in Romy Golan, *Muralnomad: The Paradox of Wall Painting, Europe 1927–1957* (New Haven, CT: Yale University Press, 2009), 182.

6. Golan, *Muralnomad*, chapter 5 ("All-Redeeming Synthesis").

7. Whitney Chadwick, "Living Simultaneously: Sonia & Robert Delaunay,"

in Chadwick and Isabelle De Courtivron, *Significant Others: Creativity and Intimate Partnership* (London: Thames and Hudson, 2005), 32.
8. Beatriz Colomina, "Couplings," *OASE: Architectural Journal* 51, no. 1 (1999): 23.
9. See Jeffrey Karl Ochsner, "The First Modern Practice? H.H. Richardson and His Office," in *Proceedings of the 81st Annual Meeting of the ACSA*, ed. Michael Fazio and Joanna Lombard, 231–35 (Washington, DC: ACSA, 1993).
10. Sandra L. Tatman, "Hoover, Ira Wilson (1871–1941)," Philadelphia Architects and Buildings, March 13, 2024, https://www.philadelphiabuildings.org/pab/app/ar_display.cfm/22704.
11. Eleanor Raymond published her book *Early Domestic Architecture of Pennsylvania* seven years earlier.
12. "Duxbury House: E. Raymond Pillsbury, Architects," *Architectural Forum* 75, no. 6 (December 1941): 402–3.
13. Eleanor Raymond, bill for "conferences, checking plans, etc.," December 1, 1938, private collection; "Alumnae Notes: General News," *CSAB* 14, no. 1 (December 1941): 26.
14. Sarah Pillsbury to John Harkness, August 20, 1940, private collection.
15. "Alumnae Notes," *CSAB* 12, no. 2 (April 1940): 31.
16. Sarah Pillsbury to John Harkness, [1940] and August 29, 1940, private collection.
17. Sarah Pillsbury to John Harkness, [1940], Vaughan Conrad Collection.
18. Sarah Pillsbury, "Aalto Furniture and Interiors Architecture," *CSAB* 13, no. 1 (March 1941): 12–13.
19. Elizabeth M'rae Boykin, "Finnish Woman Architect Helps Design National Exhibit at World's Fair," *New York Sun*, November 7, 1938; "New Yorkin maailmannäyttelyn Suomen osaston piirustuskilpailu," *Arkkitehti / Finnish Architectural Review* 8 (1939): 117; Ritta Nikula, "Aino Marsio-Aalto," in *Profiles: Pioneering Women Architects from Finland*, ed. Ulla Markelin, 56–59 (Helsinki: Museum of Finnish Architecture, 1983); Sarah Menin, "Embracing Independence: The Finland Pavilion, New York, 1939," in *Aalto and America*, ed. Stanford Anderson, Gail Fenske, and David Fixler, 141–42 (New Haven, CT: Yale University Press, 2012).
20. Sarah Pillsbury, draft of the article "Famous Finnish Couple—Alvar and Aino Aalto, Architects—Are Producing Unique Furniture in the United States," published under the byline of Susanne [Raedermacher] Wasson-Tucker in the Today's Woman section of the *Christian Science Monitor*, February 12, 1941. The drafts are in the Vaughan Conrad Collection and the article is pictured in *Artek and the Aaltos: Creating a Modern World*, ed. Nina Stritzler-Levine with Timo Riekko (New York: Bard Graduate Center, 2016), 478.
21. Pillsbury, draft of "Famous Finnish Couple."
22. Pillsbury, draft of "Famous Finnish Couple."
23. John Harkness, unpublished memoir, 11, private collection; John Harkness to Sarah Pillsbury Harkness, October 31, 1943; November 12, 1943; March 25, 1944; July 4, 1945, private collection.
24. "New Buildings for 194X," *Architectural Forum* 78, no. 5 (May 1943): 86.
25. John Harkness to Sarah Pillsbury Harkness, May 7, 1944, private collection.
26. John Harkness to Sarah Pillsbury Harkness, April 1945, private collection; "Planning with You," *Architectural Forum* 82, no. 3 (March 1945): 107–11.
27. "Building Stalls," *Architectural Forum* 83, no. 6 (December 1945): 5–6; John Harkness to Sarah Pillsbury Harkness, private collection.
28. The Smith College dormitories competition announcement is in *PP* 26, no. 9 (September 1945): 92.
29. See "Smith College Dormitory Competition," *PP* 27, no. 4 (April 1946): cover, 52–59; "Smith College Picks Winning Architects," *New York Times*, February 4, 1946; "Win Smith Prizes," *Berkshire Eagle* [MA], February 9, 1946; "Young Architects Win Smith College Competition," February 2, 1946, press release 46202-8, MoMA Archives, s://assets.moma.org/documents/moma_press-release_325503.pdf?_ga=2.29707644.2106236669.1711217684-1625942904.1710261308.
30. Regarding the Pittsburg Plate Glass competition, see "Report on the Competition," *PP* 26, no. 5 (May 1945): cover, 51–57. See also "New Yorkers Win Mention: Homes in Modern Style Featured in Architects' Awards," *New York Times*, May 13, 1945.
31. James D. Kornwolf, ed., *Modernism in America, 1937–1941: A Catalog and Exhibition of Four Architectural Competitions* (Williamsburg, VA: Joseph and Margaret Muscarelle Museum of Art, 1985), 3.
32. Bernard Michael Boyle, "Architectural Practice in America, 1865–1965—Ideal and Reality," in *The Architect: Chapters in the History of the Profession*, ed. Spiro Kostof (New York: Oxford University Press, 1977), 335–37.
33. Benjamin Thompson, quoted in Jane Thompson and Alexandra Lange, *Design Research: The Store That Brought Modern Living to American Homes* (San Francisco: Chronicle Books, 2010); Harkness, unpublished memoir, 13; Sarah Pillsbury Harkness, interview with Wendy Cox, May 28, 2010, in Wendy Cox, "Collaborative Diversity: Tracing Intentions for the Forming of the Architects Collaborative Early Housing Project Six Moon Hill" (unpublished manuscript, 2016), private collection.
34. Norman C. Fletcher to Mark Coir, July 31, 1995, Cranbrook Archives. See also Jayne Merkel, *Eero Saarinen* (New York: Phaidon Press, 2005), 50.
35. Sarah P[illsbury] Harkness, "Collaboration," in *The Architects' Collaborative, 1945–1965*, ed. Gropius and Harkness (New York: Architectural Book Pub. Co., 1966), 26. Sarah Pillsbury found her way to the Cambridge School through Mary Gay (1872–77), a "gifted" instructor of watercolor who taught at the Cambridge School as well as the Winsor School in Boston (1915–35), also attended by Pillsbury and Mary Weed. See Katherine Lord, "Report to the Corporation," 1935, Winsor School Library.
36. Sarah P[illsbury] Harkness, "A New Way of Thinking," in "Remembering Gropius: Two Colleagues Look Back," *Harvard University Graduate School of Design News* 10 (Summer 1994): 20.
37. John Harkness to Sarah Pillsbury Harkness, September 2, 1945; Sarah Pillsbury to John Harkness, May 5, 1945, private collection.
38. Jean Bodman Fletcher to Sarah Pillsbury Harkness, November 28, 1945, private collection.
39. Norman Fletcher to Sarah Pillsbury Harkness, November 28, 1945, private collection.
40. Helen Henley, "Two Girls Share as Equal Partners in Modern Architecture," *Christian Science Monitor*, January 13, 1947; Barbara Brooks Walker, "No Woman Should Stay Home: Two Cambridge Wives Solve Career Problem," *Daily Boston Globe*, March 2, 1947. See also Sarah [Pillsbury] Harkness and Jean [Bodman] Fletcher, "Architecture, Family Style: Two Women Architects Look at Today's House, Tell How They Affect Family Life," *House and Garden* 92 (October 1947), 146–49.
41. The Architects Collaborative (TAC) partners at Six Moon Hill were: Louis McMillen at 17 Six Moon Hill Road (MHR); Sarah Pillsbury Harkness / John Harkness at 34; Jean Bodman Fletcher / Norman Fletcher at 36 MHR; Robert McMillan at 38 MHR; Benjamin Thompson at 40 MHR. See "Six Moon Hill [Lexington, MA] Historic District," National Register of Historic Places registration form, December 4, 2015, chrome-extension://efaidnbmnnnibpcajpcglclefindmkaj/https://www.lexingtonma.gov/DocumentCenter/View/3860/Sixmoonhill-PDF?bidId=.
42. Sarah [Pillsbury] Harkness, "Women in Architecture—Where Are We and Where Are We Going?," lecture at Roger Williams University, November 14, 1990, typescript text in private collection. See also "Six Moon Hill: Collaborative Planning Integrates Tailor Made Houses in Co-op Subdivisions, Demonstrates New Ideas in Design," *Architectural Forum* 92, no. 6 (June 1950): 112–23; Robert Campbell, "Utopia Revisited Built by Architects Seeking a Model for Community Life, Six Moon Hill Has Thrived for 45 Years," *Boston Globe*, April 7, 1994.
43. "Program for the Proposed Willimantic Public Library by Architects' Collaborative," *Arts and Architecture* 63, no. 8 (August 1946): 28.
44. Elizabeth Bauer Mock to John and Sarah Pillsbury Harkness, Norman and Jean Bodman Fletcher, Benjamin Thompson, January 18, 1946, folder 307.2, exhibition file, MoMA Archives. For Lucia Garrison Norton Valentine, see "New College Trustee," *SAQ* 34, no. 4 (August 1943): 215; Lucia [Norton]

Valentine, "First Step Toward New Dormitory," *SAQ* 37, no. 3 (May 1946): 126.
45. TAC was further disadvantaged by James Kellum Smith, a partner in the McKim, Mead & White firm who advised Smith in 1950 that the college did not have a moral or legal obligation to TAC.
46. Two outspoken alumnae were Amanda Bryan Kane (1904–90), a trustee, and Florence Homer Snow (Ballard; 1883–1975), secretary of the alumnae association. See Lucia [Norton] Valentine to Herbert Davis, June 6, 1946, Philip Hofer to Lucia [Norton] Valentine, June 18, 1946, box 2, Office of the President, Herbert John Davis Records, Smith Archives. See also Elizabeth Bauer Mock to Benjamin Thompson, January 29, 1946 and to Miss Pease, May 24, 1946, folder 207.2, exhibition file, MoMA Archives; Philip L[ippincott] Goodwin to Mary Noyes Spelman, December 18, 1945, folder 307.2, exhibition file, MoMA Archives; "New Dormitory Group for College Lane and Elm," *SAQ* 37, no. 1 (November 1945): 6; "Prize Winning Architects," *SAQ* 37, no. 2 (February 1946): 69.
47. Elizabeth Bauer Mock, in Barbara Johnson Dry, "After College, What? Alumnae College," *SAQ* 37, no. 4 (August 1946): 198.
48. The letters of Jean Bodman Fletcher are in the Office of the President Records in the Smith Archives.
49. Lucia [Norton] Valentine to Herbert Davis, May 29, 1946, box 2, Davis Records.
50. Nicholas Adams, *Skidmore, Owings & Merrill: SOM Since 1936* (Milan: Electa Architecture, 2007), 15.
51. Unless otherwise noted, the biographical information is in "Oral History of Natalie [Griffin] de Blois," interview by Betty J. Blum, 2002, Chicago Architects Oral History Project, Ryerson and Burnham Art and Architecture Archive, Art Institute of Chicago, 2004, https://artic.contentdm.oclc.org/digital/collection/caohp/id/15893/.
52. See Susan Davidson and Philip Rylands, eds., *Peggy Guggenheim & Frederick Kiesler: The Story of Art of This Century* (New York: Guggenheim Museum Publications, 2004). See also Frederick Kiesler, multi-use chair, 1942, MoMA, https://www.moma.org/collection/works/2192.
53. Natalie Griffin de Blois, quoted in "Natalie de Blois Interviewed by Detlef Mertins," *SOM Journal* 4 (2006): 134, https://www.som.com/publication/natalie-de-blois-interviewed-detlef-mertins.
54. Morris Ketchum Jr., letter of recommendation, October 3, 1944, series I, box 1, Natalie [Griffin] de Blois Architectural Collection, Special Collections, Virginia Tech.
55. "Cracking the Glass Ceiling: A Look Back at the Career of Trailblazing Architect Natalie [Griffin] de Blois," SOM, April 2, 2015, https://som.medium.com/cracking-the-glass-ceiling-a-look-back-at-the-career-of-trail-blazing-architect-natalie-de-blois-b7ef02b28c2b.
56. For the Terrace Plaza Hotel, see "Penthouse Hotel," *Architectural Forum* 85, no. 6 (December 1946): 100–108; "Cincinnati's Terrace Plaza," *Architectural Forum* 89, no. 6 (December 1948): cover, 81–96; and M[ary] M[ix], "Barroom Art in the Modern Manner," *Architectural Forum* 88, no. 4 (April 1948): 148, 150. In 2020, the National Trust for Historic Preservation identified the hotel as one of America's most endangered historic places.
57. "Cracking the Glass Ceiling."
58. The comment of Natalie Griffin de Blois is in Edward W. Wolner, "The City-Within-a-City and Skyscraper Patronage in the 1920's," *Journal of Architectural Education* 42, no. 2 (Winter 1989): 11, which is in Series II, box 1, [Griffin] de Blois Architectural Collection.
59. The article is in the [Griffin] de Blois Architectural Collection.
60. Jennifer Dunning, "A Retrospective of Women Master Builders at Work," *New York Times*, February 25, 1977; Adams, *Skidmore, Owings & Merrill*, 126.
61. "Designers for a Busy World: Mood for Working," *Newsweek*, May 4, 1959, 99–100.
62. "The Architects from 'Skid's Row,'" *Fortune* 57, no. 1 (January 1958), 140; "Oral History of Natalie [Griffin] de Blois," interview by Betty J. Blum.
63. "Oral History of Natalie [Griffin] de Blois," interview by Betty J. Blum. See also "Penthouse Hotel," 106; "Miro Has Fun Painting Cincinnati Mural," *New York Herald Tribune*, March 7, 1948; Monroe Wheeler to Allen Thrasher, January 28, 1949, exhibition file 370–2, MoMA Archives; "Museum of Modern Art Shows Newly Commissioned Mural by Joan Miró," press release 48302-12, March 2, 1948, MoMA Archives, https://assets.moma.org/documents/moma_press-release_325592.pdf?_ga=2.96960988.2106236669.1711217684-1625942904.1710261308.
64. "We name for Glamour," *Glamour* 22, no. 4, (February 1950), 117.
65. John C. MacLean, *A Rich Harvest: The History, Buildings, and People of Lincoln, Massachusetts* (Lincoln, MA: Lincoln Historical Society, 1987), 568 lists Constantin Pertzoff but not Frances Baxter Quarton as "resident architects" who designed significant new homes in the "modern International style."
66. See Constantin Pertzoff in Modern Mass, accessed April 21, 2022, https://modernmass.com/category/constantin-pertzoff/; Baxter Quarton, interview with the authors.
67. "Professional, Practical Attitudes Combine by Architect-Housewife in Own Home Design," *Ann Arbor News* [MI], May 24, 1952. See also "Tale of a House: Architect Priscilla Baxter Neel," *a2 Modern*, April 4, 2016, https://www.a2modern.org/2016/04/tale-of-a-house-architect-priscilla-baxter-neel-2/.
68. Charles Edward Choate studied at the University of Georgia and apprenticed with several architecture firms in the South before establishing in 1892 a partnership with Wesley W. DeHaven. In the late 1890s, Choate studied briefly at Vanderbilt University before embarking on a second career as a Methodist minister, after which he designed churches and commercial buildings in the South. See Robert Craig, "Charles E. Choate," *New Georgia Encyclopedia*, August 20, 2013, https://www.georgiaencyclopedia.org/articles/arts-culture/charles-e-choate-1865-1929/.
69. AIA Historical Directory, s.v. "League, Ellamae Ellis," application for membership, April 6, 1944, https://aiahistoricaldirectory.atlassian.net/wiki/spaces/AHDAA/pages/36969716/ahd1025904?preview=/36969716/2200633362/League_EllamaeEllis.pdf.
70. See Isabelle Gournay, "Architecture at the Fontainebleau School of Fine Arts, 1923–1939," *Journal of the Society of Architectural Historians* 45, no. 3 (September 1986): 270–85.
71. Cynthia McMullen, "Always an Architect," *Wesleyan Magazine*, Winter 2013 / 2014, 16; Margaret W. Love, "Ellamae Ellis League" (MA thesis, Georgia Institute of Technology, 1981), 1–22. The thesis contains interviews with both Ellis League and Jean League Newton.
72. Ellamae Ellis League, quoted in Margaret W. Love, "Ellamae Ellis League," 13.
73. Notes on an undated letter from Jean League to Ellamae Ellis League, likely dating to her year at the Cambridge School, 1941–42, donation list, November 11–9, 2018, private collection.
74. Martha Baker, "Mother, Daughter Architect Team," *Macon Telegraph and News* [GA], July 29, 1945. Ellamae Ellis League's mother, Susie Dilworth Choate Ellis (1875–1955) was the first cousin of Augusta Choate (1874–1962), the founder of the Choate School, a day and boarding school for girls. See "Augusta Choate, School Founder," *Boston Globe*, December 14, 1962.
75. Baker, "Mother, Daughter Architect Team."
76. Ellamae Ellis League House, 1790 Waverland Drive, Macon, GA. National Register of Historic Places nomination form, April 30, 2002, https://npgallery.nps.gov/NRHP/GetAsset/NRHP/05000053_text. The original drawings for the house are in the Washington Memorial Library in Macon.
77. "Joseph and Mary Jane League House, 1849 Waverland Drive, Macon, GA," National Register of Historic Places registration form, November 26, 2008, https://www.phmc.state.pa.us/portal/communities/pa-suburbs/files/league_house.pdf .
78. Love, "Ellamae Ellis League," 31. The office was located next to a Queen Anne commercial building, which housed the Library Ballroom from 1889. By the 1960s, according to an historical marker, it was a music venue and discotheque.
79. Hudnut, "The Architectress—Part I," 111.
80. Kate Reggev, "Architect, Partner, Wife: Mid-Century Husband-and-Wife

Partnerships," in *Routledge Companion to Women in Architecture*, ed. Anna Sokolina, 201–12 (New York: Routledge, 2021).
81. Pat Kirkham, "The Personal, the Professional and the Partner(ship): The Husband / Wife Collaboration of Charles and Ray Eames," in *Feminist Cultural Theory: Process and Production*, ed. Beverley Skeggs (Manchester: Manchester University Press, 1995), 224. See also Pat Kirkham, *Charles and Ray Eames: Designers of the Twentieth Century* (Cambridge, MA: MIT Press, 2001).
82. Kirkham, "The Personal, the Professional and the Partner(ship)," 217.
83. Kirkham, "The Personal, the Professional and the Partner(ship)," 222–23.
84. Henry H[odgman] Saylor, "Progressive Practice in the Small Office," *AR* 90, no. 9 (September 1941): 69 and 72.
85. See "Eugene Klaber, 88, an Architect, Dies," *New York Times*, November 9, 1971.
86. However, during the war years, Victorine du Pont Homsey did publish exclusively in her own name, the only time in her life she did so. See "Family Hobby Rooms," *Better Homes and Gardens* 23, no. 2 (October 1944), 16–17, 79, 106; "How Will I Face My House," *Better Homes and Gardens* 23, no. 5 (January 1945), 30–31; "It's Livable; It's Expandable," *Parents Magazine* 21, no. 5 (May 1946), 52–59, 108–14; "Working in My Kitchen is a Real Joy," *Parents Magazine* 24, no. 2 (February 1949), 42–44; "I Can't Think of Anything I Would Change," *Parents Magazine* 24, no. 2 (February 1949), 40–41, 108.
87. "The Architect and His Community," *PP* 30, no. 10 (October 1949): 53–64; Devin Colman, "Modernism in Vermont: The Architecture of Ruth Reynolds Freeman," in SAH Archipedia, ed. Esperdy and Kingsley, March 15, 2024, https://sah-archipedia.org/essays/TH-01-ART019; Amy Lilly, "Vermont's First Female Architect," *Seven Days*, March 9, 2016, https://www.sevendaysvt.com/vermont/vermonts-first-female-architect-ruth-freeman/Content?oid=322111. See also AIA Historical Directory, s.v. "Freeman French Freeman," Questionnaire for Architects' Roster and / or Register of Architects Qualified for Federal Public Works, September 27, 1946.
88. "The Architect and His Community," 53–54.
89. "Two Apartment House Is Under Construction at Church, Kings Sts.," *Burlington Free Press* [VT], November 9, 1946. See also "The Architect and His Community," 64.
90. "New England Structural Company," in Ernest S. Woodaman, *Directory of Directors in the City of Boston and Vicinity* (Boston: Bankers' Service Co., 1906), 91.
91. Inge Schaefer Horton, *Early Women Architects of the San Francisco Bay Area, The Lives and Work of Fifty Professionals, 1890–1951* (Jefferson, NC: McFarland, 2010), 222–25; Philadelphia Architects and Buildings, s.v. "Martin, Clarence Augustine (1862–1944)," March 16, 2024, https://www.philadelphiabuildings.org/pab/app/ar_display.cfm/67284.
92. Dorothy Stockbridge, "Bay Island's Enduring Qualities Appreciated Anew in Building Boom," *Sarasota Herald-Tribune*, May 8, 1983.
93. Biographical note in the collection guide to the records of Helen D[ouglass] French and Prentiss French, 1932–1978, Environmental Design Archives, University of California, Berkeley, https://ced.berkeley.edu/collections/french-helen.
94. Helen Douglass French to Paul W. Ivory, January 12, 1983, Chesterwood Archive, Chapin Library, Special Collections, Williams College Archives.
95. Robert M. Toole and Alan Emmet, "Historic Landscape Report and Preliminary Landscape Master Planning, Chesterwood" [Stockbridge, MA]), December 1994, 109–7, National Trust for Historic Preservation. The drawings for the remodeling of The Canary, July 23, 1954, are in the Chesterwood Archive. In the early 1950s, Helen Douglass French also designed a gymnasium at the Tamalpais Union High School in Mill Valley, CA.
96. "A Summer Visit to Historic Houses," *St. Louis Post-Dispatch*, May 28, 1978.
97. San Francisco Planning Department, "Modern Design Historic Context Statement Case Report," January 25, 2011, https://commissions.sfplanning.org/hpcpackets/2011.0059U.pdf.
98. Nes Young, "In Home Design," *San Francisco Chronicle*, November 30, 1958.
99. Young, "In Home Design."
100. Mabel Greene, "Woman Architect Thinks Modernity Can Still Show Off Those Antiques," *San Francisco Chronicle*, November 27, 1952.
101. Greene, "Woman Architect Thinks Modernity Can Still Show Off Those Antiques."
102. Eloise Dungan, "Woman Architect Likes Man's World," *News-Call Bulletin* [San Francisco], April 19, 1960.
103. "A House with Reasons: It Grew from a Long and Careful Study of the Family's Activities, the Terrain and the Community," *Life*, June 15, 1953, 113–16.
104. "A House with Reasons," 113; "Housewife's House: Designed by a Women it Puts Kitchen in the Center," *Life*, December 24, 1956, 134–37.
105. Beatriz Colomina, "With, or Without You: The Ghosts of Modern Architecture," in *Modern Women: Women Artists at the Museum of Modern Art*, ed. Cornelia Butler and Alexandra Schwartz (New York: Museum of Modern Art, 2010), 218.
106. These wives include Maria Torch Stone, Ise Gropius, Olgivanna Lloyd Wright, and Aline Bernstein Saarinen.
107. Craig Kellogg, "Is There A D/R in the House?," *New York Times*, October 12, 2003, https://www.nytimes.com2/magazine/is-there-a-d-r-in-the-house.html.
108. Thompson and Alexandra Lange, *Design Research*, 31, 190.
109. See Esther Baum Born's curriculum vitae, 1902–1947, Ernest and Esther [Baum] Born collection.
110. Nicholas Olsberg, *Work of Ernest and Esther Born* (San Francisco: Book Club of California, 2015), 86, 210, 262; AIA Historical Directory, s.v. "Born, Ernest," nomination for fellowship, November 2, 1954.
111. "Architect Takes a Lot and a Half to Give his Plain-Seeming Row House Five Luxuries," *House and Home* 4, no. 5 (November 1953): 128–31.
112. Jen Woo, "Live Your Best Beach Life in This Historic Great Highway Home, Asking $8 Million," *7x7*, June 11, 2020, https://www.7x7.com/ocean-beach-home-great-highway-san-francisco-2646166646.html#:~:text=Situated%20right%20on%20Great%20Highway,of%20projects%20in%20the%20area.).
113. See "Ground Floor / Façade," Casa Luis Barragán, March 23, 2024, http://www.casaluisbarragan.org/eng/en_lacasa.html.
114. Elizabeth Timberman studied at Oberlin College and at the Colorado School of Fine Arts in the late 1930s and then at the Cleveland Playhouse before moving to New York, where she studied photography with Berenice Abbott in 1941 and exhibited in *Image of Freedom* at MoMA, 1941–42. Her photographs of the Luis Barragán house were published in: *Arts and Architecture* 68, no. 8 (August 1951): 25; Francisco Quiñones, "*Mi casa es mi refugio*: At the Service of Mexican Modernism in Casa Barragán," *Avery Review* 48 (June 2020), https://www.averyreview.com/issues/48/mi-casa. See her biography at the Jewish Museum, https://thejewishmuseum.org//collection/artist/elizabeth-timberman-american-1908-1988.
115. Esther Baum Born to Douglas and Helen Haskell, 1966–67, [Baum] Born Collection.
116. Ernest Born, "The Relation of Painting to Architecture" (MA thesis, University of California, Berkeley, 1922), 60–61.
117. Suzanne Stockard to Joel Louis and Marjorie Davies Stockard, [1942], private collection; "Autumn Wedding for Miss Stockard," *Boston Daily Globe*, September 1, 1942.
118. "Eastern Wedding," *Detroit Free Press*, September 30, 1942.
119. Barbara Webb, "From Bennington College to the Smith School of Architecture," *CSAB* 11, no. 2 (February 1939): 5–7. See also Mary Anne Hunting and Kevin D. Murphy, "Suzanne Marjorie Stockard Underwood," *Historic Women of the Southcoast*, accessed July 26, 1957, https://historicwomensouthcoast.org/suzanne-marjorie-stockard-underwood/.
120. Suzanne Stockard diary, September 19, 1937, private collection.
121. Stockard diary, February 28, 1936; Joel Stockard to Suzanne Stockard, private collection.

122. Stockard diary, April 15, 1937.
123. Henry Frost to Mark C. Stevens, June 10, 1942, Suzanne Stockard student file, CSR.
124. Stockard to her parents, [1942], private collection. A design for an industrial plant by Stockard Underwood and others, November 1946, is in the GSD History Collection, Student Affairs.
125. While employed in the office of Carl Koch, Stockard Underwood worked on a house for Harry Milton Lemley in Mansfield, Ohio.
126. Stockard Underwood to Julian Underwood, April 20, 1944, private collection.
127. "Variety of Houses from Identical Prefabricated Units Designed by Harvard Students," *PP* 24, no. 12 (December 1943): 80.
128. "House on Stilts," *Architectural Forum* 95, no. 6 (June 1951): 172–74.
129. Plans for the garden are in the Garden Club of America Collection, Archives of American Gardens and Images of South Dartmouth, in the Smithsonian Online Virtual Archive; see "Underwood Garden," Smithsonian Online Virtual Archive, MA321, https://sova.si.edu/search/digital?q=%E2%80%9CSouth+Dartmouth%E2%80%94the+Underwood+Garden%E2%80%9D+.
130. Stockard Underwood to her parents, private collection.
131. Both Underwoods drew plans for a house for John Burr (1949) in Mattapoisett, Massachusetts, as well as a house for Dr. and Mrs. Peter W. Sweetser (1965), the Coykendall house (1967), and the Atkinson studio (1967), all in South Dartmouth, Massachusetts. Stockard Underwood also designed the Kleiminger Farmhouse of Robert S. Rose (1960).
132. Robert Lovinger, "A Bright, Shining Life," *South Coast Today*, April 6, 1997, https://www.southcoasttoday.com/story/lifestyle/1997/04/06/a-bright-shining-life/50623159007/.
133. [Mary] Molly Weed Noyes, *Winsor* [*School*] *Bulletin* (Spring 1983): 36.
134. Gordon Bruce, *Eliot Noyes: A Pioneer of Design and Architecture in the Age of American Modernism* (London: Phaidon, 2006), 142. In the foreground of the photograph of the workspace of Mary Weed Noyes is an arrangement of the tableware she selected for use in the Cummins Gulf Stream, the interior of which she helped design. The Xerox showroom in New York is on page 219; examples of the corporate art programs she and her husband selected and installed are on page 182.
135. Frederick and Derry Noyes, interviews with Mary Anne Hunting and Kevin D. Murphy, June 20, 2017.
136. See Murphy, "The Vernacular Moment," 314–16.
137. Faith Bemis, "Alumnae Notes," *CSAB* 4, no. 2 (April 1932): 3.
138. "Other Alumnae News," *CSAB* 14, no. 2 (July 1942): 27.
139. Joseph Benjamin O'Sickey, interview, March 5, 2002, Roy Lichtenstein Foundation Archives.
140. "A City Shows How to Fight Decay," *Life* 40, no. 11 (March 12, 1956), 62–63; interview with Robert and Ann Halle Little by Avis Berman, June 23, 2004, Lichtenstein Foundation Archives.

V: The Enterprising Spirit

1. See "Miss Alice M. Carson is Wed in Greenwich," *New York Times*, October 3, 1943; "Miss Alice Carson, Lt. Cmmdr. Hiscock Wed in Greenwich, *Daily Item* [Port Chester, NY], October 6, 1943.
2. "Gift Accepted by Metropolitan Museum," *Cape Cod Chronicle*, September 1, 1983. See also Paul Kemprecos, "Evening Slippers No One Wanted Go from Yard Sale to Museum," *Cape Codder* [Orleans, MA], September 2, 1983.
3. See Sheila Hicks, "The Multi-Talented Delaunay," *Tate Etc*, no. 24 (Summer 2015), 1; Lærke Rydal Jørgensen and Tine Colstrup, eds., *Sonia Delaunay* (Humlebæk, Denmark: Louisiana Museum of Modern Art, 2022).
4. An important retrospective of the work of Terk Delaunay was *The EY Exhibition: Sonia Delaunay* at the Tate Modern in London, 2015.
5. For the needlework of Sophie Henriette Gertrud Taeuber-Arp, see Anne Umland and Walburga Krupp, with Charlotte Healy, eds., *Sophe Taeuber-Arp: Living Abstraction* (New York: Museum of Modern Art, 2021), figs. 2, 7–9, 13.
6. See Mary Douglas, *The Craftsman as Yeoman: Myth and Cultural Identity in American Craft*, Haystack Monograph 5 (Deer Isle, ME: Haystack Institute, 1994).
7. See Kathleen James-Chakraborty, "Sonia Delaunay: Media or Message?," in *Iteration: Episodes in the Mediation of Art and Architecture*, ed. Robin Schuldenfrei (London: Routledge, 2020), 105–20.
8. Kay Noguchi, "Inka Aronson Benton (1918–2015): Polymath and Activist," *Medium*, August 18, 2020, https://medium.com/anne-t-kent-california-room-community-newsletter/inka-aronson-benton-1918-2015-polymath-and-activist-8ff84d9b0936, originally published in *Anne T. Kent California Room Newsletter* (Marin County Free Library).
9. Irene Aronson-Sanna Benton to Henry Frost, June 17, 1942, student file, CSR.
10. Henry Frost to Irene Aronson-Sanna Benton, June 20, 1942, student file, CSR.
11. Christopher Reed, "Introduction," in *Not at Home: The Suppression of Domesticity in Modern Art and Architecture*, ed. Christopher Reed (London: Thames & Hudson, 1996), 9.
12. Mark Rothko and Adolph Gottlieb to Edward Alden Jewell, June 7, 1943, *Federation of Modern Painters and Sculptors* (blog), accessed March 18, 2024, https://fedartnyc.tumblr.com/post/82412858602/a-letter-from-mark-rothko-and-adolph-gottlieb-to-the. See also Potvin, *Bachelors of a Different Sort*, 122.
13. For a review of the literature on women designers working in a modern idiom, see Penny Sparke, "Introduction," in *Women's Places*, ed. Brenda Martin and Penny Sparke (London: Routledge, 2003), xi–xv. Among subsequent important monographic presentations of women designers was the exhibition *Charlotte Perriand: Inventing a New World* (1920) and its accompanying publication: Jacques Barsac et Sébastien Cherruet, *Le Monde nouveau de Charlotte Perriand, sous la direction de Pernette Perriand, Jacques Barsac et Sébastien Cherruet* (Paris: Foundation Louis Vuitton and Gallimard, 2019). See also Libby Sellers, *Women Design: Pioneers in Architecture, Graphic and Digital Design from the Twentieth Century to the Present Day* (London: Frances Lincoln, 2018), 7–15.
14. Alice Rawsthorn, quoted in Sellers, *Women Design*, 15.
15. A file for Alice Morgan Carson containing a curriculum vitae and other useful biographical information is in her personnel record, box 79, job 55–4, Office of Strategic Services (OSS), National Archives and Records Administration.
16. See "The Museum of Modern Art Announces Receipt of Major Gift from the Estate of William A. M. Burden," press release, November 1985, MoMA Archives, https://www.moma.org/momaorg/shared/pdfs/docs/press_archives/6254/releases/MOMA_1985_0108_107.pdf.
17. Alice Morgan Carson, "Fanciful Arrangement," *New York Times*, March 15, 1936; "Palm Beach at Gardens," *New York Times*, January 13, 1935.
18. Henry Frost to President [William Allen] Neilson, January 6, 1930, CSR.
19. The blueprints by Alice Morgan Carson for the Reed landscape project, December 6, 1938, are in carton 104 in the Wilson Rahn Papers. Permelia Pryor Reed was the aunt of Jacques Frazier, the husband of Carson's sister Marion Elise Carson Pryor.
20. "Vacation Houses," 62–65. Carson's S. (Samuel) Robert Glassford house is also illustrated in Nelson and Wright, *Tomorrow's House*, figs. 135–36 and in James Ford and Katherine Morrow Ford, *Design of Modern Interiors* (New York: Architectural Book Publishing, 1942), 55, 73, 95. Mention of the house is in the "Alumnae Notes," *CSAB* 12, no. 3 (August 1940): 15; "Alumnae Notes," *CSAB* 13, no. 1 (March 1941): 24.
21. Permelia P[ryor] Reed, *A Kaleidoscope of Jupiter Island from the Year 1931* (Hobe Sound, FL: privately published, 1978), 15.
22. "Vacation Houses," 62.
23. See "Other Alumnae News," *CSAB* 14, no. 2 (July 1942): 28.
24. "Museum of Modern Art Exhibits New Rugs by American Artists," press release 42609-39, June 30, 1942, MoMA Archives, https://www.moma

.org/momaorg/shared/pdfs/docs/press_archives/806/releases/MOMA_1942_0048_1942-06-30_42630-43.pdf.
25. Wright, "On the Fringe," 284–90.
26. The exhibitions on which Alice Morgan Carson worked at MoMA include *Organic Design in Home Furnishings* (1941), *Wartime Housing* (1942), *The Americas Cooperate* (1942), *Useful Objects in Wartime* (1943), *Five California Houses* (1943), and *Brazil Builds* (1943) as well as the competitions for inter-American industrial design (1940–41) and National Posters for National Defense (1941).
27. Harold J. Coolidge Jr. to Chief of Civilian Personnel, December 9, 1943, Carson personnel record, OSS; "Museum of Modern Art Selects Forty-Seven Buildings of Best Modern Design Built in U.S.A. Since 1932," press release 44412-14, April 12, 1944, https://www.moma.org/momaorg/shared/pdfs/docs/press_archives/930/releases/MOMA_1944_0016_1944-04-12_44412-14.pdf.
28. Tim Wood, "In Memoriam: Chatham's 'Godmother of Zoning' Dies," *Cape Cod Chronicle*, March 22, 2001; "Alice Morton Carson Hiscock '25," *Choate Rosemary Hall* (Summer 2001).
29. The rug stitched by the Reeds sold at auction in January 2021: "The Denbigh Farm Carpet," Stair, accessed March 18, 2024, https://www.stairgalleries.com/news-insights/insights/denbigh/. See also Jeanette Lovensheimer, "Alice Morgan Carson," *Needle Arts* 31, no. 1 (March 2000): 10–13; Armida L. Taylor, "Original Designs by Alice Morgan Carson," *Needle Arts* 34, no. 5 (December 2003), 24–28. In 2000, Samuel Reed gave the collection of patterns by Carson to the Embroiders' Guild of America.
30. "Permelia Reed—Châtelaine of Hobe Sound," *Connecticut Nutmegger* 18, no. 3 (December 1985), 29. In 2021, a set of Biedermeier chairs with the label: "Miss Alice Carson … Designs worked by Mrs. Reed" was sold at Doyle, https://doyle.com/trusts-estates.
31. Jewish Virtual Library, s.v. "Davenport, Marcia (1903–1996)," accessed June 29, 2021, https://www.jewishvirtuallibrary.org/marcia-davenport.
32. Marcia Davenport, "Patterns of Pleasure," *New York Times*, June 2, 1974.
33. The Brooklyn Bridge design (pattern #413) and the purse (#1077) are in the Embroiders' Guild of America, which also published *Needle Arts*.
34. Anne Tyng, curriculum vitae, Tyng file, Records of the Alumnae Association; Philadelphia Museum of Art, Educational Activities at the Museum (1947–1948), 6, Archives of the Philadelphia Museum of Art.
35. Anne Tyng, Child's Furniture and Toy Construction, patent no. 2,551,071, May 1, 1951, https://patents.google.com/patent/US2551071A/en.
36. Tyng Toy promotional brochure, Anne Griswold Tyng Collection, Architectural Archives, Stuart Weitzman School of Design.
37. See Robert Goldwater in collaboration with d'Harnoncourt, *Modern Art in Your Life* (New York: Museum of Modern Art, 1949), 26–30.
38. "Tyng Toy," *Everyday Art Quarterly: A Guide to Well Designed Products*, no. 8 (Summer 1948): 5.
39. See "An Exhibit of Education with Toys," *San Francisco Chronicler*, September 23, 1951; "Toys, 1951–1952," box 72, folder 11, State Department Exhibitions, 1949–1952, American Federation of Arts Records, Archives of American Art, Smithsonian Institution.
40. See "The Toy (1951) and House of Cards (1952)," in Tamar Zinguer, "Architecture in Play: Intimations of Modernism in Architectural Toys, 1836–1952" (PhD diss., Princeton University, June 2006), 155–93; Beatriz Colomina, "Reflections on the Eames House," in *The Work of Charles and Ray Eames: A Legacy of Invention*, ed. Donald Albrecht (New York: Harry N. Abrams in association with the Library of Congress and the Vitra Design Museum, 1997), 129.
41. Betty Pepis, "Children Offered a Knock-Down Set," *New York Times*, February 22, 1950. See also "Make It and Break It," *Star Tribune* [Minneapolis], May 7, 1950; "Put Together Toys from Plywood Parts," *Popular Mechanics Magazine* 94, no. 2 (August 1950), 107.
42. "Furniture in Capsules," *Time*, September 7, 1942. See also Irwin Spear, "Buy Furniture in Packages Nowadays," *Christian Science Monitor*, February 10, 1943.
43. See "Jewelry with a Stretch Uses Coil Spring Idea," *New York Herald Tribune*, July 5, 1949; "New Jewelry Goes Native," *Chicago Daily News*, June 28, 1949; Virginia Bohlin, "Young Hub Wife Makes Jewelry, Chic Furniture," *Boston Herald Traveler*, October 3, 1949.
44. Franziska Porges Hosken, "Hatred and Chaos in Europe," *SAQ* 39, no. 2 (February 1948): 90.
45. "Awards," *SAQ* 31, no. 4 (August 1940): 421. Even before graduating, Franziska Porges produced *The Merry Ski Book* (New York: Transatlantic Arts, 1939) with humorous, colorful illustrations, which she advertised in *SAQ* 31, no. 1 (November 1939), 111.
46. Franziska Porges Hosken to Henry Frost, January 28, 1941, student file, CSR.
47. "This Young Couple Used Taste, Time, Talent, Instead of Dollars," *House and Garden* 95, no. 2 (February 1949), 92–93, 122.
48. Franziska Porges Hosken, "The Short Story of Hosken Inc. (1948–1951)," 1–3, Franziska Porges Hosken Collection, GSD; "The Lives They Lived: Fran Hosken," *Weinberg Modern* (blog), December 30, 2008, https://weinbergmodern.tumblr.com/post/126097767526/the-lives-they-lived-fran-hosken; Porges Hosken, "Hatred and Chaos in Europe." Katherine Kaford Papineau, "Katherine Morrow Ford: Designs for Living," in *Routledge Companion to Women in Architecture*, ed. Anna Sokolina (New York: Routledge, 2021), 233, states that Katherine Morrow Ford resigned from the magazine in 1951 because of its change in editorial direction from covering modern houses to more traditional examples.
49. The stacking stools are pictured (without attribution) on the cover of *House and Garden* 100, no. 5 (November 1951).
50. Porges Hosken, "The Short Story of Hosken."
51. In Porges Hosken, "The Short Story of Hosken," 2, see the section "That was the idea and objective. Now to the reality."
52. W. O. Ollman to Franziska [Porges] Hosken, July 7, 1950, Porges Hosken Collection; *Good Design Master Checklist*, 1952, MoMA Archives, https://assets.moma.org/documents/moma_master-checklist_325812.pdf?_ga=2.28861823.2106236669.1711217684-1625942904.1710261308;
53. An image of the multiuse table is in the Franziska Porges Hosken Collection.
54. Interestingly, in the Porges Hosken Collection is an article on the Ash Street house of Philip Johnson, "House without Nails Is Being Bolted and Glued Together," *Cambridge Sun*, April 23, 1942.
55. Betty Pepis, "Good Design Show Spans Wide Range," *New York Times*, January 11, 1952.
56. "Franziska and James Hosken for Hosken, Inc. Designs, 1947–1952, Price List," *Weinberg Modern* (blog), March 24, 2024.
57. Riane Eisler and David Loye, "Fran Hosken: Crusading Global Humanitarian" *The Humanist* 42 (September / October 1982): 15; Fran [Porges] Hosken, "The Life of an Idea," *Sunday Herald Traveler*, November 23, 1969.
58. These materials are in the Porges Hosken Collection.
59. See Reginald Isaacs, *Walter Gropius: Der Mensch und sein Werk* (Berlin: Mann, 1983–84); Reginald Isaacs, *Gropius: An Illustrated Biography of the Creator of the Bauhaus* (Boston: Little, Brown, 1991).
60. Franziska Porges Hosken provided cover designs and drawings for Smith College's *Reunion Book, Class of 1940* (1945) and sent sketches of six dress types (private collection) to Joan Leslie (Warland), a Cambridge School / Harvard alumna. In the Porges Hosken Collection are designs for a Bata shoe store (1963), offices and conference rooms at Brandeis University (c. 1965) in Waltham, Massachusetts, and a lobby for Mitre Corporation (1960) in Bedford, Massachusetts. Also see Franziska [Porges] Hosken, "Brandeis University; A Planned Campus," *Arts and Architecture* 82, no. 12 (December 1965), 16–19; "About Franziska Porges Hosken," Porges, March 17, 2024, http://www.porges.net/FamilyTreesBiographies/PorgesFranziskaHosken.html.
61. "About Franziska Porges Hosken."
62. Bohlin, "Young Hub Wife Makes Jewelry."

63. Among other projects, in 1975, Franziska Porges Hosken founded the Women's International Network (WIN) and produced its quarterly journal on women's health issues. See "She Studies Societies That Brutalize Women," *New York Times*, February 28, 1978.
64. Porges Hosken, "Hatred and Chaos in Europe."
65. Claire Zimmerman, *Photographic Architecture in the Twentieth Century* (Minneapolis: University of Minnesota Press, 2014), 7.
66. "San Francisco Golden Gate," *Architectural Forum* 70, no. 6 (June 1939): 463–500. Unless otherwise noted, the photographs by Esther Baum Born of California buildings are in the unprocessed portion of the Ernest Born and Esther [Baum] Born collection in the College of Environmental Design at the University of California, Berkeley.
67. See Kenneth H. Cardwell, *Bernard Maybeck: Artisan, Architect, Artist* (Santa Barbara, CA: Peregrine Smith, 1977), 211–12, 231.
68. "Frank Lloyd Wright Designs a Honeycomb House," *AR* 84, no. 1 (July 1938): 59–74. Photographs by Esther Baum Born were also published in George Patton Simonds, "House for William Roger Stoll, Hayward, Calif.," *Architectural Forum* 71, no. 1 (July 1939): 54–55; Michael Arthur Goodman, "House for Dr. James B. Graeser, Oakland, California," *Architectural Forum* 70, no. 1 (January 1939): 14–15.
69. "To the Historians of Architectural America," *Architectural Forum* 73, no. 4 (October 40): 90–91.
70. Kenneth Caldwell, "Ernest and Esther Born: Born to Design; A Couple from the San Francisco Bay Area Advanced the Cause of Modernism Using Architectural and Graphic Expertise," *AR* (May 1, 2016), https://www.architecturalrecord.com/ /articles/11629-ernest-and-esther-born.
71. "The Frances Lehman Loeb Art Center at Vassar College Presents: Making a Life in Photography: Rollie McKenna," press release, *Vassar News*, accessed March 20, 2024, https://www.vassar.edu/news/frances-lehman-loeb-art-center-vassar-college-presents-making-life-photography-rollie-mckenna.
72. Jessica D. Brier and Mary-Kay Lombino, "A Vassar Homecoming for Photographer Rollie McKenna '40," *Vassar News*, March 10, 2024, https://www.vassar.edu/news/vassar-homecoming-photographer-rollie-mckenna-40. See also Jessica D. Brier, *Making a Life in Photography: Rollie McKenna*, exhibition catalog (New York: Scala Arts Publishers, 2024).
73. Sarah Pillsbury Harkness to John Harkness, private collection. "The Aaltos, Mr. and Mrs., As Furniture Designers," *Boston Evening Transcript*, November 11, 1940, states that Eliot Noyes suggested Sarah Pillsbury and Louisa Vaughan as the Boston agents of Artek. For Clifford Norman Pascoe, see "Pascoe's Progress," *Fortune* 34, no. 3 (September 1946), 156, 159; "Queens Factory Space Leased," *New York Herald Tribune*, June 8, 1941. In a letter to Frederick Gutheim and his wife, Mary, July 28, 1940, Frederick Gutheim Papers, Avery Library, Elizabeth Bauer Mock explains that the plywood pieces were carved in a factory in Three Rivers, Wisconsin, but all products were finished and assembled in New York.
74. Sarah Pillsbury, "Aalto Furniture and Interior Architecture," *CSAB* 13, no. 1 (March 1941): 11.
75. Sarah Pillsbury to John Harkness, August 15, 1940, private collection. See also "Architects to Make Furniture," *New York Times*, July 2, 1940.
76. The Churches to the Aaltos, February 8, 1941, correspondence files, Alvar Aalto Museum. The letter is in the handwriting of Elizabeth Montagu Roberts Church.
77. Pillsbury to Harkness, August 15, 1940; Clifford Pascoe to Louisa Vaughan and Sarah Pillsbury, September 16, 1940, Vaughan Conrad Collection.
78. Sarah Pillsbury to Louisa Vaughan, August 20, 1940, Vaughan Conrad Collection.
79. "Alumnae Notes," *CSAB* 9, no. 1 (January 1937): 5.
80. Louisa Vaughan student file, CSR.
81. Sarah Pillsbury to Clifford Pascoe, [1940], Vaughan Conrad Collection; Sarah Pillsbury, "Aalto Furniture and Interior Architecture," *CSAB* 13, no. 1 (March 1941): 12; James Ford and Katherine Morrow Ford, *Design of Modern Interiors* (New York: Architectural Book Publishing, 1942), 22.
82. Pillsbury and Vaughan, balance sheet, July 31, 1941, Vaughan Conrad Collection.
83. "Furniture Designed by Famous Finnish Architects to be Distributed in New England," press release, November 2, 1940, Vaughan Conrad Collection.
84. Sarah Pillsbury, draft of announcement, Vaughan Conrad Collection and Pillsbury, "Alto Furniture and Interior Architecture," 13.
85. Rhoda Nichols Martin, "Alumnae Day Trip," *CSAB* 11, no. 1 (November 1938): 5–6.
86. Pillsbury, "Aalto Furniture and Interior Architecture"; see the advertisement "Aalto Furniture Now Available," *Harvard Crimson*, [October 30, 1941], Vaughan Conrad Collection.
87. The Artek-Pascoe furniture is pictured in Constantin Pertzoff's living room in "'Permanent Investment' Core Surrounded by a 'Temporary Investment' Shell," *PP* 25, no. 9 (September 1944): 72. Sarah Pillsbury made a list of "engaged girls" to whom she could send cards, which is in the Vaughan Conrad Collection. James Ford and Katherine Morrow Ford, *Design of Modern Interiors* (New York: Architectural Book Publishing, 1942), 18, 22, 54.
88. The accounting records are in the Vaughan Conrad Collection.
89. "Paine Furniture Company Has Colonial Exhibit," *Daily Boston Globe*, March 3, 1946.
90. Sarah Pillsbury to John Harkness, private collection. For the Artek distributorships in Boston, see Kristin Purtich, "Pillsbury and Vaughan: Artek in Boston, and Cristina Nute, Inc. Boston, Massachusetts, 1940–49," in *Artek and the Aaltos: Creating a Modern World*, ed. Nina Stritzler-Levine with Timo Riekko (New York: Bard Graduate Center, 2016), 478–84. See also "Miss Cristina K. Nute is Engaged to Robert J. Simmons; Plans February Wedding," *Boston Globe*, February 4, 1951; "Christine Nute is Bride of Robert J. Simmons in N.Y.," *Boston Globe*, February 25, 1951.
91. Sarah Pillsbury to John Harkness, private collection.
92. A Knoll advertisement in the *Boston Globe*, May 10, 1950, lists Nute and Ralph Rapson as the retail distributors of Knoll in Boston. Her company was not "officially closed" in November 1949 as Kirstin Purtich states in *Artek and the Aaltos*, ed. Stritzler-Levine with Riekko, 483.
93. Christina Nute, "Modern Gets an Audience on Boston's Beacon Hill," in *Artek and the Aaltos*, ed. Stritzler-Levine with Timo Riekko (New York: Bard Graduate Center, 2016), 482.
94. Christina [Nute] Simmons obituary in *Shore Line Times* [New Haven], January 28, 1988.
95. "3 New Shops to Feature Aalto Line," *Retailing: Home Furnishings*, December 9, 1940, 6; "New Decorator's Shop Shows Work of Famous Finn," *Washington Post*, December 1, 1940.
96. Churches to the Aaltos, February 8, 1941.
97. Thomas Dolliver Church to Alvar Aalto, September 23, 1947, Aalto University Archives.
98. See Lisa Napoles, "A New Outlook: Baldwin Kingrey in Chicago," Docomomo US newsletter, August 13, 2014, https://docomomo-us.org/news/-a-new-outlook-baldwin-kingrey-of-chicago; John Brunetti, *Baldwin Kingrey: Midcentury Modern in Chicago: 1947–1957* (Chicago: Wright, 2004).
99. "Class News," *SAQ*, 41, no. 2 (February 1950): 123. Mary Dolan Rapson, obituary, *SAQ* 87, no. 2 (Winter 2000–2001): 86. See also Jane King Hession, Rip Rapson, and Bruce N. Wright, *Ralph Rapson: Sixty Years of Modern Design* (Afton, MN: Afton Historical Society Press, 1999), 88–93.
100. Louisa Vaughan's grandmother, Ellen Gardner Loring (1860–1937) was a half-sister of Olga Eliza Gardner Monks (1869–1944), the mother of Olga Monks Perzoff.
101. Caleb Hornbostel, "Store Design: Architectural Record's Building Types Study Number 188," *AR* 111, no.7 (July 1952): 154.
102. The plans for the house by Louisa Vaughan Conrad, August 4, 1950, are in a private collection.
103. "School and Faculty Notes," *CSAB* 13, no. 1 (March 1941): 20.
104. New Design fact sheet, 1947, Dorothy Noyes Berking Papers, private collection.

105. "Year's Work," *Interior* 108, no. 1 (August 1948), 80. Dorothy Noyes and Robert Rosenberg are also listed as designers in "New Designs in Furniture and Accessories are Hospitably Displayed in a Renovated New York House," *Architectural Forum* 89, no. 1 (July 1948): 104–8. In 1948, Noyes was named one of ten outstanding young achievers for her "remarkable" store in "Women of the Year," *Mademoiselle* 28, no. 3 (January 1949), 95–97. Noyes and Rosenberg collaborated in 1949 on a brownstone renovation in New York; see "Today's Elaborate Decorating and How It Grew," *New York Times*, February 25, 1956; "Light Remodeling: More style than Space Makes Much of a Brownstone," *Interiors* 109, no. 9 (April 1950), 96–99.
106. For the Meyer May house, restored and owned by Steelcase Inc., see https://meyermayhouse.steelcase.com/tour-the-meyer-may-house/.
107. David T. Van Zanten, "The Early Work of Marion Mahony Griffin," *The Prairie School Review* 3, no. 2 (1966): 12–13, 16; *Western Architect* 19, no. 10 (October 1913).
108. "Wedding Anniversaries to Be Celebrated with Informal Parties This Week: David Ambergs Will Observe Sixtieth Year," *Grand Rapids Press* [MI], June 17, 1936.
109. See "Design Laboratory, New York," *American Magazine of Art* 29, no. 2 (February 1936), 117.
110. Edith Perlman faculty file, Newcomb College, Tulane University Archives.
111. Mary Roche, "3 Women Embark as Home Planners," *New York Times*, December 3, 1947; "Intra Views," *Sarah Lawrence Alumnae Magazine* 13, no. 2 (Spring 1948), 10; "East Coast" *Everyday Art Quarterly*, no. 7 (Spring 1948), 2, cover.
112. The other consultants were Rita Davidson (writer / planner), Betty Lundquist (photographer), Oliver Lundquist (designer), Abel Sorensen (designer, United Nations Headquarters planning staff), as well as an accountant and a lawyer.
113. New Design, "All-Purpose Family Room," 1948, Dorothy Noyes alumna file, Sarah Lawrence College Archives; Mary Davis Gillies, "I'd Like to Move Right In," *McCall's* 77, no. 10 (July 1950), 82–84, 117; "Innovation in Design," *Brooklyn Daily Eagle*, April 2, 1950; Betty Pepis, "One Among Many," *New York Times*, April 9, 1950; "Three Builder's Houses in Which Architect Design Paid Off Handsomely," *Architectural Forum* 93, no. 2 (August 1950): 126–27. See also "T-Shaped House," in Mary Davis Gillies, *McCall's Book of Modern Houses* (New York: Simon and Schuster, 1951): 32–37.
114. Raye Hoffman, "New Design, Inc., Offers Something New in Furnishings and Accessories Field," *Picture and Gift Journal* 86, no. 7 (July 1949): 8–9. See also "The House in the Museum Garden: Marcel Breuer Architect," *Museum of Modern Art Bulletin* 16, no. 1 (1949); Lewis Mumford, "Design for Living," *New Yorker*, June 1949, 72–76; Dorothy Noyes to Marcel Breuer, May 31, 1949, Marcel Breuer Digital Archive, https://breuer.syr.edu/xtf/view?docId=mets/9066.mets.xml;query=new%20design;brand=breuer. See also *The House in the Museum Garden*, exhibition folder 405.2, MoMA Archives.
115. "New Design Is for Sale," pamphlet, private collection.
116. According to a letter from G. Holmes Perkins to Joseph Hudnut, December 1943, G. Holmes Perkins Collection, Architectural Archives, Weitzman School, Georgia Hencken Perkins worked for Rose Ishbel Greeley in Washington, DC, before going to the OSS; following the war, she was an interior decorator in Cambridge. See Barbara J. Richbert, "Georgia H. Perkins, Decorator," *Philadelphia Inquirer*, November 26, 1994. None of her engagement / wedding announcements mention the Cambridge School, where she met her husband, who was a design critic and instructor in architectural history. See "Alumnae News Notes," *CSAB* 5, no. 4 (June 1933): 14.
117. See Ford and Morrow Ford, *Classic Modern Homes of the Thirties*, 97–99.
118. Georgia Hencken Perkins, interview with David Contosta, January 17, 1990, 30, Chestnut Hill Conservancy, Philadelphia.
119. Hencken Perkins, interview with Contosta, January 17, 1990; "A New Curriculum," *CSAB* 7, no. 3 (May 1935): 1–2.
120. "Fenced In, a Little Store Designs for Space," *Architectural Forum* 104, no. 6 (June 1956): 153.
121. Olga Gueft, "Modern on Chestnut Hill," *Interiors* 115, no. 3 (October 1955), 128.
122. Gueft, "Modern on Chestnut Hill"; "Furniture Shop," *Architectural Forum* 77, no. 2 (August 1942): 86–88.
123. Teresa Fankhänel, *The Architectural Models of Theordore Conrad: The 'Miniature Boom' of Mid-century Modernism* (New York: Bloomsbury Publishing, 2021).
124. Helen Baxter Perrin, "In Case You Kids Are Interested," June 16, 198[?], scrapbook, private collection.
125. According to clippings in the scrapbook of Helen Baxter Perrin, the housing exhibition was shown at the Century of Progress in Chicago (1933) and Macy's (1934). Natalie Gordon, "Our Gracious Ladies," *Boston Traveler*, March 6, 1942, private collection states the exhibition was also at the Museum of Science and Industry at Rockefeller Center in New York.
126. Lefkowitz Horowitz, *Alma Mater*, 152. A photograph of the building, taken by George H. Davis near the time of its completion, is in the Raymond Photograph Collection, Historic New England. See also "Fortieth Anniversary: Tau Zeta Epsilon, Wellesley College," 1929, Wellesley College Archives.
127. Fankhänel, *The Architectural Models of Theordore Conrad*, 14.
128. See the Personals in *PP* 7, no. 5 (May 1926): 319; Baxter Perrin, "In Case You Kids Are Interested"; Gordon, "Our Gracious Ladies." See also Helen Baxter Perrin, "Seeing Is Believing: The Value of the Model to the Home Builder," *HB* 63, no. 1 (January 1928), 56, 96.
129. Baxter Perrin, "In Case You Kids Are Interested."
130. Alan Fisher, email to Mary Anne Hunting, August 15, 2021.
131. John R. Clarke, "Margaret Fisher: An American Modernist," *Woman's Art Journal* 24, no. 1 (Spring / Summer 2003): 11; Margaret Fisher to Walter L. Fisher, November 12, 1931, private collection. See also "The Racine County Court House," *Architectural Forum* 56, no. 2 (February 1932): 151–60.
132. "[Margaret Fisher] Gives Amusing Sketch of Her Life," *Saint Paul Pioneer Press* [MN], April 21, 1939.
133. Philip Johnson, Foreword to *Work of Young Architects in the Middle West*, exhibition catalog (New York: Museum of Modern Art, April 3–30, 1933); press release, April 8, 1933, MoMA Archives. See also "General Houses Completes Steel Home on North Shore," *Chicago Tribune*, March 26, 1933; Terence Riley, "Portrait of the Curator as a Young Man," in *Philip Johnson and The Museum of Modern Art*, ed. John Elderfield (New York: Museum of Modern Art, 1998), 53; and AIA Historical Directory, s.v. "Fisher, Howard," application for membership, July 11, 1949, https://aiahistoricaldirectory.atlassian.net/wiki/spaces/AHDAA/pages/36934696/ahd1013886?preview=/36934696/2216329999/Fisher_Howard.pdf. A second demonstration house by Howard Fisher erected at the Century of Progress (1933) was featured in Ethel Power, "Echoes from the Chicago Fair," *HB* 74, no. 3 (September 1933), 92.
134. Henry Frost to Margaret Fisher, April 3, 1929, private collection.
135. "What's Latest in Home Building Goes on Display: National Show Will Last 9 Days," *Chicago Daily Tribune*, May 17, 1936.
136. Margaret Fisher to Mabel Taylor Fisher, February 14, 1938, private collection.
137. In 1938, the Philips Memorial Gallery purchased from the Fisher exhibition *Landscape, New Mexico* and *Girl in Yellow Sweater*.
138. Florence S. Berryman, "Margaret Fisher at Phillips Gallery," *Sunday Star* [Wash ington, DC], February 5, 1939. After her first solo exhibition Margaret Fisher had three others: at the St. Paul School of Art (1939), Quest Galleries (1939) in Chicago, and Museum of Fine Arts, Houston (1940). Her group shows in the 1940s include venues at the Illinois State Museum in Springfield (1940), Kalamazoo Institute of Arts in Michigan (1944), Phillips Gallery (1944), Art Institute of Chicago (1945–49), and Milwaukee Art Institute (1946).
139. "Art Noters," *Washington Post*, January 29, 1939; Eleanor Jewett, "First Exhibition Reveals Artist of Great Skill," *Chicago Tribune*, December 23, 1938.
140. Margaret Fisher to Henry Frost, [1939], student file, CSR.
141. See, for example, Mary A. Mitchell, "Work of Illinois Artist on View Here," *Saint Paul Pioneer Press*, April 16, 1939; Peter Kendall, "Margaret

Fisher, 92, Artist, Benefactor of Art Institute," *Chicago Tribune*, July 16, 1990. See also "Margaret Fisher: An American Original in Her Mid-70s," *Boston Globe*, October 20, 1973; Agnes Mongan, introduction to *Margaret Fisher: Drawings, Watercolors, Gouaches* (Cambridge, MA: Busch-Reisinger Museum, 1973).

142. Monica Kirkpatrick Johnson, Kristie Long Foley, and Glen H. Elder Jr., "Women's Community Service, 1940–1960: Insights from a Cohort of Gifted American Women," *Sociological Quarterly* 45, no. 1 (Winter 2004): 457.

143. Robert A. Little, "Thanks World," 1990, 114–15, private collection.

144. Marianne Pachner, "Cleveland Art Gallery Gives Talent a Break," *Dunkirk Evening Observer* [Chautauqua, NY], January 16, 1947; "Members of New Ten Thirty Gallery Attend Opening," *Cleveland News*, September 18, 1946; and a draft for an "open letter" about the gallery (private collection).

145. Grace V. Kelly, "Ten Thirty Opens to Lovers of Art," *Plain Dealer* [Cleveland], September 18, 1946; Ann Halle and Robert Little, interview with Avis Berman, June 23, 2004, Ten Thirty Gallery file, Lichtenstein Foundation Archives.

146. Exhibition history, Ten Thirty Gallery file, Lichtenstein Foundation Archives.

147. Violet A. LaFarge, "Katonah Art Gallery Explains Its Operation," letter to the editor, Katonah Museum of Art Archives.

148. John Barnes, interview with Mary Anne Hunting, March 4, 2022.

149. John I. H. Baur, "Why a Katonah Gallery?," fundraising brochure, 1968, Katonah Museum of Art Archives.

150. George Gordon King, interview with Mary Anne Hunting, May 18, 2020. The museum hosted a symposium, titled "Edward Larrabee Barnes: A Celebration of His Life and Career" on March 20, 2004 and two exhibitions on Edward Barnes: in 1958 (with I. M. Pei and Frederick Kiesler) and in 2015, *A Home for Art: Edward Larrabee Barnes and the KMA*.

151. See Mary Anne Staniszewski, *The Power of Display: A History of Exhibition Installations at the Museum of Modern Art* (Cambridge, MA: MIT Press, 1998); Nina Stritzler-Levine, "Curating History, Exhibiting Ideas: Henry-Russell Hitchcock and Architectural Exhibition Practice at the MoMA," in *Summerson and Hitchcock: Centenary Essays on Architectural Historiography*, Studies in British Art 16, ed. Frank Salmon (New Haven, CT: Yale University Press, 2006), 33–67. See also Marcia Brennan, *Curating Consciousness: Mysticism and the Modern Museum* (Cambridge, MA: MIT Press, 2010).

152. See Kathleen D. McCarthy, "Museums and Marginalization," in *Women's Culture: American Philanthropy and Art, 1830–1930* (Chicago: University of Chicago Press, 1991), 111–45.

153. McCarthy, "Museums and Marginalization," 142.

154. Cornelia Butler and Alexandra Schwartz, eds., *Modern Women: Women Artists at the Museum of Modern Art* (New York: Museum of Modern Art, 2010), 34.

155. Juliet Kinchin, "Women, MoMA, and Midcentury Design," in *Modern Women: Women Artists at the Museum of Modern Art*, ed. Cornelia Butler and Alexandra Schwartz (New York: Museum of Modern Art, 2010), 285–86, 299 n. 10.

156. Michelle Elligott with Romy Silver, "Modern Women; A Partial History," *Modern Women: Women Artists at the Museum of Modern Art*, ed. Cornelia Butler and Alexandra Schwartz (New York: Museum of Modern Art, 2010), 514–21; "Modern Women: A Partial History," MoMA, March 24, 2024, https://www.moma.org/interactives/modern_women/history/.

157. Ernestine [Marie Fantl] Carter, *With Tongue in Chic* (London: Michael Joseph, 1974), 27. See also Alan Powers, "Exhibition 58: 'Modern Architecture in England,' Museum of Modern Art, 1937," *Architectural History* 56 (2013): 277–98.

158. Russell Lynes, *Good Old Modern: An Intimate Portrait of The Museum of Modern Art* (New York: Atheneum, 1973), 115.

159. See "Young Architects State Rival Show," *New York Times*, April 21, 1931; [Fantl] Carter, *Tongue in Chic*, 20–21.

160. [Fantl] Carter, *Tongue in Chic*, 27.

161. [Fantl] Carter, *Tongue in Chic*, 28.

162. See Sigfried Giedion, *Space, Time and Architecture: The Growth of a New Tradition* (Cambridge, MA: Harvard University Press, 1982 [1941]), 696–706. Sigfried Gideon does not list a conference in 1936. However, Ernestine Fantl Carter not only describes the experience in *Tongue in Chic*, 47, but MoMA's publicity office produced a letter announcing her return from the meeting, October 8, 1936, https://www.moma.org/momaorg/shared/pdfs/docs/press_archives/347/releases/MOMA_1936_0043.pdf, as well as a press release, 11436-32, https://www.moma.org/momaorg/shared/pdfs/docs/press_archives/354/releases/MOMA_1936_0050_1936-11-04_11436-32.pdf. While Fantl Carter states that Richard Neutra recommended her as the American delegate, MoMA maintains it was Walter Gropius.

163. [Fantl] Carter, *Tongue in Chic*, 49.

164. [Fantl] Carter, *Tongue in Chic*, 49.

165. [Fantl] Carter, *Tongue in Chic*, 33.

166. Lynes, *Good Old Modern*, 118.

167. Elodie Courter, alumna file, Wellesley College Archives.

168. "Circulating Exhibitions," *Bulletin of the Museum of Modern Art* 7, no. 5 (September 1940): 11.

169. Lynes, *Good Old Modern*, 107, including the caption under photograph.

170. Robert Osborn, *Osborn on Osborn* (New Haven, CT: Ticknor and Fields, 1982), 85–86.

171. Alice Morgan Carson to Fran[ces] Rich, September 24, 1942, series 208, folder 4, exhibition records, MoMA Archives.

172. Marguerite Young, "Glass, Paper, and Plastics Magically Replace Things 'You Can't Get Now,'" *Burlington Daily News*, March 12, 1943. See also Alice Morgan Carson, "Useful Objects in Wartime," *Museum of Modern Art Bulletin* 10, no. 2 (December 1942): https://assets.moma.org/documents/moma_catalogue_2733_300164646.pdf?_ga=2.267870285.2106236669.1711217684-1625942904.1710261308.

173. Eugenia Sheppard, "Useful Objects for Households Put on Display," *New York Times*, November 21, 1945.

174. For brief biographies on Greta Daniel and Mildred Constantine, see Thomas Hines, *Architecture and Design at the Museum of Modern Art: The Arthur Drexler Years, 1951–1986* (Los Angeles: Getty Research Institute, 2019), 42, 44.

175. See "About U," Museum Folkwang, accessed March 24, 2024, https://www.museum-folkwang.de/en/about-us; Olga Gueft, "Greta's Era," *Interiors* 121, no. 12 (July 1962), 51.

176. Press release, no. 85, December 17, 1958, MoMA Archives, https://assets.moma.org/documents/moma_press-release_326135.pdf?_ga=2.29797628.2106236669.1711217684-1625942904.1710261308.

177. Press release, no. 85, December 16, 1958; "Greta Daniel, 1905–1962," *Craft Horizon* 22, no. 4 (July 1962), 9; Lynes, *Good Old Modern*, 322; Mildred Constantine, interview with Sharon Zane, April 11, 1991, 42, in "The Museum of Modern Art Oral History Program," MoMA, https://www.moma.org/momaorg/shared/pdfs/docs/learn/archives/transcript_constantine.pdf.

178. Constantine, interview with Zane, 36.

179. "Skidmore, Owings & Merrill: Architects, U.S.A.," *Museum of Modern Art Bulletin* 18, no. 1 (Fall 1950): 11, https://assets.moma.org/documents/moma_catalogue_2411_300062082.pdf?_ga=2.189243624.2106236669.1711217684-1625942904.1710261308.

180. "Cracking the Glass Ceiling: A Look Back at the Career of Trailblazing Architect Natalie de Blois," *Medium*, April 2, 2015, https://som.medium.com/cracking-the-glass-ceiling-a-look-back-at-the-career-of-trailblazing-architect-natalie-de-blois-b7ef02b28c2b; "Oral History of Natalie de Blois," Ryerson and Burnham Art and Architecture Archive, March 12, 2002, https://artic.contentdm.oclc.org/digital/collection/caohp/id/15893/https://digital-libraries.artic.edu/digital/collection/caohp/id/15893/.

181. Philip C. Johnson, *Mies Van der Rohe* (New York: Museum of Modern Art, 1947).

182. Mildred Constantine, "In Memoriam," *AR* 175, no. 6 (May 1987): 69.
183. Constantine, interview with Zane, 43.
184. Constantine, "In Memoriam," 69.
185. Elizabeth Bauer Mock to Catherine Bauer Wurster, CBW.
186. Elizabeth Bauer Mock to Catherine Bauer Wurster, July 29, 1940, CBW.
187. Alfred Barr to Catherine Bauer Wurster, June 30, 1941, carton 2, folder 34, Bauer Wurster Papers; Elizabeth Bauer [Mock] Kassler, interview with Joan Ockman, May 12, 1995, Temple Hoyne Buell Center for the Study of American Architecture, Columbia University.
188. See also Hines, *Architecture and Design*, 22–24.
189. Stephen C. Clark, foreword to *Museum of Modern Art Bulletin* 13, no. 3 (February 1946): 3.
190. Catherine Bauer Wurster to Elizabeth Bauer Mock, September 9, 1944, CBW. The book *Built in USA* is an important reference source for MoMA: the history / purpose of the architecture department is in the preface; an index of architects, exhibitions, and publications is in the back matter.
191. Wendy Lesser, "The Importance of the Personal," *Places Journal*, September 2022, https://placesjournal.org/article/elizabeth-bauer-mock/.
192. Elizabeth Bauer Kassler, curriculum vitae, c. 1990, private collection.
193. The term *tastebreaker* was used to describe avant-garde artists by MoMA curator and director James Johnson Sweeney in "Tastemakers and Tastebreakers," *Georgia Review* 14, no. 1 (Spring 1960): 90–100.
194. In addition to an outline of her life provided by her daughter Phoebe Knapp (private collection), see "Elizabeth-Ann Knapp, A Former Architect, 76," *New York Times*, January 26, 1990; "Memorial: J. Merrill Knapp '36," *Princeton Alumni Weekly*, November 24, 1993, 40, https://paw.princeton.edu/memorial/j-merrill-knapp-'36.
195. "Thomas D. Campbell Dies at 84; Wheat Grower and Innovator," *New York Times*, March 19, 1966; "Overview of the Collection," Campbell Farming Corporation Records, 1918–1975, Archives West, https://archiveswest.orbiscascade.org/ ark:/80444/xv96804.
196. The photographs are in a private collection.
197. "Bulk of Estate of Gen. [Thomas Donald] Campbell to Grandchildren," *Albuquerque Journal*, April 1, 1966; Tom Cook, "Last of the Big Spread," *Billing's Gazette* [MT], August 17, 1992. See also Curt Eriksmoen, "'Henry Ford of Agriculture' Was Born in North Dakota," *Grand Forks Herald* [ND], November 6, 2005; "Charm, Courage, and Campbell," in Hiram M. Drache, *Beyond the Furrow: Some Keys to Successful Farming in the Twentieth Century* (Danville, IL: Interstate Printers and Publishers, 1976), 95–166; "Thomas Donald Campbell (1882–1966)," Social Networks and Archival Context, University of Virginia Library and National Archives and Records Administration, https://snaccooperative.org/ark:/99166/w6x07f1p.
198. "Overview of the Collection."
199. Melissa Adams, "Sevilleta an Outdoor Lab for Researchers," *Albuquerque Tribune*, July 1, 1981. See also Tom Butler, *Wildlands Philanthropy: The Great American Tradition* (San Rafael, CA: Earth Aware Editions, 2008), 114–15.
200. Thomas D. Campbell house, 2405 Belmont Road, Grand Forks, ND, National Register of Historic Places registration form, September 29, 1987, https://npgallery.nps.gov/NRHP/GetAsset/NRHP/87002010_text.
201. According to Drache, *Beyond the Furrow*, 135–36, Thomas Campbell made all his men shave daily as well as shower and change after work, not merely as sanitary measures but also as "psychological devices, designed to prevent the old fashioned 'farm hand' attitude from creeping into the Campbell organization." See also "Camp Four, Fort Smith, Montana," National Register of Historic Places registration form, December 6, 1991, https://npgallery.nps.gov/NRHP/GetAsset/NRHP/91001940_text.
202. See "Campbell Farming Corporation Camp 4," Big Horn County Museum, accessed March 19, 2024, https://www.bighorncountymuseum.org/structure/campbell-farming-camp/.
203. "Students, 1932–1933," *Bulletin of the University of New Hampshire* 24, no. 6 (February 1933): 277; Amy Gilley, "Women's Contributions to the Historic American Buildings Survey, 1933–1941," *CRM: The Journal of Heritage Scholarship* 5, no. 2 (Summer 2008): 39–63; "WPA Historic American Buildings Survey of New Hampshire Papers," c. 2000, MC 33, Special Collections, University of New Hampshire, https://library.unh.edu/find/archives/collections/wpa-historic-american-buildings-survey-new-hampshire-papers-1935-1941.
204. *Old-Time New England* 41, no. 1 (July–September 1950): frontispiece.

VI: Houses and Housing

1. Elisabeth Coit, *Twenty-Fifth Anniversary Report Radcliffe Class of 1913* (Cambridge, MA: Crimson Printing, 1938), 30; Elisabeth Coit, "The Smaller Airport," *PP* 18, no. 11 (November 1937): 739–41.
2. Wolfgang Langewiesche, *I'll Take the High Road* (New York: Harcourt, Brace and Co., 1939), 191.
3. Langewiesche, *I'll Take the High Road*, 222, 227.
4. "Girl Architects Organize a Firm," *New York Times*, March 8, 1914.
5. "Approved Ideas of Social Settlement Work Made Use of in Wilson Memorial," *Ithaca Journal* [NY], January 22, 1915; "Women Architects Win Chicago Prize," *New York Times*, March 6, 1915; "Mrs. [Halsey] Wilson Memorial Homes," *American Contractor*, September 18, 1915, 83.
6. Lewis Mumford, notes on Clarence Stein, box 69, folder 30, Edith Elmer Wood Papers, Avery Library.
7. Eleanor Manning O'Connor, "Architecture as a Profession for Women," *Simmons Review* 16, no 3 (April 1934): 71; Lois Wait, "People You Ought to Know: No. 56: Miss Eleanor Manning," *Boston Herald*, July 9, 1929.
8. Images of Old Harbor Village are in C. W. Short and R. Stanley-Brown, *Public Buildings: A Survey of Architecture Projects Constructed by Federal and Other Governmental Bodies Between the Years 1933 and 1939 with the Assistance of the Public Works Administration* (Washington DC: United States Government Printing Office, 1939), 660.
9. See Eleanor Manning O'Connor, "Building for National Welfare," *National Altrusan* 12, no. 7 (March 1935): 5.
10. "Elisabeth Coit, 94, Architect and a Specialist on Housing," *New York Times*, April 8, 1987; Coit, *Twenty-Fifth Anniversary Report*; Elisabeth Coit to Karen Sue Hilty, May 12, 1973, Papers of Elisabeth Coit, Schlesinger Library (henceforth Coit Papers).
11. Peter Pennoyer and Anne Walker, *The Architecture of Grosvenor Atterbury* (New York: W. W. Norton, 2009), 188; Elisabeth Coit, "Architecture as a Profession for Women," *Radcliffe Quarterly* 20, no. 2 (May 1936): 15–18.
12. Pennoyer and Walker, *Architecture of Grosvenor Atterbury*, 46–49. The list of important office staff members on page 49 includes Coit, but no other women.
13. Elisabeth Coit, notes to John Moore, April 16, 1982, Coit Papers. See also Marcia Mead, "The Architecture of the Small House: As Influenced by Our Modern Industrial Communities," *Architecture* 37, no. 6 (June 1918): 145.
14. Coit, notes to Moore.
15. Coit, *Twenty-Fifth Anniversary Report*; Coit to Hilty.
16. "G. Atterbury, 87, Architect, Dead," *New York Times*, October 19, 1956.
17. AIA Historical Directory, s.v. "Coit, Elisabeth," application for an Edward Langley Scholarship, March 11, 1937, https://aiahistoricaldirectory.atlassian.net/wiki/spaces/AHDAA/pages/36781973/ahd1008262?preview=/36781973/2214462685/Coit_Elisabeth.pdf.
18. Grosvenor Atterbury, "The Economic Production of Workingmen's Homes," in the *Report of the Regional Plan of New York and Its Environs of the Russell Sage Foundation* (New York: Russell Sage Foundation, 1930), 1–39; "Concrete Houses," *New York Times*, May 7, 1944; "Mass Production of Housing Urges," *New York Times*, February 13, 1931; Pennoyer and Walker, *Architecture of Grosvenor Atterbury*, 175–79, 254–56.
19. See "The Sage Foundation House," [editorial], *Cement Age* 11, no. 6 (December 1910): 311–14; "Studies in Economic Construction," *Cement Age* 11, no. 6 (December 1910): 315–24; Coit, notes to Moore; Elisabeth Coit, "$25 a Month for Your Own Home," *Woman's Day* 2, no. 5 (February 1937), 9–12;

Elisabeth Coit, "Prefabrication Comes of Age in Wartime," *Citizens Housing Council of New York Housing News*, April 1943.

20. "Women and Town-Planning," *Woman's Journal* 13 (August 1928): 21.

21. Sue Hendler with Julia Markovich, *"I Was the Only Woman": Women and Planning in Canada* (Vancouver: University of British Columbia Press, 2017), 40–43. While the authors discuss the historical situation in Canada, their conclusions apply to the United States as well.

22. Eleanor Manning to Charles J. Livingwood, February 2, 1923, and Livingwood to Lois Howe and Eleanor Manning, October 20, 1922, box 29, John Nolen Papers, collection no. 2903, Division of Rare and Manuscript Collections, Cornell University Library.

23. Millard F. Rogers, Jr., *John Nolen & Mariemont: Building a New Town in Ohio* (Baltimore: John Hopkins University Press, 2001), 73–77, 82.

24. See Mead, "Architecture of the Small House," pls. 185.

25. Elisabeth Coit, "Notes on European Low-Cost Housing, 1935," *Radcliffe Quarterly* 19, no. 4 (October 1935): 243–47.

26. See "Local Woman Wins Architect Scholarship," *New York Times*, June 14, 1938; "Local Woman Wins Architect Scholarship," *Boston Globe*, June 14, 1938. The Langley Scholarship that Coit received for 1937–38 was renewed for 1938–39. Of the seven winners in 1938, she was the only woman.

27. Elisabeth Coit, curriculum vitae, May 21, 1982, Coit Papers; "Notes on Design and Construction of the Dwelling Unit for the Lower-Income Family, Part I," *Octagon* 13, no. 10 (October 1941): 10–30; "Notes on Design and Construction of the Dwelling Unit for the Lower-Income Family, Part II," *Octagon* 13, no. 11 (November 1941): 7–26.

28. See Mary Otis Stevens, "Elisabeth Coit: Low-Income Housing," in *Women in American Architecture: A Historic and Contemporary Perspective*, ed. Susana Torre (New York: Architectural League of New York and Whitney Library of Design, 1977), 100–102.

29. Coit, "Notes on Design and Construction … Part I," 10.

30. Coit, "Notes on Design and Construction … Part I," 14.

31. Coit, "Notes on Design and Construction … Part I," 14.

32. Coit, "Notes on Design and Construction … Part I," 14–15.

33. Coit, "Notes on Design and Construction … Part I," 19.

34. Coit, "Notes on Design and Construction … Part I," 16. A summary of the *Octagon* articles is in Elisabeth Coit, "Housing from the Tenant's Viewpoint," *AR* 91, no. 4 (April 1942): 71–84. Her findings are also discussed in a talk entitled "Design and Construction of Dwelling Units for the Lower-Income Family," February 17, 1941, Coit Papers.

35. Stevens, "Elisabeth Coit: Low-Income Housing," 102; AIA Historical Directory, s.v. "Coit, Elisabeth," application for membership, October 13, 1953; Clarence S. Stein to Jury of Fellows, October 9, 1953, AIA Historical Directory.

36. Stevens, "Elisabeth Coit: Low-Income Housing," 100.

37. AIA Historical Directory, s.v. "Coit, Elisabeth," application for membership.

38. Eero Saarinen to Committee on Fellows, in AIA Historical Directory, s.v. "Coit, Elisabeth," application for membership.

39. Marjorie Farnsworth, "Her Career Was Blueprinted at 10," *New York Journal American*, July 11, 1953. See also Anthony P. Musso, "Millbrook's Migdale Estate Designed after Scottish Castle Enjoyed by Carnegie Family," *Poughkeepsie Journal* [NY], May 7, 2019.

40. "Through the Microphone: Art Broadcast," *Hartford Courant* [CT] December 29, 1930; "An Architect's Home—By Almus Pratt Evans, of New York," *PP* 22, no. 2 (February 1941): 101–11. See also Almus Pratt Evans, "Exposition Architecture: 1983 Versus 1933," *Parnassus* 5, no. 4 (1933): 17–22.

41. For more on Saul Edelbaum and Ida Brown Adelberg Webster, see their page on *NC Modernist*, accessed March 19, 2024, http://www.ncmodernist.org/edelbaum.htm.

42. The firm was recognized for its niche of modern houses for Jewish clientele.

43. Women in Architecture Committee of the AIA Baltimore Chapter, "Early Women of Architecture in Maryland," accessed March 19, 2024, https://www.aiabaltimore.org/baltimore-architecture-foundation/early-women-of-architecture-in-maryland/.

44. For information about the theses see chapter I, note 000.

45. Pearlman, *Inventing American Modernism*, 159; Frost, "The Twenty First Year," *CSAB* 8, no. 1 (November 1935): 4.

46. See Dorothea L. MacMillan, "Houses and Housing Exhibition," *CSAB* 12, no. 2 (April 1940), 4–8; "Houses and Housing Exhibition to Open March 1 at Somerset," *Boston Herald*, February 23, 1940. The exhibition had been part of the *Art in Our Time* exhibition commemorating the opening of the new MoMA building in 1939. See Frederick Gutheim and John McAndrew, "Housing" in *Art in Our Time* (New York: Museum of Modern Art, 1939), 311–17.

47. The Delaware projects for Victorine du Pont Homsey's relatives include Andelot house (1931–; alterations) for Lammot du Pont Copeland in Worton; Louviers (1935; alterations) for William Winder and Alletta Belin du Pont Laird in Rockland; house for Henry Belin Robertson (1936) in Centreville; Mt. Cuba (1937–) for Lammot du Pont Copeland in Hockessin; a house (1937–) for Francis V. du Pont in Greenville; and a beach house (1939–) for Alexis Felix du Pont in Dewey. The firm also restored Eyre Hall (1933) for Henry du Pont Baldwin in Northampton, VA and designed a house (1939) for Lammot du Pont Jr. in Rockland, MD.

48. "Housing Development," in "Recent Work of Victorine and Samuel Homsey," *Architectural Forum* 73, no. 3 (September 1940): 166–67. The pattern book is in the Homsey Papers, Hagley Library. The Homseys also constructed a nursery school and a recreation center at the golf course for employees and families.

49. "Greenbelt, Maryland, Historic District," National Historic Landmark nomination form, March 22, 1996, https://npgallery.nps.gov/NRHP/GetAsset/NHLS/80004331_text; AIA Historical Directory, s.v. "Klaber, Eugene H[enry]," application for membership, November 14, 1921, https://aiahistoricaldirectory.atlassian.net/wiki/spaces/AHDAA/pages/36943577/ahd1024155?preview=/36943577/2199617664/KlaberEugeneH_memb.pdf.

50. See "PBA Awards School Bldg. Contracts for $237,587 to Be Built in 4 Months," *Greenbelt Cooperator* [MD], July 21, 1944; "Architect Hopeful for School by October," *Greenbelt Cooperator*, June 23, 1944.

51. "Maintenance Buildings, Greenbelt, Maryland, FPHA, Region III," *PP* 25, no. 3 (March 1945): 71–72; "Greenbelt, Maryland, Historic District."

52. "Philadelphia Tries Modern Planning," *Building and Modernization* 5, no. 1 (January 1937): 8–11; "Mrs. Elizabeth Fleisher, Architect, Dies," *Evening Bulletin* [Philadelphia], June 10, 1975.

53. Elizabeth Hirsh Fleisher speaking at her fortieth Wellesley College reunion (1954), quoted in "Famous Architect: Elizabeth Hirsh Fleisher '14," October 1975, alumna file, Wellesley College Archives.

54. Fleisher, Stephens & Fleisher, "Sixteen Houses, Howland Street, Philadelphia, Pa.," *Architecture* 73, no. 5 (May 1936): 292.

55. Dorothy C. Kahn, "25,000 Dwellings in Phila. Are Unfit, Survey Discloses," *Philadelphia Inquirer*, December 31, 1936.

56. John F. Bauman, "Safe and Sanitary without the Costly Frills: The Evolution of Public Housing in Philadelphia, 1929–1941," *Pennsylvania Magazine of History and Biography* 51, no. 1 (January 1977): 121.

57. "Queen Lane Housing project, City's Sixth to Be Dedicated," October 24, 1954, private collection; "Housing Project to be Dedicated," *Philadelphia Inquirer*, October 24, 1954; "Roth & Fleisher, Philadelphia Architects," *Charette: Tri-State Journal of Architecture and Building* 36, no. 3 (March 1956): 10, cover. The Queen Lane apartments have erroneously been attributed to Thaddeus Longstreath, an employee of Roth and Fleisher; see Ryan Briggs, "Bidding Farewell to Queen Lane, Looking Ahead for PHA," *Hidden City*, September 12, 2014, https://hiddencityphila.org/2014/09/bidding-farewell-to-queen-lane-looking-ahead-for-pha/.

58. Horace Fleisher, "Current Work in Progress: Some New Approaches to Philadelphia Playground Design," *Landscape Architecture* 45, no. 2 (January 1955): 63.

59. John F. Bauman, *Public Housing, Race, and Renewal: Urban Housing in Philadelphia, 1920–1974* (Philadelphia: Temple University Press, 1987), 113.
60. John F. Bauman, "Row Housing as Public Policy: The Philadelphia Story, 1957–2013," *Pennsylvania Magazine of History and Biography* 138, no. 4 (October 2014): 425.
61. "PHA Implodes Queen Lane High-Rise," Philadelphia Housing Authority, September 13, 2014, http://www.pha.phila.gov/pha-news/pha-news/2014/pha-implodes-queen-lane-high-rise.aspx.
62. Edith Elmer Wood, "The Ideal and Practical Organization of a Home," *Cosmopolitan* 26 (April 1899), 659–64.
63. Note about [Edith Elmer] Wood, student file, Smith College Archives; Eugenie Ladner Birch, "Edith Elmer Wood and the Genesis of Liberal Housing Thought, 1910–1940" (PhD diss., Columbia University, 1975), ii.
64. "Graduates of the New York School of Social Work," June 1933, New York School of Social Work Records, Columbia University Archives, 21; "Degrees Conferred During 1919–1920," *Columbia University in the City of New York Catalogue, 1920–1921* (New York: Columbia University), 305.
65. Edith Elmer Wood, "Reminiscences of a Housing Reformer," *SAQ* 11, no. 1 (November 1919): 29–32; Edith Elmer Wood, "What Is a House? VI: Constructive Housing Legislation and Its Lesson for the United States," *JAIA* 6, no. 2 (February 1918): 58–67.
66. Edith Elmer Wood, *Housing Progress in Western Europe* (New York: E. P. Dutton, 1923), 3.
67. Carol Aronovici to Edith Elmer Wood, July 12, 1932, and Edith Elmer Wood to Carol Aronovici, 1932, box 63, folder 7, Elmer Wood Papers.
68. University Extension, "A New Course on Housing: Applied Problems in Development and Management," 1939–40, box 63, Elmer Wood Papers.
69. Joseph Hudnut to Nicholas Murray Butler, January 21, 1935, Joseph Hudnut files, 1926–1936, Columbia University Archives.
70. Edith Elmer Wood, "Report of the Committee in Housing of the Association of Collegiate Alumnae," 1919, box 21, folder 1, Elmer Wood Papers.
71. Edith Elmer Wood to Elisabeth Coit, March 18, 1939, and Elisabeth Coit to Edith [Elmer] Wood, March 6 and May 11, 1939, box 69, folder 10, Elmer Wood Papers.
72. Mumford, notes on Stein.
73. See Catherine Bauer "Housing: Paper Plans, or a Workers' Movement" as well as Edith Elmer Wood, "The Housing Situation in the United States," in Carol Aronovici, ed., *America Can't Have Housing* (New York: Museum of Modern Art for the Committee on the Housing Exhibition, 1934).
74. Catherine Bauer Wurster to Edith Elmer Wood, July 30, 1941, and Edith Elmer Wood to Bauer Wurster, August 23, 1941, Elmer Wood Papers.
75. Mumford, notes on Stein.
76. R. L. Duffus, "What Modern Housing Means and Why It Is Delayed," *New York Times Book Review*, December 23, 1934.
77. Duffus, "What Modern Housing Means"; Catherine Bauer Wurster to Joseph Hudnut, December 17, 1943, box 15, CBW.
78. An excellent account of the career of Bauer Wurster is in Barbara Penner, "The (Still) Dreary Deadlock of Public Housing," *Places Journal* (October 2018), https://doi.org/10.22269/181030.
79. J.J.P. Oud to Catherine Bauer, March 9, 1931, box 24, CBW.
80. Catherine Bauer, draft, "Mass Production in America," box 7, CBW.
81. Catherine Bauer, "Biographical Records Questionnaire," February 19, 1930, Vassar College Archives; Catherine Bauer, travel diary, 1926–27, box 4, CBW.
82. Catherine Bauer, draft, "Modern Department Stores," 10, box 7, CBW.
83. Catherine Bauer, "Machine-Age Mansions for Ultra-Moderns," *New York Times*, April 15, 1928. The *Fortune* articles (in Lewis Mumford's name only) are "Housing in England," *Fortune* 6, no. 5 (November 1932), 32–37, 82, 84; "Machines for Living," *Fortune* 7, no. 2 (February 1933), 78–80, 82, 84, 87–88; "Taxes into Housing," *Fortune* 7, no. 5, (May 1933), 48–49, 86, 88–89.
84. Lewis Mumford first discusses the concept in *The Story of Utopias* (1922). See John L. Thomas, "Lewis Mumford: Regionalist Historian," *Reviews in American History* 16, no. 1 (March 1988): 158–72.
85. Catherine Bauer, "Who Cares About Architecture?," *New Republic*, c 66, no. 857 (May 6, 1931), 326.
86. "Houser Wins Guggenheim Award," *AR* 79, no. 5 (May 1936): 341.
87. See "Modern Department Stores," box 7, CBW; "Mass-Production Design in America: The Word and the Thing," box 7, CBW; "Typenware in Amerikia," box 7, CBW; "Photography: Man Ray and Paul Strand," *Arts Weekly* 1, no. 9 (May 7, 1932), 193.
88. Catherine Bauer, "The 'Exuberant and Romantic' Genius of Frank Lloyd Wright," *New Republic*, July 8, 1931, 214. See also Neil Levine, introduction to Frank Lloyd Wright, *Modern Architecture: Being the Kahn Lectures for 1930* (Princeton, NJ: Princeton University Press, 2008).
89. Bauer, "The 'Exuberant and Romantic,' " 214.
90. Catherine Bauer, "Exhibition of Modern Architecture: Museum of Modern Art," *Creative Art* 10 (March 1932): 201.
91. Catherine Bauer, "Pre-View … Or Post-Mortem?," in *Architecture in Government Housing* (New York: Museum of Modern Art, 1936).
92. See MoMA, "Architecture and Design," accessed March 19, 2024, https://www.moma.org/collection/about/curatorial-departments/architecture-design.
93. The MoMA projects Catherine Bauer worked on include: the housing section of *Modern Architecture: International Exhibition* (1932); Catherine Bauer, "Cities and Houses," in *Art in America in Modern Times*, ed. Holger Cahill and Alfred H. Barr Jr. (New York: Reynal and Hitchcock, 1934); Catherine Bauer, "Housing: Paper Plans, or a Workers' Movement," in *America Can't Have Housing*, ed. Carol Aronovici (New York: Museum of Modern Art for the Committee on the Housing Exhibition, 1934); Bauer, "Pre-View … Or Post-Mortem?"; Catherine Bauer, "Elements of English Housing Practice," in *Modern Architecture in England* (New York: Museum of Modern Art, 1937); and the "Houses and Housing" section in *Art in Our Time* (1939). She also contributed to the exhibitions *Stockholm Builds* (1941); *America Builds* (1944); *U.S. Housing in War and Peace* (1944); and "Built in USA" section in *Art in Progress* (1944). She was also a juror for the Industrial Design Competition for Home Furnishings (1941) and the International Competition for Low-Cost Furniture (1948).
94. Catherine Bauer, *Architecture in Government Housing* (New York: Museum of Modern Art, 1936).
95. See "Acknowledgements," in *Modern Architecture: International Exhibition* (New York: Museum of Modern Art, 1932), 11; Terence Riley, *The International Style: Exhibition 15 and The Museum of Modern Art* (New York: Rizzoli / Columbia Books of Architecture, 1992), 60.
96. See the Architecture column in *Arts Weekly* by Henry-Russell Hitchcock and Catherine Bauer on April 16, 1932; Bruce Brooks Pfeiffer and Robert Wojtowicz, eds., *Frank Lloyd Wright and Lewis Mumford: Thirty Years of Correspondence* (New York: Princeton Architectural Press, 2001), 16.
97. Philip Johnson to Catherine Bauer, June 13, 1934, carton 2, CBW.
98. Catherine Bauer Wurster to Alfred Barr, April 28, 1941, carton 2, CBW.
99. Catherine Bauer Wurster to Joseph Hudnut, June 25, 1945, carton 15, CBW.
100. Joseph Hudnut to Catherine Bauer Wurster, October 11, 1943, and January 4, 1940, carton 15, CBW.
101. Joseph Hudnut to Catherine Bauer Wurster and Bill Wurster, May 9, 1944, carton 15, CBW.
102. Catherine Bauer to Joseph Hudnut, September 13, 1943, carton 15, CBW.
103. See Pearlman, *Inventing American Modernism*, 147–51. See also "Joseph Hudnut, Architect Dead," *New York Times*, January 17, 1968.
104. "$30,000 in Grants $20,000 in Prizes in International Competition for Design of Low-Cost Furniture," press release 48105–1, January 25, 1948, MoMA Archives, https://www.moma.org/momaorg/shared/pdfs/docs/press_archives/1237/releases/MOMA_1946-1948_0111_1948-01-05_48105-1.pdf.
105. "Housing's White Knight," *Architectural Forum* 84, no. 3 (March 1946): 116.

106. Elizabeth Bauer Kassler to Frederick Gutheim, 1992, box 138, Frederick Gutheim Papers, American Heritage Center.
107. Catherine Bauer Wurster to G. Holmes Perkins, May 29, 1945, carton 15, CBW.
108. Anishi Patel, "UC Berkeley Hosts Virtual Toast to Honor Bauer Wurster Hall Reaffirmation," *Daily Californian*, December 20, 2020, https://www.dailycal.org/2020/12/10/uc-berkeley-hosts-virtual-toast-to-honor-bauer-wurster-hall-reaffirmation/.

VII: Creating Community

1. Raymond Williams, "Community," in *Keywords: A Vocabulary of Culture and Society* (New York: Oxford University Press, 1983 [1976]), 75.
2. Williams, "Community," 76.
3. Williams, "Community," 75.
4. Coit, application for the Langley Scholarship.
5. "Where the Hills Look Like Mountains," Yorktown Museum.
6. Holly Rivlin and Nancy Sherwood Truitt, "Croton Heights: From Revolution to Soirees; A History of Croton Heights," 2019, Croton Heights Community Association, Yorktown Museum; Halsey William Wilson, letter announcing the opening of Croton Heights Inn, July 8, 1926, Yorktown Museum. See also Creighton Peet, "A Mousetrap in the Bronx," *New Yorker*, October 29, 1938, 28; "Halsey William Wilson," *Wilson Library Bulletin* 28, no. 8 (April 1954): 665–67.
7. Halsey William Wilson, "To All Property Owners at Croton Heights," December 17, 1941, Yorktown Museum.
8. Coit, application for the Langley Scholarship; Edith May Phelps, "The Story of Croton Heights as I Remember It," December 1976, Yorktown Museum. See also John Lawler, *The H. W. Wilson Company: Half a Century of Bibliographic Publishing* (Minneapolis: University of Minnesota Press, 1950).
9. Elisabeth Coit's house for Mary Burnham is illustrated in "30 Houses Costing Under $10,000," *House and Garden* 78, no. 2, section 2 (August 1940), 29 and "House of Miss Mary Burnham, Yorktown Heights, N.Y.," *Architecture* 73, no. 5 (May 1936): 271. Coit also did house plans for Wilson (1925), Mary B. Worley (1926), C. W. Polkes (1927), Agnes Cowing and Jessie Douglass (1927), Edna May Turner Folks (1938), Misses Rose & Manning (1930), Mrs. Fred H. Conklin (1941), Edith May Phelps (addition, 1937), Alberta Worthington (alteration, 1937), Minnie E. Waite (alteration, 1931), and Tracy D. Mygatt and Frances Witherspoon (n.d.).
10. Austin P. Evans, "God Almighty Hates a Quitter," *Columbia Library Columns* 2, no. 1 (November 1952): 14.
11. James Ford, "1932 Better Homes in America Small House Architectural Competition," *AR* 73, no. 3 (March 1933): 216; "Prize-Winning Homes Stress Compact Layouts," *New York Times*, February 26, 1933; "Yorktown Homes of Historic Distinction: Small House Design Award Winner (1932)," Yorktown Landmarks Preservation Commission, September 26, 2018, https://www.tapinto.net/towns/yorktown/articles/yorktown-homes-of-historic-distinction-small-house-.design-award-winner-1932. See also Dolores Hayden, *Building Suburbia: Green Fields and Urban Growth, 1820–2000* (New York: Pantheon Books, 2003), 117–18; Janet Hutchison, "The Cure of Domestic Neglect: Better Homes in America, 1922–1935," in *Perspectives in Vernacular Architecture II*, ed. Camille Wells, 168–78 (Columbia: University of Missouri Press, 1986). The Anna B. Van Nort house is also pictured in Lewis A. Coffin, *American Country Houses of the Thirties* (Mineola, NY: Dover Publications, 2007 [1934]), 152.
12. Myra B. Young Armstead, "Revisiting Hotels and Other Lodgings: American Tourist Spaces through the Lens of Black Pleasure-Travelers, 1880–1950," *Journal of Decorative and Propaganda Arts* 25 (2005): 140; Andrew W. Kahrl, "The Land Was Ours: Black Beach Resorts in the Jim Crow Era," lecture at Guild Hall, East Hampton, NY, August 4, 2018; Mark S. Foster, "In the Face of 'Jim Crow': Prosperous Blacks and Vacations, Travel and Outdoor Leisure, 1890–1945," *Journal of Negro History* 84, no. 2 (Spring 1999): 136.
13. For the early history of the development of Oak Bluffs, see Ellen Weiss, "Robert Morris Copeland's Plans for Oak Bluffs," *JSAH* 34, no. 1 (March 1975): 61–62.
14. Young Armstead, "Revisiting Hotels and Other Lodgings," 143.
15. Ronald J. Stephens, *Images of America: Idlewild, the Black Eden of Michigan* (Charleston, SC: Arcadia Publishing, 2001), 77; Patrick Dunn, "Michigan's Black Eden: A Short History of Idlewild, Second Wave, Michigan," *Model D Media*, October 6, 2020, https://www.modeldmedia.com/features/Idlewild-mnrtf-series-14.aspx; "Idlewild Historic District [MI]," National Register of Historic Places inventory nomination form, June 7, 1979, https://npgallery.nps.gov/GetAsset/c051b73e-45db-474a-ad40-462073dbf535.
16. Grace Lynis Dubinson, "Slowly, Surely, One Plat, One Binder at a Time: Choking Out Jim Crow and the Development of the Azurest Syndicate Incorporated" (MA thesis, Georgia State University, 2012); Dreck Spurlock Wilson, ed., *African-American Architects: A Biographical Dictionary, 1865–1945* (New York: Routledge, 2004), 280–82.
17. Paul Ruffins, "The Soul of Summer," in *Sag Harbor Is: A Literary Celebration*, ed. Maryann Calendrille (New York: Harbor Electronic Publishing, 2006), 77. See also Sandra E. Garacvia, "On Long Island, a Beachfront Haven for Black Families," *New York Times Style Magazine*, October 1, 2020.
18. Jacqueline Taylor, "Amaza's Azurest: Modern Architecture and the 'New Negro' Woman," in *Suffragette City: Women, Politics, and the Built Environment*, ed. Elizabeth Darling and Nathaniel Robert Walker, 33–56 (New York: Routledge, 2019); Jacqueline Taylor, *Amaza Lee Meredith Imagines Herself Modern: Architecture and the Black American Middle Class* (Cambridge, MA: MIT Press, 2023).
19. "Samuel Meredith Dies by His Own Hand Early Today," August 30, 1915, [from an unidentified newspaper,] Amaza Lee Meredith Papers, Special Collections and Archives, Virginia State University.
20. Taylor, "Amaza's Azurest," 38, 40.
21. Richard Guy Wilson, "Building on the Foundations: The Historic Present in Virginia Architecture, 1870–1990," in Charles E. Brownell, Calder Loth, William M. S. Rasmussen, and Wilson, *The Making of Virginia Architecture: Drawings and Models, 1719–1990* (Richmond: Virginia Museum of Fine Arts, 1992), 104.
22. Colson Whitehead, *Sag Harbor: A Novel* (New York: Anchor Books, 2009), 4, 64, 95–97.
23. Whitehead, *Sag Harbor*, 72.
24. Whitehead, *Sag Harbor*, 81, 95.
25. Amaza Lee Meredith to Edna Colson, Colson-Hill Family Papers, Special Collections and Archives, Virginia State University.
26. Ruffins, "The Soul of Summer," 78; Wendy Schuman, "A Place in the East Hampton Sun for Affluent Blacks," *New York Times*, September 5, 1976; Jerry Komia Domatob, *African Americans of Eastern Long Island* (Charleston, SC: Arcadia Publishing, 2001), 83.
27. Amaza Lee Meredith to Edna Colson, June 24, 1950, Colson-Hill Papers.
28. Amaza Lee Meredith, list of master drawings in a letter to Edna Colson, Colson-Hill Papers; Whitehead, *Sag Harbor*, 80.
29. "Sag Harbor Hills, Azurest, and Ninevah Beach [NY], Subdivisions Historic District," National Register of Historic Places registration form, March 25, 2019, https://ncshpo.org/wp-content/uploads/2020/07/SANS-NR.pdf; Stan Gale, interview with Mary Anne Hunting and Kevin D. Murphy, November 14, 2022.
30. Amaza Lee Meredith to Maude Meredith Terry, October 14, 1964, Meredith Papers.
31. According to a letter from Maude Meredith Terry to Amaza Lee Meredith, June 30, 1953, Meredith Papers, Amaza Lee Meredith and Edna Colson provided a portion of her investment: "I have no tangible assets to contribute, but I just could not withdraw myself irrevocably because of that—which the group does not even guess. So perhaps you and Edna could allocate half of your present funds (nothing additional) to cover my insufficiency."

32. Amaza Lee Meredith, "Suggestive House Plans [and] Ideas for Evelyn Leroy Parker's Home at Azurest North," August 1975, Meredith Papers.
33. "Six Moon Hill," *Architectural Forum* 92, no. 6 (June 1950): 113.
34. "Six Moon Hill," 113.
35. Sarah Pillsbury Harkness, quoted in Campbell, "Utopia Revisited."
36. Barbara T. Alexander, "The U.S. Homebuilding Industry: A Half-Century of Building the American Dream," John T. Dunlop Lecture, Harvard University, October 12, 2000, http://www.jchs.harvard.edu/sites/default/files/m00-1_alexander.pdf.
37. Joan Goody, et al., *Building Type Basics for Housing*, 2nd ed. (Hoboken, NJ: John Wiley and Sons, 2010), 38–39.
38. Sarah Pillsbury Harkness, "Women in Architecture—Where Are We and Where Are Going?," lecture, Roger Williams College, November 14, 1980, private collection.
39. "Six Moon Hill," 113.
40. See Murphy, "The Vernacular Moment."
41. Ken Tadashi Oshima, "The Modern House in the Postwar Period: Part 3: Building Utopia at Six Moon Hill, The Fletcher House," *Architecture and Urbanism*, no. 321 (June 1997): 6, states that when the TAC partners began construction, the house owned by Walter Gropius in nearby Lincoln, MA (1937) was already part of "the regional context" for TAC members, and thus they repeated his window and door treatments. The larger issue posed by the involvement of Gropius in TAC but that does not consider the role of Eleanor Raymond, nor of gender, is posed by Michael Kubo, "The Anxiety of Anonymity: On the Historiographic Problem of Walter Gropius and the Architects Collaborative," in *Terms of Appropriation: Modern Architecture and Global Exchange*, ed. Amanda Reeser Lawrence and Ana Miljački, 24–49 (Abingdon, UK: Routledge, 2018).
42. Sarah Pillsbury Harkness, "Eleanor Raymond, Walter Gropius and the Legacies Left to Us," lecture, Boston Architecture Club, March 18, 1992, private collection.
43. Helen Henley, "Two Girls Share as Equal Partners in Modern Architecture," *Christian Science Monitor*, January 13, 1947.
44. "Six Moon Hill," *Architecture Forum*, 121–23; Walter Gropius and Sarah P[illsbury] Harkness, eds., *The Architects Collaborative, 1945–1965* (Teufen AR, Switzerland: Arthur Niggli, 1966), 41.
45. Keith N. Morgan, "Six Moon Hill," in Keith N. Morgan with Richard M. Candee, Naomi Miller, Roger G. Reed, et al., *Buildings of Massachusetts: Metropolitan Boston* (Charlottesville: University of Virginia Press, 2009), 438; Gropius and P[illsbury] Harkness, *The Architects Collaborative*, 48.
46. Lily Geismer, *Don't Blame US: Suburban Liberals and the Transformation of the Democratic Party* (Princeton, NJ: Princeton University Press, 2015), 25–30.
47. Inga Leonova, "Constantin Pertzoff and the Quest for American Orthodox Architecture," *Wheel* 1 (Spring 2015): 40; "Miss Monks Wed at Two Services," *Boston Daily Globe*, September 2, 1937, 18. Olga Monks Pertzoff's mother, Olga Eliza Gardner Monks (1869–1944), was a daughter of George Augustus Gardner (1829–1916), whose brother, John Lowell Gardner Jr. (1837–1898) married Isabella Stewart Gardner in 1960.
48. "'Permanent Investment' Core Surrounded by a 'Temporary Investment' Shell, Description by Constantin A. Pertzoff, Architect," *PP* 25, no. 9 (September 1944): 71. The article also illustrates the exterior and interior of the Pertzoff house.
49. "Erna Herrey Dies at 76," *New York Times*, October 8, 1980. Herrey applied her expertise in physics to resolving highway issues and advised sculptors on materials.
50. Hermann Herrey, Constantin Pertzoff, and Erna M. J. Herrey, "An Organic Theory of City Planning," *AR* 80, no. 4 (April 1944): 133–40, quote at 133 (emphasis in the original).
51. Kay Sieverding, "Lincoln Sells Historic Hollingsworth House," *Concord Journal* [MA], September 20, 2012.
52. Barbara Sampson, "Silver by Lincoln's Florence Hollingsworth Up for Bid at Auction," *Lincoln Journal* [MA], April 10, 2015; Martin Willis, "Modernistic Silver in Lincoln Massachusetts," *Antique Auction Forum* (blog), April 22, 2015, https://antiqueauctionforum.com/blog/modernistic-silver-in-lincoln-massachusetts/.
53. A letter from Sarah Pillsbury to John Harkness, January 10, [c. 1945] private collection, confirms the closeness of their relationship: "I got a letter from Ann Halle Little. I must say it was damn nice of her."
54. "Report to People Who May Be Interested in Buying Part of the Land Which Jim Hughes Is Considering Selling," Spring 1950, manuscript, private collection.
55. Frances P. Taft, "Folk Tales of Pepper Ridge Road: I, 1950–1970," and "Folk Tales of Pepper Ridge Road: II: 1950–2000," private collection.
56. In addition to the Little house, the others (all on Pepper Ridge Road) designed by Robert Little were for Sanford and Marcia Ketchum (#3), 1951; John and Louise Robbins (#2), 1951; Dr. Charles and Martha Hickox (#10), 1952; John M. and Trudy Keeler (#11), 1953; Seth and Frances Taft (#6), 1954; William and Leza McVey (#18), 1955; and Henry and Isabel Haiman (#16), 1958. Later houses include one for Robert L. and Rosie Groves (#1) by Charles Haertling in 1966; a prefabricated Deck-Built house (#14) for Robert and Gretchen Larson in 1969; and a house for John M. and Betsy McEwan (#12) in 1975 by William L. Steck.
57. Michael O' Mallet, "Pepper Pike's One-of-a-Kind Community," *Plain Dealer* [Cleveland], November 8, 2006.
58. "Robert Andrews Little," in *Harvard College Class of 1937 Twentieth Anniversary Report* (Cambridge, MA: privately printed for the class of 1937, 1957), 233; Taft, "Folk Tales of Pepper Ridge Road: I, 7.
59. The house of Robert and Ann Halle Little was published in "House Planned for the Fun of Growing Up," *House and Garden* 107, no. 2 (February 1955), 50–57; "A House That Works," *House and Home* 4, no. 2 (August 1953), 110–15.
60. Registry of Deeds, Grafton County, New Hampshire, no. 763, February 28, 1948, 435–37.
61. Margaret King Hunter, "A Design for Living—or Building," *Wheaton Alumnae Quarterly* 36, no. 3 (July 1957): 14–15.
62. Registry of Deeds, Grafton County, New Hampshire, no. 788, July 6, 1949, 47–49.
63. Registry of Deeds, Grafton County, New Hampshire, no. 788.
64. "Four Small Houses in E. H. and M. K. Hunter, Hemlock Hill, Hanover, N. H.," *AR* 114, no. 5 (November 1953): 154–65, cover. Plans for the house of Roy P. and Dorothy M. Forster are in folder 10 in the Edgar H. and Margaret K. Hunter Architectural Papers, Special Collections, North Carolina State University.
65. According to the deeds, though, Donald H. and Elizabeth Morrison purchased a parcel, but did not build and instead sold it, in 1955, to the Forsters who built a house designed by the Hunters at 18 Hemlock Road.
66. Margaret Hunter, letter to the editor, *New Hampshire Architect* 4, no. 8 (March 1953): 14; Lisa Mausolf, "Mid-20th Century Residential Architecture in NH: 1945–1975," report prepared for the New Hampshire Department of Transportation, 2019, 38–46, https://nhsl.ptfs.com/knowvation/app/consolidatedSearch/#search/v=grid,c=1,q=qs%3D%5Bdublin%5D%2Cbrowse2%3D%5B"Historical%20Resources"%5D%2Cbrowse1%3D%5B"Natural%20and%20Cultural%20Resources"%5D%2CqueryType%3D%5B16%5D,sm=s,l=library1_lib,a=t.
67. Margaret Hunter writing in the *Granite State Architect* 1 (April 1964), quoted in Mausolf, "Mid-20th Century Residential Architecture," 45.
68. Historic American Engineering Record, "Deer Isle-Sedgwick Bridge, Spanning Eggemoggin Reach between Sedgwick & Deer Isle at Route 15, Sedgwick, Hancock County," ME, HAER-ME 66, Library of Congress, http://www.loc.gov/pictures/item/me0314/.
69. Philip Conkling, "A Practical Visionary, Remembering Emily Muir," *Maine Magazine*, May 2017.
70. Conkling, "A Practical Visionary."

71. "Emily Muir: Mistress of Conscience," interview, *Island Journal* 4 (1987): 52.
72. "Emily Muir: Mistress of Conscience," 52.
73. Peg Myers, "Emily Muir's Lasting Legacy Includes Crockett Cove Woods," *Island Heritage Trust* [newsletter] 13, no. 1 (Spring 2003): 3.

VIII: Singular Statements

1. Alison Brooks, quoted in Dagmar Richter, "On Success and Career and Conditions Therefore," in *Architecture: A Woman's Profession*, ed. Tanja Kullack (Berlin: Jovis Verlag, 2011), 121.
2. "House Without Nails Is Being Bolted and Glued Together Here," *Cambridge Sun*, April 23, 1943.
3. "House Without Nails"; "Houses," *Architectural Forum* 79, no. 6 (December 1943): 89–93.
4. Raymond, "The House of To-morrow," 18.
5. "Useful Household Objects under $5.00," 1938, Exhibition History, MoMA Archives, https://www.moma.org/calendar/exhibitions/2745.
6. Patrick Tracy Lowell Putnam and Mary Farlow Linder Putnam, "Our Camp on the Epulu in the Belgian Congo," pamphlet, c. 1933, Field Museum of Natural History; "Noted Explorer to be Woman's Club Speaker," *Orangetown Telegram* [Spring Valley, NY], March 1, 1946.
7. According to the *CSAB* 1, no. 1 (January 1929): 1, Mary Farlow Linder received a "first mention" in a three-week landscape exchange problem ("A Shore Estate" for a banker of international prominence).
8. "Buried in Chilmark," *Vineyard Gazette* [MA], December 24, 1937.
9. "Patrick Putnam Dies in Africa," *Vineyard Gazette*, December 25, 1953.
10. Putnam and Putnam, "Our Camp on the Epulu."
11. Putnam and Putnam, "Our Camp on the Epulu."
12. "Dude Ranchers in the Belgian Congo: They Sing Africa's Praise and Safety," *Vineyard Gazette*, October 8, 1937; "Alumnae Notes," *CSAB* 10, no. 1 (October 1937): 12.
13. Martin Birnbaum, "Mambau: An African Experiment," *Geographical Magazine* 5, no. 5 (September 1937), 339–42.
14. On the "turn to the organic" making an impact on artistic media, see Romy Golan, *Modernity and Nostalgia: Art and Politics in France between the Wars* (New Haven, CT: Yale University Press, 1995), 61–84.
15. Gael Minton, email to Kevin D. Murphy, March 11, 2023. See also William Morgan, *Monadnock Summer: The Architectural Legacy of Dublin, New Hampshire* (Boston: David R. Godine, 2011), 15; Wolfgang Saxon, "Newell Brown, 82, a Labor Aide in Eisenhower's Administration," *New York Times*, May 1, 2000; Alice Osborn Brown, Dublin, New Hampshire, House Survey, 1976-77-78.
16. Typed notes in the Bemis family archive, author and date unknown.
17. Calder Loth, ed., *Virginia Landmarks of Black History: Sites on the Virginia Landmarks Register and the National Register of Historic Places* (Charlottesville: University of Virginia Press, 1995), 17–19.
18. "Gropius House Chronology, 1938–69," Historic New England, accessed March 24, 2024, https://www.historicnewengland.org/property/gropius-house/; "Samuel Meredith Dies by His Own Hand Today," August 30, 1915, Meredith Papers.
19. "Alumnae News Notes," *CSAB* 6, no. 2 (January 1934): 10; "Alumnae Notes," *SAQ* 26, no. 2 (February 1935): 207.
20. Elizabeth Wiley Dunlap, American Society of Landscape Architects, Committee for Women in Landscape Architecture questionnaire, November 28, 1977, student file, CSR; "Architecture a New Field for Women: Eleanor Raymond and Mary P. Cunningham are Architects and Landscape Architects," *Chicago Tribune*, June 16, 1923.
21. "Alumnae Notes," *SAQ* 10, no. 2 (February 1919): 177; "Alumnae Notes," *SAQ* 13, no. 2 (February 1922): 210; "Society, Social and Home News for Women," *Journal and Tribune* [Knoxville], December 29, 1921; "Knoxville Girl in Art Field," *Knoxville Sentinel*, January 15, 1922; "Ten Years Ago Today," *Knoxville News-Sentinel*, October 15, 1933.
22. "Alumnae Notes," *SAQ* 15, no. 1 (May 1924): 370.
23. "Mrs. Frank Creekmore," *Knoxville News-Sentinel*, April 8, 1951.
24. Elsie Prentiss Briggs, "1918's Jobs and Hobbies Exhibit Raises a Few Questions," *SAQ* 29, no. 4 (August 1938): 373–74.
25. Elizabeth Wiley Dunlap, questionnaire, student file. On the Stran-Steel house, see Louise Bargelt, "Wood or Brick Can Be Utilized for the Exterior," *Chicago Daily Tribune*, June 4, 1933; "Stran-Steel House, Chicago World's Fair—1933," *AR* 75, no. 1 (January 1934): 18–19.
26. *Knoxville News-Sentinel*, January 21, 1934.
27. Timothy Mennel, "'Miracle House Hoop-La': Corporate Rhetoric and the Construction of the Postwar American House," *JSAH* 64, no. 3 (September 2005): 340–61.
28. "Alumnae Notes," *SAQ* 22, no. 1 (November 1930): 96.
29. See Stephen C. Porter, "Memorial to Richard Foster Flint, 1902–1976," Geological Society of America, 1978, https://geosociety.org/documents/gsa/memorials/v08/Flint-RF.pdf.
30. Colin M. Caplan, *A Guide to Historic New Haven, Connecticut* (Charleston: History Press, 2007), 44.
31. "House for Richard Foster Flint, New Haven, Connecticut," *Architectural Forum* 67, no. 3 (September 1937): 210–11.
32. Carina Eaglesfield Mortimer kept up her connections with Cambridge School alumnae, for example, by designing a house for *House Beautiful* when Ethel Power was editor; see "Home Builders' Service Bureau," *HB* 61, no. 5 (May 1927), 674.
33. "Carina [Eaglesfield Mortimer] Milligan, 88, Stricken While Swimming," *New Canaan Advertiser* [CT], September 14, 1978; AIA Historical Directory, s.v. "Milligan, Carina E[aglesfield], application for membership," April [?] 1930, https://aiahistoricaldirectory.atlassian.net/wiki/spaces/AHDAA/pages/35731879/ahd1030662?preview=/35731879/2197913651/Milligan_CarinaE.pdf.
34. Henry Frost to Herbert Gibson, October 11, 1937, Eaglesfield student file, CSR.
35. By "stilts," Eaglesfield Mortimer was referring to the pilotis by which the Villa Stein-de Monzie is supported. See Alice T. Friedman, "Being Modern Together: Le Corbusier's Villa Stein-de Monzie," in *Women and the Making of the Modern House: A Social and Architectural History* (New York: Abrams, 1998), 93–125.
36. Carina Eaglesfield [Mortimer] Milligan, "An Architect Remembers," 1974, TS, 22, Eaglesfield and Taggart Family Papers, Indiana Historical Society.
37. Martha Hale Shackford, ed., *Wellesley Verse, 1875–1925* (New York: Oxford University Press, 1925), 185. In correspondence of May 24 and June 1, 1940, Carina Eaglesfield Mortimer sent Van Wyck Brooks a list of her other Connecticut houses to see (Van Wyck Brooks Papers, Rare Books and Manuscripts, Kislak Center for Special Collections, University of Pennsylvania).
38. "Exhibition of Photographs of Work by Three Women Architects of Connecticut," March 6–20, 1938, Yale University Art Gallery Archives; Eaglesfield [Mortimer] Milligan, "An Architect Remembers," 15.
39. Jack LeMenager, "Adaptability Key to Longevity," *New Canaan Advertiser*, May 8, 1975.
40. When the Richard Foster Flint house was published in *Architectural Forum* 67, no. 3 (September 1937): 210–11, as part of a national survey of houses, Carina Eaglesfield Mortimer was the only woman practitioner whose work was represented.
41. See Patrick Sullivan, Mary Beth Reed, and Tracey Fedor, *The Ranch House in Georgia: Guidelines for Evaluation* (Stone Mountain, GA: New South Associates, 2010).
42. Jean League to Ellamae Ellis League, July 1942, Jean League Newton Papers, box 1, Harvard University Archives.
43. Morrow Ford and Creighton, *Quality Budget Houses*, 45. See also "House: Macon, Georgia, League, Warren & Riley, Architects," *PP* 34, no. 7 (July 1953): 102–4.
44. After her marriage in 1954, Ellamae League Newton continued to work in Georgia, where, like other women architects, she also moved into allied fields such as historic preservation.

45. Sarah Schaffer, "A Civic Architect for San Diego: The Work of William Templeton Johnson," *Journal of San Diego History* 45, no. 3 (Summer 1999): 166–87.
46. For the work of William Templeton Johnson, see Save Our Heritage Organization, "The SOHO Annual Historic Home Tour Weekend," 2008, 10–13, https://www.sohosandiego.org/tourbooklets/2008HomeTourWeb.pdf; "Architect Wednesday: William Templeton Johnson, November 18, 2020," Coronado Historical Association, 2020, https://coronadohistory.org/blog.
47. Anne Petersen, "Women Architects Few but Versatile," *New York Times*, April 11, 1937; "Mrs. Clara Johnson of Claremont Dies," *Progress Bulletin* [Pomona, CA], October 27, 1969; and "Mrs. W. T. Johnson Gets Divorce," *New York Herald Tribune*, February 17, 1931.
48. The Bertram F. and Katherine Webster Wilcox house (1939) and the John C. B. and Edith V. M. Moore house (1940), both designed by Moore (of Moore and Hutchins [1937–73]), are claimed as the first two modern houses in Pound Ridge, NY, in *Modern in Pound Ridge: 20th-Century Architecture and Lifestyle* (Pound Ridge Historical Society, 2017).
49. "Roth & Fleisher, Philadelphia Architects," *Charette*, 10, cover.
50. Elizabeth Hirsh Fleisher to Wharton Esherick, June 1, 1953, Wharton Esherick Museum.
51. Anne Tyng, "Synthesis of a Traditional House with a Space-Frame," *International Journal of Space Structures* 6, no. 4 (1991): 273.
52. Tyng, "Architecture Is My Touchstone," 7.
53. Tyng, "Architecture Is My Touchstone," 7.
54. Mary Palache Gregory, "Notes by Herself," Charles O. and Mary (Palache) Gregory files, Papers of the Palache Family, Schlesinger Library. See also Mary Palache Gregory, "The Oxford Summer School—Summer 1928," *CSAB* 1, no. 2 (January 1929): 9–13.
55. See Susanna Terrell Saunders, "Georgianna Goddard King (1871–1939): Educator and Pioneer in Medieval Spanish Art," in *Women as Interpreters of the Visual Arts, 1820–1979*, ed. Adele M. Holcomb and Claire R. Richter (Westport, CT: Praeger, 1981), 219–21.
56. Terrell Saunders, "Georgianna Goddard King (1871–1939)," 225.
57. Mary Palache Gregory, "Pots and Pans and Books," lecture to Bryn Mawr alumnae, November 1951, Mary Palache Gregory alumna file, Bryn Mawr Archives.
58. See Mark Alan Hewitt, *Domestic Architecture of H. T. Lindeberg* (New York: Acanthus Press, 1996).
59. Mary Palache Gregory to Charles Gregory, January 1928, (Palache) Gregory files.
60. Palache Gregory to Gregory, January 1928.
61. Calvin Woodard, "Charles O. Gregory," *Virginia Law Review* 74, no. 1 (February 1988): 3–10; "Charles Gregory, 84: Arbitrator, Was Acting Secretary of Labor," *Boston Globe*, March 27, 1987.
62. Palache Gregory, "Notes by Herself."
63. Robin Horton, "Mary Palache Gregory: Some People Take Pictures … She Paints," *Leisure Weekly*, February 5–12, 1981, Palache Gregory alumna file.
64. Cora Baird Jeanes, biographical note accompanying Palache Gregory, "The Deanery Revisited," *Bryn Mawr Alumnae Bulletin* 24, no. 2 (Winter 1954): 8–9.
65. Mary Palache Gregory, obituary, *Monadnock Ledger-Transcript* [NH], February 22, 1996.
66. These projects include the Mrs. Josiah Harmar house (1947) in Jaffrey, NH, and the Ian Hahn house (1948), in Vineyard Haven, MA, both documented with correspondence, November 8. 1932, (Palache) Gregory files.
67. "Room—Kitchens in America's New Homes," *Portland Sunday Telegram* [ME], July 5, 1953.
68. Mary Palache Gregory, "Speaker Describes Modern Problems Facing Builders," (Palache) Gregory files.
69. Palache Gregory, "Notes by Herself."
70. Palache Gregory, "An Evocation, Written Up from Notes Made Over a Decade," typescript, c. 1967, 2, private collection.
71. Le Corbusier, *Toward an Architecture*, trans. John Goodman (Los Angeles: Getty Research Institute, 2007 [1923]), 21. The fascination of modernists with the grain elevator is discussed in Reyner Banham, *A Concrete Atlantis, U.S. Industrial Building and European Modern Architecture, 1900–1925* (Cambridge, MA: MIT Press, 1986), 109–79.
72. Palache Gregory, "Speaker Describes Modern Problems."
73. Loretta Ford, "Prim Without—Spectacular Within," *Boston Globe*, October 15, 1962.
74. Nathalie Swan, letter to the art editor, *New York Times*, December 18, 1938; Edward Alden Jewell, "Decade of the Bauhaus," *New York Times*, December 11, 1938; Alfred H. Barr Jr., letter to the art editor, *New York Times*, December 25, 1938.
75. For the list of firms where Nathalie Swan Rahv worked, see chapter II, note 000.
76. Liane Lefaivre, "Living Outside the Box: Mary Otis Stevens and Thomas McNulty's Lincoln House," *Harvard Design Magazine*, Spring / Summer 2006.
77. Susana Torre, "Building Utopia: Mary Otis Stevens and the Lincoln, Massachusetts House," in *Impossible to Hold: Women and Culture in the 1960s*, ed. Avital Bloch and Lauri Umansky, 29–33 (New York: NYU Press, 2005).
78. Mary Otis Stevens, quoted in Lefaivre, "Living Outside the Box."
79. Torre, "Building Utopia," 34.
80. Stevens, quoted in Lefaivre, "Living Outside the Box."
81. Lefaivre, "Living Outside the Box."

Conclusion

1. See, for example, H. Peter Oberlander and Eva Newburn, *Houser: The Life and Work of Catherine Bauer* (Vancouver: University of British Columbia Press, 2000).
2. Knowles, ed., *Our Beloved Betsy*, 45.
3. "Historic District Commission Meeting Notes," Lincoln Historical Commission, August 9, 2016, available through www.lincolntown.org.
4. Diego Hernández, "Inside a Demolished Brutalist House: The Lincoln House," *Archdaily*, June 11, 2021, https://www.archdaily.com/963219/inside-a-demolished-brutalist-house-the-lincoln-house.
5. "Historic Macon Acquires Historic Ellamae Ellis League House," Middle Georgia CEO, March 22, 2022, middlegeorgiaceo.com/news/2022/03/historic-macon-acquires-historic-ellamae-ellis-league-house/.
6. Katherine Ott, Susan Tucker, and Patricia P. Buckler, *An Introduction to the History of Scrapbooks* (Philadelphia: Temple University Press, 2006), 2.
7. Ellen Gruber Garvey, *Writing with Scissors: American Scrapbooks from the Civil War to the Harlem Renaissance* (New York: Oxford University Press, 2013), 207.
8. Elizabeth Bauer Kassler to Catherine Bauer Wurster, 1956, CBW.
9. A guide to the Amaza Lee Meredith Papers, 1912, 1930–1938, a collection in Special Collections and Archives, Virginia State University Library, https://ead.lib.virginia.edu/vivaxtf/view?docId=vsu/vipetsoooo5.xml;query=;#series6.
10. Taylor, "Original Designs by Alice Morgan Carson," 24–25.
11. Pietro Belluschi, "Should You Be an Architect," quoted in *"That Exceptional One": Women in American Architecture, 1888–1988* (Washington, DC: American Architectural Foundation, 1988).
12. See Mary D. Sheriff, "'So What Are You Working On?' Categorizing the Exceptional Women," in *Singular Women: Writing the Artist*, ed, Kristen Frederickson and Sarah E. Webb (Berkeley: University of California Press, 2003), 49.

Bibliography

Collections

Aalto University Archives (Otakaari, Finland)
Alvar Aalto Museum (Jyväskylä, Finland)
American Institute of Architects (Cleveland, Ohio), Historic Resources Committee
American Institute of Architects Archives (Washington, DC), Historical Directory of American Architects
Andover Historic Preservation (Andover, Massachusetts)
A[rchitectural] A[ssociation School of Architecture] Archives (London)
Archives of American Art, Smithsonian Institution
Archiv města Plzeň (Czech Republic)
Art Institute of Chicago (Illinois), Ryerson and Burnham Art and Architecture Archives
Art Institute of Chicago, Ryerson and Burnham Libraries
Associated Architects, Architecture Archives (Birmingham, UK)
Athenaeum of Philadelphia (Pennsylvania), archives
Bennington College Archives (Bennington, Vermont)
Beverly Willis Architecture Foundation (New York)
Biblioteka Publiczna m.st. Warszawy, Dziat Informacyjno-Bibliograpficzny
Bryn Mawr Archives (Bryn Mawr, Pennsylvania)
Canadian Centre for Architecture (Montreal, Canada)
Chesterwood Museum (Stockbridge, Massachusetts)
Chestnut Hill Conservancy (Chestnut Hill, Pennsylvania)
City of Cambridge Inspectional Services Department, Records Room (Cambridge, Massachusetts)
Cleveland Architecture Foundation
Cleveland Institute of Art
Cleveland Public Library, Fine Arts and Special Collections
Colorado College (Colorado Springs), Tuft Library, Special Collections
Columbia University Libraries (New York): Avery Architectural and Fine Arts Library; Temple Hoyne Buell Center for the Study of American Architecture
Cornell University Library (Ithica, New York), Division of Rare and Manuscript Collections
Cranbrook Center for Collections and Research (Bloomfield Hills, Michigan)
Dartmouth College Archives (Hanover, New Hampshire)
Embroiders' Guild of America (Louisville, Kentucky)
Fairfax Regional Library, Virginia Room
Filson Historical Society (Louisville, Kentucky), Special Collections
Fondation Le Corbusier (Paris, France)
Frederick Kiesler Foundation (Vienna, Austria)
Getty Research Institute (Los Angeles), Research Library
Greenbelt Museum (Greenbelt, Maryland)
Hagley Museum and Library (Wilmington, Delaware)
Harvard University (Cambridge, Massachusetts): Graduate School of Design, Frances Loeb Library, Special Collections; Art Museums Archives; Schlesinger Library, Radcliffe Institute; Law School
Historic Beverly (Massachusetts)
Historic New England (Boston)
Indiana Historical Society (Indianapolis)
Josef and Anni Albers Foundation (Bethany, Connecticut)
Katonah Museum of Art (Katonah, New York)
Knox County Public Library (Knoxville, Tennessee)
Library of Congress (Washington, DC), Prints and Photographs Division
Mariemont Preservation Foundation (Mariemont, Ohio)
Massachusetts Historical Society (Cambridge)
Massachusetts Institute of Technology (Cambridge): Institute Archives and Special Collections, MIT Libraries; MIT Museum
Metropolitan Museum of Art (New York): Costume Institute
Museum of Modern Art (New York): Architecture and Design Study Center; Archives
National Archives and Records Administration (Washington, DC), Records of the Office of Strategic Services
National Gallery of Canada (Ottawa), Library
National Library of Australia (Canberra)
Newberry Library (Chicago)
New-York Historical Society (New York)
New York Public Library: Library for the Performing Arts; Brooke Russell Astor Reading Room for Rare Books and Manuscripts
North Carolina Museum of Art (Raleigh)
North Carolina State University Archives (Raleigh)
Pound Ridge Historical Society (Pound Ridge, New York)
Royal Institute of British Architects (London)
Roy Lichtenstein Foundation Archives (New York)
Sarah Lawrence College Archives (Bronxville, New York)
Simmons University Archives (Boston)
Skidmore, Owens & Merrill (Chicago and New York)
Smith College Archives (Northampton, Massachusetts)
Smithsonian Institution (Washington, DC): Archives of American Art; Cooper-Hewitt, National Design Museum, Drawings, Prints and Graphic Design Department

Staatsarchiv (Kanton Basel-Stadt, Switzerland)
Stanford University Libraries (Stanford, California), Department of Special Collections
State Library of New South Wales (Sydney, Australia)
Swedish Center for Architecture and Design (ArcDes; Stockholm, Sweden)
Syracuse University Libraries (Syracuse, New York), Marcel Breuer Digital Collection
Town of Lincoln (Massachusetts), Board of Assessors
Tulane University (New Orleans), Newcomb Institute, Newcomb Archives
Ubu Gallery (New York)
University of Arizona (Tucson), Center for Creative Photography
University of California, Berkeley: College of Environmental Design Archives; Environmental Design Library; University Archives, Bancroft Library
University of California, San Diego, Special Collections and Archives
University of Cambridge (Cambridge, UK), Fitzwilliam Museum
University of Chicago, Special Collections Research Center
University of Illinois Archives (Ubana-Champaign)
University of Liverpool (UK), Special Collections and Archives
University of Michigan (Ann Arbor), Special Collections and Archives
University of Minnesota (Minneapolis), Archives and Special Collections
University of New Hampshire Library (Durham), Special Collections
University of New Mexico Libraries (Albuquerque), Center for Southwest Research and Special Collections
University of Pennsylvania (Philadelphia): Stuart Weitzman School of Design, Architectural Archives; Kislak Center for Special Collections
University of South Carolina (Columbia), South Caroliniana Library
University of Virginia Archives (Charlottesville)
University of Wisconsin Archives
University of Wyoming (Laramie), American Heritage Center
V&A Theatre and Performance Collections (London)
Vassar College Archives (Poughkeepsie, New York)
Vermont Division for Historic Preservation (Montpelier)
Virginia State University (Petersburg), Special Collections and Archives
Virginia Tech (Blacksburg), International Archive of Women in Architecture, University Libraries
Warsaw University of Technology
Washington Memorial Library (Macon, Georgia), Middle Georgia Archives
Wellesley College Archives (Wellesley, Massachusetts)
Wellesley Historical Society
Western Regional Archives (Ashville, North Carolina)
Westford Historical Society (Westford, Massachusetts)
Wharton Esherick Museum (Malvern, Pennsylvania)
Wheaton College Archives (Wheaton, Massachusetts)
Williams College (Williams, Massachusetts), Chapin Library, Special Collections
Yale University Library (New Haven, Connecticut), Manuscripts and Archives
Yorktown Museum (Yorktown, New York)

Selected Bibliography of Secondary Sources

Adams, Nicholas. *Skidmore, Owings & Merrill: SOM since 1936*. Milan: Electa Architecture, 2007.

Affron, Matthew, Mark A. Castro, Dafne Cruz Porchini, and Renato González Mello, eds. *Paint the Revolution: Mexican Modernism, 1910–1950*. Philadelphia: Philadelphia Museum of Art, 2016.

Albrecht, Donald, ed. *The Work of Charles and Ray Eames: A Legacy of Invention*. New York: Harry N. Abrams in association with the Library of Congress and the Vitra Design Museum, 1997.

Aldrich, Chilson D. *The Real Log Cabin*. New York: Macmillan, 1929.

Allaback, Sarah. *The First American Women Architects*. Urbana: University of Illinois Press, 2008.

Allen, John. *Berthold Lubetkin: Architecture and the Tradition of Progress*. 2nd ed. London: Artiface, 2012.

Ames, Meriam. *Rancho Santa Fe: A California Village*. Rancho Santa Fe, CA: Rancho Santa Fe Historical Society, 1993.

Anderson, Dorothy May. *Women, Design, and the Cambridge School*. West Lafayette, IN: PDA Publishers Corp., 1987.

Banham, Reyner. *A Concrete Atlantis: U.S. Industrial Building and European Modern Architecture, 1900–1925*. Cambridge, MA: MIT Press, 1986.

Barnes, Edward. *Edward Larrabee Barnes, Architect*. New York: Rizzoli, 1995.

Berkeley, Ellen Perry, ed. *Architecture: A Place for Women*. Washington DC: Smithsonian Institution Press, 1989.

Betsky, Aaron. *Queer Space: Architecture and Same-Sex Desire*. New York: William Morrow and Co., 1997.

Biederman, Marcia. *Popovers and Candlelight: Patricia Murphy and the Rise and Fall of a Restaurant Empire*. Albany, NY: SUNY Press, 2018.

Bjone, Christian. *First House: The Grid, the Figure, and the Void*. New York: Wiley, 2002.

Bloch, Avital, and Lauri Umansky, eds. *Impossible to Hold: Women and Culture in the 1960s*. New York: NYU Press, 2005.

Bogner, Peter, and Gerd Zillner, eds. *Frederick Kiesler: Face to Face with the Avant-Garde: Essays on Network and Impact*. Basel: Birkhäuser, 2019.

Born, Ernest. "The Relation of Painting to Architecture." MA thesis, University of California, Berkeley, 1922.

Born, Esther [Baum]. *The New Architecture in Mexico*. New York: Architectural Record and William Morrow, 1937.

Boutelle, Sarah Holmes. *Julia Morgan, Architect*. Revised ed. New York: Abbeville, 1995.

Brennan, Marcia. *Curating Consciousness: Mysticism and the Modern Museum*. Cambridge, MA: MIT Press, 2010.

Brienza, Laura Brienza. *Discovering Vintage Washington, DC: A Guide to the City's Timeless Shops, Bars, Restaurants and More*. Guilford, CT: Globe Pequot, 2015.

Brook, Clayton McClure, ed. *A Legacy of Leadership: Governors and American History*. Philadelphia: University of Pennsylvania Press, 2008.

Brownell, Charles E., Calder Loth, William M. S. Rasmussen, and Richard Guy Wilson. *The Making of Virginia Architecture: Drawings and Models, 1719–1990*. Richmond: Virginia Museum of Fine Arts, 1992.

Brownlee, David B., and David G. De Long. *Louis I. Kahn: In the Realm of Architecture*. New York: Rizzoli, 1991.

Bruce, Gordon. *Eliot Noyes: A Pioneer of Design and Architecture in the Age of American Modernism*. London: Phaidon, 2006.

Brunetti, John. *Baldwin Kingrey: Midcentury Modern in Chicago: 1947–1957*. Chicago: Wright, 2004.

Butler, Cornelia, and Alexandra Schwartz, eds. *Modern Women: Women Artists at the Museum of Modern Art*. New York: Museum of Modern Art, 2010.

Butler, Tom. *Wildlands Philanthropy: The Great American Tradition*. San Rafael, CA: Earth Aware Editions, 2008.

Calendrille, Maryann, ed. *Sag Harbor Is: A Literary Celebration*. New York: Harbor Electronic Publishing, 2006.

Cantarow, Ellen. *Moving the Mountain: Women Working for Social Change*. New York: Feminist Press, 1980.

Caplan, Colin M. *A Guide to Historic New Haven, Connecticut*. Charleston, SC: History Press, 2007.

Cardwell, Kenneth H. *Bernard Maybeck: Artisan, Architect, Artist*. Santa Barbara, CA: Peregrine Smith, 1977.

Carter, Ernestine. *With Tongue in Chic*. London: Michael Joseph, 1974.

Chadwick, Whitney, and Isabelle De Courtivron. *Significant Others: Creativity and Intimate Partnership*. London: Thames and Hudson, 2005.

Cheng, Irene, Charles L Davis, and Mabel O Wilson, eds. *Race and Modern Architecture: A Critical History from the Enlightenment to the Present*. Pittsburgh: University of Pittsburgh Press, 2020.

Cole, Doris. *Eleanor Raymond, Architect*. Philadelphia: Art Alliance Press, 1981.

———. *From Tipi to Skyscraper: A History of Women in Architecture*. New York: G. Braziller, 1973.

Cole, Doris, and Karen Cord Taylor. *The Lady Architects: Lois Lilley Howe, Eleanor Manning and Mary Almy, 1893–1937*. New York: Midmarch Arts Press, 1990.
Colquhoun, Alan. *Modern Architecture*. Oxford: Oxford University Press, 2002.
Cunningham, Phyllis Fenn. *My Godmother Theodate Pope Riddle: A Reminiscence of Creativity*. Canaan, NH: Phoenix Publishing, 1983.
Currey, Josiah Seymour. *Manufacturing and Wholesale Industries of Chicago*. Chicago: Thomas B. Pool, 1918.
Daly, Reginald A. *Charles Palache, 1869–1954: A Biographical Memoir*. Washington, DC: National Academy of Sciences, 1957.
Darling, Elizabeth, and Lynn Walker, eds. *AA Women in Architecture 1917–2017*. London: AA Publications, 2017.
Darling, Elizabeth, and Nathaniel Robert Walker, eds. *Suffragette City: Women, Politics, and the Built Environment*. New York: Routledge, 2019.
D'Emilio, John, and Estelle B. Freedman. *Intimate Matters: A History of Sexuality in America*. 3rd ed. Chicago: University of Chicago Press, 2012.
Domatob, Jerry Komia. *African Americans of Eastern Long Island*. Charleston, SC: Arcadia Publishing, 2001.
Drache, Hiram M. *Beyond the Furrow: Some Keys to Successful Farming in the Twentieth Century*. Danville, IL: Interstate Printers and Publishers, 1976.
Dubinson, Grace Lynis. "Slowly, Surely, One Plat, One Binder at a Time: Choking Out Jim Crow and the Development of the Azurest Syndicate Incorporated." MA thesis, Georgia State University, 2012.
Dvosin, Andrew James. "Literature in a Political World: The Career and Writings of Philip Rahv." PhD diss., New York University, 1977.
Elderfield, John, ed. *Philip Johnson and the Museum of Modern Art*. New York: Museum of Modern Art, 1998.
Esperdy, Gabrielle. "The Incredible True Adventures of the Architectress in America." *Places Journal* (September 2012): https://doi.org/10.22269/120910.
Etlin, Richard A. *Frank Lloyd Wright and Le Corbusier: The Romantic Legacy*. Manchester: Manchester University Press, 1994.
Ford, James, and Morrow Ford. *Classic Modern Homes of the Thirties*. New York: Dover Publications, 1989.
Ford, Katherine Morrow, and Thomas H. Creighton. *Quality Budget Houses: A Treasury of 100 Architect-Designed Houses from $5,000 to $20,000*. New York: Reinhold Publishing, 1954.
Fowler, Cynthia. *Hooked Rugs: Encounters in American Modern Art, Craft and Design*. New York: Routledge, 2016.
Friedman, Alice T. *Women and the Making of the Modern House*. New York: Harry N. Abrams, 1998.
———. *American Glamour and the Evolution of Modern Architecture*. New Haven, CT: Yale University Press, 2010.
Garvey, Ellen Gruber. *Writing with Scissors: American Scrapbooks from the Civil War to the Harlem Renaissance*. New York: Oxford University Press, 2013.
Geismer, Lily. *Don't Blame US: Suburban Liberals and the Transformation of the Democratic Party*. Princeton, NJ: Princeton University Press, 2015.
Gibans, Nina Freedlander, and James D. Gibans. *Cleveland Goes Modern, Design for the Home, 1930–1970*. Kent, OH: Kent State University Press, 2014.
Giedion, Sigfried. *Space, Time and Architecture: The Growth of a New Tradition*. Cambridge, MA: Harvard University Press, 1982 [1941].
Gilley, Amy. "Women's Contributions to the Historic American Building Survey, 1933–1941." *CRM: The Journal of Heritage Stewardship* 5, no. 2 (Summer 2008): 39–63.
Gillies, Mary Davis. *McCall's Book of Modern Houses*. New York: Simon and Schuster, 1951.
Girouard, Mark. *Sweetness and Light: The Queen Anne Movement, 1860–1900*. Oxford: Clarendon Press, 1977.
Golan, Romy. *Modernity and Nostalgia: Art and Politics in France between the Wars*. New Haven, CT: Yale University Press, 1995.
———. *Muralnomad: The Paradox of Wall Painting, Europe 1927–1957*. New Haven, CT: Yale University Press, 2009.
Goldhagen, Sarah Williams, and Réjean Legault, eds. *Anxious Modernisms: Experimentation in Postwar Architectural Culture*. Cambridge, MA: MIT Press, 2002.
Goldsmith, Margaret Olthof. *Designs for Outdoor Living*. New York: George W. Stewart, 1941.
Goldwater, Robert, in collaboration with René d'Harnoncourt. *Modern Art in Your Life*. New York: Museum of Modern Art, 1949.
Goody, Joan, Robert Chandler, John Clancy, David Dixon, and Geoffrey Wooding. *Building Type Basics for Housing*. 2nd ed. Hoboken, NJ: John Wiley & Sons, 2010.
Gropius, Walter. *Scope of Total Architecture: A New Way of Life*. New York: Harper and Row, 1943.
Gropius, Walter, and Sarah P. Harkness, eds. *The Architects Collaborative, 1945–1965*. New York: Architectural Book Publishing, 1966.
Gruskin, Nancy Beth. "Building Context: The Personal and Professional Life of Eleanor Raymond, Architect, 1887–1989." PhD diss., Boston University, 1998.
Hall, Jane. *Breaking Ground: Architecture by Women*. London: Phaidon Press, 2019.
Hartman, Jan Cigliano, ed. *The Women Who Changed Architecture*. New York: Beverly Willis Architecture Foundation and Princeton Architectural Press, 2022.
Hayden, Dolores. *Building Suburbia: Green Fields and Urban Growth, 1820–2000*. New York: Pantheon Books, 2003.
———. *Grand Domestic Revolution: A History of Feminist Designs for American Homes, Neighborhoods, and Cities*. Cambridge, MA: MIT Press, 1981.
Held, Roger L. "Endless Innovations: Frederick Kiesler's Theory and Scenic Design." PhD diss., Bowling Green State University, 1977.
Heporauta, Arne et al. *Aino Aalto*. Jyväskylä, Finland: Alvar Aalto Foundation and Alvar Aalto Museum, 2004.
Hession, Jane King. *Elizabeth Scheu Close: A Life in Modern Architecture*. Minneapolis: University of Minnesota Press, 2020.
Hewitt, Mark Alan. *Domestic Architecture of H. T. Lindeberg*. New York: Acanthus Press, 1996.
Higonnet, Anne. *Margarett Sargent: A Modern Temperament*. Wellesley, MA: Davis Museum and Cultural Center, 1996.
Hines, Thomas S. *Architecture and Design at the Museum of Modern Art: The Arthur Drexler Years, 1951–1986*. Los Angeles: Getty Research Institute, 2019.
Holcomb, Adele M., and Claire R. Richter, eds. *Women as Interpreters of the Visual Arts, 1820–1979*. Westport, CT: Praeger, 1981.
Hollister, Paul. *Beauport at Gloucester: The Most Fascinating House in America*. New York: Hastings House, 1951.
Horta, Inge Schaefer. *Early Women Architects of the San Francisco Bay Area: The Lives and Work of Fifty Professionals, 1890–1951*. Jefferson, NC: McFarland, 2010.
Hunting, Mary Anne. *Edward Durell Stone: Modernism's Populist Architect*. New York: W. W. Norton, 2013.
Jacobs, James E. *Detached America: Building Houses in Postwar Suburbia*. Charlottesville: University of Virginia Press, 2015.
Jacobs, Jane. *Death and Life of Great American Cities*. New York: Random House, 1961.
James-Chakraborty, Kathleen. *Erich Mendelsohn and the Architecture of German Modernism*. New York: Cambridge University Press, 1997.
———. "Sonia Delaunay: Media or Message?" In *Iteration: Episodes in the Mediation of Art and Architecture*, ed. Robin Schuldenfrei, 105–20. London: Routledge, 2020.
Jencks, Charles. *The New Paradigm in Architecture: The Language of Post-Modernism*. New Haven, CT: Yale University Press, 2002.
Johnson, Philip C. *Mies Van der Rohe*. New York: Museum of Modern Art, 1947.
Kantor, Sybil Gordon. *Alfred H. Barr, Jr. and the Intellectual Origins of the Museum of Modern Art*. Cambridge, MA: MIT Press, 2002.

Katz, Sandra L. *Dearest of Geniuses: A Life of Theodate Pope Riddle*. Windsor, CT: Tide-Mark Press, 2003.
Kentgens-Craig, Margret. *The Bauhaus and America: First Contacts, 1919–1936*. Cambridge, MA: MIT Press, 1999.
Kiesler, Frederick, and John Kiesler. *Ten Years of American Opera Design at the Julliard School of Music*. New York: New York Public Library, 1941.
Kornwolf, James D., ed. *Modernism in America, 1937–1941: A Catalog and Exhibition of Four Architectural Competitions*. Williamsburg, VA: Joseph and Margaret Muscarelle Museum of Art, 1985.
Kostof, Sprio, ed. *The Architect: Chapters in the History of the Profession*. New York: Oxford University Press, 1977.
Kullack, Tanja, ed. *Architecture: A Woman's Profession*. Berlin: Jovis Verlag, 2011.
Larsen, Agnessa. *Graffiti on My Heart: An Autobiography, 1926–1937*. Seattle: Peanut Butter Publishing, 1994.
Lawrence, Amanda Reeser, and Ana Miljački, eds. *Terms of Appropriation: Modern Architecture and Global Exchange*. Abingdon, UK: Routledge, 2018.
Le Corbusier. *Vers une architecture*. 2nd ed. Paris: Éditions G. Crès et Cie, 1925.
Lewisohn, Sam A. *Painters and Personality: A Collector's View of Modern Art*. New York: Harper, 1948.
Loth, Calder, ed. *Virginia Landmarks of Black History: Sites on the Virginia Landmarks Register and the National Register of Historic Places*. Charlottesville: University of Virginia Press, 1995.
Lynes, Russell. *Good Old Modern: An Intimate Portrait of the Museum of Modern Art*. New York: Atheneum, 1973.
Marcus, Sharon. *Between Women: Friendship, Desire, and Marriage in Victorian England*. Princeton, NJ: Princeton University Press, 2007.
Markelin, Ulla, ed. *Profiles: Pioneering Women Architects from Finland*. Helsinki: Museum of Finnish Architecture, 1983.
Martin, Brenda, and Penny Sparke, ed. *Women's Places: Architecture and Design, 1860–1960*. London: Routledge, 2003.
McCarthy, Kathleen D. *Women's Culture: American Philanthropy and Art, 1830–1930*. Chicago: University of Chicago Press, 1991.
McCleod, Mary, and Victoria Rosner, eds. *Pioneering Women of Architecture*. New York: Beverly Willis Architecture Foundation. https://pioneering-women.bwaf.org.
McCoy, Esther. *Five California Architects*. Los Angeles: Hennessey and Ingalls, 1975.
Mongan, Agnes. *Margaret Fisher: Drawings, Watercolors, Gouaches*. Cambridge, MA: Busch-Reisinger Museum, 1973.
Moore, Honor. *The White Blackbird: A Life of the Painter Margarett Sargent by her Granddaughter*. New York: Viking, 1996.
Morgan, Keith N., with Richard M. Candee, Naomi Miller, Roger G. Reed, eds. *Buildings of Massachusetts: Metropolitan Boston*. Charlottesville: University of Virginia Press, 2009.
Morgan, William. *Monadnock Summer: The Architectural Legacy of Dublin, New Hampshire*. Boston: David R. Godine, 2011.
Murphy, Kevin D. "The Vernacular Moment: Eleanor Raymond, Walter Gropius, and New England Modernism between the Wars." *Journal of the Society of Architectural Historians* 70, no. 3 (September 2011): 308–29.
———. "'Secure from All Intrusion': Heterotopia, Queer Space, and the Turn-of-the-Century American Resort." *Winterthur Portfolio* 43, no. 2 / 3 (Summer / Autumn 2009): 185–228.
Museum of Modern Art. *Architecture and Furniture: Aalto*. New York: Museum of Modern Art, 1938.
Nelson, George, and Henry Wright. *Tomorrow's House: A Complete Guide for the Home- Builder*. New York: Simon and Schuster, 1945.
Oberlander, H. Peter, and Eva Newbrun. *Houser: The Life and Work of Catherine Bauer*. Vancouver: UBA Press, 1999.
O'Gorman, James, ed. *Hill-Stead: The Country Place of Theodate Pope Riddle*. New York: Princeton Architectural Press, 2010.
Oles, James, ed. *South of the Border: Mexico in the American Imagination, 1914–1947*. Washington, DC: Smithsonian Institution Press, 1993.
Olsberg, Nicholas. *Work of Ernest and Esther Born*. San Francisco: Book Club of California, 2015.
O'Rouke, Kathryn E. *Modern Architecture in Mexico City: History, Representation, and the Shaping of a Capital*. Pittsburgh: University of Pittsburg Press, 2016.
Osborn, Robert. *Osborn on Osborn*. New Haven, CT: Ticknor and Fields, 1982.
Osorio, Ernestina. "Intersections of Architecture, Photography, and Personhood: Case Studies in Mexican Modernity." PhD diss., Princeton University, 2006.
Ott, Katherine, Susan Tucker, and Patricia P. Buckler. *An Introduction to the History of Scrapbooks*. Philadelphia: Temple University Press, 2006.
Otto, Elizabeth. *Haunted Bauhaus: Occult Spirituality Gender Fluidity, Queer Identities, and Radical Politics*. Cambridge, MA: MIT Press, 2019.
Otto, Elizabeth, and Patrick Rössler. *Bauhaus Women: A Global Perspective*. London: Bloomsbury Publishing, 2019.
Pelkonen, Eeva-Liisa, and Donald Albrecht, eds. *Eero Saarinen: Shaping the Future*. New Haven, CT: Yale University Press, 2006.
Porter, Austin, and Sandra Zalman, eds. *Modern in the Making: MoMA and the Modern Experiment, 1929–1949*. New York: Bloomsbury Visual Arts, 2020.
Potvin, John. *Bachelors of a Different Sort: Queer Aesthetics, Material Culture and the Modern Interior in Britain*. Manchester: Manchester University Press, 2014.
Pound Ridge Historical Society. *Modern in Pound Ridge: 20th-Century Architecture and Lifestyle*. Pound Ridge, NY: Pound Ridge Historical Society, 2017.
Randl, Chad. *A-frame*. New York: Princeton Architectural Press, 2004.
Rapson, Rip, and Bruce N. Wright. *Ralph Rapson: Sixty Years of Modern Design*. Afton, MN: Afton Historical Society Press, 1999.
Raymond, Eleanor. *Eleanor Raymond: Architectural Projects, 1919–1973*. Boston: Institute of Contemporary Art, 1981.
Redgrave, Corin. *Michael Redgrave: My Father*. London: Fourth Estate, 1996.
Reed, Christopher, ed. *Not at Home: The Suppression of Domesticity in Modern Art and Architecture*. London: Thames & Hudson, 1996.
Report of the Regional Plan of New York and Its Environs of the Russell Sage Foundation. New York: Russell Sage Foundation, 1930.
Rhoads, Linda Smith. *Amelia Peabody*. Boston: Amelia Peabody Charitable Fund, 1998.
Rivera, Diego, with Gladys March. *My Art, My Life: An Autobiography*. New York: Dover Publications, 1991 [1960].
Rogers, Millard F., Jr. *John Nolen & Mariemont: Building a New Town in Ohio*. Baltimore: John Hopkins University Press, 2001.
Saarinen, Aline B., ed. *Eero Saarinen on His Work*. New Haven, CT: Yale University Press, 1962.
Saarinen, Eero, *Challenge to an Architect: Deere and Company Administrative Center*. New Haven, CT: Yale University Press, 1964.
Schildt, Göran. *Alvar Aalto: The Mature Years*. New York: Rizzoli, 1989.
Schulze, Franz. *Philip Johnson: Life and Work*. New York: Alfred A. Knopf, 1994.
Schwitalla, Ursula, ed. *Women in Architecture: From History to Future*. Stuttgart: Hatje Cantz Verlag, 2021.
Sellers, Libby. *Women Design: Pioneers in Architecture, Graphic and Digital Design from the Twentieth Century to the Present Day*. London: Frances Lincoln, 2018.
Shackford, Martha Hale, ed. *Wellesley Verse, 1875–1925*. New York: Oxford University Press, 1925.
Shand-Tucci, Douglass. *The Crimson Letter: Harvard, Homosexuality, and the Shaping of American Culture*. New York: St. Martin's Griffin, 2003.
Sheeler, Charles. *Charles Sheeler: Paintings, Drawings, Photographs*. New York: Museum of Modern Art, 1939.
Shipway, Verna Cook, and Warren Shipway. *Mexican Interiors*. Santa Monica, CA: Hennessey and Ingalls, 2007 [1962].
Skeggs, Beverly, ed. *Feminist Cultural Theory: Process and Production*. New York: Manchester University Press, 1995.

Sokolina, Anna, ed. *Routledge Companion to Women in Architecture*. New York: Routledge, 2021.

Spathopoulos, Wanda. *The Crag: Castlecrag, 1924–1938*. Blackheath, Australia: Brandl & Schlesinger, 2007.

Staniszewski, Mary Anne. *The Power of Display: A History of Exhibition Installations at the Museum of Modern Art*. Cambridge, MA: MIT Press, 1998.

Stephens, Ronald J. *Images of America: Idlewild, the Black Eden of Michigan*. Charleston, SC: Arcadia Publishing, 2001.

Stephenson, Gordon, and Christina DeMarco, eds. *On a Human Scale: A Life in City Design*. Fremantle, Australia: Fremantle Arts Centre Press, 1992.

Stern, Jewel, and John A. Stuart. *Ely Jacques Kahn, Architect: Beaux-arts to Modernism in New York*. New York: W. W. Norton, 2006.

Stratigakos, Despina. *Where Are the Women Architects?* Princeton, NJ: Princeton University Press, 2016.

Stritzler-Levine, Nina, with Timo Riekko, eds. *Artek and the Aaltos: Creating a Modern World*. New York: Bard Graduate Center, 2016.

Taylor, Jacqueline. *Amaza Lee Meredith Imagines Herself Modern. Architecture and the Black American Middle Class*. Cambridge, MA: MIT Press, 2023.

"That Exceptional One": Women in American Architecture, 1888–1988. Washington, DC: American Architectural Foundation, 1988.

Thompson, Jane, and Alexandra Lange, *Design Research: The Store that Brought Modern Living to American Homes*. San Francisco: Chronicle Books, 2010.

Torre, Susana, ed. *Women in American Architecture: A Historic Contemporary Perspective*. New York: Whitney Library of Design, 1977.

Travisano, Thomas, with Saskia Hamilton, eds. *Words in Air: The Complete Correspondence Between Elizabeth Bishop and Robert Lowell*. New York: Farrar, Straus and Giroux, 2008.

Tyng, Anne, ed. *Louis Kahn to Anne Tyng: The Rome Letters, 1953–1954*. New York: Rizzoli, 1997.

Umland, Anne, and Walburga Krupp, with Charlotte Healy, eds. *Sophie Taeuber-Arp: Living Abstraction*. New York: Museum of Modern Art, 2021.

Valentine, Norton, and Alan Valentine. *The American Academy in Rome, 1894–1969*. Charlottesville: University Press of Virginia, 1973.

Venturi, Robert, Denise Scott Brown, and Steven Izenour. *Learning from Las Vegas*. Cambridge, MA: MIT Press, 1972.

Walker, Meredith, Adrienne Kabos and James Weirick. *Building for Nature: Walter Burley Griffin and Castlecrag*. Castlecrag, Australia: Walter Burley Griffin Society, 1994.

Waterman, Laura, and Guy Waterman. *Forest and Crag: A History of Hiking, Trail Blazing, and Adventure in the Northeast Mountains*. Albany, NY: Excelsior Editions, 2019.

Welch, Diane Y. *Lilian J. Rice: Architect of Rancho Santa Fe, California*. Atglen, PA: Schiffer Publishing, 2010.

Whitehead, Colson. *Sag Harbor: A Novel*. New York: Anchor Books, 2009.

Wilson, Dreck Spurlock, ed. *African-American Architects: A Biographical Dictionary, 1865–1945*. New York: Routledge, 2004.

Woolf, Virginia. *A Room of One's Own*. London: Hogarth Press, 1929.

Wright, John Lloyd. *My Father Frank Lloyd Wright*. Mineola, New York: Dover, 1992.

Wright, Olgivanna Lloyd. *Frank Lloyd Wright: His Life, His Work, His Words*. New York: Horizon Press, 1966.

———. *The Shining Brow: Frank Lloyd Wright*. New York: Horizon Press, 1960.

Zinguer, Tamar. "Architecture in Play: Intimations of Modernism in Architectural Toys, 1836–1952." PhD diss, Princeton University, 2006.

Zipf, Catherine W. *Professional Pursuits: Women and the American Arts and Crafts Movement*. Knoxville: University of Tennessee Press, 2007.

The text's extensive citations of journals, magazines, newspapers, and internet sites are documented in the notes.

INDEX

ILLUSTRATION CREDITS

Architectural Archives, Stuart Weitzman School of Design, University of Pennsylvania (figs. 2.24, 2.25, 5.4, 5.5, 8.14, 8.15)

Archiv města Plzeň (fig. 2.14)

Archives of American Art, Smithsonian Institution / photograph by Elizabeth Timberman (fig. 4.20)

Athenaeum of Philadelphia (figs. 2.8, 2.9, 2.10, 2.11, 2.12, 2.13, 2.15)

Billy Rose Theater Division, New York Public Library / Vandamm Theatrical Photographs (fig. 3.10)

© Brian Lanker Archive, National Portrait Gallery, Smithsonian Institution (fig. 3.1)

Chestnut Hill Historical Society / photograph by Edmond B. Gilchrist Jr. (fig. 5.13)

Center for Southwest Research and Special Collections, University of New Mexico Libraries (fig. 5.19)

© Damora Archive, all rights reserved / photographs by Robert Damora (figs. 1.11, 1.12, 4.21, 6.4; frontispiece)

Department of Drawings and Archives, Avery Architectural and Fine Arts Library, Columbia University / photographs by Joseph W. Molitor (figs. 2.30, 4.7, 7.10)

Department of Prints, Photographs, and Architectural Collections, New-York Historical Society (fig. 2.22)

Division of Rare and Manuscript Collections, Cornell University Library. (figs. 1.3, 7.1)

Embroiders' Guild of America (fig. 5.3)

Environmental Design Archives, College of Environmental Design, University of California, Berkeley (figs. 1.1, 4.14)

© Esther Born Estate, courtesy of the Center for Creative Photography, University of Arizona, (fig. 2.32)

© Ezra Stoller/ESTO (figs. 4.5, 4.6, 4.24, 4.25, 5.10, 5.11, 7.6, 7.7; cover)

© Fitzwilliam Museum, University of Cambridge (fig. 2.16)

Frances Loeb Library, Harvard University Graduate School of Design (figs. In.5, 2.17, 5.7)

Freeman French Freeman archive / photograph by Richard Garrison (fig. 4.13)

Germantown Historical Society / photograph by Bradley Maule (fig. 6.7)

Greenbelt Museum (fig. 6.6)

Hagley Library (fig. 1.13)

Harvard Law School, Harvard University / photograph by Walter R. Fleischer (fig. 4.1)

Harvard University Archives, Pusey Library (fig. 1.20)

Historic New England, (figs. In.1, In.2, 1.14, 2.2, 3.11)

Institute Archives, MIT Libraries (fig. 6.3)

© J. Paul Getty Trust, Getty Research Institute / photograph by Julius Shulman (fig. 8.19)

Jerry Cooke Archives, Briscoe Center for American History / courtesy of Special Collections and Archives, Kent State University (fig. 5.16)

Knox County Public Library / photograph by Jim Thompson (fig. 1.10)

Manuscripts and Archives, Yale University (fig. 8.18)

Margaret Fisher Archive (fig. 5.15)

© Metropolitan Museum of Art / Art Resource, NY (fig. 5.1)

Middle Georgia Archives, Washington Memorial Library / photograph by Gabriel Benzur (fig. 4.10)

© Morley Baer Photography Trust, Santa Fe. All rights reserved. Used by permission/ courtesy of Environmental Design Archives, College of Environmental Design, University of California, Berkeley (fig. 4.15)

Municipal Archives, City of New York (fig. 6.5)

Museum of the City of New York / photograph by Wurts Brothers (fig. 6.2)

© Museum of Modern Art / SCALA / Art Resource, NY (fig. 2.1)

© Museum of Modern Art / SCALA / Art Resource, NY / photograph by Soichi Sunami (fig. 2.26)

New Haven Preservation Trust (fig. 8.8)

Photograph by Jessica Lewis / courtesy of Andrew Leary (fig. 8.9)

Photograph by Jim Thompson (fig. 8.7)

Photographs by Kevin D. Murphy (figs. In.6, 4.9, 4.11, 7.9, 8.5, 8.16)

Photographs by Maura McEvoy (figs. 7.11, 7.12)

Photograph by Michael Borowski (fig. 8.6)

Photograph by Sam Robertson Little (fig. 6.8)

Photograph by Walter Elliot (fig. 8.10)

Photograph by Ye Craftsman (fig. i.4)

Photograph courtesy of the Cleveland Architecture Foundation Collection (fig. 4.26)

Photograph courtesy of Connecticut College Libraries (fig. 2.28)

Photographs courtesy of Larry Weinberg (figs. 5.6, 5.8)

Photograph courtesy of Mark Vasquez (fig. 4.19)

Photograph courtesy of the Town of Lincoln [MA] Building Department (fig. 7.8)

Prints and Photographs Division, Library of Congress (figs. In.8, 1.7, 2.19, 2.20, 5.21)

Prints and Photographs Division, Library of Congress / photographs by Gottscho-Schleisner (figs. 1.18, 2.6)

Ryerson and Burnham Art and Architecture Archives, Art Institute of Chicago (fig. 5.14)

Schlesinger Library, Harvard Radcliffe Institute (figs. In.7, 2.29, 6.1, 7.2, 8.11, 8.12, 8.17)

Smith College Special Collections / photographs courtesy of Smith Archives (figs. 1.4, 1.9)

Special Collections, Field Museum of Natural History (fig. 8.1)

Special Collections and Archives, Virginia State University (figs. 7.3, 7.5)

Special Collections and Archives, Virginia State University / photograph courtesy of Jacqueline Taylor (figs. 7.4, Co.3, Co. 4)

Special Collections and University Archives, University Libraries, Virginia Polytechnic Institute and State University (fig. 4.4)

Vermont Division for Historic Preservation / photograph by James V. Detore (fig. 4.12)

Wharton Esherick Museum (fig. 8.13)